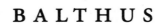

BALTHUS

BALTHUS

A Biography

NICHOLAS FOX WEBER

ALFRED A. KNOPF NEW YORK 1999

THIS IS A BORZOI BOOK
PUBLISHED BY ALFRED A. KNOPF, INC.

Copyright © 1999 by Nicholas Fox Weber

www.randomhouse.com

Library of Congress Cataloging-in-Publication Data
Weber, Nicholas Fox.
Balthus : a biography / Nicholas Fox Weber. — 1st ed.
p.   cm.
Includes bibliographical references and index.
ISBN 0-679-40737-5
1. Balthus, 1908–   2. Painters—France Biography.   I. Title.
ND553.B23   W43   1999
760'.092—dc21
[B]   99-28422
CIP

Manufactured in the United States of America
First Edition

For the two sisters,
Charlotte and Lucy

CONTENTS

Chapter One   A BIRTHDAY   3

Chapter Two   MITSOU   19

Chapter Three   TRANSFORMATION   56

Chapter Four   THE BOMB   88

Chapter Five   NARCISSUS   95

Chapter Six   PIERO   107

Chapter Seven   PERAMBULATIONS   130

Chapter Eight   THE STREET   150

Chapter Nine   THE PIERO OF PARIS   186

Chapter Ten   THE GUITAR LESSON   205

Chapter Eleven   THE WINDOW   249

Chapter Twelve   CATHY DRESSING   283

Chapter Thirteen   ALICE   302

Chapter Fourteen   DERAIN   314

Chapter Fifteen   MIRÓ   347

Chapter Sixteen   SURREALISM À LA COURBET   358

Chapter Seventeen   THE CHILDREN   374

Chapter Eighteen   THÉRÈSE   388

Chapter Nineteen   BATTLEFIELDS AND CHÂTEAUX   402

Chapter Twenty   THE THREE SISTERS   458

Chapter Twenty-One   AN OBSESSION IN DISGUISE   475

Chapter Twenty-Two   THE VILLA MEDICI   491

Chapter Twenty-Three ROSSINIÈRE   550

Chapter Twenty-Four CAT AT THE MIRROR   585

AFTERWORD 593

NOTES 605

SELECTED BIBLIOGRAPHY 619

ACKNOWLEDGMENTS 623

INDEX 627

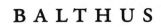

BALTHUS

A BIRTHDAY

I treated art as the supreme reality and life as a
mere mode of fiction.

—OSCAR WILDE[1]

I

WHEN BALTHAZAR KLOSSOWSKI turned six, he had a large birthday party in his family's apartment in Paris. Birthdays were a funny business for "Baltusz"—as everyone called him. Since he had been born on February 29 in 1908, his family did not know precisely when to celebrate except on leap years. Nonetheless, as the boy anticipated his friends' arrival, he was in high spirits. He had a plan.

It was a cozy home full of art and books—in a building on the Rue Boissonade, near the Boulevard Montparnasse in the fourteenth arrondissement. Baltusz's parents were both painters, his father an art historian as well, and along with Baladine's winsome watercolors and Erich's vigorous oils hung canvases by Cézanne and Delacroix, as well as a Géricault drawing and Japanese woodcuts. Baltusz's little friends entered dressed in their finery, in his eyes "all very beautiful with their white lace collars."

Once the nurses and governesses left the children on their own, the birthday boy took charge. Addressing the other youngsters, Baltusz announced that the time had come for them "to eat badly." There was a chocolate cake, and they all plunged in. Everyone got his collars and cuffs filthy with frosting. Everyone except for Baltusz, who remained spotless. When the nurses and governesses returned, all the other children were chastised or slapped, while Baltusz escaped punishment.

The story was told to me a lifetime later by the eighty-two-year-old Balthus—the Count de Rola—in the sitting room of his vast eighteenth-century chalet in a small French-speaking village in the Alps. "It's part of my bad side," he explained, referring to the way he had trapped others into temptation while keeping himself clean.

"A very naughty boy, and until now he has never changed," laughed his forty-eight-year-old Japanese-born wife, Setsuko, who had encouraged him to tell me the tale.

I had met both of them for the first time that afternoon. Balthus's reputation was that he loathed writers on art and would not grant interviews. In an era when many successful artists preen like movie stars, he has managed to give the impression that he prefers to live in isolation, as if the occasions when he has been quoted or photographed are accidental slips. In 1977, at the time of a rare Balthus show in New York—the first in a decade—Robert Hughes wrote of the artist in *Time* magazine that "at 69 he has no public face"[2] and that there were no anecdotes about him in circulation, thanks to his own careful control. I had scant hope that he would alter his reclusive pose for me.

John Russell had begun his introduction to the catalog of the 1968 Balthus retrospective at the Tate Gallery with the statement, "What is private must remain so: that is Balthus' attitude, and it is at his insistence that this catalog contains no biographical matter. 'The best way to begin,' he said when apprised of our customs, 'is to say: "Balthus is a painter of whom *nothing is known*. And now let us have a look at the paintings." ' " That statement, often cited since, has become the gospel on the artist. It is especially provocative given the eroticism and deviltry and sinister overtones so many viewers see in his paintings of comatose teenagers and seemingly spent naked women.

When his major retrospective opened in Paris at the Centre Pompidou in 1983, critics in search of a lead on the work from Balthus himself could do no better than to fall back on his 1945 pronouncement, "I refuse to confide and don't like it when people write about art." The exhibition catalog, although rendered heavier than the combined volumes of the Paris phone book by its many essays and reproductions, presented no straightforward biographical data. It was pointed out that the largest book on Balthus, done with his cooperation, did not even provide his birth date. And the people in Balthus's constellation acted as if they had signed a secrecy oath. To a journalist from *Le Monde,* the artist's son Thadée declared politely that he would not speak about his father because his father did not want people to; moreover, he shared Balthus's view that to talk about painters was not to talk about paintings. Pierre Klossowski, the artist's brother, himself a famous writer and leading intellectual figure—known for his lifelong devotion to the work of the Marquis de Sade—explained that to discuss Balthus would give him migraines. Sylvia Bataille, an old friend who was the widow of Balthus's acquaintance the "excremental philosopher"[3] Georges Bataille and the mother of one of Balthus's early mistresses, allowed that Balthus would never forgive her if she spoke. Other close acquaintances, expecting approaches because of the fanfare over the Pompidou show, disconnected their telephones.[4]

But Balthus had readily acceded to my request that I come see him about the book I wished to write about him. On that first occasion, as we sat side by side on an eighteenth-century sofa, he was gracious and compliant, answering all of my questions and offering numerous anecdotes. Although he had forbidden my turning on a tape recorder, he had sanctioned my use of notebook and pen, and voiced no objection to my writing continuously. The story of his sixth birthday party, told with a great grin on his face, seemed, however, clearly a warning. Balthus could manage to get everyone else in trouble while keeping only himself above the fray, and he delighted in doing so.

II

INITIALLY BALTHUS FAILED to answer the letter I sent him from Connecticut saying I had been asked to write a book on him and would like to meet him. So, having learned his phone number from Swiss information—it was listed under "Klossowski"—I steeled up the nerve to dial it early one morning about a month before that first visit in 1990. When someone with a gravelly yet tremulous voice answered the phone in slow and refined cadence, I asked, in my best high-school French, "Est-ce que je peux parler avec le Comte de Rola?"

"C'est lui-même!" the voice bellowed back authoritatively.

From then on, this man of such terrifying reputation, so ferocious in his portrait photos, was the height of graciousness. First he suggested that we switch to English. This, he offered, was his first language; he was one-quarter Scottish, he told me, and as a child had had a Scottish nanny. He said that I might call on him, as if it were a matter of course. Solicitous about my travel plans, he scheduled a Monday morning three weeks hence that suited me well. The count gave me meticulous instructions on how to change to the small mountain train in Lausanne. He wondered if I knew his part of Switzerland, and seemed particularly pleased when I said that when I was in college I had dated a girl in Gstaad, only half an hour away; like a concerned older relative, he asked me her family name. He did not know these people, but when I explained that they could hardly ever use their large Gstaad chalet anymore because they now had to spend over half their time in another canton for tax purposes, he chuckled knowingly.

I arrived in Rossinière on the afternoon prior to our scheduled rendezvous. Walking through the village to the one *pension* that was open in a season suitable for neither hiking nor skiing, I was struck by the resemblance of everything around me to certain Balthus paintings. People in this mountain hamlet were walking through the small town square and talking in the sole café as if they had been absorbed in the same routine forever. This seemed a place where time had been frozen—not out of nostalgia or the deliberate veneration of an earlier epoch, but because modern madness had not crept in. Every poster and vista bespoke childhood pleasures—chocolate and snow. There was something magical in the atmosphere, yet also inaccessible, the people remote in a particularly Swiss way.

It seemed as if everything was fitting in place. But when, as instructed, I phoned on the morning of our appointed visit, Balthus was irritated. He could not understand who I was. He then explained in a laughing voice that he had hearing problems and needed to install an instrument "like a small shrimp"— pronounced *scha-rimpp,* the intonations of Breslau tinging the more dominant London cadences—into his ear. Then, with a return to emphatically British pronunciation, he declared that I should come in the afternoon. He greatly looked forward to meeting me "at last"—these last two words uttered in a dramatic adagio.

I should have no trouble finding the house, Balthus assured me. "It is the biggest house in the village, the largest chalet in all of Switzerland," he said with a hint of boastful little boy in his voice.

When I arrived at Le Grand Chalet, it seemed, indeed, the size of one of the Alps surrounding it. I was let in by a uniformed butler. But then there was further confusion. No one seemed to know where the count was, and as I sat alone in the large living room—looking intently at a framed photo of the thirteen-year-old Balthus between his mother and Rainer Maria Rilke, who was her lover at the time—I heard a lot of running around, followed by a prolonged silence. This lasted nearly half an hour.

Finally Balthus entered. The gaunt figure in a Japanese vest, flannel shirt, and baggy tweed pants limped on his cane. It was he who began the conversation. "So here I am: a disabled old man," he uttered with a smile, sounding like a Shakespearean actor playing Lear at the end. I protested that he looked fit and healthy. He politely contradicted me, insisting, "No. That is the truth." The brief exchange seemed to set the tone of our encounter: there was to be no glossing. Balthus insisted on candor and honesty, and he would be the one to have the first and last word.

We talked in the elegant salon and had high tea in the dining room. Setsuko periodically joined us, as if she were checking me out; it was during one of these interludes that she urged her husband to tell me about his sixth birthday party. By the end of the afternoon, we had had more serious discussion than I had dreamt possible about Balthus's art and life. He made me feel privy to a range of unknown details—who was who in his paintings, the correct facts of his ancestry, the details of his friendship with Picasso. Our rapport was facilitated by his perfect idiomatic English, which he spoke with a distinguished Oxonian accent, although certain words took on a surprising, guttural German ring.

But in the course of that day, despite my joy at the depth and range of our conversations, I became increasingly struck by how haggard my subject looked. Although his ornate vest might have been worn by an emperor, his other clothing was frayed and tattered—as if he were too old to bother to replace them. His skin was pale and translucent. He was animated, but seemed merely to be hanging on to life.

IN THE EVENING, HOWEVER, there was a change. Balthus and Setsuko invited me to join them for dinner with some other guests at eight. The Filipino butler—named Leonardo, much to his employer's delight—was now in a white jacket and white gloves, more formal than his daytime uniform. He again led me into the living room, and again I waited.

On this occasion, however, little time elapsed before the Count and Countess Klossowski de Rola walked in together. Balthus was in an exquisitely tailored gray flannel suit with intricately shaped, Edwardian-style lapels. It hung easily on his lean body. The jacket cuffs were rolled up a turn, so that he seemed both very formal and completely casual. He wore an English-style shirt of bold stripes, a solid tie, and a plaid vest with brass buttons. Setsuko was ravishing in a gold brocade kimono, flecked in a deep red that she had matched with her nail polish.

Together they were a flawless composition: her cheeks a broad plane in opposition to the sharp angles of his Voltairean profile and beak of a nose. He was, indeed, a count: with just a touch of Dracula. She was an Oriental potentate, reserved and statuesque.

The other dinner guests soon arrived. A jolly, white-haired English couple named the Devenishes, they had been the previous owners of Le Grand Chalet. The five of us had drinks in the living room. Setsuko offered pistachio nuts from a large silver dish and announced with a look of unabashed delight that these were "true Iranian pistachios—brought by the Aga Khan."

Soon the second of the two Filipino menservants, Virgilio, also clad in white jacket and gloves, announced dinner. As we walked down the hall to the dining room, Balthus whispered to me that he was as amused by Virgilio's name as by Leonardo's. Looking especially gleeful, he added that his servant reminded him "of Friday in *Robinson Crusoe.*"

Everyone was in high spirits throughout the long meal. The Devenishes explained to me that they were former innkeepers, and that under their owner-ship Le Grand Chalet had been a hotel. This had been so since the nineteenth century, when Victor Hugo had stayed there. Mr. Devenish said that when they sold the place to Balthus, they had no idea who he was. In fact, for most of the thirteen years Balthus had been in Rossinière, the local population sim-ply thought Balthus was a retired businessman who painted as a hobby—until the recent appearance of an article in *Paris Match.*

Balthus invited me to stay for a brandy after the other guests left. As if I were the old acquaintance and they the new people, he asked if I agreed that they were "quite amusing." "I rather like Devenish," he said in a slightly patronizing way. And then, as if to assure that we were brethren in taste, he inquired, "Don't you?" When I replied that I had appreciated the Devenishes' way of including me, Balthus said that that was simply because they were innkeepers and it was part of their profession.

THE SECOND DAY IN ROSSINIÈRE, however, did not go nearly as well. Balthus was having stomach problems and could not see me in the morning when I arrived according to plan; Setsuko said that she or he would call me that afternoon to say if I might come later on. When neither of them had phoned by 6 p.m., I decided that I had been naïve in assuming that yesterday was really the start of something and had been as successful as it appeared; clearly Balthus had changed his mind about me, and that would be my sole audience.

Waiting at the silent guesthouse, I was also irritated with myself over one tactical error I had made. I had suggested to the count, toward the end of that first wonderful afternoon and in anticipation of the evening ahead, that, American-style, he might stop calling me "Mr. Weber" and use my first name instead. To this he had replied, with a slight frown and a glare more the domain of boarding-school headmasters than of avant-garde artists, "But I am European." I did not want to be out of line again by taking the initiative. However, when I finally disobeyed instructions and telephoned myself, Setsuko went out of her way to make clear that the reason she had not called was very specifically because with Balthus's stomach things might improve at any moment. They were both very sorry. Her husband would phone me the next morning, and I should wait for the call.

I would subsequently learn that Pierre Matisse used to spend two or three days at a time cooped up in his room at the Hotel Hassler in Rome—having breakfast, lunch, and dinner delivered by room service, even when his young wife yearned to go out if only for an hour's jaunt to a simple trattoria—while awaiting Balthus's phone calls. Those were the years when Balthus was the director of the Villa Medici, a few hundred yards from the sumptuous Hassler. Matisse, who was Balthus's dealer, was hoping to be summoned to the artist's studio to see any paintings Balthus might have finished since the previous visit. This was in the mid-1960s, when Balthus's work had only recently begun to fetch big prices, and since he had a notoriously limited output—sometimes, in that period, not even completing a picture a year—Matisse was always eager to see what he might have to offer clients. At the time, it was a new development that Balthus was doing better than earning his bare subsistence, and one might have expected the artist to welcome the man who sold his paintings. But it didn't work that way—as I knew even before I had heard Balthus's voice or set foot in his chalet. For Balthus's paintings had made it clear that I was dealing with someone for whom power and control were paramount issues.

YET THE NEXT DAY Balthus cheerfully told me—when I phoned him just before lunch, since he had again failed to call me as promised—that he was quite a bit better. He and Setsuko had just returned from an outing to the bank in Château-d'Oex, about twenty minutes away. He explained that he always accompanied his wife on such errands, that he never allowed her to go to the bank only with a driver; a woman required the presence of her husband for financial transactions. Balthus said he was just recuperating from the journey, and then was planning on ringing me. In any event, I should come over at 3 p.m.

Again we had a wonderful, easy afternoon. We sat on the delicate sofa in the living room as Balthus chain-smoked and answered some of my questions about his art, which we looked at in a large Skira book opened on the coffee table. A penetrating light, bouncing off the snow-covered mountains, streamed in from behind. With his hollow cheeks, aquiline nose, wide, dark eyes, and taut, wrinkled skin, Balthus had the authority of age and the intensity of the wisest, most seasoned intellectuals. His speaking was metered, the diction precise; his erudition and the meticulousness of his word choice and ideas made him seem the source of irrefutable truths.

Most of the time, Balthus was encased in cigarette smoke, but in the brief intervals between cigarettes, he was as scent-free as a little boy. It was as if he really belonged to childhood, which I knew to be his preferred period of life—and had indeed had no more birthdays than his leap-day birth date allowed. It seemed that his inner workings and even his skin, as soft as it was creased, were those of a youth who spent most of his time in the mountain air. If there was any odor at all that emanated from the octogenarian, it was—for reasons I cannot explain—the very slight aroma of English butterscotch candy.

This impression of innocence was confirmed that second afternoon when Setsuko joined us in the dining room at five for tea. We ate pancakes with some Vermont maple syrup I had brought as a gift on my arrival day—and which they said was especially exotic to them because they had never been in America. Balthus was like a schoolboy as he downed his afternoon snack. But then the couple spoke in Japanese. I felt as if I were being handled. After conferring in this private code, Setsuko switched to English to say her husband wondered if I would like to stay for a simple dinner later on. There would be no need to go back to the *pension* to change, as this would be more informal than our evening two days earlier. And would I come again tomorrow?

I explained that I could not change my arrangements to fly back to the States the next day but would love to return. We all agreed that this would make sense about a month later, after Christmas and New Year's. During the holidays, they would be inundated with their adolescent daughter and her friends and with Balthus's older children from his first marriage, as well as by in-laws and their young granddaughter and, they were both happy to say, the artist's ex-wife, Antoinette. Setsuko explained that they were all close friends; Antoinette had woven all the needlepoint chair covers on which we were sitting. We should discuss all this when I came back.

The second journey to Rossinière ultimately proved as complex to organize as my second afternoon with Balthus; the Klossowskis repeatedly scheduled and canceled it, with me always being the one to make the phone calls. But I did end up back at Le Grand Chalet six weeks later, in January 1991, this time staying in the house, talking with the artist morning, noon, and night for ten days.

III

What a wee little part of a person's life are his acts and his words! His real life is led in his head, and is known to none but himself. . . . Biographies are but the clothes and buttons of the man—the biography of the man himself cannot be written.

—MARK TWAIN[5]

BALTHUS AND SETSUKO and their staff of four made me feel wonderfully at home on that second visit. Their friendship became so convincing that I found it awkward when, over drinks one evening, Balthus told me that he wanted my text to contain no biography.

I responded that I wished for no misunderstanding, that indeed my book would include elements of biography—although I fully understood his stance that his paintings and his life were separate issues. I explained that my primary hope was to gain access to his point of view, not to establish spurious links between his personal history and his work. But at the same time I wanted him to realize that I intended to write at least summarily about his past.

Balthus grinned mischievously. From then on, if he was speaking of friends or personal experiences and I was not taking notes, he would remind me to get my notebook.

I even had the bad taste to put my legal pad down on the dining room table, pushing aside a finger bowl. Balthus and Setsuko, rather than making me feel that this violated their highly decorous way of life, appeared to respect the compulsive note-taking as part of a quest they well understood: the desire to understand what an artist is thinking about, to capture the painter's own thoughts and glean his intentions as he articulated them rather than as other people might have erroneously perceived them. They wanted to debunk the Balthus myth, they said, and they felt I might help. Balthus repeatedly insisted that his art has been grossly misread. It is neither erotic nor mysterious, he told me time and again. He trusted that I would do better than reiterate those usual clichés about his work, and would help convince people of their fallaciousness.

The reaction of people who had known Balthus for a long time—some of whom I met while I was staying with him—was that this unexpected cooperation with me reflected a recent change. Balthus, apparently for the first time, had become ambivalent about the issue of his life as a subject. He had mellowed and, like many people in old age, had come to enjoy reminiscing far more than he used to. The deaths of most of the major acquaintances of his lifetime had sharpened his awareness that stories and memories die with a person if they remain unrecorded, and had made him more tolerant of new, younger people eager for his stories. Additionally, after years of privately savoring her husband's recollections, Setsuko now wanted her privilege shared by a larger audience. She hoped to avert the eventual loss of Balthus's tales and point of view.

It seemed an ideal situation. Balthus and I were soul mates. Together we would help rectify errors and preserve history. The aged artist had, for whatever reasons, decided to open up to someone the age of his sons.

DAY AFTER DAY, BALTHUS and I discussed his work as we looked at reproductions of it. The artist has painted fewer than two hundred oils in all, and has sold almost every one of them, so Balthus and I depended exclusively on the various books and catalogs of his work as visual refreshers; only two relatively minor oils, both reacquired, were in the house at the time. And although a couple of fine watercolors—a landscape and a still life, both reflective of the most refined and least salacious aspects of his work—were in the downstairs, public rooms, the oils were sequestered on the bedroom floor above. Not only had Balthus clearly been happy enough to sell virtually all of his entire output, but, he told me, the reason he had no paintings by himself at Le Grand Chalet was "I couldn't stand it; it would be too great a shock. I would think, 'Did I really make these mistakes?' "

Yet the artist had no trouble recalling every element of his paintings, now dispersed all over the world. Whatever the limitations of their reproductions, he knew the colors and textures and intricacies in unnerving detail. While many aged painters are amazed or confounded by what they have done, for Balthus there were no surprises.

I IMMERSED MYSELF in the idyllic life of the Count de Rola. The meal schedule was like clockwork—breakfast at 9:30, lunch at 1:00, tea at 5:00, dinner at 8:00—and every meal was an occasion. The silver was always impeccably polished and the china glistening. Balthus's family and visitors always included me in their conversation as if I were completely accustomed to their very cosmopolitan universe. At the same time, I got to observe the artist's other side as well. Aided only by his cane, the hobbling octogenarian, visibly bony and frail, would, either in late morning or just after lunch, wend his way across the road on the outskirts of this modest Swiss village. There, in the simple garage converted into a studio with northern light, he would resume the struggles of his day's work. The worldly nobleman of the night before now became the image of the honest workman: consumed by the love of his craft. Persevering against the unachievable goals of his work, he accepted the solitude of his métier as he went about the battle that painting has always been for its truest practitioners.

The studio was sacrosanct territory that few people have ever been allowed to enter, however, and once we reached its door I would go my separate way. For nothing should interfere with his work. Balthus was doing his utmost to fight the limitations of age to put paint on canvas as well as he could. He told me that he had suffered three minor strokes and recently had an operation, and that he had to conserve all of his energy to paint. Everything was geared to the supremacy of his art and to the hours of solitude when he might summon the strength to pursue it.

Then, one afternoon toward the end of my second visit, Balthus at last permitted me into his studio. There were few objects in this private sanctum, save the necessary furniture and crafts of the trade, and countless pots of paint containing colors that Balthus, dissatisfied with the usual store-bought tubes, ground himself. Beyond these, there was a large photograph of Giacometti in the corner, a book on Courbet, and lots of objects for still lifes.

On the easel in the center of the room stood a large, unfinished canvas. Balthus told me he was not yet pleased with the form of the central figure, but did acknowledge: "I managed to get the head at its place. After that I had to leave it to go have an operation. But I was pleased when I saw it again that the head was at this place."

In spite of the artist's own reservations, I burst out that the sight of this latest, unfinished canvas gave me an inestimable thrill. He wanted to know what I found so engaging; I answered that even in this rough sketch the figures were real presences and embodiments of vigor. Balthus countered that he could only see all the work that still had to be done. Smiling pleasantly, he told me that now I should leave him to use his limited strength and the remaining daylight to resume work.

IV

Why do I forgive his behavior? Because he was a storyteller. That was his life and work and business and vocation and avocation. It was impossible for him to retell anything exactly as it had happened, just as it is impossible for Picasso to produce a photographic likeness. There are three sides to every story— yours, his, and the truth.

—Garson Kanin, *Remembering Mr. Maugham*[6]

BALTHUS'S PAINTINGS are a product of the same sort of manipulative seduction that has consistently governed his handling of many aspects of his life. Their unsettling character derives in part from the contradictions within them. Like the artist, and like the varying versions of his life's story, they are full of discrepancies; the parts and effects don't all jibe. This is one of the reasons that, in spite of Balthus's counsel to the contrary, I have come to find the art and the person inseparable. The qualities evinced by Balthus in his splendid chalet—the mix of exquisite visual judgment and aesthetic refinement with the compulsive need for deliberate falsification—exist in the paintings as well. Balthus is a real and honest painter whose art reveals both his ferocious diligence and his extraordinary talent; his perpetual withholding and contrived elusiveness are equally present. The personages in these paintings are also like their creator: thoughtful, and seemingly wrapped in a cocoon of sensuousness—while at the same time exulting in their own wickedness and devoid of conscience.

YEARS BEFORE I MET BALTHUS, I had heard about what it was like to pose for this gentleman tyrant from Jane Allen, a woman from Connecticut whose portrait Balthus painted in 1937. Mrs. Allen was a crusty Yankee lady in her mid-seventies when she happily regaled me with her story of being painted by Balthus. Her "Dr. Jekyll and Mr. Hyde" take on the artist has been borne out time and again.

Mrs. Allen's husband at that time was Paul Cooley, assistant to A. Everett Austin, Jr.—the pioneering director of the Wadsworth Atheneum in Hartford, Connecticut. Both Austin and James Thrall Soby—a sort of adjunct curator to the Atheneum, and the first American to collect Balthus's work—were very keen on the young painter. Cooley caught the bug, and had the idea that his new bride should have her portrait done by Balthus on their honeymoon in Paris. The rich young couple had made arrangements for Pierre Matisse to introduce them to the twenty-nine-year-old painter. But once they got to Paris, Matisse disappointed the newlyweds with word that Balthus was tired of doing portraits. The artist no longer needed to take commissions.

Matisse warned the Cooleys that, although they might meet Balthus, they were never to utter the word "portrait": it would enrage him. So, halfway into a four-month honeymoon, they met Balthus with the understanding that the introduction was being made simply because they were interested in his art.

Within minutes of their meeting, however, Balthus told Jane Cooley that she reminded him of his English mistress—and that he would like to paint her portrait. He also said that he loved the suit she was wearing, and that she should be painted in it. At the time, Jane was a beauty of the Hedy Lamarr type as well as quite a stylish dresser, so the response may not have been a total surprise. She and her husband, having by then rearranged their original travel plans thinking that the portrait was off, now jumped at the chance to change everything again to accommodate the proposal. Within a day or two, she began to sit for Balthus.

Jane Cooley posed willingly for the portrait, but the experience was sheer torture. The young bride found the sittings painful and uncomfortable, and Balthus "cruel" and "horrible" to her. Every day for an entire week, she had to position herself at the very edge of a table, and she was miserable.

"Sadistic and tyrannical" from his subject's point of view, Balthus insisted that she not alter the angle of her back by so much as half an inch, even though the ache was excruciating. She argued politely, and then declared her agony, but he was brutal with her about her need to hold the pose exactly.

Finally she could bear the ordeal no longer. Having wanted nothing more than to have her portrait painted by Balthus, she now told the artist that he was being wretched. He had to understand that she was about six weeks pregnant, which was one of the reasons she was so extremely uncomfortable. She had initially been afraid to reveal this fact for fear Balthus would find her undesirable and stop the portrait, but now she was too desperate to continue concealing it.

Balthus warmed up the moment she confronted him and gave the reason for her pain. Expecting to be rebuffed, Jane Cooley was astonished when the

Portrait of Jane Cooley, 1937, oil on canvas, 92 x 65 cm

artist instantly became as considerate and obliging as possible. From that point on, he treated her totally differently; he seemed thrilled by her news, and became gentle and solicitous. Now he frequently brought her water and urged her to rest whenever she wanted. The portrait was finished in the opposite mood from that in which it was started. Balthus's solicitude and courtliness often equal his power to deceive and torment. The only consistency is that he is always the person in charge.

The portrait—which I often saw at the house of Jane Cooley's daughter—is painted somewhat in the manner of André Derain's work of that same period. It presents interior space as a thrilling sequence of planes and imbues its female subject with a haunting, arresting force. Full of erotic tension thanks to the way Balthus positioned Mrs. Cooley's buttocks against the sharp corner of a wooden table, it gives this tweedy lady unexpected spice. Moreover, her image and surroundings are painted with the grip and flare of Balthus at his finest.

Jane Cooley did not like it, however. It was unflattering, and she looked old. She and her husband kept it in a closet back in West Hartford.

When the Cooleys divorced about fifteen years later, Paul kept most of the artworks, and Jane was happy to have him take it. After another decade had passed, though, she realized the importance of this particular picture and asked for it back. She told me that she was amazed by what she found. Oddly enough, the portrait Balthus had done of her when she was in her twenties looked very much the way she began to appear a quarter century after he had painted it. This astonished people—that the painting of Jane as a young bride so accurately resembled her as a middle-aged woman.

It seems that he could merge ages in a single portrait, just as he could reveal virtually opposite sides of his personality in the process of painting it. There is no barrier between youth and age, and the unexpected can be counted on to happen.

Balthus, meanwhile, was glad to have news of Mrs. Cooley when, over fifty years after that meeting, I told him I knew her. But what surprised me, given her report that he had insisted she dress for the portrait as she had for their initial meeting, was that his sole comment to me about Jane Cooley was that "she wore a frightfully bourgeois outfit." He told me he had never found her looks particularly interesting, and seemed to derive a certain satisfaction in learning that, while remaining handsome, she had become quite weather-beaten and matronly with age: engaging and fun but, for some of us in that American outpost, distinguished above all by her having been the woman who posed for Balthus.

·   ·   ·

BALTHUS HAS CREATED HIMSELF in the mode of his heroes. Obsessed, he has imitated their artistic style, restated their subject matter, and even fashioned his own appearance in an effort to become the people he has wanted to be.

In the 1930s his idol was Antonin Artaud; by the 1950s it had become Lord Byron. To varying degrees, he tried to transform himself into each of them. But although as a painter he has borrowed heavily from Poussin, Hogarth, Seurat, and others, his foremost artistic mentor has consistently been Piero della Francesca. When he was eighteen years old, Balthus spent most of a summer copying Piero's art in Italy, and he has revered it ever since. Its textures and tones and attitudes have permeated his own work. So have the precise characters; the profiles of certain of Piero's biblical personages have reappeared, transformed, on many of Balthus's little boys and girls allegedly plucked from contemporary Paris. No wonder, then, that Balthus often claimed to me that he wanted the ignorance surrounding Piero's personal history to apply to him as well.

Piero is someone about whose life virtually nothing is known; his date of birth can be no further pinpointed than within a ten-year span. There is practically no information about his heritage or early upbringing. Balthus told me he wished the same were true of him. He wanted "no biographical details. Even to correct is not necessary. Biography of people like Gauguin and van Gogh has pushed people to conclusions that are wrong. I'm always enchanted that one doesn't know anything about Piero della Francesca, for example. One doesn't even know when he was born."[7] Factual information simply distracts from the real issues of painting.

Such lack of information about the creator forces people to concentrate on the art, Balthus rightly pointed out. Anonymous art—Hellenistic bronzes, Romanesque portals—is no less powerful because its makers are unknown to us. On the contrary, the absence of facts often intensifies its impact. Encounters with paintings, he said, are visual experiences—not literary, historical, or psychological undertakings. Like most true painters, Balthus deplores the practices of art history and modern museology—the wall texts and earphones that overload people with irrelevancies about the artists' grandparents or the commerce of their hometowns. He loathes interpretation and extrapolation when they supplant the power of simple, immediate responses.

That is how the artist would have us approach his work, and it is a pure and appealing idea. One is tempted to leave Balthus's life alone, and simply to follow his counsel that all that matters is the artist's point of view as he expresses it. On the other hand, Balthus has managed to leak out just enough material—his noble title; the amazing chalet and his Italian castle, both of which he has permitted to be shown in glossy magazines—to make us eager to know more. While saying habitually that he does not grant interviews, he has, over the years, given many. As long as he was the one controlling the presentation of his past and the consequent interpretations of his art, he readily violated his own rules.

In the modern era, the lack of information that is the luxury of Piero or the sculptors at Vézelay is no longer a reality. And Balthus's paintings are provocative; they invite curiosity. Why is that music teacher pressing so hard into her pupil's upper thighs just below the girl's naked genitals? Why does the child look ecstatic in her torture? One cannot help wondering about the creator of this art—who has made himself all the more intriguing by his deliberate elusiveness.

CHAPTER TWO

MITSOU

Don't ask me to explain too much! "The only valid thing in art
is that which cannot be explained," I once wrote. I still feel this
very strongly. To explain away the mystery of a great
painting—if such a feat were possible—would do irreparable
harm, for whenever you explain or define something you
substitute the explanation or the definition for the real thing. . . .
Believe me, there are certain mysteries, certain secrets in my
work which even I don't understand nor do I try to do so. . . .
Mysteries have to be respected if they are to retain their power.
Art disturbs: science reassures.

—GEORGES BRAQUE[1]

I

THE LETTER ADDRESSED Rainer Maria Rilke as "Madame" and remained
unsigned. But these mistakes did not keep Rilke from finding its contents
"entirely charming."

What mattered to Rilke was that the author of the letter, Pierre Bonnard,
was "full of praise for my dear collaborator," the fourteen-year-old Balthus. So
wrote Rilke to Balthus's mother, Elizabeth Dorothée Klossowski—"Baladine"
to those who knew her paintings; "Merline" or "Mouky" to Rilke alone,
depending on whether he and she were in their French mode or their German
one. For the previous two years, Baladine had been the object of Rilke's passionate devotion, but also the source of agonizing conflict; Rilke insisted on
isolation for his work, compelling them to live separately.

Early adolescence is the period of life on which Balthus would dwell forever after. The leitmotif of his art has been children—mostly girls—just at the
onset of puberty, full of anticipation and uncertainty. His artistic approach,
like his subject matter, would also have the primary characteristics of that time
of latency. Emotions are intense without being clear. Like the nubile girls he
repeatedly chose to portray, Balthus as a painter appears possessed by overwhelming yet dormant yearnings. The ardor is palpable, but its sources disguised, perhaps even to its bearer.

Balthus, about
twelve years
old

It is no wonder that the ages of eleven through thirteen would hold a life-long grip on Balthus. His mother and Rilke's affair, his own connection with the magical poet, the love and endorsement that Rilke heaped on him, and the burgeoning of his prodigious talents made Balthus's experience of that time in childhood extraordinary—as unlike the norm as the rest of his life would be. And the rude shock of reality that hit when he turned fourteen, the pains inflicted by historical and economic truth, gave him further reason to turn back to the blissful years preceding—and escape into fantasy forever after.

Bonnard's letter had arrived on a glorious December day in the Valais, at the thirteenth-century château that Rilke and Baladine had discovered together the previous summer and that she had made habitable for him. The year was 1922, and Baladine and Balthus and his older brother, Pierre, were by now living in Berlin. Rilke had begun his letter to her with the wish that he could slide a little bit of the Swiss sunlight into the envelope. What he could fit in was a tidier version of Bonnard's letter that he copied over for the boy, since he felt that the original was not sufficiently legible.

Rilke and Balthus had recently published a book together. Balthus had drawn its forty illustrations, and Rilke had written the preface—his first work in French after decades of composing in German. Balthus had made the drawings two years earlier; they narrated, wordlessly, the tale of a child and a stray Angora cat. It was based on events that had occurred on an outing to the château at Nyon, at a time when Rilke was with Balthus and his mother.[2] The eleven-year-old boy had found and loved a cat that then ran away. The cat had become part of his everyday life: alongside him in bed, on the dining room table, with the rest of the family staring at the candles on their Christmas tree. The final image, of the little boy crying, wiping away his tears with his hands, was a vivid self-portrait. The young artist showed himself grieving and vulnerable, at a loss for action. It was both the first and the last time he would let the world see him quite so helpless.

BALTHUS'S DRAWINGS FOR *Mitsou* are animated with the fervor of an intense child eager to tell his tale. They are also extraordinarily articulate for the work of someone so young. The pen strokes are bold and decisive, the imagery and atmosphere clear. The opening drawing, in which the boy finds the cat on a park bench, conveys the excitement and terror of human discovery. The flurry of thick and thin brushstrokes charges the atmosphere. In a single dash Balthus has contorted the boy's mouth. Thick, raised eyebrows and a sharply angled cheekbone heighten the look of amazement. The boy leans toward the animal. He points eagerly with one arm, while pushing the other into his pocket to gain composure. By contrast, the cat faces forward, frontal and symmetrical, frozen like a statue, visibly unperturbed. Three short strokes give it a bland expression. The young artist has used the black ink and blank paper to show the animal squarely in the sunlight, accentuating the ability of cats to make themselves comfortable and assume center stage. The sphinxlike creature appears stolid and regal while adorable, detached, and in total command of itself.

Balthus has put this action in a charming setting. Vines meander up a wall behind the bench. The boy and cat are in a courtyard, separated by a gate and stone wall from small-scaled buildings and a tree in full bloom. Like the cut of the little boy's jacket, the scene is worldly, and refined.

In the following image, the little boy has picked up the cat; now he is the one in charge, smiling and standing erect as he firmly holds the limp creature. He presents the animal to two ladies—presumably one is his mother, the other a governess or relative or friend; next to them and a man we assume to be his father, the boy holds the animal tenderly on board a ferryboat on Lake Geneva.

From *Mitsou*, 1922

He plays with it at home: on the handsome checkerboard floor of the entrance hall and in rooms with attractive country furniture and gaily patterned wallpaper. The cat has a nice life: playing with a ball, knocking over a pitcher, looking for mice, putting himself at ease where he does not belong, sprawling on pillows.

Oddly, the boy ties the cat to a leash to walk it in the garden. This is the sort of image that will appear in the artist's mature work—it is remarkably like a sketch that Balthus, now an urbane Parisian, penned almost thirty years later on a placemat at the Catalan Restaurant. In that later drawing, a large creature who is half horse and half man straddles a miserable rocking dog—a toy but very much alive—with a little boy's face. The poor creature underneath, who looks as if his back is about to be broken, is harnessed through his mouth, and the horse-man holds the reins—in reversal of a horse's usual situation. Balthus has always claimed to have very little understanding of this sort of imagery—whether it is the constrained cat in *Mitsou* or this pathetic creature serving his master on the Catalan paper tablecloth. But as the cat lunges toward a bird under a large flowering plant, the boy restrains it with the leash. He wants control, and uses this unusual means to achieve it.

Similarly, in about 1922, shortly after he created *Mitsou,* Balthus made an extraordinary drawing of a man walking with a child on a leash. The man carries a butterfly net. The subject is capture—be it with that net or with the dreadful connector attached to the child's collar. It is capture that eludes the child in *Mitsou.* As a mature artist, he would gain the power to hold others captive. His quarry, of course, would consist mainly of beautiful women; he would evoke them as he wanted them—frozen in space, naked, without pubic hair, seductive, immobilized for the savoring. And he would have his way with his public as well. Meanwhile, as the little boy in *Mitsou,* Balthus knows that cats sometimes flee; they are agents of their own will. The former stray plays with a ball and mauls a bird. It assumes regal poses in prime locations all over the house—on tabletops covered with breakable objects, and on an ottoman in Balthus's father's studio where, as if perched on a throne, it poses for a portrait. Then the cat disappears, only to be found on a patch of grass outside.

But just when everything seems to be going well again, the boy appears to have a premonition of further trouble. Following the ultimate moment of well-being in front of the Christmas tree—Balthus's mother's arm around him, the cat at his side, the other woman and the father figure nearby—the cat is gone. The anguished boy searches underneath the bed—and then, with a candle, in the basement and outside. The final image is a drawing of the boy wiping the tears from his eyes.

*Drawing on
Catalan Placemat,*
October 19, 1949,
ink, 37.5 x 32.5 cm

Untitled, c. 1922,
ink, 21.5 x 16 cm

The sequence of events and the shifts in mood are all conveyed with few lines, but they are told very clearly. Balthus uses gesture and pose astutely. At one moment the cat is rigid as bronze; elsewhere it is flaccid. At other times it is poised in action. In the way they stand or sit, people appear anxious, amused, relaxed, astonished. The mother points her finger with authentic parental authority; the little boy squats and leans with a child's particular nonchalance. This eye for the way people look, and the degree to which physical and psychological attitude coalesce, would remain a major factor in Balthus's art.

Details establish the cast of characters. The women, with their hats and handbags, have all the appurtenances of pleasant bourgeois ladies. The child in his handsome clothing is well cared for. And the success with which Balthus has rendered the settings makes the story plausible. The recesses under beds and tables have depth; the wallpapers and floorboards are real. The outdoor passageways have a direction.

Telling as the drawings are, they never look labored. They are fresh and breezy. No wonder Rilke and Bonnard were both enchanted. The young boy's art had an aliveness and clarity they sought in their own work. Balthus's style may have a slightly naïve, folk-art quality, but he achieved a reality of appearances. In territory familiar to Bonnard and Rilke—a European milieu in which daily living was uniquely cultivated—Balthus, too, responded intensely to the drama, internal and external, of everyday events. The eleven-year-old draftsman caught the interplay of sunlight and darkness, the mingling of excitement and grief.

THE EVENTS OCCURRED, and he drew them. Discussing *Mitsou* with me over seventy years after he made it, Balthus told me, repeatedly, that he had no idea why he has been attracted to certain subject matter; nor is it important. The only significant issue is how successful he is at capturing nature and making worthwhile artwork.

"I don't see what one can say about my paintings," he was quoted as saying in 1967 in the glossy French magazine *Réalités*—after his customary disclaimers about how he never grants interviews. "After all, if they are good, they should say whatever it is for themselves. It's very exceptional that writers on art actually help one to see. And poets—Baudelaire apart—are particularly dangerous; they tend to use others' works to talk about their own. . . . The trouble is that people have become so much more interested in the artist's 'personality' than in his work. What can it matter what Picasso eats?"[3]

"I have absolutely no idea why I paint or what I paint. I am not the symbol of my generation, or of any generation. I do not paint to interpret or transmit messages; I simply paint. I do not want to be a voice. My subjects do not speak. I do not wish to discuss the human condition in my art at all."[4] So Balthus declared in a 1983 interview in *Connoisseur*.

"It's difficult and boring to talk about my paintings. They're just what they are," he said to me one sunny morning, with a world-weary look on his face and a slight nod.

It is, of course, hard to believe that Balthus's lifelong obsession with the imagery of naked young women really just comes from outside of him—and that there is no meaning to his leashed cats or to any other of the themes of *Mitsou*.

Yet Balthus was most vehement in our conversations, day in and day out. "They're always trying to see something erotic in my painting, which I never understood." He reiterated the same complaint to me on countless occasions, with an absolutely pitiable look on his face.[5]

Balthus ridiculed what he gathered were rumors that he had a thing for little girls. He seemed puzzled that anyone could suggest that some of his figures were somnambulists, or that the characters he conceived of as ordinary little girls might be mistaken for dwarfs. Ever since the time of that early book of drawings with which he made his artistic start, he maintained, his imagery was simple and straightforward.

"People have a very strange conception of me. I don't see what they mean; people see all sorts of things for which you can't be responsible. They like to be disturbed by something."[6] He implicitly credited me with the intelligence to go beyond such self-involvement and misperception.

WHEN I REFERRED TO John Russell's theory that *The Passage du Commerce Saint-André*—a major canvas of 1952–54—represents the "three ages of man," Balthus said this typified the gratuitous interpretation inflicted by writers on art. "I wonder if people aren't too much full of literature. What I tried to do is something rather Mozartian—the familiarity of daily life. The old man, I think, was Armenian, whom I passed every day to get my baguette. The old woman was one of those older women you see everywhere in Paris. A concierge probably."[7] The seemingly hairless child at the far left, holding up a sort of toga, is, Balthus explained to me, "a little girl who was disguising herself." Her virtual twin, of whom nothing can be seen but a head in a nearby window— which various viewers have assumed to be a wig stand (a complete mistake in Balthus's eyes)—is simply another child. That apparent wig stand was, Balthus told me, a straightforward rendition of a boy's head. When I politely remarked that this head appears to hang over a windowsill, completely disconnected from a neck, and is oddly bald, the artist just shrugged his shoulders like a child who simply will not discuss something.

"What I above all saw were the colors—the color of the Armenian restaurant. I tried to use very few colors and to mix them through glazing. A glazure is a technique—a technical word in painting—you see colors and then mix them," Balthus announced perfunctorily, referring to his method of coating certain hues with transparent or semitransparent paints to modify their effects, and dismissing any more grandiose iconographic scheme as folderol.

Balthus seemed versed in all the errors that had been propagated. He told me that critics have made much of the site being around the corner from the residence of Dr. Guillotine and the location where his famous decapitation device was first tried out, on a lamb, in 1792; Jean Clair has written that the white dog clearly refers to that earlier victim. "I didn't have this in mind. I just saw a dog there once, smelling on some interesting places, smelling everywhere. In the same way, one American lecturer couldn't understand why there was a coat with a sleeve in the second-story window. These intellectuals who never look where they are, what is to be seen on a street."

The Passage du Commerce Saint-André, 1952–54, oil on canvas, 294 x 230 cm

Balthus knew this location only as a corner of the neighborhood in which he lived—and had not even been aware of the local history when he painted the canvas.

Nonetheless, I asked if the man carrying a baguette, walking away with his back to us, was a self-portrait. "Is it or isn't it? I don't know," Balthus replied. Like the figure in *The Passage,* Balthus would rather retreat than come nearer; he would deliberately shield his face. But when I then commented on the remarkable light and shadow perfectly circling the crusty baguette, Balthus was unequivocal: "That's the most important thing."

IN ONE OF OUR CONVERSATIONS about interpretation and what people see in his work, I told Balthus the remark of one New York collector that her Balthus canvas shows a woman having an orgasm. He instantly replied that her observation pertains only to the nature of her own orgasms; sex applied neither to Balthus's intentions with regard to his model's pose nor to the expression on her face.

But how typical that a rich American would get his art all wrong, he said, laughing. Balthus could hardly wait to have me tell the tale to each of the many visitors who came to Le Grand Chalet. It amused him both because it reflects the typical misinterpretation of paintings and because it suggested to him "that on Park Avenue women laugh when they are coming."[8]

Balthus allowed, however, that he had an underlying goal behind the woman's pose in this painting. It was to suggest "a general awakening." "The whole idea of awakening—becoming aware of things"—was also his primary desire in *The Room* (1952–54) (color plate 1).[9]

The Room is one of his most provocative and successful paintings; many of Balthus's later figure paintings are derivations of it. In *The Room*, a sprawling naked female has suddenly had sunlight thrown on her by a bizarre figure (a dwarf? an aged child? Alice in Wonderland?—it depends on the critic writing) pulling back a drapery. Since the first showing of this painting, pundits have been writing about what the scene represents. Balthus calmly insisted to me that, except for that very general concept of awakening, there is no significance to the subject beyond what you see. This woman whom others have deemed either dead or unconscious, victimized or sexually satiated, was, according to the man who painted her, "just a nude." The golemlike creature—to many of us a nasty, androgynous gnome—was "an ordinary little girl." Her function is simply to let in light by holding back the drapery.

As we looked together at *The Room* in a large color reproduction, the artist made me feel that there was no question that the painting was nothing more than he said. Seated next to me on the sofa, his dark eyes large and penetrating, his skin taut, his neat strands of white hair combed back impeccably, the lean and compact artist gave the impression that his mind was as precise and gritty as his appearance and language. There was no fluff or embellishment. Thus I prepared to become his coconspirator.

On such occasions in Rossinière, Balthus made me feel as if there was no chance that I would be such a fool as to see things any differently from the way he discussed them. He was counting on me to help him in getting others to realize that in his work from *Mitsou* to his most recent oils, the imagery was more straightforward and less significant than others perceived. Clearly I was too intelligent to need what he called the "walking sticks" required by most art historians; I would take his gospel at face value. Indeed, with the painter at my side, I momentarily believed that this was just an ordinary child pulling back the drapery in *The Room*—and the nude merely a contented woman in the sunlight.

The Room IS RARELY SEEN in public anymore. It is large and fragile, and its owners are loath to lend it, so most people know it only through reproductions. But because Balthus apparently gave the word that I was to be treated as part of the inner sanctum, I was subsequently allowed in to the unimaginably grand Roman flat of Gianni Agnelli, where the painting is installed in the entrance hall.

Standing before the actual, enormous canvas (some nine by eleven feet), I was overwhelmed by the texture, the modeling of the forms, and the stupendous mixture of stasis and movement. But I also came to see the "child" as a demonic amalgam of little girl and old man. Moreover, by the time I made that trip to Rome, some two years after the artist and I discussed the work in reproduction, I viewed Balthus himself as being that same combination. The naked woman struck me as a powerhouse who had been subjugated, even bludgeoned—which, I now believed, was how Balthus fantasized his ladies. The watchful cat seemed the ultimate observer: seeing all without giving away any of his own sinister secrets. He, too, represented the man who had painted him.

SHORTLY AFTER OUR CONVERSATION that had meandered from *Mitsou* to *The Room,* I asked Balthus about *The Balthus Poems,* a 1982 book by the poet and mystery writer Stephen Dobyns. I wondered what he thought of Dobyns's ideas about *Japanese at a Black Mirror,* a canvas the artist worked on between 1967 and 1976 (see page 547). Balthus quickly told me that he was unfamiliar with Dobyns's book, and neither had nor wanted it. So I explained to him that the poem about the painting suggests that the woman facing a mirror in it is anticipating her own impending death.

Balthus was startled. "The mirror is just a mirror. It's absolutely not symbolic. The picture problems of the painting are what mattered. The meaning of the painting is the painting. I was interested in getting that black."[10] The canvas took him almost ten years entirely because he wished to resolve issues like the pull of the material around the girl's waist and the tone of the lacquered chest. If people see allegory or symbolism in his paintings, Balthus could bear no responsibility for their foolishness.

Balthus told me that he regarded his task in *Japanese at a Black Mirror* as a transformation from ukiyo-e—the Japanese woodblock prints that have been extremely popular in France since the time of Impressionism. He had simply reworked the pose from the traditional one in which the woman sits upright with her knees folded underneath her.

Balthus volunteered this idea to me enthusiastically. Yet he used to insist precisely the opposite, that the influence of Oriental art was *not* significant. In 1977 Thomas B. Hess—one of the few art writers Balthus told me he personally liked and had been willing to talk to in the past—wrote of this same nude, "The impact of Japanese art [he made a journey to the islands] is apparent, even though Balthus himself, characteristically, denies it."[11]

"Everyone has been influenced by something," he declared with annoyance. "One painter painted with a brush, and so did another; so there's an influence!"

Balthus wanted to be as hard to pinpoint as his beloved Mitsou. "My point of view is extremely vague," Balthus explained with evident pleasure, his head thrown back as he blew thick rings of cigarette smoke into the air. "Je change les chemins tous les jours. What I don't like is to nail down a conception."

THE PROBLEM TODAY, Balthus complained, was that people no longer know how to react to paintings. He said that Delacroix, whose art and journals he adored, diagnosed this syndrome as a result of *"l'oeil devenu inert."* The situation had worsened since Delacroix's day. Balthus surmised that in recent years "people have stopped seeing as astutely as they once did because they are perpetually assaulted visually by television and film and computer screens; the human eye may have been weakened organically."

THAT CRITICS HAVE ALLUDED to *Lolita* in reference to his work, and portrayed him as a sort of Humbert Humbert, struck him as "stupid" and "grotesque." The use of his 1937 *Girl with a Cat* on the widely distributed Penguin paperback of *Lolita* was anathema to him. Balthus maintained that there is not a hint of lasciviousness in this portrait he made of a girl Lolita's age—in which the viewer is at eye level with the child's crotch, which is also the painter's vantage point. If we see sexuality in this rendition of a pensive child, it is our problem. Of the way that the child flashes her bare thighs at an alluring angle and flaunts her underwear-covered labia, he blithely commented, "That's how little girls sit."

Balthus's attitude is very much the same as that of the mute yet insolent creatures who have consistently populated his art, and as that of his mentor Rilke. The poet, apropos of his masterpiece the *Duino Elegies,* issued the state-

Cover of
Penguin
paperback
of *Lolita*

ment: "And am I the one who might provide a correct interpretation of the ele-gies? They extend infinitely beyond me."[12] Of his *Sonnets to Orpheus* he declared, "Where obscurity remains, it is of the sort that requires submission, not clarification." Rilke and Balthus were aligned in their view that they were not so much the creator as the vehicle by which forces beyond them were transmitted to the earth.

Balthus has chosen to return time and again to little girls as his subject, he told me, because they were a familiar, everyday sight to both him and his view-ers, "a universal theme." Additionally, "they often dress in interesting ways." These were the reasons for what others have regarded as his obsession: nothing more.

If Jane Cooley had initially bored him because her garb was "too modish," Balthus pointed out that little girls, by contrast, wear dresses that tend to be less trendy and more suitable. Their outfits reflect more innate style than do the contrived fashions of grown women. But his attraction to little girls was no deeper than that. "If their knickers show," he said again, "it is because little girls often sit in a position in which their knickers show"—not because he was lusting for them or wanted his viewers to.

PEOPLE FOREVER LOOK FOR A SCANDAL that is not there, and so they exaggerate the facts, Balthus insisted every time we talked. To make a big deal out of his lifelong preoccupation with little girls was as nonsensical as all the fuss about his being married to a relatively young wife. Balthus amplified. Writers have stretched the age difference between him and Setsuko well beyond the thirty-four years that is all it really is, he said. The artist was fifty-four and Setsuko twenty when they met, but to make the most of his involvement with adolescent girls, a number of journalists claimed he had married a teenager.

At that moment Balthus assumed his most Voltairean smile. He was particularly "amused"—whenever he used this word, it seemed to suggest the most exalted of mental states—by the version of his marriage that appeared in a Roman newspaper after he was presented with the Via Condotti prize. He generally turned down public accolades, but had treated this one differently since several heads of state, the King of Spain, and Federico Fellini had been awarded it in the past. Prime Minister Andreotti was presenting it personally.

But at the actual ceremony Balthus downplayed the acclaim by sending his and Setsuko's daughter Harumi, then twelve years old, to the podium to accept the award. It was fun for her, and got him off the hook from doing something he detested. The next day the newspapers showed a photograph of the girl delivering the prize to her father. The caption read, "Balthus and his young Japanese wife." Recounting this, Balthus threw back his head in laughter.

And then he grew rather serious. The error should not be seen as an innocent mistake. It was inspired by the human craving for gossip, the same unattractive motive that makes people act as if he has a thing for young girls.

II

"THERE IS, AFTER ALL, in the subject matter of Balthus's paintings something that goes beyond mere conviction. The subject matter in emotional terms is manifestly a matter of life and death to him,"[13] John Russell wrote at the time of Balthus's Metropolitan Museum retrospective in 1984, sixteen years after he had put forward his "three ages of man" idea.

Russell knew Balthus well enough to recognize how deliberately the artist might lead us in a direction of his own choosing. Russell told me that when he mounted a Balthus retrospective at the Tate Gallery in 1968, the largest show to date in Europe, Balthus had responded to a draft of Russell's catalog essay by drawing large X's through much of it, threatening to cancel the exhibition if the offending passages—too biographical—were not deleted. The artist did not bother to attend the opening or see the show at any point.

Another seasoned art viewer who paid no heed to Balthus's dictums and declared the imagery pivotal was Kenneth Clark. In the *New York Review of Books* in 1980, Lord Clark described Balthus as "one considerable artist who never disguised the importance that he attached to his subjects."[14]

Mitsou supports John Russell's and Kenneth Clark's views, however much those opinions contradict the artist's own declarations. The coming and going of the cat are paramount issues. Balthus started out—by instinct as a child—using art in its narrative form. Beyond being forty excellent drawings, *Mitsou* is potent visual literature.

Indeed, Balthus's achievement depends essentially on his technical virtuosity and the unique look of his paintings, and he was probably telling the truth when he insisted that his conscious decisions in planning his pictures concerned issues of rhythm, balance, surface, and the quality of light. But it is the psychological portent that ultimately gives the work its grip. Hence it was with *Mitsou,* so much so that Rainer Maria Rilke was moved to extrapolate in depth on its theme and implications.

Even at age eleven, Balthus knew a great deal about human needs and anxieties. The fate of his superlatively well-drawn cat echoes, in exaggerated form, the plight of human beings. *Mitsou* touches movingly on the issue of separation in its largest sense—on what it means to go from being protected and feeling safe to fleeing the nest and facing the world on one's own. Its young artist—whether or not he was conscious of any ambition beyond drawing lively pictures of actual events—made a powerful evocation both of childhood and of the loneliness and independence that mark its end.

Balthus knew what he had won at the age of thirteen with *Mitsou,* and he can hardly be unaware of the contribution of its human topics to his acclaim. Whatever bewilderment he feigned in our conversations at the notion that his imagery was provocative, he probably cultivated it, assiduously, with an eye for attention. There were also some compelling issues in his life that have inevitably inspired him to paint what he has painted.

HOW SPECIFIC THE SCENES in *Mitsou* were to Balthus's own childhood is an open question. Balthus made a point with me of disputing the claims of the art historian Sabine Rewald that he altered reality in those drawings. More resolute than insistent, he maintained that the matter was beyond question—that he set the action in locations true to the scenes of his actual childhood.

Rewald wrote the catalog for Balthus's Metropolitan Museum exhibition —a book the artist told me is rife with inaccuracies. With regard to *Mitsou,* Rewald says that Balthus "took some liberties" in putting himself in a "large country house, complete with servants and garden."[15] Balthus told me that the house in the book is, down to every last article of furniture, his father's home near Geneva. "It was the reality, exactly," the artist assured me with just a hint of irritation that anyone could question it. "My father had the house near Geneva, which was exactly like the house in the book." He resented the suggestion that he might have exaggerated its scale or comforts. For nothing should alter his preferred way of looking back: "My childhood was wonderful. I had a wonderful childhood."

Yet there can be no question that the eleven-year-old artist did, at the very least, carefully select the points of emphasis in his tale. For one thing, he left out his brother and is the sole child in the family. He also added a second woman the age of his mother—although her identity is not clear. If she is supposed to be a nanny—which is what she looks like—then she is there out of nostalgia more than in actuality; by the time the Klossowskis had moved to Switzerland, having been forced as German citizens to give up their Parisian life and most of their possessions shortly after the outbreak of World War I (much as Rilke had), they could no longer afford staff. On the other hand, this other woman might represent Baladine's sister, who lived nearby.

In any case, the existence in *Mitsou* of more than one father figure—the man in town, the man on the boat, and the man at home are not the same—corresponds to the truth. Balthus's parents were still married, his father periodically on the scene, but by the time he was eleven, Balthus, and fourteen-year-old Pierre, often saw more of Rainer Maria Rilke than of Erich Klossowski. Rilke was the focus of his mother's life.

III

In her person Baladine is provocative. Once you notice certain movements her large body can make, you're no longer able to take your eyes off it. A fairly accurate qualifier would be "female bird." Long legs very pleasant to look at, arched feet, hips and bust present, but a gentle figure. . . . The broad, charming face

Balthus and his brother, Pierre, c. 1913

*of a cat, thin lips rouged, eyes ash-gray. As for her hair, it is
provocative too, rather dark, sensual.*
                                    —PIERRE JEAN JOUVE, *The Desert World*[16]

RAINER MARIA RILKE had first met Erich and Baladine Klossowski in Paris
in 1907, the year before Balthus was born. Rilke was then thirty-two years old,
Erich thirty-three, Baladine twenty-one. Erich painted bold and brushy oils,
many of which were historical pastiches; Baladine made gentle drawings and
watercolors. Erich had recently written, in German, a book on the painters of
Montmartre, among them Toulouse-Lautrec and Steinlen; he was currently at
work on a book about Daumier.

A mutual friend, Ellen Key, took Rilke to the Klossowskis' house for dinner. Key was a Swedish psychologist, the author of *The Century of the Child,*
which Rilke had reviewed enthusiastically. She was known for her progressive

thinking on child rearing; Rilke had often confided to her about the misery of his own early years.

He was interested to meet a young and lively couple whose lives were devoted to art and art history. As a young man in Prague, he had written the play *Murillo;* in 1897 he had penned *On Art* in response to Tolstoy's recent *What Is Art?* In the following year he had supported himself in Berlin by doing newspaper reviews of art exhibitions, and more recently he had worked as secretary to the sculptor Auguste Rodin and begun to write extensively on Cézanne.

Shortly after Rilke's evening at their home, Erich and Baladine visited the poet in his apartment on the Rue Cassette. On that occasion Rilke stood at his writing desk and read out loud to them from his *Livre d'heures.* Several years later, Baladine and Rilke ran into one another on the Boulevard Raspail. She told him that they had two "ravishing" young sons, and invited him to call on the family in their new apartment in Saint-Germain.

Rilke and Baladine did not see one another again until 1919. In Switzerland to do a reading, impatient with a crowded household in which he was staying in Nyon, the poet had indulged his fondness for grand hotels by booking into the Richmond in Geneva. Nostalgic for prewar Paris, he looked up the tall, dark Madame Klossowska shortly after arriving there.

As German citizens, Erich Klossowski's family had been forced out of Paris during World War I. They had been sharing their apartment on the Rue Boissonade with Baladine's brother, the portraitist Eugen Spiro, who had been a member of the Berlin Secession group of modern painters; Spiro had moved back to Berlin, and the Klossowskis had followed him there. For a while Erich and Baladine and their two young sons lived in Spiro's flat, but once Erich began working as a designer for the theater, they took a place of their own. Then, in 1917, the Klossowskis separated. Baladine took the boys to Switzerland, living for most of that year in Bern, and at the end of 1917 she moved to Geneva. She had found a modest flat in a comfortable bourgeois neighborhood at 11, Rue Pré-Jérôme, a pleasant street of five-story buildings, all rough stone at ground level and plaster above. It was in this solid and orderly space with big windows that Baladine and fifteen-year-old Pierre and eleven-year-old Balthus were living when she became involved with Rilke.

A schoolmate of Balthus's at the lycée describes Baladine

as a fascinating woman with heavy expressive eyes set in the middle of a face framed by a mass of black hair. Her rapid movements were accompanied by a deep, warm voice and a captivating Slav accent. This mother is very present in her sons' life.[17]

Erich Klossowski, *Still Life with Fruit*, c. 1930, oil on canvas

Eugen Spiro, *Portrait of Erich Klossowski*, c. 1900, oil on canvas

Baladine Klossowska, *Balthus*, 1924, oil on canvas

Baladine Klossowska in 1906

When Rilke had started out on the journey to Switzerland, this striking Madame Klossowska, eleven years younger than he, was the first name in his address book. Having intended to spend five days in his luxurious hotel room on Lac Leman, Rilke stayed for fifteen.

Rilke and Baladine were both refugees yearning for Paris. For neither of them was the French capital their birthplace or where their ancestors came from, but they deemed it the center of civilization and their chosen home. They spoke French to one another and used French nicknames: Rilke became René again, and Baladine was now Merline. Their relationship quickly consumed them.

Rilke generally lived apart from his mistresses and maintained his solitude, but he found it harder to detach himself from Merline. Later in 1919, when he announced his intention to go into retreat at Schloss Berg am Irchel near Zurich, which Richard and Lily Ziegler had offered him for the winter, he acceded to Merline's pleas instead and abandoned the plan to remain in Geneva. Together the lovers went to Sierre—where Erich Klossowski, who was living in Zurich at the time, was staying with his friends Jean and Frieda Strohl. The lot of them got along famously as they traveled around the Valais together. (The visits of Balthus's ex-wife to his new household in Rossinière repeat a pattern of his childhood in both their form and their felicitousness.)

Rilke was perpetually torn between working unaccompanied at Berg or being with Merline in Geneva. On one occasion when he had managed to isolate himself, his mistress developed severe lumbago; he rushed to her, and arranged for his patron Georg Reinhart to lend her money so that she could then come to him in Berg.

Living alone with his mother and brother in their small apartment—first as a student at the International School and then at the Lycée Calvin—Balthus must have been constantly alert both to the rapture Baladine would feel after the arrival of a bunch of pansies from her lover and to her periodic despair at Rilke's insistence on their remaining apart. This intertwining of ecstasy and torment would permeate Balthus's art forever after.

DURING THEIR TUMULTUOUS separations, René and Merline wrote to one another as often as three times a day, with missives that could run fourteen pages and take up to six hours to write. Over six hundred pages of this correspondence are in print, as are numerous letters in which Rilke wrote to many of his acquaintances about Madame Klossowska and her sons. "Appear to me, pour on me, my sweet summer rain. . . . I throw myself into your arms": this was the characteristic language and ardor of the communication.

Baladine's obsessiveness, evident in those letters, would be echoed in the art of the mature Balthus, who, as a boy, had been a participant as well as a bystander.

> Often I dream in my dreams, and I see myself with you—far, far away on a long journey. Oh René, René, blessings on you! for seeing me before you when you leave me: as a fountain, as a tree, as a flower in your star shining above you—*for* you—I have kissed Balthus and told him: "This comes from far away."[18]

By return mail, Rilke wrote her, late at night after he had put out his lights and was standing at the window watching the fountain "in a lunar kingdom."

> It was your body which was the miraculous equivalent to that fountain, for it too leaps up, and all the infinite nostalgia it has ever felt has served only to enrich the intensity of its fall, which is the strength of your arms—. And I remember certain gestures of a grace so complete that they too related to the fountain, and your smile itself, never lost, returns to your mouth. How rich you are, my friend, with that wealth which can never be counted, for it is the wealth of nature, a fortunate sum which is transformed without ever being depleted.

The gush was relentless; she replied by calling him

> the entire light of my life! . . . I believed myself a happy Cinderella whose Prince Charming had been able to find the slipper—oh my evening star and my morning star in my arms! I mirror you with each movement of my body soaring toward you.[19]

RILKE'S CONNECTION WITH Baladine's sons was a major part of this relationship cast in a setting of myth and dreams. And while the poet thought highly of Pierre, he was even more affectionate toward Balthus, and admiring of the boy's art. Rarely has a child been so openly esteemed for his unique talents, or made to feel so central to a romance. Like Balthus and Pierre, Rilke had spent most of his childhood with his parents apart and his mother in charge. He felt perpetually abandoned, left to the care of an inept and corrupt maidservant until, at age ten, he went to a military boarding school. He gave the Klossowski boys the continuous support that he had lacked.

Rilke had actually abandoned his own daughter Ruth, whose mother he had long since divorced and who was only two years older than Pierre, but he became like an attentive stepfather to Baladine's sons. When, in September 1920, the twelve-year-old Balthus was not admitted to a higher class at school because he had done so poorly on his geography exam, Rilke went to meet both with the school director and with one of Balthus's masters. The problem was "caused by an extreme pedantry on the part of the school"[20]—not by the charming, brilliant Balthus. Rilke talked the boy into the next class.

A few months later, Balthus, already fascinated with Oriental art and literature, sent Rilke some illustrations for a Chinese novel. On the last day of 1920, Rilke wrote him,

> Young as you are, your artistic instincts seem to me deep enough to bear within them an unconscious judgment which, long before anything I might say, will have told you that these drawings with which, quite spontaneously, you have accompanied your memories of the Chinese novel have all the advantages of a very happy inspiration. Almost every evening lately, I have spent a half hour with your images, each time finding new reasons to delight in them. Their invention is charming, and their facility proves the wealth of your inner vision; the arrangement unfailingly enhances the excellent choice you have made, almost unknowingly, among the elements available to swift composition. . . . All right, to say no more: if we could study together this series of twelve images, we should have (you the artist—and I to whom you have given this lovely present) an entirely parallel, virtually identical joy.[21]

That effusive feedback and confirmation of his talents at this essential moment in his life imbued the boy with a self-esteem that has probably determined how he has conducted his life ever since. If on one level he was intensely fragile and vulnerable, on another he felt empowered to do anything he wanted.

BALTHUS TOLD ME, "Rilke was a wonderful man—fascinating. He had a wonderful head, with enormous blue eyes. He had a sort of dreamy voice, and an extraordinary charm." Balthus's childhood was "beautiful"—in large part because one of the greatest geniuses of the era was perpetually showering ardor on both his mother and himself.

On November 18, 1920—in the midst of the time period when he was working on arrangements for the publication of *Mitsou*—Rilke wrote Baladine:

Rainer Maria Rilke,
c. 1922

I, the "image hunter," go up into my mountains, wild, taciturn, losing myself. But you, my delicious valley, you, my heart's flute, you, earthenware vase on whom I, love's humble artisan, bestowed the inspired curve that consecrated you forever to divine usage—you, who have the innate, imperturbable patience of the landscape and the flute and the holy chalice! May you succeed, my love, in abandoning yourself to the rhythms of the seasons and of the mouth and of the hand. Let us not be satisfied with recounting a fable of the heart; let us create its myth. Is not love, with art, our only license to overreach the human condition, to be greater, more generous, more sorrowful if need be, than is the common lot? Let us be so heroically, my sweet friend—let us give up not one advantage afforded by our spirited state of being. . . .

Beloved: without telling him, embrace B. for me. I am sorry not to have done it myself; it's one of those silly discretions one scolds oneself for afterwards. When I return, I will do it, with all the tenderness I feel for him. I spoke with his publisher by telephone; we're going to

draft the contract sometime soon, only I alone will append my signature, because B., being a minor, cannot enter into any contract.[22]

That excessive emotional pitch, and the sense of being entitled to be different,
were young Balthus's norm. Rather than resist these feelings as another adolescent might have, he imbibed them as his own.

IV

THE CONTRACT FOR *Mitsou* arrived from Rotapfel-Verlag, a publisher with
offices both in Zurich and in Leipzig, on November 24. Rilke wrote to
Balthus:

> Since, according to law, my very dear B. . . . , you still live more or less
> in heaven, where no earthly commitment can reach you, I alone must
> bear the enormous weight of this authentic contract. . . .
>
> Please send me this paper after having studied it; as soon as I have
> your consent, I shall forward the duplicate I am keeping here to Mr.
> Rentsch with my signature affixed. At the same time I shall have our
> publisher return the manuscript to you, so that whenever you please
> you can add the missing drawing and the cover. I should like to see the
> work again in this final state, in order to keep it in view while I deal
> with the preface.[23]

Rilke's obsequiousness was boundless to the twelve-year-old boy he treated not
only as a talented equal and a confidant but practically as a lover:

> My valiant Château, I assure you, keeps me well. . . .
>
> My conscience tells me I am right to be here, alone with the
> demands of my work, from which exasperating circumstances have
> separated me for too long. There, with you, my nature expanded in
> that delicious freedom permitted by affection and friendship; here, it
> becomes austere and parsimonious. Let us hope it will emerge some-
> what enlarged from its voluntary prison.

After giving warm regards to Merline and Pierre, Rilke signs off:

> And as for yourself, my dear B. . . . , you know—don't you?—that
> quite frankly we love each other.
>
> To you with all my heart

Rilke and
Baladine
in Muzot

Muzot

·   ·   ·

RILKE HAD LONG DREAMED OF that château in Switzerland. He and Baladine saw a photo of Muzot in the window of a hairdresser's in Sierre. When
they then visited this thirteenth-century tower, it had crumbling plaster walls
and needed extensive repairs. The three rooms on each floor were junked up
with broken crockery and dilapidated seventeenth-century furniture. Because
of the devaluation of the German mark, Rilke could not afford the rent. But
Werner Reinhart of Winterthur agreed to take it on his behalf, and Baladine
undertook the fixing up. For Rilke had said that Muzot might protect him,
and that the Valais environment would enable him to finish the *Duino Elegies*
and move on. A château was a haven for productive isolation.

Watching Baladine and Rilke restore a multiturreted ancestral pile isolated in the countryside, Balthus developed a lifelong fondness for similar
habitats. He first fulfilled the craving in the early 1950s in a tumbledown
château in the Morvan region of Burgundy, then on a grander scale at the Villa
Medici in Rome, and more recently in both the castle-scaled Grand Chalet
and a thirteenth-century stone castello that he owns near Viterbo in Italy. His
elegant abodes complement his aristocratic style and foster the separateness he
first gleaned in Rilke.

WHILE RILKE ESTEEMED BALTHUS'S drawings for *Mitsou* and was thrilled
by what the book did for its young artist, he sometimes acted as if his contribution were the mark of a bumbler. He wrote to the poet Charles Vildrac that
his own prose, "while appearing easygoing, requires a strong hand to guide it
on occasion and, if need be, to correct it ruthlessly,"[24] while he credited "my
young friend's delightfully narrative brush which steadily advances from one
image to the next like the happy utterance of someone who can, between his
memories and his inventions, naïvely select the significant and essential feature
which sustains continuity."[25]

Rilke scholars and biographers disagree on the significance the poet
accorded to this preface. The writers who regard Baladine Klossowska as a desperate, craven creature who wanted Rilke only for herself and was an impedi-
ment to his work treat *Mitsou* as "a sort of recompense to Merline for her
patience," at best "a trifle . . . a charming effort, but in every sense a diversion."[26] The collaboration with Balthus is perceived mainly as consolation
offered by a difficult woman's lover to humor the woman's son. In the opposite
camp, Jean Rodolphe von Salis, the one of Rilke's biographers who knew the
poet personally, takes the view that Baladine gave Rilke a new clarity of mind.

Rilke had come through a tempest, but with Madame Klossowska was restored to a calm that enabled him to write. "Beyond any doubt this companion of his first years in Switzerland played a great part not only in furnishing and organizing Rilke's Valais home, but also in this success which he called a rescue."[27] In that happy scenario, *Mitsou* was a labor of love to which the poet applied himself wholeheartedly.

Balthus—glancing toward the side table on which the framed photograph of himself, his mother, and Rilke stands—told me that his mother had rescued Rilke and gotten him working again. Rilke's letters support the claim. "I am saved," the poet wrote in reference to Baladine; he credited her with his resuscitation as a writer following a fallow period. Rilke's correspondence also substantiates the concomitant view that the preface to *Mitsou* was no mere trifle.

When—on October 21, 1920[28]—an editor called to say that he was inclined to produce the book, Rilke was ecstatic. It had been his idea to present the drawings and write the preface. The editor wanted his text in German, but Rilke hoped to convince him that he would possess something far rarer if he consented to let the poet write in French. "It will afford me a very palpable joy to try my skill in this sublime language. . . . Always granted that Balthus is willing to accept my little collaboration with regard to *Mitsou*." Baladine's reply (in which she used one of the many variations with which she and Rilke spelled Balthus's name in those days) was predictable:

> As for Baltus' book, I am delighted! Heartfelt thanks, dear friend! He will howl with joy! Yes, write, write, my love, in French! One can say that an angel will walk before you.[29]

On November 26, walking his routine of 120 paces in the park at Berg, Rilke composed the preface in his mind. That evening he wrote it down. But what could be written in a single burst of enthusiasm would later be enlarged and trimmed and polished in every nuance. Even then, the results would not entirely satisfy the creator. That unwinnable battle for perfection would mark Balthus's future efforts as well.

Rilke's main problem was the shifting of tongues. He had lived in Paris, and he used French with Baladine and her sons, but to write literature in French, and attain the requisite clarity and grace, was a challenge. When he sent the text to Vildrac in Paris, beyond requesting heavy editing, he implored, with what rings as false modesty:

> I should never dare to make a public appearance with this little improvisation, which cannot come under the judgment of my artistic con-

science. . . . Save me, please, from the censure with which my work might deservedly be met.[30]

Rilke claimed he would not have seen the project through had he not felt obliged to Balthus. Yet this shift to French stuck for the remaining six years of his life and inspired one of the most beautiful phases of his poetry.

As soon as Rilke heard back from Vildrac in February, he wrote to Baladine that the proposed corrections destroyed his rhythm and that the Parisian poet wanted to replace key phrases with insignificant banalities. Rilke beseeched Baladine and her sons to help immediately. "Advise me, you as well as Pierre and Balthusz, put your heads together and compare! After all, there is no school tomorrow, so you can all concentrate on this." Years later, an aged Baladine Klossowska would reminisce, "My sons were my school and my pleasure and I was their playmate. When Rilke came, we were like four happy children."[31] By Rilke's account, they were also collaborators at work.

BASED ON A LETTER HE WROTE to the Swiss historian and diplomat Carl Burckhardt,[32] Rilke ultimately felt he succeeded in overcoming the barriers imposed by the hitherto untried language. As Rilke's recent biographer Ralph Freedman has pointed out:

> Rilke knew he had to write this *Préface à Mitsou* in order to turn the boy's efforts into an enterprise that could be taken seriously by adults, but the short prose essay also represented a turning point in his own career. It was his first public work originally composed in French, his first liberating experience in writing with some precision and elegance in the language he had chosen to adopt. He wrote proudly to Lou [Andreas-Salomé; a close confidant] just before New Year's that in writing this preface all his ideas had been translated in his mind.[33]

Mitsou was printed in Heidelberg in the spring of 1921 and appeared that summer. It was an elegant, large volume—nine by seven inches—printed on ivory paper, with each richly inked drawing surrounded by ample space. Balthus had drawn the cover by hand. The title page put MITSOU QUARANTE IMAGES PAR BALTUSZ in large type, with PREFACE DE RAINER MARIA RILKE substantially smaller. Rilke's essay bore the dedication "A mon cher Arsene Davitscho B.K." That name—for which I can find no explanation beyond Rilke's playfulness—was among the first of Balthus's many imaginary identities.

.   .   .

Perhaps one of the reasons Balthus told me he was baffled by all the subsequent commentary on his work—even by Albert Camus, Paul Eluard, Antonin Artaud, or Octavio Paz—is that none of it could ever equal Rilke's eloquent and insightful preface of 1921. No discussion since has been either as crisp or as exquisitely ambiguous as the five-page commentary that opens, "Qui connaît les chats?"

The existence of cats is "shakily hypothetical," according to Rilke. Unlike dogs, who worship and obey us, cats keep their distance. They surprise us by being suddenly "strange, brusque, and offhand." "Cats are just that: cats. And their world is utterly, through and through, a cat's world," wrote the poet in his preface to *Mitsou*. "The meaning of a painting is in the painting," declared Balthus seventy years later. Perhaps to understand why Balthus did certain things is no more possible, or necessary, than to understand why a cat at one moment runs up a tree and at the next hides on top of your old sweaters in the back of a storage closet. It does so because it likes the feeling.

Rilke reiterates in the text for *Mitsou* that cats are accessible only to the degree that they choose to be. Elegant and enchanting, they are also elusive. The same can be said of Balthus, and of his art forever after. Like the little boy's leash, any attempt to keep them in tow is a short-lived contrivance.

But Balthus is the seeker also. And for him, too, the object of the chase is uncapturable. Like a cat, the aims of his art perpetually escape the creator, however tenaciously he pursues them. So it is that Balthus has sometimes taken over a decade to complete a single picture and has declared all of his paintings failures (except on those days when he allows that perhaps the larger compositions have succeeded to a degree). For him art has been the task of trying to tame the untamable. Balthus has tried to take hold—to give his figures weight and put shadows beneath them, to gain the grip he cherishes in Masaccio—but, finally, his objectives have remained one step out of reach. This is why thousands of paintings have been lost under the relative handful—his is the smallest output of any long-lived modern master—of finished ones which he has repeatedly repainted.

After characterizing the battle of making art to me by explaining, "You don't think when you're working. You just push forward," he described the process of completion as one in which he felt even less control. "There comes a moment when a painting is like dropping an apple from a tree—when you can't go on anymore."

The task of his painting has been to fix a fleeting beauty. Balthus told me that Camus's 1952 essay on him confused him, but Camus strikes me as accurate in stating that Balthus's aim was to give "permanence to that which is fast disappearing." The swing from appearance to disappearance is the crux of *Mitsou.* It is also the dominant theme of the endless letters in which Rainer Maria Rilke and Baladine Klossowska tell one another about the sunlight in a room, or describe the degree to which some rosebuds had opened into blossoms—those flowers that they were perpetually sending one another, and that embodied the splendor and mutability of their relationship.

Balthus later painted flowers on a windowsill as they exist at only one brief moment of the morning. Canvases that he took years to complete evoke fleeting instants. Allow the second hand to advance, and his people will all have progressed elsewhere in the street; the child's reverie will have shifted in a totally different direction; the page of the novel will have been turned to a whole new chain of events. The light that boldly illuminates one area of a canvas while casting another in darkness will be somewhere else a moment from now. Structured and weighted as the paintings are, nothing lasts: except, perhaps, its rendition into art. The rest is ephemeral. The world is in perpetual, unpredictable flux. Everything alive goes through its cycles and eventually dies. Beauty is intangible. What is there is only a breath away from what is not there. So Balthus showed, and Rilke observed, in these forty drawings. Like Mitsou, things come and go.

BALTHUS THE CHILD may have been in tears about his missing cat; Balthus the man would grow not only to accept disappearance but also to embrace it.

Balthus told me that in the late 1930s he worked for a year on a text about children's literature to be published in the avant-garde magazine *Minotaure.* He tried to determine the predominant characteristics of various civilizations— what traits distinguished English stories from their French and German counterparts. With *Alice in Wonderland, Images d'Epinal,* and *Struwwelpeter* as the main examples, he had developed an elaborate theory of "English absurdity, French legalism, and German *Angstmachen.*"

Balthus recounted that after working on the essay in London, he took the boat train to Dieppe on his way back to the Continent to hand in the sole copy of the manuscript to Skira, the publisher of *Minotaure.* Looking positively exultant, Balthus told me that after arriving in Paris, he realized he had left this text on the train. "I burst into laughter"; Balthus claimed to have no regrets whatsoever at having lost all that he had done—Skira could simply wait another few years. "C'est très Balthus," allowed Setsuko. Balthus never wrote this—or any other major text—again.

Balthus eagerly gave me further examples of the phenomenon of disappearance—the fundamental theme of *Mitsou*. He described an incident concerning his painting *The Moth* (see page 479), a large canvas that depicts an animated female nude in profile, standing on her tiptoes, her arm outstretched as she tries to capture a translucent, elusive moth. The scene, cast in an otherworldly glow by the chimney lamp to which the insect has been attracted, has a dreamlike quality, as if there is some ungraspable significance to the rumpled bedding and an upside-down water goblet. Balthus told me that after working on the painting for three years in the château at Chassy, he finally took it, reluctantly, to Paris so that it could be sold. The artist felt that he still had more to do, but he owed the canvas to the syndicate of supporters who were financing his way of life at the time.

Driving from Auxerre to Paris with the packaged painting on the roof rack of his Deux Chevaux, Balthus heard a crash. Over thirty years later, he beamed at the memory. Figuring that he had finally gotten rid of the painting, he felt liberated.

A short distance down the road, however, a truck driver stopped the Deux Chevaux. Assuming that Balthus had no idea he had lost his cargo, the driver told him it had fallen off and gave the large package back to him. Balthus insisted that he was disappointed with the return. Disappearance is preferable to the struggle for an unattainable goal—as the little boy in *Mitsou* realized when he abandoned his hope of recapturing his cat.

"C'est presque Zen," Setsuko remarked admiringly.

BUT BALTHUS IS NOT JUST the boy in *Mitsou* confronting the issues of disappearance and his own lack of control; he is also the cat. Alternately intimate and out-of-reach, gregarious and silent, Mitsou resembles his maker. The changes in the cat's relationship to the world around him in the slim volume of forty drawings also anticipate, with astounding prescience, the way Balthus would approach the rest of society: first, when he was in his early twenties, as a stray coming in as if from nowhere; then, once he had found the right people, as an insider; and, finally, as a free spirit able to keep everyone else guessing.

When he was in his twenties, Balthus publicly called himself "H.M. The King of Cats." In 1935 he painted a self-portrait where a signboard is boldly inscribed "A PORTRAIT OF H.M. THE KING OF CATS painted by HIMSELF MCMXXXV" in which he stands accompanied by a large tiger-striped cat whom he closely resembles (see page 242). Balthus has rendered his features and the set of his jaw completely feline; he also emanates the same haughty confidence and inaccessibility as the animal at his side. He would repeat the image in his art over the years.

Cats were the ideal creatures with whom to identify. For their size and weight, they are extremely strong. Compared with other animals, they are solitary and independent. Like Balthus's subjects, they express themselves posturally rather than verbally.

The vulnerable boy in *Mitsou* and the dominating King of Cats are both grappling with control. The child is anguished by his failure to hold on; the mature creature grips ferociously. Although Balthus denies that it was his intent to give his imagery any psychological significance, that denial is simply another manifestation of the desire for power that, from *Mitsou* on, has always compelled him.

OF THE INSCRIPTION "A Portrait of H.M. The King of Cats painted by Himself MCMXXXV," Yves Bonnefoy—in "Balthus's Imagination"—writes, "A foreign language, then, which betrays a concern for solitude, a second language revealing a desire to set oneself aside, and the choice of English can also be interpreted as the sign of an adherence to the religion of dandyism, in its Baudelairean nuance, emphasized by the very style of the work—ascetic, stripped of sensuous indications, quite close, in fact, to the taste of French Romanticism."[34] This is the sort of analysis Balthus repeatedly counseled me to avoid. English, after all, was his first language.

But what are the facts? Balthus told me, as he has told many other people, that the reason English was his "first language" was that he was taught it by a Scottish nanny. The quality of his speaking and his grasp of its puns and poetry convinced me. Yet the primary reason for Balthus's good English was that—like his brother Pierre, who became so adept at Latin that he eventually translated *The Aeneid* and St. Augustine into French—he has always had a tremendous gift for languages. Although English was, in fact, the initial language of his relationship with Setsuko, today he also speaks Japanese with her, Italian with his former chauffeur from Rome, "mountain Swiss" with the locals who know it, English with me and others, and French with most people. If he must, he can also speak German—which is what his parents spoke to one another—and, in all likelihood, his parents' native Polish.

And it suited him well to master English as a young man. He was an Anglophile—with a strong penchant for Victorian novels and tweeds. This tongue gave him an upper hand he relished; he would insist on speaking English whenever British or American people were present, even if they, too, were bilingual and preferred to speak French.

But recollections of the nanny may have helped Balthus live out his dream of a childhood easier than the chaotic reality. His life was totally disrupted when he was six and the Klossowskis could no longer remain in Paris after the onset of World War I; it has been his lifelong task to counteract that agony.

V

TOWARD THE END OF *Mitsou,* there are three images of little Balthus holding his candle, using it to see what he can. Rilke describes these poignant moments in his preface: "How courageous he looks there in the cellar, all alone, with the candle that he carries as emblem of his search—he carries it everywhere, henceforth, in the garden, in the street." Even if Balthus is different from other people—his outfit more stylish, his back turned and his face deliberately hidden—his search suggests everyone's difficult, desperate attempt to see and understand.

Baladine Klossowska recognized from the start the profundity and power of these images by her eleven-year-old son. By Christmastime in 1921, economic necessity had forced her and the boys to move back to her brother's in Berlin. She describes to Rilke being there and reading a letter from him while the children were out. "It reminded me of the little drawing in *Mitsou* where the child holds the candle to light up every corner of the cellar. Distress—I was beginning to weep bitter tears. What could I have been looking for?"

Rilke was even more bothered by the sorrow that underlies those scenes of the boy with the candle. In a letter Rilke wrote on February 13, 1922, to Simone Brüstlein, a close friend of Baladine Klossowska's, he moved in one quick skip from extolling the success of Balthus's book to lamenting World War I and the abrupt halt it had brought to the Klossowskis' Parisian way of life.

> Please accept the book with my compliments; in the meantime, it's been sent thither and yon, and has brought me many surprisingly positive responses, also in public forums. People hardly want to believe that a boy of this age is capable of narration of such substance. There is universal agreement on this point; also, his almost remarkable expressions of loss arouse admiration: the standing while holding a candle, three times, in the room that seems so unsympathetically distant, without Mitsou—and it is indeed here, with a childlike yet already accomplished technique, that something is shown in its entirety, beyond which one can go no farther. This wonderful, brilliant, small Baltusz—and Pierre, with his strong, dark moods: what children, what boys!—and how matter-of-course would their paths have been

in the Parisian milieu, in the beautiful, spacious house in Saint-
Germain. The war, the war is still everywhere—everywhere everything
is still interrupted, divided, scattered.[35]

That shattering of Eden was something from which Balthus would never
recover. Like Rilke, he was intoxicated by the beauty he had once known—and
devastated by its tragic fate.

The idea was there in *Mitsou:* what we most love ultimately gets away or is
taken from us.

Nostalgia permeates all of Balthus's art. His paintings combine a savoring
of life's riches with an underlying sadness. Glory exists in the past—as if in a
dream, or locked in one's thoughts—more than in the here and now.

The idea was there in *Mitsou:* what we most love ultimately gets away or is
taken from us.

MY SECOND VISIT TO BALTHUS corresponded precisely with the Persian
Gulf War. At age eighty-three, he said that world events made all of art seem
pointless and irrelevant. Time and again, Balthus told visitors, and those of us
in the house with him, that the prospect of a third world war in his lifetime
made him entirely "*dérangé.*" Why on earth did one bother to paint? He could
understand nothing.

At other moments, though, his mood would shift to unabashed pleasure.
He told me that he had great admiration for Saddam Hussein. Seemingly in
dead earnest, he commended the Iraqi leader as "a genius for managing to hold
the world up at gunpoint." And he seemed to love observing the expression on
my face as he held me up at gunpoint by saying so.

But most of the time he was as horrified by war as Rilke was in that letter
where the poet amplified on the themes of *Mitsou.*

Those drawings of the boy with the candle are not just emblematic of loss
and longing, of isolation and aloneness. They are also a perfect premonition of
the act of looking that would govern this little boy's life, of the casting of light
into the darkness that would figure in so many of Balthus's paintings. They
evoke the finding, and the losing, and the attempt at illumination, that constitute an artist's, or a philosopher's, life.

At one point in the *Mitsou* preface, Rilke voices distinct skepticism about
the act of painting. "Will he be able to console himself with the picture of
Mitsou his father recently sketched? No—that had something almost premon-
itory about it, it was an evil omen, and God knows when the loss was actually
ordained!" But it seems perhaps that here the poet had unwittingly given in to
his feelings of competition toward Erich Klossowski. To view Balthus's father's
drawing of Mitsou as a sorcerer's forecast of Mitsou's disappearance is a swipe

at Erich more than at the function of picture making. For the preface is ultimately a celebration of the merits of painting. Balthus's drawings of Mitsou are quite the opposite of objects that anticipate some dreaded event; they are a means of holding on to memory. And his future work would be a means of recalling that perfect moment in his life when he was making and publishing that volume with his beloved, admiring mentor Rilke.

Art is the antidote to death and loss. Representation in pictures is the only possible means of truly establishing certain facts, of strengthening one's grip on life—given that there are no absolutes in existence itself, except for the prevalence of uncertainty.

But to lose a cat: no! that is unheard of. No one has ever lost a cat. *Can* one lose a cat, a living thing, a living being, a life? But losing something living is death!

Very well, it is death.

Finding. Losing. Have you really thought what loss is? It is not simply the negation of that generous moment that had replied to an expectation you yourself had never sensed or suspected. For between that moment and that loss there is always something that we call—the word is clumsy enough, I admit—possession.

Now, loss, cruel as it may be, cannot prevail over possession; it can, if you like, terminate it; it affirms it; in the end it is like a second acquisition, but this time totally interiorized, in another way intense.

Of course you felt this, Baltusz. No longer able to see Mitsou, you bent your efforts to seeing her even more clearly.

Is she still alive? She lives within you, and the insouciant kitten's frolics that once diverted you now compel you: you fulfilled your obligation through your painstaking melancholy.

And so, a year later, I discover you grown taller, consoled.

Nevertheless, for those who will always see you bathed in tears at the end of your book I composed the first—somewhat whimsical—part of this preface. Just to be able to say at the end: "Don't worry: I am. Baltusz exists. Our world is sound.

There are no cats."[36]

Nothing is certain, but by making art we exist. So Rilke told his young collaborator, and credited the boy with having revealed it in his forty drawings.

CHAPTER THREE

TRANSFORMATION

*I don't feel that it is necessary to know exactly who I am. The
main interest in life and work is to become someone else that
you were not in the beginning.*

—FOUCAULT[1]

*But when he saw all this finely wrought silver and the countless
refinements of a sumptuous table, when for the first time he
could admire service that was discreetly silent, it was hard for
someone of such lively imagination not to prefer this consistently
elegant way of life to that of hardship which he had been willing to embrace that morning.*

—BALZAC, *Père Goriot*[2]

I

BONNARD WAS NOT THE ONLY person impressed by Balthus's drawings in
Mitsou. Rilke gave a number of copies of the book as Christmas presents in
1921. That January the poet wrote his young collaborator that "nearly every day
brings another letter (one day I will show you the most interesting) saying
pleasant things about *Mitsou.*" His close friend Frau Gudi Nolke wrote ecstatically about "the book with the drawings by that extraordinarily gifted boy!
Everybody thanks you and is proud to possess it."[3] The publisher Kurt Wolff
wrote, "Yesterday I saw at Margot Hausenstein's a very charming and touching
little book of which you are the godfather. The talent of this young boy, his
capacity to produce an artistic expression, is wonderful and almost alarming."[4]
There was scarcely a member of Rilke's strong circle of friends and patrons
who had not come to share the poet's enchantment with the young boy's art.

The prodigy was no angel, however. While Rilke was sitting in Berg am
Irchel completing the *Mitsou* preface in honor of Balthus's thirteenth birthday,
his collaborator was playing hooky that same day in Geneva. Baladine was summoned to the school, and in the evening she demanded an explanation from

her son when he got home. Without evincing an iota of guilt, Balthus explained that he had told Monsieur Pittard, his teacher, that he had gone out with his aunt, after which, in order not to have lied, he had fled to his aunt's house.

Mother and son faced Monsieur Pittard together the next day. Leaving the classroom, Baladine saw a pastel by Balthus. She commented on it to the teacher, since she believed that with his marvelous artwork her son redeemed his sins. But her praise of the boy's picture only irritated Monsieur Pittard further. He told Baladine he could not understand her attribution of the pastel to Balthus, since he was under the impression that it was she, Baladine, who had made it. When she insisted that Balthus was the artist, Monsieur Pittard was astonished.

To give his work more value in Pittard's eyes, Balthus had said it was by his mother. Baladine reported to Rilke:

> The poor man was quite confused, and when I told this to Balthuz, he replied, "It's a good thing Mr. Rilke said in his preface that I exist; otherwise Mr. P. wouldn't believe it."—and now I'm obliged to make a present of one of my paintings to Mr. P. to bring him back to life—Oh my friend, does Baltuz exist? I myself suffer from his mischief-making—especially since we're in the country of Calvin.[5]

Rilke, however, was more amused than annoyed by his protégé's misdemeanors. Having considered his own school years "a monstrous affliction of my childhood,"[6] the poet had lax standards about what he expected of Balthus at school. Writing to Baladine, referring to an imaginary time period between midnight and the start of the next day where one might escape reality, he made light of the boy's deceptiveness:

> As for my friend B. . . . , I wasn't so wrong after all to advise him not to vanish into the "Crac," since with regard to school, he was there already. Luckily, he was found in time! I nonetheless remain convinced that "B. . . . exists," only it will always be extremely difficult to agree upon the place *where* he exists!

THE ONLY MEMORY I COULD ELICIT from Balthus about the school where Monsieur Pittard taught—the International School—was that his greatest pleasure there was playing Romeo opposite a Juliet who "was a charming Norwegian boy called Billigen." He described Billigen to me twice. On both occasions Balthus closed his eyes as if in a trance and, with a smile of amused reverie as he pictured this male/female somewhere between sleep and death, recited the line "She sleeps." Overcome by the forces of love, medicated into her daze, Juliet at that moment is the woman Balthus would paint over and over again throughout his life.

Beyond theatricals and pranks, however, school had little to offer him. At least so he told me—although this bilingual institution in Geneva is probably where Balthus became so proficient in English. In keeping with Rilke's model, Balthus would never have high regard for formal education. Having learned about art on his own in museums and churches, and having had his literary education at home, Balthus told me he felt diplomas and degrees were greatly overrated compared with direct experience.

For a prodigy in a foolish world, after all, what's the harm in skipping school and lying to the people in charge?

BALTHUS HAS DONE HIS UTMOST to keep writers about him away from the Rilke–Baladine Klossowska correspondence in which the incident about his deceit of Monsieur Pittard, and so much else about his childhood, is immortalized. When, during my second visit to him in Switzerland, I asked the artist if he had a copy of the book containing these letters—I had not yet been able to locate it elsewhere—he told me he did not own the volume or have any idea where I might find it.

The truth of that statement seems unlikely. But Balthus has always hated the idea of a close examination of this correspondence. What difference do the details of his childhood make? Who cares about the lie to Monsieur Pittard? Research into such material irritates him. It violates his rigorous standards that eschew biography; letters between his mother and her lover, and the everyday events of his youth, have no bearing on his art—which is why he X-ed them out of John Russell's initial Tate catalog text in 1968.

But Balthus has been inconsistent on this issue. Having officially declared, time and again, that the public need not—in fact *should* not—know anything about him, in 1945 he permitted Rilke's letters to *him* to be published in the French periodical *Fontaine*. He might claim he did so anonymously; the recipient of those missives was named only as "B." But most everyone knew who it was, and even if the artist coyly left out his full name, one could scarcely fail to deduce they were written to Balthus, given that the publication of those letters has been cited wherever the artist's bibliography has appeared ever since. In 1991, Balthus told me, in fact, that he was very pleased because these letters might now come out in English; indeed, in 1994 they were republished in French.

Balthus at
age fourteen
in the role
of Romeo

The real difficulty with the letters Rilke and Baladine exchanged is that they bring up aspects of Balthus's life that he does not want his public to know—and that he probably would rather not know himself. It could not have been easy for a teenage boy to witness his mother's uncontrolled ecstasy, itself adolescent, with someone other than his father—to whom she was still married. It must have been even worse to bear witness to Baladine's periodic, excruciating anguish. And beyond that, Balthus—very much Baladine's companion and soul mate, especially once they were in their Swiss exile—was probably jealous.

There is yet another aspect of the Rilke material that makes it distasteful to Balthus. These letters depict other family members whom Balthus would rather keep out of the picture. There are numerous references to Eugen Spiro, and to Baladine and Eugen's sister Gina. Very little could displease Balthus more.

The problem is that the Spiros were Jewish; Baladine and Eugen's father, Abraham Beer Spiro, was an Orthodox cantor. In 1873 Spiro, who had thirteen children in all, had moved from Kövelitz in Novgorod—near Pinsk—to Breslau, in Silesia (then part of southeast Prussia), where he sang and composed

music for services at the Old Storch Synagogue.[7] In Breslau the cantor's daughter met Erich Klossowski, a Catholic who had grown up in Ragnit, and who
arrived there in 1895 to study law at the university. Erich and Baladine had left
Breslau for Paris in 1903, five years before Balthus was born.

I brought up the subject of Balthus's Jewish ancestry—about which
the American public was informed in the 1984 Metropolitan Museum catalog
and in a related Sunday *New York Times*—on my very first afternoon at Le
Grand Chalet. I thought that Balthus would feel a certain rapport with me
when I remarked that we both descended from Jews from Breslau. But he
quickly corrected me. "No, that is wrong, Mr. Weber," he said blithely.
Behind his "it really doesn't matter" tone of voice, there was an underlying
vehemence.

Balthus ascribed the erroneous notion of his Jewishness to an innocent
mistake. "One of my father's best friends was a painter called Eugen Spiro,
who was the son of a cantor. My mother was also called Spiro, but came apparently from a Protestant family in the south of France. One of the Midi
Spiros—one of the ancestors—went to Russia. They might be of Greek origin.
We called Eugen Spiro 'Uncle' because of the close friendship, but he was not
my real uncle. The Protestant Spiros are still in the south of France."

Balthus said it was not necessary—nor would it be tasteful—to correct
these errors. He did nothing when the Met catalog appeared. "I couldn't
protest because I have so many Jewish friends that it was improper to complain." He was "not Jewish, but denying it becomes disagreeable. I have many
Jewish friends—Yehudi Menuhin, for instance, who is one of the greatest men
of our time, and who lives nearby in Gstaad—and the attitude would be mis-
interpreted." On the other hand, he was completely cognizant that I was writing down his every word, and he periodically glanced in the direction of my
notebook with visible pleasure as he straightened out his history.

He went over the material again with a few new embellishments, just to
make sure I got it right. "My mother was born Spiro, and Eugen was a close
friend of my father's. My mother was close to that family—having the same
name—but in fact she was connected with the Narischkin family." This time
she was—he gave no reason but had a look of piety on his face that made the
case irrefutable—Roman Catholic. Again he suggested that the name Spiro
might have been of Greek origin. I nodded my head in agreement and wrote
all of this down diligently, but I mentally questioned this last claim; while
Spiro is a Greek first name, as in the case of Spiro Agnew, it is not a Greek last
name. Spiro, in fact, is a variation of the name Shapiro, which is almost always
Jewish.

. . .

I WAS A RECEPTIVE AUDIENCE in that first meeting, still too enchanted to be receiving the gospel from the elusive Balthus to question him. I knew that newspapers and exhibition catalogs often made mistakes of the sort Balthus claimed they had made about the various Spiros. Only later did I recognize that the artist had fabricated the story about the confusion of the name.

Initially Balthus succeeded in getting me to take the position that this error about his being Jewish, while nothing he would be so unattractive as to fuss about, might now be corrected. He eased me into his camp by lamenting that Sabine Rewald, who had written the Met catalog, was a dry and turgid art historian, essentially unresponsive to the qualities of his art and factually inaccurate, on whose work I might improve. As for the other writer about his Jewish background, James Lord—whose 1983 piece, "Balthus: The Curious Case of the Count de Rola," which appeared in *The New Criterion,* was once the talk of almost everyone interested in Balthus—Balthus said that Lord's commentary resulted from a vendetta because Lord had not been invited to a dinner following the opening reception for a big Giacometti exhibition at the Villa Medici. Balthus, in fact, wanted Lord at the party, but it was a small, official event, and he was not, unfortunately, in charge of the guest list. Yet "poor Jimmy Lord" had maligned him for the slight ever since. Balthus encouraged me to believe that my access to the individual himself beat my previous reliance on secondary sources.

Just as in his paintings Balthus can persuade us to overlook the distortions and believe the truthfulness of the scenes—utilizing his brilliant craftsmanship and technique to make unreality plausible—he does the same in his speaking. Sitting there in his spacious salon flooded with winter sunshine; looking at me head-on with his dark, intense eyes; ingratiating himself with his polished, yet seemingly natural, manners: he was entirely convincing. He did not allow an iota of drama or tension to enter his voice. He had the aspect of a phlegmatic professor patiently elucidating a time-proven principle to a young student. The reason these issues meant a lot to him—as they obviously did—was his determination, in life as in art, to get things right. He would not drop the subject.

With the tone of a historian determined to explain the phenomenon of rumors, Balthus said that "it was the trend to deprecate in Poland old families by considering them Jewish." He gave as an example the case of the king Poniatowski. For a while it was the "fashion"—Balthus uttered the word disparagingly, clearly distinguishing both himself and me as members of the

intelligentsia who knew better than to succumb to the latest style—to make
the king's mother Jewish. Balthus then made the point that of course "today
nobody would mind anymore," that there was nothing wrong about the king's
mother being Jewish, only that it was historically inaccurate.

II

ON THAT SAME DAY Balthus first corrected the error concerning his Jewish
background, he told me, toward evening, more about his mother. This time
she descended from an old Russian family called "the Raginets."

Balthus also said she was "a famous beauty." That also seems to reflect
more how Balthus would like things to have been than how they were. Baladine in photos has a powerful and fascinating appearance, but her face does
not conform to most European standards of beauty. With her large nose and
thick dark hair, she looks remarkably like Balthus himself as a teenage boy; and
the features that made him so handsome are less suited to a female.

Balthus was more accurate when he then mentioned that his mother lived
separately from his father. Yet in citing the reason for their estrangement, he
again prevaricated. He said it was solely because of Rilke. In fact, Baladine and
Erich Klossowski had stopped living together over a year before Rilke first
came calling in Geneva. But it was important for Balthus, at the point when I
got to know him, to maintain the fiction that his childhood was nothing but
"wonderful"—the word he consistently used to describe his youth.

ON MY SECOND VISIT to Balthus, he again raised the subject of his lineage.
But now there was an addition to the tale: one of the reasons his mother had
become friendly with Eugen Spiro and his siblings, whom she purportedly met
when she was studying art in Breslau, was because of this coincidence of their
having the same name. This denial of his Judaism was so crucial that, to support it, he had invented a construction as precisely premeditated, and elaborate, as the composition of his large canvases.

Again in the history teacher's voice, Balthus added that his mother was
connected with the Romanovs. She was also Alsatian. This, I would later learn,
was truly the case with Rilke's mother, who came from a prominent Alsatian
family that moved to Prague—which probably explains how Balthus came to
pick that particular corner of Europe, aside from its being a place where both
of Baladine's primary languages were spoken.

As many times as Balthus discussed the matter, he invariably emphasized
that of course if he were Jewish he would not mind being known as such.

When I was staying at Le Grand Chalet, Balthus was quite steamed up about an erroneous attribution he said Sabine Rewald had recently made for Christie's in New York. I did not feel that he was truly rattled by it; he seemed, rather, irritated in a way he enjoyed. Mrs. Rewald said that Balthus had done a very early painting of a dog that he was certain he had never seen before—even though he did, in fact, know the person who owned the dog portrayed, which may in part explain the misattribution.

Balthus told me that he had recently written to Sotheby's and Christie's to issue a warning that Mrs. Rewald should not be permitted to issue or deny authentication of his work. Yet either he was never, in fact, in touch with the houses himself as he had told me, or they disregarded his request, because, as recently as September 1993, Tana Matisse, the widow of Balthus's lifelong dealer, complained to me about Sabine Rewald having authenticated, for Sotheby's, a "Balthus" drawing Mrs. Matisse recognized as being clearly false. Mrs. Matisse took on the auction house about this matter, reminding the authorities there that when an artist is still alive, he should be the source of authentication, and pointing out Mrs. Rewald's error.

In the past few years, I have come to hear so many points of view concerning the authenticity of Balthus's drawings that it is hard to know where the truth lies. For years, various visitors to his studio witnessed the artist trampling or tearing up his sketches. James Thrall Soby wrote of a visit to Balthus's studio in Chassy in the 1950s where drawings were strewn all over the floor, with Balthus destroying them with every footstep. When Soby asked why, the artist said he did not want evidence left of his unpremeditated, less formal art. He only changed this practice and began to sell drawings in the 1960s, Balthus told me, when, needing funds to cover the costs of receptions for the exhibitions he organized at the Villa Medici, he consented to the sale of these impromptu studies for that purpose. This is why the generally accepted theory about Balthus's drawings of the 1950s and earlier is that most of the authentic ones on the market were those that left Balthus's studio against his wishes: the group allegedly stolen by his son Stanislas. (On this purported incident, a full account will come later.)

When Balthus first told me that he had never let his drawings out until after he arrived at the Villa Medici, I asked him why it was therefore the case that a number of drawings from earlier years, particularly the 1950s, are in private and public collections all over America. The artist quietly shrugged his shoulders as if he had no idea what the answer was.

I suppose I could hardly have expected Balthus to come clean and admit that the reason a lot of those drawings got out of Balthus's studio was that Stash had taken them—any more than he might tell the whole story about the

drawings that have been sold as Balthuses but that are said to have been made
by Frédérique Tison. Many people feel that a number of so-called Balthus
drawings—often depicting the dreamy young girls deemed to be the artist's
signature—were actually drawn by Frédérique. Frédérique is the daughter,
from a previous marriage, of Pierre Klossowski's wife Denise. Besides being
Balthus's stepniece, she lived with him in the late 1950s. Frédérique and
Balthus were together in the château at Chassy from 1956 until he was summoned to the Villa Medici six years later, when, after a period of overlapping
with Setsuko, she returned to Chassy—where she has remained ever since.

One theory—told to me by a young artist who knows Balthus well, and
who is also a friend of Frédérique's—is that Frédérique makes fake drawings
that Balthus then willingly signs, as a sort of recompense for having abandoned
her for the Villa Medici and Setsuko. Happy to help his old girlfriend make
some money, the artist has no qualms about his role in the sham being perpetrated on the sort of greedy, unseeing people who buy artworks. It may not
trouble him, either, that havoc has resulted: lawsuits; awkward situations when
Sabine Rewald or Tana Matisse has declared one or another drawing fake but
other experts have rightly declared the signature real; consternation at the auction houses.

This was pretty much what Balthus suggested to me when, after lashing
out at the art of the other Surrealists, he praised Giorgio De Chirico. Balthus
knew the Italian well after the heyday of Surrealism—during the Villa Medici
years when he and De Chirico would often go to cafés in Rome together.
Setsuko beamed at the mention of De Chirico's name; she, too, was "very
amused by him."

What they enjoyed was his attitude toward the world. "De Chirico was
very interesting and frightfully funny," Balthus allowed with a grin. "I liked
him because he was extremely amusing. And reaching old age, he decided to
have fun. He declared that everything was fake."

Balthus elaborated. Toward the end of his life, De Chirico would claim
that his actual works had been painted by someone else. He also told people
that if they bought someone else's fakes of his work, he would sign them as if
they were genuine—especially if this enticed those collectors who had come to
him for authentication to purchase later, authentic works that he had previously been unable to sell. De Chirico's mockery of his audience and assumption of power without so much as a passing nod at truth had Balthus's
complete approval.

By falsely authenticating Frédérique's drawings, if that is what he did,
Balthus may have achieved two goals: a similar duping of the public for whom

he had no respect, and financial support for his former mistress. The approach is in line with his early assertion to Monsieur Pittard that his own work was by his mother.

There are other possibilities. In 1994 a friend of Balthus's told me he had been commandeered by Balthus and Setsuko to hire lawyers and intervene in New York to put an end to Sabine Rewald's claims that Frédérique Tison was faking Balthus's art. Balthus told his young friend that Frédérique had merely added a few lines and a "B" to some of his early sketches. If those improvements helped Frédérique to sell a few things, it was not for Sabine Rewald to interfere with his act of gallantry toward a former mistress.

Yet in the summer of 1993 Balthus complained bitterly to another acquaintance visiting him in Rossinière about the problem of Frédérique's fakes. (Both of the artist's friends who told me these stories have asked to remain nameless.) This time the artist and Setsuko asked their intermediary, who knew Frédérique as well, to telephone her and try to put an end to the practice. The visitor, however, knew Balthus too well to take the situation at face value. As they sat smoking and drinking relaxedly, Balthus's friend candidly told him that most of the drawings the artist was claiming were fake "could not possibly be fake because they were too poor. Anyone falsifying Balthus's work would have done a better job." Clearly these works of which there were now too many on the market were genuine, but they were discards. Either these were simply inferior sketches that the artist had tossed away, but not actually destroyed, and that Frédérique had subsequently found kicking around the château, or these were works Balthus had sold during his Villa Medici years.

Balthus's intimate told me that the artist had concurred with a laugh. Balthus's problem with some of the drawings now being offered was their embarrassing lack of quality, not their authenticity. Balthus admitted these must all be in his hand; indeed, anyone forging his drawings would have done a better job than to produce these mediocre sketches now being hawked. Having initially defended the drawings in an act of gallantry toward a former mistress, Balthus had then reversed himself and tried to disseminate the idea that they were fakes rather than own up to his authorship of inferior work, the friend told me. "Balthus loves saying anything like that; he loves mystifying people," explained another acquaintance of the artist's who has known him for thirty-five years when we discussed the matter.[8]

No wonder, then, that one court of law has declared Balthus incompetent to validate or invalidate his own work. The artist's capricious attitude toward authentication is not succeeding in duping some savvy jurists. In 1995 *ARTnewsletter* ran an article, "Court Rules on Balthus Drawing," that opened, "A

New York State appellate court recently ruled that an artist's repudiation of his own creation is not sufficient, in and of itself, to establish that the work of art is fake."[9] The Gertrude Stein Gallery on upper Madison Avenue had sold the drawing *Colette in Profile* to the dealer Arnold Herstand, who subsequently sold it for $51,000 to Claude Bernard in Paris. Bernard showed a photograph of it to Balthus, who declared the work a fake.

Outside experts, however, concurred that the drawing was a genuine Balthus. The Gertrude Stein Gallery, it seems, had bought it from Frédérique. The court said that unless Balthus was extradited and testified at a trial, there was no guarantee of his credibility. It was assumed that his motive might be revenge against Frédérique, and that the Stein gallery was not accountable.

But there was another factor as well—one that apparently eluded the appellate court judge. This was the artist's fondness for amusement at any cost.

AND SINCE THE "FALSITY" that most annoys Balthus about Sabine Rewald is, he told me, her presentation of his Jewish background—which led to that information passing into the canon of literature about Balthus—it is especially hard to know whether to trust the artist on his declaration of her "erroneous attributions." Time and again, he complained to me about her having helped perpetuate the heinous "biographical error." At times he was gentle about it— the poor dear had been thrown by the confusion about the two Spiros, an understandable mistake. At other moments he was condescending—she was doing the same silly sort of thing as those who "accused" (Balthus's word) the Poniatowskis of being Jewish.

III

> *People take for gospel all I say, and go away continually with false impressions.* Mais l'importe! *it will render the statements of my future biographers more amusing. . . . (One will represent me as a sort of sublime misanthrope. . . . Another will portray me as a modern Don Juan; and a third . . . will represent me as an* amiable, ill-used gentleman. . . . *Now, if I know myself, I should say, that I have no character at all. . . . But, joking apart,) What I think of myself is, that I am so changeable, being everything by turns and nothing long,—I am such a strange* mélange *of good and evil, that it would be difficult to describe me.*
>
> —LORD BYRON[10]

*Ay me! What perils do emiron the man that meddles with Lord
Byron!*

—Unknown[11]

*Then battle for Freedom wherever you can,
And, if not shot or hanged, you'll get knighted.*
—Lord Byron[12]

LIKE ALL SUCCESSFUL LIARS, Balthus intersperses the falsities not just with
truths but with a dose of obscure or confidential information that makes you
feel like an insider with rare access to what others do not know. It is much the
same as what he does with his paintings, where in certain details he is disarmingly faithful to the truth of appearance so as to be able to carry off a major feat
of deception.

When Balthus told me about how his mother had installed Rilke in his
château in the Valais, and provided details on the poet's stays at Muzot, his elucidation of the facts was so straightforward and correct, his memory so in line
with what I knew to be the truth, that it was hard to believe he could ever lie. If
anything, he downplayed the esteem in which the poet held him. Moreover, in
talking with me about this pivotal relationship of his youth, he made me feel as
if I had assumed the exclusive role of young confidant and spiritual kin—as if I
might become the Balthus to his Rilke.

But in spite of his occasional lapses into modesty and truthfulness, on the
issue of his background Balthus has long been an inventor possessed. The artist
told me he had a Scottish grandmother. His father's mother, who died before
he was born, was "a Gordon of Bight." Hence he was related to Lord Byron.
Even the name was not correct; George Gordon, Lord Byron, was the son of
Captain John Byron and Miss Catherine Gordon of Gight. But accuracy
scarcely figured; a day after Balthus told me that the Scottish grandmother was
on his father's side, he said she was his mother's mother.

Balthus developed the Scottish obsession as a young man immersed in
Wuthering Heights. It grew as he came to read Byron and then visited Scotland
with Cyril Connolly. Whether or not Connolly believed the claim, he helped
perpetuate it. The writer—who also erred, perhaps at the artist's behest, in having Balthus born in 1910—wrote, "His grandmother was Scottish, a Gordon of
the family of Lord Byron, some of whose dandyism he has incorporated into
his slender Baudelairean physique." The Byron idea flourished as part of
Balthus's own legacy mainly in the 1940s and 1950s—just before he was going
full tilt with his current claim that he is "the Count de Rola."

Even once he had added that Polish title to his list of dubious aristocratic
credentials, he kept up the Scottish side. I was fascinated to discover a 1967

article by John Russell in which the usually perspicacious critic referred to "the fact of Madame Klossowska's being a distant relative of Byron."[13] By the time I talked with Russell about these matters in 1992, he had, much to Balthus's annoyance, informed his *New York Times* audience of Baladine's Jewish lineage—and laughed uproariously when I pointed out to him that Cyril Connolly had written that Balthus was related to Byron. "Cyril probably did that as a joke," Russell suggested. But once upon a time, Russell, too, had been duped.

In his 1979 book, the first on Balthus, the distinguished art historian Jean Leymarie kept up the notion of Balthus's Byron link while treading lightly. Balthus's spokesman wrote, "Among his ancestors was a Scottish lady connected with the family of Byron, that intrepid and self-reliant hero-figure who haunted him as an incarnation of the aristocratic, freedom-loving spirit."[14] It was a smart move to avoid the specifics of a grandmother, but probably a giveaway that the link was more psychological than genetic.

As with all of his personal myths, Balthus was remarkably successful in foisting this chosen identity on the public at large. The rare journalists with whom the artist consented to talk in that Scottish period almost all helped to disseminate the idea. One writer, Alexander Watt, wrote that when Balthus, recuperating from war wounds in 1945 and 1946, lived in Switzerland at the Villa Diodati—once inhabited by Byron—the painter could feel essential links with his own heritage. Watt wrote:

> It is interesting to note that Balthus attaches importance to the theory
> of ancestral memory. This coincides with the mystic and sensitive
> vision that is inherent in his Scottish ancestry.[15]

Balthus had initially moved to Switzerland for reasons having nothing whatsoever to do with atavistic memories of Lord Byron. In 1943 he had moved from Champrovent—in the French countryside—to the Swiss city of Fribourg, where he stayed until the war ended. Both his Jewish and his Polish heritage posed problems in France. Gestapo law dictated that one was Jewish only if one had at least three Jewish grandparents or actively practiced the religion, so Balthus was not actually in danger. Yet in spite of that, he must have felt that it was wiser not to remain in France. For one thing, he knew full well that his mother was at risk. In the eyes of the Nazis, Baladine was Jewish, even if her sons were not. Accompanied by Pierre, she had to go into hiding during the occupation of Paris: Baladine and her older son lived secretly in friends' houses. Eugen Spiro ended up with his wife at Les Milles Deportation Camp (where he befriended Walter Benjamin).[16] For Balthus, Switzerland was not so much a way of tapping into "the mystic and sensitive vision . . . of ancestral memory" as it was a device for avoiding ancestral reality. Beyond that, the move to Diodati nurtured his fantasy that his emotional connection to the lonely, irresistible, free-spirited Byron was genetic.

JAMES THRALL SOBY ALSO MENTIONED the Byron idea in a pivotal catalog essay he wrote in 1956 for Balthus's first major show anywhere, in New York at the Museum of Modern Art. Soby, however, presented the notion in a manner that suggests we would do well to read between the lines. "His grandmother, he says, was a Gordon from Scotland, somehow, but in any case appropriately, related to Lord Byron,"[17] Soby writes. Soby's graceful approach seems to honor, with ironic amusement rather than judgment, Balthus's fondness for fiction. As if to justify the artist's claims, while subtly implying their falseness, Soby offers that "there is a strong Byronic cast to Balthus's own temperament; he shares to the full the English poet's aristocracy of spirit, contempt for convention and essential solitude of creative mind."[18]

The mainstream press in America, however, bought into the Byron idea quite literally, with no irony whatsoever. Although Balthus's Scottish ancestry has virtually disappeared from recent commentary on the artist, it was regularly included for some two decades following the Second World War. In 1949 *Time* informed its readers that the French artist descended from Lord Byron "through a Gordon grandmother." The same magazine, twelve years later, in a text that accompanied a particularly dashing photo of Balthus in front of his multiturreted château at Chassy, reported, unequivocally, that Balthus was "descended from the Gordons of Scotland, the most notable of whom was Lord Byron."[19]

And in recent times, although the Gordon/Byron note has been mostly dropped, Balthus has still played the Scottish-nurse card and evinced Byronic disdain even if he has not invoked the poet's name. To an interviewer from *Newsweek,* the artist declared in 1993: "When I was an infant, I had a Scottish nurse. The first sounds I emitted were in English." Apparently it was an important point—enough so that this habitual opponent of biography was adamant. He then uttered one of his greatest falsities ever with the self-contradictory statement: "I don't think about what the world thinks of my painting. I don't care what the world thinks."[20]

AT DINNER ONE NIGHT during my stay at the Grand Chalet, Harumi told her father that Loulou, the wife of Balthus's son (Harumi's half brother)

Thadée, did not believe the claims of Scottish lineage. Harumi teased her father affectionately about this, as if she, too, were skeptical. But rather than show typical teenage hostility, she was light-toned and smiling; she seemed aware of her father's fragility.

Balthus scoffed and feigned astonishment. Probably annoyed to have Loulou's doubts raised in front of me, he said he could not imagine what her problem was. He looked so sad and offended—like a child who had had something taken away—that it was hard not to feel a bit sorry for him. Perhaps because Loulou de La Falaise is herself from the sort of aristocratic French family to which Balthus aspired, the source of the critique may have been especially wounding.

But at least the press has consistently behaved. When Balthus was appointed director of the French Academy of the Villa Medici in Rome in 1961 and the story and his name made the major French papers, *L'Express* reported not only that the artist was a great-nephew of Lord Byron but that Balthus's parents were Rilke and a Polish countess. What a victory it was for Abraham Beer Spiro's grandson.

DURING MY VISITS TO HIM, Balthus was occasionally White Russian, slipping "my cousins the Romanovs" into the conversation. And on one occasion he proffered a link to a family almost as prominent in Poland as the Romanovs were in Russia by referring to Prince "Stash" Radziwill as a cousin. The artist let this one drop when he told me how he put a stop to a book being written about him for Doubleday. The writer was Olivier Marc, a friend who had done a book on Setsuko. The new volume was supposed to focus on the places where Balthus lives or has lived, and he and Setsuko decided it had gotten out of hand. Balthus telephoned the editor to say that the project could not continue. Recounting this to me, he appeared unable to remember the editor's name; acting as if it were inconsequential, he identified her simply as "the former sister-in-law of my cousin Stash Radziwill." Supplying the editor's name for him, I thought that Balthus evinced a look of sheer triumph at being one of the few people alive who might be able to forget the name of Jacqueline Onassis.

BALTHUS TOLD ME he was fond of Guy Davenport's *Balthus Notebook,* a slim volume, published in 1989, of reflections stemming from his work. He called its commentary an exception among the texts about him. But on the several occasions when he mentioned the book, he invariably went out of his way to fault its dependence on the "incorrect biographical information" provided by Sabine Rewald's Metropolitan Museum catalog, which led Davenport to make a reference to Balthus being, "a Jew by the Gestapo's reckoning."[21] Davenport concomitantly described the artist "painting meadows in the Rhône Valley . . . and children playing a card game called patience" during World War II with an awareness of the concurrent tragedy of children being marched from the Warsaw Ghetto to a train bound for Treblinka.

It is a lovely idea of Davenport's. Balthus's *Landscape at Champrovent* (color plate 3)—a vast panorama that shows the rolling hills of the Rhône region, the ridge near the river, and the Colombier mountains in the distance—is one of Balthus's most bucolic compositions, ineffably serene. The artist started it in 1941—shortly after he was demobilized as a soldier—and completed it in 1943, when concentration camp atrocities were at a peak in, among other places, the Poland where Balthus's Jewish ancestors come from. The canvas seems an ode to the beauty of life in peacetime, to the tranquillity and eternal values of which millions were being systematically deprived with a cruelty so incomprehensible that for Balthus the sole way of dealing with the crime was to show what he hoped might live forever.

The shimmer on tree branches, the solidity of the mountain peaks, the clean air of the blue sky, the recession of forms in space, are glorious. The Balthus canvas is peace itself—a paean to the beauty of life and to the workings of the universe. Light and shadow bespeak the extraordinary relationship of the earth to the sun. This superbly constructed canvas has a religious serenity, an ethereal, paradisiacal calm. Yet this is a very real space; the fields seem truly covered in grass, and the space recedes authentically. Balthus shows himself to be the Claude Lorrain of his time, and he puts as much poetry into the rows of trees leading into the landscape as Mozart does into a chord progression.

In addition, there is a charming vignette of seductiveness in the foreground. The farmer's daughter—Georgette—lies there in a summer afternoon reverie. Her short, tight skirt is hiked all the way up her thighs. It's as if, whatever his subject, however religious the atmosphere, Balthus could not resist being Balthus: off-color, a bit risqué. The woman has the usual Amazon legs of most of his female subjects, and we feel we are being invited to look up her skirt into the suggestive shadow between them. Lying there in the sunlight, she teases us. She gladly assumes her slutty pose, yet gazes off as if she is oblivious to her effect. Impervious to outside reality, she has escaped into her own private world of sensuous pleasure to which this painting is such a moving ode. Davenport's stance makes sense: her attitude, and this painting, was a sensitive artist's way of dealing with the tragedy that was then befalling him.

But all that Balthus would discuss with me about Davenport's observation was what he insisted was the factual error based on "that ridiculous confusion of the Spiros, and the modern fashion for making people Jewish." He remarked again on how this erroneous conclusion was based on false information. As one of his oldest acquaintances later pointed out to me, the artist had become so attached to this notion of not being Jewish that he may actually have come to believe it—like the Scottish nanny. In fact, many of Balthus's close friends told me they were sure he now believed his myths; their sole question was whether Setsuko believed them, too.

HOWEVER RESPECTFUL BALTHUS may have been when talking about his "dear Yehudi," he periodically voiced a flagrant anti-Semitism when I was staying with him. More than once in my presence, he characterized William Lieberman—who, as chairman of the Department of Twentieth-Century Art, conceived his show at the Met—as "a horrid little Jew." A painting conservator got the identical appraisal. At Sunday dinner, Balthus reminded his family, as he clearly had many times previously, that since he grew up as a Polish Catholic he still believed that the Jews crucified Jesus.

My having told Balthus and Setsuko that I am Jewish seemed to increase rather than decrease his pleasure in making these remarks. When he suggested to his son Stanislas, who lives in Malibu, and to me that the solution to the problems of Israel would be to relocate it in its entirety to California, he looked particularly pleased with himself and wore much the same grin as when he described himself coaxing his boyhood friends to smear themselves with chocolate from a birthday cake. A number of Balthus's American collectors who were directly responsible for the artist's current well-being—Joseph Hirshhorn among them—were from much the same background as Balthus on his mother's side. But Balthus had little interest in them—they were clearly not on the same echelon as owners of his work like the Agnellis or Stavros Niarchos—and I felt certain that snobbery was the reason. Their love for his painting could not offset the undesirability of their backgrounds.

A LETTER THAT RILKE WROTE to Dory von der Mühll in 1922 makes clear just how difficult it was for the Klossowski boys to be Jewish in Europe in the 1920s. Approaching Mrs. von der Mühll about the possibility of her brother providing financial help to Balthus and Pierre, he writes:

> I myself can already see two objections: the thoroughly unfavorable moment (the inhibiting restriction on private ownership is now

spreading through Switzerland, which has long since happened elsewhere)—and the other circumstance which was previously a hin-
drance, when we, in the case of another "emergency," considered your
brother could be taken into our confidence: it remains to be mentioned that although the K. children have Jewish blood from their
mother, are thoroughly Catholic on their father's side: the K. family,
even the branch that later emigrated to Silesia, were members of the
Polish nobility; this composition of the blood, which is further determined by the fact that the Jewish origins can be traced back to the very
oldest Spanish-Jewish bloodlines—the Spiros belong to the greatest
ruling families of Spanish Jewry's history—has probably contributed
to the brilliant talents of Pierre and Baltusz: it is responsible for superb
tensions and creates a strong background for their mental contribution.[22]

It seems strange that Balthus did not, in later life, follow Rilke's lead and,
rather than deny his Jewish background, claim it in all its Sephardic
grandeur—unless that chic detail, which is otherwise impossible to substantiate, was simply a Rilke embellishment. There is no knowing what Rilke actually said in Balthus's presence about Jewishness, but to other people the poet
sent out mixed signals. As a young man, the poet had a part-Jewish fiancée and
a number of Jewish friends. He was by no means indifferent to the matter of
whether someone was Jewish, but if at times he voiced the anti-Semitism that
was the norm among his fellow Germans in Prague when he was growing up,
on other occasions he expressed a particular liking for what he considered to be
Jewish traits. "From the Jewish actress Hedwig Bernhard—who was to die in
Auschwitz—to later crucial love relationships, he was attracted by a 'Jewish
temperament' and responded to it not only sexually but also intellectually.
Still, he repeated with conviction common slogans about the corrosiveness of
the Jewish intellect and its hostility to a creative spirit."[23] To various people, for
example, Rilke referred to the poet Franz Werfel as a "Jew-boy"; he lamented
what he termed Werfel's "decidedly Jewish attitude toward his work."[24]

Were it not that it also reflects self-loathing, Balthus's "ugly little Jew"
remarks seem not so far from Rilke's contemptuous—and contemptible—
"Jew-boy." On the other hand, Rilke seems to have had no problems at all with
Baladine's Jewishness.

What, therefore, about his heritage made Balthus not just deny but also
denigrate it? Some of his wealthy, aristocratic friends—like the Vicomtesse de
Noailles—were also part Jewish. Perhaps—although some will say this is being
far too generous to the artist—another key element was that, in Balthus's own

experience, to be Jewish was to be at risk for tragedy. It rendered him vulnera-ble—as susceptible to loss as a child whose cat has run away. Like poverty, which at fourteen Balthus experienced in so dire a form that he barely had a roof over his head, a Jewish lineage symbolized hardship. His solution later in life was to invent a past devoid of the difficulties that had caused such pain.

By rejecting his mother's heritage and embracing his father's Polish Catholicism, Balthus was making a significant choice. The wish to disassociate himself from his mother—the person to whom he may have felt so guiltily close—may, indeed, have been a central motive for Balthus's sham.

Baladine, in the pivotal years of her son's adolescence—the period of life that has been the obsessive theme of his art ever since—was both attached to the boy and completely distracted because of her romantic obsession. Balthus was her genius, her companion, and the puzzle that preoccupied her, yet she was even more obsessed with someone else. One suspects that her beloved son was, for all of his closeness to his mother's lover, furious.

THE TEENAGE GIRLS and slightly older women Balthus has painted all his life strike me as a fusion of himself and his mother in the era of Rainer Maria Rilke. And the style in which he has painted this combination of his irresistible adolescent self and his passion-consumed mother suggests ambivalence as much as ardor. Ever since his childhood Balthus has used his art to anesthetize, distort, and even victimize these characters not only in order to immortalize their beauty but also so as to control them utterly.

IV

BALADINE KLOSSOWSKA did not have the means to survive on her own with her two sons in Geneva. Erich Klossowski, who was in Munich with the National Theater, provided little financial support. At the start of 1921, Rilke scrambled to help his lover by covering the cost of her shipping two paintings to Berlin so that Eugen Spiro might try to sell them. Rilke lamented to his friend Nanny Wunderly-Volkart, "Now everything is collapsing at once" for Baladine; he was astonished that "contrary to expectations" no Swiss collector could be found to buy these artworks, especially the Delacroix, which he con-sidered "a captivating little picture, characteristic of the great master in a very special way."[25]

The poet tried to help his fellow refugee make ends meet, yet nothing was enough. When taking care of Baladine in the flat on the Rue Pré-Jérôme when she was suffering crippling pain from lumbago, Rilke arranged a loan for her from his friend Georg Reinhart—a member of the same family that was paying his rent at Muzot. But when she recovered from her ailment and joined her lover in Bern, it was clear to both of them that she would have to return to Germany.

In April 1921, a month after the incident with Monsieur Pittard, Baladine and her sons moved to Berlin. They were taken in again by Spiro and his wife in their apartment, which was where they periodically camped for over the next two years. They went back to Switzerland for long holidays when Baladine would stay with Rilke at Muzot and the boys with friends, but then, like refugees being forced into exile, they invariably returned to Germany out of sheer necessity.

The Spiros had a small son, Peter. From the moment he arrived in Berlin, the thirteen-year-old Balthus mesmerized his young cousin. Shortly after their arrival, Baladine wrote Rilke, "He plays the devil in the baby's room. You can't imagine the things he makes up to excite this poor little boy, who stares at him terrified, who simultaneously loves and fears him."[26] Balthus kept Peter transfixed and terrified with a wax samurai he made of Peter's same size. Baladine, having seen him create it, reported to Rilke, "You really feel yourself in the presence of a miracle when you watch him at work."[27] Similarly, in his last weeks, Balthus had fashioned a wax page with black hair and melancholy black eyes. When he would carefully put the creature to bed and stand it up in the morning, the page took on such life that Baladine felt that "if one day he woke up with an immortal soul, I wouldn't be at all surprised."[28] Balthus also made himself such marvelous costumes out of little scraps of material that on one occasion his mother opened the door of his room and found that, instead of his usual fine brown hair, Balthus had black curls and had been transformed into Sinbad. She was alarmed but impressed; wherever he was, Balthus had the imagination and competence to create a new reality.[29]

BALADINE AND BALTHUS and Pierre were at Eugen Spiro's from mid-April to mid-June 1921 and again from November of that year until the following July, and Baladine and Balthus (this time without Pierre) were at Baladine's sister Gina's, also in Berlin, between December 1922 and July 1923. They made their desperate sojourns because they were dependent on family income in Germany, and the rate of exchange was so bad that they could no longer continue in Switzerland. Away from a French-speaking country, they were like people in transit, never culturally at home.

It was during their return to Switzerland in the summer of 1921 that Rilke and Baladine found Muzot and she began to rehabilitate it for him. After convincing Rilke that the thirteenth-century château was the place for him, although it was badly run-down and had no electricity, she planned the renovation, whitewashed the walls, did cementing and plastering, refurnished the rooms, and hired a housekeeper. Balthus, meanwhile, enjoyed splendid days with family friends in the mountain village of Beatenberg.

If Rilke had been willing to have Baladine, Pierre, and Balthus live with him at Muzot, they could have remained in Switzerland. He could not tolerate his rural retreat thus "overfilled," however. But without Rilke, their return to Berlin for the winter of 1921–22 would have been more arduous. For even if he effectively exiled them, he organized a further loan of 3,000 Swiss francs from Reinhart to be sent in installments to Baladine, primarily for the boys' schooling.

For Rilke, the solitude paid off. Alone at Muzot, that February he composed six of his ten *Duino Elegies*—considered his masterpiece. Meanwhile, he remained keenly aware of both Klossowski boys. Referring to further financial support he had commandeered on their behalf from Andreas Weininger, he wrote to Nanny Wunderly-Volkart:

> That Weininger, so large and resourceful, helped, was a wonderful thing for the two young K[lossowskis]. The older one, indescribably encouraged by this support, has already begun to study for his exams at the Ecole des Etudes Sociales [School of Social Studies], the younger is more than ever engrossed in his paintings and gets by with the peculiarly direct instinct of his subversive talent.[30]

And referring to some maquettes Balthus was making for a Chinese play at the Staatstheater in Munich, where Erich Klossowski was working at the time, Rilke wrote:

> Strohl told me that Baltusz really has received the proposed commission to provide a work for the large National Theater in Munich!!! He is working in all happiness dear boy, and a part of the decoration should soon be complete and delivered! (What glory at fourteen years!)[31]

Balthus subsequently sent some of these for Rilke to see, and Rilke heaped praise accordingly. The play was ultimately not produced, but the young artist's first of many forays into set design must still have felt like a great step forward.

In July 1922 Baladine and her sons returned to Switzerland. Balthus

Rilke, Baladine, and Balthus in 1922

arrived at Muzot a few days after his mother, but then went back to Beatenberg, where, on August 17 or 18 (both dates emerge from Rilke's correspondence, so it is impossible to be conclusive), Rilke and Baladine joined him.
The trio had a blissful holiday until September 6. Rilke wrote to Frau Gudi
Nolke that those weeks in the mountains had conjured some of the happiest
times of his own youth—in large part because of the joys of being with "the
author of *Mitsou.*" But again it seemed that Baladine and Balthus would have
to return to Germany, while Pierre was now old enough to be on his own.

Although not willing to provide the solution, Rilke expressed further
anguish at the prospect of their going back to Berlin. He again wrote to his
friend Frau Gudi Nolke:

Ever since, with her two talented boys, she [Madame Klossowska] has
had to leave Geneva (where she lived so bravely) these children's lives,

like her own, have been broken off, and as we all know—nowhere do pain and care gnaw their way in more greedily than into a fractured surface of life. I'm really extraordinarily worried about her and the boys, Baltusz and Pierre.[32]

Desperate that Baladine and Balthus be spared "the ever increasing terrors of a Berlin winter," Rilke asked Mrs. Nolke to take Baladine and Balthus into her house. The poet involved himself to the extent of finding out the cost of lighting and heating the room that Balthus and Baladine would share in Frau Nolke's house. Baladine could do housework, and Balthus would be an ideal playmate for the Nolke children.

But Gudi Nolke did not think it right for Baladine to be her maid, even though Rilke assured her that this was the sort of job Baladine wanted to take. Mrs. Nolke proposed instead that Baladine teach French—both the language and an introduction to its literature.

To that suggestion, however, Rilke reacted with slight apprehension. Since Baladine and Balthus conversed entirely in French, she could clearly teach the language, but literature was ill advised.

> As for an introduction to the history of French literature, I must confess that is another matter. . . . Baltusz (who knows quite a lot—mostly, strange to say, about China and Japan) might turn out to be a good deal better informed, and his mother would hardly dare treat the subject in his presence, for fear of being contradicted at any moment with the most sturdy superiority.[33]

On the other hand, Rilke had no fear that Balthus would be arrogant to anyone other than his mother. The boy would contribute to the life of the household

> in all sorts of ways, with his uncommonly adaptable capacities, especially as he has long been used to testing them in life-sized emergencies. His considerable artistic talent, which, like his mother's, though of a different nature, is always essentially and uninterruptedly productive, might contribute something too.

Recognizing the desirability of having the boy and his mother come to live with her, but at the same time seeing Rilke's point about the hazards of Baladine trying to teach literature when Balthus would constantly be correcting her, Mrs. Nolke accepted the concept of their coming with Baladine instructing in French language alone. Everyone agreed to the plan.

Rilke's trenchant descriptions of the fourteen-year-old Balthus to Mrs. Nolke correspond precisely with the man the child grew into:

> It might be very nice for the children to have dear little Baltusz as school- and playmate. When we went to see him at Beatenberg in September, he was just painting Chinese lanterns, with a flair for the Oriental world of form that is amazing. Then we read the little Book of Tea; one can't imagine where he gets all his assured knowledge of Chinese Imperial and artistic dynasties. . . . I can't help thinking what it would mean to this boy, so strangely oriented toward the East, to talk to Asa [the Japanese governess]!

Time and again, Rilke's observations have been validated long after the poet's death. The boy who Rilke recognized as "so strangely oriented toward the East" would not only be profoundly influenced by Chinese landscape painting and Japanese woodcuts in his work, and even by Japanese theater, but would also end up being sent to Japan by André Malraux to explore current folk art there, and would spend his final days in the most pagodalike of chalets with his young Oriental wife (of noble lineage, so he assures people) presiding over the house in her exquisite kimonos.

Rilke recognized not only who Balthus was but what he needed. The most sage of guardians, the poet stressed the importance of Balthus having amiable young companions around him for the winter. This "would preserve much of his innocence, and a happiness still natural to his age would save him from looking upon grown-up cares as the only important and decisive things." Time at the Nolkes' would also allow Balthus opportunity for reflection—that sacred act. To be allowed to remain a child, unimpeded by responsibility, free to play and drift, able to invent rather than be bound by "grown-up cares": this Rilke recognized as Balthus's most important need.

But the arrangements that Rilke had so carefully made for Baladine and Balthus suddenly fell through on November 30. Baladine panicked because of the unexpected news that railway fares to Germany would more than double within two days. She and fourteen-year-old Balthus quickly packed up, and left precipitately for Berlin. Of this Rilke wrote:

> I have hardly ever had such a ghastly feeling that I was letting someone I loved fall into the abyss: for this is what Berlin must mean to poor Mouky Klossowska, for many reasons: a bottomless abyss, and continually being pushed further down it. . . .
> It is painful to see these delightful, intensely gifted children living

at the caprice of fortune, alternately on the emptiness and the over-
fullness of unorganized life. It was an enrichment for me to have little
Baltusz here.[34]

On December 4 Rilke wrote Anton Contat, a friend whose wife was a painter,
and described Balthus and Pierre's situation.

If on the one hand their very pronounced artistic faculties seem to correct the fatal irregularity of these two boys' development, on the other
one cannot help being disturbed by the notion of how charming it
would have been to be able, under more or less normal circumstances,
to nourish and sustain, quite deliberately, their talented natures so
greedy for any vital instruction. Then, too, in a world which increasingly fluctuates between excessive anxiety and equally excessive profit,
what will be the fate of those who by instinct can make nothing but
art?[35]

But such concern did not prevent Baladine from becoming intensely bitter toward the person she felt could have prevented this turn of events and kept
her and Balthus from being forced yet again into the abyss. Ralph Freedman
points out:

On the train back to the bitter north and during the long, cold winter
that followed, Merline expressed her pain and anger. Unfortunately,
none of these letters has survived. When, after his death, Rilke's execu-
tors returned her communications, as they did to all his correspon-
dents, Merline destroyed her own notes and letters written between
December 1922 and May 1923. No doubt, the depth of disappointment, despair, even rage at being literally shipped back to the place she
loathed by a man who professed to love her, was too naked to be pre-
served.[36]

If the importance of Rainer Maria Rilke in the lives of Madame Klossowska and her sons was far from over, it would never again be the same.

V

IN HIS ART, BALTHUS HAD PROVIDED himself with the trouble-free afternoons of which he was deprived during his own adolescence. The paintings
give teenagers the privilege to dream and read without interruption; one need

The Mountain, 1937, oil on canvas, 245 x 353 cm

have no concern that their comfortable armchairs will be taken out from under them.

Yet Balthus's characters often look exhausted or sad, their mood desultory. In *The Mountain*—a 1935–37 reconstruction of those Beatenberg holidays when Balthus was visited by Rilke and Baladine—the group assembled for a supposedly playful outing seem half dead. They are self-absorbed to the point of being totally out of reach. Forever fixed in a life that Balthus knew to be imperiled, they do not savor it easily.

For as Rilke reiterated time and again, those long interludes back in Berlin when Balthus was between ages thirteen and fifteen were returns to an abyss.

THE CANON OF ART HISTORY, however, has put a very different slant on those winters in Berlin between the publication of *Mitsou* and Balthus's move to Paris at age sixteen—and of the artist's consequent connections to German art. When Balthus had his first exhibition in New York in 1938, the review of it in *ARTnews* related his work to that of "Neue Sachlichkeit practitioners like Dix and Schrimpf."[37] In the Metropolitan Museum catalog, Sabine Rewald refers similarly to the painters of the Neue Sachlichkeit, and to an affinity between Balthus's work and that of Georg Schrimpf. Timothy Hyman, in an article that appeared in *Artscribe* in 1980 and then in the *London Magazine*, pinpoints the time period in the Spiros' apartment as the source of these artistic connections. "The Berlin years are the most shadowy of all. It seems likely the boy had some art training there, and through Meier-Graefe (who would start writing on Beckmann in 1925) he would surely have been made aware of the *Neue Sachlichkeit* to which Balthus's own later neorealist aesthetic can easily be related. Certainly by the time he arrived in Paris in 1924, the sixteen-year-old may have been more formed than has been understood, and formed at least as much by German as by French culture."

At the end of my first visit with Balthus, he gave me Hyman's article to take back to America as a sort of homework. He made no comment on it himself; he just said he thought I would want to see it. When I returned to Rossinière six weeks later, he asked me—in the most politely inquisitive voice—what I had thought. I answered that I hoped he did not mind my saying so, but I had found Hyman's ideas absurd. The piece suffered from stringing together too many facts without a real feeling for Balthus's art; the notion of his connection to the Neue Sachlichkeit seemed wrong.

I had passed a test. Balthus allowed that my response gave me license to keep working with him. Hyman's article was full of even more mistakes than most of the error-filled literature on him; for example, it put Setsuko at the age of twelve years when Balthus began to court her. Even worse, it was "a concentration of incorrect theories" that exemplified "the traps into which art historians fall" that had nothing whatsoever to do with the artist's intentions.

The octogenarian told me he had spent little more than six months in Berlin and that it had no major effect on him. In fact, not only were all the Klossowskis in exile in Berlin for about three years during World War I, but Balthus was again there for a total of about sixteen—not six—months in the 1920s.

Yet even if Balthus did live in Berlin for far longer than he now says, no one knows better than the artist himself how irrelevant and distasteful modern German art was to him. Berlin was clearly not the stylistic breeding ground into which assorted pundits on Balthus have turned it.

Balthus was emphatic that, in spite of his admiration for Grünewald, he has rarely cared for any aspect of German art. He also told me that, even though Erich Klossowski wrote in German for German publications, his father "hated German painting of all periods." Both of them detested its stridency and statement-making—and loathed German Expressionism. Max Beckmann was "a terrible painter." Indeed, while the poses and facial expressions of

Balthus's characters may suggest a resemblance to German art of the 1920s, the textures, spatial depth, light, and animation are unrelated.

Culturally and politically, Balthus has consistently linked himself with France, his birthplace. Although he was a lackadaisical member of the Communist party in the 1930s, he told me proudly that he left it at once when Stalin made his alliance with Germany. He served in the French army and is pleased that he is known as a French painter. I rarely heard Balthus sound as resolute.

In Switzerland, Balthus now lives almost as near to the German border as to France and Italy, yet he travels in almost every direction except the north. When he was offered a major retrospective at the Kunsthalle in Düsseldorf in 1977, he turned it down flat, urging them to mount a Poussin exhibition instead. I find myself wondering if this vehemence against Germany stems, ironically, from his ill-disguised Jewishness.

IF THERE WAS ONE PAINTING that significantly affected Balthus during those miserable Berlin winters, it was Caravaggio's *Amor Victorious* in the Kaiser Wilhelm Museum; he would repeat Cupid's brazen pose in many of his own later paintings. Balthus also loved a Signorelli that was destroyed during the war, and the Chinese and Indian collections at the Museum für Völkerkunde. The greenness of Berlin—its beautiful trees and large parks, the memorable zoo on the Kurfürstendamm—appealed to him as well. He was by no means closed to the entire experience; but for composition or color or the handling of surfaces, his mentors have never been artists of the German tradition.

OUR CONVERSATION STEMMING from Timothy Hyman's article led Balthus to say that, although he disdained most work by art historians, he had the highest regard for certain writing on art by artists. "Delacroix's journals, for example, are wonderful." The reason that art historians get things so wrong, he said, was that they do not understand the artist's point of view. It was a cautionary remark.

IN THE YEARS WHEN BALTHUS was being buffeted from country to country and made to live in a place whose culture he abhorred and resisted, Rainer Maria Rilke, however much he had disappointed Baladine, continued to make his protégé feel valued and superior.

Rilke saw Balthus as above the usual human fray. While the poet feared that a second move to Berlin would be so traumatic for Pierre that he persuaded Baladine to make arrangements for her older son to remain in Geneva, he believed, "For Baltuz, it's something else, he will survive in his dreams, and will transform any reality according to his creative needs."[38] The poet gleaned the inner necessities and disregard of ordinary reality that would underlie Balthus's art and his way of life forever after.

Not only did Rilke recognize that the altering of reality was essential both to Balthus's art and to his emotional survival, but he encouraged the ambiguity that is its consequence. Inaccessibility and inscrutability had been their mutual themes in *Mitsou*. The coming and going of creatures and ideas, the uncertainty of everything, the lack of dependability, were to be accepted, not overcome.

The imperceptibility of what is concealed from us, of what exists and yet cannot be grasped, was, for Rilke, splendidly echoed by the rare fact of Balthus's birth date. The boy's birthdays, or their nonoccurrence, obsessed the poet, who always penned Balthus a long letter at that point in the year. With the deliberately vague date of "toward the end of February," in 1921 Rilke wrote his young friend:

My dear friend B. . . . ,
   Many years ago I knew an English writer in Cairo, a Mr. Blackwood, who in one of his novels advances a rather attractive hypothesis: he claims that at midnight there always appears a tiny slit between the day ending and the day beginning, and that a very agile person who managed to insert himself into that slit would escape from time and find himself in a realm independent of all the changes we must endure; in such a place are gathered all the things we have lost (Mitsou, for instance) . . . children's broken dolls, etc. etc. . . .
   That's the place, my dear B. . . . , into which you must insert yourself on the night of February 28, in order to take possession of your birthday, which is hidden there, coming to light only every four years! (Just think how worn out, in an exhibition of birthdays, other people's would be compared with this one of yours which is so carefully tended and which is removed only at long intervals, quite resplendent, from its hideaway.)
   Mr. Blackwood, if I am not mistaken, calls this secret and nocturnal slit the "Crac": now I advise you, if you want to please your dear mother and Pierre, not to vanish into the Crac, but only to look around there when you are asleep. Your birthday, I am certain, will be very close by and you'll see it right away, and perhaps you'll have a

chance to catch sight of other splendors as well. When you wake up on March 1, you'll be filled with these admirable and mysterious memories, and instead of your own celebration, you will generously provide one for everyone else, by sharing your moving impressions and describing the magnificent state of your rare birthday, missing but intact, and of the finest quality.

This discreet birthday which most of the time inhabits an extraterrestrial space certainly entitles you to many things unknown here on earth (it seems to me more important and more exotic than the Brazilian uncle). What I wish for you, my dear B. . . . , is that you'll be capable of acclimatizing some of these things on our planet so that they can grow here, despite the difficulties of our uncertain seasons.

This extraordinary message from Balthus's mentor—his artistic hero and the most down-to-earth of his three parent figures—gave license to ideas that have dominated his thinking ever since. He was rare, his situation practically unique. The world of sleep was as real as any other. There is no accessible truth.

EARLY IN OUR ACQUAINTANCE, Balthus told me a story about Francis Bacon, to which he then often referred. Balthus identified his subject as "the real Francis Bacon" to distinguish him from the modern English painter who, in his eyes, does not so qualify. Bacon had been writing a history of mankind. "From his window, Bacon witnessed two people quarreling, and one of them was killed. He was a prisoner in his house, and saw it out his window. Yet the way in which other onlookers related the incident afterwards was totally different from what he saw. That's why he gave up writing the history of mankind. 'I've seen that now. How can I write about people who are dead for one thousand years? How can I write about something?' " Bacon abandoned the project because there are no certainties, Balthus explained.

The mutability of perceptions was to be relished, not lamented. Balthus's stance was that we should savor inexplicability, rather than foolishly try to decipher and unravel the inherent haze of life. More than once, Balthus complained to me that the greatest problem in this regard was psychoanalysis. Although he was pleased to let me know that he was a friend of Jacques Lacan's, whom he consulted about his malaria-induced hallucinations, Balthus felt that psychoanalysis is based on a pointless, and inevitably unsuccessful, attempt to fathom the unknowable. It encourages false conclusions—like people declaring his art erotic. It leads to ridiculous conjecture—like the silly efforts to figure out why that nonexistent eroticism is there. One cannot, and should not, try to be definite about what is going on in one's life, any more than in his paintings.

In recent interviews, Balthus has been given to antipsychoanalysis quips of a sort that fit in fairly clearly with the most philistine side of the recent trend of Freud-bashing. But what has now become a seemingly simplistic dismissiveness may have, earlier on, had a serious intellectual basis. The artist's hero Rilke had had a complicated and fascinating experience of psychoanalysis. When he was in his mid-thirties, Rilke had decided to go into treatment. He intended to do so with Dr. Victor Emil Freiherr von Gebsattel, a colleague of Lou Andreas-Salomé's, with whom he was alternatively lover and close friend. Andreas-Salomé herself had attended lectures by Freud and become an analyst.

Rilke then changed his mind. He decided that analysis would sap his creativity and that his work served many of the same purposes as this medically inspired process. Andreas-Salomé concurred. Astonishingly for an analyst, she discouraged the poet from starting with Gebsattel. She even went so far as to lie and suggest that Gebsattel "treated very few patients and those for short periods only."[39] Her motive was probably her fear of what analysis for Rilke would reveal about her, but she gave as her main reason the notion that treatment might stultify the poet in his work. Rilke came to subscribe to this notion so completely that even when, in 1913, he attended the Third Psychoanalytic Congress in Munich in order to be with his lover, he avoided meeting Freud, although Freud, whose son Ernst revered the poet, tried more than once to see him.

In Setsuko's presence, Balthus did not credit the analytic process with the same sort of intrinsic value suggested by Rilke's considerations; nor did he give as profound a reason for shunning it. He suggested, repeatedly, that psychoanalysis was unworthy—and intellectually dangerous. But in fact, in his earlier years—when most of the people he knew treated Freudian thought with respect and admiration—Balthus, like Rilke, may well have been one of those people who believed in "the primary efficacy of 'self-treatment' " through his work.[40] He, too, may have been afraid that greater self-knowledge and mental hygiene would have prevented him from working through his fantasies and neuroses in the manner he chose—which was to paint them. Not that Balthus would ever have voiced such sentiments at the stage of his existence in which I found him, but one can easily imagine him having had such views earlier on.

AT TEA ONE DAY when I was visiting, Setsuko began mocking psychoanalysis with particular zeal and amusement. She laughingly declared it a ridiculous

New York phenomenon. Sitting at the dining room table, she told me, as if it were the funniest thing she had ever heard, about a friend of hers whose husband went to his analyst every morning before work. In Japan, she explained, people accepted the idea that sometimes they are sad and have problems, and that is that. When I defended the Freudian method, she asked me point-blank if I had ever been in analysis; caught off guard, I answered yes.

I felt that this information, which Setsuko invariably passed to her husband, contributed to Balthus's being even more depreciatory than before about psychoanalysis when we saw one another two and a half years later. It was the day after the opening of his 1993 exhibition in Lausanne. When we talked that May afternoon in the lovely flower gardens behind the Grand Chalet, I sensed that the artist was issuing me a sharp warning. With new urgency, he said that psychoanalysis is "the curse of modern thought." And, in almost the same breath, he added that for some silly reason people find his art "erotic."

Surely Balthus had calculated that my involvement with analysis would color my way of looking at his painting and cause me to probe in precisely the manner he deplores. Our conversation was limited because there were a number of other guests present as well, but he was still resolute in his attempt to steer my course in his preferred direction.

CHAPTER FOUR

THE BOMB

During my first visit to Rossinière, Balthus and Setsuko urged me to read the writer Ananda Coomaraswamy. He was their ultimate "*porte-parole*," Setsuko said, using the French term that literally translates to "carrier of the word" and roughly means "spokesman" or "mouthpiece." When Setsuko said that Coomaraswamy's books would guide me toward her husband as he wished to be understood, Balthus nodded affirmatively.

Stanislas Klossowski de Rola—clearly under his father's close edit in the four-page preface that is, appropriately from the artist's point of view, the sole text of *his* Balthus book—quotes Coomaraswamy extensively in his opening paragraph. Stanislas advises that we all adapt Coomaraswamy's position that "the student of art . . . must rather love than be curious about the object of his study."[1]

Coomaraswamy—a combination of art historian, philosopher, Orientalist, and linguist—was curator of Indian art at the Boston Museum of Fine Arts. He wrote many highly theoretical books and maintains that painters are their sole appropriate spokespeople. "It will not be 'educational' to interpret," he writes.

Balthus's "*porte-parole*" warns viewers against thinking of artists as "expressing themselves"; the worthwhile aim of art is the use of formal means to achieve a purity and religiosity. Balthus concurred entirely. He told me that he was a "religious" artist. When I asked him to amplify, he said that if I did not understand, he could not help me further.

Ananda Coomaraswamy writes, "If a poet cannot imitate the eternal realities, but only the vagaries of human character, there can be no place for him in

Balthus and Setsuko in 1998, by Raphael Gailliarde

an ideal society, however true or intriguing his representations may be."[2] These "eternal realities," Balthus suggested, are what he has tried to capture—far more than any specifics of his own life—which is why he finds any examination of his private persona so annoying.

Balthus's best paintings do, indeed, capture the eternal truths: how light falls, how children sit, how cats stare. Yet even in his most rudimentary sketches, something else beckons us.

EVERY EVENING DURING MY VISIT to the Grand Chalet in January 1991, Balthus and Setsuko and I would repair to the library after dinner for coffee or tisane. In front of the large fireplace, with a fire periodically poked by one of the smiling Filipino servants, we would eat dark chocolates and discuss books or art. On some occasions we were joined there by Harumi or Stanislas, depending on who was home. Then, because these were the days in which the Persian Gulf War was being fought, we would often go upstairs to the small, narrow television room so that we could watch the news on the French network that broadcast CNN.

The TV room was off a long corridor of the type one would expect to find in a large inn or small hotel rather than a private home. There were a dozen doors spaced at fairly even intervals on both sides of the dark expanse. One of these led to Balthus's bedroom; another to Setsuko's; another to the spacious, beautifully appointed bed-sitting-room in which I was staying.

One night after we had been watching the news, Balthus and I headed down the corridor together toward our rooms. Somehow we got back to the subject of Coomaraswamy. I referred to the Indian's statement about a bomb but could not recall the exact words. Balthus, however, knew them verbatim.

Like someone reciting a religious credo, he recited, with impeccable recall: "The bomb, for example, is only bad as a work of art if it fails to destroy and kill to the required extent."[3] He enunciated these words with a look of profound delight on his face—as if he were purring.

Know your intentions, and realize them. If you have attained your goal, then your artwork is a success. If that goal is to baffle, or subjugate, your viewer, it scarcely matters, so long as you achieve what you set out to achieve. What counts is for the artist to be as competent and sure of his tools as the maker of a bomb.

AFTER OVER TWO YEARS of agonizing flights to the Spiros' apartment in Berlin, Baladine Klossowska managed to cobble together a year for her family back in Switzerland. In the course of this winter of 1923–24, the mother became more convinced than ever of Balthus's talents. She wrote Rilke, who was in the process of completing the *Duino Elegies* at Muzot:

> At the house I've *admired* what he's done. He is a great, great artist. He has shown me his picture and the ceiling; I had no idea what I was looking at! I told myself, when I saw those four apostles this morning, that what I had in front of me was a wonder, a prodigy. . . . Today, looking at his paintings, *I told myself that perhaps everything is merely an interregnum* and with such talents something has to happen, one *cannot despair.*—Once again, my very dear friend, B.'s paintings have tremendously impressed me . . . and I am terrified by the idea that he

might fall ill. Especially because at the age of fifteen he is doing things which could be the work of a great painter.[4]

Baladine wrote this letter in late November 1923, when she was visiting Balthus in Beatenberg. Because the lad was too thin, and ate better when his mother stayed with him, she settled in, although she had initially intended only to remain there a few days. Not only was she acting upon her maternal instinct to nurture her son, but she was also advancing a genius—much as she had done by fixing the crumbling plaster for Rilke at Muzot.

She worshiped Balthus: "This child is marvelous and braver than a grown-up—than I am, for instance," she explained.[5]

While tending to her son, she made a portrait of him, and then sent it to Rilke. Her lover praised it as her best work ever: "*delicious,* of an incomparable tenderness and melancholy charm." Every emotion, every trait, was apocalyptic. They would rarely ever be otherwise for Balthus.

IN FEBRUARY 1993 the man who says he never gives interviews or allows himself to be quoted in print publicly reminisced in considerable detail about that winter in Beatenberg in a statement he made to Prince Sadruddin Aga Khan—the source of the pistachio nuts. These intimate recollections appeared in *Alp Action,* a special advertising supplement to the European edition of *Newsweek.*

Gazing toward windows in winter, at the mountains beyond, I discovered the great art of Chinese painting. Watching the peaks, I could see things appear, disappear and reappear as I entered a singular state of mind. Then I came across a book on Chinese and Japanese art and I realized that these works had been painted by people who, while gazing through a window, had experienced the same change of perspective. As an artist I was fascinated by this and I realized that for me, the mountains were, truly, where it all began.

The grandeur of the mountains first entered my consciousness at age four, when my parents' cook took me shopping. Mrs. Quiblier had a poster of Mont Blanc in her dairy shop, and when I saw it I felt a yearning for mountains. During my youth, we also spent a great deal of time in the Alpine town of Beatenberg, which, incidentally, was well known to the Russian nobility. Everyone, even Dostoevski, had at some time been to Beatenberg, where there were very old and very grand palace hotels that have now all disappeared. My most profound childhood memories derive from the mountains, which are the source of all my sensitivity.

One special memory involves a feast called the distribution of cheese, a great celebration marking the end of summer. To commemorate the event, the Alpine communities of Beatenberg and Sigriswil came together each year on the 15th of September, each receiving its share of cheese. In the evening, we descended from Beatenberg and sometimes spent the night sleeping in hay. One strange night, I recall, a boy began telling the most extraordinary ghost stories and showed me what he said were the tracks of the Devil's hooves, though I thought they might have been left by a goat or a cow. At the time, I thought it strange that people from Switzerland, such a developed country, still nurtured traditions of ghosts. But even when I settled in the Villa Medici in Rome, I never stopped missing the mountains. I painted them from the city, where I could see the light of the mountains, as in a dream.

These days, things have changed. There are high-rise buildings in Beatenberg, and this lovely Alpine region, like so many others, has been doomed by its very splendor because it attracts the whole world and too many hotels. The region is poised for the ultimate destruction of beauty, because we live in times when everything is for sale.

The statement is pure Balthus: as he was as a child, and as I have always found him to be at Rossinière. His words combine his deep affinity for the Orient, his genuine love for nature, his fascination with ghost stories, and his loathing of the way the world is changing. At the same time, it drops quiet hints about the affluence of his childhood, with no reference to the very real anxiety. And his penchant for grandeur is palpable; that aside about the Russian nobility and the palace hotels, while never actually claiming direct experience of them, falsely suggests that he had a connection to their world. There is no intimation whatsoever that the mountain village was Balthus's refuge in a time of turmoil.

Balthus's concluding message, however, does ring true to the most salient and stirring aspects of his art. The celebration of beauty is tempered by tragedy; the world destroys what it has; enchantment is fleeting. Little wonder that for Rilke, Balthus's charm, tenderness, and melancholy were incomparable.

TENSIONS BETWEEN RILKE and Baladine were at a peak that winter. Rilke, suffering from the early stages of serious illness, was struggling to preserve as much energy as possible for his work. He continued to insist on his solitude. But Baladine longed to be with him at Muzot. She would not go back to the Spiros in Germany and, ever eager to cross the mountains to be with her lover, stayed instead at Beatenberg. Rilke wrote to Nanny Wunderly-Volkart that Baladine was "stubborn, selfish, insensitive, and forward."[6] Meanwhile, Baladine wrote him almost daily, imploring her great love at least to progress to *tu* and *du* from *vous* and *sie* in his letters to her. But while she longed for renewed intimacy, Rilke spent most of his time pursuing his interest in recent French literature and focusing on his own writing.

Balthus fared well in Beatenberg that winter, but he could not—yet—escape to the mountains permanently. The prodigy would be turning sixteen on February 29, 1924. And whatever conflicts the poet was experiencing with his protégé's mother, he still gave Balthus his full affection. Rilke concluded that the time had come for him to go to Paris.

The poet felt that this was the best possible move for Balthus's development as an artist. He had similarly steered Pierre in his career as a writer. To help organize the Klossowski boys' lives in Paris, Rilke had enlisted the support of André Gide. The two writers had been friends since 1910, when each had come to know, and translate, the other's work. In November 1922 Rilke had written Gide:

> You know of my interest in these two sons of my friend Klossowski. It is only natural that I should think so often of them now, especially since their gracious mother is spending some of her vacation here with me. Young Baltusz (with whom I once collaborated) is also in Switzerland.[7]

Within a year, Gide arranged for Pierre to enter the Ecole Dramatique of the Théâtre du Vieux-Colombier, directed by Jacques Copeau. Pierre initially stayed at Gide's house, a plan to which Gide had happily consented solely on the basis of Rilke's recommendations for this gifted young writer.

Now Rilke launched Balthus in an equivalent fashion. But both he and the artist of *Mitsou* opted for a different route. For Balthus, a school would have nothing to offer. Rather than waste time with any institution, he should be free simply to paint.

There was no question that he was worthy of it. He was immensely gifted as a draftsman. On Balthus's actual birthday, Rilke wrote Baladine:

> Baltusz's drawings are very fine. It is amazing how he has sensed the life of the body, I should say, the current of its vitality; it's like a

welling-up of life of which Baltusz has realized both the freshness and
the constant agitation, the unconscious stream fulfilled and renewed
within the bed of this form.[8]

It gave Rilke vast pleasure to see the young genius embark on his new course. A
week later, he wrote:

> I think of Baltusz, and I am really so happy for him! A fine date to
> arrive in Paris: March 7! . . . Gide's letter is charming; how delighted
> he will be with Baltusz.

So the talented youth headed to the art center of the world, under the guidance, both emotional and practical, of Rainer Maria Rilke.

CHAPTER FIVE

NARCISSUS

Sin of self-love possesseth all mine eye,
And all my soul, and all my every part;
And for this sin there is no remedy,
It is so grounded inward in my heart.
Methinks no face so gracious is as mine,
No shape so true, no truth of such account,
And for myself mine own worth do define,
As I all other in all worths surmount. . . .
—WILLIAM SHAKESPEARE, SONNET 62

Baladine Klossowska was soon in trouble with the Swiss police. She had failed to deposit her passport, which was German, with the authorities in Sierre when she arrived there at the start of summer in 1924. She turned to Rilke for help. The poet did his best to resolve the situation, beseeching influential friends to intervene on Baladine's behalf, explaining that she had never before had to take care of such matters for herself and was preoccupied with the precariousness of her and her sons' situation.

> Madame Klossowska is quite alone, and doubtless the dimensions of her mistake seem larger upon reflection. The two children are in Paris, invited there by André Gide, who was so kind as to express an interest in their fate; but it is not yet certain that they will be able to remain there and arrange a future for them suitable to their talents.[1]

Immediately after Easter, just when Anton Contat appeared on the verge of solving her problems at Rilke's bidding, Madame Klossowska fled to Paris. She should have straightened out her situation with the Swiss police first. But the pressures were beyond her control, Rilke explained. She simply had to be with Balthus and Pierre.

Once she managed to join her sons, Baladine saw the degree to which Rilke's efforts on their behalf was already paying off. She happily reestablished her home base at 15, Rue Malebranche, a studio and living space near the Luxembourg Gardens where she had lived before the disruption of the war.

It was up to Rilke to resolve her problems with the Swiss bureaucracy; she could think about little other than her boys. In October she was overjoyed by further encomia for Balthus's work from Pierre Bonnard. Bonnard had paid a call on Baladine. He praised her watercolors and they exchanged works, but what touched her above all was "the lively interest he took in Baltusz's paintings and compositions. He was delighted with what Baltusz was doing." Bonnard was so impressed that he had Balthus take the work to the Galerie Druet on the Rue Royale, in order to present it to Maurice Denis and Albert Marquet, as well as to Eugène Druet himself.

That distinguished group was intrigued by the work of this youth who had never had a painting lesson. Maurice Denis told the prodigy, "All you lack is a matter of 'savoir faire'; as it is, you succeed, but with roundabout devices you can do without." He invited Balthus to come visit him for a chat.

Baladine reported to Rilke that at that get-together Bonnard said of Balthus's work, "I know nothing about painting but I find what he does very beautiful and *extraordinary*." Everyone at the gathering commended Balthus for having started to copy Poussin at the Louvre—something his mother had done when he was a toddler. They deemed this just the right step in training his eye for composition. Following that session at Druet's, Bonnard said to Baladine Klossowska, "He is an artist, a real artist!" She could hardly wait to repeat all of this to Rilke, whose admiration for Balthus she knew would never waver whatever the vagaries of her lover's feeling for her.

The man "of whom nothing should be known" alluded to Bonnard's admiration for his work in an interview in *Le Figaro* in 1989. Called "Balthus Parle"—the suggestion being "at last," although there have been similar articles here and there since the 1940s—it covered an entire page of the daily Paris newspaper.[2] Here Balthus let it be known that he had had an exhibition at age fifteen for which Bonnard had written a catalog preface. In truth, the entire extent of this "exhibition" and "preface" was this one-time, informal showing of a handful of works to three other people when the boy was sixteen, and Bonnard's remarks to Baladine. Yet even if Balthus ultimately felt the need to transmogrify the details of those occurrences for the sake of the Paris newspaper readers, the actual events truly constituted a stunning start.

To his mother, Balthus in those early days in Paris was "very soigné and *very beautiful*." She was thrilled about his success, and happy to have him receive the advice of the masters—even though it completely contradicted

Pierre Bonnard in 1937

what she and Rilke had told him. "The odd thing," she wrote Rilke, "is that we have always told him just the opposite: not to undertake compositions at so young an age. Here Bonnard and Denis say that he must do as much of such things as he can."[3]

In 1925 Balthus took the counsel to heart by copying Poussin at the Louvre. What he learned in this way would become a mainstay of his art. Here Balthus developed Coomaraswamy's "formalism," the structure and precision of arrangement that would guide his painting methodology as well as his life.

Rilke had arranged for his young protégé's support in this endeavor by organizing funding from the Berlin industrialist Richard Weininger and his wife. At the poet's behest, the Weiningers also financed Pierre Klossowski in the same time period. Rilke frequently wrote to these generous patrons throughout the year to tell them how much it meant to these two gifted boys to have this time for quiet work and development. The poet, sounding very much as Balthus would half a century later, bemoaned recent changes in modern society—which he felt was being damaged in two directions at once by

Bolshevism and American culture. "The education the Klossowski brothers would receive, and the artistic insight it would engender, might fortify them to resist these destructive trends in contemporary life that flattened the uniqueness of the creative spirit."[4] Without their support, he told the Weiningers, Balthus and Pierre's progress would not have been possible. But such talented youths warranted the effort, he wrote the Weiningers. "Young Baltusz is what he was from the beginning, a real artist, a painter of talent, possibly of genius."

Rilke and Baladine began to spend a lot of time together again. The poet arrived in Paris at the start of 1925 and immediately sent his Merline "a huge bouquet of flowers."[5] He took rooms at the Hôtel Foyot, near her place on the Rue Malebranche. For the next seven months, they enjoyed day after day of seeing one another: at home in her studio apartment; walking around the city; and visiting Rilke's friends from the worlds of literature and society, among them Paul Valéry, Jules Supervielle, the Princess Marthe Bibesco, and the Countess Anna de Noailles. It was René and Merline's most prolonged period together, and the final one.

There were those in Rilke's circle who were skeptical about the relationship. In his diary that year, Harry Kessler complained of Rilke having "seemingly allowed himself to be completely ensnared by Madame Klossowska."[6] Rilke's old friend Annette Kolb "viewed Merline's frequent presence at his side with a jaundiced eye—the great poet caught in 'that Klossowska's coattails.' "[7] Regardless, Rilke and Baladine left Paris in August 1925 to go first to Burgundy and then, via Muzot, to Milan. It was a summer holiday they both seemed very much to enjoy until Rilke fell victim to food poisoning in a resort on Lake Maggiore, after which they canceled the Milan segment of their journey and returned to Sierre, where Merline took care of René at the Bellevue.

A deeply saddened Merline left her lover at Muzot in early September. Something in her may have recognized that this was the last time they would see one another. Standing at the station on the occasion of Baladine Klossowska's departure for Paris, Rilke "believed he had outgrown the very relationship that had been one of the important vehicles of his transformation."[8] A couple of days later, seemingly cognizant of the finality of that farewell, Baladine wrote him, "Oh, René, how small you became, seen from my train, and how unreachable. My heart is overwhelmed."[9]

IT WAS DURING THIS LAST flourishing of his mother and Rilke's relationship that Balthus copied his first painting by Poussin in the Louvre: *Echo et Narcisse.*

Moreover, he intended the copy to be a fiftieth-birthday present for René. To honor his mentor and teach himself composition and spatial organization, he chose perfectly.

Balthus devoted much of 1925 to the undertaking, which provided a level of instruction no school could match. Poussin understood surfaces and texture, high drama and subtle nuance. He was a master of the careful relating of a complex array of elements. Balthus had found the ultimate guide to show him how to order life's diversity with overriding control, taste, and poetry.

Of all of Nicolas Poussin's major canvases at the Louvre, *Echo et Narcisse,* the smallest, held particular appeal for the copyist. Matisse had made a version of the painting, between 1892 and 1896, having similarly been drawn to the canvas, which was so immediate and personal compared with Poussin's larger, more complex pictures. The dramatic scenario of *Echo et Narcisse* is focused and concentrated. Poussin has impeccably articulated the state of being and the physical position of each of the major figures. His rendering of Narcissus is the consummate expression of a lifeless body. The weight of the youth's legs and torso is palpable; his arms hang entirely limp. Echo, even though she is fading away in the process of her transformation into stone, appears splendidly relaxed, recumbent on her rock. She seems surprisingly at ease— sadomasochistically, perhaps—with both her own and Narcissus's fate. Cupid is feisty.

Knowing Balthus's subsequent work, we can see the degree to which Poussin's canvas nourished his imagination. The seventeenth-century painting offered an exquisite, melancholy rendition of a dead, sexy young man—whose exact position Balthus would repeat, albeit on women, in his own work for years to come. Poussin's half-dead Echo is the prototype of even more of Balthus's women: those modern Parisians mimicking the mythical creature's dream state in their way of being somewhere between this world and the next.

There is a direct line between Echo and Narcissus and the characters in Balthus's art. Poussin's personages are both beautiful, both victims of misfortune, and they suffer from unrequited love. With their great bodies, they are incredibly tempting and seductive. But, sadly, they are never united. Poussin has depicted these godlike creatures as isolated and alone; such self-love and unfulfilled passion would permeate Balthus's world. Unfulfilled passion is, after all, the romance that prevails in Balthus's paintings. Beauty does not prevent—but, rather, seems to invite—aloneness.

Yet for all of the tragic separateness, Poussin's painting surface abounds in rhythm, and the forms relate to one another as if by divine plan. Echo's arms loop musically, their arrangement in counterpoint to Narcissus's. A visual link is established between the two characters by the way the lines of their legs flow into one another and connect through the void between them. The curved vertical of the central tree neatly balances the sloping mass of Narcissus's body. The angles gyrate; Cupid's spear, his torch, and the various tree trunks have been worked out for maximum effect.

Such systems and connections would soon underlie Balthus's own work. Qualities of *Echo et Narcisse* pertain to Balthus's mature figure compositions as well as to his landscapes. In the manner of Poussin, he would develop an eye that encompasses everything. Poussin's lighting would also find its echoes in Balthus's art. Like theater spots, it falls clearly on the figures. The main body of the painting is divided into dark and light areas. A somber foreground leads to an ambient sky. Sunlight glows behind the foliage. The effects clarify the details and lend poignancy, even a slight eeriness, to the strange scene.

Poussin's details have a vividness the seventeen-year-old student would forever do his best to achieve. The narcissus blossoms are lovely and delicate, their yellow stamens and white petals catching the light. Their jewel-like luminance would occur in bouquets Balthus painted at Chassy in the 1950s. The flames of Cupid's torch truly glow, much like the fire that would rage in Balthus's 1945–46 *Beaux Jours*.

In his placement of every element of the composition, Poussin was a model of dexterity and competence. He knew where to leave space around figures, and how to enliven a canvas with bold forms. He made the people dominant, and kept his landscape recessive while thoroughly descriptive. The painting is supremely well ordered—and, at the same time, rich in its nonstop motion. It also makes plausible an altered state of being, with "the dreamlike suspension of the figures and the languid nature of their pose."[10]

The young artist with his easel set up in the Louvre intuited, or deliberately studied, all of this. Like Poussin, he would spin extraordinary tales in which everything had its right place. He, too, would achieve the bizarre while maintaining tremendous reserve in its expression. Poussin was a classicist, a geometrician, an artist in consummate control of characters out of control. He could neatly orchestrate disarming images in which people exist as if in a dream state: dazed, dead, or in the process of metamorphosis. Balthus would also deliberately illustrate discomfiting and ambiguous themes.

Poussin borrowed Narcissus's pose from a sixteenth-century Pietà by Paris Bordone. Balthus would, ten years later, repeat the image, with some minor changes, in *The Mountain* and in *The Victim*. Poussin's Narcissus instructed Balthus greatly, much as Bordone's dead Jesus had inspired Poussin. These were exquisite renditions of creatures struck dead just while their physical

Nicolas Poussin, *Echo et Narcisse*, c. 1629–30, oil on canvas, 74 x 100 cm

beauty was at its peak. The imagery was melancholic to the point of tragedy, but the splay-legged victims, whether comatose or dead, were highly alluring specimens of humanity, of strong body and sumptuous flesh.

At the same time, immersing himself in the Poussin, Balthus found a perfect single-painting course in how to paint. *Echo et Narcisse* was an exemplar of brilliant construction and impeccable articulation. We feel the space perfectly. Nature is graceful, color and form exquisite. Poussin depicts drapery masterfully; after all those months at the Louvre, his copyist learned the same skill to such an extent that it would last him all his life.

Years later, Balthus would still be quoting Poussin. The girl in the 1940 *Cherry Tree* would be a modern version of the harvester on a ladder in Poussin's *Autumn*. How like Balthus to select the creature with her back turned. Poussin's art offered any number of models for bold and brazen characters or for straightforward heroes; Balthus latched on to one of the rare quirky ones, the mysterious one, the oddball. But none of Poussin's prototypes would prove as true to Balthus's needs and passions as Echo and Narcissus, so gorgeous yet forever lost.

. . .

T<small>OWARD THE END</small> of November, Baladine wrote Rilke:

> I went to the Louvre today to see Baltusz's lovely copy; he's beginning
> to have a public. His copy resembles Géricault's painting—Pierre,
> who came later, said the same thing as soon as he saw it. I am proud of
> Baltusz, René, he'll be a great painter, you'll see; as you know, he's
> copying *Narcisse*. . . . I'm ecstatic about Poussin's picture, can't stop
> marveling at the mastery and the expression of each brushstroke.
> Actually, one can't be sure it's actually painted, but perhaps breathed
> by some god; the same kind of enchantment produced by pure music.
> The lips already dead utter divine words.[11]

Balthus finished the work just after Christmas. He inscribed it in the rock: "A
René." Baladine immediately wrote the intended recipient; "My dear René,
this copy is a wonder as both matter and spirit, as you will see."[12] She continued to effuse in letter after letter.

Even before he took possession of the work, Rilke wrote Balthus, who was
about to turn eighteen, "This *Narcisse* makes me proud and happy that it will
eventually come to enrich my immediate surroundings with its composite tenderness and with that admiring *summa* to which it testifies." On the other
hand, because of the importance of the copy, he wanted Balthus to take his
time sending it.

> But first it must stay with you so that you can show it to the
> friends of your friends, and also so that by seeing it more you will be
> inspired with the will to make other splendors according to the old
> masters or according to the harmony established between your imagi-
> nation and whatever happens to you in life.

Nothing could have been more fitting than for Balthus to paint *Echo et Narcisse* as a gift to Rainer Maria Rilke. For in January 1925 Rilke had written the
poem "Narcisse," which he dedicated to Balthus.

> Encircled by her arms as by a shell,
> she hears her being murmur,
> while forever he endures
> the outrage of his too pure image. . . .

Wistfully following their example,
nature re-enters herself;
contemplating its own sap, the flower
becomes too soft, and the boulder hardens. . . .

It's the return of all desire that enters
toward all life embracing itself from afar. . . .
Where does it fall? Under the dwindling
surface, does it hope to renew a center?[13]

Narcissus, at the time of the events chronicled in Ovid's *Metamorphoses* and alluded to by Rilke, was sixteen: Balthus's exact age. Ovid had described the youth destroyed by self-love as

Enchanted by the charms which were his own.
Himself the worshiped and the worshiper.[14]

BALTHUS PRESIDING OVER grand dinners at the Villa Medici, using *Le Figaro* to disseminate chosen details about himself to an eager public, keeping the world at a precisely calibrated distance: Ovid's words were an apt prediction of his dedicatee's future life.

As for Echo—the woman who could initiate no sounds, but could only repeat what she heard from others; who ended up betrayed by Narcissus, vanished in the forest as a disembodied echo: isn't this the role to which Rilke's young friend would perpetually relegate those who tried to get close?

THE NARCISSUS MYTH is not only a parable of self-worship, and of the concomitant exclusion of the other people in one's orbit. It is also an evocation of the way in which vision—both optical and psychological—is constantly fleeting. Narcissus's attempt to embrace his image in the well is like the little boy's efforts to hold on to Mitsou, and Balthus's later attempt to evoke the seeable world in paint on canvas:

O foolish innocent! Why try to grasp at shadows in their flight? What
he had tried to hold resided nowhere.

Narcissus's cry—"I am entranced, enchanted / By what I see, yet it eludes me, error or hope becomes the thing I love"—could have been, at almost any point in his life, Balthus's unspoken lament, whether his focus was on himself or on the world beyond.

In Ovid, metamorphosis is perpetual. Rilke's poem thus focuses on transformations—of the boy into a flower, and of Echo into stone. Balthus would similarly shift realities as he altered personas, and invoke the ongoing process of appearance and disappearance in his art. Rilke's "dwindling surface" describes the still lifes, urban scenes, and portraits Balthus painted for decades after Rilke dedicated these words to him.

His bathers have only a moment ago stepped out of the tub, as if in the process of birth. His peaches and apples have just ascended to their peak of ripeness—and are also on the very verge of withering. People in *The Passage* (1952–54) move from shop to home; they are between places more than at places. All that is certain is change and flux; the cycle of diminishment and emergence is continuous.

Rilke's poem has the sense of gain and loss that would underlie Balthus's painstaking process of painting and repainting a single work over a period of years. The surface dwindles; the center is renewed. Trying to capture the essence of what is there before our eyes in the Rotterdam *Card Players*, Balthus added so much paint that the unframed canvas weighs four hundred pounds.

IN A LETTER THAT RILKE WROTE to Balthus primarily to extol the merits of the *Narcisse* copy, the poet dwelt further on the matter of how little we can know or apprehend. Balthus's eighteenth birthday, or lack thereof, only a few days away, provided the perfect starting point. The date was February 24, 1926:

> Once again, my dear B. . . . , you must organize a little festivity for yourself with the eleven imperceptible intervals between the strokes of midnight on February 28. Few persons, certainly, possess such pure, such untouched material with which to compose their birthday; yours, rare as it is, is a true collector's item. Make for yourself, therefore, out of the minuscule elements of its absence a lovely personal substance on which other people, on the morning of March 1, can rest their eyes and their good wishes. And may the new year be useful and usable for your deepest needs, known or unknown to yourself.

To be someone who has no need to pin everything down gives one a certain nobility. The recipient of that letter was in complete agreement that atmosphere and personal preference outweighed the tedious notion of irrefutable facts. Fealty to his own shifting fantasies would suit him far more than enslavement to reality.

IN MY DAYS AND NIGHTS with Balthus in Rossinière, his dark eyes sparkled especially on the many occasions when we discussed literary fiction. Toward the end of our long lunches in the spacious dining room, or in front of the fire in the library after dinner, the artist would recite Poe with daunting accuracy and recount Chinese folktales in splendid detail. He spoke of characters in nineteenth-century novels as if they were the most real people of all. The personalities conjured by Stendhal and Chateaubriand were his close acquaintances.

At those moments he always sat still, in rapt concentration; he seemed far more comfortable than when the subject was either his own past or his art. The realm of imagination—a world that could be constructed from kernels of truth leavened by fantasy and invention—was where he was most at home.

At age sixteen, contemplating Poussin's and Rilke's images of the dying Narcissus giving birth to the flower and of Echo turning into a rock, he was equally centered. The lack of plausibility gave him no trouble. Explanations for the scene or its ramifications were beside the point. Part of the majesty of art comes from its power to transform, to create sights and forms of perception that never existed before. Facts are not the issue. Rather than engage in the tiresome, and futile, attempt to capture and impale truth, no more attainable than a missing cat, one should succumb to the enchanting spell of the made-up.

IN THE SPRING OF 1926, Balthus made a copy of Poussin's *Concert*. He was schooling himself intensely in French art. At the same time, Claude Lorrain, David, Ingres, Delacroix, and Théodore Géricault begin to exert their lifelong influence on him. Géricault had been the subject of a major exhibition at the Galerie Charpentier on the centennial of his death in 1924, the year of Balthus's arrival in Paris. The fierce romanticism of this "*maudit*"—that category of artists distinguished as thrillingly "damned"—his captivating imagery, and his marvelous ability with paint wooed its eager young viewer. Géricault, too, had mastered the craft of painting by copying Poussin in his own independent way; at least one such study was in the Charpentier show. That exhibition also had in it *Portrait of Louise Vernet as a Child,* called *Child with a Cat* as well, a painting of the daughter of the painter Horace Vernet. This marvelous canvas depicts a child not yet ten years old but surprisingly womanly with her mature

Jean-Louis-André-Théodore Géricault,
Portrait of Louise Vernet as a Child (also called *Child with a Cat*),
c. 1822, oil on canvas, 60.5 x 50.5 cm

pose and Empire dress. Mademoiselle Vernet, transfixed in a sort of reverie, holds a knowing, sphinxlike cat on her lap. She seems very much the predecessor of Balthus's paintings of Thérèse done when Balthus was living back in Paris fourteen years later—in 1938, the same year this painting passed permanently from the estate of Madame Philippe Delaroche-Vernet into the collection of the Louvre.

Géricault was a stirring mentor: for the sheer assurance and authority with which he worked, and for the virility and completeness of his painting. Each work presented dramatic subject matter in a rhythmic, engaging way.

Yet for the art Balthus now wanted to imbibe, Paris was no longer the answer. The time had come to go to Italy.

CHAPTER SIX

PIERO

*Piero della Francesca seems to have been opposed to the mani-
festation of feeling, and ready to go to any length to avoid
it. . . . In the Borgo San Sepolcro fresco the Resurrected Christ,
a sturdy stevedore. . . . looks straight ahead of him, dazed and
as if waking from a refreshing sleep. . . . One is almost compelled to conclude that Piero was not interested in human
beings as living animals, sentient and acting. For him they were
existence in three dimensions whom perchance he would gladly
have exchanged for pillars and arches, capitals, entablatures
and facets of walls.*

*Indeed, it is in his architecture that Piero betrays some-
thing like lyrical feeling. He paints what he cannot hope to
realize, his dream of surroundings worthy of his mind and
heart, where his soul would feel at home. . . .*

*One may venture to ask whether it is not precisely Piero's
ineloquence, his unemotional, unfeeling figures, behaving as if
nothing could touch them, in short his avoidance of inflation,
which, in a moment of exasperated passions like our [sic] today,
rests and calms and soothes the spectator and compels gratitude
and worship.*

—BERNARD BERENSON[1]

I

FOR FIVE YEARS, Balthus had been haunted by the urge to make a journey
to Italy. He wrote to friends that just hearing "Arezzo" would make him shudder; he equated its effect with that of the sound of the name of an inamorata.
He approached the trip with fear; it might let him down. But rather than disappoint him, the weeks that followed provided lessons that would guide and
compel him for the rest of his life.

Piero della Francesca's name had been in the air in the Klossowski household ever since Balthus had begun to look at art. The early Renaissance Italian
had long been a favorite of Erich Klossowski's. In 1920 one of Erich's friends—

Hans Graber, a professor in Basel—wrote a pioneering book on Piero which he sent a couple of years later to Balthus in Beatenberg. Baladine responded so strongly to Piero's imagery that she wrote to Rilke—in one of her letters in which she alternated between French and German in her fervor to find the words that could best evoke the intensity of her emotion—

> The day before yesterday I saw a reproduction of Piero della Frances-ca's *Noli me tangere.* That head of the Magdalen, almost grimacing with grief, with terror as she falls to her knees, slipping over the flowers of that garden, suffering and fainting. And he, the Christ, with an arrogant, unpitying gesture, as if he scarcely recognized her—I was terrified, a sort of dread clutched my heart.[2]

So this was the grip a painting might have!

Balthus, meanwhile, prized Graber's book. When he was sixteen, he lent it to Rilke—who soon wrote that he was savoring it. Now the young painter needed to know the originals. When a friend invited him to Florence for the summer of 1926, he was desperate to go. The trip would take him to the work of Masaccio, Fra Angelico, and, above all, to Piero.

IN SPITE OF THE ESTEEM in which the Klossowskis and Rilke held Piero della Francesca, for the eighteen-year-old Balthus to make a pilgrimage to his work in 1926 was a brave and independent move. Piero was not the taste of the day. In his thirty-nine volumes on Italian art, John Ruskin—in Balthus's youth still the reigning authority on Italian art—had given the fifteenth-century painter only a parenthetical reference. Ruskin and his followers found Piero's work antithetical to their taste. Their preference was for the decorative flourishes and overt sentimentality they found in Botticelli.

Rather than address Piero's painting, Ruskin had mentioned Piero only in connection with the issue of students taking their masters' names. Piero was different for having used his mother's; as Vasari had been the first to report, he had done so because it was his mother, Francesca, who had trained him as a painter. Even if Balthus enjoyed and, perhaps, to some degree identified with this detail Ruskin had latched on to—while Erich was also a painter, Baladine was the parent with whom he spent more time—it had little to do with the primary draw of Piero.

Piero's work has no lack of emotional depth, but achieves its force with the utmost reserve. It also emphasizes modeling more than line, and keeps details at a minimum. Like the art Balthus would come to admire by more recent practitioners—especially Courbet and Seurat—it extols balance and solidity. There is a strong sense of stasis and order; figures and objects are anchored and stable. The precise pictorial architecture creates a distinct impression of depth. Conscious geometry underlies both the overall composition and the individual figures. The paintings—and in this respect they are like Poussin's—give to visual experience a sublime classical order that deliberately counterbalances the vagaries of the human psyche.

No wonder Balthus, when talking to me about Piero at age eighty-two, was visibly still in the thrall he felt at eighteen. To embrace the haze of life, one must first establish an atmosphere of plausibility. Ambiguity is its most telling when cloaked in harmony.

For a young artist to obsess over Piero in 1926 was counter to the prevailing trends not only because Piero was then among the old masters out of favor. At that moment in the history of art, the tendency was to avoid the past altogether. Painters and sculptors of various schools above all sought newness and novelty. They wished to shatter boundaries, not learn from what others had already achieved. Some were taking the Cubists' dissolution of form or the Fauves' unabashed emotionalism to new extremes. The Dadaists closed the book on history. The general emphasis was on art that gave voice to the inner self, and that broke new ground.

Heading to Florence and Arezzo, Balthus was turning in an opposite direction. The idea of intentionally exposing his own personality held no appeal for him. Tastefulness was central. Piero offered deliberation and structure. In the havoc of the 1920s, to seek out the art of Piero della Francesca was to gravitate toward order and discipline: the route of steely control.

Its cultivation of human experience and high degree of visual refinement made Piero's art the ideal. Its organization and miraculous appearance had a magnetic attraction on Balthus. And it provided a disguise.

IN JULY 1926 BALTHUS BEGAN his pilgrimage toward the originals of those Piero frescoes he had savored in reproduction. En route from Paris to Florence, he stopped at Muzot for an overnight stay with Rilke for what would be, as he perhaps realized, their last meeting. The occasion was profoundly significant for both of them. On July 8, 1926, Rilke sent a telegram to Merline, who was in Paris: "Happy to have Baltusz here and with him a little of you & the Rue Malebranche. He leaves tomorrow morning.—René."[3] In 1898 Rilke had briefly lived in Florence, and he must have been delighted to think of his protégé on his way there.

From Florence a few days later, Balthus described this visit to his mother: "I spent some delicious hours with René, what a springboard to jump into

Italy from!"[4] Baladine liked these words so much that she quoted them when she wrote Rilke on July 14 to describe this "charming letter from Florence" from her "charming boy."[5]

"What a springboard to jump into Italy from!"[6] The unbridled enthusiasm evokes Balthus's persona more than any of his bigotry or pseudoaristocratic nonsense. If he deplores or scoffs at all he deems second-rate, he does so in part because he has long been so genuinely euphoric, and reverential, when the object of his feelings is brilliant and beautiful.

In the power of the art of Arezzo—and in the charms of the hill town itself and the surrounding countryside with its cypresses and vineyards and olive groves—the journey exceeded Balthus's wildest imagining.

BALTHUS SPENT THREE WEEKS in Arezzo, from which he made outings to Sansepolcro, and then returned to Florence, where he stayed for a month with American friends he had met in Paris and who lived on the Piazza Santa Croce. These were young painters he knew through Stanley William Hayter, the painter and printmaker. Hayter was "like an older brother for me . . . a marvelous man," Balthus told me: words far more affectionate than any I ever heard him utter about his actual brother.

The trip to Italy was financed by Jean Strohl. Strohl, a professor of zoology who lived in Zurich, was a friend of Erich Klossowski's, of Gide's, and of Rilke's patrons the Reinharts. The Strohl and Reinhart families knew lots of artists, Bonnard and Xavier Roussel among them; Jean Strohl was happy to support the journey of such a promising young painter.

Balthus told me that Professor Strohl was a wonderful man "who knew everybody." When he was eighteen, he wrote Strohl and his wife frequently from both Arezzo and Florence; these letters reveal a tremendous rapport between the young artist and his patrons. Balthus was rapturous, and extremely articulate. He described his thrill over Piero's frescoes and his love affair with Italy in general. He told his patrons that, having been haunted by the desire to make this journey, he had considered it dangerous to anticipate it, putting himself at risk of disappointment. Now his ecstasy was almost beyond measure—at seeing the cypress trees that were like toys, at the balance and precision and unprecedented harmony of Piero's frescoes in Arezzo, at the divine mystery of this art. He wrote that the Arezzo frescoes conjured thoughts of Valéry and of "The Lady and the Unicorn"—but that no adjective was sufficient to describe them.

Balthus also recounted to the Strohls how he would—as discreetly as possible—observe schoolgirls playing on the Piazza Santa Croce. He would sketch these girls at night. But in spite of his effort not to attract their notice, the youngsters would often surround him. Writing about this, the eighteen-year-old artist repeatedly used the word that, in my days with him, was always the ultimate accolade for any person or any experience: "amusing." Watching the children play on the piazza was amusing. And he would amuse himself "enormously" by making little girls jump over a rope and studying the acrobatic pirouettes they would perform in the process.

Sabine Rewald quoted a few of these letters in a doctoral thesis she wrote for New York University on Balthus. But, alas, none of these fragments can appear within this text, because of Balthus's prohibition against such usage.

It is, however, a blessing that at least the excerpts remain on microfilm (the only form in which Mrs. Rewald's thesis can be read, according to its author's stipulations), for a strange fate has now befallen those letters.

These letters to Professor and Mrs. Strohl that so tellingly document Balthus's pivotal first journey to Italy belonged to the Geneva-based art dealer Jan Krugier, whose adoptive mother was the niece of Jean Strohl's wife. An outgoing and highly insightful individual, Jan Krugier is a gallery owner of rare taste and seriousness whose exhibitions and connoisseurship I have long admired. Krugier, who has known Balthus for practically his entire life, discussed these letters and other matters with me at the New York branch of his gallery. It was he who, in the early 1980s, let Sabine Rewald read them. Subsequently, as requested, he sent the same material to Jean Leymarie.

Leymarie was, at the time, the director of the Villa Medici. It was perfectly natural for him—Balthus's heir in that directorship, and a substantial authority on the artist—to see the correspondence.

Several months later, however, Krugier asked for the return of his collection of letters. Leymarie was terribly upset. He explained that Balthus had recently visited Rome. Leymarie had shown the painter the stack of letters and left him in a room to read them. Now they had disappeared. The archive has not resurfaced since.

FORTUNATELY, HOWEVER, Jan Krugier still has several Balthus copies of Piero's frescoes which the young artist sent to Jean Strohl in appreciation for having financed the journey, and that subsequently were passed on to the gallerist. These small canvases may have nothing to say about the pirouetting schoolgirls, but they are immensely informative about the exchange between the early Renaissance master and the eighteen-year-old prodigy.

Balthus told me that he considers the process of making copies a complete necessity for a young painter. He pointed out that for many centuries this was a tradition in Chinese as well as Western art; that Piero probably copied Masaccio, and that Michelangelo certainly did. Copying is one of the greatest learning tools open to the artist.

Yet Balthus did not "copy" Piero della Francesca's compositions in the manner of academically trained art students attempting precise facsimiles. Rather, he created his own versions of Piero's scenes. Both in Arezzo, where Piero's *Legend of the True Cross* fresco cycle is, and in Sansepolcro, where the *Resurrection* is, Balthus made small, sketchy oils that are like lively conversations between two painters five centuries apart. Balthus's studies reveal both the education that Piero's art gave its young admirer and the remarkable freedom and license he took with his beloved model.

Humbled as Balthus was by the sublime force of those frescoes, he nevertheless transformed Piero with independence and savoir faire. The young artist fastened on the nuances of Piero's organization and control of form but took them his own way. Balthus forsook most of the details and iconography. He dwelled, rather, on the action, the quality of rhythm, the positioning of Piero's broad planes. His renditions of Piero's highly finished, entirely resolved scenes are fresh and breezy sketches. Concentrating where he chose and avoiding a multitude of elements either because he could not master them or because he did not care about them, Balthus left most of the faces featureless and relied on posture to evoke the drama of the scenes.

The eighteen-year-old's version of the Sansepolcro *Resurrection* testifies to this combination of respectfulness and self-confidence with which he responded to his artistic hero. In love with the past, the young artist made his own, highly personal selection of its offerings. He was devoted—but not enslaved.

What he gleaned from Piero was not a specific period style but, rather, the qualities that ally Piero with Poussin, or, for that matter, with Chardin and Cézanne. The fresco at Sansepolcro offered Balthus a strong vertical against a strong horizontal, a colorful panoply of curves played out against that grid, a profound mix of passion and control.

BALTHUS'S SUBSEQUENT ART—whether it shows little girls' underpants or a cat grinning demonically—is consistent with this copy he made in a small rural *pinacoteca*. Whatever the psychological factors, Balthus has been brazen yet refined, bold and delicate at the same time. Marveling at the riches before his eyes, he has not hesitated to use his imagination in his handling of them.

As he looked at Piero's *Resurrection,* Balthus's first instinct was to block out the forms. He focused on the major issues of the composition and stayed away from questions of surface. He maintained the strong frontal design and the solidity of forms. He also kept the two vanishing points, suggesting two different origins of vision, so that we see the sleeping soldiers' heads from below but are at eye level with Christ's. Regarding Christ, we feel as if we are in the apse of a church. With the Piero as with the subsequent themes of his own invention, Balthus concentrated on the figures and objects, giving them a larger-than-life presence. Generalizing Christ's facial features by practically eliminating them, he used gesture to make Christ triumphant. And he kept his palette minimal: displaying an austerity, a taste for limitations of means and materials, to which he would adhere forever after.

That self-imposed limitation of his color range is one of the few aspects of his painting method which Balthus was willing to acknowledge in our conversations. In general, he would not talk about how he paints; nor, he told me, does he discuss this with anyone else. But his preference for a deliberately small color vocabulary is something he pointed out. It is apparent as far back in his work as in this version of Piero's *Resurrection*. The nuances Balthus could extract from a few hues are evident in this panel he made at age eighteen. Simply but cogently, he worked the darks against the lights. In interpreting Piero, Balthus balanced limited colors just as he orchestrated a few bold forms. The pale rosedust wash of Jesus' robe, in contrast to the guards' darker tones, makes Jesus truly ethereal; that same hue, translucent in Jesus' flesh, effectively establishes its bearer's otherworldliness. Similarly, Balthus played the light emerald of the hats against the darker green of the robe.

He also created a range of reds by having the light hit the red shoulder strap of the guard in the right foreground so that it becomes a needed crimson accent. The sharp dashes of red on the flag and on Jesus' wound add to the potent rhythm of the painting and make the reality of the scene jump out at us. Balthus would incorporate the same sort of rich and telling tonality in his later work. While never abandoning his overview, he would treat the act of painting as a series of small imperatives—and continue to reap the benefits of the lessons learned within the thick plaster walls of Sansepolcro.

ONE OF THE HALLMARKS of most of Balthus's major pictures is their sharp division into two major areas of light and dark. What Piero implied in this regard, Balthus took further. In Balthus's small panel, the tomb and everything in front of it are dark, as if in earthly shadow; Jesus and the background landscape are more luminous, bathed in light physically and spiritually.

The paradisiacal trees on the right, fresh and brushy, are much like the trees that would appear in Balthus's later scenes of Paris—in the parks where

Piero della Francesca, *Resurrection of Christ*, 1463–65, fresco, 225 x 200 cm

Copy after Piero della Francesca's "Resurrection," 1926, oil on wood, 29 x 31 cm

young children play with hoops—and in stage sets he would design in the
1950s for performances of Mozart. Balthus doesn't just paint nature; he paints
its powers of liberation, the release it affords the human soul. While true to
Piero's prototypes, his trees have an added springiness; what was statuesque is
now dancing.

On the other hand, Balthus has taken Piero's less leafy trees on the left and
denuded them. Perhaps it was only a formal decision, but it is as if he was
driven toward the theme of death. Instinctively, he has disarmed us by adding
an element that is quirky and unexpected—and morbid.

While Piero's Jesus has taut skin that we can practically touch, Balthus's is
more frankly painterly; the fifteenth-century version seems a reproduction of
life itself, whereas in its twentieth-century interpretation the breastbone is suggested in what is clearly a single stroke of pigment. The arm is patently a
sketch, a candid assertion of painting, not a simulation of living reality. The
flag is just a splash of white in the sky, fading into the blue. But hasty as its formation appears to be, it is, with its red cross, a strong optical anchor.

Informal though the brushwork may seem, the scene is cogently evoked.
Balthus gives the mountains their sweep. He achieves the mass and solidity of
the tomb. It is palpably man-made and inescapable, which is essential for the
tale. Balthus has made postures as telling as possible. So Jesus is nobly erect; he
emerges strong and confident, with that undeniable presence that the walking
figures of Balthus's friend Giacometti would ultimately possess. The guards, on
the other hand, are supine to the degree of complete lassitude. This ability to
conjure the way in which people carry themselves—or sprawl or laze—and to
make it establish personality and attitude, would prevail in Balthus's future
work.

In spite of Balthus's deceptive informality, Piero's well-defined structure
prevails. The speedy brushstrokes honor the grid. Lively and fluid as Balthus's
rendition appears, it is also rigid and hieratic. The forms line up within a hori-
zontal/vertical/diagonal system. That obeisance to ancient guidelines suited
Balthus's temperament, as it always would. So did the deliberate sense of measure. When, within a decade, his subject matter would turn from traditional
biblical imagery to scenes full of sex in which many of the characters either
attack or recoil, he would continue to give priority to form. Balthus needed all
the rules and structure possible to counteract both his emotional intensity and
the sheer abandon of his subjects.

IN MOST OF THE MAJOR ARTISTIC and psychological developments of the
twentieth century, spontaneity and freedom have supplanted the premedita-

tion and training that were previously deemed essential. For Balthus, on the other hand, compositional structure and a highly developed code of behavior—both associated with earlier times—have always been paramount. Every line of his canvases relates to the underlying pencil grid that precedes the paint; his way of life adheres to ancient guidelines for conduct. Piero helped provide the model.

Another aspect of Balthus's traditionalism, reinforced by his Piero pilgrimage and at such a remove from many concurrent artistic movements, is the dominance of highly legible human figures throughout his art. People and their actions and emotions—more than abstract or theoretical issues—are at its center. Balthus told me emphatically—however laconic his manner, however seemingly untroubled his attitude, a look of gravity was there—that his work "always stems from nature." More than nature itself, human experience is his starting point. His landscapes are not the mountains and valleys alone so much as the earth observed, or cultivated, by people. To view his work is to have a spiritual and physical confrontation with the human drama; it is like watching living theater.

Yet even though Balthus made the setting in his *Resurrection* secondary to the human events, the natural environment rings true. The clouds are nothing more than three dashes of paint, but they are real clouds. Such clarity would always be his goal. The soldier's staff catching the light adds plausibility to the scene; as such, it is like the baguette carried by the solitary man in *The Passage du Commerce Saint-André*. Part of the central lesson Balthus learned from Piero, and would return to time and again, was that a dash of light caressing a straight object could provide both allure and a vital resemblance to reality.

As he copied Piero's frescoes, Balthus evidently came to recognize the merits of premeditation in creating art. Careful planning was essential to the balance and the underlying mathematical precision that give the frescoes their pure, timeless beauty. It was this divine, abstract grace that inspired him to the lofty comparisons to Valéry and a string of superlatives when he wrote to the Strohls declaring that, for all his enthusiasm, his attempts to verbalize his response to this art would never be adequate. His only recourse was to paint them.

And so he made those sketches evoking Piero's rich order, capturing the Italian's series of echoes, striving for his eloquence. Totally engaged, Balthus embraced the tasks of painting as Piero presented them. Copying the *Resurrection,* when he re-created the relationship between the guard on the left, wrapped in a circle, and the one on the right, swinging around, Balthus absorbed rhythms and balances he would never forget. The young artist continued the lesson he had begun with Poussin about how to get the folds of drapery to fall correctly; that early learning would be recalled throughout his subsequent art in the many towels draped over chairs, and in sheets hanging off beds. This is the possibility of art: a painter can take human life and its props and transform the juxtapositions into magic.

II

IN 1989, AND AGAIN IN 1992, Balthus and Setsuko went to London for the openings of gallery exhibitions of her work. Setsuko—who, like her husband, uses her single name professionally—is a competent figurative painter whose charming, somewhat lightweight work has a distinctly Japanese cast. Her still lifes, vases of flowers, interiors, and paintings of cats almost all have a predominantly golden yellow palette. Their subject matter reflects the rural elegance and worldly style in which the couple lives: Queen Anne chairs, Persian rugs, backgammon boards, Japanese black-iron teapots, baskets full of fruit, and vases of flowers from the gardens at Le Grand Chalet.

This work has been bought by Balthus and Setsuko's fellow elegant habitués of the Swiss Alps like Audrey Hepburn and the Prince and Princess Aga Khan. Setsuko's paintings are pleasing and very well executed, if somewhat stultified, and it is no surprise that her shows sell out quickly, with the prices ranging from about $15,000 to $25,000 per work. In a way, her canvases are like tame, affordable, trouble-free Balthuses: perfect for gracing well-appointed interiors.

Balthus told me that he considers his wife to have enormous natural gifts: an instinct for composition as well as an inherent gracefulness. The artist said he turns to her "for her feeling for composition and her way of applying colors." That gallant, supportive approach is, on the one hand, easy to understand because Setsuko is such a marvelous aide-de-camp to her husband. She is also enviably confident of her own artistic skills, and although her talents are limited, her sense of her own worth combines with a certain ability to make the paintings attractive. Yet it also seems extraordinary that the former soul mate of Antonin Artaud and Giacometti, those ceaseless explorers of the raw underpinnings of human existence, might now content himself with the essentially thin, and completely self-satisfied, art of pussycats and objets d'art bathed in their artificially golden light. There is little question that the polite Palm Beach veneer of his wife's art, and the emotional veil that overshadows it, would have horrified Balthus's friends from the old days.

Balthus adores his highly intelligent and cultivated wife, and has become extremely helpful to Setsuko and her career. When I asked why he had agreed to have their houses (not only Le Grand Chalet but also their castle in Italy and the rooms Balthus restored at the Villa Medici) published in *House & Garden,* the French *Vogue,* and so on, Balthus told me he consented to this only for Setsuko's sake. Thus he was willing to overcome his distaste for publicity—his evident devotion betraying just a hint of condescension that she should need such aid.

Having failed to make the journey for his own, larger exhibition at the Tate when he was considerably younger and more fit to travel, the attentive husband attended both of Setsuko's London vernissages. Balthus told me he was delighted to find that London was still the way it has always been— civilized and on a human scale, unlike Paris, which he considered nearly destroyed. Besides, he and Setsuko had a lot of friends there; Balthus mentioned especially Lucien Freud, whom he said he had "taken care of" years earlier in Paris. On the 1989 visit, Balthus sat for a portrait by Freud—who, I believe, was the first person to draw him since Baladine.

But the greatest pleasure of all in London for Balthus and Setsuko was, they said, their visit to the National Gallery in Trafalgar Square to see Piero's *Nativity* and *Baptism of St. John.* For Balthus's passion for the artist who overwhelmed him in Arezzo has been lifelong. The Piero pilgrimages are a framing element of his artistic life—at age eighteen after the glorious stay with Rilke, at age eighty-four with his stunning young Japanese wife at his side.

BALTHUS CLEARLY could have written a catalogue raisonné of Piero from memory. He was pleased that, because I came from America, I could bring him firsthand reports on the Pieros at the Frick in New York, the Gardner in Boston, and the Clark in Williamstown. He knew them well in reproduction, but lamented not having seen the originals. Balthus told me he felt a certain "malaise" about the one at the Clark; the composition and the folds seemed wrong. Here he sounded suspicious of American culture in general—as if in a place called Massachusetts they would not recognize a true Piero della Francesca anyway.

When Balthus spoke about recent restoration work on Piero's frescoes, his brow furrowed. Since he rarely betrayed emotion—and never raised his voice or altered the evenly metered gait of his speaking—those wrinkles suggested a high level of feeling. He did not approve "at all" of the way the Arezzo paintings had been cleaned, he said. Yet this was not because he was uniformly opposed to conservation work. He liked the restoration of the Masaccios and Masolinos in the Brancacci Chapel. Balthus told me that these, too, were

Sctsuko, *Summer Afternoon*, 1990, gouache, 100 x 70 cm

among his favorite paintings in the world. He had copied several of these in 1926 when he returned to Florence after Arezzo; a few years later, he gave one of his Masaccios to André Derain, who cherished it.

What came Balthus's way from the contemporary scene, he treated more as evidence of human folly. He and Setsuko sometimes opened their morning post in front of me. Looking at the announcements they receive from the Centre Pompidou and other showplaces of modernism, they acted as if it were all one big joke. Why deliberately create such ugliness? asked the count and countess. They named Andy Warhol, John Chamberlain, and Duane Hanson as particularly beyond their comprehension. The only art worthy of a journey must be of a caliber and excellence of another order.

WHAT THRILLS US when we are eighteen sometimes retains its hold. Young females like those schoolgirls jumping rope on the Piazza Santa Croce have

never lost their sway on Balthus. Nor has the nature of art as it presented itself
to him in the work of Piero della Francesca.

Ever since those summer weeks in Italy, Balthus's art has resembled Piero's
in the precision of its arrangement and in its stately tempo. In *The Street* (1933)
and *The Passage du Commerce Saint-André* (1952–54), in the various versions of
The Three Sisters (the 1950s and 1960s) and the canvases of girls looking out
windows or staring into mirrors (including the most recent one, completed in
1993), time is frozen—as if in the "Crac" identified by Rilke. The world—in all
its storm and pageantry—has been immobilized much as it was at Arezzo.
Sights both wondrous and unsettling have been taking place for quite a while
and should continue uninterrupted into the future. Just as Balthus conducts
his daily ritual in the tranquillity afforded by rural isolation, life is a careful
progression: the speed is andante at most.

Having been hurled about by the miserable circumstances that had forced
him and his mother and brother repeatedly back to Berlin, Balthus found relief
and security in Piero's careful, metered unfurling of events. Even when World
War II was destroying civilizations, he painted scenes of utter peacefulness in
which everyone seemed to have all the time in the world just to watch the grass
grow and listen to the sound of waterfalls. He would never want to move faster.

PROCESSIONAL GRACE CAN, of course, be a marvelous cloak for fury. It tem-
pers innuendo and violence—while not completely denying or concealing
them. This, too, was a lesson Balthus learned from Piero della Francesca.

Consider what unfolds to the slow march rhythm of the *Legend of the True
Cross,* from which Balthus copied many passages in Arezzo. Adam announces
his own impending death, with the melancholy Eve behind him. Then he
appears as a rigid corpse, his family torn asunder by grief. Beleaguered men
carry the beam of sacred wood to bury it, while failing to see the mouth of hell
yawning at their feet. Horsemen who clash ferociously look as if they are under
a spell.

Judas, threatened with starvation until he reveals the whereabouts of the
cross, seems dazed as he is lowered into a dry well. He has the same glazed look
worn by the people in Balthus's paintings; nothing in his face will betray either
his sins or his fears. Even as Judas's hair is pulled, he remains expressionless, as
if resigned to his conduct and his pain. Similarly, his torturer's emotions are
indecipherable. The events are extreme, but the participants engage in them
enigmatically, with emotional distance. It was an example from which Balthus
learned some lifelong messages: about how to paint his subjects, and how to
behave in public.

Decorum and restraint prevail in the midst of high drama. And violence is expressed through gesture and pose rather than by any hint that the people involved know the state they are in. This is the approach Balthus would apply with consummate skill. Even more than Piero, he would control tumult with artifice. He would, meticulously, ration what observers might glean beneath the surface—first luring them into what is patently a highly charged scenario and then throwing a gauzy screen over all the excitement.

Balthus's card-playing boys, adolescent girls, and city dwellers are the direct descendants of Piero's workmen and Judas. So is the artist himself, with his sterling facade. The rest of us cannot penetrate the emotions or get beyond the masks. The apparent isolation in which Balthus has deliberately encased himself and his subjects enhances their strength. The people with whom Piero populated his chapel at Arezzo, the characters in Balthus's paintings, and Balthus himself all gain—through their detachment—tremendous power. At the same time, their distance and separateness diminish us, their viewers.

EVER SINCE THE END OF World War II, when he first began to acquire interesting ancestry, Balthus has tried to make himself into the people he envied as a youth: titled, non-Jewish, of particularly distinguished lineage—sometimes Byronic, sometimes czarist. Having chosen his heritage and convinced himself that it is his own, he has, like the most studious of actors, performed the privileged part impeccably—right down to the requisite soupçon of simplicity. He has imitated everything he has wanted to be, and done his utmost to become the objects of his admiration. The same can be said for his artistic technique. He has had more than one role model, but the mentor he has followed the most assiduously has remained Piero della Francesca.

Not that Balthus would have us see him this way. Talking with me, he denied the notion of direct influence with a flick of the wrist—as if of course we were in agreement that this was the piddle of art history. I had asked him what he thought of John Russell's statement in his Tate catalog that the man carrying wood in *The Street* (color plate 4) derived from Piero's man shouldering the cross at Arezzo, and Russell's illustration of the fresco detail to support his argument. Balthus belittled the point with a quizzical laugh. Then, bearing his patient professor's look, he remarked to me that people carry wood, that there is a natural way of placing a board on your shoulder, and that he intended no specific reference to his beloved Piero.

But the visual evidence is all on Russell's side. Examine the work, put it together with what you know of Balthus's personality, and it is clear that Rilke's protégé took his unabashed admiration for his fifteenth-century hero to the degree of trying to be, in certain ways, Piero's modern reincarnation. The Italian painter was not the only person Balthus would imitate to the point of becoming him—we will see some other, wilder models he would latch on to for briefer periods—but with regard to how he paints, Piero was and is the most lasting of his chosen selves.

Perhaps he was in the same sort of unconscious trance in which he shows his subjects, but Balthus has paraphrased Piero throughout his art. The boy on the left in *The Street* (1933) has an uncanny resemblance to the figure of Eve in *Adam Announcing His Death* at Arezzo. They have the identical eyebrows, full lips, flattened nose, wide cheeks, and strong indentations under their mouths. In addition to being practically the same person thanks to their features, they have in common that they both look as if they harbor a secret. They hold some knowledge unavailable to the rest of us. And the other boy in *The Street,* the one walking toward us with his hand across his chest, is, equally, Piero's version of one of Adam's sons, only now in modern Parisian dress.

THE PROFILED HEAD OF THE GIRL in Balthus's *Nude in Front of a Mantel* (1955) has features virtually identical to those of one of the members of the Queen of Sheba's retinue. The same delicate chin tucks into the girl's neck. Balthus's subject, like Piero's, gazes ahead transfixed. And these women painted five centuries apart have been revealed in much the same way. A soft light falls on their cheeks and caresses their curves, giving them the sheen of porcelain. Balthus's girl—in relief just as Piero's women are—has the same milky flesh and smooth perfection of her ancestor from Arezzo. She, too, emerges detached and beautiful.

ALAS, THIS 1955 *Nude in Front of a Mantel* is one of the most difficult of all of Balthus's paintings to see, although it is now almost always on view in a major public museum. The large canvas hangs in the Robert Lehman Collection at the Metropolitan Museum of Art in New York. Not only is it illuminated entirely by artificial light, in direct violation of the artist's wishes for the viewing of his work, but—worst of all—it is under glass. When it went to the 1980 Balthus show at the Venice Biennale, where it appeared on the catalog cover, witnesses saw the artist himself reduced to despair at the moment it arrived for installation. Balthus stormed around, shaking his cane in rage; here was one of his treasures imprisoned behind glass that deprived it of all its nuance and subtlety.

The 1955 painting, to begin with, has a distance about it; compared with the brazen adolescent girls of Balthus's prewar years, this girl with her hands in her hair is more of a stylized relief figure, her profile muted, her surroundings a stage set more than a room. But behind the shimmering glass that disturbs and deadens the treasure it traps, there is some fine painting. The girl stands with true weight and equipoise, her feet authentically planted. The light and shadows on her lovely flesh and within the fireplace are completely real and, at the same time, soothing.

Balthus first fell in love with this deliberate artificiality under the vaults of the apse at Arezzo. He learned how to formulate that cool and distant beauty, and how to conceal emotion—both his own and his subject's—when he was eighteen years old.

ONE OF THE REASONS BALTHUS doesn't want us looking at his origins and sources may well be that they offer too many clues to much that he would rather keep shadowed in mystery. Piero's prototypes help unravel the enigma of some of Balthus's most puzzling paintings.

In this regard, I have a theory that I did not dare bring up with the painter himself. It is that Balthus's extremely discomfiting 1952–54 *Room* derives directly from Piero della Francesca's equally baffling *Madonna del parto*.

The face of the woman in *The Room* is practically identical to that of Piero's Virgin. Her private domain is similarly revealed by a smaller creature holding back the drapery. But in Balthus's transformation, the woman who was in an elegant dress in the Renaissance has been stripped bare. Piero had her standing regally; Balthus has vanquished her. Now the former Holy Mother lies stunned. Her limp right arm suggests she is a victim, although the splay of her left leg reveals her to be available for sex. Piero's magisterial setting has become an ordinary room.

Yet for all that has changed, the *Madonna del parto* and *The Room* have similar effects. We are swayed and moved by their remarkable painterly beauty; at the same time, we struggle with a feeling of being left in the dark. The enigma is deliberate. In the Piero, why is her hand on her belly? In the Balthus, what has happened to her? Like cats, the facts are provocative yet out of reach.

One possibility that scholars have raised about Piero's offbeat fresco, located in Monterchi, is that the Madonna is pregnant. Such an image is practically unique in Italian art, and no one can be certain that Piero intended it, but it has been surmised that Mary points to her womb in what might be the sixth month. One of the reasons I think Balthus had the *Madonna del parto* in mind is that the woman in *The Room*—naked except for her shoes and socks— also looks pregnant. The shape of her bare abdomen, like this facial resem-

Piero della Francesca, *The Queen of Sheba, Kneeling with Her Retinue,* detail from
The Queen of Sheba's Visit to Solomon, 1452, fresco, overall size: 336 x 747 cm

blance, makes Balthus's girl an updated, overtly sexualized version of that
fifteenth-century Madonna.

Kenneth Clark has pointed out that this, of all of Piero's paintings,
"reminds us of the finest Buddhist sculpture in its calm detachment, and
is even more oriental in its outlines."[7] We know these to have been Balthus's ideals as well. His dramatically exhausted figure in *The Room* shares that
distance—and Easternness. Much as she is the image of spent passion, she
is also like a statue. And the artwork that contains her is a fine and stirring
object.

The *Madonna del parto* is considered a memorial to Piero's mother, who
was born and married in Monterchi. *The Room* might easily be read as Balthus's
portrait of his mother—one of many. This is the Baladine Klossowska we know
from her letters to Rilke—consumed by her own passions and longings.

Piero's Madonnas are some of the strongest females ever painted. They are
not the tender earth mothers of many Renaissance Madonnas but creatures of

Nude in Front of Mantel, 1956, oil on canvas, 190 x 164 cm

steely strength, composure, and fortitude. Balthus's women, however young and unformed some of them may be, have similar power. While Balthus and Piero were both artistically reserved, they gave their women an unreserved forcefulness.

As for the character in *The Room* who resembles a terrifying dwarf—the little girl with the aged face and the miniaturized build of a middle-aged man; the character of whom Balthus told me, with his most taciturn look and a declaration that the point was beyond debate, that she was just a girl, and that if people called her a dwarf, or said there was anything odd about her, that it reflected their own hang-ups, but had no bearing at all either on him or on the actual painting—it seems to me that this is his own transformation of the angels in the *Madonna del parto.* Like those angels, Balthus's golem in 1950s schoolgirls' clothing stands firmly anchored with its legs wide apart—in a position that we now associate with classical ballet. It wears slippers almost identical to those on Piero's angels. The light from the window behind creates a glow like a cap over the poor character's bangs that can be read as a grotesque parody of the angels' halos. Balthus's weird invention appears to be his own, highly personal version of those biblical supporting actors. In Renaissance art, they almost always look female, although they were, historically, male; Balthus has taken the angel type one step further and turned it into an impersonator.

In the *Madonna del parto,* the angels, holding open drapery so that we may see the scene better, serve as revealers. Pulling back curtains, throwing light on a subject, they have the same function as the artist. The angels' heir, the weird creature in *The Room,* is a stand-in for Balthus himself. An amalgam of middle-aged man and young girl, the different ages and opposite sexes converging in one puzzling being, this representative of the artist is both revealer of an enigma and creator of an even greater one. Unique, unfamiliar, and unforgettable, the anomaly is meant to keep us guessing.

The androgynous gnome is a mix of youth and old age, childishness and wisdom. The nude on the divan also combines birth and death. Life is starting up inside her, yet she appears halfway out of the world, as if in a coma or at the edge of death. The stages of existence are as simultaneously evident in Balthus's art as in the man himself.

BALTHUS TOLD ME, OF COURSE, that *The Room* is simply a painting of a nude in a room with a girl at the window. People hold back curtains. They naturally situate their feet firmly—which is why the "child" stands as it does. This is life—not artistic quotation or poetic analogue. He painted what moved him, without knowing why. What concerned him were the problems of texture and color and light and form—not symbolism or meaning. Yet he did allow that the pulled-back curtains of *The Room* are an invitation to seeing, a form of opening. For Balthus perpetually beckons and excites us—even as he refutes our conclusions.

III

PIERO'S CLEAR PERSPECTIVE, spatial geometry, and delicate balance of convex and concave that were the eighteen-year-old Balthus's ambrosia moved him to develop standards and techniques that have guided him ever since.

Piero della Francesca, *Madonna del parto,* c. 1460, fresco, 260 x 203 cm

In those few weeks in Arezzo and Sansepolcro, he discovered how he would paint. He learned how to model figures delicately in relief. Like Piero, he would populate his paintings with fully frontal faces, on heads that were relatively large proportionate to the rest of the body. Compelled by the look of assurance behind Piero's work, he made its arrangements his own. Piero's design precision and controlled observation became his models. Balthus emulated Piero's motionless gravity and his delicacy, as well as his mix of opulence and austerity. He has worked to achieve the Italian's clear delineation of sunshine, and his use of light to envelop forms. He has strived for Piero's impeccable judgment in the subtle tones of his carefully related, pale, cool colors. Balthus learned that such a palette creates a quiet, detached majesty; it helps provide the elegance, and the air of remoteness, vital to figures absorbed in their own worlds.

So Balthus would give the colors of *The Street* a softness—the muted, dignified tonality—much like the cast of *The Victory of Heracles* at Arezzo. These earthy, yellow-tinged hues provide the action of *The Street* with a look of extreme significance—as if these happenings have been going on for quite some time and now are fixed forever. *The Street* shows everyday occurrences, but the people in it have noble stature, like biblical characters. So do the hikers in *The Mountain,* and most of Balthus's adolescents. The well-controlled, subtle, atmospheric palette that he learned from Piero is a primary source of that momentousness.

From Piero, Balthus developed a color sensibility that lends both reality and unreality. The palette that makes the personalities in Piero's frescoes simultaneously genuine and fictitious provides Balthus's people and scenes with their dreamlike aura. The muted, powdery fresco colors help create Balthus's unusual combination of palpable presence and elusiveness.

Whatever his subject—children languishing in dark interiors, the splashily tiled Turkish Room of the Villa Medici in Rome, mountain landscapes, naked bathers stepping out of the tub—Balthus has always put his colors in quiet discourse with one another. They resonate subtly under the pervading calm cast by muted sunlight. The system of responses—a splash of yellow-green in the foreground echoing the identical tint in the distant hills, the orange of a flower the same as that in a nearby tapestry pattern—works like the balancing of forms. Blacks, ochers, and russets correspond just as arcs, spheres, and cylinders do. These were among Piero's most potent lessons.

In Balthus's art as in Piero's, the restrained colors and precise geometry classicize the experience. Balthus's imagery—even though he denies this—is often sexually violent, yet he handles the subject matter as if it were a formal occasion to which one should have received an engraved invitation protected by a tiny square of tissue paper. The underlying systematization asks us not to recoil. A breast hangs out, a lance pierces, a child flashes her inner thigh, but the tone in which the story is told suggests that the teller is unfazed and we should be, too. Following his Italian sojourn, Balthus would depict lust and brutality, yet he would veil it—and, perhaps, disguise it from himself—by making it look staged. If it is theater, then we don't have to take it as real. The techniques whereby he achieved that glorious artifice were at his beck and call in Piero's marvelous frescoes.

Balthus became as careful in his placement of colors and forms through-out his paintings as he would eventually become in his application of the rules and schemata with which he controlled his personal image. He gave to *The Street* a careful orchestration of cylindrical, columnar shapes much like that of Piero's rendering of the Queen of Sheba's visit. He could depict the most provocative, unsettling subject matter—as in the 1937 *White Skirt,* in which his sitter, looking as if she has been hit over the head, collapses in an armchair with her blouse open, her breasts so tight in her bra that she seems in bondage—while precisely halving the composition horizontally just as Piero did in his ineffably tranquil London *Baptism* and in so many of the Arezzo frescoes.

Balthus's approach is the exact opposite of that of realist photography or Expressionistic painting. With those styles, horrors are conveyed in a cry of anguish. The voice unsettles us as much as the subject does. When Balthus and Setsuko speak of the current art scene, they deplore art in which the shock is explicit. Bluntness is out of the question, deliberate unattractiveness inexcus-able. To hear the Count and Countess de Rola speak, you would not think that Balthus's own work had ever made anyone uncomfortable. You would assume his paintings were as tame, and harmlessly decorative, as hers are. Art should have nothing to do with hardship, except for the struggles implicit in the act of painting. Formality and propriety are the ultimate virtues. This is what Edmund Burke called "the decent drapery of life"—of which, for Balthus, his mentor Piero della Francesca was early on, and remains, the greatest exemplar.

In *De Prospettiva Pingendi,* Piero della Francesca wrote:

> Painting contains within itself three principal parts, drawing, compo-sition, and coloring. By drawing we mean the profiles and contours within which they are contained. By composition we mean how these profiles and contours may be situated proportionately in their proper places. By coloring we mean how to give things their colors as they appear, light or dark, according as the light varies them.[8]

Piero's word for "composition" is *commensuratio,* whereas Alberti's, in *Della pittura,* was *composizione.* This distinction is key to why Balthus fastened on Piero with such zeal, and to what he has been emulating for more than seventy years. Balthus has, unflaggingly, sought measure and proportion—the quali-ties it took to commensurate for other, less ruly forces—in both his art and his self. What he has suppressed is another matter.

CHAPTER SEVEN

PERAMBULATIONS

*In all memory there is a degree of falseness; we are all exiles from
our own pasts, just as, on looking up from a book, we discover
anew our banishment from the bright worlds of imagination
and fantasy.*

—JOHN LANCHESTER, *The Debt to Pleasure*[1]

I

BALTHUS AND HIS MOTHER would never see Rainer Maria Rilke again.
The moment on the train platform in Sierre in September 1925 was the last
time Merline and René would gaze into one another's eyes; Balthus's stop-off at
Muzot en route to Italy was the final occasion when the coauthors of *Mitsou*
would enter the marvelous mutual territory in which art and the intangible
reigned supreme.

In 1926 the poet was traveling between Muzot and friends' houses and
grand hotels while battling a mysterious and devastating illness—which was
probably undiagnosed leukemia. Baladine, in Paris, seemed more aware of the
effect of the symptoms of his declining health on her and on their relationship
than on Rilke himself. As Rilke succumbed to increasing weakness and exhaustion, she wrote him that November, "Has nothing bad happened between
us? . . . Tell me that it's still good between you and me. Are you so ill that all
love for me stands still?"[2] Baladine must have felt utter dismay in the ensuing
week when she did not hear from him, and then when she finally received a
birthday telegram that failed to answer her questions and that, although polite
and concerned about her and her sons, addressed her with the formal "vous."

The last letter Rilke ever wrote was to Baladine Klossowska on December
23, 1926. Here, too, she was "*vous.*" Her former lover warned her, "If your loving heart were to counsel you to come, you would be ill advised." No one was
permitted in, he instructed. The poet slipped into a coma at midnight on
December 28, and revived briefly at 3:30 in the morning only to fall back dead.

Rilke was buried on Sunday, January 2, 1927. It was bitter cold but brilliantly sunny in the mountains. The interment followed a short Catholic church service in which music by Bach was performed on violin and organ. In his 1992 essay "Balthus et la Suisse," Jean Leymarie reports that Balthus attended that funeral, at the side of Rilke's faithful editor Anton Kippenberg, his devoted supporter Werner Reinhart, and his intimate friend Nanny Wunderly-Volkart—and that Balthus then remained for several days near Muzot contemplating the beauty of the Valais in the winter. Perhaps this was so. But no other account of Rilke's funeral—including several contemporary reports that list all of the attendees—mentions Balthus's presence. And one of these histories makes specific reference to the absence of Balthus's mother; in spite of the occasional communication, Rilke had deliberately reduced their connection in his final months.

Balthus cared enough for Rilke, and the poet for him, that the idea of the young painter standing there at the grave is easy to imagine. The image of a saddened Balthus, staring out over the snow-covered mountains, ruminating over the death of his mentor and his mother's great love, is irresistible.

STARTING IN 1925, when he was seventeen, Balthus had begun to make oil paintings in which he depicted ordinary Parisians of all ages going about their daily activities—walking, playing, doing errands, gazing at their surroundings. He continued this work in Paris with renewed zeal after his inspirational trip to Italy.

The subject matter was the same he had first explored in pen and ink at age eleven in his telling evocations of the life of city squares and parks in *Mitsou*. Balthus had an affinity for charming, quiet vignettes within urban settings. In a fast-paced metropolis, he would dwell not on the hustle and bustle or the latest evidence of modernism but on the neighborhood scenes that make corners of cities like small towns. It was in these locales where he could most intensely feel the poignancy and humor of human existence.

Ordinary daily living was the subject he would depict, in however different a tone, forever after. Initially he concentrated on the way children spent their time—like those girls jumping rope on the Piazza Santa Croce. He had an eye for how women look, and for their awareness of their appearance and their methods of drawing attention to it. If he painted a shopgirl in a hat, he seemed able to evoke all the hopes she attached to that hat. The nuances of vanity—evident both in clothing and comportment—were clear. He could suggest a man's position in society not just through what he wore but also by how he carried himself. Balthus applied a novelist's sense of detail and a painter's eye to the subtle aspects of the human comedy.

When Balthus first painted his whimsical interpretations of everyday life in the mid-1920s, he used a style similar to that of his champion Bonnard. His method in those years resembled Bonnard's in the apparent freedom of the brushstrokes and the look of dappled sunlight. The young Balthus prized the notion of capturing the first impression of the scene before his eyes.

The goal—allegedly—was to present visual experience, not comment on it. Balthus claims that he neither embellished his subject matter nor put a personal slant on it. He told me that his lifelong task has always been to paint what he sees and to suspend judgment. Yet, just as his later work reflects a particular vision of the world, his early canvases had a bias that was definitely comic. Balthus's initial renditions of everyday life mocked personality types and often lapsed into snide caricature. Whether inadvertently or by plan—and in spite of his claims to the contrary—he depicted, and perhaps saw, the world in a highly personal, subjective, and deprecatory way.

The Quays, which Balthus painted in 1929 when he was twenty-one, shows a group of people standing and walking along the Seine. A bridge and some Parisian buildings are part of the setting, in which a picnic basket and wine bottle take up the foreground. It was precisely the sort of scene that artists throughout Europe had been painting for decades. This twenty-one-year-old could represent his subject matter with considerable success. Without formal training, Balthus could deftly establish near and far, articulate the cityscape, make clear at what angle the hay was heaped on a distant horse cart, and focus sunlight on people's faces and on the wickerwork of the picnic basket.

A young man leaning over a wall puts his weight on his forearms. The men walk with a robust stride; a woman standing is properly immobile. The painting has an underlying kernel of truth: this is what human civilization looks like. Apparently with very little effort, Balthus has made everything plausible.

He also painted the world seductively. A range of soft and subtle colors permeates the rich impasto. On close viewing, the gray pavement yields a variety of tones, and the powdery sky is an amalgam of purples, blues, and grays. The woman's blouse radiates iridescent blue. The free and brushy rendering and lively colors give the scene a forceful immediacy. It has spark and animation. The tone reflects a reverence toward the world, but also the insouciance possible only through polished style. The young Balthus already had panache.

Balthus combined the styles of Bonnard and of some of the Impressionists, yet even in this early stage his work had a unique quirkiness. The cast of characters is unlike anyone else's. This is not just a scene in a city; it is a satirical exposition of how people look and conduct themselves. They are quite odd. We focus on them more than we would on ordinary mortals because of the

The Quays, 1929, oil on canvas, 73 x 59.8 cm

tragicomic expressions on their oversized faces. One man has a nose that is positively putty-like. The hair of the solitary woman is not simply puffed in the manner of the day; the front of it billows like a soufflé, while her bun resembles a pom-pom. A parody of propriety, this lady is clearly misguided in her judgment as to how to put herself together. Self-impressed and tasteless to the point of being asinine, she is a type that will be a leitmotif in Balthus's art. Everyone is a caricature; Balthus had subtly evoked a corner of modern Paris with Balzac-like incision.

Balthus told me that *The Quays* was "just a scene and nothing more." The sole acknowledgment he offered of his own cynical wit was a sort of half smile. Yet his depiction of "just a scene" is almost ludicrous.

Balthus's particular slant is especially apparent in the way the woman with puffed-up hair holds her cat. The animal, hanging limply, looks miserable; no cat wants to stay this way for five seconds. Yet in spite of the cat's uncomfortable position, the woman smiles merrily and stands firmly. She is completely indifferent to the agony she is causing. An utter fool, she represents the stupidity and blindness of bourgeois society—the object of Balthus's dupery and mockery for the rest of his life.

The old crone has the temerity, and gall, and ignorance, to think that she can grasp the kin of the elusive Mitsou—the artist's alter ego. The creature who wins our heart is this emblem of Balthus himself: the poor and beleaguered victim, the free spirit that will not be tamed or made to fit into the oppressive and rule-bound society that surrounds him and tries to hold him in its pathetic grip.

There is only one person in *The Quays* who does not appear silly or bizarre. That exception is the solitary figure walking away from us with his back turned and his face invisible. Different from the others, this is Balthus himself. The artist confirmed this in conversation with me.

Tall and lanky, he conceals his persona. With his hands in his pockets, he appears utterly taciturn. He has seen the world, but now he turns his back on it. Like Balthus's self-portrait as the man carrying a baguette in *The Passage du Commerce Saint-André,* his identity comes from what he has seen, his strength from his ability to cloak himself completely. This slow-going, surefooted witness relates to the world on his own terms.

II

FROM LATE 1930 UNTIL THE SPRING of 1932, Balthazar Klossowski performed his military service. He was stationed with the French army, in the Seventh Regiment of Tirailleurs, at Kenitra in Morocco—a country he told me he loved although he contracted both dysentery and malaria there.

Balthus was fascinated by the desert landscape he saw on tours of duty in the southern reaches of Morocco, and he relished the chance to glimpse the world that had intrigued him in *The Thousand and One Nights*—whose translator, Dr. Mardrus, he had met in Paris. Above all, he liked Fez. He was moved by the maze of angled passageways and the intense urban bustle of the Medina in that atmospheric Arab city. When he was there, he managed the feat, unusual for a European, of learning to speak and understand some Arabic. He came to feel, he says, very much at home. Fez struck him as being like the medieval Arezzo of Piero's frescoes. Thus it seemed in his eyes to belong to an earlier epoch, which gave it undeniable charm.

Balthus told me he still cherishes the memory of that North African

Medina. The perfection of his recollections is the reason he has never dared return there; he would rather keep it wonderful in the world of his mind than find it changed.

The actual time in Morocco was not easy, however. Of frail constitution, Balthus struggled with the rigors of military life. In contrast to the memories he voiced to me, the letters he wrote as a soldier reveal his feelings of loneliness and isolation.

In that period of reflection and longing, of fascination and alienation, Balthus developed a new way of expressing his vision of the world. He never had time to paint during the year and a half in Morocco, but the anxieties of his time there, and the strong and uncompromising North African light, had a lasting effect on his art.

Morocco, particularly Fez, can be as wet and gray as it can be Mediterranean and sunny, but its light is clear and distilled. The flowers and faces and minarets illuminated by the North African sun, even on a cloudy day, have sharp optical definition. Most significantly for Balthus, the light in that part of the world elevates the objects it illuminates beyond apprehensible reality into another sphere of being.

Edith Wharton, after visiting Morocco in 1925, depicted its light as having a "preternatural purity which gives a foretaste of mirage." It is "the light in which magic becomes real. . . . To people living in such an atmosphere, the boundary between fact and dream perpetually fluctuates. . . . Buildings, people, customs, seem all about to crumble and fall of their own weight: the present is a perpetually prolonged past. To touch the past with one's own hands is realized only in dreams; and in Morocco the dream-feeling envelops one at every stage."[3] What the American writer gleaned there exactly describes the qualities with which Balthus imbued his art following his sojourn with the military.

"The result of Morocco was washing away an Impressionist vision of things. Perhaps the cleanness of the light," Balthus said to me. Balthus's army experience indeed marked his break from Impressionism and its use of loose brushwork to create a mottled atmosphere and color fluctuations. The paintings he began to make in the course of 1932, and all of his subsequent work, are more focused, their forms more precise, than previously.

But with the appearance of clarity came the ambiguity and intentional haze identified by Edith Wharton.

THE HIATUS FROM PAINTING—his life's blood—for a year and a half, and his experience of the army, caused a hardening in Balthus. More than the surface of his pictures turned brittle. After his return from Morocco, he became more exacting and definite than he had been as the painter of his earlier, light-hearted Parisian scenes. He lost his lyricism, and gained remoteness and self-assuredness. He mastered the structure and finish he wanted to put on things. Before Morocco, Balthus had painted ordinary life by using a charming, light-infused Impressionistic technique and treating his subjects humorously. Now he took control and turned deliberately elusive. His style crystallized. He became more formal and posed, and estranged, in both his work and his persona. The unguarded if volatile enthusiast had evolved into a person who would live out his life as if by a conscious scheme.

After his return from Morocco, Balthus's work, like his characters, developed a glaze, both physical and emotional, and took on the quality of being intensely studied. Passion underlies the rhythms and the vehement organization of the forms, but something is not available to us. That sense of concealment makes us uncomfortable, in part because we are left wanting to know what is going on. For a while these pictures engage us totally with their sheer elegance, their considerable visual impact, and the expertise of their technique; but then they put us on edge.

IF MOROCCO HAD BEEN ARDUOUS, Balthus's homecoming was not all that much easier. When he returned to Paris after completing his military service in the spring of 1932, he longed to paint but did not have enough money to survive doing so. Unwilling to take a job, Balthus could not survive in the French capital.

Fortunately, there was a solution. The twenty-four-year-old Balthus had a friend, Robert de Watteville, who lived in Bern. De Watteville, who had written about Morocco, was sympathetic to the young painter and asked him to come and stay at his parents' house. Again Switzerland proved a haven. It also became further associated in Balthus's mind with luxury and stability—which would increase its allure later in Balthus's life. The de Wattevilles had a large and lovely mansion in which the young artist could live well at no cost.

Not far away from this gracious house in Bern, Balthus discovered the work of another artistic mentor whose voice would help him develop his own. Shortly after arriving in Switzerland, Balthus saw the eighteenth-century Swiss portraitist Joseph Reinhardt's Swiss Peasant Costume Cycle. Over a hundred of these canvases, depicting lively local characters in the colorful garb indigenous to each of the many Swiss cantons, crowded the staircase of the historical museum. These canvases were an unusual learning tool for a young artist fully aware of all that was going on in Paris at the time, but Balthus set to work.

Joseph Reinhardt, *Hanss Mast and Liesabett Zbinder,*
1795(?), oil on canvas, 70 x 50 cm

Reinhardt's pictures are charming in their crude force as well as their quality of confidence, but the characters are for the most part dour and taciturn,
encased behind facades, posing as if frozen in place. Some are downright
weird, epitomizing deranged country types. Others are particularly funny:
women smoking pipes; sisters in bright red tights and dirndls who appear
practically committable; taciturn personalities capable of anything. Balthus
would have picked up on the humor of the work, and at the same time must
have been lured by the strong forms, sure-handed drawing, and rich palette.
He also could not have been impervious to the odd raciness behind the proper
fronts of the men and women shown together in the paintings of couples.

In one from the Kanton Bern, for example, the lust between Hanss Mast
and the fifteen-year-old Liesabett Zbinder is palpable in spite of their wooden
faces. The robust Hanss looks extremely virile in his knee breeches, obviously
delighted to be arm in arm with the buxom Liesabett, about a quarter of his

age, with her bulging breasts and vixen's face. It was a brilliant and independent eye that could discover this art and let it nourish him to such a degree that it would permeate his own paintings forever after.

Balthus found Reinhardt's work vivid and truthful. He admired the portraitist's skill at grouping figures, and must also have liked Reinhardt's mix of sophistication and primitiveness. Based on what we know of Balthus's taste and what we see in Reinhardt's canvases, it is not a far reach to suppose that the young copyist was also riveted by the peculiarities of Reinhardt's stalwart peasants, frozen in their silent folk dances, looking incredibly like the sort of creatures who might leap from the barn-dance floor and go dismember corpses with an ax.

The former acolyte of Poussin and Piero concentrated intensely on the task of recapitulating and interpreting Reinhardt's portraits. Entirely possessed by the act of painting, he worked long days and sometimes painted for seven hours at a stretch. He noticed that when he was working he forgot everything extraneous to the issues of making pictures. He wrote to the Strohls that with a brush in his hand, he did not have to endure the doubts and anxieties about life which plagued him the rest of the time. It was a discovery he loved. Now more than ever he was convinced that to make art was his only possible goal in life.

Balthus made ten copies after Reinhardt's work. Like his canvases based on Piero, these borrowed from the originals while not replicating their exact appearance. The young copyist was true to Reinhardt's rhythms and to the careful positioning of the leaning peasants, but his strokes are sketchier and his "copies" are bolder and looser than their models.

More than his mentor, Balthus enlarged the subjects' heads. He thereby intensified the human presence. Balthus's Reinhardts, unlike their prototypes, are practically caricatures. The Swiss peasants are now rendered more puckish and high-spirited. With glimmers in their eyes, they look more aware of the impressions they make than do the sterner types on whom they were based. What Reinhardt had done in earnestness, Balthus did with the self-conscious bias of the satirical observer.

If he had a prayer of making a go of it as a painter, Balthus needed to sell these copies. Fortunately, he found a patron. Margrit Bay, a friend in Beatenberg, tried to find buyers for them but failed, so she ended up paying for them herself. The fledgling artist considered her act of support a lifeline.

Lots of people Balthus knew had cautioned him that painting was an unrealistic profession. He was embarking on a hazardous course. But as he worked on the Reinhardts, he came to recognize, as never before, that to stifle his own creativity would destroy him. As he explained in letters of unabashed ardor and intensity, he had to be an artist.

III

THAT FALL OF 1932, Balthus painted his first significant portrait. Shortly after arriving at the de Watteville household, the young artist had become intrigued by Robert's sister Antoinette. In five years, after a tumultuous courtship, he would marry her. Soon after glimpsing her for the first time, he painted her picture, somewhat in the manner he had developed when doing the Reinhardt copies.

When I stayed with Balthus and Setsuko in Rossinière, one of the two Balthus oil paintings in the vast house—aside from the one in progress in the studio—was this small portrait of Antoinette. The painting evokes a major, glowing moment of the artist's youth; it is a vision of first love. Additionally, its possession is the solution to a problem.

Balthus told me that this riveting, disarmingly simple image is both one of his earliest extant canvases and one of the most recent. With the pleasure of someone telling a charming anecdote, he said that the original 1932 portrait had been stolen—from the studio he had in Paris at the Cour de Rohan between 1937 and 1954. In the late 1970s, however, it resurfaced in New York, and so he bought it back. Seeing it again, the artist deemed certain improvements necessary. He changed the background color and redid the face. In so doing, he gave his subject the new translucency with which he had come to imbue his most recent figures; at the same time, he kept her the young Antoinette.

The alterations after a hiatus of fifty years afforded Balthus a chance to make a gift with a twist he relished. He had given the work to Stanislas, his and Antoinette's son, who in turn had left the painting at Le Grand Chalet where all the family might enjoy it. Balthus recalled that he had prefaced the presentation to his son with the remark, "I have a wonderful Christmas present for you. You know it, but you don't know it." Stanislas—tall, sunken-cheeked, his hair pulled back in a ponytail—was at his side when Balthus told me this story. As we stood in front of the 1932–82 canvas, they both grinned at the memory. It seemed perfect: this idea of something both recognizable and altered, gone but now recovered. I shared their delight in the tale.

There is, however, more to the history of this small canvas than I knew when Balthus recounted these events to me. James Lord told me that in the early 1960s he was walking along the Rue Bonaparte in Paris one day when he noticed an unframed Balthus drawing on an easel in the window of an antiques shop. It wasn't initialed as Balthus's drawings often are, but Lord recognized what it was and went in to ask the price. The antiquarian responded to Lord's inquiry by bringing out an entire portfolio of Balthus drawings; when I dis-

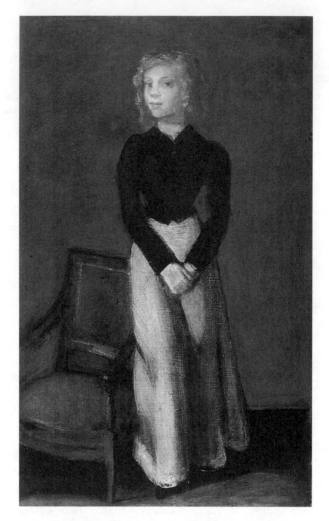

Antoinette, 1932–82, oil on canvas, 70 x 50 cm

cussed this with Lord in Paris in 1992, he recalled that there were between twenty and thirty.

Lord immediately telephoned Eugene Victor Thaw in New York. Thaw was a well-established art dealer and collector who specialized in works on paper. Lord periodically bought artworks in Paris for Thaw: he knew that Thaw was friendly with Pierre Matisse and so would have an inside track on the Balthus market. He quoted Thaw the very low prices being asked for these drawings and asked what he should do about them. Thaw's instructions were unequivocal: "Buy them all."

Lord returned to the antiquarian and did so immediately. To his surprise, the seller then offered him more drawings. This time he added that he might be able to come up with an oil painting and some watercolors as well. Gene Thaw and Pierre Matisse ended up jointly buying this entire cache of Balthuses—including the oil and watercolors.

Once Thaw had sent Lord the necessary funds and Lord had paid the antiquarian and shipped the work to New York, Thaw and Matisse went about preparing an exhibition of these previously unknown Balthuses at Thaw's gallery on East Seventy-eighth Street. But long before the scheduled opening of the show—late November 1963—they sent photos of all of the work to Balthus so that the artist could provide certificates of authentication. Balthus instantly realized that these pieces had all come from his studio, although he had not even noticed that they were missing. The small painting—which was the 1932 portrait of Antoinette—had been there as well. Balthus told Pierre Matisse that all of this work had been stolen by his son.

Lord and Thaw both gave me identical accounts of these events. Stanislas had desperately needed money from the antique dealer to cover some personal debts, and had long since spent what the dealer had paid him by the time the ruse was uncovered. Balthus said that Thaw and Matisse could keep the draw ings. He would not sign them, but neither would he repudiate them or challenge the ownership. The art dealers, however, had to satisfy one demand in exchange for his cooperation. Balthus asked Thaw and Matisse to return the portrait of Antoinette and absorb the loss of the amount they paid for it— about $4,000. The dealers willingly did so; even with that concession, they made a small fortune on these stolen Balthus drawings which they were able to sell easily for far more money than they had paid.

The exhibition was a coup. The catalog had an erudite introduction by John Rewald. The show, which also depended on loans from a few private collectors, gave the public its first look ever at a range of Balthus's drawings. Starting with his early illustrations for *Wuthering Heights,* it also included studies for some of his best-known paintings, and recent watercolors of flowers and landscapes. Since Balthus had always kept his preliminary sketches to himself and treated them as private notations, this was a unique event.

Balthus's statement to me that the early portrait of Antoinette in front of us had been stolen and then had resurfaced in New York was completely correct. He certainly could not have been expected to mention that the thief had been his son, who was standing there at his side. But Lord's addenda—which Thaw subsequently corroborated to me—made it a very different sort of scenario. This meant that Balthus, who redid *Antoinette* in the early 1980s, had repainted it almost two decades after the nasty incident—not right after he had recovered the picture, which is what he suggested to me. And the recipient of the gift was its thief. The style of it all—ironic, carefully thought-out, counter to all norms of bourgeois behavior—is one hundred percent Balthus.

Was the gift an acknowledgment that Stanislas had mended his ways? Did it serve as a form of thanks for Stanislas's book, in which Antoinette's portrait was reproduced in color for the first time? Was this Balthus's way of saying that filial love transcends all? Or a message from a father to his son that stealing is really okay? Perhaps it was simply a capricious act—for which the motives are as unknowable as when a cat settles on you to purr just when you think it is about to claw you.

THE NATURE OF THE ALTERATIONS Balthus did and did not make fifty years later to that painting from 1932 tells a lot about his life's work. Essentially, the style he had developed as Reinhardt's young copyist still looked acceptable to him and was of a piece with all he had done in the meantime. He felt a need to tinker with the original, but was content to forgo any more sweeping changes. In the period between 1932 and 1982, the evolution of modern art had encompassed an encyclopedia's worth of styles, but Balthus had remained essentially the same artist he started out as.

In this respect, it made complete sense when Balthus told me that his

Giorgio Morandi, *Still Life,* 1947, oil on panel, 43 x 60 cm

favorite of his contemporaries has long been Giorgio Morandi. The choice is especially significant in a century when the high-speed movement of Cubism, Futurism, Constructivism, and Abstract Expressionism have been at the forefront. Morandi was, Balthus explained, "one of the greatest painters of the century. Extraordinary economy. Doesn't need any tricks."

Balthus and Morandi share the relative consistency of almost all of their meticulous, slow-paced work. Both of them evolved stylistically, but within a tight sphere. Having found something he cared about when he was quite young, each was content to devote his life to it, with few divergences. While Balthus had, at the time of my visits, none of his own art on view in the main sitting rooms of Le Grand Chalet, he treated the Italian's fine still-life drawing he has in his drawing room as a sort of icon. Having led me to believe that he could barely tolerate the presence of his own two watercolors hanging less conspicuously in Le Grand Chalet—they are there, he maintained, only because Setsuko insisted—he voiced a collector's pride in both this drawing and Morandi's subdued landscape watercolor in the foyer of the visitor's bathroom. Along with a Bonnard print and works by Balthus's parents and a couple of his favorite students, little else was on view.

Balthus told me he deeply regretted that he and Morandi never met. But even if Morandi admired the quiet grandeur and visual serenity of Balthus's finest achievements, the Italian would probably have perceived Balthus's work as troubling and erotic. Since Morandi, who lived modestly with his sisters in Bologna, completely eschewed the high life, they would probably have had less in common than Balthus liked to imagine.

Balthus nevertheless deliberately established his link to Morandi by virtual paraphrase. Although he assiduously maintained to me that he has avoided specific reference to other artists in his work, particularly when he was living in Italy in the 1960s, he put distinctly Morandiesque details in his work. The arrangement of cup and vase on a tabletop at the right of the 1963–66 *Turkish Room* (page 532) so closely resembles Morandi's still lifes that Jean Leymarie and other writers have called it a direct and intentional quotation. Balthus told me that this was not the case—that Leymarie was wrong in this matter—but given the authority he had over Leymarie's text, and the visual evidence, this is probably just another instance of Balthus's changing his story simply to be confounding. Ever since his own move to Rome in 1962, Balthus has used the Italian's tonality, his particular matte beige and white and terracotta. Like Morandi, he has cloaked the objects in a soft haze, muting their edges while making them powerfully present in a uniquely artful way.

Even when he was still at Chassy, Balthus had assumed Morandi's voice in the still-life vignettes behind his nudes—to considerable effect. The Morandi-like progression of bottles on the sideboard in the 1958 *Young Woman Getting Ready for the Bath* added a deliberate propriety and foil to the sexiness. The chunky pitcher, shaped just like one of Morandi's, on the mantel in the 1955 *Nude in Front of a Mantel* teeters on the edge of pure imitation. Of course, when I asked about these references, Balthus just smiled elusively and blamed the assumption on Sabine Rewald.

But the visual evidence is strong. That Balthus's method of painting in 1981 could be so close to what it was in 1932 makes clear why Morandi was another of his chosen voices.

THE YOUNG ANTOINETTE of Balthus's portrait epitomizes the artist's feminine ideal. She has the look of both a young matron and an eight-year-old. The child and the mature woman are simultaneously present in her combination of girlish ease and total self-command. Her allure seems instinctive, yet she is rather coy.

The painter, too, is both ingenue and sophisticate. His rendering of Antoinette's flattened hands and of her arms in their black sleeves is awkward and primitive. But elsewhere his painting technique reflects a high degree of polish. The work has an authority; the surfaces read clearly. The style combines a childlike freshness with the expertise of a savvy painter.

The child-woman Antoinette is decidedly elegant. Her simple black waistcoat and white skirt—now more accentuated than in 1932, thanks to Balthus's repainting of the background in a matte, orangy red—become her with dignity. Balthus knew the blend of ingredients that makes a true aristocrat. Antoinette is regal in her erect bearing and easy stance. She is self-assured without flaunting it. The artist has rendered his inamorata's legs under her skirt—the right one bent and weight-bearing, the left slightly twisted and balletic—to display this quiet strength.

A YEAR LATER, IN *Cathy Dressing,* Balthus would transform this refined Antoinette into a vamp and a conqueror. There she holds her right leg at almost exactly the same angle as in her aristocratic portrait, but to a very different purpose: in the guise of Cathy from *Wuthering Heights,* she brandishes her nudity.

The Reinhardt-like portrait of 1932, however, has a deliberate simplicity, a courtliness, a controlled grace. Sunlight luxuriates on the subject's face. It also highlights some of her clothing, the chair against which she leans, and the wooden floor. This is a happy domestic scene; life is bountiful.

Antoinette embodied the young artist's highest standards and represented some of his paramount goals. He was almost as attracted by aristocracy as by oil paint and young women. In time he would specialize in the intricacies of all three; and master them all. In this luminous early canvas, we can already discern their allure for the struggling young artist.

BALTHUS MADE HIS FUTURE bride's face wider than her waist, her head larger than her upper torso. The distortion is extreme. Yet as with most of Balthus's deceptions, we do not initially discern anything awry. At first glance, the viewer falls sway to the glowing, angelic presence. Enchantment precedes our understanding of its components or recognition of its causes: this is a sequence Balthus has long understood.

We are warmed by the glow that emanates from the small canvas before we realize that this light is an audacious contrivance. Balthus overpainted pure white on the arm support of the chair, in Antoinette's eyes, over her mouth, and on her hands. Unrealistic though the dazzling tone is—no human flesh is so snow-white—we take it to be the truth.

We believe the lies because the rest is so convincing. In part as a result of his recent study of Joseph Reinhardt, at age twenty-four Balthus had already developed the wherewithal to establish position and to articulate the human body with consummate authority. By putting a distinct shadow behind Antoinette's right arm, he brought it forward—just in front of the left—with precision.

The sense of reality is sufficient that we tend to overlook the areas where it is lacking. Consider the hands. In virtually all of his work, hands are Balthus's most pronounced failing. In general, he either makes them complete blurs or renders them so that they resemble claws. Antoinette's are vague and awkwardly formed. Yet we read them as hands and condone the clumsiness. Balthus gets away with his fudging because the canvas is convincing as a whole. Having learned his lessons at Arezzo about the painting of white drapery, he deftly evokes Antoinette's skirt. Over her right leg, it is opaque and stretched taut by the flesh tacitly underneath it. Where it hangs freely, it is slightly translucent so that a bit of the background shows through. These details flawlessly duplicate real visual experience.

Elsewhere this exacting canvas is an artist's sketch far more than an imitation of life. The armchair is more brushwork than velvet. The floor is a shorthand notation. The point where floor and wall meet shows through the alleged mass of the chair.

Balthus would no sooner justify his decisions about where he is exact and where he is approximate than he would attempt to explicate the loveliness of Antoinette's powdery blue eyes. If some of us consider analysis a means toward understanding, this particular artist regards it as destructive to real experience—and disrespectful of his wishes. It is no more possible, or wise, for the layman to dissect a painting than for the listener of music to cite the reasons why Mozart—Balthus's favorite composer—selected a certain chord at a given moment.

Extend the same courtesy to the man himself. That we choose to do otherwise reflects our own needs more than objective insights. If we wish to see Balthus's manipulative interplay of truth and lies, visual and personal, as all connected, this says more about us than him. So he would have us believe and fear.

IV

BALTHUS RETURNED TO PARIS from Bern in the fall of 1932. He wrote Jean Strohl that the mere presence of Antoinette overwhelmed him. She was his ideal of a young girl. Yet he knew he was an unacceptable suitor. His beloved became engaged to a diplomat, and a bitter, anguished Balthus felt himself to be at the edge of losing all reason. Painting offered his sole chance of emotional recovery and comfort. Besides, if he made a name for himself as a painter, he might have more success at approaching Antoinette, and increase his chances at entering the solid Swiss world from which she came.

Back in France, Balthus stayed at first with Pierre and Betty Leyris, close friends of both him and his brother Pierre. Like Pierre Klossowski, Pierre Leyris was a gifted linguist and translator. Betty—an English music-hall girl who had come to France as part of the song-and-dance group called the Blue Bells—had muscular legs that made her an ideal model for Balthus, and within the next two years he made several paintings of her. The most remarkable was the powerful, intensely sexual *Alice,* which would provoke reactions ranging from titters to outbursts of horror to wild approval at his first gallery show.

I spent an afternoon with the Leyrises in Meudon in the winter of 1991. Both of them knew Balthus for most of his life—from his days of penury to his subsequent success and current wealth. Our conversation was pivotal to my coming to grips with the many sides of my subject. Sitting in their cluttered, book-lined living room—it resembled the digs one would expect of a retired Sorbonne professor—the Leyrises discussed their old friend with rare perspective and insight. While Betty was suffering from confusion and memory loss—although she still had some vivid recollections of Baladine Klossowska—Pierre Leyris, a man of substantial intellect, perceived as clearly as anyone the difference between the truth and the lies in Balthus's life, and recognized the reasons behind the lies. Unlike so many of Balthus's close acquaintances of the eighties and nineties—be they his daughter Harumi or the singer David Bowie—who would go no further than to declare the brilliant poseur ununderstandable, or the writers who invariably fell back on the hackneyed "mysterious," Leyris put the pieces together.

Pierre Leyris stressed Balthus's phenomenal intelligence and intense seriousness as a painter. He emphasized to me that from the thirties onward, the artist had fervently approached the tasks of painting with the most heartfelt sense of urgency. Balthus's devotion to his craft, and the diligence with which he undertook his daily tasks, was beyond dispute.

Pierre Leyris disapproved of, yet understood, Balthus's elevation from struggling, impoverished youth to high-living, bogus aristocrat. However absurd the subsequent role-playing and silly the external garb, the person he housed in a period of dire struggle has remained an earnest painter, genuine technician, and brilliant linguist. To Pierre Leyris, the fiber underneath justified the gloss on top—at least in part.

On the other hand, Leyris clarified the dissembling and the fraud. He elaborated movingly on the pathology of Balthus's periodic reincarnations. First as the virtual doppelgänger of Antonin Artaud, and then, in a completely different guise, as this or that aristocrat of impressive lineage, Balthus had repeatedly presented evidence of what Leyris diagnosed as his "mimetic personality."

Leyris was keenly aware of where this came from. Balthus's early years had, indeed, been a tremendous struggle. I was, Leyris reassured me, completely correct about all the facts concerning Eugen Spiro. And the Klossowskis were as desperately dependent on Baladine's brother as all of the Rilke letters suggested. Leyris added the information, which Balthus almost certainly would have found annoying, that Spiro wanted to do a portrait of the great Jewish theologian Martin Buber, for which reason he went to Palestine.

Betty Leyris then added some telling details to my hazy portrait of Baladine. Balthus's mother, I learned, was "very matter-of-fact and earthy, as practical as she was romantic." She had "quite definite ideas on how to keep house." Erich Klossowski was opinionated to the point of being harsh. He "criticized Balthus's lack of color and told him he painted 'black things.' " Leyris linked these traits to their younger son's becoming "someone of incredible imagination and will, who could metamorphose into any creature he wanted to be."

Balthus lived with the Leyrises both in 1932 after his return to Paris from Bern and again during the Second World War, when the artist and Antoinette and Pierre and Betty all found refuge from the occupied French capital in

Champrovent in Savoie. In the intervening time, they often saw each other at
least once a day. By the time I got to know the Leyrises, there had been a complete schism between them and Balthus, but Pierre Leyris was more circum-
spect than bitter on the subject of his old friend. And he was one of the few
sources on Balthus who could actually elucidate facts. Much of my information about the artist's intriguing, brutal Artaud phase, discussed later on—as
well as on Balthus's reinvention of his childhood—came from this close friend
of those early decades.

FOLLOWING HIS STAY with the Leyrises in 1932, Balthus moved into a single
skylit room in the attic of a handsome five-story house on the quiet Rue de
Fürstemberg near the corner of the Rue Jacob, just behind the church of Saint-
Germain-des-Prés. Alain Jeaneret, a cousin of Le Corbusier, lent him the
space. This was not, however, because of any particular connection between
Balthus and the architect; Balthus made a point of letting me know that at age
twenty-two, when he was "terribly insolent," he had told Le Corbusier that
"his design for a stadium for half a million people looked like a soup bowl.
And a soup bowl enlarged is a soup bowl."

The young artist's new digs were in the heart of the small Left Bank district where Picasso and other well-known painters lived and where the avant-
garde galleries were. But what appealed to him as much as the bohemianism of
the milieu was that this was in many ways an ordinary, quiet Parisian neighborhood. The network of narrow, bending passageways created an intimate
and charming enclave for people to shop, walk to work or to school, and go
about their everyday lives. If the young artist had one eye on the exceptional—
he would quickly get to know some of the most original and inventive thinkers
of the day—he also cherished the ordinary sights of bourgeois existence. They
were his daily bread. Living at a slow, old-fashioned, metered pace, he set out
to capture quotidian life in the unique way in which he saw it.

The nature of Balthus's surroundings would consistently permeate his art.
In the thirties the painter was a close friend of the poet Pierre Jean Jouve, who
vividly described that studio on the Rue de Fürstemberg and the effect of the
laconic atmosphere of this little corner of Paris.

I saw Balthus again after his military service in Africa—lodging in an
attic room in the Rue de Fürstemberg. He had found the *site* which
corresponded to his formula, to everything he wanted to do and was
already achieving with characteristic intensity. From his window, were

it not for the houses around a courtyard as severe and dry as a David, he could have seen the studio and garden where Delacroix died. The strange Rue de Fürstemberg with its tiny square, behind the seventeenth-century Abbey of Saint-Germain-des-Prés, afforded nourishment for his mind, along with many other little streets of a neighborhood so antiquated and odd, so easy to confuse with the elements of a dream.[4]

THAT PROXIMITY TO DELACROIX'S last studio mattered deeply to the young artist. Balthus used to joke to friends about being protected by the spirit of the great Romantic, whose door he could see clearly from his solitary attic window. Delacroix was one of his role models and standard-bearers—marvelous both for the bravura of his paintings and for his statements on art. The young Balthus could walk the same ground and envision the Romantic living and painting only a few meters across the passageway.

At the Louvre, Balthus stood rapt before Delacroix's canvases as well as the art of his other nineteenth-century heroes. Corot's poignant, elegantly crafted paintings of young girls reading moved him both as art and as tender evocations of his favorite species engaged in one of his most cherished pastimes. Balthus prized the drama of the art of all of these painters, their sheer painterly know-how and their verve and flair. He quickly set about refashioning their vision according to his own personal taste and idiosyncrasies as surely as—later on, when the opportunity presented itself—he would appropriate for himself the life of a nineteenth-century nobleman.

CHAPTER EIGHT

THE STREET

A man who boasts that he never changes his opinions is a man committed always to follow a straight line, an idiot who believes in infallibility. There are no such things as principles, only events; no laws, only circumstances. Your exceptional man adjusts to events and circumstances in order to control them. . . .

"To have a mistress and rank close to royalty," he said to himself, "that is a sign of power."

—BALZAC, *Père Goriot*[1]

I

IN 1934 THE GALERIE PIERRE in Paris gave the twenty-six-year-old Balthus his first solo exhibition. Eight years had passed since his summer in Italy. The small gallery—a showplace for Surrealism and other contemporary movements—presented just seven paintings all in the vein that had developed in the young artist's work over the previous eighteen months. They catapulted their viewers to a level of excitement and engagement that has scarcely subsided both for Balthus's followers and for his detractors ever since.

Not all of these canvases could be viewed by just anyone. The artist had insisted that one painting—*The Guitar Lesson*—be kept in a back room, covered with a curtain and available only to selected individuals. It presented a scenario too sexually violent and offbeat for the public at large. As it is, the work that *was* available for general viewing set most people on their ears.

Four of the paintings on public view displayed a sexuality more explicit and forthright than even the most savvy gallerygoers were used to. This new art was lewd in a quirky, idiosyncratic way, its provocative images having been achieved with astounding technical mastery and visual richness.

Balthus's manner of painting distinctly evoked Piero della Francesca—as well as several other painters ranging from Poussin to Courbet to Seurat. It

1. *The Room*, 1952–54, oil on canvas, 270 x 330 cm

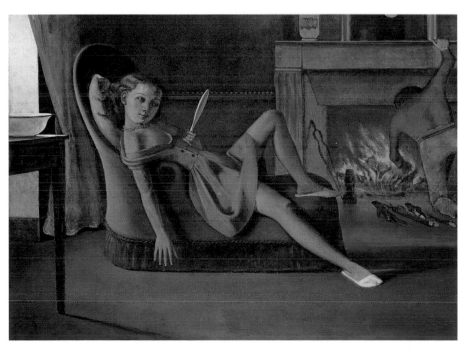

2. *Les Beaux Jours,* 1945–46, oil on canvas, 148 x 199 cm

3. *Landscape at Champrovent*, 1942–45, oil on canvas, 96 x 130 cm

4. *The Street*, 1933, oil on canvas, 193 x 235 cm

was, nonetheless, unique. The young artist with his strident single name had invented a style unlike anyone else's. Balthus's work blended deliberate distortions with uncanny realism. It mixed vigor and lassitude. A peculiar combination of primitivism and refinement animated its extraordinary scenarios. As people walked into Pierre Loeb's little Left Bank establishment, where, as it was, they expected the unexpected and avant-garde, this vivid presentation of discomfiting subject matter was guaranteed to stop them in their tracks as nothing had before.

In *Alice,* a woman combing her hair faces us head-on while her strapless slip falls below one of her large bare breasts. This copious, sagging breast begins at the midpoint of her chest and hangs practically to her belly, while its covered mate appears to be less than half its size. It is as if "Alice's" body has been pulled and compressed even more torturously than the hair she is trying to untangle. Her tight and binding undergarment is so short that her labia visibly bulge below its hem. Her pubic hair catches the light within the dark shadow in which her inner thighs are dramatically cast.

The model—Betty Leyris—stands resolute with her left foot on a chair seat. She has gargantuan legs, sturdy as iron. While bending one of them upward, she emphatically rests the other leg, perfectly straight, on the floor. Her thick and muscle-bound thighs are almost as wide as her waist underneath the sheer translucent slip. Disproportionate to the rest of her body, these legs seem to endow her with a gigantic physical and sexual power.

To look at this canvas is to experience a confrontation. Yet at the same time, the viewer is made to feel oddly distant. The palette is subdued, and the surfaces seem composed of layer upon layer, as if they had been worked on for years. The startling scenario appears to exist behind coatings of old, yellowed varnish. An erotic force envelops us, yet the model is entirely uninterested in her impact. She is deep in reverie, out of touch with any thoughts or reactions but her own. Like the man who painted the picture, she is able to be phenomenally provocative without appearing to care one iota. She seems contemptuous of the people she excites.

In another of the Galerie Pierre paintings, *The Window,* the female subject again has her left breast bared and the right one clad. But otherwise she is dressed with a decorousness that makes the exposure of her naked flesh all the more shocking. Her smart outfit also indicates that her position backed against a windowsill is a complete invasion of her usually dignified existence.

The woman is horrified. She raises her right hand in frantic defiance. Her dress pulled down brutally, she has been forced against her will to the edge of a life-threatening precipice. The painter—unseen, but imagined in our eyes—is the attacker. His brush might as well be a dagger: a lethal, phallic weapon.

Here the woman is the painter's victim; in *Cathy Dressing,* she is his conqueror. The second-largest canvas at the Galerie Pierre, *Cathy Dressing* depicts
a woman brazen, powerful, and dominant. Like a cross between a stripper and
one of Lucas Cranach's Venuses, Cathy is aware of the power of her milky flesh
and unabashed sexuality to hold her audience captive. The dressing gown
hanging over her shoulders frames rather than conceals the stunning nakedness of her lithe, tapered body. Her black high-heeled slippers, in which she
stands bare, elevate her forthright presentation of herself and emphasize her
coquettishness.

Unlike *Alice* and *The Window,* this painting is not of a woman alone.
Cathy is one of three figures in a narrative. She is having her hair combed by an
old-fashioned lady's maid who is proper to the point of being a lunatic. This
dour character descends directly from the spinster type holding a cat so ridiculously in *The Quays.* While the younger woman is totally wanton, the older
epitomizes repressiveness. The maid's tight gray bun is in marked contrast to
the seductress's flowing blond tresses. Her gray and black uniform and white
apron invoke rules and restraint, while the younger woman's large, naked, tip-
tilted breasts (they zoom outward like well-tuned instruments of power)—and
the hairless genitalia, curvaceous hips, and graceful legs that she displays so
confidently—embody lust and the freedom to enjoy it. Her daring to put herself on display like this in the presence of that grim maid adds to her
unabashed sense of self.

A somber, inward-looking man, recognizable as Balthus himself, sits on a
simple side chair near the woman and maid. But he does not look at them; his
slitted eyes and furrowed brow make clear his concentration on his own inner
world. This scowling, swarthy fellow has a strained and troubled relationship
to this scene in which he is present but excluded. With his thick black hair and
his black and gray clothing, he exists in a state of darkness in exact opposition
to the lightness of the female temptress. She knows, and flaunts, her power; he
sits hunch-shouldered and brooding. The man appears isolated and very much
alone. He wraps his hands intensely around one of the posts of the chair back.
Although they are at the height of his chest and at a safe remove from his
crotch (which has been painted with the flare of Géricault)—and although the
artist would deny the point vociferously—the position of these hands suggest
that he is masturbating.

In the largest painting of all—the 76-by-94-inch *Street*—everyone wears
clothes, and no one has even had her dress torn off (color plate 4). The scene
shows nine carefully clad characters going about their everyday lives in a quiet
Parisian neighborhood. The painting style and overall atmosphere were unlike
anything that had ever been seen before, but the subject matter was very much

in keeping with the large Parisian scenes of Seurat, Caillebotte, and Bonnard. At least so it seems for the first moment or two.

But then the details begin to jar. A couple of the characters are halfway between being real and being made of wood. Are they people, or objects, or creatures that might exist only in dreams? And then there is the little creature in the foreground who is a cross between a grotesque little girl, Humpty-Dumpty, and one of Piero's angels. This character in her unflattering green stocking cap is like a heavy-set dwarf with the countenance of an old lady.

An assault is taking place on the left-hand side of the canvas, where a girl in a red cardigan is trying to escape a demonic boy who has come upon her from behind. The boy, gripping her left wrist firmly with his left hand, has wedged his right calf between her legs to hold her in place. And in 1934 that attack had more to it than it does now. The vignette was painted out when Balthus sanitized the painting in the 1950s—of this, more later—but originally the boy could be seen grabbing the hem of her hiked-up skirt with his right hand and plainly groped her genitals. The position of his hand is no longer the same, but his face still bears the expression of simultaneous lust and satisfaction it had before the boy's creator folded his fist and moved it, just a bit more properly, sideways onto the girl's thigh.

Aside from the canvas that was on view only for the select few in the back room, the two remaining paintings in that first show were portraits. Since no precise list remains, we cannot be sure which two they were, but whenever the young artist painted the human face in this early period, his idiosyncratic renditions were unusually severe and cutting. Balthus would eventually soften his portraiture to accommodate his well-heeled clients (while maintaining the requisite degree of acidity and innuendo to ensure that his sitters would look "painted by Balthus"), but not yet.

In this handful of paintings at the Galerie Pierre, the twenty-six-year-old artist showed his real colors. He would continue to paint for over half a century to come, but here was the real person and artist he would subsequently cloak under so many layers. For this reason, I shall focus in depth on these few paintings and the issues they raise. Their echoes, as well as the traits Balthus found it necessary to cover up with such vigilance, would underscore his later life.

IN BALTHUS'S IDEAL WORLD of artistic perception as he characterized it to me, what people would have noticed most about all of these canvases at his first exhibition would have been the way they were painted. What merited attention was the subtlety of their old-master palette, their compositional richness, and their success as evocations of earthly existence. Most viewers, however, dwelled more on the subject matter. For some, it prompted delight; for many, it resulted in consternation or horror.

Yet even though Balthus was condescending about such responses to the stories revealed in these paintings—if people were more visually alert and intellectually sophisticated, he said, they would give the artistic qualities primacy and see the subject matter as nothing but a tool—he feigned no surprise at them. He told me that when he was young he wanted to shake up the public. He said that he considers that instinct to shock natural for a person in his twenties. It belonged to this period in his life only; he has long since lost his wish to affront. But he would have us believe that this very conscious wish to startle his viewers is the sole reason he depicted images of sexual aggressiveness.

He has rationalized it all. To say that he made sexual violence his theme only because he wanted to engage people and conjure a little mischief is a handy way of discounting the savagery and anguish that pulsate in these canvases. The ploy is almost as good as the confusion about Uncle Eugen.

THE COGNOSCENTI HAD PRAISED *Mitsou,* and Bonnard and his friends had admired Balthus's copy after Poussin, but between 1926 and 1934 Balthus had not managed to get very far with the public. He had known for a long time that his artistic skills were those of a genius—Baladine and Rilke had told him so repeatedly, and Bonnard and others confirmed it. But just to paint well was not enough. His relatively tame work of the period between 1923 and 1933 was charming, but not sufficient for him to make a life for himself as a painter.

The shock value of those paintings at the Galerie Pierre instantly brought Balthus the first glimmer of the attention for which he yearned. He did not immediately sell work, nor was he written about by the popular press, but one or another of this small group of canvases inspired fascinating and enthusiastic commentary by writers as significant as Pierre Jean Jouve and Antonin Artaud. Among a certain group of people, the name on everyone's tongue that season was "Balthus."

FROM THE START, THERE WAS a discrepancy between the reasons for the attention Balthus attracted and those he claims he would have preferred.

The most important review of the Galerie Pierre exhibition was by the Cubist painter André Lhote in the influential *La Nouvelle Revue Française.*

Even what appeared to be the calmest of the series of canvases, which a young painter, Balthus, exhibited, betrayed a sexual obsession not without a turbid but quite overwhelming lyricism.

Lhote pointed out that these paintings reveal sexuality without necessarily stimulating it. In this he gleaned an essential truth about Balthus's approach to females; he would paint women as seductresses without making them seductive and arrest our attention while leaving us always feeling in want. One might conclude that this was his means also of neutralizing the effects of his mother's allure.

But even though Lhote was a painter, he did not grasp Balthus's fascinating style or the appearance of the paintings. He described Balthus's use of a "careful *trompe-l'oeil* technique, derived from douanier Rousseau and restored to honor by Max Ernst." The critic failed to acknowledge the textural richness and the other aspects of Balthus's way of painting that made him closer kin to painters of the seventeenth century like the brothers Le Nain than to Max Ernst.

What he did perceive accurately was the psychological atmosphere. Lhote characterized the people in Balthus's work as "impassioned 'automata' possessing a 'hysterical rigidity, a certain disturbing hieratism.' " The critic's conclusion was "It is good for the age-old hypocrisy of men to yield somewhat to the pathos of sexual anxiety."[2]

Balthus decries observations of this sort as having nothing to do with his intentions. He told me repeatedly that there is nothing convoluted, or dream-like, or mysterious in his straightforward depictions of everyday life. Yet what Lhote, his first critic ever, found was what most viewers—from uninformed onlookers to sophisticated scholars—have consistently felt to be the content of Balthus's art. Balthus must have realized how essential the disconcerting imagery was to his success. By the time of his exhibition at the Galerie Pierre, he had found an identity that worked.

BALTHUS HAD THIS FIRST exhibition because Pierre Loeb, the owner of the Galerie Pierre, had seen *The Street* when Wilhelm Uhde had taken Loeb to the artist's studio in 1933. Uhde was a friend of Henri Rousseau's and a writer on French art with a good eye for modern paintings. Balthus was living and working at the time in his attic on the Rue de Fürstemberg, just around the corner from Loeb's gallery at 2, Rue des Beaux-Arts. *The Street* was barely dry when Uhde guided him there. Facing this large scene of workers, children, and well-put-together young ladies—all going about their everyday activities in this same Left Bank neighborhood—Loeb instantly found it to be a revelation:

> Above all, it's been a very long time since I've seen such frankly realist work which has given me an impression not only of formal plenitude, but which fully satisfies the expectations of a new expression. I was spellbound by the remarkable ensemble of scenes from which this *Street* emerged.
>
> In a warm blond light which bathes the composition, various persons circulate; I don't know where the scene occurs, but this street seems to be the one leading from the Place Fürstemberg, where the artist lived, to the Rue Jacob.
>
> The figures here are immobilized, like those of *La Grande Jatte*, but in a "snapshot" and no longer in a "pose." They are not caught in motion, in action, like those of Degas, but as though petrified on the spot.
>
> That mason, all in white, is the axis of the picture; he is passing through it like a ghost. The other figures graze each other, meet though without seeing each other, even the main actors of this curious scene which takes place under the eyes of the baker's assistant whose mind is elsewhere, as is that of the ageless child pursuing her inner reflections while playing with a ball.
>
> A young boy steps forward. His gaze is lost in a dream. The swaying of his arm is immobilized in an automaton's gesture, while the little girl unconsciously steps aside in order not to break into this dream and to pursue her own.
>
> A woman leaves, carrying a sleeping child whose dreams are troubled.
>
> We seem to be watching some strange dream in which everyone is a somnambulist; an anxious atmosphere emanates from this perfect composition whose plastic equilibrium and rhythm so perfectly harmonize with its conception.
>
> We had already experienced a sensation of discomfort, even of malaise, when confronted by the "absent" stares of certain faces by Picasso, of anxiety when meeting the gaze of Derain's lifeless or haggard eyes, drained of all expression. But this astonishing picture might mark an intermediate stage between the escape into dreams and the return, by means of somnambulism, to tomorrow's reality.[3]

Balthus must have been pleased to have been offered an exhibition, but Pierre Loeb, like André Lhote, admired *The Street* for the wrong reasons. The artist told me repeatedly that he has never understood why people refer to the characters in his paintings as looking as if they are sleepwalking. Anguish and malaise had nothing to do with his intentions. His goal was not an atmosphere of torment or alienation; it was, Balthus maintained, a simple celebration of the wonders of daily existence.

Whereas Balthus in the 1960s was known to say he considered all of his paintings "utter failures," he also told me, his eyes sparkling, that he has always considered *The Street* his first important painting. A modest smile of victory on his face, he allowed that in this monumental canvas, his largest to date, he had at last succeeded in realizing his intentions. He had managed to articulate the setting and the characters in it. The issues were composition and rhythm, color and texture: concerns of the eye and the brush, devoid of narrative subtlety or psychological innuendo. The goals he had set for himself when copying the work of Poussin and Piero were now within his grasp.

IN *The Street*, BALTHUS ALSO DID what he does in the presentation of his own life, and in all of his subsequent work. He combines a straightforward exposition of the truth with extreme distortions of reality. Nature is the starting point—but then it is cloaked and enhanced by an elaborate process of deception. Honest facts coexist with elegant embellishment and complete invention.

Because of the sheer quality of its painting—the convincing surfaces, the success of the spatial illusion, the meticulous details, the craft that enables you to breathe the air and sense the enclosure—this large canvas convinces you that the scene is entirely real. You are in a corner of a Parisian neighborhood, looking at everyday life. Then comes the discordance.

What at first seems natural soon strikes you as contrived. The fellow walking toward you is like a mechanical toy that has been wound up; you expect his arm to move in fits and starts. The creature held in the crook of a woman's arm is like a grown-up man in little boy's clothes. The woman elegantly clad in black with red trim is both a fashion plate of her era and like an acolyte in papal robes. The childish figure in the foreground wears hausfrau slippers: the shoes of an old lady. Bizarrely, the girl being groped looks unaware of what her attacker is doing, as if she is in a religious trance—while no one else appears the least bit aware that she is being accosted in their midst.

With all of these gambols and twists, the large canvas was both the culmination of the first phase of Balthus's mature work and a foray into new territory.

II

BALTHUS HAD PAINTED AN INITIAL rendering of *The Street* in 1929, prior to his pivotal trip to Morocco. A backward glance at it shows the young painter still raw and groping before he developed the layers and devices evident on the easel when Wilhelm Uhde and Pierre Loeb walked into his studio four years later. The setting is the same as in the later rendering, the cast and arrangement of characters similar. But in his first essay on the theme, Balthus was not yet the master craftsman who had figured out how to hold the world in the palm of his hand.

On the left in the earlier painting, a bearded grandfather figure in topcoat and bowler clasps the hands of a little boy and girl walking with their arms and legs asunder. They make an amusing trio, the old man rigidly correct, the children too young and free to have any sense of order or direction. Those children are innocent and charming, the boy in shorts and a hat with a pom-pom, the girl in a skirt and flowered hat. There is already a very Balthus-like power play going on. That rigidly erect, properly dressed grandfather, the epitome of bourgeois propriety, virtually drags the children, who are eager to break away into their own helter-skelter world of play. The stalwart old man is unfazed by the rambunctious youths. The issue is control, and he has it. Four years later, an incident of patent sexuality and aggressiveness would be depicted in the same work. In the 1933 *Street,* the trio of the old man and children has been replaced by the altogether uninnocent pair of teenagers. Now a deranged young man—although Balthus says he is perfectly normal—tries unabashedly to grope beneath the hiked-up skirt of the young woman with the massive legs.

The female in this later vignette is both real and from another world. She resembles a Renaissance angel who either has just landed or is about to take flight. The model for her may well be the archangel Gabriel—which would make her male in spite of her female appearance. But she might also be a mockery of the Virgin; the expression on her face is much like that of Mary in many versions of the Annunciation. The young man is simply a demonic heathen.

The old man and youngsters in the 1929 *Street* serve as background figures, like many inhabitants of Vuillard's or Bonnard's city squares. The teenagers who replaced them in 1933, however, are brought sharply to our attention. Whereas the man and children walk in front of a blank doorway the

The Street (first version), 1929, oil on canvas, 130 x 162 cm

same color as the surface of the pavement, and hence blend into a homogenous whole, the malicious teenage boy goes about his antisocial act in front of a bright, eye-catching wooden panel—in what is apparently the same, previously muted doorway—that frames his body and crowns his head underneath a riveting, smooth expanse of solid black. In four years Balthus had come not just to develop new dramatic personae but to paint them arrestingly. He had gained both the freedom and the sense of self to allow some of his own issues to come to the surface.

In his second version of *The Street*, Balthus got rid of the quaint, horse-drawn cart on the cross street, as well as of several indistinct figures, and added two new personages, both highly defined, in the foreground. The vestiges of nineteenth-century Impressionist life gave way to elements that were both completely contemporary and uniquely Balthusian. He retained several members from his original cast of characters: the baker, the workman shouldering a wooden board, the woman with her small child in the crook of her arm, and the wide-cheeked boy strolling imperiously out of the picture and toward us so that we feel that either he is about to enter our world or we his. Yet the boy has now been moved back. And with his change of position, the viewer has been pushed away. Our first encounter is no longer with the boy. The nearest figure in the 1933 *Street,* a well-dressed woman facing away from the picture plane, meets us only with a cold shoulder. The result is that where previously we had a sense of engagement, now we encounter a barrier; the obfuscation is deliberate.

There are two new presences in the foreground. One is this stylishly dressed woman of whom we see only the back; all that we can know of her is what we can deduce from her gait, her hand gesture, and her carefully conceived clothing. The other new figure at center stage—one of the most bizarre of all of Balthus's characters ever—is even more off-putting. In fact, she defies description.

I asked Balthus about the strange proportions and form of this lumpy, pernicious being who seems simultaneously young and old and, while predominantly female, also male. The artist answered, as if there could be no possible question about it, that she is "simply a little girl." He seemed astounded at the notion that she might be anything else. But to the rest of us she is unlike anyone we have ever before seen, unsettling and haunting. Like the terror holding back the drapery in *The Room*—a figure her creator also insisted to me was just an ordinary child—she is the prototype of a particular Balthusian golem that appears periodically throughout his art and that most of us would hope not to encounter either in life or in our dreams.

BETWEEN 1929 AND 1933, Balthus had not just developed new character portrayals. To achieve the pinnacle represented by the 1933 *Street,* he also changed his manner of painting. The early version of *The Street,* like his other small canvases of the late 1920s, is relatively small and has a mottled surface composed of a series of numerous small brushstrokes. The bearded man wearing a bowler, a Cézanne look-alike, was painted in an approximation of Cézanne's middle style. Rilke had been passionate about Cézanne; it's no surprise that Balthus gave Cézanne's doppelgänger such authority and stature in his canvas, and worked for a while in a Postimpressionist manner. The horse pulling the carriage was almost identical to those in the small oil sketches of Georges Seurat—another of Balthus's artistic models.

While the second, bigger, bolder *Street* is more riveting, everything about it is less accessible. Balthus has found his voice—or has adopted other people's voices—and has polished his act; at the same time, he has learned to cover his tracks. His new blend of primitivism and finesse, of old-master coloring and modernist compression of space, deliberately befuddles us. The artist has taken command and simultaneously cloaked himself.

His surfaces have grown smooth, the light sharp and raking. The forms are crystalline, as if fixed in relief in a frieze. Each figure looks like a mannequin in front of a backdrop. A precise geometry dominates. The rich and lively rhythms are syncopated.

The result is a painting that guarantees you will look twice. The newer *Street* arrests the viewer. However charming those earlier canvases of the 1920s are, and however much they convey the pleasures of looking at people going about their lives amid pleasant Parisian scenery, the 1933 painting both rivets and unnerves us.

SINCE BALTHUS SEEMED TO REGARD the 1933 *Street* as the painting that sums up who he is, we discussed it more than any other work. Time and again, Balthus would tell me that he could not understand the use of words like "strange," "dreamlike," or "somnambulistic" with regard to it.

If Balthus is telling the truth, he has always regarded the environment and characters in *The Street*—and the settings and personages of all of his art ever since—as nothing more or less than straightforward reality viewed by the light of day. He saw something, and he constructed a picture based on it. So he would have the world believe, and so, perhaps, he believes himself. Often in rebuttal to assertions that he is up to something else, he has maintained to numerous journalists and fellow artists the idea that this is nothing but ordinary everyday life. If we think the people in these paintings are puppets or dwarfs or signboards, that's our problem. The imagery of *The Street* comes from the typical moments of quotidian life; sleep or hypnotic trances have nothing to do with it. The Count de Rola discussed *The Street* in exactly the way that old people consider a faded family photo: a summoning of the neighborhood he once inhabited in the good old days.

I have spent hours observing viewers commenting on *The Street* at the Museum of Modern Art in New York; like Pierre Loeb and Pierre Jean Jouve, they instinctively feel that there is something bizarre going on with this assemblage of Parisians. But they are outsiders, Balthus reminded me. Its maker quietly insisted that *The Street* is an evocation of a simple, bucolic world that he deeply misses today.

Yet in *The Street* as in all of his art, Balthus's characters exist as if in a dream. Balthus gives them shadows that anchor them in space; he works tirelessly on their textures that fix them—but like dreams and cats, they are finally elusive. We don't know who they are, and like Balthus, they don't know who they are.

· · ·

ALONG WITH "DREAMLIKE," the other word about which Balthus periodically launched into a diatribe during our discussions of *The Street* was "mysterious." He considered it absurd to apply either to him or his paintings. He
stated his case calmly, even logically—almost as if the fallacy of "mysterious"
amused him more than it annoyed him. But he was resolute: he regarded the
notion of secret or cabalistic elements as patently ridiculous.

Balthus was even more adamant on this point when my daughters and I
were visiting him in Rossinière the day after the opening of his Lausanne exhibition in May 1993. Standing in the garden behind Le Grand Chalet, its rear
facade like a Chinese temple, Balthus was on this occasion sporting a Missoni
vest. An attentive host, he was chatting warmly with diplomats and making
sure that his daughter's friends were getting enough at the buffet table. Suddenly he took me aside with a look of urgency on his face and said he must set
the record straight on a matter of pivotal importance. He simply could not
grasp why people called his work mysterious. That and erotic: they had no
bearing on the real nature of his paintings.

"Mysterious" has, indeed, been immensely overused for Balthus—a too
convenient escape valve, hackneyed and meaningless. For those of us to whom
a single blade of grass, or any form of communication, defies adequate explanation or total comprehension—in spite of whatever information or explanation science or religion may provide—everything has mystery.

Balthus and his work are enigmatic, but its puzzlement is a ploy. The haze
and ambiguity are intentional. The mixed signals Balthus initially developed in
The Street are part of a scheme he has cultivated ever since.

IN ALL OF OUR CONVERSATIONS, of course, Balthus told me that, to the contrary, his aim has consistently been clarity. He explained miscomprehension of
that point in the same painstaking way he unraveled the myth of his Jewish
background.

So if Pierre Loeb depicted *The Street* as a scene of anguished phantoms
sleepwalking in a strange dreamlike state, the problem, Balthus told me, was
Loeb himself. Loeb was the first person to bring Balthus's work before the public, yet—either because of this or in spite of it—the artist loathed him. He
characterized the dealer as "a typical outsider" lacking any true vision of what
really matters to painters. Worst of all, Loeb used this art he did not understand as a vehicle for his own identity. Balthus disparaged the dealer as "a self-
anointed martyr to modern art."

For all I knew, everything Balthus told me about Pierre Loeb was entirely justified. Yet his contempt was so blatant that I wonder if one of Loeb's unpardonable sins was that Balthus felt beholden to him, the other travesty being that Loeb was Jewish. Had a French or Polish aristocrat said or done something Balthus disliked, it would have been a pardonable foible. For although the Galerie Pierre launched Balthus, Pierre Loeb's name evoked only the vivid memory of an act of unpardonable chicanery Balthus says the dealer committed a couple of years after the exhibition.

When Balthus produced this vignette in the course of my first visit to him, I took it at face value. I did not yet know that it is impossible to determine whether any events related by Balthus are fiction or fact. He spoke with a mix of pathos and authority that was utterly convincing. Now, all I am certain of is that Balthus recounted his saga with an eye to the effect it would have. With the Count de Rola, truth is as elusive as his beloved Mitsou.

BALTHUS'S AGENDA IN characterizing his first dealer was to portray himself as the generous but hapless innocent—the young ingenue struggling for good in a corrupt world—and the gallerist as a conniver.

With a look teetering on disgust, Balthus leaned back on the settee and launched in. In front of the splendid large living room windows of the Grand Chalet, their vast grid of small panes overlooking the frozen lake and tracks for the mountain train in the snowy valley below, he seemed an oracle. Pierre Loeb, Balthus declared, had approached him about two years after that 1934 Galerie Pierre exhibition to say that Joan Miró was having a birthday. Miró's studio was in the same building as the Galerie Pierre, and both Loeb and Balthus liked the Spaniard personally and admired his work. Loeb asked Balthus to paint a portrait of Miró, which Loeb then intended to give to Miró as a present.

In countless sittings in 1937 and 1938, Balthus worked and reworked the portrait, which shows Miró holding his young daughter. But in spite of all the travail and his own impecuniousness, he only asked Loeb a low symbolic price for it because he knew—or thought he knew—that Loeb was making the painting a gift to Miró.

A few days after Loeb took possession of the completed portrait, Balthus eagerly asked him how Miró liked it. Loeb's reply, Balthus told me—his face now betraying out-and-out revulsion—was simply that he had sold it to the Museum of Modern Art. Balthus said he had never forgotten or forgiven that act of deceit.

When Balthus told me this story, I felt terrible for him. I pitied not only his loss of deserved money and his thwarted generosity but also his feeling of betrayal at an age when he was especially vulnerable and trusting. Loeb's offense typified the sort of thing art dealers do to struggling painters, and evoked my deep sympathy.

Months later, however, I discovered that the Modern had purchased *Joan Miró and His Daughter Dolores* directly from the New York dealer Pierre Matisse. Matisse sold it on behalf of Balthus in the 1938 exhibition that was the artist's first American show. Pierre Loeb had no part in the sale. In his unpublished memoirs, James Thrall Soby, the American collector who had recently become one of Balthus's most ardent supporters and patrons, described the precise sequence of events by which this esteemed painting entered the collection of the Museum of Modern Art:

> Balthus painted what is to my mind one of the greatest portraits of our century, the *Joan Miró and His Daughter Dolores* of 1937–38. I bought this remarkable picture the moment I saw it at Pierre Matisse's gallery, but Pierre phoned me the same afternoon and asked me if I would release it to the Museum of Modern Art because Alfred Barr liked it as much as I did and even found a donor, a fairly rare occurrence in those earlier days of the Museum's history. It was the first time Pierre and Alfred had asked such a favor of me and I naturally said yes.[4]

Records at both the Modern and the Matisse gallery corroborate that the museum bought the painting from that New York gallery—not from Pierre Loeb.

There is, of course, the remote possibility that Balthus's story has an iota of truth. Maybe Pierre Loeb did betray the artist in some way, and only the details are wrong. Consider this possibility: Loeb might have said that the painting would be a gift, and then, after getting it cheap, tried to put it on the market. Then Balthus might have demanded it back and sent it to Pierre Matisse, who sold it—at a fair price—to the Museum of Modern Art. To skip a couple of stages in the progression from Pierre Loeb to the Museum of Modern Art might easily reflect a loss of memory that would be quite natural with old age.

More likely, however, Balthus developed his version of the tale to suit some purpose. Another strike against Loeb—beyond his being a Jew and the artist's savior—is that he was a primary ally of the Surrealists, whose tenets Balthus came to repudiate. In any event, to alter the facts has never troubled Balthus so long as the manipulation has the desired impact. It is no more unnatural than organizing the composition of a painting or modifying his ancestry. What matters is only the success of the bomb in achieving its goal.

III

Please do not expect me to speak to you of my inner labor—I must keep it silent; it would be tiresome to keep track, even for myself, of all the reversals of fortune I will have to undergo in my struggle for concentration. This sudden shifting of all one's forces, these about-faces of the soul, never occur without many a crisis; the majority of artists avoid them by means of distraction, but that is why they never manage to return to the center of their productivity, whence they started out at the moment of their purest impulse. At the onset of every work, you must re-create that primal innocence, you must return to that ingenuous place where the angel found you, when he brought you that first message of commitment; you must seek through the brambles for the bed in which you then slept; this time you won't sleep: you will pray, wail—anything; if the angel condescends to come, it will be because you have persuaded him, not with your tears, but by your humble decision always to start afresh: ein Anfanger zu sein.

—RAINER MARIA RILKE[5]

IN THE 1960s, before many other writers had attempted to tackle the issues surrounding Balthus's work, the artist's brother, Pierre Klossowski, wrote a pivotal article that focused on *The Street*—and the painting often regarded as its sequel, the 1952–54 *Passage du Commerce Saint-André*. Printed in both English and French, it has been quoted frequently in catalogs of Balthus's exhibitions ever since.

Pierre Klossowski called these paintings "tableaux vivants"—"living pictures." As such, they are inventions intended to evoke visions tempered by personal psychology. Klossowski explained, "*Painted* space, visual simulacrum of physical space, restores the *felt* space which had vanished in physical space; but this simulacrum has the capacity to restore and unfold the past experience in the form of an extended object, the picture, present with other objects in physical space."[6]

Discussing that specific notion with me, Balthus merely shrugged his shoulders. His bemused grin suggested that he regards his brother as a dear but woolly-headed fellow. Balthus told me he subscribed neither to Pierre's complex linguistics nor to the theories behind them. To its maker, *The Street* presents tangible, indisputable reality. Ordinary everyday conduct—alas, of a type that has generally disappeared—has always been his subject. Other observations, and esoteric interpretations of his work, are gratuitous. If I now repeat the point, it is because this was the abiding concept that Balthus, day in and day out, emphasized.

Looking at a glossy reproduction of his early masterpiece as we sat together on the sofa, Balthus became nostalgic about this villagelike corner of Paris where girls "still dressed with an independent sense of style. Today those girls would wear blue jeans," he lamented.

Those empty byways were mainly for the use of pedestrians in those kinder, easier days before traffic sullied the streets. Instead of the noise of cars, one heard everyone singing, as in London, and the sounds of people hawking their produce and wares. You listened to street vendors in the nearby market stalls on the Rue de Buci extolling the glories of their fish fresh from the Mediterranean or their vegetables brought in that morning from Provence.

As Balthus declared in 1992, in some statements by him cobbled together as a preface to his exhibition catalog for the Musée Courbet, "I have never felt obliged to reveal anything of myself in my painting, but only to manifest life and what is sacred in life." Just as all of his art is meant as a celebration of ordinary daily living, the goal of *The Street* and *The Passage* was to convey the urban ideal of such quiet neighborhoods in which a constant cast of characters regularly traverses the same passageways.

People should get places by walking. Declaring this to me as if it were the essence of his art, Balthus looked up in the direction of the main motorway that links Rossinière with the highways to Geneva, Zurich, and Bern. He began to bemoan the current tendency of people to isolate themselves in their cars and spend so much time on the road. The new communities of matched holiday chalets in Switzerland epitomize the destruction of the way of life that he sought to capture in *The Street* and *The Passage*. He deplores these "new houses, and only for weekend people, not even used during the week, and destroying the countryside, just for winter sport." Life is no longer integral; work and recreation and observation, which should all occur simultaneously, are now separated.

Suddenly Balthus stopped talking and looked again at the color plate of *The Street* in the book opened on the delicate eighteenth-century tea table before us. Inhaling deeply from yet another long white Dunhill cigarette, he seemed on the verge of letting an ever-extending growth of ash fall directly on his rough twill pants. Without releasing the ash, which had grown to the point where its further suspension seemed impossible, he explained that television, like the superhighway, is responsible for the demise of our culture. He dropped the ash neatly into the ashtray; surely it could not have lasted a thousandth of a second longer. The old way of life beats the modern, he said. What *The Street* and *The Passage* are meant to present is a richer, more deeply felt way of living that has now, tragically, evaporated—in part because TV has replaced it.

The artist could hardly have devised an agenda with which I was more in agreement. It was marvelous to think of *The Street* as a celebration of urbanism and connectedness, and for a while I succumbed to the temptation.

I had the sense that even when he was painting *The Street* in 1933, Balthus may already have had a foreboding of the ultimate passing of the life he cherished and intended to convey in it. It was as if he anticipated his own nostalgia. Cats run away; childhood ends. Constructing his canvas, he probably knew that urban life would not remain the same. For even though what he was painting was the current reality of a rather ordinary Parisian crossroads that, he told me, he saw every day near the Rue de Fürstemberg, he re-created it with a tone of sobriety and foreboding. In its ceremonial pace and muted palette, *The Street* has the look of memory rather than the flush of current experience. That is the perpetual voice of all of Balthus's work: enchanted yet melancholy. The splendors are noticeably short-lived.

BALTHUS ENUMERATED TO ME the specifics of the life revealed in *The Street* as if each paving stone near the bare-bones digs of his early years had a certain magic. What others find ambiguous, its creator regards as a source of crystalline facts. The wooden panels and multipaned window belonged to a bistro; all the bistros at that time had this sort of wood and these windows. Across the way from that bistro—on the cross street that forms the backdrop to the scene—the arrangement to the left consists of open shutters on either side of a large window. The round sign cut off by the top of the canvas is for a coiffeur. The structure directly behind the boy and girl on the left is a vitrine—a shop-window—with decoration in it.

Yet having insisted in our conversations that his paramount goal was to communicate such specifics—not just in *The Street* but throughout his work—Balthus appeared quite indifferent to his failure to achieve this purpose. He gave the impression of being amused, rather than disappointed, by the way that I, like so many other people, have misread his renditions. Was this just *politesse*, or was this a tacit admission that his reality is different from other people's?

Does he really see the stocking-capped grotesque in the foreground of *The*

Street as an ordinary child, as he claimed to me? Is that bizarre character pulling back the drapery in *The Room* truly "just a little girl, my dear Nicholas"?

Why—if verisimilitude is really Balthus's all-or-nothing goal—did he appear to be totally unannoyed by outright mistakes when we discussed *The Street?* Was this yet another facade? Or did he take deliberate pleasure in the muddle?

More used to saloon doors in Western movies than to the way Parisian vitrines were decorated in the 1930s, I saw the broken arch underneath the black area on the left as the tops of swinging doors rather than as window decoration. I thought that the first of the open shutters on the cross street was a mailbox. I told all this to Balthus. Courteously and patiently correcting me, he seemed unfazed by these misperceptions. He acted, in spite of his claims about his high standards for visual communication, as if they were irrelevant. It was apparently unimportant to him whether the discrepancies stemmed from his lack of success at articulating the scene or from my being a visual dolt. The artist acted as if these supposed misreadings mattered no more than when *The Moth* fell off the roof of his car.

The viewers' confusion, in fact, may be desirable. Balthus keeps even rudimentary facts inaccessible and sometimes skews the simplest, most straightforward information. At times, for example, he has refused to tell writers the year of his birth, while on other occasions he has provided it incorrectly. Sometimes he would make himself older, sometimes younger; his only apparent motive was to keep people guessing. Occasionally, as a foil, he would give the right year.

The personages Balthus has created have the same false verisimilitude; they, too, give an appearance of straightforward reality while being elusive and confusing. The people he paints have that artificial posture and aloofness—the controlled, impenetrable cool—of Balthus himself. Our confusion is irrelevant to them, except to the degree that they may savor it.

Like emperors, Balthus and these characters he has invented use silence as a key tool of their power. They know what they want to know. If we have questions, or make erroneous assumptions, it's not their problem. He and they share a cloak of aristocratic indifference to the world that is looking at them. They delight in befuddling their audience—before whom they appear proudly indifferent. The pose, of course, is there only to cover an obsession.

IV

BALTHUS'S WORLD FAILED to conform to any prosaic, bourgeois notion of truth even when I was pursuing the apparently simplest matter: the identity of the crossroads in *The Street.*

When I asked Balthus what the precise setting was, he told me that the canvas represented an imaginary combination of two thoroughfares, the Rue de Buci and the Rue de Seine, both near his studio on the Rue de Fürstemberg. This contradicts most of the literature on the painting. Many writers—among them other people who also got their information directly from the artist himself—have pinpointed the scene as being, very specifically, the junction at which the Rue de Bourbon-le-Château runs into the Rue de Buci. It is a harder situation to resolve, and the confusion about it more significant, than one might think.

Among the writers who claim that *The Street* is a rendition of that terminus of Rue de Bourbon-le-Château is Jean Leymarie. Leymarie, who has often functioned as Balthus's chosen apostle, is the author of the most substantial picture book on the artist. This is the coffee-table tome that Balthus and I often had open before us so that we could study its excellent plates. Produced in 1979 by the distinguished firm of Skira, Leymarie proudly declared it a collaboration with the artist and, as such, a breakthrough; the writer says at the start that "this long-awaited book is the first which he has allowed to be published on his work." Leymarie's *Balthus* has now appeared in two large-format editions, as well as in smaller paperbacks in both French and English, all widely distributed. In this sanctioned source on the artist, the writer has exchanged his liberty for a willingness to take the approved course. The book promotes the atmospheric haze, the un-pin-downable aura, Balthus cherishes. It also disseminates the artist's biography precisely as Balthus would like it to be known. Leymarie is by no means a toady; he is a highly gifted, intelligent, and original writer with a keen and intensely informed feeling for paintings. But all of his "facts" and observations have been developed under Balthus's watchful eye.

In return for this compliance, Leymarie has long enjoyed a position as Balthus's official spokesperson. It is he who has been granted the coup of providing the text for a colorful spread on the artist in *Paris Match* and writing articles about Le Grand Chalet, the castle in Italy, and Balthus's redecoration of the Villa Medici for *House & Garden*—of course while maintaining the usual tale of Balthus's elusiveness and removal from society. The price, however, has been a degree of disparagement in the French art world. The second time I stayed with Balthus, Dominique Bozo, then the director of the Centre Pompidou, came to call one day. Setsuko very kindly made arrangements for the two of us to go, after lunch, to Gstaad to visit Basil and Elise Goulandris, who own one of the very greatest of Balthus's landscapes—the magnificent and serene 1979 *View of Montecalvello*—which is on view in their Swiss chalet along with their important van Goghs, late Cézannes, and other modern masterpieces. As we followed the winding mountain roads in the Klossowski de Rolas' Audi station wagon, Bozo and I discussed the matter of how people write about Balthus. He was frankly amazed to learn that I was ensconced at the Grand Chalet, and said that this was clearly a result of Balthus's recent and surprising mellowing. Bozo told me that he always felt that Balthus and Leymarie had "a kind of S&M relationship." It was precisely the term I subsequently heard from an astute gallery owner who has known both the artist and the writer for years. There was no question as to who held the whip.

In the opening of his book, Jean Leymarie instantly submits to a Balthusian contradiction that is fairly ridiculous. First declaring that he will follow the artist's idea that we should "approach [the work] in silence, as if it were that of an unknown author," he then, as if oblivious to the inconsistency, immediately furnishes us, in spades, with the image this "unknown author" would have us believe. "Let us state his name and identity, with their full resonance and the aura surrounding them. In the world he is Count Balthazar Klossowski de Rola, descendant of an old Polish family of many branches, and by nationality a Frenchman. In the realm of painting he is Balthus, an ideogram of two well-tuned syllables fraught with far-reaching echoes."

During my stays in Rossinière, Setsuko—more than Balthus—mentioned Jean Leymarie both as a close friend and as the ultimate authority on her husband. Initially they both proposed, with Setsuko being the more adamant one, that I might collaborate in some way with the Paris-based scholar. He was, at that point in 1991, talking with Balthus about a book of which the working title was "Balthus Speaks"; although Balthus and Setsuko both disparaged those exact words, they said that the title was true to the book's concept. Since Leymarie and I were clearly after the same sort of information, we should be at Le Grand Chalet together to work with Balthus.

We did, in the course of the following year, attempt unsuccessfully to coordinate visits by Leymarie and me to Le Grand Chalet, although clearly a collaboration would have been a mistake.

Masked as Balthus has always been, Leymarie puts further veils around the masks. Here are some characteristic bits from that text that so many people eagerly awaited, and that still remains the gospel:

> Some artists are providentially singled out as bearers of the Golden Bough. They abide, pilgrims of eternity, keepers of the spirit, servants of beauty, traversing their time and all its transitory flux and reflux, set on a steady course, intent on timeless values. . . .
>
> With a lofty delicacy and an obstinate observance of good manners, Balthus holds aloof from the trivialities of fashion and publicity; he avoids any confusion between the social sphere, in which he shines

easily, and the private domain in which the work of creation is carried out in seclusion.[7]

When Leymarie's book first came out in 1979 and broke the Balthus barrier, I, as a Balthus initiate and like many other Balthus enthusiasts, soaked up that sort of thing with gusto.

Above all else, Leymarie perpetuates Balthus's beloved haze:

> The emotion peculiar to painting, since it takes possession of us inwardly, has the effect of doing away with words, or reviving within us the coenaesthesia [sic] anterior to speech.[8]

No wonder that Douglas Cooper, in a 1979 review, calls Leymarie's book—written, after all, when the author was Balthus's appointed successor as director of the Villa Medici—an "act of bureaucratic homage," and refers to the author's language as "a special kind of gobbledegook" and an "outpouring of flowery nothings."[9] Gabriele Annan, in the *Times Literary Supplement*,[10] gives Leymarie more of a break by suggesting that "perhaps to obfuscate rather than illuminate was a deliberate act of friendship," but while she praises the reproductions in this well-produced Skira volume, Annan writes of "the few facts suspended like bits of vegetable in the thick soup of his throbbing prose." Adding to the sense of impenetrable confusion, Leymarie's book, in its original form, is unpaginated. This is consistent with the failure of this mélange to give precise facts like the year of Balthus's birth—and its cultivation of cloudiness and inaccessibility.

The Skira book, nonetheless, is full of valuable theories and thoughtful appreciation of Balthus's art. Jean Leymarie is an insightful viewer of paintings. And he is informed about what Balthus would have us believe are his sources and connections. For all the manipulation to which the author has wittingly or unwittingly submitted, the compliance and genuine friendship that gained him a rare position on the inside track enabled him to be a source of a lot of accurate information on the artist.

It is curious, therefore, that what Balthus told me on several occasions about the setting of the painting he treated as his most major accomplishment should differ from what Jean Leymarie says on the subject. Given Leymarie's close access to the painter, if Leymarie cites as the location of *The Street* the Rue de Bourbon-le-Château at the corner of Rue de Buci—along with the statement that the building on the right of the canvas has been borrowed from another location—this information should be definitive. Yet Balthus contradicted it. While explaining to me, more than once, that the scene is an invention combining elements from the Rue de Buci and the Rue de Seine, he never mentioned Bourbon-le-Château—a street he knew intimately, since it is only a three-minute walk from the Rue de Fürstemberg. Balthus said that *The Street* did not specifically re-create a single given spot.

The issue here concerns only a small detail, but it exemplifies Balthus's approach to all factual information. Is it Jean Leymarie or I whom the artist misled? Because Balthus has long treated Leymarie as a close friend, I initially assumed that I was the one he would more readily deceive.

After all, not only did Balthus arrange for Leymarie to follow him as director of the Villa Medici, but to me he voiced great admiration for Leymarie's text on Impressionism and for his knowledge of art in general. Yet Balthus is ultimately loyal to no one. He has the sort of perceptiveness that enables him to home in on everyone's essential flaw—sitting there taking in the gospel, I was surely not exempt from this—and has cultivated that form of negative insight to the ultimate extent. He certainly did not spare this acolyte who has been so dutiful to him. Balthus referred both to "dear Jean's" excessive poeticism, and to his being "too respectful, too enchanted." In talking with me, the artist, with considerable condescension, criticized Leymarie's writing on him as being too worshipful. Having demanded fealty, he now mocked it; in one of our very first conversations he labeled Jean Leymarie's book "slightly too hagiographic. There's too much admiration." Balthus told me that Leymarie would have done better to be cooler and more objective about him. It seemed a courtly way of telling me that he would not expect such worship from me. But the device probably had to do with numerous more subtle subplots as well, even if at that stage of the game I was still too naïve to recognize them.

For when Leymarie dared show any sign of independence, Balthus criticized this, too. He also complained that Leymarie is too interpretive, particularly in his recent writing. He said Leymarie's comments on his artistic quotations were gratuitous—where, for example, did Leymarie get that idea that he was deliberately including Morandi still lifes or Hogarth cats within his canvases?

I nodded my head politely when Balthus asserted the improbability of those last two claims, but of course there is no question as to their validity; the visual evidence makes them irrefutable. And my hunch is that, once upon a time, Balthus admitted the Hogarth and Morandi references to Jean Leymarie—and that I was the one to whom he was now reconstructing the truth. This flip-flop pattern would correspond to his contradictory statements, a decade apart, to Tom Hess and me about the relationship of the "Japanese Girl" paintings to Oriental art. On the issue of the intersection in *The Street*, I was certain that Jean Leymarie also based his claims on what the artist had said to him—as well as on his own observation of the neighborhood. He must have been right that this was the Rue de Bourbon-le-Château slightly transformed, not, as Balthus told me, an amalgam of two other locations.

JAMES THRALL SOBY, WHO OWNED *The Street* for over forty years, similarly calls it "an imaginative transcription of a scene on the Rue [de] Bourbon-le-Château."[11] Like Leymarie, Soby probably got his idea from the artist himself, since he certainly must have discussed the painting when he visited Balthus in Chassy and when he made arrangements for its repainting.

(Balthus told me more than once that he could not remember if he had ever met Soby—whom he associated with me since we were both from Connecticut, and because I said my wife and I had met the writer-collector and first seen *The Street* in the stair hall of his Greek Revival house in New Canaan, where it hung until 1979. I know, however, from Soby's memoirs and some Balthus-Soby letters that Soby visited Balthus in France for several overnight visits in the 1950s. In this instance, I attribute no motive to Balthus's confusion—only the memory lapse of even the sharpest octogenarian.)

Sabine Rewald, in her Metropolitan Museum catalog, concurs with Leymarie and Soby, and adds that what has been brought in from another location was a bistro from the Rue Bonaparte. And Jean Clair—like Jean Leymarie, among the most highly regarded art scholars in post–World War II France—also says *The Street* is the Rue de Bourbon-le-Château. In an article published in the magazine *Beaux-Arts* at the time of Balthus's Centre Pompidou exhibition, Clair went so far as to include a photograph of the precise view of this street that he claims Balthus painted. But Clair also made one patently incorrect statement—which was that Balthus had his studio on the Rue de Bourbon-le-Château—thereby opening up to question the correctness of his other claims.

A VISIT TO THE ACTUAL Rue de Bourbon-le-Château where it intersects the Rue de Buci does not settle the matter. The Rue de Bourbon-le-Château indeed has a bistro on that corner in an equivalent location to that of the bistro in *The Street;* the angles of the junction and spatial scale are the same; and some of the windows on the Rue de Buci at this intersection are like some of the windows on Balthus's cross street. But the similarities stop there. The windows that are of the same scale and dimensions as the windows on the *premier étage* (second floor to Americans) in Balthus's painting are on the *deuxième étage* (third

story) at the actual location. Additionally, while certain windows on the real
Rue de Bourbon-le-Château have cornices over them, in *The Street* they do
not. The buildings may have been altered between 1933 and now, but no one
would have lowered a course of windows by a floor or removed heavy plaster
cornices. Moreover, while the scene of *The Street* does bear some resemblance
to the cited corner of the Rue de Bourbon-le-Château, Parisian architecture is
so homogenous—with its generic bistro paneling and awning design and shop
fronts—that Balthus's site could be any number of locations.

So *The Street*, LIKE EVERYTHING ELSE in Balthus's life, is a mixture of invention and reality, of fact and game. The borderlines are impossible to
discern.

Francis Bacon's unwritten treatise pertains again. At age eighty-three, the
painter, making me—as he has made a number of people before me—feel that
I was the chosen apostle, the pet selected to receive the truth he had been
unwilling to reveal before (and that I therefore had an obligation to relay
according to his presentation of it), claimed he had invented a scene based on
two specific sources. Four knowledgeable art historians—all of whom also had
direct access to this painter, and all of whom knew the neighborhood in which
he worked—pinpointed this location as elsewhere: a specific intersection on a
street quite different from the ones he cited to me. Balthus would say that
none of these details make any difference. All that matters is the painting.

On the other hand, he enjoys reminiscing, with great specificity, about
the details of the old neighborhood of which he regards the painting as a
record. It would be nice to know what he really started out with in this painting, how whole the cloth is from which he made up the facts, and what the
process of transformation was by which the known world became the basis of a
work of art.

Is the identification of the setting for *The Street* as the Rue de Bourbon-le-
Château—as declared by all those competent art historians—simply a case of
misinformation getting repeated, as so often happens when a printed source
gives facts incorrectly and other texts lamely follow suit? Or is Balthus's need to
mislead people so compulsive that he cannot even identify the scene of a picture the same way twice? Does Balthus perpetually invent new information
simply because he enjoys fiction? Or is it because, as a painter, he feels bound to
take a deliberate stand against the annoying insistence of scholars on specifying
and explicating places and objects? Above all, to what degree have his manipu-
lations—and his will to blend fact and fiction—affected the way he paints?

What is certain about *The Street* and its location is that Balthus *transformed* reality, whatever his model was. In all probability, what the artist really did was to base his painting on the Rue de Bourbon-le-Château, its angles widened, and then alter the details of the buildings—the fenestration, the moldings. His primary goal was not to encapsulate a specific spot; it was to fashion an artwork. That that artwork should be visually charming, that it should appeal to the eye as music does to the ear, was more important than that it should record a given crossroads of the web of streets behind Saint-Germain-des-Prés.

ONE DECEMBER AFTERNOON IN 1991, I went to the Rue de Bourbon-le-Château to consider yet again its validity as Balthus's source. An extraordinary event occurred there which in my mind is connected with the purpose of my mission that day.

I was in Paris with my eight-year-old daughter Charlotte, who knew scarcely a word of French. I had left her happily ensconced in a hairdresser's chair about two blocks from Bourbon-le-Château before I walked over there. It was a gray but mild day. Notebook in hand, along with a reproduction of Balthus's painting to refer to, I could see how Balthus had distorted the dimen sions and angles both to serve the purposes of his picture and to impose drama and intensity.

Suddenly an incredible gust of wind swept through the neighborhood. In a matter of a minute or two, it had evolved into a tempest almost on the scale of a tornado. I was desperate to get back to my daughter, but shop signs, wooden fruit crates, and wastebins were literally flying around the streets, and it instantly became clear that I had no choice but to join all the other panicked people by rushing into the entranceway of the nearest building.

Someone slammed shut the heavy steel door of this old Parisian four-story structure to keep out the wind. The door squashed my finger, and as I tried with the other hand to open it just enough to release my finger, other people pushed with even greater force to keep the door closed. I shouted to open. The effect of my cries was only to make people exclaim angrily that to release the door would be dangerous. When I finally got them to open it, my finger, miraculously, was not broken.

After about five minutes, the storm had passed. I rushed, as if in a night-mare, in the direction of the beauty salon where I had left my child. When I had last seen her half an hour earlier, she had all the excitement of a pretty young girl about to have her first Parisian hair trim—with not another thought on her mind. I hardly dared imagine what had happened since then. On the way to the salon, I passed broken windows, cars with shattered windshields, iron fencing pulled out of the ground, heavy benches bent almost beyond recognition, and several people knocked to the ground, bleeding from fresh cuts inflicted by the flying debris.

When I got to Charlotte, she was looking contentedly in the mirror. She seemed very pleased by the new way her soft, dark blond hair framed her face and fell on her back. All she knew of the tornado was that at one point everyone had rushed to look out the windows of the salon and that for some unexpected reason her hairdresser had suddenly stopped trimming her hair.

Charlotte was stunned when we then walked around the neighborhood. I, meanwhile, found myself wondering how much power Balthus really wielded. Precisely when I was doing the sort of research that my subject would have derided, I had come precariously close to real catastrophe. This was the sort of occurrence that belongs to the poems and stories of Balthus's beloved Edgar Allan Poe, a gale more ferocious than those that sweep through the moors of his favorite *Wuthering Heights*.

Meanwhile, my daughter had been every bit as self-absorbed as the girls her age in Balthus's many paintings of them. Focused on her own looks, enjoying the power of appearance, she remained blissfully impervious to the world around her. Like the girls of Balthus, she evinced a charm and spell more eternal and lasting than the rubbish and destruction strewn all over the streets. Should I just accept *his* truth as the real truth and consider this a warning?

V

In the street people put on a face so that strangers won't read their souls.
—THORNTON WILDER, *The Eighth Day*[12]

With their chins high and their half-shut eyes looking at the hills, the woods, the sky, the horizon—anywhere but at their companions—they slouched along in seeming bland oblivion.
—ELIZABETH MARSHALL THOMAS, ON SEEING MALE
CHEETAHS CROSSING AN AFRICAN PLAIN[13]

VIEWERS IN FRONT OF *The Street* at the Museum of Modern Art say they can taste the bread. We are in the sixth arrondissement. We feel enclosed by the same juxtaposition of plaster and wood that surrounds the nine characters. We sense with total authenticity what it is to step up on the curb, to carry a board, to press against another person, to anchor one's feet for stability—the momentary occurrences that constitute human aliveness. Perhaps this celebration is what Balthus meant when he referred to himself as a religious painter.

The carpenter who holds center stage moves at a brisk stride; Balthus establishes this in the leg angles and muscle tension. With his outstretched arms, he grasps the wood capably; he knows how to perform his task. This vigorous character is analogous to Balthus himself.

The surface of the plank of wood carried by this man is a major victory. Undisguisedly oil paints applied to canvas with free and animated brushwork, this wild amalgam of white, yellow, gold, and red, with some astonishing accents of green, is a far cry from a deliberate re-creation of reality. But the device works; at a distance it is a piece of wood. Balthus has rendered it so convincingly that we feel that he and the carpenter are kin in their firm control of materials and their competence. In the grand sweep of the composition and the bold play of the horizontals, verticals, and diagonals, Balthus, like his subject, has made strong, energetic moves.

The Street isn't the world as one would actually find it; it is civilization with decor and costumes by Balthus. The artist has carefully constructed his canvas so that one's eye easily connects the characters and their setting. The various elements are flawlessly coordinated. Balthus has related the details of the garments and the architecture. He has framed the head of the woman nearest us—seen from behind in her handsome outfit of black with red piping—with a distant shop facade painted the exact same red and black that she is wearing. A musical sort of linkage, this resembles the use of a series of notes to echo or transpose an earlier phrase, or the repetition of a chord; the placement accentuates her powerful, thunderous impression.

Balthus constantly relates shapes and colors to such strong effect. The position of the red and black architrave in the distance around the identically colored hat in the foreground joins the nearest and farthest points of the painting. In that way it is a deliberate reminder of the ultimate flatness of the canvas, a statement that art is a contrivance and an illusion. An exquisite visual passage, it also extols the beauty of that artifice. And it helps give the impeccably turned-out woman, perhaps just an ordinary shopgirl, the charm and impact of the most meticulously put-together lady in all of Paris. Balthus's subjects invariably have what it takes to catch your eye—and to possess you.

The pink and green stripes on the scarf of the woman carrying a little boy appear—their size, angle, and colors, although faded, are the same—in the panel of the building she approaches. The sign over the woman's head also contains, if on a different scale, these diagonal bands of pink and green. And their colors are identical to those worn by the bizarre girl playing in the left foreground. These are systems within systems.

The broken-arch pediment over the head of the young molester on the left serves as a neat framing device surrounding the top of his head. It puts him, like the woman in red and black and the woman with the striped scarf, in visual harmony with the setting. The shape of the head of the character being carried is echoed by the lantern above him; they are similarly crowned as well.

Balthus's use of black and red throughout this painting lends balance and order; it also heightens the visual drama. As in sixteenth-century Spanish painting, the black has power and elegance. On the lower right, the broad expanse of the back of the well-dressed lady works in conjunction with the skirt of the woman who carries a boy in the crook of her arm as a sequence of major black notes: concentrated and emphatic. They balance the black plane created on the upper left in the void of the shopwindow, and the concomitant blacks of the paired schoolgirl and schoolboy. Smaller areas of black punctuate the passageways, the window glass of the bistro, and two picture windows on the cross street. All of this well-situated and opaque darkness—antithetical to the more luminous, translucent yellows and ochers that dominate the painting—helps give *The Street* its rhythm. The beat is like the continuum of footsteps and the ongoing pulse of city life.

Small doses of red offer a vibrant accent to counteract the black expanses. It adds a necessary light touch to the outfit of the woman at the right. By appearing in the jersey underneath the pinafore of the girl on the left, it clarifies what is where, and lends vibrancy and drama to the pairing of her and her assailant.

That identical red in the pom-pom leavens the seriousness of the saucer-shaped black body of the tam. Spots of red elsewhere make pivotal stopping points. Visually, through the complex interplay of colors and forms, there is total unity. Yet on the level of human attitudes and relationships, Balthus has created a troubled universe in which nothing fits. Inaccessible emotions are offset by the aesthetic organization. It is like Balthus himself.

We think we know what we are looking at, and it is immensely attractive. But then we have no idea. Initially welcoming and enticing, *The Street* throws us off. What at first is warm and pleasant and accessible becomes, as we emerge from our own carefully induced dream state, nerve-racking. Seduced by the lush surface and plentitude of artistic effects in this large painting, sucked in by its false similarity to the real world, we then find ourselves on completely shaky turf.

Seeking resolution, we are driven to know more. As with all of Balthus's art, it is the picture itself that impels us to violate his recommended attitude of passive acceptance and to delve into the territories that he perversely insists have nothing to do with his work.

In truth, Balthus's rendition of his old neighborhood is not at all a salubrious, placid scene. The sweep of the angled curb at the left, the catapulting perspective of the street itself, startle us like a ride at an amusement park. This dramatically foreshortened pavement in *The Street* brings forward, at high speed, a scene that by contrast is somewhere between deeply lethargic and frozen. We zoom in and come to a full stop; ferried to splendid territory, we are then told we may go no further. Our experience of the two simultaneous tempos induces tension. So does our awareness that we have been both invited in and kept at arm's length. Seeing one corner of the neighborhood, we are left wanting to look around a bend where we can never turn; we sense the space of the cross street, but we will never see it. We have enough information about the inhabitants of the canvas to be enticed, but then we feel the limits that restrict our knowledge of them. Everything looks momentous—as if a major event either has just occurred or is about to—but all the players conceal the details and keep the facts clandestine.

Looking at this painting, we have subjected ourselves to the devices of a master magician and manipulator. The rewards are bountiful: a glorious visual experience, a rich piece of chocolate cake. But then we lose control, for Balthus has seen to it that he alone is in charge.

It is the human drama that is most off-putting of all. Each of the nine figures in *The Street* has some trait that imprints the character on our minds. Like the personalities in a dream, they seem totally plausible during our initial encounter with them; it is only when our state of consciousness changes that we recognize how weird they are.

These people in *The Street* intersect visually—the little girl's hoop in front of the carpenter, the well-dressed woman partially blocking the boy with bent arm—yet even those who are paired with someone else occupy their own insular worlds. These are isolated and estranged individuals engaged in some sort of performance more than in natural, intuitive living. Each is disconnected, immersed in his or her own thoughts or actions. Their mouths are clamped shut, as if they are locked in an irrevocable silence. Any effort they make toward the world is only for their own benefit.

What we do grasp of their human interaction is unsettling and sinister. A boy accosts a girl in broad daylight, but the characters who bear silent witness to this act are entirely indifferent to it. The faces of three of these bystanders are hidden from us; the four who can be seen ignore the violence that is taking place only a few feet away from them—that is, unless their apparent obliviousness can be seen as a deliberate stance. As encompassing a view as *The Street* provides, the painting is about not seeing, and not getting the whole story. No one looks at anybody else. The boy assaulting the girl in red and black is transfixed, impervious to his effect on other people. For all his brutality and the violence of his grip on the girl's wrist, he reveals only inner repose. His victim, rather than looking startled, appears resigned. She is the image of martyrdom with her winglike arms and otherworldly gaze.

People engage only with themselves. The boy near center stage—the fellow with the lascivious mouth and rather militant walk—looks in our direction, but his eyes roll upward and completely miss contact with ours; everyone else has his or her eyes shut or stares downward.

More awkward than natural, this pudgy, malformed lad bends his right arm as if saluting—or else holding something in, keeping it beneath the surface. He has wide-open eyes, yet his thoughts have nothing to do with the scene through which he has just progressed.

BALTHUS TOLD ME that when he was working on *The Street* he would periodically walk around the neighborhood near his studio to gather impressions for the painting. In the course of those strolls, he selected the faces or clothing that suited him best. Then, back in his studio, he painted from memory, transforming his cast of characters at will.

This has remained his working method in general, except in the case of specific portraits. Although he has often sketched from live figures, when painting oils in the studio he has not had people in front of him, and has consulted no source but his own mind.

These characters based on actual people but metamorphosed by imagination are both real and frightening. What holds us rapt has been illuminated in as clearly contrived a way as in a stage play. The shadows made by people's legs suggest multiple light sources, all from the left, while the facts and the setlike facades have been lit head-on. The artifice of these particular Parisians is accentuated by the way the face of each glows like that of an actor under individual spotlights. They pose as if performing a pantomime. But they become our reality for the stretch of time we are looking at them.

Strange as everyone else in *The Street* is, the chef is the most detached, solitary figure of all. Yet for all his remove, he grabs our attention by force of his parodic flatness and compression, and his bizarre proportions. Only a few feet away from the other characters, he has no business being half their size. But Balthus insisted to me that this is quite simply a real person; there is nothing more to it.

Sabine Rewald claimed that the chef in *The Street* is a flat, freestanding wooden restaurant sign. Many people have seen it as such—Ted Morgan, in his 1994 *New York Times Magazine* article on Balthus, wrote that the chef was plywood. But "the chef," Balthus told me, his voice rising assertively, "is a chef."

The scale and flatness of this creature, as well as the form of his legs, certainly make him as plausibly an advertising tool as the person Balthus now claims him to be. How could he be that size if he were real? Unless, of course, he was a midget or a small boy in men's clothes—with a troubled old man's face: all of which is possible with Balthus as the creator.

And the lad in the crook of the woman's arm looks like a ventriloquist's dummy. One of those children who already appears the way he will when he is eighty, he is all the stranger because he faces us squarely but reads a document that he holds far to his left; his tiny pupils are angled theatrically in the most remote corners of his eyes. We have no idea what the document is—a letter, a newspaper, a comic book. Balthus's characters have concerns that we cannot possibly penetrate; they are as inaccessible as the artist himself.

The boy and the chef are as stiff as inert material and as pale as ghosts. No wonder the boy has been "mistaken" for a puppet just as the chef has been construed as a sign. The squat girl with a stocking cap—angel, Humpty-Dumpty, a court dwarf—is still less plausible. Yet Balthus shrugged his shoulders at my queries about her as if it were absurd to suggest that she is other than a normal child.

EVEN MORE THAN THE faceless carpenter, the chef is a neat, serious professional whose occupation depends on his expertise in combining the correct ingredients. And this distant, remote outsider evinces unflappable resolve.

When I therefore asked Balthus whether he was one of the people in *The Street,* he again shrugged his shoulders and answered with silence. Unyielding, unrevealing, and unapproachable, as intractable as a piece of wood, he seemed at that moment more than ever like both the chef and the carpenter.

The artist to whom Rilke dedicated the poem "Narcissus" has, I believe, represented himself in almost every one of his paintings. The autobiography is not apparent at first; it is a case of self-portraiture in costume. Androgynous, commanding, elusive, conducting themselves imperiously while betraying a certain fragility, hiding their vulnerability behind masklike faces: the wily cats, the self-obsessed girls, the demonic boys, and the haughty and gracious socialites all seem to be extensions of the Balthus I grew to know. At times Balthus's persona is present in a roaring fire or a well-aimed knife; these inanimate objects represent parts of his psyche. Above all, the nubile young girls who have been his lifelong obsession are an aspect of the artist himself.

At first I wanted to take at face value the gospel of the master as he elaborated it to me, and to believe that he depicted all his teenage women just because they were universally familiar types and because youth interested him.

He asserted this "fact" time and again in our smoky chats on the sofa—with
the truth of his words seemingly guaranteed by the winter sunlight suffusing
his powerful, imposing face. Yet the more I have looked at his work and
learned about the man, the clearer it has become that his obsession with those
girls is not just with an "other"—passionate as he unquestioningly is about
adolescent girls—but also part of his complete immersion in himself.

Balthus's girls are Balthus? The savvy, secretive, masculine/feminine adolescent who has dominated his art is a self-image? The artist might roar, yet I
maintain that the creatures who are so ardently coveted by this narcissistic man
are their creator in another form. Those girls are the same age he was when
tragedy and beauty coincided so powerfully in his tumultuous life. This was
when, as Rilke and Baladine's genius, he basked in their esteem—but also suffered from the complexities of the love affair that was so all-consuming for his
mother and took her from him. Because of the realities of poverty and inflation, Balthus never had the serenity necessary for the successful completion of
his own adolescence.

As for the other group of women Balthus has painted repeatedly—the
victims and dreamers, in their twenties, seemingly overcome by their emotion—these are stand-ins for his mother. I see them as Baladine herself, but
also as the Baladine whom Balthus resembled and with whom he identified.

Balthus is also powerfully present as the invisible person seeing his art.
He looms as the being through whose eyes we have come to view these unique
arrangements and without whom we could not possibly be encountering
them. Every image, as well as the vision that encompasses them, stems directly
from his own psyche. The artist himself may insist that we not ask questions
about who he really is, but whether he admits it or not, he has made one
painting after another, starting with *The Street,* that vehemently begs the
question.

THE BIZARRE CHARACTERIZATIONS of people are not all that make *The
Street* discomfiting. The blinded windows that loom ominously throughout
the large canvas also make vivid that there is a lot we do not know and cannot
find out. The artist presents either blackened, opaque glass or panes behind
which curtains or shades have been drawn. As in conversation, he puts up
deliberate stopping points. You think you have been taken inside a secret
world, where you see people as they really are, when in fact a slew of barriers
remain; it is the same pattern as when Balthus reminisces about his childhood
or an early friendship and seems like someone in a trance who is letting his

associations flow completely freely, when in truth there is not a prayer he will let slip one unintended word.

Someone with the discrimination of a propaganda artist has determined what we can and cannot see. Balthus gives us, in his art as in his life, as much information as he wants: nothing more, nothing he cannot control. If this leaves us squirming, *tant mieux.*

When I asked the creator of this scenario about the violence in it, he asked what on earth I meant. Like the characters in this canvas, we, too, should look straight ahead and not see what is going on.

In *The Street,* BALTHUS went further than before with the distortion of scale and proportions that had already been evident in his work before he went to Morocco. The relationship of the body parts of the boy reading is completely out of whack. At first glance, we know that something strange is going on but cannot quite fathom what; the incongruity is subtle. But soon we realize that the masklike face of this "child" is the same size as his chest. His visible hand is two-thirds the size of the face. His calves are gargantuan, and his knee almost as wide as his shoulders.

Peculiar proportions became one of the elements that gave Balthus's work its unique stamp. His characters often have elephantine limbs. Either they resemble cones standing on their points—tapered at the ankle, bulging above— or they are straight and massive like tree trunks. Compared with the distortions of Cubism or the other transmutations of twentieth-century art, Balthus's work is realistic, but in spite of its initially old-fashioned appearance, it is actually radical and irreverent. Like Giacometti, Balthus worked from the human figure but reinvented it. Giacometti elongated; Balthus reproportioned. In both cases, the original, unusual beings they invented have superhuman force.

Throughout his art, not only has Balthus widened calves to empower his subjects physically, but he has consistently enlarged their heads. The mammoth faces make his characters appear to have enormous inner worlds. Their oversized brains give them a vast capacity for rationalization and invention.

These distorted features also suggest Balthus's childlike perspective on the world. The artist has often said that he wishes he could always have remained a child and is grateful for his rare birth date as a means of shaving off three-quarters of his age. His work maintains that child's vantage point, from which adults' legs are particularly large; Balthus paints them almost as if seen by an infant on the rug.

Babies and toddlers, of course, have proportionately big heads; the widest

part of the body coming through the birth canal is the head. With their gargantuan faces lumbering over narrow shoulders, many of Balthus's characters
thus resemble newborns. These characters—conceived, after all, in his own
image—are wise and infantile in much the way he is.

Writers in the 1930s referred to the heads in Balthus's paintings—above all
those in *The Street*—as encephalitic. That frightful disease, however, can
hardly be claimed as part of the artist's conscious program. An unconscious
wish to keep everyone childlike seems far more probable. The dual ages of the
figures in *The Street* and in his subsequent paintings serve the great purpose of
helping to eradicate the distinction between the stages of life.

THOSE LARGE HEADS and the deliberately immature vantage point in
Balthus's art call to mind *Alice's Adventures in Wonderland*—both Lewis Carroll's text and John Tenniel's illustrations for it. *Alice in Wonderland* was one of
the three books Balthus studied for his essay on illustrated children's literature.
Stanley William Hayter, the English-born printmaker and painter who was a
close friend of Balthus's in Paris and helped him stretch the canvas for *The
Street,* has said that in 1933 Balthus declared that the boy walking toward us
was based on a character from *Through the Looking-Glass.*

When I raised this point in Rossinière, Balthus told me that the boy simply resembled someone he saw in his neighborhood; there was no basis in
Lewis Carroll. He added that, in any case, artistic sources make no difference
and are irrelevant. But what he told Hayter in 1933 was probably true.

One of the reasons Balthus has since recanted on the subject of his debt to
Carroll and Tenniel may be that, on the subject of influence, he's been pushed
too far. Critics have now further pinpointed the boy as Tweedledee, the other
young man as Tweedledum, and the girl being grabbed as Alice. The figure in
white has been identified as Lewis Carroll's carpenter without the walrus. It
may in part be out of reaction to these overreaching analogies that Balthus
entirely shut off the subject of Alice with me.

Yet Lewis Carroll—particularly as he was illustrated by Tenniel—is pivotal to Balthus's work, and not just to *The Street.* Alice pulling back the curtain
that covers the small door that leads to the rabbit hole was probably a partial
model for the figure that has just opened the drapery in *The Room.* In his Tate
catalog essay, John Russell has pointed out that Balthus's dreamy-eyed girls
with their cats—a type he developed in the late 1930s—resemble the large-
headed Alice sitting with "Kitty" in a Victorian armchair at the start of
Through the Looking-Glass. There is no question that this is the case.

Balthus deems this sort of analysis gratuitous, but beyond the distinct visual resemblance, there was also a major psychological affinity with *Alice*. Consider the questions posed at the close of *Through the Looking-Glass*. Alice is trying to figure out who dreamed it all—she or the Red King. She consults her cat, but the creature responds only by licking her paw. Alice is desperate for answers; none are forthcoming.

> "Oh, Kitty, *do* help settle it! I'm sure your paw can wait!" But the provoking kitten only began on the other paw, and pretended it hadn't heard the question.[14]

The image of that cat feigning deafness is followed by Carroll's last line: "Which do *you* think it was?"

Balthus has spent his whole life as both the impassive cat and the ambitious narrator of this story. If the reader/viewer, like Alice, insists on asking questions and trying to unravel mysteries, the writer/painter has no intention of obliging with an answer. He will either ignore the question or be blithely inconclusive in his response.

To provide simple solutions is to diminish beauty. *Alice in Wonderland* occurs

> where Childhood's dreams are twined
> In Memory's mystic band.
> Like pilgrim's wither'd wreath of flowers
> Pluck'd in a far-off land.

These are Carroll's words before his narrative commences; his epitaph following the second volume leaves us no closer to solid facts or certainty. Alice's adventures have taken us somewhere tangentially based on the real world, but this fictional territory is not to be entirely grasped. It is, rather, in the realm of dream and memory.

Perhaps this far-off haze is the only truth there is.

> Ever drifting down the stream—
> Lingering in the golden gleam—
> Life, what is it but a dream?[15]

So Balthus has maintained, both by how he has painted and how he has lived. With *The Street*, he first laid claim to this far-off land as his territory of choice.

CHAPTER NINE

THE PIERO OF PARIS

In *The Street,* Balthus became Piero della Francesca in twentieth-century Parisian dress. To consider the issue is to violate the artist's own dictates at every step, but its validity is self-evident.

When I asked him about John Russell's idea, supported with illustrations in the 1968 Tate catalog, that the carpenter shouldering his wooden plank in *The Street* derives directly from the figure, also clad in white, carrying the wood of the cross in Piero's chapel in Arezzo, Balthus replied, "One could so endlessly find sources. Painting has always come out of painting. In the Middle Ages, every painter was influenced by another painter. There was a model for all the subjects. Carpenters carry wood. Period.

"In Paris a man carrying a board was something so usual that even without Piero you had to close your eyes not to see it. But art historians need walking sticks," Balthus wistfully lamented, his cigarette moving up and down between his lips as he spoke.

Yet he used a myriad of details from the Arezzo frescoes in his painting of ordinary, contemporary life—whether or not he realized he was doing so.

The tam worn by the little boy being carried closely resembles the saucer-like hat worn by Piero's Judas. Surely Balthus was not impervious to the ironic touch of restating it with a pom-pom in *The Street,* to the humor of adding this childish ornament to the headgear of a traitor. Balthus's little creature also wears a collar of exactly the same design and proportions as the Arezzo Judas. This odd character of puzzling identity is truly Piero's traitor as a little boy living in modern Paris, the joint creation of an early Renaissance master and the young hellion who worshiped him.

The Greek cross on the well-dressed woman's hat echoes the cross on the flag in another of Piero's Arezzo frescoes: *The Victory of Heracles*. Its light-infused, pale tomato red is almost precisely the same hue as the background of that flag, and it functions similarly as a powerful, vibrant, upbeat element in the overall composition. There is also an uncanny resemblance between the central teenage boy in *The Street,* the one walking toward us with his right hand across his waist—and one of Adam and Eve's children at Arezzo. As facial types, both this boy and the assailant of the girl in red, practically his doppel-gänger, have features identical to those of many of Piero's characters: the same full lips, flattened noses, wide cheeks, and perfectly arched eyebrows. Like Piero's heads, these faces are compelling more as artistry than as specimens of nature.

Throughout his subsequent work, Balthus would continue to use this very limited repertory of facial types—as if his design agenda always mattered more than the appearance of specific individuals. Rather than create new people, he made everyone conform to the model of a round, masklike disk with perfectly organized, symmetrical features and the eyes ludicrously wide apart. The people seem predetermined and calculated—copied from something rather than possessed of their own independence and force.

Balthus's youths—not only those in *The Street* but also a number of his subsequent creations, the most striking being his 1976 *Katia Reading*—descend directly from the facial type Piero gives to the first figure in the Queen of Sheba's retinue, the turbaned man in Solomon's retinue, Constantine's lieu-tenant, Judas, Adam's children, and various other personages. If Balthus did not intentionally have the relationship in mind, the only other plausible expla-nation for the close resemblance is that he was so hypnotized by those early Renaissance faces as to be unaware of the trance in which he re-formed them. The figures in *The Street,* with their globular heads and wide eyes, were by no means the ordinary French street types of the time; they are Piero's biblical characters reincarnated.

BALTHUS'S BOYS AND GIRLS are the heirs of Piero's figures in more than their physiognomies. They also share the look Piero gave his subjects of knowing something we do not know. Transfixed, all these creatures both belong to our world and exist outside of it—with their cache of private information.

Piero's figures impart majesty to their everyday deeds. Balthus's "ordinary" Parisians do the same. Each person in *The Street* is sure of what he or she is doing—be it mischievous, playful, or diligent. Balthus has made their actions momentous by locking them into his or her own microclimate with the still-ness of children playing "Statues."

Piero della Francesca, *Judas,* detail from *The Discovery and Proof of the Cross,* 1452, fresco, overall size: 336 x 747 cm

Piero della Francesca, *Men Carrying the Wood,* detail from *The Burying of the Wood,* 1455, fresco, overall size: 356 x 190 cm

A master choreographer, Balthus has put all the people in *The Street* in tight geometric relationship to one another. Seven of them—all except for the girl under attack and the boy being carried—are strong columnar forms, locked in position like units of architecture.

That ordering, the faces themselves, and the dignified movement all make the creator of *The Street* Piero della Francesca's filial heir. By becoming, in his own way, Piero, Balthus could obtain the control and quiet majesty, as well as the visual sumptuousness, he craved.

THE HUES OF BALTHUS'S CANVAS are much the same as that of *The Victory of Heracles* at Arezzo. The tonality is practically identical. There is a softness to the coloring, a sense of distance, a refinement that lends noble stature to the subject matter.

Piero's elegant reserve is evident. Using a limited palette, Balthus, too, has put his colors in quiet discourse with one another. The resonance of the colors is paralleled by the interaction of the forms. In a precise program, arcs, spheres, and cylinders have a similar impact on one another as do blacks, ochers, and russets. *The Street*, like *The Queen of Sheba's Visit to Solomon,* has been divided carefully, the spaces neatly delineated and divided, the columns worked out in an orderly sequence. Balthus's painting, like Piero's *Flagellation,* can be described by Kenneth Clark's words: "space created and space filled."

AS A YOUNG ARTIST in a modern metropolis, Balthus, rather than embrace the present, looked to history and gave Paris in the 1930s the scale and pace of Piero's fifteenth-century Borgo Sansepolcro. In Rossinière I was struck by the degree to which Balthus the artist has completed the process; here he has not only halted time but turned the clock backward. This is a community where he knows everyone, if not as names than at least as types. On weekday mornings, workmen in caps carry their tools and buckets to their barns and workshops. Women have their market bags. Schoolchildren walk their usual routes. An old-fashioned train whistle offers its loud shriek like clockwork. The details of daily existence provide the structure and purpose of life.

Wood is everywhere. It is the main material for both building and heating, visible in the roof shingles, ornate balconies, siding, and beams of the local houses as in the stacks of firewood everywhere. In planks and logs, it is piled high; catching the sunlight, those planks bear the same rich grain as the board in *The Street* which recollects the cross being carried at Arezzo. The other dominant materials are stone and plaster: of ancient tradition, solid, resistant to age. Balthus's paintings may hang in the Centre Pompidou, but in his own life

Balthus in 1933, by Man Ray

he has no taste for the chrome and glitz of contemporary Paris. Since the French capital no longer offers Piero's tempo, Balthus has found a mountain hamlet that does.

WHEN BALTHUS FINISHED *The Street* at the age of twenty-five, he wrote to friends that it was his first important painting. Discussing the canvas with me, Balthus took an approach like that of certain aged parents toward their children. They are not sure if their offspring are successes, but the progeny are, for better or worse, their legacy to the world.

Yet when I insist that the painting was an unusual accomplishment for someone aged twenty-five, Balthus disagreed. Seurat was no older when he painted *La Grande Jatte,* he pointed out.

The comparison was relevant. Seurat was an artist who periodically painted monumental group scenes, the same sort of summation pictures that Balthus has occasionally made. As numerous observers have written, *The Street* is very much in the tradition of *La Grande Jatte.* Every element of these complex compositions is obeisant to the grid. Balthus admired Seurat's rigor, his perpetual compliance with the vertical/horizontal arrangement, and the intricate relationship he developed among the parts. Seurat was a supremely self-disciplined craftsman and observer, detached and astute: the stance Balthus also desired. Like Seurat, by locking everyone within a visual nexus, Balthus froze time and ordered experience in a well-crafted mechanism—operated by him alone.

But Seurat was not the only artist Balthus pointed out to me as doing more than he had by the age of twenty-five. Masaccio was younger when he painted the Brancacci Chapel; Mantegna produced some of his finest work at sixteen. One of the reasons for the early success of people like Seurat and Mantegna, Balthus explained, is that these artists had the advantage of having had minimal formal education. Nowadays school keeps young people from doing anything important. In earlier times, they might have become painters' apprentices at the age of eleven or twelve. They would have painted out of necessity and avoided the debilitating effects of too much education.

Balthus often reiterated to me that the sole education that mattered in his own development was the simple act of looking—at good art, and the world around him. People should enjoy and cultivate their powers of observation—not accumulate facts or gratuitous theories.

No one bought *The Street* from the Galerie Pierre. Most of its admirers—young poets, fellow artists, and others on the fringes of Parisian life—could not afford it, while the sort of Parisians who had enough money to purchase such a large painting found it too scandalous.

But even without a purchaser, *The Street* had admirers. Antonin Artaud and Pierre Jean Jouve were among the literary figures who soon wrote about its effects on them; Albert Camus eventually followed suit. The Surrealists became so fascinated by the large canvas in the show at the Galerie Pierre that they asked Balthus to let them exhibit it in the Minotaure exhibition held in Paris later that year; they hung it there in the section with work by Picasso, Brancusi, Duchamp, Klee, and Kandinsky.

Then, just over two years after the exhibition closed, *The Street* was pur-

Georges Seurat, *Sunday Afternoon on the Island of La Grande Jatte*,
1883–85, oil on canvas, 6 ft. 9¾ in. x 10 ft. 1¼ in.

chased—surprisingly, by an American. James Thrall Soby, just two years older
than Balthus, was an adventurous young collector with a taste characterized by
Alfred Barr as "bold enough to confront the formidable." The heir to fortunes
made from the machine that returned change on pay telephones and from a
tobacco business that sold cigars called "the German lovers," he had only
recently come to discover that what he wanted to do with his life was to
acquire, curate, and write about paintings.

Soby had seen *The Street* in Balthus's exhibition at the Galerie Pierre in
1934. He had not purchased it then, but neither had he been able to get it out
of his mind. For two years, he had "brooded about it almost constantly."[1]
Astonished but relieved to see that it had not been sold by the time he returned
to Paris in late 1936, he bought it instantly.

Soby had assumed that the reason no one else had obtained *The Street* was
because of its size. This had been his problem; in 1934 he had been living in a
suburban home where there was no wall that could easily accommodate a
painting that measured almost 6½ by 8 feet. But now he had moved to a Greek
Revival house in Farmington, Connecticut, where he had room for it.

Pierre Loeb told Soby that for most people size had not been the primary
issue. The difficulty that had turned buyers away had been what Soby later

termed the "passage which even the French, usually calm about such matters, found hard to take: the depiction of the young man at the edge of ecstasy reaching over the hem of the girl's hiked-up skirt toward the young girl's genitals."

That scene was a pivotal factor for the young American as well, but in his case it was favorable. He delighted in the shock value. Like Balthus, James Thrall Soby was a young man with a lively sense of humor and a deep pleasure in upsetting the bourgeoisie. He was keyed up by—in his own words—the "young girl being seized by the crotch by a strangely Mongolian-looking young man who has come up behind her, his face taut with easily decipherable excitement." He savored the idea that it might create problems with the U.S. Customs office in Hartford, which was to be its port of entry into the country. Soby had imported many paintings there, and seemed pleased that *The Street* would bolster his reputation for eccentricity.

When the customs authorities opened the crate containing *The Street*, however, they simply acknowledged that it was an original work of art and hence duty-free. One official even told Soby that this was the first painting the collector had brought in that the official really liked. Like Balthus, Soby was a keen, and somewhat sardonic, observer of the audience for paintings. It was not lost on him that a work both more realistic and more salacious than other examples of contemporary painting was the biggest hit with someone to whom most recent art was anathema.

Soby had bought Balthus's painting above all because he admired it, but his pleasure was enhanced by the way it confounded its viewers even more than had the rest of his modern paintings in his living room in Farmington. Most of his friends and neighbors were bridge players or golfers for whom even Matisse had been beyond comprehension; the licentiousness of *The Street* was beyond them.

Off in a Greek Revival house on an elm-lined rural road in a country to which Balthus had not been and which he would never visit, the racy subject matter was therefore having precisely the effect the artist now says he intended.

For he wanted to shock. That, above all, was the motive behind all of his extraordinary subject matter. So Balthus, in hindsight, insists.

That the eroticism or violence might be innate, or that they even exist in his work: to these notions, the creator offered a resounding no. Day after day, wording it in various ways, Balthus reiterated to me that to call his work erotic is to misunderstand it, to see it as violent is to miss the point completely.

Yet however ardent his disclaimers, Balthus's art is blatantly about sexuality and power. In the earlier paintings, those themes are brazen; in his later art, they are sheathed in veils and guises. The vignette in the left-hand corner of

Detail of
The Street
of 1933
prior to its
repainting
in 1955

The Street—Balthus's generic, Piero-like boy, transfixed in a dream world, lost in reverie, attacking a girl his own age, reaching under the skirt of her gargantuan legs while she reacts by freezing in her own, out-of-it, mannerist mode—is what Balthus's art, and the man himself, are all about. The power and thrill of lust, and a panoply of elegant subterfuges through which to deal with physical desire, has consistently pervaded Balthus's art ever since *The Street* and those six other paintings, some of them even more blatant than this one, caused such a stir at the Galerie Pierre in 1934.

So although I have had the distinct pleasure of hearing one of the most talented artists of our century, one of the most courtly and erudite citizens of the modern world, elucidate his views as to what is and is not shown in his work, I should believe him no more than when he, calmly and skillfully, lies to me about his heritage and a range of other subjects.

And even if the reason Balthus repeatedly gave me for the salacious subject matter of his early work was that he wished to be deliberately provocative because he knew that the more subtle aspects of the painting would be lost on most people, and that this was his device to get people to pay attention and attract the larger audience, I think that the subject matter is part of a far deeper inner agenda.

BALTHUS MADE THE CASE to me that in *The Street* as in all his other work, he was showing life as it really was. Boys in grade school often lift girls' skirts. They rarely go so far as to actually grab their victims' genitals, but it's what they are thinking of.

He allowed himself to go no further in this commentary, however. He would not consider that the act of raising the hem stems from a wish to embarrass and humiliate and degrade. Nor would he contemplate the idea that, as the painter of the scene, he was one with those teenage boys. Yet in the boy's treatment of the girl in *The Street,* we may very well be seeing the essence of Balthus's much discussed, lifelong attitude toward women.

The young man is patently ecstatic, while the girl—whom I also see as a partial self-portrait as well as (not inconsistently) the object of his passion—is harder to read. The other seven characters in the painting, technically near this scandalous encounter, are entirely impervious to it. Lust and indifference thus juxtaposed were guaranteed to evoke titillation, discomfort, or a blend of the two.

Balthus would have us believe he painted these various modes of behavior because he wished to entertain; he was young, eager to evoke a reaction. It is a most convenient out. His own emotional necessity—to behave like the malevolent boy while the rest of the world walks by glazed—is equally behind all this.

WITHOUT QUESTION, BALTHUS succeeded in his goal of attracting attention to his art. Soby's cohorts Henry-Russell Hitchcock and A. Everett Austin, Jr., reacted like schoolboys. Hitchcock was an architectural historian and champion of the pioneering International Style, Austin the director of the Wadsworth Atheneum and hence the impresario for such modern and startling events as the world premiere of Gertrude Stein and Virgil Thomson's *Four Saints in Three Acts.* They were hardly unsophisticated. But the two often clowned around in front of *The Street* in its owner's living room. They liked to stand directly in front of the scandalous passage and assume in their own way the role of the naughty teenagers.

If people like Henry-Russell Hitchcock and Chick Austin cavorted in front of *The Street,* it should come as no surprise that the owner of the painting soon had serious problems with the reactions of real schoolboys. In the late 1930s Soby's adopted son—who had previously been in the custody of the boy's mother, the collector's first wife—moved into the house in Farmington where Soby was living with his second wife. Peter was five years old. Soby and his wife were eager to put Peter's life on an even keel, and it didn't help when the boy's friends began to titter wildly over *The Street*. Neighborhood children carried home tales of the naughty painting at their playmate's house. Their parents began to telephone Soby to ask what on earth these kindergartners were seeing in Soby's living room.

The collector attempted the defense that Giovanni Bellini's *Feast of the Gods*, on view in the National Gallery in Washington, had equally explicit imagery—even if it was cloaked in mythological dress and the participants took less visible pleasure in their frolicking. But the argument carried little weight in a New England town. Soby later wrote:

> The neighborhood clamor didn't subside nor did the number of very small visitors to my living room. Moreover, with childhood's instinct for getting right to the point, the kids would gather in front of the "questionable" passage, as though there were nothing else in the large composition worth looking at. I finally decided that it wasn't fair to my small son to have his father thought of as unmoral, if not immoral, and I reluctantly took the picture down.[2]

At first Soby had considered putting a screen in front of *The Street* so that it would simply be out of view when Peter had friends over. He discussed the possibility with Russell Hitchcock, but every time they tried to work on its design, they simply ended up drinking and laughing in front of the painting. Finally Soby stored *The Street* in a fireproof vault he had built adjacent to the garage.

Balthus's masterpiece remained out of view for a number of years. It only emerged from its hiding place in the early 1950s when Soby was visited by the Reverend James L. McLane, another of Balthus's American champions. Soby knew that Father McLane had hung several of the artist's most provocative paintings of young girls in his church in one of the poorest sections of Los Angeles. He admired the reverend's courage, and he felt shamed when McLane "bawled [him] out for three hours for being so cowardly as to hide a great painting away in a darkened vault."[3] McLane was unmoved by Soby's explanation that he had done this for his son's sake. The reverend insisted that "the painting is perfectly innocent, and, besides, your son is a child and not supposed to know what great art is. Nor are his friends or his friends' mothers."

Several years later, Soby wished that the Reverend McLane were still alive

Henry-Russell Hitchcock and Chick Austin in front of
The Street, c. 1938, Soby House, Farmington, Connecticut

to defend *The Street* to the authorities at the Museum of Modern Art in New York. Soby had become active as a curator there and was organizing a Balthus exhibition scheduled to open in 1956. It was the first major museum show any-where of the artist, who at that point still had a limited audience, and whose work had been publicly seen only at infrequent gallery exhibitions in Paris and New York. Soby thought it essential to include *The Street* in this show; he intended to bequeath the painting to the Modern. But he knew enough about the prevailing attitudes at the museum to realize that Balthus's large canvas was too lurid to be allowed on view.

When Soby was in the process of organizing Balthus's show, he wrote to the artist and explained the problem. He dropped the hint that several restor-ers had offered to alter the troublesome passage, although of course he would not allow anyone but Balthus himself to touch the picture. In spite of this diplomatic approach, he feared that the mere suggestion of a change would end a friendship that had by that time acquired great meaning for him.

To Soby's astonishment, Balthus wrote back that if the collector would send him the canvas, he would gladly repaint the passage. "When I was young,

I wanted to shock. Now it bores me," Balthus wrote. In my visits with him thirty-five years later, Balthus was still uttering precisely the same statement, which he remembered practically verbatim: "I wrote one of my rare letters to James Thrall Soby to explain that when I painted this part of my work it was of course a sort of provocative intention. This was when I felt for the first time the need of attracting attention on me, which after that I tried to avoid." With these few words, uttered with a sage's smile, he seemed satisfied that he could sweep the brazen candor of his early work under the rug.

Balthus's statement that he wanted to be provocative, and his admission that he used the imagery to do so, contradicts all of his claims that the subject matter was irrelevant. As astute a person as Balthus can hardly have believed that such imagery would serve his alleged intention of having the visual, formal elements hold center stage in his art. His insistent denial of the weight of his thematic content defies all reason. Surely he knew that this passage in *The Street,* like Alice's gaping pudenda and the crotch views of his other paintings, would attract the sort of response it evoked in people like Austin and Hitchcock. They, after all, were intellectually at the extreme upper end of his viewing public. Balthus could hardly have painted themes more certain to make people wonder about the painter, the very response he claimed to disparage.

Balthus was tacitly acknowledging that the subject matter of art, the very element he has consistently denigrated, had considerable weight. And the notion that he has always painted in a vacuum—for his own nefarious reasons, unclear even to himself, and with no awareness of the larger audience—is a shibboleth. On the contrary, anyone who once wanted so desperately to shock, and then is willing to repaint a painting to get past the censors and temper its effects, cares deeply about the perception of others. To manipulate and affect the observers of his art has been of paramount importance to him.

THAT LETTER WHICH Balthus wrote to James Thrall Soby in June 1956 is now owned by the Museum of Modern Art. The missive is tactful and courtly to a fault. No one could be more considerate and engaging than the man who characterized himself as a former mischief-maker. Because of Balthus's prohibition against printing material from his letters, the document cannot be quoted further. The reader may, however, picture small pages scrolled in neat fountain-pen script, addressed from "Château de Chassy, par Blismes Nièvre." Dated in French, the letter, except for a few interludes, is written in charming English. Balthus opens with heartfelt thanks to Soby for having lent *The Street* to an exhibition in France, and the most contrite apologies for not having written sooner. He then explains that he has indeed obliged the collector by changing the gesture of the boy. Balthus allows that this was a difficult task. His problem was that the composition of the picture was based on such a complex and intricate series of mathematical relationships. But he had no trouble with the idea of altering *The Street*, except for the effect of the revisions on its visual system. To move the angle of the boy's hand meant a lot only because of the geometric issues: the need for parallels and certain juxtapositions and rhythms.

Balthus told Soby that, on the other hand, he was quite happy to revise the painting. He never thought that the primary issue of *The Street* should be its infamous naughty incident. The artist justifies the image of the groping by explaining that as a youth he believed in scandal. Now, however, he felt scandal to be a worn-out subject, best discarded.

Indeed, precisely as Balthus would have us believe, visual and painterly issues had become—and to a degree always were—his preeminent concern. He was first and foremost a designer and craftsman. On the other hand, the dominating, isolated, secretive teenage boy in *The Street*—taking his pleasure regardless of its effect on his object of prey, acting in his own private world— shows more about Balthus than he subsequently wanted anyone to see.

Toward the end of the summer in which Balthus agreed to revise the painting, James Soby, his third wife, and Alfred Barr visited the artist at his château to see the revision of *The Street* and to discuss other matters concerning the exhibition at the Modern. In spite of Balthus's letter, Soby was still apprehensive when he arrived at the great stone dwelling near Autun. The collector, in fact, had become afraid that Balthus's possible resentment of the request would have inspired him to paint out the entire canvas. Balthus instantly sensed his visitor's concern. To put Soby at ease, he immediately dragged the large painting into the living room. Soby saw that "the Mongolian boy's hand had been moved very slightly to a less committed position on the young girl's body, though his eyes were tense with the same fever." Not only was the man's hand moved upward, but the extended fingers were bent inward, folded safely over the girl's dress.

Those few days in Chassy were memorable for Balthus's loyal patron. The artist gave him and his wife a tour of the château, which had been a hunting lodge. Soby was particularly fascinated by the basement, where enormous hooks hung from the ceiling so that stags, boars, and other game could be suspended for curing. He was highly entertained one evening when everyone dined at the nearby Hôtel du Barrage, which is where the Sobys and Barr were staying. With the Italian proprietor, Balthus sang "very long, in fact interminable, duets from various operas. It's difficult to remember which of the two men had the worse and less accurate voice, but neither lacked courage or volume, and they bellowed heartlessly."[4]

Balthus had cause to sing. He was just emerging from a long period of financial struggle. Having scarcely been able to afford the modest rent at Chassy when he had moved to the tumbledown château two years earlier, he was now beginning to enjoy sales and recognition that Soby's show would further clinch. His title and longer name were, here and there, beginning to take hold. And he was painting well and living a life of ease that he had not always enjoyed.

ONCE JAMES THRALL SOBY acquired the large canvas in 1936 and brought it home to Connecticut, the audience for Balthus's work grew on that prescient collector's side of the ocean—so much so that the United States, particularly the East Coast, became Balthus's primary center of support for decades to come. To a large degree, Soby was responsible for this, steering museums and fellow collectors to Balthus's work and acquiring further major paintings. The other reason that so many of Balthus's paintings have ended up in America is that, starting in 1938, Pierre Matisse, with his gallery in New York on East Fifty-seventh Street, was Balthus's primary dealer worldwide. Until Matisse's death over fifty years later, they remained closely allied, and as of this writing, Balthus maintains strong ties to Matisse's widow.

The relationship between Balthus and Pierre Matisse may hold a longevity record for an artist-dealer connection. The norm is for artists who do not initially sell well (as was the case when Balthus first showed with Matisse in the late 1930s) to leave their galleries in despair or to get booted, and for successful ones (as Balthus became in the 1960s) to move elsewhere in search of a better deal. Balthus and Pierre Matisse, however, remained faithful to one another. Balthus told me that he considered Matisse an unusual and wonderful man. He felt that Matisse, as the son of an artist, grasped the issues that really mattered to a painter; it was irrelevant that Henri Matisse was someone whose work Balthus did not especially esteem. From Pierre Matisse's point of view, Balthus was often not easy to work with, but he deemed him a masterful painter and had the tenacity to survive the hardships of their relationship. Ultimately Balthus was also a significant moneymaker for Matisse.

In talking with me, however, Balthus always seemed skeptical about this new world from which I hailed. He made me feel like a traveler in a Henry James novel—the sort whose New England background amuses but baffles the inhabitants of a palazzo.

Having declined all previous invitations to visit America, when he did plan a trip there for his 1984 Metropolitan show, he was so put off by the exhibition catalog and checklist that he decided not to go to New York for its opening, although it had been scheduled on his rare birthday that year. He was further upset by the critical attacks on him in the American press once the show was up. Considering how urbane and erudite Balthus was, I found him to be amazingly unaware of American culture in general. He claimed never to have heard of F. Scott Fitzgerald or George Gershwin. On the other hand, he did know the names of the various Hollywood collectors—Billy Wilder as well as Tony Curtis—who owned his work.

Shortly after I arrived in Rossinière on my first visit, Balthus showed me a *House & Garden* with an article about a luxurious New York apartment in which one of his recent canvases had been hung near an Andy Warhol. He told me when the article had appeared several years earlier, "I was absolutely furious and was going to write Pierre that he should never sell any more paintings to Americans." Balthus said that Pierre Matisse became so ill at just this time that the artist felt he could not make the request, but he had seriously intended to ban all further sales of his work on my side of the Atlantic—that they killed his work.

YET BALTHUS ALWAYS HAD a weak spot for the American who had had the courage—as well as the funds in the middle of the Depression—to buy *The Street*. Soby was the rare case of a collector who was also a sage critic. His writings not only helped significantly to establish the audience for Balthus's art but reflected considerable insight. The first of these was an essay Soby wrote for the catalog for Balthus's first Pierre Matisse exhibition in 1938. It was a difficult task to offer perspective on such disarming paintings by an unknown thirty-year-old artist, but Soby was already a respected voice on the American art scene, and his unequivocal support, articulately justified, was persuasive:

> Here is a young painter who . . . must be judged for now as a major artist—perhaps the first one to appear since the generation which produced Picasso, Chirico and Duchamp. . . . When a painter in his twenties can communicate original ideas with such terrific force, and on such a large scale, as Balthus has done, he must be appraised as a painter who may give direction to a whole epoch in art; he must be accepted or rejected as one would accept or reject a Cézanne or a Picasso, not as one would *discover* or tolerate a Boudin or a Modigliani.[5]

Soby viewed *The Street* as the linchpin of this assessment, the ultimate Balthus, both for its charms and for the struggles it reveals and inspires:

The special point about a picture like "La Rue" . . . is not that it is a large and malignant picture, but that it is almost wholly a new one. There have not been many in modern times: among others, the "Grande Jatte" was one, and before that, the "Raft of the Medusa." To my mind "La Rue" is another.[6]

Two decades later, in his MoMA catalog essay, Soby, again without ever allowing that he was its owner, focused on this painting he was fortunate enough to see all the time, whether in his living room or squirreled away in the vault.

The large picture abandons impressionism for a stylized, monumental and much more solid handling of color and form. The figures have an hypnotic intensity, as though seen in a dream or viewed on a moving-picture film which abruptly and inexplicably has stopped on its sprockets. It seems likely that at this time Balthus was especially impressed by Seurat's ability to freeze contemporary life at a moment of poetic and ageless dignity; the figure of the chef in *The Street* is closely related to Seurat. The other figures are puppet-like in their sleepwalking irrationality, yet at the same time alive and majestically composed.[7]

In observations that apply to *The Street,* Albert Camus similarly assessed Balthus's presentation of time in an essay he wrote for Balthus's 1949 exhibition held at Pierre Matisse's.

A painter's style is essentially a certain way of conjugating the natural with the impossible, of presenting that which is perpetually in process of becoming, and of presenting it in an instant which is endless. . . .

Balthus . . . fixes the emotion and the scene both at once, so precisely that one has the impression of gazing through glass at figures which a kind of spell has turned to stone, not forever but for one-fifth of a second, after which their motion will be resumed. That fifth of a second is still going on as I write: that's the point and then we realize that nature, if we look at it during that instant of silence and stillness, is even stranger than the strange monsters that take shape in men's imagination. What is before us is indeed reality, the most familiar sort of reality. But we learn through Balthus that until now we did not know how to see it, that our homes, our friends, our streets concealed disturbing aspects to which we closed our eyes. We learn, above all,

Working on Albert Camus's *L'Etat de siège*, in 1948.
From left to right: Jean-Louis Barrault, Arthur Honnegar, Balthus,
Maria Casarès, Albert Camus

that the most ordinary reality can assume the unfamiliar, remote air,
the soft resonance, the muffled mystery of a lost paradise.[8]

The year before Camus wrote that essay, Balthus had designed the sets and costumes for Camus's play *L'Etat de siège*, directed by Jean-Louis Barrault. Camus
admired Balthus tremendously; he eventually bought the artist's 1951 *Italian
Landscape*. One would expect them to have been soul mates. Yet Balthus told
me he really did not agree with Camus's commentary. Just as Soby's notion of
sleepwalking figures in a hypnotic trance does not line up with the artist's insistence that *The Street* must be seen as a straightforward celebration of everyday
life, Camus's sense of the disturbing and the remote, laments Balthus, has
nothing to do with the artist's intentions.

Balthus told me he does not understand the notion of frozen time, only
the construction of the picture. There is no "mystery." This was his Paris. Its
music was the trafficless silence punctuated only by the street vendors' cries, its

forms and people as you see them. These were the good old days: nothing more or less.

Truth. Invention. For Balthus there is no distinction between them.

> *But there is one memory of that Lughnasa time that visits me most often; and what fascinates me about that memory is that it owes nothing to fact. In that memory atmosphere is more real than incident and everything is simultaneously actual and illusory. In that memory, too, the air is nostalgic with the music of the thirties. It drifts from somewhere far away—a mirage of sound—a dream music that is both heard and imagined; that seems to be both itself and its own echo; a sound so alluring and so mesmeric that the afternoon is bewitched, maybe haunted, by it. And what is so strange about that memory is that everybody seems to be floating on those sweet sounds, moving rhythmically, languorously, in complete isolation; responding more to the mood of the music than to its beat. When I remember it, I think of it as dancing. Dancing with eyes half closed because to open them would break the spell. Dancing as if language had surrendered to movement—as if this ritual, this wordless ceremony, was now the way to speak, to whisper private and sacred things, to be in touch with some otherness. Dancing as if the very heart of life and all its hopes might be found in those assuaging notes and those hushed rhythms and in those silent and hypnotic movements. Dancing as if language no longer existed because words were no longer necessary.*
>
> —Brian Friel, *Dancing at Lughnasa*[9]

THE GUITAR LESSON

To accomplish the tour de force in its entirety, it remained for the author only to divest himself (as much as possible) of his sex, and to make himself a woman. This resulted in a marvel; for, in spite of all his zeal as an actor, [Flaubert] could not but infuse his virile blood into the veins of his creation, and Madame Bovary, for what there is in her that is the most forceful and the most ambitious, and also the most of a dreamer, remained a man.

—BAUDELAIRE[1]

I believed, from the time I could reason, that nature and fortune had joined together to heap their gifts upon me; I believed it because people were foolish enough to tell me so, and this ridiculous prejudice made me haughty, despotic, and angry. It seemed that everything must give in to me, that the whole world must flatter my whims, and that it was up to me alone to conceive and satisfy them.

—MARQUIS DE SADE[2]

I

ANOTHER OF THE PAINTINGS in Balthus's 1934 Galerie Pierre exhibition which James Thrall Soby brought to America was ultimately deemed too scandalous to hang at as allegedly enlightened an institution as the Museum of Modern Art. But unlike *The Street,* it could not merely have one salacious passage repainted so that it might be shown publicly. Even in the libertine 1980s, Balthus's painting was considered so immoral that censorship prevailed and the public was denied access to it forever. The painting was *The Guitar Lesson* (color plate 5).

The imaginative fantasy on flagrant display in this large canvas was an original and cruel scenario that linked sex and violence inexorably, in a seemingly safe and well-appointed bourgeois sitting room. *The Guitar Lesson* shows a stormy sexual encounter between a dominating, tyrannical woman—she seems to be in her twenties—and a girl about twelve years old, whom the older creature is sadistically inducting into the life of flesh. The child appears stunned but not entirely unhappy. Both of the players are lost in the glories of all-consuming, obsessive passion.

A music lesson has just been interrupted. A guitar is lying on the floor. The woman has thrown the girl across her lap and yanked her dress up over her navel. The child is naked from navel to knees, while her lower legs are covered in high socks. With her right hand, the ferocious instructress pulls back a clump of her victim's long, flowing hair. The pain must be excruciating. The older woman digs the fingers of her left hand—which look like talons—into the upper part of the girl's inner thigh, just below the child's bulging vulva.

With her left hand, the pupil has grabbed the teacher's silky gray dress by the neckline just below the ample bosom that is in such marked contrast to her own undeveloped chest. Exactly like the women in two of the other paintings in the Galerie Pierre show, the instructress is in Balthus's favorite pose of one breast exposed, the other covered. The bare one is taut and muscular. An erect nipple juts out from it at a high angle. It is more like a weapon than a source of nourishment. Because of the extent of exposure, the painting resembles a Madonna, but this is a mockery of the Virgin.

The Guitar Lesson is, in fact, a neat blend of Madonna and Lamentation: an erudite, modern-dress, erotic version of Renaissance prototypes. It hearkens back to classic renderings of both the beginning and the end. At the same time, it is a laden sexual encounter. It invests that traditional imagery with the most rabid human cravings and gives unabashed sadomasochism a vivid life virtually unprecedented in the history of art.

II

Today we enjoy the freedom to read, read most anything, whether by a literary master or by a hack with a flair for using "dirty" words. Even the cinema permits us to observe couples performing the sex act. When it comes to sculpture and painting however there is still an aura of the forbidden connected with presenting them to the public. Monarchs, aristocrats and millionaires have always had access to these forbidden treasures of art. So has the Church and State. To be sure, these collections are not at the disposal of the general public. . . . The strange thing is that, so far as we know, none of the keepers of this unholy assortment of art has ever run amuck, has never become a rapist or a degenerate, which is alleged might happen to the man in the street were he exposed to such works. The rich

collector, the expert, the critic of art, the clergy, the censors
might view such work without fear of moral derangement, but
not the ordinary man. L'homme moyen was regarded as a
potential sex maniac who had to be hedged in with all manner
of restrictive prohibitions.

HENRY MILLER[3]

WHEN *The Guitar Lesson* WAS shown at Pierre Loeb's gallery, its twenty-six-year-old creator had conspired with Loeb to hang the painting behind a covering in the back room of the gallery, like an elegant peep show for selected eyes only. Then, several years following this clandestine presentation at Loeb's, James Thrall Soby acquired *The Guitar Lesson* from the Paris dealer Pierre Colle. If *The Street* was too risqué for visitors even in the privacy of Soby's Connecticut living room, this new painting had to be held under tighter wraps. *The Guitar Lesson* was never shown with the rest of Soby's collection at Hartford's Wadsworth Atheneum and other locations, and its owner eliminated it completely from his writing on Balthus.

Soby saw the painting only in his storage vault. After a while there was no point in owning it. In April 1945, about seven years after he acquired this extraordinary canvas, the collector, courageous as he was, swapped it with the painter Roberto Matta Echaurren for one of Matta's own works. When, a few years later, Matta's ex-wife married Pierre Matisse, *The Guitar Lesson* became part of the gallery's collection. It remained there, in private storage, seen by virtually no one, until the late 1970s. Its existence was known to Balthus aficionados—who had either seen it in 1934 or at least gotten wind of it and the furor it caused—but hardly anyone ever viewed the actual work or knew its whereabouts.

Then, in 1977, Pierre Matisse presented it to the public during a Balthus exhibition—much awaited, the first after a ten-year hiatus—at his New York gallery. The painting was the talk of New York. For one month, throngs of people—the majority of them students and young artists—crowded into the small exhibition space on Fifty-seventh Street. The area in front of *The Guitar Lesson* was always thick with viewers. This, above all, was the work people had come to see.

Hilton Kramer told me that when he asked Pierre Matisse if it wasn't gratifying to have students always congregating in front of the canvas, Matisse replied that the difficulty was in getting them to leave the gallery at closing time. But in any event, they were all there the next morning waiting for the gallery to reopen. *The Guitar Lesson* exerted a virtually unprecedented magnetic attraction on the viewing public.

Having clearly anticipated that it would be the pièce de résistance, Pierre

Matisse had *The Guitar Lesson* as the full-color frontispiece of the exhibition catalog—the first time it had ever been reproduced. Opposite the riveting, disturbing image, there was an essay by the film director Federico Fellini, which was translated by Luigi Barzini.

Fellini had been one of Balthus's regular visitors and close friends in the Villa Medici period. The juxtaposition of his text with the reproduction of that stunning painting is pure Balthus. The essay reads more as if it were written by an elderly Roman history professor than by the maker of *La dolce vita* and *8½*. You might expect Fellini's commentary to be fluent and spicy; on the contrary, it is measured to the utmost, almost impenetrably vague, and exceedingly high-toned.

The implication is clear, and perfectly in accord with the wishes of the Balthus of 1977—in contrast to the troublemaker of 1934. The goal was no longer to shock the bourgeoisie. Instead, Fellini acted as a spokesman for the Count de Rola. Rather than dwell on the androgynous seductress strumming the inner thighs of her exposed, ecstatic victim, Fellini steers toward spheres supposedly loftier than the realm of sexual urges.

The director focuses first on "the feeling for that accumulation of history that is Balthus," declaring that "history is no longer for him an objective and indifferent catalog, but is rather present, alive, and renews itself in a time that is only to be found in his conscience." We feel that Balthus is, above all, the calculator and craftsman, the artist and organizer with a distinct agenda and the dexterity to realize it. Indeed, he is the equivalent of the seductive teacher in *The Guitar Lesson*—served perfectly by his friend Fellini's words:

> Every image is the result of the patient search for "that" form; the irreplaceable caliber of that form, the exact and unalterable tone of a color are obtained, one would say, by cutting away from the material, with delicate scalpels, the veils which still alter the balance that the author already perceives in its entirety and is trying to reach by degrees.[4]

Fellini's commentary ignores the real-life context of the painting and focuses only on the formal, but the meticulous know-how he attributes to Balthus the painter is clearly akin to that of the enthralled, enthralling music teacher.

AT THE TIME OF THE EXHIBITION at Pierre Matisse's, numerous magazine and newspaper reviews referred to the canvas. But none dared show it. The critics explained that the shock would be too great. The distinguished Thomas

Hess devoted most of his Balthus article in *New York* magazine to a brilliant and insightful description of the painting, but explained, without giving any further reason, "I dwell at some length on *The Guitar Lesson,* even though it can't be illustrated in the pages of *New York.*"[5] Clearly this was more than even a supposedly sophisticated audience could handle.

Then, the year following that first presentation of *The Guitar Lesson* in his gallery, Pierre Matisse tried to donate it to the Museum of Modern Art. Given the attention the initiation scene had generated during its singular public showing a few months earlier, its owner was thoughtful and generous in subsequently trying to make it available to the public at all times. He wished it to be a memorial to his late wife, Patricia. This was intended as a monumental tribute: to a woman he wanted to honor, to an artist he had loyally represented for almost forty years, and to the recipient institution—a museum that had both done great honor to his father and recognizably improved the experience of living in New York. Pierre Matisse, who had a large collection of work by a range of major modern painters, had deliberately selected one of his masterpieces.

Blanchette Rockefeller—Mrs. John D. III—who was then chairman of the board at MoMA, did not approve, however, when she saw the painting at a small presentation of Pierre Matisse's recent gifts to the museum. Even in a place where Picasso's *vagina dentata* hangs unchallenged and Amedeo Modigliani's and Gaston Lachaise's forthright interpretations of the nude body are boldly exhibited, *The Guitar Lesson* was declared to be too obscene and sacrilegious to be displayed. Blanchette Rockefeller could sanction no such immorality. Having kept Balthus's painting in storage for almost five years, MoMA returned it to its unsuccessful would-be donor in 1982.

In the wake of the so-called sexual revolution, Americans have become increasingly hysterical about the issue of children and sex. If Balthus has not only come to feel alienated by the vulgarity of American interior decoration but also become paranoiac about the national attitude toward anything suggestive of children's sexuality in art, he has good reason to feel fearful. If Mrs. Rockefeller's power was extraordinary, her attitude was symptomatic. In 1994 a respectable New Jersey businessman who was taking a course at the International Center of Photography shot, in a single fifteen-minute session, a series of images of his six-year-old daughter in the nude. The photo-processing lab reported this to the authorities, and the man's three children were rushed to the police station, where they were interrogated "about good touches and bad [and] the existence of God." Their father was handcuffed, jailed, "and ever

after that forbidden further contact with the daughter he had photographed."[6]
It was almost a year before the man could prevail against the state and obtain
permission to return home.

Such incidents are directly related to the fate that has befallen one of the
greatest paintings of our century. In a less censorious world, Balthus might not
have been driven repeatedly to say that he wished he had never painted *The
Guitar Lesson.* But with his antennae for public taste and his wish to avoid further opprobrium, he kept the work out of his Pompidou-Metropolitan retrospective, and has assured its isolation for years to come. What the public has
lost is a painting as brave and brilliant in its artistic technique as in its narrative.

WHEN *The Guitar Lesson* WAS notably absent from Balthus's Centre Pompidou retrospective in 1983–84, *Le Monde* explained that the painting was missing at the insistence of the artist, who considered it "an initiatory painting
reserved for the eyes of a small elite." Dominique Bozo, the museum director,
lamented in the catalog that two essential canvases that they had hoped would
be in the show were not there, the other one besides *The Guitar Lesson* being
The Room of 1952–54.

The Centre Pompidou director went to great lengths, odd for an exhibition organizer, to point out to his public how deprived they were:

> *The Guitar Lesson* too, for reasons which we do not entirely share,
> reveals fifty years after it was painted, how much Balthus's work still
> disturbs and profoundly troubles us today. First shown in 1934 at
> Pierre Loeb's gallery, but not in the gallery's main exhibition space, it
> reappeared in public only in 1977 at the Pierre Matisse Gallery in New
> York. Anglo-Saxon puritanism then obliged Tom Hess to apologize for
> being unable to reproduce the painting in his article in *New York,*
> though only after a long and exact description: "I dwell at some length
> on *The Guitar Lesson,* even though it can't be illustrated in the pages of
> *New York,* because of the intensity of its image." This canvas, which
> Balthus actually regards as initiatory and which was doubtless
> intended only for certain "privileged viewers, in secrecy" and was per-
> haps prematurely subjected to the gaze of the public at large, recently
> suffered a misfortune which has "obliged the painter to prevent its
> divulgation"! Its reappearance, then, must occur at some future date.
> Yet it seemed to us, seeing it again quite recently, that this highly
> charged image, sustained as it is by an exceptional plastic quality, is
> obviously one of the great classics of the twentieth century. It is with

enormous sadness that we have had to forgo its presence here, for it seemed to us that the painting, as one discovered when confronted by the actual canvas, if not independent of the image, does suppress the possible misunderstanding of the reproduction and in fact ensures its disturbing coherence.[7]

While emphasizing the significance of the loss, Bozo provides no satisfactory reasons for the absence of the pivotal canvas. The museum director exercises a Balthusian elusiveness about the omission. He establishes that *The Guitar Lesson* has been excluded because the painter himself inveighed against its presence, but one is at a loss to know what the mechanics of this deliberate self-censorship were.

Balthus, after all, no longer owned *The Guitar Lesson*. Its owner was a free agent. But who was the owner at that point? Had Balthus instructed this person not to lend it? If so, why was the painter against its inclusion? Why would the owner comply? And what, precisely, was the forbidden fruit?

In his comments, Bozo implicitly blames American taste for the predicament to which the more enlightened French were now subjected. Bozo was right; if the Museum of Modern Art had accepted *The Guitar Lesson*, it would have been able to lend the painting.

Of course, Bozo, while alluding to the restrictions on *New York* magazine, diplomatically avoids making any specific reference to MoMA. The French museum director would not have risked antagonizing the administration of an institution with which he needed to collaborate regularly. Officials at MoMA probably would have been highly embarrassed to let it be known that pressure from one rich trustee had prevented their acquisition of this extraordinary Balthus painting.

Bozo also avoids stating that the person exercising the ultimate control was, as usual, Balthus. Just a few years earlier, Pierre Matisse had had Balthus's go-ahead on the presentation to MoMA. Still the owner, Matisse would inevitably have followed Balthus's instructions with respect to the Pompidou. Yet again, it was the artist himself who chose to keep *The Guitar Lesson* under wraps.

ONE MIGHT SAY THAT the exhibition organizers and Pierre Matisse were properly honoring an artist's rights.

Yet to listen to Balthus, the authorities at the Centre Pompidou failed to do him justice. Balthus complained to me that the Parisian curators were oblivious to his way of seeing. The Pompidou lighting was disastrous. In our conversation one day, his paintings were "murdered"; the next day they were "slaughtered." Balthus only painted in the natural luminosity of daylight; the glare of spotlights obliterated the subtle tonality he had painstakingly achieved. The Centre Pompidou was, he said, a "horrible place, *horrible* place." He termed his show there "a massacre, absolutely killing everything. All those relationships of color killed by electric light. You couldn't see *The Passage du Commerce* at all, there was such a strong light on top, with all the rest in the dark. The way people look at painting now is so surprising and so strange that sometimes one asks oneself whether it's worth showing paintings."

He continued, "Paintings shouldn't be seen in electric light. The first paintings I saw in electric light were in Paris, probably 1925. A Cézanne show at the Salle Pleyel—toward the Bois [de Boulogne]. There was an art gallery in the same building, a *sous-sol,* and I saw for the first time Cézanne with electric light, and they looked like reproductions."

Balthus also generally detested the architecture of the galleries in which the work was installed in Paris. If on one level Bozo had generously honored his wishes, on the essential issue of visual presentation the museum director had let the artist down brutally.

IF BALTHUS BELIEVED, first and foremost, that he should be judged not for his subject matter but for his ability to paint, he did himself an enormous disservice by excluding what is arguably the greatest evidence of his technical virtuosity. To prevent its being seen was an act of petulance—MoMA had turned it down; therefore the public did not deserve to see it—that worked against the artist's own interests. Balthus must have known that hordes of Parisians, like those crowds that stood four or five people deep at all hours in 1977 at Pierre Matisse's, would have loved the canvas. It is as if he was punishing the world, and himself, because of Blanchette Rockefeller and her cronies.

On the other hand, Balthus may by this time have wanted to stay clear of scandal as assiduously as he had once sought it. Maybe the Count de Rola didn't want the parents of the other children at his daughter's Swiss school tittering. So he willingly succumbed to the dictates of the bourgeois establishment he had once deliberately offended.

As always, he had a story and a reason for his actions. What Balthus insisted to me is that the explicitly sexual side of his art causes people to focus on the wrong things. Yet as a former model of Balthus's—an old friend who knew him well—pointed out to me, the real danger of *The Guitar Lesson* is that it lays the truth bare. This very beautiful, stirring painting lacks the convenient cloak of hazy ambiguity. Everything is visible, clear as day. This, more than anything, was what the Count de Rola wished to avoid.

.   .   .

DOMINIQUE BOZO'S PREDICTIONS of the future reappearance of *The Guitar Lesson* are unlikely to come true. The 1977 Pierre Matisse Gallery show was, in all likelihood, not only the first but also the last time the painting will ever be seen by more than a few individuals. That month will probably be the only occasion in any of our lifetimes when *The Guitar Lesson* might be viewed other than by private invitation.

A couple of years after its return from MoMA, Pierre Matisse sold the painting to the film actor-director Mike Nichols. Tana Matisse, Pierre's widow—his third wife from a late marriage, forty years his junior, the diligent keeper of his flame—provided this history for me. Than, in the late 1980s, when the prices for Balthus's paintings had gone higher than ever before, Nichols sold *The Guitar Lesson* through the Zurich gallery Thomas Ammann. Ammann soon resold it to a person of vast wealth who keeps it privately and intends never to sell or lend it. And so today *The Guitar Lesson*—the extraordinary painting that might have belonged to a major public museum had it not been for the censorship of one influential trustee—is virtually off the map.

One of the few other paintings to be treated as such was Courbet's 1866 *Birth of the World*—a graphic and exquisitely painted between-the-knees view of female genitalia. The original owner of the painting, the Turkish diplomat Khalil Bey, had always kept it cloaked much as *The Guitar Lesson* was at Pierre Loeb's gallery. But the Courbet then became the possession of the psychoanalyst Jacques Lacan—whom Balthus knew, and in whose collection he would have seen it uncovered. And now it belongs to the Musée d'Orsay in Paris, where it is shown freely.

The Courbet is out there, and the secret chambers at Pompeii have been unlocked. But Balthus's canvas is unique in the extent to which it has been held captive. Having almost consistently been kept off limits to the world at large, now—even if its prison is known—it will probably remain in hiding forever.

THE FIRST TIME THIS "initiatory" canvas came up in our discussion, Balthus told me that he had no idea where it was or who owned it. But two days later, once he had apparently become more comfortable with me, he allowed he had heard various rumors of its whereabouts. Squinting his eyes, he strained to remember. Oh yes, it had been for sale in Switzerland, after "some film person" owned it—he could not, however, remember the name. I suggested Mike Nichols; I did not yet know that this was the case, but I knew Nichols owned other of Balthus's paintings, including a splendid version of *The Three Sisters,* and I could imagine him owning *The Guitar Lesson* as well. Balthus looked quizzical and merely asked if there weren't "also a Nicholson."

In our next conversation about *The Guitar Lesson,* however, the artist recalled quite a bit more. He allowed that the canvas might now belong to a Greek shipping magnate. But who knew in which residence the wealthy Greek had it? And perhaps by now it had gone somewhere else; he was not sure.

Then, one morning toward the end of my second visit to him, Balthus named the owner of *The Guitar Lesson.* He wore an expression of unequaled delight as he let the elegant appellation roll off his tongue and slowly enunciated its mellifluous syllables. Balthus was patently thrilled to play a part in this international tycoon's world. What a coup that this painting he had made when he could scarcely afford the rent on his one-room studio was now treasured by someone of such prominence.

But I must never let on that I knew. The collector's name had to be kept private, Balthus told me. This idea that the information was clandestine enchanted Balthus almost as much as the billionaire's stature.

Citing the location of the painting as the lair of someone as secretive and powerful as an Ian Fleming character, Balthus had his little-boy look of glee. It was a fine solution after the abuse of those hand-wringers and culture vultures at MoMA.

THE FLEMING COMPARISON is mine, but I thought of it because Balthus proudly told me that he was a friend of the "terribly amusing" Fleming in the 1930s. Moreover, he was a tremendous fan of all the James Bond books. Now he had made it sound as if *The Guitar Lesson* belonged to Dr. No.

The painting's seclusion and inaccessibility rather delighted its maker. Balthus, after all, had insisted on its initially being viewed only by the select few in the back room at Pierre Loeb's. Besides asserting that he wished he had never painted the canvas to begin with, he repeatedly claimed to me that although *The Guitar Lesson* was nothing more than the sort of thing you do when you are young and intend provocation, it has led to major misunderstandings about his work. So why not keep it out of bounds to the public at large? This was a better proposition than having the painting displayed in an artificially lit museum space where ignorant audiences would make lots of irritating remarks.

Yet at other moments Balthus was highly annoyed that *The Guitar Lesson* had escaped his grasp. Its fate was typical of the wounds inflicted on artists by the art world—according to Balthus's construction, yet again, of his own victimization. Here, too, the artist was presenting himself as the earnest and naive good guy of whom cannier people took unfair advantage. It was like his depiction of Pierre Loeb's alleged maneuvers with *Joan Miró and His Daughter Dolores* (a sequence of events that I had subsequently come to believe had not actually occurred as Balthus had described it). He told the tale in a way meant to show how an artist could lose control of his own work, how paintings could become a commodity in a way that had nothing to do with their creator.

Then Balthus would resign himself to these events and become philosophical about them. Disappearance is inevitable, he reminded me. Consider what happened to Mitsou, and to that canvas that fell off the car roof.

AFTER MY SECOND STAY with Balthus, Tana Matisse made the initial steps necessary for me to see *The Guitar Lesson*. Balthus must have authorized this and given me the equivalent of security clearance. As with my initial visit to Le Grand Chalet, I was welcomed into a private and secret universe.

The arrangements for my actual visitation with the hidden painting had the ring of adventure and intrigue. I felt as if I were organizing the transfer of hot loot with gangsters. Mrs. Matisse told me that I had to understand that, in deference to both Balthus's and the owner's wishes, I could pass on the information about the whereabouts of *The Guitar Lesson* to no one whatsoever. I should not even cite the city.

Yet once the secrecy was established, I was treated like royalty. I phoned the owner's office as instructed and reached the designated business assistant, who explained that I would be met at the owner's residence. We settled on a mutually convenient time, and I was assured that I could have as long as I liked with the work.

WHEN THE APPOINTED DAY CAME, I entered a mythic world. In 1934 the back room that housed the painting was a tiny space behind a small gallery. Half a century later, *The Guitar Lesson* has ended up in a secret domain of unfathomable opulence. Its present place of hiding is as different from its original lair as Le Grand Chalet is from the garret on the Rue de Fürstemberg.

As the gates lifted for my visitation, it struck me that the painting in its current situation is like Balthus himself. It is extremely secure and protected. It abides in reclusive luxury. It belongs to the top echelon of society, the world of those who know both how to attract the spotlight and how to avoid it. It lives like rare, forbidden fruit. It may be visited by the select few, but by the time you are in its hiding place, you feel as if you are having an audience with royalty and are ignited by the mere act of gaining access.

The doorman was expecting me at the address I had been given for a vast flat in the heart of one of the finest residential districts in one of the largest cities in the world. The elevator doors opened onto a vestibule from which I reached a dark entrance hall the size of a small ballroom. I was met there by the owner's employee, an amiable fellow in a dark suit, who quickly led me off to the left, but even at our rapid pace I took in the otherworldly figures looming from a large El Greco. The man guided me down several corridors that were practically the length of theater aisles. Doors on both sides revealed multiple chambers in which I glimpsed French furniture, Courbets, some well-known Cézannes, a large early Matisse I had often seen lent anonymously in major exhibitions, and old masters. Heading beyond them, I felt as if I were going to see the most secret treasure in the trove.

We finally arrived at an elaborately paneled bedroom, furnished like rooms at Versailles. Under the coffered ceiling, Balthus's "initiative" canvas hung in the sleeping alcove. Like a piece of erotica, it is displayed alone on a wall so it can easily be viewed from the large bed canopied in stiff brocade. If one were on one's back on that splendid bed, the painting would be to the right. On the opposite side, large windows—framed by heavy draperies, tasseled and fringed—look out on a spectacular urban vista. The Modigliani portrait between those windows seems to have been induced into its drugged stupor by *The Guitar Lesson* across the way.

This private chamber of the exotic potentate—I knew, after all, who my Dr. No was, even if I could divulge the name to no one—was not, however, without its mundane touches. Next to the lavish Louis XIV bed, on the delicate marquetry table, stood, in plain view, a king-size container of Preparation H. It was almost as large as the delicate base of the porcelain lamp next to it. And at the foot of the bed there was a VCR on a scale generally found in bars packed with sports fans. I imagined a film version of *The Guitar Lesson,* directed by a master of pornography and starring skilled sybarites, being shown on it.

The owner's employee told me to sit on the bed and take as much time as I wished studying the painting. I could have asked for no better circumstances to be before the sacred altar. A butler arrived with a silver tray and served me a large, steaming cappuccino topped with bittersweet chocolate shavings. Perhaps all artistic masterpieces should be kept this way; it certainly beat the usual frantic search for 500-lire coins to drop into a machine for a few minutes of poor light on a Renaissance masterpiece in a cold and damp Italian church. For two hours, in perfect comfort, I studied Balthus's masterpiece and took notes.

FOR SEVERAL YEARS, on the infrequent occasions when I mentioned my magical audience with *The Guitar Lesson* to anyone, I honored the terms of secrecy of the visitation. I planned to write about the painting without ever saying where it was—even what city it was in. I knew, after all, that the billionaire owner of this once unsalable masterpiece of erotica had residences in Paris, New York, and London (a penthouse at Claridge's), as well as Villefranche and Saint-Moritz, and a yacht he kept in the Aegean. For all I knew, he moved it from place to place—or took it wherever he went, like a portable altarpiece.

There was, I must admit, something nice about this feeling of being an insider, and I relished my complicity. It was much the way I felt when I first interviewed Balthus and thought, like all of his interviewers, that he was talking to me when he would not do so to others.

I felt duped therefore, when, having kept my word about not revealing where Balthus's early masterpiece was (and probably antagonizing a couple of friends by not revealing its location), the allegedly never-to-be-known information appeared in a 1994 *New York Times Magazine* article on Balthus. This was yet another of the many pieces where the author acted as if the reclusive artist had at last granted a rare interview. Whether Ted Morgan, who wrote the article, had breached a promise by divulging this information about *The Guitar Lesson,* or whether yesterday's top secret was today's common knowledge, I could not be sure, but I felt foolish and undermined. Now any reader of the Sunday *Times* might learn that the salacious canvas was in the New York apartment of Stavros Niarchos. The fact is not of vast significance, but in guarding it so carefully, I seem to have been as controlled, as held in thrall, as the child in the painting.

III

"I bargained for humiliation," she said. "If I had to choose between unhumiliated boredom and humiliated fulfillment, even for a short time, I took the latter. I had no illusions about him; I expected to be smacked and brutalized, but it is his aura that takes me to bed, to sofa, to the kitchen table, not a man. I find myself possessed by a notorious whirlwind so heedless that it cares not what it leaves behind. It is not pleasure he takes with me, but proof."

—PAUL WEST, *Lord Byron's Daughter*[8]

THE GIRL IN *The Guitar Lesson* hangs, with her left hand, from the neckline of the teacher's dress. In doing so, she turns the gray satin of the low-cut, old-fashioned garment into a sort of sling that cradles the older woman's excited breast. Is this child grabbing the fabric to brace herself? A desperate attempt to keep from falling?

Or has she deliberately denuded that breast out of lust? Would she like to finger the teacher's erect nipple? Has she been forced to straddle the woman's lap, or is she there by choice?

The scenario offers multiple readings. Perhaps the teacher is an unabashed seductress, the pupil a hapless victim holding on for dear life. Or maybe the girl is stripping the teacher out of clear and conscious longing. The way her right hand falls to the ground suggests that she is helpless; by using her left hand to hold back the teacher's dress and practically tweaking the erect nipple of the mature instructress's bulging right breast, she also participates enthusiastically.

In either case, confronted by that angular peak of a bosom, the young initiate is stunned. The child is overwhelmed both by this organ that represents her own future, that embodies her own incipient sexuality and the womanliness that awaits her, and by the sensation the teacher is inducing high within the girl's inner thigh.

The girl responds to the violent pulling of her hair and the invasive gouging of her thigh with both rapture and anguish. Balthus has seen to it that the specifics of her emotions are inaccessible. Wearing almost the identical outfit as the creature under attack in *The Street*, she is in a similarly disconnected state. She is dazed: somewhere between misery and ecstasy. Like her twin in *The Street*, she appears alarmed but anesthetized.

The teacher, too, is a conflux of emotions. Her face mixes rapture with scorn. While she eagerly contemplates her prey, she is entirely self-absorbed. Is the scene an act of punishment? Is the teacher seducing the girl or chastising her? Is this retribution for the child's sexual impulses; has the older woman taken violent action against the younger one because, a moment beforehand, the child attempted to touch the woman's breast and is still trying to do so? Is the teacher gleefully introducing her protégée to a world of violent pleasure? Whether the instructress is contentedly forcing and inspiring the child's action—or, with equal pleasure, inflicting pain on her for it—is ambiguous.

THE MOTIVES AND FEELINGS are hazy, but in plastic values, the scene could not be clearer. The two bodies have been stretched to the utmost. The girl's torso is pulled as if on a rack—so that her pelvic bone is pushed upward, her pudenda thrust forward, her thigh stretched to the breaking point. Only her right arm and her hair lie limp. Balthus has fixed the locking figures in position, sharpening it all with his precise use of light and dark.

The teacher evades us, but not herself; *she* knows precisely what she is doing. Whatever the exact sequence of events here, the older woman is control

itself. She manipulates the child with the authority of an expert worker of marionettes, holding the girl's hair and thigh just so. She has experience; she has
probably given this sort of lesson before.

She uses her charms to full effect. Possessed of the elegance of a Boucher
nymph—and dressed with marvelous style in her coquettish dress, of the
shepherdess mode an eighteenth-century courtesan might have worn to a
country dance—she is a stunning demon. Her stylish looks add panache to
her diabolical squint. Moreover, the woman has tremendous physical strength.
She is built like a monster. Her oversized arms have the grip of steel vises. Her
strong legs lock firmly into place underneath the girl. To exert maximal force,
she twists herself like a coiled spring. Her powerful torso in its sculptural contrapposto interlocked with that of the passive, dazed, limp child make a
dynamic, galvanic pairing—like Bernini's *Rape of Persephone* or *Daphne and
Apollo.*

Strong as her body is, it is the teacher's face that dominates the painting.
Her large head with its mass of hair has the same width as her shoulders; the
addition of her hair brings it out to the shoulders' dimensions completely.
These proportions—typical for Balthus's work, but even more pronounced
here—lead us to concentrate on the protagonist's face. The huge scale of people's heads makes it seem that their bodies are what they are and do what they
do in response to the mind. The cerebral dictates the physical. All the gripping
and grabbing and posing are the result of precise mental calculation. The
sadism is carefully thought-out.

As with *The Street,* in *The Guitar Lesson* it is as if time has suddenly been
frozen. This is an in-between moment—like the "Crac" between midnight of
February 28 and the start of March 1 about which Rilke wrote to the young
Balthus at the time of his nonexistent birthdays. The occasion exists more in
imagination than in fact. The reality of the present eludes us; we more readily
grasp what has previously taken place and what will soon occur. While the
details of the current scene beg many questions, we apprehend without difficulty the lesson that was interrupted by rage and lust, and the possibility of
ecstatic lovemaking to follow.

Yet Balthus has painted the imaginary interlude so brilliantly that the
stormy scene has the superreality of a dream image. It is as palpable as it is
ambiguous. The concentrated and isolated figures grab our attention like
actors holding center stage in theater or film. Every element of the painting
converges to intensify the central event. The upholstery tacks, wallpaper
stripes, and floorboards, all in sharp focus, point to and frame the stunning

encounter. The dark split in the guitar handle between the tuning pegs echoes the naked genitals above.

The vividness of the setting that encases this extraordinary drama is one of the devices through which Balthus makes *The Guitar Lesson* really happen. Balthus the set designer has controlled it as carefully and knowingly as he has directed the action. It is the physical reality of the scene that makes the psychological issues rise to the surface so powerfully. Without the essential success of the painted canvas as a convincing illusion, and without its rich and alluring appearance, none of the other considerations would come into play as forcibly. However much the situation may be an invention, Balthus has captured the appearance of life. The surfaces shine or absorb luminosity as they would in actual life. The clear and raking light that falls on the wainscoting makes it palpable. The shadows read so tellingly that we feel they have been cast by actual objects.

The details have the effect of heightening our attention. The striped silk wallpaper with its contrast of lime and rust alerts us. And consider the floor. Balthus found the optimal means of evoking its wooden planks. They are precisely the golden yellow of highly varnished pine or oak. The artist has diligently put in every line of separation between the individual boards. He has used these lines to establish a one-point perspective system that is his own variation of Piero's model. The floorboards veer at a sharper angle from the left of the canvas than from the right, so as to throw our vantage point distinctly off-center—close to the right-hand edge of the canvas, almost in line with the girl's knees. Every device brings the viewer in.

The rendering of the texture of this wood justifies what Balthus has repeatedly said over the years about the futility of formal education for painters. Observation, direct experience, and experimentation—rather than anyone else's instruction—had indeed been crucial to his success. Untaught, he developed an impeccable means of making wood both beautiful and real— with a thin speckling of brown on top of yellow. He achieved this by lightly flicking the dark color over the lighter, perhaps using a sponge to apply and remove the colors as necessary. The hue and intensity are flawless. The wooden floor practically has a ceramic glaze, like that of spatterware, but it is precisely what it is supposed to be. All the accoutrements are equally real. The pull of fabric across the teacher's left breast—the one that is still clad—is authentically taut. We believe in her billowing puffed sleeves, the satin pleats and seams, the wrinkles at her left armpit. The young Balthus had already mastered the tricks of the trade to be as convincing as possible.

.   .   .

IN THE EXQUISITE LAIR in which *The Guitar Lesson* now hangs, the Modigliani opposite it and the two other Modiglianis and a Toulouse-Lautrec on view in the adjacent sitting room are all marvelous creations, but they also are all art objects—designed, enticing, quite different from life itself. *The Guitar Lesson,* on the other hand, is not a canvas; it is an event. Sitting there on the brocade bedspread as I looked at Balthus's early masterpiece, I felt as if the two women were actually engaged in their act of passion before my eyes.

The previous time I had seen the canvas—fifteen years earlier, amid throngs of art students, elderly painters, and curiosity seekers at Pierre Matisse—I had had much the same feeling, and felt that everyone else did as well. We were viewing not just an artwork but a real occurrence: highly charged, perplexing, a mixture of exciting and embarrassing.

Initially we do not consider the artistic factors that made each element so plausible, any more than, when first seeing someone we know, we count the hair follicles or skin creases. Without identifying the devices whereby the feat is achieved, we feel that we are actively witnessing this bizarre, masculine woman attack a young girl who exhibits a range of responses. Flemish Renaissance masters like Jan van Eyck painted their Annunciations to make clear that the Immaculate Conception really took place. They articulated every windowpane and cast the Virgin and Gabriel in crystalline light so as to leave no doubt of the truth of the miraculous event. The young Balthus similarly found the means to make us believe the scenario of *The Guitar Lesson.*

For all his psychological elusiveness, he painted in order to impart precise information. The guitar and the girl's and woman's feet make shadows on the floor so that we know their exact angles. The teacher has braced both of her legs for optimal power. Her position is that of someone playing a cello or a double bass more than a guitar; indeed, she handles the girl like a large string instrument, squeezing the child's inner thigh with the extended fingers of her left hand as she might press strings for a chord, stretching her right arm and folding the fingers of her right hand as if she were bowing, and then pulling the girl's hair to the tautness of tightened bow strings. Metaphorically, she makes precisely the music she wants.

The expert instructress uses her hands like tools. She deftly squeezes her powerful fingers into the girl's thigh near the child's hairless mons veneris. Those fingers excite and dominate at the same time.

Meanwhile, the position and tension of the girl's limbs make the child appear both active and passive. Her left leg dangles; she has succumbed. With the right, however, she supports herself. Balthus establishes both pressure and its absence in the placement of her feet and repeats the pattern with her arms. Every angle denotes either resignation or desire.

Similarly, he uses her hair to evoke her duality of feeling. Most of the girl's thick locks cascade downward, loose in their fall, suggesting abandon. But then these are the strands being pulled forcibly by the teacher—their tightness echoed by the taut strings of the guitar on the floor. With her clenched fist, the instructress yanks the child's hair with such violent energy that the pain is palpable. The teacher's sharp tugging, and the indentations visible where she is pressing her fingers into the child's inner thigh, gives the moment a screaming anguish that counters the languor invoked by the girl's flowing tresses and collapsed right arm.

Yet for all this detail, it is again apparent that Balthus could not, or did not care to, paint human hands. The teacher's left hand resembles a bird's claw, with talons. The palm is too broad and puffy, the fingers too tapered and too alike, for a person's. The wrist is proportionately too wide. This appendage belongs to a beast of the jungle. On one level, however, that discrepancy is appropriate. If as representation this arm and hand are all wrong, as invention they succeed. Like the woodenness of the baker in *The Street,* we accept them—and all of Balthus's distortions—as part of the whole. Like a detail in a dream that will never jibe with our experience of real life, it coheres within the unique nexus of Balthus's art.

THE WORD "AWAKENING" that Balthus cited as the underlying goal of his 1952–54 masterpiece *The Room* pertains equally to *The Guitar Lesson.* Its characters are relentlessly alert to the moment, and so are we when we look at it. A psychic intensity accompanies the physical high pitch. Desire, fear, and satisfaction are as vivid as the bones and musculature. In time Balthus would learn to conceal, to disguise, to dissemble. He would envelop his subjects, and his viewer, in a cloud. But here everyone is awake.

Every detail of the painting accentuates the greatest of all sources of awakening: sexuality. The violent lifting of the girl's dress adds drama to the exposed nakedness of her genitals. The decorousness of the bows at her neck and in her hair and the presence of her schoolgirl's white socks contrast the rawness of the scene in the way that seemingly innocent details add punch to pornography. The noticeable absence of her underpants (which Balthus always referred to, in our conversations, as the more English "knickers") is another spicy detail. They are neither around her ankles nor on the floor; perhaps she was never wearing any. The dropped guitar takes on erotic portent: a curvaceous form that gets played across its dark, gaping hole. It is all so real that, just as we feel we might actually look around the corner in *The Street* and see another scene, we can readily picture the girl's naked buttocks against the lining of her skirt.

Actions and feelings are at their pinnacle and frozen in place for the savoring. There is no subtlety. Lust has won; the teaching of music has come to a full stop. The teacher's breast—a porcelain-textured, pure, milky white—zooms forward decisively. Her erect nipple catches the light sharply. The girl's genitals are deep red, as are the teacher's fingertips that press the child's thigh; blood has rushed to these points. The girl's labia pulse.

With her legs emphatically splayed, the teacher holds the girl in a wrestling lock. The older woman wears delicate black velvet shoes, but this ladylike touch merely emphasizes her powerful athleticism. Strong-boned, fully muscled, she commands her formidable strength ably, and uses it unabashedly. The teacher authoritatively cradles the girl's backside on her upper thighs and across her crotch. Balthus has designed her body so that she does this with maximum efficiency. While the upper half is oversized, the lower half is miniaturized and diminutive; her arms are as long and thick as her legs. By enlarging the teacher's head, reducing her scale waist-down, and stretching her legs, Balthus has made her titanic. The contrivance of her vast head enables her to dominate the scene.

As manipulator and painter, Balthus is remarkably like his stunning slit-eyed music teacher: imperious, disdainful of normalcy. He makes his creatures as he wants them; their plausibility matters far less than his personal aims. The painter has his protagonist's daring, her power and control. And she has his seductive know-how. In their understanding of sexual response, the painter and the music teacher are one and the same.

If *Mitsou* depicts the pain of emotional separation and loss, *The Guitar Lesson* shows complete and absolute possession. The person who painted it, like the creature he has invented, will do whatever is necessary to achieve that steel grip.

WHEN I HAD MY PRIVATE VIEWING of *The Guitar Lesson* in Niarchos's apartment, the girl's flesh was so plausible that it made me feel guilty, as if I were pressing *my* fingers into her thighs. I could not for a minute buy Balthus's idea that these sensations reflected my own lascivious desire rather than his intentions. The discomfiting sight of this half-comatose child submitting to tyranny felt like a nasty imposition, not a happy choice. The violation of a girl close in years to my own daughters was heinous. But the effects of Balthus's virtuosity had left me no room for escape.

.   .   .

THE GIRL'S POSE CLEARLY derives from the Avignon Pietà at the Louvre. Among other things, *The Guitar Lesson* is a sexualizing of Jesus and Mary. The teacher cradles the child like Mary in a classic Lamentation format, while her single bared breast echoes the familiar nursing Madonna pose.

In the context of the times, however, this sort of heresy was not so unusual. Religious mockery was the height of vogue for the Surrealists. In the 1930 film *L'Age d'or,* Salvador Dalí and Luis Buñuel created sequences in which a pope has his naked big toe sucked and the Marquis de Sade's protagonist from *The 120 Days of Sodom* appears in the guise of Jesus Christ. Max Ernst had recently painted a large image of the Virgin Mary enthusiastically spanking a bare-bottomed Jesus.

But Balthus's strategy is entirely different from Ernst's. Like the Marquis de Sade and other stylish technicians of sexual violence, he has set his fantasy in a nicely appointed domestic context. His unfailing worldliness and refined taste add luster to the savage behavior on view. The green and red wallpaper played against the yellow floor would, in someone else's hands, be garish, but Balthus makes it fashionable. The elegant, impeccable trappings give the tale its spin.

The cosmopolitan Balthus has treated his lurid tale with both sangfroid and playfulness. Emotions might be squalid or tawdry, but not one's clothing.

EVEN MORE THAN the satins and velvets, the piano makes the setting of *The Guitar Lesson* a real, bourgeois home.

A piano requires neatness, repetition, and practice. It depends on training and refinement. In these ways it is both opposite and similar to the tempestuous scenario of the two women. The instrument suggests propriety, but it is also a provider of sensuous pleasure; properly harnessed, it can transport you into another realm. This well-conceived tool, expertly handled, is a vessel of intense passion. To achieve its power, it requires a level of expertise and discipline comparable to that which the teacher is now applying in another arena of sensuous pleasure. Know your devices; cultivate your skills; keep the elements in order; play your instrument properly. Then—Balthus seems to be saying—rapture awaits.

For a painter of his ability, it was a fairly straightforward matter, this making of the piano. But Balthus chose to go about it in a way both childish and tricky. Relative to the people and the chair, the instrument is ridiculously small—a dwarf piano. The keys are as unrealistic as the proportions. They are

zebra-striped—alternating black and white, of equal size and scale, directly
next to one another—a far cry from real piano keys, in which the black sharps
and flats are smaller and sit atop the larger white ones.

Yet the shorthand works. The piano seems quite real. Balthus knows how
to communicate through deception; the sexual scenario is so riveting that few
viewers would ever notice that he has had us on in the rendition of the piano.

Perhaps Balthus made those piano keys a sham for the same reason that he
put the teacher in a sort of costume. The devices announce that the scene is an
illusion. It's make-believe, an act. We must take it with a grain of salt. This
music lesson should be regarded as a fantasy, not as an event that actually
occurred.

If *The Guitar Lesson* is theater, after all, then the cruelty of that vicious
teacher and the submission of her victim do not have to be taken quite as seriously as they would if we treated the painting as realistic. Don't fret, this is not
really molestation and child abuse in which the paralyzed victim is having her
share of pleasure. This is a painting about painting, a pose, nothing we have to
worry about.

REVOLUTIONARY, *The Guitar Lesson* also established the extent of the artist's
links to the past. The prevalent artistic styles of the day would not have sufficed; he needed the traditional techniques whereby he could re-create surfaces
and evoke details in a way that would enable him to convince. His deep,
muted hues—reminiscent of Chardin and Géricault—position the painting
within a known tradition. Balthus laid down a red ground at the onset that
gives the paint its rich tonality; that timbre is especially remarkable in light of
the prevalent palette of most artwork in 1934. Painters as diverse as the Surrealists, Matisse, and Kandinsky (then also in Paris) were all using brighter,
sharper colors. Their work had a distilled, concentrated, up-to-date look.
Balthus achieved his intensity in a very different way: one that deliberately
depended on an expressive means mankind has known for centuries.

The look of artistic heritage is vital. Like the fiery people in the painting,
whose faces and poses link them to a range of Renaissance prototypes, the colors, too, come from somewhere. As with Balthus himself, it is of the utmost
importance that everyone and everything have a certain ancestry.

Yet, also as with the artist, that ancestry, while obviously very fine, is
impossible to pinpoint. The colors in *The Guitar Lesson* stem from earlier art
without having a precise equal in anyone else's palette. Although similar in
hue, they are lighter than Géricault's, deeper than Piero's. The scarlet of the
girl's jacket might exist in a Courbet hunting scene or an English portrait, but

there it would be juxtaposed to the greens of the forest and the pale wash of a blue sky. Here it abuts yellows and other reds. Like Balthus, the palette of this painting derives from a range of prototypes but ends up being unique.

BALTHUS HAS CREATED the teacher in *The Guitar Lesson* with a rapid and knowing brush. The twenty-six-year-old painter appears to have dashed out her vicious slits of eyes and then, with a couple of quick strokes, to have shadowed them sinisterly. In a similar coup, Balthus has used a single, decisive, well-aimed line to tighten and clench the teacher's steely jaw. These features may have required repeated attempts and hours of concentrated work, but they look as if they were done by someone who hadn't a question in the world.

The teacher's eyes allow only the merest squint; the student, too, sees little. Within her barely open eyes, her pupils are locked in place as if she is in a trance. We, the witnesses, have been made to see every lurid detail in clear light, but the participants cannot look.

Balthus is the one in control. Having determined to expose his viewers to an incident sure to excite them—either to titillate them or to make them supremely uncomfortable—he has also chosen to permit the participants to avert their vision.

TOTALLY IN CHARGE, tackling the most provocative subject he would ever attempt, Balthus did some of his best painting. The artist might occasionally hit his stride again, but here—frankly engaged by violence and the depiction of dominance—he was at a peak. Later in life, cloaked beneath layers of facade, Balthus would not be the same. The elegant nobleman of the 1970s and 1980s, embraced by his coterie and aware that any painting he produced was worth a fortune, would be considerably diminished in strength and skill. Visually and psychologically, his work would become too labored, its way of being disturbing too intentional. In his recent art, Balthus seems enigmatic and sexually provocative by design—as if his goal is to paint a Balthus. In *The Guitar Lesson,* he was unself-consciously himself.

One of his latest attempts to deflect viewers from this truth was a statement on *The Guitar Lesson* in a 1996 interview with David Bowie:

> This one I painted because I was very hard up and I wanted to be known at once. And at that time you could be known by a scandal. The best way to get known was with scandal. In Paris.

Balthus would rather blithely declare himself a cad and a schemer than own up to one of his rare moments of unabashed candor.

IV

"ALL ART IS AT ONCE SURFACE and symbol. Those who go beneath the surface do so at their peril. Those who read the symbol do so at their peril."[9] So Oscar Wilde writes in the preface to *The Picture of Dorian Gray.*

"It is the spectator, and not life, that art really mirrors," declares Wilde. And so Balthus claimed to me time and again. If viewers find *The Guitar Lesson*—or the paintings he made of young girls twenty, thirty, and forty years later—shocking or titillating, repulsive or seductive, they reveal only their own psyches, not his.

How fervently Balthus presents himself as the passive, harmless observer and counsels us to accept his work as beautiful fictions, psychologically irrelevant. The credo is Wilde's: savor the aesthetic enchantment and leave the rest alone.

THE COUNT DE ROLA—leaning back on the settee in his mix of silk and twill, blowing smoke rings into the palatial sitting room of his eighteenth-century chalet—made himself clear to me. Living as an actor, inhabiting a stage set, painting people as if in costume plays, he has chosen his own course: everyday existence as a fancy dress party.

The duo in *The Guitar Lesson* are also performers. They, too, act out their private fantasies. Like their creator, they cast a spell without ever really meeting our eye or engaging with us. They betray passion yet remain veiled and impenetrable.

The Guitar Lesson is loaded with signals without answers. The girl's knees glow almost as red as stoplights. They look rouged; they are either scraped or blushing. Why is there so much color to them? Has she been kneeling for some previous sexual rite or punishment? Or is their hue simply a reminder of her age, that kids get scraped knees? Or would Balthus claim that the color simply went to the knees because she was placing her weight on them? Does Balthus have any idea why he made them this color? Was this just his caprice of the moment? Had he seen a little girl near the Rue de Fürstemberg with unusually red knees and used her as his imaginary model?

Yet it is hard to believe that someone as precise about his details, personal and artistic, did not have some purpose—concealed though it may be—in accentuating both the rosiness and the nakedness of those knees with the white socks folded down just beneath them. Even though Balthus today would have us forget this painting entirely, and would probably write off the color of the knees purely as a necessary touch of red on that part of the canvas, it is hard to buy his and Oscar Wilde's pronouncement that it is only because of our own hang-ups that we see something more and are curious about its origins.

Or should we leave the artist in charge, just as the music teacher is?

After all, it is a delight to be this seducer's prey. To allow oneself to be conquered, however confounding the submission, is shown in *The Guitar Lesson* to be a glorious pleasure. Even if the young initiate is holding on to that plunging neckline for dear life, her struggle is over and she is resigned. The viewer of the painting should be similarly entranced. To be forcibly overwhelmed—to be manipulated sensually and violently—is, in this painting, to be transported to a new peak of experience, a hitherto unimagined high point. How marvelous to succumb, whatever the proportions of pain and delight may be.

THE TEACHER IN *The Guitar Lesson* is Balthus himself. I do not mean this metaphorically; she is a self-portrait in drag. After an hour of sitting on the canopied bed in Niarchos's lair and studying the painting, I realized this with a jolt.

I had been staring at the teacher's face and trying to reckon with her personality. This powerful expert on sex held me rapt with her alluring appearance and her visible will to exact total control. Then I saw—without any question whatsoever, although I had not recognized the fact before—that it was Balthus's own face. The features are identical to what we see in photos and self-portraits from the period when he painted this picture; the look of determination is exactly what I had come to know in Rossinière. The satin-clad music teacher with her milky white breast and thick long coif is not simply Balthus; she is Balthus less disguised than in many of his other roles.

She has Balthus's pointed chin, sharp jaw, large narrow nose, strong cheekbones, and thin lips. Her eyes have the same cattish squint as his. Her skin has his pallor. This is the same face with which he showed himself in *The King of Cats* and *Cathy Dressing*. And the music teacher has Balthus's personality—intense, mischievous, seductive, domineering, irresistible. She achieves to a tee the artist's goal of being the one in charge, able to make the recipient of his charms submit with minimal resistance and enjoy the submission.

Like Balthus as a painter and a man, the teacher taunts as she seduces. Introducing her prey to the world of pleasure, she makes the receiving of her delights a complex, uncomfortable process. The enthusiast of Balthus's paintings may not actually succumb like the child bent across the teacher's lap, but the controlling, withholding Balthus commands his viewer's reactions as surely as the teacher manipulates her victim's awakening to sex. In *The Guitar Lesson*, the providing of thrills is perilously close to the administration of punishment; pain and happiness are kin. The same can be said of the act of observing Balthus's art: it is an excursion into aesthetic glories forever halted by uncertainty and discomfort.

The protagonists in *The Guitar Lesson* are as alarmed and bothered by their situation as they are gratified. Having gotten where she is by her own devices, the teacher appears tortured. Perhaps shame and guilt accompany her sadism; she may be as masochistic and self-punishing as she is hedonistic and commanding. Whatever the cause, her face betrays conflict. Similarly, the girl, while slightly enthralled and rhapsodic, is also miserable.

The scenario links wish fulfillment with punishment. The teacher both introduces the girl to pleasure and takes her over her knee for it. Balthus's much loathed Sigmund Freud provides some insight here in his discussion of punishment dreams: "They fulfill the wish of the sense of guilt which is the reaction to the repudiated impulse."[10]

Balthus introduces such guilt throughout his work—in the explicit wickedness of sex in *The Guitar Lesson*, and in the more subtle nuances underlying the tone of his later work. Sex becomes naughty; pleasure and punishment and violence often exist in tandem. Physical pain is often seen as part of erotic pleasure. And the characters that seem so sexual are often equally demonic.

To study the child's face, by the way, the viewer practically needs to look at the canvas upside down. Then, from the proper angle, we realize that the girl is the same character as the boy in *The Street*—which is to say Piero della Francesca's Eve from Arezzo. She has the identical dimple below the full lips, the Romanesque arched eyebrows, the flat forehead, the nose plane. Time and again, Balthus paints the same people—in a fantastic range of guises. There are only a few archetypes, and the issues are recurrent.

A PEN-AND-INK DRAWING Balthus made in 1949 corroborates that the female teacher is really just Balthus at a clever remove. In this *Study after "The Guitar Lesson,"* the aggressor—now stripped to the waist—is male. His face has virtually the same features as that of the teacher in the 1934 painting. Only now, with short hair—and the slightly feline, demonic cast Balthus traditionally gives himself—the dominator is unquestionably the painter himself.

In this drawing, the Balthus character holds by his teeth a piece of mate-

Study after "The Guitar Lesson," 1949, ink, 28.5 x 19.1 cm

rial that supports, like a sling, the nude girl sprawled across his lap. Stretched taut around the small of the girl's back, this harness is a unique, and highly clever, contrivance for domination. The man in charge is that much more of a brute for his ability to use his teeth to support the weight of the woman's torso. With his head almost directly above the girl's genitals, at which he stares avidly, he resembles a lion about to savage its prey.

The man who told me repeatedly that there is no eroticism in his art, who constantly denied (while perpetually bringing up) allusions to Humbert Humbert, who depicts himself as the beleaguered aesthete, has in both of these versions of *The Guitar Lesson* openly displayed the lust that consumes him. He routinely protests when others claim it, but he shows himself ravaged by passion. His obsession is with the female body just on the brink of womanhood: as seen both from her own point of view and by her seducer. And what was so overt in the early work would, in more subtle form, underlie all of his art through the years.

The autobiographical fantasy of *The Guitar Lesson* must have been a happy one for its maker. The teacher has won the battle with a victory that is as absolute as it is original. Mitsou may have gotten away, but now the love object has been captured. Balthus would keep her that way.

THERE WAS, INDEED, one young woman whom Balthus would have liked to have had in his lap when he was painting *The Guitar Lesson*. She was not prepubescent, and there is no saying whether he wanted to pull her hair, but he certainly craved more of a grip than he had. Antoinette de Watteville may have consented to sit for her portrait and accept Balthus as a friend of the family's, but in 1934 she was not yet returning the degree of affection he felt for her.

"Blonde, beautiful, wide-eyed, voluptuous, serene in the self-assurance of her physical and social distinction,"[11] Antoinette was everything the young artist adored. Balthus wrote his friends that she embodied the spirit of youthful femininity. Their age difference was insubstantial—she was twenty to the artist's twenty-four when they met—yet, Balthus confided, he saw her as the ideal, quintessential young girl. He said she conjured an atmosphere of delicious hot chocolate: the perfect taste of sweet, unblemished youth.

Antoinette also had rank and fortune. The de Wattevilles were one of the most prominent ancestral families in Bern, their mansion grand and opulent. Balthus was enamored, but to no avail. Antoinette has said subsequently that, at the time, she did not want to be married to a poor painter.[12] It has been reported that she smirked at Balthus condescendingly.[13] Whatever the extent or the causes of her dismissal of him, Balthus was stung by the rejection.

As the artist who has entered a fine household and taken its resident maiden by storm, the Balthus doppelgänger in *The Guitar Lesson* is a stand-in for the person the painter wanted, but was not yet permitted, to become. A single woman was not all Balthus wished to conquer, and he did not necessarily intend to have her quite so brutally. But, exaggerated though it may be, the position of the music teacher is an apt equivalent for what Balthus desired. He wanted to take hold, to be the one in command.

Yet the student, too, partially represents Balthus: spellbound, seduced, held captive by a strong woman psychologically if not physically. Had Antoinette shown a sign of wanting to take him by force, he would probably have been delighted. Balthus put his face on the conqueror, but the schoolgirl was also a form of self-portrait. By his own admission a perpetual adolescent, he readily identified with the young initiate into the world of sensuous and aesthetic response. As with most sadomasochistic fantasies, the dreamer was both players at the same time.

V

WHENEVER BALTHUS BROUGHT Ian Fleming into the conversation, he would invariably raise his eyebrows and label him "amusing," sometimes elevating him to "frightfully amusing" or "terribly amusing."

James Bond's inventor was among Balthus's favorite acquaintances of the 1930s, both because of the writer's creative intelligence and because of his upper-class English ways. But Fleming, particularly in that time period, had other sides to his character which make Balthus's lifelong fondness of him—and the wry grin he made when recalling the writer—all the more curious. Fleming

> may have been intelligent, charming and witty . . . but he was also a gold-plated phoney, a chancer, a ruthless, brutal womaniser, a sadist, a pompous snob, a toady, a chauvinist, a nihilist, an opportunist, an egocentric devoid of shame or guilt who cuckolded his best friends without a second thought, a miserable man with an emotional age of a 12-year-old. . . . He kept a collection of pornography, mostly about flagellation, and showed it to women he brought to his flat. Although most of it depicted men as the victims being beaten by women, Fleming reversed these roles in real life and mercilessly wielded the whip himself. . . . Luck favoured him when he met Ann Rothermere. As a girl she had written in her diary, "Why do I like cads and bounders?" In Fleming she found the cad of her life. He determined to "whip the devil" out of her. Her friends noticed that she was always black and blue when Fleming was around, and the letters between the couple are peppered with loving phrases such as "10 on each buttock"; "I want you to whip me and contradict me"; and "Be prepared to drink your cocktails standing for a few days after my return."[14]

We will never know how well Balthus really knew Fleming. It is possible that he only saw the Englishman in passing and trumped up their connection to impress me. But to use the word "amusing" as the operative adjective for this sort of character is a fairly singular taste. *The Guitar Lesson* makes clear, however, that for Balthus—at least in his fantasy life—there were, quite literally, no holds barred.

IN THE SAME TIME PERIOD when Balthus was painting his scene of the androgynous music teacher and her young novitiate, Pierre Klossowski was devoting himself to a study of the Marquis de Sade. In 1933 Balthus's brother published—in the *Revue Française de Psychanalyse,* a quarterly journal produced "under the high patronage of M. le Professeur S. Freud"—a psychoanalytic study of Sade. Each of the Klossowski boys addressed the issue in his own way, but they had emerged from the same childhood with a mutual interest in the sort of fantasies of power and dominance that got their name from the infamous marquis.

In the years since he had left Geneva, Pierre had flourished under the tutelage Rilke had arranged for him. Following his work with André Gide, he had established himself as a writer and translator. In 1930 he had collaborated with Pierre Jean Jouve, who had been a neighbor of the Klossowskis on the Rue Boissonade before the war, on a German-to-French translation of *Les Poèmes de la folie* by Hölderlin. That same year, Pierre had become secretary to the psychoanalyst René Laforgue. By the time the Princess Marie Bonaparte persuaded him to publish this psychoanalytic study three years later, he had acquired a considerable reputation for his extensive interest in the writings of both Freud and Sade.

In his essay on Sade, Pierre Klossowski explores Sade's childhood development as a key to the understanding of his work. He acts in complete contradiction to Balthus's counsel that it is heresy to consider the psychological sources of an artwork and to analyze the origins of its emotional content.

Pierre proposes that the Marquis de Sade had "a negative Oedipus complex." The author of *The 120 Days of Sodom* was, according to the young writer, motivated primarily by an early hatred for his mother rather than the typical male hatred for the father. He characterizes the mother image in Sade's work as a "tyrannical idol." He points out that "it is the ideal of the devoted self-sacrificing woman that Sade is determined to destroy."[15] For that reason, "With fierce delight Sade undertakes the minute description of scenes in which the mother is humiliated before the very eyes of her children or by the children themselves."[16]

Pierre Klossowski must certainly have been aware that his own brother was, in his paintings, depicting in elaborate detail related scenes of humiliation. Every major painting in Balthus's 1934 show focused on creatures fitting

Pierre's description of the Sadean female. In *The Window*—the canvas in which a woman the age of a young mother has been pushed, terror-stricken, against the open sill—the painter himself is her apparent attacker. In *The Street,* the scene now amended depicts a female similarly in the throes of a humiliating experience. Both as tyrants and victims, the women in *Alice* and *Cathy Dressing* are precisely the types Pierre Klossowski identified as occurring in the Marquis de Sade's work as a result of the marquis's wish to subjugate his own power-house of a mother. Cathy lords her sexuality and uses it to torment her hapless admirer, Balthus himself. She is, in a sense, the victor in the scene, yet the artist has denigrated her totally by making her vain and ridiculous. Alice appears to have stripped herself and freely chosen her brazen pose, but she nonetheless looks sullen and miserable—like human meat at a slave auction.

The ultimate personification of what Klossowski calls Sade's "*idole tyran-nique*" is the teacher in *The Guitar Lesson.* Moreover, she is, generically and specifically, a mother image; by looking like Balthus, she closely resembles Bal-adine Klossowska. When Balthus was twelve and he was photographed on sev-eral occasions with his mother and Rilke, he and Baladine appear strikingly similar: with identical large noses, thin mouths, deep-set eyes, hollow cheeks, and nearly the same thick black pageboy-length hair. Whatever his deliberate intentions were, Balthus made the teacher an amalgam of himself and his mother.

The object of humiliation in this canvas—the girl on the teacher's lap—is the prototype of the character Balthus would continue to subjugate, albeit far more subtly, for the rest of his painting life. She embodies the female who would be his lifelong obsession, whom he would present in an endless array of poses. These seductive girls in their formative years would tend to appear slightly anesthetized. Beyond displaying the usual absentmindedness of teenage girls, they seem to have been temporarily stunned. Overwhelmed by their own sensuousness, these alluring creatures are lost in their own worlds, inaccessible except to the rare soul mate. Balthus was preoccupied by enchant-ing, enchanted, women who were often on the brink of puberty physically, and, even if older, acted with the self-absorption that belongs to adolescence. The artist had to ennoble and devour such females.

Is this young lady—that initiate in *The Guitar Lesson* who in effect would be the subject of Balthus's art forever after—yet another version of Baladine? Is she a portrait, deliberate or inadvertent, of the young mother who, when her sons were teenagers, wrote Rilke that she considered herself one of the chil-dren? The look of unconsciousness indeed describes Baladine—in the state of mind to which she was driven by her passion for the irresistible poet who was her lover during the period when Balthus and Pierre might have wished her to be more adult and attentive to their adolescent needs.

Or is the girl in *The Guitar Lesson* simply Antoinette, succumbing at last? Perhaps so. Or a version of the artist—initiated at a tender age into blazing sexual awareness? The essay Balthus's brother wrote contemporaneous to the creation of the painting allows both for the confluence of all of these characters into a single image and for a connection between this extraordinary painting and its maker's own early experience.

VI

THE ENGAGEMENT BETWEEN A BIOGRAPHER and a living subject is one of the most fraught of all human relationships. To keep my freedom—once I realized I was writing about someone as unscrupulous as he is brilliant, almost as talented at lying as he is at painting—I pretty much stopped meeting with Balthus.

My biggest problem was the way I enjoyed him and revered him whenever we were face-to-face; his charms blinded me to his faults. If I had given in to his nearly irresistible promise of friendship, I would ultimately have violated that relationship even more extremely than is already the case.

But even once I ceased accepting the invitations to Rossinière, I still returned there often in my mind. Writing about identity in *The Guitar Lesson*, I pictured Balthus reading it in the library of Le Grand Chalet. The problem is poor Nicholas's, Balthus would kindly allow with a look of compassion and understanding. The disappointed artist had hoped I wasn't "one of those psychological types." He thought I knew better. Perhaps *my* mother was an *idole tyrannique;* the issue was clearly personal.

"My dear Nicholas, what on earth does an obscure essay of Pierre's have to do with me? I am a painter. Consider only the rhythms and textures." This would be his approach; it was the way he fended off views he found distasteful. Rather than evince fury, he would look down his nose at me with a mix of patient understanding and condescension. *The Guitar Lesson,* Balthus would remind us, was merely a youthful prank. As for my notion that it presents, in undisguised form, the artist's lifelong mind-set, I believe he would simply have reverted to his statement that he wishes he had never painted it.

However, if you, the reader, had wanted to follow Balthus's own guidelines and consider the artist only according to his dictates, you would have thrown down this book long ago. Since you have not done so, I hope you will be willing to venture further into forbidden territory suggested by Pierre's tren-

Pierre Klossowski

chant analysis of the Marquis de Sade's personal background. For Balthus's brother offers insights that may be of as much value to understanding the Klossowski boys as "the divine marquis."

PIERRE'S AWARENESS of the absent father—and of the consequent hostility toward the powerfully present mother—may well have come from personal experience. Following the separation of the Klossowskis, Erich played a minor role in his sons' lives compared with that of Baladine, Rilke, and Rilke's circle. Yet in many ways the distant father was, at least so far as Balthus was concerned, the ideal one. Of the two parents, Erich was the more accomplished painter, a successful set designer, and an esteemed writer on art. By his younger son's standards, he also came from a far better background.

Balthus once made a point of telling me that, contrary to what several people have written, he always adored his mother. Yet various friends of the artist have reported to me that in the 1940s and 1950s, he was visibly ashamed of her. When Balthus and Baladine attended the same parties in Paris, he avoided her. Balthus himself recalled to me that whereas Pierre was with their mother at the point in 1969 when she was dying, he was absent. And Balthus has certainly gone to considerable lengths to cover up, deny, and repudiate his mother's background. While it is unclear whether he rejected his Jewish heritage because he connected it with Baladine—or whether he disassociated himself from his mother because she was a reminder of his Jewish origins—there is no question that he turned against his maternal lineage.

In his essay on Sade, Pierre Klossowski elaborated on the process by which the sons of absent fathers can turn on their mothers and develop an abiding need to dominate all females. The literature of Sade provided his examples:

> It is impossible to find more typical examples of the antimaternal complex: Bessac has no father, but instead of transforming his filial condition so that he takes the role of his mother's second husband (positive Oedipus complex), he represents, on the contrary, the absent father's virility and natural cruelty, he *avenges* that absence, so to speak; whereas in the Oedipus complex the father's suppression makes possible the reestablishment of the primitive union of mother and son, the *suppression of the mother performed jointly by the father and the son*—as presented in the story of Brisa Testa—by exploding the latent rivalry between mother and son, reveals the community between the son and the father.[17]

Not only is the teacher in *The Guitar Lesson*—which is to say Balthus himself (even if it is Balthus in imitation of the very mother about whom he had such mixed feelings)—guiltlessly satanic, but she appears to get, and give, considerable pleasure as she inflicts horrendous pain on the girl by pulling her hair and pressing those talons into her bare thighs. And the child is almost as determined as the teacher; the violent act is the means toward ecstasy. This is the beginning of a chain. She, too, will grow from being a little girl in her cardigan and pinafore into a mature woman in seductive silk. Evil passes from generation to generation.

For Pierre Klossowski, the explanation for this phenomenon lay in the creations of Sade. The mother who is seen to have inflicted forms of punishment has inspired her victim to create characters who represent her in her willfulness and tyrannical impulses. The victim now succeeds in subjugating the former tyrant by giving her a nasty portrayal. Everyone is oppressor and oppressee, on through the generations. It fits that each of the figures in *The Guitar Lesson* has dual identities: the teacher is both Balthus the conqueror and the mother whom he avenges; the schoolchild is both Balthus the victim and the embodiment of that female he now gladly subjugates.

In "The Atmosphere of Evil in de Sade's Work," Pierre Klossowski quotes Saint-Fond from Sade's *Juliette:*

> I may very well be deceived as to what I am calling *evil*. What I am so characterizing with regard to myself is apparently a very great *good* with regard to the being who brought me into the world; and if I receive evil from others, I enjoy the right of doing evil to them in return, and even the aptitude for doing evil to them first; so from now on *evil* is a good for me, as it is for the author of my days with regard to my existence; I am happy for the evil I do others as God is happy for the evil he does me; there is no mistake except in the notion attributed to the word; but in reality, where there is both *evil* as necessity and *evil* as pleasure, why should I not call it a good?[18]

When Balthus the intense young man painted *The Guitar Lesson,* he still knew the sharp sting of helplessness and defeat to which he had given such poignant voice as the child creator of *Mitsou.* The only way to handle his suffering and sense of loss was to become a conqueror. Having felt harm, he would now inflict it—in keeping with the pattern Klossowski identifies. So the once anguished child transformed himself into the all-powerful teacher. The same cycle is evident in the response of the teacher's captive; the schoolgirl, rather than simply remaining passive, pulls back her instructress's dress and tweaks the nipple she has just exposed. Having been awakened violently to sex, the child is herself a happy seductress in the making.

Balthus's brother, in analyzing Sade, characterizes early life as a series of disappointments. First, the love union of the mother and child runs aground. Then comes the realization that nature is destructive, and the development of a universal ingratitude. The response is to seek revenge.

People are victimized; so Balthus illustrated in his paintings. Downtrodden by historical circumstance, his response was to dominate the way the music teacher does—and thus avenge himself. And as was true for the Sadean character quoted by his brother, he might redefine the usual notions of good and evil in the process.

Having gone from the luxurious Parisian existence his family had enjoyed

Pierre Klossowski,
Portrait of Balthus,
1956, pencil

before World War I to the subsequent exile in which his mother was reduced to the possibility of domestic servitude—and then, after the hardship of the army, having been under true financial duress while his friends, mostly privileged and noble, were cavorting around him—the final humiliation occurred when he was spurned in love. The victim would strike back by seducing.

HE WOULD SUCCEED UTTERLY. Socially down-and-out, Balthus would one day ascend to the point of dominance he had initially witnessed from a position of submission.

It did not take long for him to begin to exert the power and allure of the music teacher. A marvelously talented painter and a strikingly handsome man, Balthus had the wherewithal to charm and enchant. With the 1934 exhibition, Balthus took the helm in making himself central and getting others to take notice.

His mother and Antoinette had both put him in second place, but through the sorcery of paint, Balthus had commenced his ascent. If attention was what he craved, he could have been no more successful than with this show at Galerie Pierre. Some people deplored it, and others were moved to the depths of their being; few were mute. At age twenty-six, Balthus had everyone running and guessing—as he has ever since.

KLOSSOWSKI'S PROSE ABOUT his brother is difficult to penetrate, as complex and layered as Balthus's art. It is little wonder that Balthus told me he found Pierre's writing on him obtuse and imcomprehensible. Yet the older sibling occasionally hits on some piquant truths. Pierre's intellect, his knowledge of the facts, and his psychoanalytic insightfulness merge in certain observations that, for all their obtuseness, reflect a unique understanding of the complex character with whom he shared that extraordinary childhood. Pierre wrote, cogently, of his brother:

> A double violence is perpetrated in his struggle to insert his own vision into our world: the violence he does to his own sensibility, and that which he does to things in snatching them from the life of the world with which he himself lives at odds. . . . He does violence to his own sensibility, to certain infantile nostalgias, to certain aristocratic claims; hence to his own pathos when he snatches things from life and sets them outside of life into an ontological reality.[19]

When we know the background and can mentally footnote and explicate the references, we feel that Pierre grasps both Balthus's vulnerability and chicanery, while having the utmost regard for his genius as a painter. The older brother discerns the real person, anguished and anxious, from the poseur who has resorted to deception as his only means of coping with life.

IN THE OVERT SELF-PORTRAIT Balthus painted the year after *The Guitar Lesson,* he not only calls himself "H.M. the King of Cats" and makes himself look the tyrant, but he even puts a circus whip on a stool at his side. Its lash is curled over its sturdy handle, ready for action. The whip is the key to his identity; it rests on top of the signboard that bears his name.

The artist has come a long way from being the little boy in *Mitsou.* With both elbows bent, the imperious wielder of the whip holds one hand authoritatively on his hip while clenching the other in a determined fist. This is not someone who will be left in tears, or from whom any animal will get away. The sad child is now a despot who has found the perfect means of taking charge. He has become a cat himself—a sphinx, a slayer, the one who comes and goes at will. Beyond that, he is now the king of the species: the master—rather than the victim of the four-legged creature nuzzling his leg.

In this feline self-portrait, Balthus's head is proportionately far too large for the rest of his body. If his splayed left leg were reconciled with the right, it would be considerably longer. The cat's head is also too big. These distortions give the painting intense drama. The enlarged, masklike faces and the raking light that highlights some surfaces while leaving others in obscurity make the canvas pure theater. If in his life Balthus has lived out in the wings, in this example of his art he has put himself at center stage. Not only is he the king and the ringleader, but he is a performer, and the star at that.

This character is not merely swarthy, sinister, and domineering; he is emphatic about the point with that revealing signboard which is no mere signature but the declaration "A PORTRAIT OF H.M. THE KING OF CATS painted by HIMSELF, MCMXXXV." Balthus may now insist that what interests him is the painting itself, not self-portraiture—that we should consider only the object, not its creator—but here he has printed that lettering as precisely, and with the same desire to establish identity, in a way that will outlive him and last through the centuries, as Chardin does when he creates the illusion of his name etched deeply in stone.

H.M. the King of Cats regards the world not dissimilarly from the way the teacher does in *The Guitar Lesson.* He is more than in charge. He demands, and has acquired, a maniacal sense of control. With good looks, he seduces; with strong arms and a steely grip, or a whip, he conquers. He is sardonic, elegant, and powerful.

The whip—Balthus could hardly have picked a less subtle symbol— pertains not so much because Balthus hoped to inflict pain as because he wished to terrorize. That was the word his mother had used in her letter to Rilke in reference to the way he taunted his baby cousin in Berlin, dominating little Peter with his costumes and game-playing. Balthus's goal has been consistent all his life: to hold his audience captive by keeping them unsure about what to expect. His weapon, of course, has been the charm of his person and his art.

As a child he lost Mitsou. He could not hold on to what he wanted. He was swept from home to home and city to city, victimized by war, cast among the Jews in a spare bed in a room that was not his own, denied a commission he thought he had in Beatenberg. Cherished by his mother and her lover, he

The King of Cats, 1935, oil on canvas, 71 x 48 cm

also watched as the obsessed Baladine wept at Rilke's insistence that she keep her distance, as she begged for some more stable living situation, as she mourned their separation and her lack of a higher position in the poet's life.

In letters from Morocco, Balthus was hopelessly gloomy and depressed. Following that, he was so poor that he did not know if he would be able to continue painting. If he was lucky enough to be able to sleep in the large house of aristocratic friends, he did not feel as if he really belonged there. But in his painting, and in his image and fantasy of himself, he would not merely take charge; he would make his prey submit.

VII

A POET, ESSAYIST, TRANSLATOR, and draftsman, Pierre Klossowski is held in high regard within a relatively small circle even if he never became the international celebrity Balthus has become. His work has been widely read as well as translated and written about extensively, even if its audience has primarily been academic. And its popularity continues; in 1996 Klossowski and his views on Sade were the subject of two important symposia at the Institute of Contemporary Art in London.

When he was a child, Pierre's first grammar book was in Latin. The erudite scholar translated Virgil into French while still a young man. Since then he has also translated Kafka, Kierkegaard, Klee, Rilke, and Heidegger, and has written fifteen books of his own.

It has been a rigorous life. Just before World War II, Pierre Klossowski began a novitiate with the Benedictines, which was followed by one with the Dominicans. But he lasted only three months in the religious community.

Then, in 1947, he married a war widow who had been deported to the concentration camp at Ravensbrück because of her activities in the Resistance. For many years, Pierre depended on his wife, who worked as a translator and proofreader, to survive. Even when their circumstances improved in the 1980s, Pierre and Denise Klossowski made few changes in their lifestyle. Characteristically, Pierre has never tacked "de Rola" onto his name—let alone used a title to which, as a "count's" elder brother, he would presumably be entitled.

In conversation with me, Balthus referred to his brother amiably if condescendingly. While making clear that Pierre's work was not to his taste, he suggested that there was no problem between the two of them. Mutual associates of theirs told me, however, that for a number of years there has been no connection between the two. I was told that when Pierre was very poor, Balthus closed the door on him at the Villa Medici. Yet information is hazy; the family

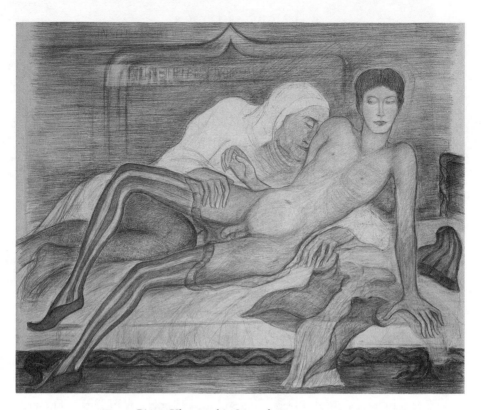

Pierre Klossowski, *Scène du jeune ogier et
du Commandeur de Saint-Vit,* 1982, pencil

Pierre Klossowski, *Roberte au passage Choiseul,* 1979, pencil

doesn't talk, Balthus doesn't give straight answers, and Pierre will not discuss Balthus with researchers.

In the thirties Balthus and Pierre had certainly been very close. They had in common their extraordinary acuity, their gift for language, and their tremendous creativity, and they traveled in the same circle. The two had shared a childhood beyond anyone else's ken: unique in its stimuli as well as its hardships, dominated intellectually by their father figure Rilke.

But the current lack of relationship between the brothers is understandable. Pierre lives modestly with his wife in government-subsidized housing. In many ways the essence of the modern French intellectual, Pierre is said by friends to be aghast at his younger brother's use of a title. Balthus is equally appalled by the overt eroticism of Pierre's rather simplistic drawings and the undisguised sadomasochistic obsession of his writing. Not only does the Count de Rola disparage this sort of thing, but it has had the nasty effect of muddying the waters with respect to how people regard *his* work. Beyond that, there are complexities that arose because of Balthus's affair with Pierre's step-daughter.

Since the war, Pierre has been closely allied with many major French intellectuals, including Roland Barthes, Michel Foucault, and Georges Bataille. Barthes, for example, would, in the 1940s, go to the Klossowskis' apartment to play four-handed piano with Denise. The place he has held in the lives of these people is summed up by a statement from the philosopher Gilles Deleuze. Deleuze declared that all of Klossowski's work "strives towards a single goal: ensuring the loss of personal identity, dissolving the ego; that is the splendid trophy that Klossowski's characters bring back from a journey to the edge of madness."[20]

Since he wrote that essay in 1933 in which he was one of the first people to take Sade seriously and to revive interest in Sade's work, "the divine marquis" has been Pierre's lifelong passion. Over the years, he has authored essays ranging from "Sade et la Révolution" in 1939 to "Signe et perversion chez Sade" in 1966 to "L'Androgyne dans la représentation sadienne" in 1977. In 1947 Pierre wrote the book *Sade, mon prochain.* His own fiction writing—like *Roberte ce soir* and *The Revocation of the Edict of Nantes*—is known for its vivid sadomasochistic passages and the elaborate schemes he has devised in which women are brutalized and violated.

As with Balthus, Pierre's work has been interpreted in various ways. Many observers consider it misogynistic and pornographic, but he claims it to be mystical. The main character of his fiction, Roberte—who is based on his wife, Denise—assumes various identities in his tales and goes through a series of sexual encounters in which she is raped and humiliated, and others in which she

Pierre
Klossowski,
Dans le parc,
1977, pencil

is the seducer. The writing is overtly salacious, but—as with Balthus—it is
hard to determine where reality is. "Like the tableaux vivants imagined and
staged by de Sade's libertines, Klossowski's words and images betray an obsession with representation itself: representations of plays, of drawings, of drawings of scenes from plays, books about books. They are a theater of simulacra
in which everything is represented, and nothing is real."[21]

In 1970 Pierre published *La Monnaie vivante*, which "describes a utopian
stage in economic development in which the medium of exchange will not be
currency, but living beings. The gold standard will give way to a pleasure standard, and producers will be paid in boys and girls. A graphite drawing dating
from 1969 illustrates the process by depicting *The Recuperation of Surplus Value*
as an act of sodomy."[22] This work was greatly admired by Foucault, who considered it "a distillation of Blanchot and Bataille." But in 1973 Pierre appalled
the previously enthusiastic Foucault by suggesting that the way to deal with

5. *The Guitar Lesson*, 1934, oil on canvas, 161 x 138.5 cm

6. *The Window,* 1933, oil on canvas, 160.6 x 112 cm

7. *Cathy Dressing,* 1933, oil on canvas, 165 x 150 cm

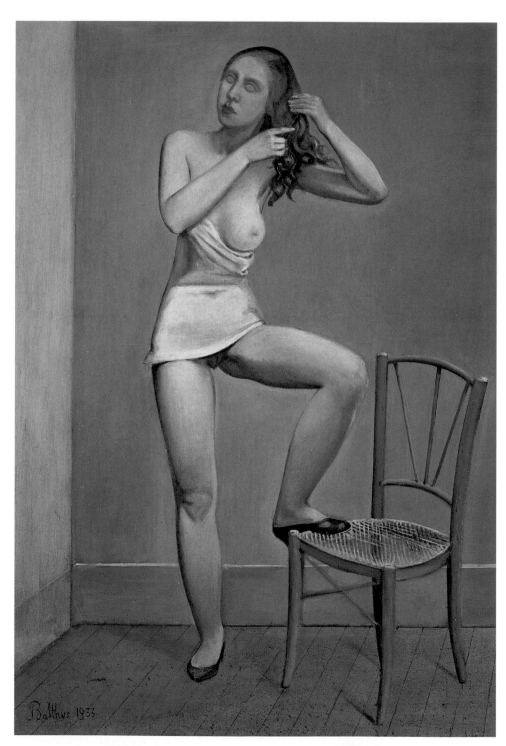

8. *Alice,* 1933, oil on canvas, 175 x 125 cm

the C.R.S.—the Compagnies Republicaines de Securité—in demonstrations would be to arm a platoon of "thirty very handsome young men" with sticks; this elite corps of police would be so struck by their beauty that they would become immobilized.[23] The wicked wit and intrepid originality are similar to Balthus's; sometimes it seems as if the sole goal of the Klossowski brothers is to be perverse.

But Pierre's style and Balthus's are hardly the same. Like Balthus, Pierre drew quite a bit as a child, and in recent years he has become known for his highly erotic drawings and paintings. Artistically weak, the drawings depict craven naked men with erections and seductive women bound and harnessed. If as a writer and modern intellectual Pierre is a serious and highly esteemed force—with many essays and books having been devoted to him—as a visual artist he lacks Balthus's skill and subtlety, and emphasizes subject matter in the way that Balthus deplores. Androgyny and sadomasochism are made florid.

Moreover, Pierre's drawings are like a statement declaring that the Klossowski boys are obsessively erotic: almost as inconvenient for Balthus as his brother's unwillingness to be a Count de Rola.

Yet, blessedly—and in spite of his own work on Sade—Pierre Klossowski is no more in favor of a comparable investigation of his own intellectual formation than Balthus is. In spite of the several books that have been written about Pierre, he has consistently resisted efforts to establish the family biography. Pierre has been slightly more lax than his brother in permitting chronologies of his life to appear in several publications, but he has said that he fears biography because it furnishes keys that are too facile—and that he does not want his work to be interpreted on the basis of his individual experience. Pierre Klossowski has had, he explains, a life of strolling around, and whereas his own experience has been full of discontinuity, the problem with biography is that it tends to fix, unify, and classify.

SO FOR WHATEVER REASON, Pierre and Balthus Klossowski have denied us access to their extraordinary childhood or subsequent experiences. They believe, they both say, in creative achievement, in the end products, not in the vagaries of psychological conjecture about how they got there.

Yet both Pierre and Balthus have made sure that anyone writing even cursorily about them mentions Rilke and some of the other luminaries of their youth. The rule is merely that after the name-dropping, all investigation stops. As young men, both Balthus and Pierre developed consuming obsessions, yet they are determined that no one find out too much about their origins.

The resistance may come from the intellectual rigor they both claim; it may derive from reasons we will never know. The secrets of life in that flat in Geneva will probably never be unlocked. Balthus's and Pierre's experiences, beyond those of which we are certain, may all have been purely psychological; there may have been something more. What is clear is that—with their impassioned, possessed, and adoring mother, and a cast of characters that included Rilke and Gide—the young painter who created *The Guitar Lesson* and the young writer who grappled zealously with the Marquis de Sade had a youth quite unlike anyone else's.

> There were moments when he looked on evil simply as a mode through which he could realize his conception of the beautiful. . . .
>
> There are moments, psychologists tell us, when the passion for sin, or for what the world calls sin, so dominates a nature, that every fibre of the body, as every cell of the brain, seems to be instinct with fearful impulses. Men and women at such moments lose the freedom of their will. They move to their terrible end as automatons move. Choice is taken from them, and conscience is either killed, or, if it lives at all, lives but to give rebellion its fascination, and disobedience its charm.[24]

For Balthus, as for that beautiful, striking seductress in *The Guitar Lesson,* evil was exquisite.

CHAPTER ELEVEN

THE WINDOW

I

*The primitive, so-called sympathetic nervous system is a won-
drous thing we share with all other species that owe their continued existence to being quick on the turn, fast and hard into
battle, or fiery in flight. Evolution has culled us all into this efficiency. Nerve terminals buried deep in the tissue of the heart
secrete their noradrenalin, and the heart lurches into acceler-
ated pumping. More oxygen, more glucose, more energy,
quicker thinking, stronger limbs. It's a system so ancient, developed so far back along the branchings of our mammalian and
premammalian past that its operations never penetrate into
higher consciousness. There wouldn't be time anyway, and it
wouldn't be efficient. We only get the effects. That shot to the
heart appears to occur simultaneously with the perception of
threat. . . .*

—IAN MCEWAN, *Enduring Love*[1]

DURING ONE OF THE rare interludes when they were both staying at
Muzot and enjoying a respite from the tumult of their separations, Rainer
Maria Rilke and Baladine Klossowska made an outing to the Swiss city of Fribourg. In the course of that journey through the mountains, they decided to
collaborate on a book in which his poems and her illustrations would appear
side by side. Its theme was windows.

The slight, elegant volume was published by the Librairie de France in
1927, the year after the poet's death. Called *Les Fenêtres*, it consists of fifteen
poems dedicated to "Mouky et à Baladine." Each poem is printed in distinctive hand-cut type, with lots of plain white space around it. Interspersed
among the poems are ten of Madame Klossowska's etchings.

The women created by Balthus's mother are all locked in trances. The
first, in profile, is framed by window mullions. Fixing her hair, she is completely detached from the act, as if absorbed in private thoughts. Another

woman rests with her hands on a windowsill and looks off absently into the distance. She is in a spell, possessed by intense emotions of which we will never know the specifics. In one plate, a nude woman sprawls, seemingly overwhelmed, on a daybed. She is in a sensual paradise, with a vase of flowers at her side and birds visible through the skylight above. Elsewhere women lean and wave, and shutters open to unseen vistas.

The subjects are all transfixed; so, apparently, was the woman who created them. Baladine's rather limp, awkwardly articulated etchings have an adolescent quality. These pleasant but flowery pictures appear to have been drawn in a semihypnotic state of bliss.

The manner and technique of Baladine's window illustrations probably had little value for Balthus by the time he became truly serious about making his own art in the early 1930s. But his mother's imagery and arrangements would nonetheless appear repeatedly in his work throughout his life. Time and again, he would pose women identically, surrounding them with many of the same details. His characters, too, would be in a state somewhere between reverie and agony.

WINDOWS—THE VEHICLES by which daylight enters rooms, the man-made framework that establishes the perimeters of what we see—would also be a leitmotif of Balthus's painting. The artist must have known the meaning and symbolism his mother and Rilke ascribed to these forms. Windows suggest unknown territory. They open to distant information that, while present, is hazy. The walls around them create barriers that block entire areas from view. Balthus would often show adolescent girls languishing against a windowsill and gazing out through these openings to the outdoors that invoke the necessity of losing oneself to imagination.

Other central themes of Rilke's poetry—the mirror and the rose especially—would repeatedly figure in the vocabulary of Balthus's art. But the window, not just within the canvases but as the embodiment of the canvas itself, had particular portent.

RILKE WAS OBSESSED with windows. Walking around Bern and Fribourg in the early 1920s, he had decided that a serious history of them ought to be published. He felt that their shape determines our idea of the world. They help provide clarity, put us in charge, and diminish the risk of loss. They offset the incapacity and tenuousness he lamented in the preface to *Mitsou*.

A lover's never so beautiful
as when we see her appear
framed by you; because, window,
you make her almost immortal.

All risks are canceled. Being
stands at love's center,
with this narrow space around,
where we are master.[2]

By revealing a visual world that required no explanation and demanded
nothing beyond itself, Rilke's windows celebrated the act of seeing that Balthus
would describe as the ideal of his art:

She was in a window mood that day:
to live seemed no more than to stare.
From a dizzy non-existence she could see
a world coming to complete her heart.[3]

Yet windows could also be treacherous. They have the capacity to bring on
qualms and make us anxious at the edge of a precipice:

You propose I wait, strange window;
your beige curtain nearly billows.
O window, should I accept your offer or,
window, defend myself? Who would I wait for?[4]

It is, above all, that role that these openings in the walls assume in Balthus's art.

ONE OF THE SEVEN PAINTINGS in Balthus's show at the Galerie Pierre was
The Window (color plate 6). He painted it in 1933, six years after the publication of his mother and Rilke's volume. The canvas presents a desperate woman
pushed against a window ledge. She raises her right arm in a frantic gesture of
protest and self-defense. With her left hand, she braces herself against a fall.
The woman bares a breast; it appears that someone has violently grabbed her
blouse by its frilly neckline and pulled it down on one side. Everything else
the woman is wearing is still in place. She faces her unseen attacker in abject
terror.

Viewing *The Window*, we take the role of the assailant—unless we are one of those rare people for whom this painting stirs up nothing at all, or who can turn away from it with moral repugnance or a virtuous sense of shock. The act of seeing this canvas implicates us. As when we look at *The Guitar Lesson*, we feel ourselves to be something between naughty and evil.

The woman looks as if she is being threatened with a lethal weapon. We picture the painter, whose vantage point we share, wielding a knife. Whether this was a deliberate comment on the role of the brush or an inadvertent revelation, Balthus was showing the act of painting to be a means of terrorizing. He could subjugate his portrait subject and hold her captive through the devices of his studio: the same means that ultimately enabled him to conquer a large audience. Art is a power struggle, a process of personal metamorphosis, a means of taking command and astounding the bourgeoisie. Like the teacher in *The Guitar Lesson*, an artist must both thrill and intimidate.

The Window again makes blatant the artist's need to prevail. He would later cloak and soften his approach, but he remained consistent in this compulsion to force alluring women to take the poses he commanded. Even inanimate objects must succumb to him. Tables would be locked in position, however awkward the angle; bed linens would be twisted this way and that. He would make beauty his prey.

WHEN THE ACTUAL MODEL for *The Window*, Elsa Henriquez, "first arrived at Balthus's studio in the Rue de Fürstemberg, he opened the door dressed in his old army uniform, a dagger in his hand and a scowl on his face. He grabbed her blouse and tried to pull it open. Elsa recoiled in horror, just as Balthus intended."[5] The reticent young woman, educated at a convent, did not, however, actually bare her breast. Her exposure was a personal embellishment Balthus added to the painting to suit his own tastes after the fact.

The Window is another of Balthus's personal fantasies. The horror-stricken woman is the captive of the celebrant of her beauty, like a butterfly specimen squashed between two pieces of glass. Having come into the room dressed as a seductress, she has ended up being the victim.

Elsa's intense rhythm and springiness contrast markedly with the permanence of the setting. The rigorously constructed space—both of the very real room, which is graphically solid and fixed, and of the neighborhood, which summons a world of order—accentuates Elsa's tumult and vulnerability. The brute who has yanked her blouse and pushed her against the window ledge has made her his squirming prisoner. The woman looks as if she is about to be flattened or impaled—as if the force looming over her is big enough to crush her.

Like a tool of bondage, her wide yellow belt is as tight as possible around her cinched waist. Her tapered skirt is stretched as much as the fabric will permit. Her breast seems to have been squeezed out.

Balthus has set up a situation where we blame the victim. The lacy, plunging neckline and beguiling brooch inform us that the woman arrived on the scene intending to allure. Her most arresting device is that oversized scarlet hairband with its billowing ruffles. Luminous and airy, this hairband resembles a halo—as if this is a saint who is being raped. On the other hand, it is also a coy device of its wearer's. This puffy tiara is the sort of thing one of Manet's demoiselles might have worn. Like the flower in Olympia's hair, it is a tool for enhancing appearance. Along with Elsa's tight skirt with its flared hemline, it is one of the ingredients that have driven her attacker to frenzy. The implication is that anyone who decks herself out like this deserves what she gets. The underlying premise, as in so many of Balthus's scenes, is that the woman wants to submit; she has set herself up to be violated. In keeping with a basic pornographic assumption, Balthus's women aim to seduce. Then the *manipulatrices* suffer the consequences.

BALTHUS, IN FACT, ASCRIBES a certain guile to women of every age. We see it in his shopgirls dressed with a mission; we see it in his young teenagers. They all have devices and a purpose.

I was struck by a remark Balthus made to his seventeen-year-old daughter one Saturday evening when I was in Rossinière. Harumi was late coming into the dining room for dinner; the rest of us had already been seated for about fifteen minutes. Preparing for a party in Gstaad, she had taken the extra time to change her hairstyle for the third time that day, and had dressed for the event in skintight pants and a low-cut blouse.

"Harumi, est-ce que tu va séduire le chauffeur?" her father asked her with a wry smile.

Of course, it was in jest; the driver was the amiable Leonardo. There was not a chance Harumi would make moves on him. By suggesting seduction, Balthus was, I thought, mocking its possibility. Earlier that same day he had told me, with his most approving smile, that his Filipino servants were "beautiful people. They are like children."

For some reason, I continued—for several years afterward—to hear that sardonic question over and over in my mind, as if it were a key to something. It became like certain phrases you repeat time and again when free-associating in the process of psychoanalysis; you know it is important, without being entirely certain why.

On reflection, what was remarkable was the pleasure Balthus took in asking the question—and his relish at the quick and lively smile with which his daughter responded to it. Harumi was far too sophisticated to be taken aback; she enjoyed this sort of banter with her father. Indeed, she may well have been on her way to seduce some socialite that night.

Balthus visibly delighted in the exchange of mischievous grins with the gorgeous Harumi and in the reference to the "chauffeur" who would be driving her to Gstaad. The luxury must have represented the fulfillment of dreams he had when he was fourteen. Clearly Balthus also got a charge from the very idea of seduction.

WHEN WE FACE THE ACTUAL painting of *The Window,* the young woman's exposed skin is alluringly silken. The astounding verisimilitude of this and other surfaces instantly takes us in. But within moments, nothing else is quite right. As usual, Balthus, having first made himself credible, distorts freely. He has transformed his subject's body to suit himself. Her large breasts start too far down—on the lower half of her chest—while their nipples are too high. Her hip is lower and longer than it could possibly be. Her head is stretched, her forehead too wide. Just below her knee, the woman's left calf is two-thirds the width of her waist.

She emerges as both dominator and victim. Her overly solid limbs and spiraling hips give her the brute force of the teacher in *The Guitar Lesson.* She could break wood or crush rocks with those legs. Yet for all her mass and strength, she is helpless. Her feet are off the ground; her arms and legs are flying this way and that; her left hand alone is her sole means of support. She raises her pitiful right hand—half the size of the left—with its fingers bent so as to be useless. This pathetic gesture is all the defense she can summon in her state of panic. And she has a black eye.

What made Balthus come up with the scenario of *The Window?* At his most forthcoming with me, he allowed that although he did not know why, subject matter of this ilk "interested" him. More often, he shrugged his shoulders and declared the issue irrelevant to the real concerns of a painter. Yet, entering the territory Balthus perpetually scorned, knowing that the artist would disparage me for saying so, I believe it is likely that Elsa was a stand-in for Baladine Klossowska. The real Elsa was only fifteen when she posed for this painting, yet she resembles Baladine in her hair and her solid, sturdy body. Either intentionally or unconsciously, Balthus thus empowered himself to push his mother through the very sort of opening that was hers and Rilke's last mutual obsession. The painting is a son's revenge. Now he could bare the maternal bosom with which she had betrayed him. And he could hold her at knifepoint against the very sort of window ledge where, throughout his adolescence, she pined endlessly for the man with whom she had replaced his father. The setting was the same as in her and Rilke's book: in front of one of those windows about which she waxed so lyrical with her lover.

If you accept this reading of the painting, then Balthus is the perfect exemplar of what his brother termed the "negative Oedipus complex." He has taken the side of the absent, thwarted father and vanquished his mother—or her representative—on his father's behalf. Now, with this painting, it is her son, the all-powerful painter, to whom Baladine must answer.

Rather than have us consider such an interpretation, Balthus has, of course, consistently resorted to the rubric that he painted his provocative themes of the 1930s simply because he knew what it took to captivate his audience. But the idea that "only the picture problems were of interest"—as he so often insisted to me—does not fly. The painted canvas was his means for dominating certain women—Antoinette de Watteville, Elsa Henriquez, his mother—and paralyzing them.

THAT VIOLENT CONQUEST ENABLED Balthus to summon his artistic skills at their most profound. Technically and aesthetically, *The Window* is superb. The view out Balthus's window on the Rue de Fürstemberg excels both as a rich urban vista and as an intricately conceived, rhythmically dynamic artistic sequence. As in *The Street*, Balthus has carved out the rooftops and gables and construction details of Parisian architecture with trenchant accuracy. He cares about roof tiles almost as deeply as the Dutch masters did, and has rendered them painstakingly with a personal and ingenious shorthand. He found the paint colors that authentically evoke the earthy red-brown tones of clay and brick. The vents and smokestacks and dormers are crystalline in the cool light.

It isn't only the view outside that the deft twenty-five-year-old painter caught and imbued with charm. The open window shutter and the drapery on the right are entirely convincing. The total conception of the painting is equally impressive for so young an artist. *The Window* is a bold composition on a large, noble scale. It has the elaborate construction that the committee of elder artists had first commended to Balthus when he was copying Poussin. Before using the picture space as a setting for human drama, the artist laid it out in advance and articulated its broad angles as well as the interstices. He made real the distinction between inside and out by establishing them in contrasting light zones, and then, with remarkable assuredness, splashed the bright outside light throughout the darker interior wherever it might naturally fall.

Yet significant as the setting is, it functions primarily as background to the people who occupy it. Like Roger van der Weyden as opposed to his predecessor Jan van Eyck, Balthus brought human life to the fore while integrating it in the visual world at large. Balthus captured the lurid details of Elsa even more forcibly than the quotidian aspects of the setting. He achieved this in part because he has the French eye for clothing; he knows its effects, and has related the different elements like a master couturier. The skirt material truly pulls across Elsa's thighs. Her body within is twisted with sharp physical tension. Elsa's shoes, with their gratuitous bows, augment her coquettish side. The green stripes of her blouse are coordinated with a similar color in her skirt. The lace fringe of her low-cut blouse—a style that Balthus called "pleasantly old-fashioned" in his limited comments to me about the painting (he confined himself mainly to pleasantries on how Elsa was dressed)—is another example of the degree to which she honed her own image before being yanked out of her area of control.

Elsa's red cheeks—brighter in the actual painting than in reproductions of it—are startling. She may be highly, rather ridiculously rouged—or blushing with the extreme change of skin color more typical of a child. If the former, then the redness is the result of her attempt to make herself attractive; if the latter, then she has an oddly young side and is agonizingly flushed with discomfort. There is also the possibility that she has been slapped. Our inability to discern whether this redness stems from a deliberate plan of Elsa's or if, on the contrary, it is inadvertent and reflects the shock of being caught off guard or the pain of having been struck, is akin to our uncertainty in *The Guitar Lesson* as to whether the girl is anguished or delighted. The signals are bold, yet we cannot read them. Like the red knees of the girl in *The Guitar Lesson*, Elsa's luminous cheeks startle us while making us feel that some key information has been withheld. The painter has imposed this ambiguity on the viewer, and led us to lose our bearings in the same way that he has reduced Elsa to confusion. He does to his viewers what he does to his women: excite and stun.

THIS DISTURBING CANVAS that Balthus conceived in his historic corner of Paris during the heyday of Surrealism hangs today in a football-crazy university town surrounded by the sprawling landscape of rural Indiana. When I made my pilgrimage to see it, the journey seemed far more unlikely than my visits to see Balthus's other early output. Also conceived in near-poverty, those other canvases nonetheless seemed more at home residing in the lavish residences of people like the Niarchoses and the Agnellis than they would in the American Midwest. On my way to Bloomington, I stopped at a roadside diner frequented mainly by truck drivers. Downing the breakfast special, I felt like Humbert Humbert going off to see Lolita in a trailer park; it seemed nearly impossible that a player in such a worldly and urbane drama would end up *here*.

But Bloomington has a fine small museum, in spite of I. M. Pei's refusal to put daylight in the right place. When I got to *The Window*, I was instantly overwhelmed by its artistic effect, and was happy to see it near one of Picasso's surreal women painted a year later. Balthus's painting is wonderfully lively, its tormented subject an intensely beautiful woman. The ravishing Elsa, caught in her web, emanates force.

Yet in little time, I came to feel that my reaction was that of an aesthete. After half an hour of note-taking, I spoke with one of the female student guards responsible for *The Window* in its current home. The painting, which she regards as "confrontational," angers her. Some of its other attendants told me they avoid looking at it because of the pain they experience from its "cold, alienated" tone.

The Window got to Indiana initially because the painter William Bailey, who taught there one summer, encouraged its purchase, which was subsequently backed by several of his fellow figurative painters then in the university's art department, all of whom agreed that it was a masterpiece. To its admirers it remains a jewel. But for many of the visitors to Bloomington, the canvas ranges from being upsetting to deliberately demeaning.

So Balthus achieved his goal: the painting deals a shock. Unlike other avant-garde works, *The Window* remains as provocative as when it was painted.

IF THE BALTHUS I CAME TO KNOW, both in person and in his late work, greets visitors with a dagger—even proverbially—it could hardly be better concealed. Was the persona adopted in my presence, so gentle and courtly, a sham and a cover-up? Had he truly outgrown his violence of the 1930s, or was that sinister, bizarre side so visible in *The Window* merely an act developed to shield his gentler core? Or is the reverse true, and the sweetness and refinement of the 1990s a front for the inherent cruelty?

What becomes unquestionable in Bloomington is that at least once upon a time Balthus acted with unabashed zeal in trapping and flattening an alluring woman. He did not flinch from the intensity with which he portrayed her as a culprit and then punished her for it.

What is also clear in Bloomington are the precision and exactitude, as well as the rare understatement, with which Balthus elected to render his unusual personal narrative. Balthus constructed his canvas mainly in a reserved and limited palette of yellow-beige, terra-cotta, and dark greens. The difference between these choices and the dominant mode of the time is especially apparent in the painting's current setting because of its proximity to Picasso's 1934 *Artist and the Model.*

The subject matter of the Picasso is surprisingly similar to that of *The Window.* Picasso's model, her string of beads in place but her breasts bared, has been pushed backward with violence. Yet here the artist has used a new and individuated language all his own. And he has fashioned his victim in strikingly modern colors. Those hues have the effect of making us feel we are looking at something other than at the real world conveyed by Balthus's tones with their earthy underpinnings. And Picasso's painterly vocabulary distances us further; his woman's subjugation is not as upsetting to the viewer as is Balthus's.

The Cubistic forms and expressive colors make the Picasso as much a statement about painting as a real image. What Balthus lays out blatantly is here obscured. Abstraction cloaks the psychological immediacy and permits the viewers to feel removed. Balthus's technique, on the other hand, brings us face-to-face with real life. The confrontation is not just Elsa's and Balthus's; it is our own.

II

I have tried to imbue the characters in my tragedy with the same sort of fabulous amorality that belongs to lightning as it strikes, and to the boiling explosion of a tidal wave.

—ANTONIN ARTAUD[6]

If crime lacks the kind of delicacy one finds in virtue, is not the former always more sublime, does it not unfailingly have a character of grandeur and sublimity which surpasses, and will always make it preferable to, the monotonous and lackluster charms of virtue?

—MARQUIS DE SADE[7]

TWO YEARS LATER, Balthus painted another woman at a window—only now the creature in distress appears about to fling herself over the sill of her own volition.

This large, rich, dark canvas was a portrait of Lady Iya Abdy. The diaphanous creature with flowing blond hair is dressed stunningly in a long maroon gown, with billowing sleeves and a full, flowing skirt, by the French designer Madame Grès. With one bare foot elevated on the baseboard, the angel-like actress looks as if she has just alighted yet will soon fly off again.

Her contrived gesture betrays a self-conscious theatricality. The pose is contorted, even by Balthus's standards. With her left hand, she pulls back a transparent, gauzy curtain. She leans awkwardly, her head pressed into her right forearm, her right hand holding a clump of her own wavy hair against the window casement. This is clearly painful. Lady Abdy is more demonic than terrorized, but like the woman in *The Window,* she looks as if she is being forcibly pushed by an invisible agent.

Balthus painted the portrait in 1935, the year following his exhibition at the Galerie Pierre. This was around the time he was designing the sets for *Les Cenci,* a play by Antonin Artaud in which Iya Abdy played the role of Beatrice, its principal character, who is raped by her father and subsequently plots his murder. *Les Cenci* was the first production of Artaud's "Theater of Cruelty." These new connections—with Artaud, with Artaud's radical concept of the-ater, with the playwright's circle—were changing the young painter's life.

Iya Abdy was a fine-boned, beautiful, fair, and blond Russian woman who had, after a brief marriage, divorced Sir Robert Abdy, the fifth baronet so named, in 1928. She had been at loose ends until getting involved with the Theater of Cruelty, which she had helped to launch by joining Robert Denoël, Artaud's publisher, in finding financial backing for *Les Cenci.* Although she had done little acting before, the new venture suited her perfectly by providing her with the opportunity to be onstage, which she had been yearning to do.

Balthus had been instrumental in much of this. He had introduced Lady Abdy to Artaud and told Artaud about the version of *Les Cenci* by Percy Bysshe Shelley on which Artaud had loosely based his play. With Antonin Artaud—sinister, ferociously imaginative, passionately devoted to Balthus—the young painter entered into a powerful, symbiotic relationship.

They first met late one afternoon in 1932 when both were taking a break from their work at a Left Bank café. Balthus later told people that this initial encounter occurred at Artaud's instigation. Whether this was actually the case or was, in retrospect, wishful thinking on Balthus's part, it makes for a nice story. Balthus, according to an account for which he furnished the "informa-tion,"

> was sitting one day on the terrace of Les Deux Magots. Artaud hap-pened to be there and scrutinized him carefully. He went over to the unknown young painter, introduced himself, and said he would be happy to make his acquaintance. In Artaud's eyes, Balthus incarnated

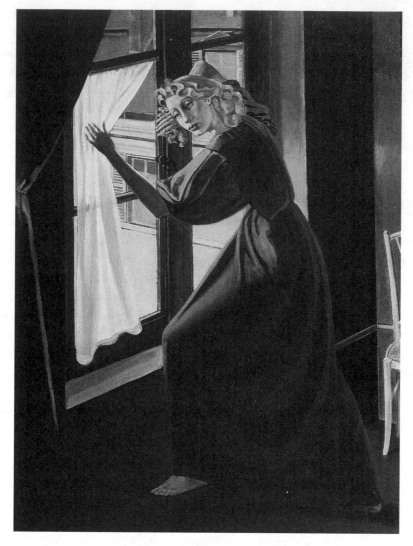

Lady Abdy, 1935, oil on canvas, 186 x 140 cm

the image of his double. Moreover, their physiognomies were so alike
that their friends would take one for the other.[8]

When I met with Pierre Leyris in Meudon, he amplified on the significance of
Artaud's and Balthus's resemblance. Leyris says that Balthus's "force of character was such that he could turn himself into the person he wanted. Once he
latched on to an image—the sort of creature he wanted to be—he could metamorphose into the same." In the transformation in which I knew Balthus, he
had convinced both himself and the world that he was an elegant European

Antonin Artaud,
1934, crayon,
24.1
x 20.3 cm

Antonin Artaud, *Self-portrait,*
c. 1915, charcoal, 15 x 10 cm

noble—the refined, Aryan, aristocratic Count de Rola—but in the mid-1930s, the persona he chose was altogether different. His model was the brilliant, deranged Antonin Artaud. He absorbed elements of Artaud's appearance and personality as if they were in his own genes. As Pierre Leyris explains, this phase in which Balthus sought to become Artaud was the artist's "very dangerous period."

Yet the Artaud role came to Balthus naturally. He and Artaud initially had a lot in common not just in appearance but also in personality. Artaud was "an erudite, melancholy French aesthete, of extraordinary, if alarmingly morose, facial beauty."[9] The description would have applied equally to Balthus. Both Balthus and Artaud were gaunt and hollow-cheeked, with dark, deep-set eyes, similar large, angular noses, and shocks of black hair.

A drawing of Artaud that Balthus made during the rehearsals for *Les Cenci* is easily mistaken for a self-portrait. They were at the Café du Dôme, and Balthus drew it on a piece of Dôme stationery. One of his most frequently reproduced works, it appeared first in the May 1935 *Bête Noire* edited by Tériade and Maurice Raynal, and it has been in practically every major publication on Balthus. What makes it so remarkable is that not only does Artaud have Balthus's face, but he has the artist's primal force. The fiery, bone-lean visage belongs to someone who holds secret knowledge.

Born in 1896, Artaud, like Balthus, had been a prodigy. At the age of fourteen, he had started a magazine. He then went on to do theater work under the actor-director Georges Pitoëff—who was also esteemed by Rilke and to whose performances Rilke had taken the Klossowski boys when they were both teenagers in Geneva. Artaud had joined the Surrealists, but in 1926 had been excommunicated from the movement because his fellow members considered him to be concerned only with his own mind and private literary interests rather than with the world at large. Balthus would have identified with the rejection.

Artaud claimed to be uninterested in human relationships. Content to be solitary—a "*maudit*" or "infernal creator" in the tradition of Baudelaire and Rimbaud—he was Balthus's sort of outsider. He compared himself to the sinister Usher, whom he played in *The Fall of the House of Usher*. Like Balthus, the actor-writer-director was brazen and completely original. The same year the Surrealists expelled him, the impassive, mournful Artaud was Massieu in Carl Dreyer's haunting silent film *The Passion of Joan of Arc;* as the monk who tells Joan she will be burned at the stake, he could hardly have been more demonic, or more handsome.

Before founding the Theater of Cruelty, Artaud publicly attacked Western theater. He lamented its focus on psychological and social issues. Pro-

foundly moved by an Oriental theatrical group that had visited Paris, he preferred their emphasis on gesture over words. Artaud declared that language was
flawed compared with nonverbal communication and direct experience. Com-
plaining that in most plays problems were stated and then settled, Artaud felt
that art need not necessarily provide solutions.

Artaud was especially affected by a performance of Balinese dancing he
saw in July 1931 in an exhibit of works from the Dutch colonial empire at the
colonial exhibition in the Bois de Vincennes. Its appeal lay in its lack of words
and its dependency on light, color, and movement. Artaud agreed with the
concept of a religious or magical role that non-European societies accord to
art, and prized primitive rites in which spectators are awed and terrified. Theater, in turn, should induce trances in its audience and disturb their mental
tranquillity.

These tastes, which captivated Balthus when he met Artaud, coincided
with the young artist's own beliefs. Balthus often spoke to me of his admiration for the silences of Oriental culture, and for Chinese mythology with its
symbolism. He disdains language much as Artaud did; he, too, eschews resolution and summary statement—in deference to ambiguity and open questions.

While Balthus has never explicitly embraced Artaud's goal of putting his
audience into a trance, he has implicitly adopted that approach as well. The
glazed characters in Balthus's paintings stare off into space in their own nonverbal worlds; viewers of these paintings become transfixed in the same way.
Atmospheric haze prevails. Visual absorption supplants steadfast conclusions.
This is precisely what Artaud advised: an attitude toward human behavior in
which normal morality and rationality are insignificant.

FEW MAINSTREAM ART CRITICS in Paris had bothered with Balthus's exhibition at the Galerie Pierre in 1934, and those who did dwelled mainly on the
scabrous subject matter. Even the other painters and art viewers who were
buzzing were not necessarily saying what Balthus wanted them to say. But in
an article that appeared in *La Nouvelle Revue Française* shortly after the show
closed, Antonin Artaud recognized the young artist for certain qualities
Balthus himself believed in.

Artaud's five short paragraphs thereafter became among the few texts on
his work that Balthus has tolerated. It has been reprinted in the Tate and Centre Pompidou catalogs and quoted in other sanctioned publications. It
acknowledges sex and violence more than the artist's current taste allows, but it
also zeroes in on the painterly method. Artaud's commentary treats Balthus's
work as the embodiment of the writer's own wish to fix certain images in all

their power and to evoke a physical and psychological atmosphere through visual rather than verbal representation:

> Balthus paints, primarily, light and form. By the light of a wall, a polished floor, a chair or an epidermis he invites us to enter into the mystery of a human body. That body has a sex, and that sex makes itself clear to us, with all the asperities that go with it. The nude I have in mind has about it something harsh, something tough, something unyielding and—there is no gainsaying the fact—something cruel. It is an invitation to love-making, but one that does not dissimulate the dangers involved. . . .
>
> What we have here is the technique of J. L. David's day in the service of an inspiration that is entirely of our own time; an inspiration full of violence that is just right for our diseased epoch. These are times in which the artist is perforce a conspirator. If he uses "reality," it is the better to crucify it.[10]

RAINER MARIA RILKE had understood and explicated the drawings of the adolescent Balthus as no one else could; Antonin Artaud was the seer of the next decade. In an essay about Lady Abdy in which Artaud discussed Balthus's portrait of her, the writer recognized, as Rilke had, both Balthus's extraordinary artistic ability and his unique relationship to the world around him. Artaud elucidated the way in which the artist entered into, and became, his subjects. His connection with what he painted was the same as with some of his acquaintances; to discern Balthus from the "other" was often impossible.

> Balthus has painted Iya Abdy the way a primitive might have painted an angel; with as sure a technical mastery, with an identical understanding of the spaces, lines, lights, and hollows which constitute space; and in Balthus's portrait, Iya Abdy is alive; she cries out like a writhing sculptural figure in a tale by Achim von Arnim.
>
> It is the face of Iya Abdy and it is her hands which the light devours, but another being, who is Balthus, seems to have inserted himself beneath this countenance and within this body, like a sorcerer who might take possession of a woman with his soul while he himself is stabbed in his bed.
>
> And this same Balthus who makes Iya Abdy into a mysteriously incarnate ghost has made a stage set for my play *The Cenci* that might

well be for ghosts, as awe-inspiring as a ruin in a dream or a gigantic
ladder.

For he, too, is a creature of noble breeding. A kind of forgotten
hero; and it is good that the incredible subject of *The Cenci* should be
the occasion on a stage for the encounter of gigantic beings.[11]

Rilke had focused on the young artist's espousal of elusiveness and of the hazi-
ness of visual and psychological truth. Artaud identified the quality of sorcerer,
and dwelt on his eradication of traditional boundaries. Balthus needed either
to become the people who obsessed him or to possess them.

III

WHEN BALTHUS MET HIM, Artaud had recently published *Héliogabale,* a
study of an infamously cruel and tyrannical Roman emperor. The book was
illustrated with six small designs by André Derain. In his post-Fauve years,
Derain had become one of the most independent artists in France, coura-
geously traditional. Rejecting modern trends in favor of an allegiance to the
lessons of Courbet and to a dependence on nature as the beginning and end of
his art, the gifted and witty Derain was a great favorite of Balthus's. Derain's
illustrations for Artaud's book were little more than thumbnail sketches, but
Héliogabale represented a collaboration between two contemporary voices
Balthus admired almost above all others.

The hallmark of the reign of the flamboyantly homosexual Heliogabalus
was an imaginative cultivation of sexual perversions. The first section of
Artaud's book, "Cradle of Sperm," opened:

> If, around the corpse of Heliogabalus, dead and unburied and slaugh-
> tered by his own police in the latrines of his palace, there is an intense
> circulation of blood and excrement, there is around his cradle an
> intense circulation of sperm. Heliogabalus was born at a time when
> everyone slept with everyone else; and we will never know where nor
> by whom his mother was actually impregnated.

Artaud wrote Jean Poulan of his fondness for sexual hyperbole. "There are
excesses and exaggeration of images, wild affirmations; an atmosphere of panic
is established in which the rational loses ground while the spirit advances in
arms."[12] The same description suits *The Guitar Lesson, The Window, Lady
Abdy*—and *The Street* as it looked in 1934, prior to its subsequent revision.

Artaud's words pertain equally to Balthus's 1952–54 *Room*—as well as to those
other rare paintings in which the view to elegance has not completely obliterated the underlying hysteria.

Artaud wrote of his 1934 hero, "Heliogabalus, the homosexual king who
wants to be a woman, is a priest of the masculine. He realizes within himself
the identity of opposites. . . . Heliogabalus is man and woman."[13] Artaud
developed a similarly androgynous character in *Le Moine*, where the temptress
who leads the monk astray is a female dressed as a young boy. Talking with me,
Balthus denied the notion of such ambiguity in his paintings, yet throughout
his art there are characters with dual identities or indecipherable gender: the
manly teacher in *The Guitar Lesson*, the little girl/male gnome in *The Room*,
the masculine female in *Large Composition with Raven*. In the 1968–73 *Card
Players*, the sex of the two children is so difficult to discern that while some
viewers regard the painting as showing a boy and a girl, I believe it depicts two
boys: Balthus and Pierre Klossowski as children. Often, Balthus's children
sport pageboy haircuts—as he did at age twelve—that could belong to either
sex. Characters who appear at first to be unquestionably female so closely
resemble the angels of Renaissance art that they thus become male.

In *Le Moine*, a monk meets an innocent young girl, kills her mother, then
kills her, and finally discovers that they were his mother and sister. In *Le Jet de
sang*, scorpions emerge from under the skirt of a nursemaid who nourishes
small, shiny beasts in her vagina. In some of Artaud's other writings, women
are threatened with dismemberment, destruction by vampires, and strangula-
tion. He believed that terror and cruelty govern our fundamental instincts.
Balthus has been insisting for years that he has none of the taste for sexual violence and sadism about which Artaud was so unabashed, but Balthus's art begs
the question.

Artaud felt that the imagery of dreams was evidence of an inherent
human violence, the true eroticism of our psyches. When dreams are
"imprinted with terror and cruelty,"[14] they have a liberating effect. The plots of
Artaud's writings derived from a blend of his fears and fantasies—all of which
he connected with the intrinsic human condition. While Balthus consistently
maintained to me as to his other interlocutors that his work neither presents
nor explores the unconscious, his art offers sharp testimony that he and Artaud
were in the same camp. Balthus's unsettling canvases of the 1930s—when the
artist allowed himself the most candor—provide liberation in the spirit of
Artaud.

To recognize rather than dispute the psychological depth and adventurousness of his art is to come to grips with both its true nature and its greatest

Man Ray,
Antonin Artaud,
1926

value, however much Balthus now declares otherwise. Balthus's early paintings possess the expansive and, ideally, guiltless quality that Artaud identified and celebrated in our dream life. Regardless of their maker's reluctance to say so, their revelation of the human psyche is their most profound asset.

As in the artistic production of those non-European cultures embraced by Artaud, primal forces dominate undisguised. Balthus's work joins the seemingly barbaric side of the human mind with the decorous. By now denying the violence of his art—indeed, by succumbing, as the Count de Rola, to complete Europeanization—Balthus is effectively negating one of the great merits of his work. For his art is a celebration of anger and turmoil as much as of grace and tranquillity. Its achievement is in showing the degree to which opposite forces commingle. Uncontrollable cravings thrive in the most ordered, unruffled settings. In keeping with Artaud's mandate, Balthus could reconcile these polar opposites of human existence. Fantasies of murder enter the drawing room.

CONSIDER, BY CONTRAST, MATISSE. When Matisse's characters take tea in the garden or play at a checkerboard, all is innocent and lovely; there is no suggestion whatsoever of violence. This was, in fact, at a great remove from the truth. I once discussed these idyllic scenes of Matisse's family life with his son Pierre, who gave me an account that Balthus had probably heard as well. Pierre told me that just before his father painted those happy domestic vignettes, he and his brother would be fistfighting or throwing each other into the prickers in the rose garden. They played checkers with such apparent innocence only because they were ordered to do so when posing for their father; the atmosphere was complete artifice.

Henri Matisse may have painted his young son's piano lessons as pleasurable events, but by Pierre's account, his study of the piano was an unmitigated torture. When Balthus shows children playing a game, on the other hand, they are indeed schemers and fighters. Throughout his art, the malevolence is patent. He clearly accentuated—rather than disguised, as Matisse had—the violence and repression inherent in life. Precisely as Antonin Artaud recognized, Balthus's more candid renditions of childhood experience, startling and unsettling though they are, are closer to the painful realities of life's earliest years, the frustrations and power issues. For all of Balthus's insistence on his own "wonderful childhood," in his art he went far beyond the illusion of simplicity.

ANTONIN ARTAUD WROTE:

> Apart from a few very rare exceptions, the general tendency of the era has been to forget to wake up. I have attempted to give a jolt to this hypnotic sleep by direct, physical means. Which is why everything in my play turns, and why each character has his particular *cry.*

Attempting to alert others, Artaud once gave a performance at the Sorbonne in which he deliberately acted out his own death by plague. He presented himself with contorted face, dilated eyes, and cramped muscles. Everyone laughed, then hissed, and finally walked out in noisy protest, banging the door as they left. The dramaturge explained the event to Anaïs Nin. He had wanted the audience to experience the plague itself "so they will be terrified, and awaken. I want to awaken them. They do not realize *they are dead.*"[15]

Balthus shared with Artaud both that disdain for the misty-eyed world at large and the goal of firing people up. Most people were numb, they believed. Balthus joined his double in wishing to force confrontation on these sorry souls. Intentionally or not, Balthus painted Artaud's two archetypes: the sleep-walkers, and the people who look as if they have awakened screaming from a nightmare. And like Artaud, he willingly resorted to violence to induce the cry.

BALTHUS'S WORK GRIPPED Artaud largely because it examined the thrill of violence as if through a magnifying glass. At the same time that he wears masks, and masks the personages in his art, Balthus is the great unmasker.

In his Galerie Pierre review, Artaud laments "our diseased epoch." The explanation for that term is offered in his writing about the Theater of Cruelty in which he states, "If confusion is the sign of the times, I see at the root of this confusion a rupture between things and the words, ideas, and signs which represent them."[16] Artaud saw Balthus as having a rare ability to eradicate that rupture. As signs representing life, paintings should reveal life as it really is: replete with its inherent violence, power plays, and craving for seduction. For Artaud, Balthus's art achieved the task at which almost all other contemporary paintings failed.

Artaud wrote that theater should "force the sensibility and the mind to undergo a kind of organic alteration which helps rid poetry of its customary gratuitousness."[17] Balthus made paintings with precisely that capability. And he also espoused Artaud's skepticism about words, insisting that there is no use in trying to bridge the unmanageable gap between spoken or written language and visual images. Paintings must be accepted like cats: as being beautiful and alluring yet elusive and, ultimately, incomprehensible. They are what they are; to deal with them intellectually is to miss the real experience.

Artaud mistrusted the whole notion of "civilization." He felt that "civilized" people had distanced themselves from the innate forces in life in favor of various artifices; he viewed intellectualization—and the imposition of logic, systems, and forms—as diversions and escapes. For Artaud, Balthus was one painter who did not accede to the corrupting influence of abstract thought, who remained close to the mythical and the pagan. So for the rest of his stormy, often mad life, Artaud would passionately turn to, and write about, Balthus.

If Antonin Artaud had lived to see his clone and soul mate become the Count de Rola, with the poses and veneer Balthus adopted for himself and his art once he assumed that position, the founder of the Theater of Cruelty probably would have recoiled. On the other hand, he might have heartily approved.

Balthus, after all, had turned himself over completely to an exalted state of gesture and myth. And in their powerful symbiotic connection, the two sunken-cheeked, angular young men with their shocks of black hair were united above all in their ferocious zeal to stretch and intensify earthly existence.

IV

THE STAGE, TRADITIONALLY, is a place where an individual assumes the part of someone else and commands an audience. Theater was Balthus's natural domain.

As a child in Berlin during the First World War, Balthus had thrilled at the news that his father's sets and costumes at the Lessing and Deutsches Künstler theaters had drawn applause the moment the curtain rose. When Balthus was fourteen, he had submitted his own set designs for a Chinese play at the Munich Staatstheater: the ones that made such an impression on Rilke even if they were not used. He fared better as a young adult. A few months after the 1934 Galerie Pierre exhibition, Balthus designed the sets and costumes for Jules Supervielle's adaptation of *As You Like It* at the Théâtre des Champs-Elysées. These were well received, with Antonin Artaud among their admirers. Artaud singled out Balthus's dark woodland scenes of bold trees with thick foliage in his review of Supervielle's production that November in *La Nouvelle Revue Française:*

> All of Balthus's forests in this production are deep, mysterious, filled with a dark grandeur. Unlike other stage forests, they contain shadows, and a rhythm which speaks to the soul: behind the trees and the lights of nature, they evoke cries, words, sounds; they are all imaginary conceptions in which the spirit breathes.[18]

This was clearly the person to design the sets for *Les Cenci.*

CONTEMPORARY CRITICAL RESPONSE deemed Artaud and Balthus's one actual collaboration a fiasco, but historically it was a remarkable production. In a 1933 essay in which Artaud cited his purpose in launching the "Theater of Cruelty," he explained that this was to be his vehicle for expressing his horror of the contemporary Western world in general and of the bourgeois realism that dominated its theater. His theater company would awaken people to the cruelty inherent in life. Artaud's initial intention was for it to stage Elizabethan melodramas, a tale by the Marquis de Sade, and the story of Bluebeard. *Les*

Cenci, performed in 1935 with Balthus's sets and costumes, ended up being the company's sole, short-lived endeavor.

Artaud depended on two sources for the story of the Cenci family. Besides Shelley's five-act verse tragedy, he had Stendhal's *Chroniques italiennes,* which contains a factual account of the historical events based on trial records. The central character—the monstrous Italian Renaissance nobleman Cenci—is so obsessed by his longing for his daughter that he tortures and rapes her. Artaud himself played the role. At the beginning of the play, he states his raison d'être: "I have one aim left in life: to fashion more exquisitely refined crimes."[19] But in the course of the endless bloodbath of the play, the villain ends up the victim; eventually Cenci is killed by assassins his daughter hires.

In staging this macabre drama, Artaud's goal was to show "the things . . . which human speech is incapable of expressing, and to find things that no one can say, however great may be his natural sincerity and the depths of his self-awareness."[20] Rather than through dialogue, this could be achieved with "a whole language of gestures and signs in which the anxieties of the age will blend together in a violent manifestation of feeling."

The sets were vital to that objective. Artaud called for scene 1 to be "a deep, winding gallery."[21] Scene 2 was "a moonlit garden."[22] Next, when an orgy occurs, "the scene resembles that depicted in *The Marriage of Cana* by Veronese, but is far more savage in atmosphere." Act 2 opens in "a room in the Cenci Palace, containing a great bed in the centre."[23] Its second scene occurs in "an indeterminate place. Waste land, corridor, stairway, gallery, or any other setting."[24] After that, there are no further specific instructions. But with Balthus, the playwright got precisely the results he wanted.

THE 1935 PERFORMANCE of *Les Cenci* took place at the Théâtre des Folies-Wagram, an enormous music hall reached via a long, narrow corridor. Today it is the Théâtre de l'Etoile. Jean-Louis Barrault—who would eventually become, both as an actor and as a director, one of the great names in French twentieth-century cinema—helped Artaud produce it. In rehearsal, Barrault played the part of Béatrice's younger brother Bernardo, although he dropped out before the actual performance. By one account, the problem was that Barrault had other commitments that created a scheduling conflict; by another, he quit acting because he could not tolerate Lady Abdy. Roger Blin also assisted in the production and played the part of one of the two deaf-and-dumb murderers. Roger Désormière composed the music, for which he used modern instruments and broadcast, through loudspeakers, prerecorded sounds of machinery, cathedral bells, and thunder. For Balthus, a relatively fresh arrival on the

Parisian art and theater scene, this was a high-ranking and exciting team in which to be included.

The twenty-seven-year-old artist was equal to the task. His set designs corresponded to the atmosphere the playwright had in mind. In the eyes of viewers as perspicacious as Pierre Jean Jouve and Artaud himself, Balthus's schemes were symbolically apt, and effective in their simplicity and forcefulness.

The artist developed two main sets that were altered throughout the course of the play. The first was an imaginary palace in which, as in a dream, the architectural elements did not quite go together. In the Italian style, according to Jouve it resembled

> an enormous palace-prison à la Piranesi, but where an inner discord, contained within the conflict of colors and certain fragmentations of the forms, produces the dissonant sonority we nowadays expect.

The background, intended as a setting for scenes of torture, consisted of scaffolding, suspended ropes, and mysterious ladders going from nowhere to nowhere. Like ruins, the foreground had a disjointed grandeur. It had the trappings of a royal abode—staircases, columns, arches, and porticoes—without the reality: good practice for someone who would eventually adopt a noble past without solid foundation.

In the second set, used for the final scene, Balthus incorporated a number of symbols that appear throughout Artaud's work. There was a wall of blind windows, darkened or shuttered. Flames suggested major destruction. And there was a wheel, to which Béatrice Cenci was attached.

Some of those motifs would recur in Balthus's work forever after. In a less jarring way, they would continue to have the impact Balthus discovered when making these strident set designs. Blind windows and raging flames would remain central to his artistic vocabulary. Regardless of the bourgeois fittings that surrounded them, they would impart some of the same discomfort they brought to the *Cenci* backdrop. And even though, in Balthus's later art, there would be no wheels to which characters might be affixed for torture, there would be plenty of women held captive and immobilized by other, less flagrant means.

In his program notes, Antonin Artaud proclaimed that Balthus had a perfect grasp of his spirit and intentions. The playwright characterized the first setting as "a phantom decor, grandiose, like a ruin in a dream, a huge ill-proportioned ladder."[25] Artaud referred to the painter as "one of the strongest personalities of his generation who understands wonderfully well the symbolism of both form and color: green, the color of death, yellow, the color of a bad

From left to right: Pierre Asso, Cécile Bressant, Julien Berthau,
Iya Abdy, and Antonin Artaud in *Les Cenci*

Sketch for "Les Cenci," 1935, China ink, 30.5 x 38.1 cm

death, he used this symbolism in his choice of costumes."[26] Against the austere colors of the set, Balthus put Béatrice in a black dress to exhort the assassins to kill her father, while cladding some of the killers in red and green.

In *La Nouvelle Revue Française,* Pierre Jean Jouve described Balthus's designs in such a way that they seem to exist before us, and discussed their significance to this production. Jouve treated *Les Cenci* as a collaboration between Balthus and Artaud, a devastating and effective representation of "our inner life":

> There is a great deal to be written about the secret symbols at work here beneath the surface of visible reality—as may be similarly observed in Balthus's paintings. Thus: the scaffolding like a gigantic ladder and the round columns silhouetted against the sky which raise the Cenci Palace to an alarming height but still bear their own signification; the red curtains hanging like "iron rags" or clots of dried blood; the broken arches suspended in space. The fabrics of the costumes afford a brilliant contrast to this grandiose background, though the "living" substances never triumph over the inert matter of the stone facades, the staircases, porticoes, wheels, and ropes.
>
> Antonin Artaud's direction continuously animates this space in the most creative fashion: here we are constantly "at work." The complex lighting, the movements of individuals and groups, the sound effects and the music all convince the spectator that space and time together form an *affective* reality. Artaud's will, united with Balthus's, is everywhere: excruciations appear in the somber rhetoric of Artaud's own performance and in the incandescent beauty and childlike, primitive action of Iya Abdy.[27]

"This theater is not made to please," Jouve concluded. "Artaud constantly plays against the house and wins. The spectator is continually upset, and sometimes hurt, by the sharpest tension."[28] That shock to the audience, the nerve-racking battle between artist and viewer, is the essence of the work of both Balthus and Artaud.

Les Cenci OPENED ON MAY 6, 1935, with an evening gala sponsored by such prestigious society figures as H.R.H. Prince George of Greece and the Princess de Polignac. Even though the opening and the production included numerous luminaries, and intellectuals like Jouve commended its pioneering force, most of the critics in Paris gave it terrible reviews. Radical though the philosophy behind it was, the play came off as an old-fashioned melodrama. And Artaud's performance as Cenci was considered too extreme.

After seventeen performances, *Les Cenci* closed. The Theater of Cruelty was finished. In January 1936 Artaud, utterly depressed, left for Mexico—in quest of a place not destroyed by Western culture.

V

Man is made to live in the convulsions of anxiety, or the lethargy of ennui.
—VOLTAIRE, AS QUOTED IN ANDRÉ MAUROIS'S *Byron*[29]

IN MEXICO, Antonin Artaud came to feel that he had always been on the right track in believing "that madness, utopia, the unreal, and the absurd will constitute reality."[30] In the northern mountains, he participated in the rites of the Tarahumaras and joined them in taking peyote for days on end. He became obsessed with tarot cards and other aspects of the occult; the irrational world of the spirit became his reality. He also converted to Catholicism.

Yet having given up and denounced his Paris life, Artaud still maintained his relationship with Balthus. From Mexico, he stayed in frequent touch with both the painter and Jean-Louis Barrault. As Artaud became increasingly crazed over the years, Balthus and his work would be both part of the madness and an anchor within it.

MOST OFTEN, WHAT THE dramaturge had on his mind when he wrote to Balthus and Barrault from Mexico were his desperate financial straits. Fortunately, as he explained to his friends, he was able to make some money by writing newspaper articles. One of those essays, which appeared on June 17, 1936, in the Mexican paper *El Nacional*, was entitled "La pintura francesa joven y la tradición." Concentrating on the current situation in French painting under the domination of Surrealism, and on Artaud's belief system about painting since the Renaissance, its linchpin figure was Balthus.

Initially published in Spanish and soon translated into French (although it has never been translated into English), "La pintura francesa joven y la tradición" has remained an essential document in the limited canon of literature about Balthus. Of the writers on Balthus, Artaud was the one who talked with him the most—even more than Rilke. He saw the painter virtually every day of 1934 and 1935, and his account is both personal and astute.

Artaud's essay identifies Balthus as a pioneer and radical at that moment in the history of painting. This text also depicts the forces that for Balthus were so tumultuous, perhaps of such unbearable intensity that the artist's only way of handling them and emerging with his sanity intact subsequent to that period was to take the opposite course from Artaud himself. Artaud embraced his furies until they devoured him, whereas Balthus retreated under multiple protective shells. Reading this 1936 essay, we come to understand the origins of the layers in which the Count de Rola is now so securely encased.

Artaud opened "La pintura francesa joven y la tradición"[31] by citing the young painter Balthus as the leading force in the current reaction against Surrealism. His essay contrasts the differing ways in which Balthus and the Surrealists approached reality. Artaud emphasizes the role of unconscious thought as the primary source of Surrealism, calling Surrealist painting a negation of the real in whose conception there was no difference between the world of dreams and that of reason. He viewed Balthus's vision, on the contrary, as inexorably linked to reality.

It is an explanation that makes perfect sense when one considers how Balthus talked about *The Street* and *The Passage* not as images of sleepwalkers or contrived scenarios but, rather, as forms of everyday reality: familiar street corners with the neighborhood habitués hanging around. Balthus's world, unlike that of the Surrealists, is not an imaginary one. It presents—if in a highly personal, offbeat way—Balthus's reality. His paintings may not show your everyday universe, but they represent his. His women are not the bizarre creatures of the Belgian Surrealist Paul Delvaux's beauty contests; they are— even if blatantly sexualized, even if they look abused—real women. His takeoff point was daily life as you and I know it; he would never have been remotely interested in Magritte's sort of imagery of a sky seen through an eye or the simultaneous occurrence of nocturnal darkness and daylight.

> The forms of Surrealist culture exist in hallucinatory light. Struggling against such divorce and destruction, Balthus confronts the world *starting from appearances;* he accepts sense-data, he accepts the data of reason as well; he accepts these things, but reforms them; I should prefer to say that he recasts them. In a word, Balthus starts from the *known;* in his painting there are universally recognizable elements and aspects; but the *recognizable* in its turn has a meaning which not everyone can reach or, indeed, recognize.

Artaud recognized Balthus as a total revolutionary—both against Surrealism and against academicism of every form.

To situate his friend's work in the context of world art, the playwright declared that a certain artistic tradition was lost at the time of the Renaissance and had never previously been regained. "Painting has fallen under the anecdotal domination of nature and of psychology. It has ceased being a means of revelation and become an art of simple descriptive representation. It has lost that raison d'être, at once secret and universal, which made it, in the true sense of the word, *magical.* The culprits who betrayed that power were Titian, Michelangelo, and Giorgione."

On the contrary, pre-Renaissance—so-called primitive—painting had this force that then evaporated. "The faces in primitive painting transmit the soul's vibration, the profound efforts of the Universe." Artaud credits Cimabue, Giotto, Piero della Francesca, and Mantegna with evoking "actuality," with being near to the mysterious essence of being. "It is to this magical and esoteric tradition that a painter like Balthus belongs."

Artaud considered Balthus, his mirror image, to be the twentieth-century heir to early Renaissance painting—with the "sacred and hieratic primitivism" of those earlier painters. Because of this, Artaud responds to Balthus as if to a hallucinatory drug. He cannot get over what he sees. What others might find bizarre—what makes others uncomfortable—was to Artaud, the author of *Héliogabale,* the creator of the Theater of Cruelty, an expression of truth.

Linking his doppelgänger to artists of the era of Cimabue, Artaud writes:

> There is, in their representations, a kind of esotericism, a sort of enchantment, and by its lines the human figure becomes the fixed sign and transparent filter of a certain magic. This is Balthus's procedure, which will reject the anarchic abandon and the more or less inspired disorder of so-called modern painting, and give us landscapes, portraits, groups which have their own code and of which the symbolism is not immediately apparent. Balthus has painted mysterious groups, a street down which parade the automatons of our dreams; he has achieved concentrated portraits in which, as though on an astrological chart of the heavens, a color, a flower, a metal, fire, earth, wood, or water permits the person represented to regain a true identity.

Artaud, as a poet, felt he was forever dealing with ungraspable ephemera. Artists like Balthus and Uccello, however, had the enviable control whereby they might dominate their own thoughts and impulses by capturing them on canvas.

Like Rilke and Jouve—and, later on, Camus and Paz—Artaud is yet another major literary figure to be profoundly moved by the individualism and unique forcefulness of Balthus's art. Artaud wrote in "Pintura":

Similarly, in a Balthus portrait, the figure evokes the element it most resembles in its life, character and spirit. . . .

He manages to impart life to objects in a light he has made his own. One might say that there is a Balthus color, a Balthus light, a Balthus luminosity. And the characteristic of this luminosity is above all to be *invisible.* Objects, bodies, faces are phosphorescent without our being able to say where the light comes from. In this realm Balthus is infinitely more skillful than Goya, Rembrandt, or Zurbarán, than all the great agonists of that painting which rises out of the darkness glaze by glaze to the light.

Allied to the science of color, Balthus possesses a science of space. He immediately knows just where to place on a canvas the touch that vibrates, following in this the great tradition of painting according to which the painted canvas is a geometric space to be filled. But within this painted, vibrating space, within this invisible illumined space, it is Balthus's personality which summons the colors and shapes and upon them imposes his somber seal. He curdles them, as we say that an acid ferment curdles milk.

It is not Balthus who works with ochers, tawny reds, earth greens, bitumen, and lacquer blacks, but it is a fact that the world he sees sustains itself within this minor range.

Balthus's bitter chromatics signifies chiefly that the life of our time is bitter. In his agile yet concentrated forms, Balthus proclaims the bitterness and the despair of being alive. . . .

With his angular and constricted drawing, his earthquake chromatics, Balthus, who has always painted hydrocephalic creatures with fleshless legs and long feet—which proves that he himself has difficulty supporting his own head—Balthus, when he has ultimately assimilated all his *sciences* of painting, will assert himself as the Uccello or the Piero of our time or even more as a Greco who somehow wandered into it.

IN 1937 ANTONIN ARTAUD returned to France from Mexico. He was soon certified mad, and was locked up in mental hospitals for the next nine years.

This was a time of incarceration more than medical care. When Artaud got out in 1946, he was ravaged by shock treatments that left him toothless and emaciated. His cheeks even more sunken than before, he appeared defeated by life; he died two years later, seriously crazy and addicted to drugs.

Throughout his decline, the dramaturge remained loyal to Balthus. While he was hospitalized, Artaud kept chaotic journals in which the artist's name periodically emerged. In the moments of respite when he was semicoherent and well enough to write more than haphazard notes, he often made Balthus the subject of his ramblings.

While some of Artaud's writing from his later years was reprinted in the 1983 catalogue for Balthus's exhibition at the Centre Pompidou, there is one essay by Artaud that has most certainly *not* been included in those publications sanctioned by the artist. Written in 1947, this is Artaud's reminiscence about Balthus in his first studio on the Rue de Fürstemberg—and the suicide attempt the artist made, or appeared to make, a few months after the Galerie Pierre show.

In 1934 the two were such close friends that they saw each other virtually every day. It was Artaud's habit to drop in daily between 6:30 and 7 p.m.

> He lived in a studio in the Rue de Fürstemberg, a sort of shed on the roof, made of scaffolding, as if framed for eternity, where it seemed he would never stop climbing up and down, or rather remaining at the top of this scaffolding where something eternal or sempiternal was hammered together.
>
> > for in the Rue de Fürstemberg there is a brothel and there is also a chapel where some kind of filthy free-masons come to pray out of a huge emblazoned breviary apparently there are descendants there and relatives of some sort of a sect of old Rosicrucians, old initiates dressed and undressed, but who are dressed and undressed only upon entering and leaving the old house in the Rue de Fürstemberg, for with regard to the remainder of the interior they are purely and properly,
> > which is to say very
> > co
> > cho
> > WOE TO ANYONE seeing herein a shadow of pornography, woe and curses.

For there was on one side the life of balthus who had to live, to pay for the roof over his head, his sleep, his three meals a day, his work-site, that is, the place where he could work, and then the work itself, its value, its effectiveness.

It is well known what the undertow is:

that elastic motion the sea imparts to its own loins.

well, this article is like such a motion which I impart to myself in order to regard myself

in the depths of my own past.

and to regard myself regarding

> Balthus
> BALTHUS
> The same Balthus
> Balthus

Balthus dreaming in the depths of his own past.

The same Balthus all alone and who tried to commit suicide one evening, and whom I found all alone in his bed and to his left on a chair a little vial of 15 grams of Sydenham laudanum, and beside the vial a photograph. I looked at the vial, the photograph, and Balthus was hardly breathing at all, and it seemed to me that the allusion was too strong, too crudely strong for me to be able to accept it.

Suicide by laudanum was too much too banal, and suicide on account of a woman, suicide because of a lover's despair for me to be able to accept it and admit it.

I had gone into the room to see Balthus the way I came to see him every evening around 6:30 or 7. The door was never closed in the evenings. Balthus was lying on his bed as he used to do sometimes, but somehow sunk into his own sleep, more than sunk: one can say

> buried
> actually
> BURIED.

He was no longer breathing, he was dead, not dead like someone already buried in his coffin, but dead like someone.

And that was how I saw that terrible black corpse, black and poisoned, whom I confuse with a young man lying on his bed, dead and intoxicated on a certain bed in the Rue de Fürstemberg, in a house next door to a brothel, and who in the depth of the first judgment was fulminating and one after the other released, what he ought never to have done and which was the first sin, to paint in the anchored astral spirit all the paintings lining the wall and which seemed to be finished, when it takes a hundred million eternities and applications each one added to the next in order to produce what Balthus in fact better than Poussin, Corot or Courbet has produced: a callused hand of life, of an illuminated exterior which is not filmed but painted.

Artaud was something of an expert on laudanum. Anaïs Nin, his occasional lover, describes him with "his mouth with the edges darkened by laudanum, a mouth I did not want to kiss."[32] Artaud understood the use of this morphine-based medicament sufficiently to recognize that Balthus had been careful not to take too much.

Artaud was also guided by his intimate knowledge of Balthus's nature. He deduced that this overdose was a staged act that Balthus was sure to survive. Moreover—as Artaud realized when he walked into the studio that fateful afternoon—the painter had timed his maneuver meticulously. Balthus knew that his friend would be arriving, as he always did like clockwork, at what would be precisely the right moment to rescue him.

When he found Balthus lying there, Antonin Artaud instantly called Pierre Leyris to the scene. Leyris described this to me when I met with him in 1992. When he arrived in the artist's studio flat on the Rue de Fürstemberg, he, too, immediately recognized the overdose as a dramatic gesture more than a genuine attempt to take his own life.

Balthus had arranged his body and the photograph at his side as skillfully as if he had painted the scene. The comatose state was both real and a pose. Lying on that bed in his studio, Balthus resembled the major prototype of his art: limp, dazed, overwhelmed by circumstance. As always, Balthus was playing with perceptions, manipulating the psychological and visual elements to garner the desired response, focusing on how others would see him more than on his inner self.

But even if the scenario was a contrivance and Balthus meant to be discovered, he was still in a serious condition and required medical help. Together Artaud and Leyris rushed their friend to the doctor. Balthus was treated and in little time returned to his life as usual, but it had been a close call.

Describing this incident, Pierre Leyris provided a fascinating aside. The doctor was Jewish—and someone whom Balthus liked and respected very much. Leyris mentioned this to me as a specific example of the duplicity of Balthus's perpetual anti-Semitic quips. In the 1930s there was no possible way for the artist to cover up his Jewish half—Baladine and Pierre Klossowski were still too much in the picture—and Balthus had close Jewish associates. This is one of the reasons Balthus's presentation of himself later in life struck Pierre Leyris as so particularly pathetic.

. . .

As Pierre Leyris pointed out to me, even in his "dangerous, mimetic phase" Balthus never lost sharp consciousness of his devices. If Balthus wished to become—and simultaneously endear himself to—Antonin Artaud, what better way to do so than to take his look-alike's favorite intoxicant, touch the level of danger and extremis Artaud cherished, and finally be rescued by Artaud himself?

CHAPTER TWELVE

CATHY DRESSING

"I'd not exchange, for a thousand lives, my condition here, for Edgar Linton's at Thrushcross Grange—not if I might have the privilege of flinging Joseph off the highest gable, and painting the housefront with Hindley's blood!"

      —HEATHCLIFF, IN EMILY BRONTË'S *Wuthering Heights*[1]

Men and women who, perhaps naturally very calm, and with feelings moderate in degree, and little marked in kind, have been trained from their cradle to observe the utmost evenness of manner and guardedness of language, will hardly know what to make of the rough, strong utterance, the harshly manifested passions, the unbridled aversions, and head-long partialities of unlettered moorland hinds and rugged moorland squires, who have grown up untaught and unchecked, except by mentors as harsh as themselves.

      —CHARLOTTE BRONTË[2]

As for poetry—well, poetry comes into Balthus' painting in the picture called "Cathy Dressing," where the body of a young girl in love imposes itself in dreamlike fashion upon a canvas that has the realism of Courbet's "Atelier." Imagine, in life, an artist's model suddenly metamorphosed into a sphinx, and you will have some idea of the impact of "Cathy Dressing."

      —ANTONIN ARTAUD[3]

I

ANTONIN ARTAUD AND Pierre Leyris were not the only people who might recognize what ailed the drugged, unconscious artist with that photo at his side. Even a complete outsider who had happened into the Galerie Pierre a few months before could see, if he knew how to read the clues, evidence that Balthus was suffering from unrequited love.

The man who has repeatedly claimed he should be "an artist of whom nothing is known" had created a canvas that was pure and candid autobiography. What was part theater in that overdose of laudanum was—as Balthus's double well recognized—also a manifestation of pain. The painting laid bare the source of his anguish.

The "unsatisfaction of his desire" cited by Artaud referred, of course, to a woman. A dozen years earlier, Balthus could scarcely bear his powerlessness when, for all his wit and charm, he could not put his hands around the beloved cat who had fled from him forever. Now the free-spirited love object eluding his grasp had plunged him to even greater depths. Artaud and Jouve esteemed him much as Rilke and Baladine had, but not everyone was under his sway. For a Byronic hero, the situation was intolerable.

The painting that recorded Balthus's torment was *Cathy Dressing*—the representation of a scene from *Wuthering Heights.* In late 1932 Balthus had begun to make a series of pen-and-ink illustrations for Emily Brontë's 1848 novel. In those drawings and in this large canvas, the artist repeatedly cast himself as Heathcliff. Every image of the swarthy misfit is a straightforward self-portrait.

Catherine Earnshaw, the high-born young lady who spurns Heathcliff, is represented by Antoinette de Watteville, the Swiss aristocrat who repeatedly rejected Balthus's advances. It was Antoinette whose photograph had fallen to the floor out of Balthus's limp hand when he took his overdose of laudanum.

BALTHUS'S PSYCHOLOGICAL REALITY and what he read in a nineteenth-century novel became indistinguishable; he readily conflated his own life with a work of fiction, himself and Antoinette with Brontë's anguished pair. And Heathcliff was a brilliant role to assume. He was sexy, ferocious, and unlike anyone else. Able to transform himself from victim into victor, Brontë's anti-hero moved from a low rank and early poverty to wealth and entitlement. His rise gave him power over the world that had oppressed him.

Balthus had first read *Wuthering Heights* when he was fourteen. The book became an obsession. Already passionate about the English language and its literature, now he would be satisfied only if he could make them an integral part of his life. Brontë's highly charged but hazy narrative was the ideal vehicle. Her gripping account of nightmarish violence alternates between flashbacks and so-called actuality; the text is a sequence of stories within stories, memories interspersed with present horrors. Dreams, fantasies, and the shaky, unsettling reality of life all merge. And underlying all the complex shifts and layers is a romantic adventure in which the underdog prevails. The novel mirrored both Balthus's way of seeing and his aspirations. His connection to *Wuthering Heights* and his identification with Heathcliff determined the tone and appearance of his art, and shaped his personal comportment, from then on.

WITH THE INSIGHT OF ONE who really understands the creator's interaction with his or her act of creation, Somerset Maugham wrote about Emily Brontë's relationship to *Wuthering Heights* in a way that applies directly to Balthus's attitude to his own work—most especially *The Guitar Lesson:*

> Why did Emily need to hide herself when she wrote this powerful, passionate and terrible book? I think because she disclosed in it her innermost instincts. . . . I think Emily put the whole of herself into Heathcliff. She gave him her violent rage, her sexuality, vehement but frustrated, her passion of unsatisfied love, her jealousy, her hatred and contempt of human beings, her cruelty, her sadism. . . . I think Emily loved Catherine Earnshaw with Heathcliff's masculine, animal love; I think she laughed when, as Heathcliff, she kicked and trampled on Earnshaw and dashed his head against the stone flags; and I think when, as Heathcliff, she hit the younger Catherine in the face and heaped humiliations upon her, she laughed.[4]

Maugham's observations about Brontë pertain to Balthus's approach in *The Street, The Window, The Guitar Lesson,* and numerous other paintings to come:

> I think it gave her a thrill of release when she bullied, reviled and browbeat the persons of her invention, because in real life she suffered such bitter mortification in the company of her fellow creatures; and I think, as Catherine, doubling the roles, as it were, though she fought Heathcliff, though she despised him, though she knew him for the beast he was, she loved him with her body and soul, she exulted in her power over him, and since there is in the sadist something of the masochist too, she was fascinated by his violence, his brutality and his untamed nature. She felt they were kin, as indeed they were, if I am right in supposing they were both Emily Brontë. "Nelly, I am Heathcliff," Catherine cried. "He's always in my mind: not as a pleasure, any more than I am always a pleasure to myself, but as my own being."[5]

Maugham also points out that while *Wuthering Heights* is "a love story," it is "perhaps the strangest that was ever written, and not the least strange part of it is that the lovers remain chaste."[6] This last statement further explains its appeal for Balthus. The machinery of love in Balthus's universe seems to be one of watching and attraction more than of consummation. The ultimate goal is supremacy—far more than tenderness and intimacy. So it appears, anyway, in Balthus's art—as well as in most of what we know of his personal life prior to the mellowness of old age.

Wuthering Heights contained ingredients that would remain central to Balthus and his art forever. Brontë set her action in vast country houses with fires blazing in their open hearths. The characters are in a frenzy of emotion. Rejection, domination, and submission—at times extremely violent—are pervading themes. No wonder Balthus was inspired to develop imagery and poses in his illustrations that would recur throughout his subsequent art. Much of his life's work can be seen as illustrations of Brontë's novel.

IN HIS 1979 BOOK ON BALTHUS, Jean Leymarie put forth the notion that Balthus "was familiar with the Yorkshire moors long before he illustrated *Wuthering Heights* in 1933."[7] We have no idea how or why, but apparently we are supposed to take Leymarie's word that this was so.

It was not the first time that the idea had been propagated. In his 1956 Museum of Modern Art catalog, James Thrall Soby had written, "In youth Balthus spent much of his time visiting in England."[8] The artist must have told him as much.

In one sense this was perfectly true. As a teenager Balthus had been a voracious reader of English novels, and he was one of those fortunate people for whom the world of books was more real than his actual surroundings. His imagination sustained him. When Balthus and Baladine were living out of suitcases in the Spiros' small flat in Berlin, the boy may have been mentally skipping steps on the grand staircase of an English mansion. On an army base in Morocco, he might have liked to envision the butler pouring his port.

But there is no reason whatsoever to believe that Balthus actually got to England in those years. His whereabouts throughout his adolescence are documented on a week-to-week basis in Rilke and Baladine's correspondence, and whereas his stays in Beatenberg and Geneva and Berlin and Muzot and Paris are discussed so specifically that we can practically say where he was on any given day, there is no mention of any journey across the channel.

Balthus was so in love with the world of *Wuthering Heights* that it is not surprising that he eventually chose to acquire this personal connection to it. But it is almost pathetic that in 1994, upon the republication of his *Wuthering*

Heights illustrations in a highly deluxe edition published by Sidney Shiff's Limited Editions in New York, the "artist of whom nothing is known" declared in an afterword:

> In 1922, when I was fourteen years old, my dearest friend the late Bill Hayter introduced me to two Yorkshire lads who kindly invited me to stay with them in Leeds. In their company I discovered the wild beauty of the moors around Hawarth which left an indelible impression upon me. . . . Thus, when many years later, I decided to yield to the compulsion to illustrate *Wuthering Heights,* the vivid memories of that wondrous first journey to Yorkshire were an important source of inspiration.[9]

There is a chance that some ten years after 1922—in the early 1930s, when Balthus returned to Paris from the army—he made a junket to the British Isles at just about the time he was developing his Brontë illustrations. Although there is no contemporaneous documentation of such a trip, it is not impossible. The journey at age fourteen with those "two Yorkshire lads," however, is probably no more real than Heathcliff's dream of conjugal bliss with Cathy in the moments when Heathcliff is completely alone and Cathy is in the arms of someone else.

PHYSICALLY, HEATHCLIFF WAS practically Balthus's double: "a tall, athletic, well-formed man," with "decision of feature" and readily visible intelligence. Like Balthus, the deep-voiced hellion generally dressed in dark clothes. With his shock of black hair, his sunken cheeks, his sallow skin, and his "eyes deep set and singular,"[10] he could equally have been Antonin Artaud.

Those remarkable eyes were "that couple of black fiends, so deeply buried, who never open their windows boldly, but lurk glinting under them, like devil's spies."[11] They had two deep lines between them, and "thick brows, that instead of rising arched, sink in the middle." Both Heathcliff and Balthus had features that were like their single names: compact and intense, with no element wasted or gratuitous.

Separate Christian and surnames would never have had the same mystique or punch. That one pared-down appellation, however, provided a sense of sheer strength and suggested an unknown, unknowable past. Its bearer needs nothing more, and has less visible baggage than other people.

At one extreme, Heathcliff would be "rough as a saw-edge, and hard as whinstone! The less you meddle with him the better." Yet he had a cultivated side as well. "A half-civilized ferocity lurked yet in the depressed brows and eyes full of black fire, but it was subdued; and his manner was even dignified: quite divested of roughness, though too stern for grace."[12] Brontë's descriptions are equally of the young Balthus.

HEATHCLIFF WAS THE WANDERING child brought into an established household in which other children, their lives remarkably stable, seemed to have everything going for them—all the property and sense of place implicit in their last names. This was Balthus's situation exactly—when he and his mother were on the verge of moving in with the Nolkes, and again when he stayed with the Wattevilles in Bern.

When he first encountered Heathcliff, Balthus instinctively identified with certain aspects of the teenage misfit's personality and envied others. Brontë's demonic hero started as a blow-in from nowhere, but he would ultimately come to control everyone around him—a power Balthus sometimes had, but which periodically failed him. The only way, in fiction or in real life, to deal with early deprivation was to return victorious. Heathcliff managed—with little conscience—to elevate himself with admirable success. The character once degraded eventually becomes lord of the manor.

Nelly Dean, the housekeeper in the novel, gives Heathcliff some pivotal advice on how to emerge from his subjugation.

> You're fit for a prince in disguise. Who knows but your father was Emperor of China, and your mother an Indian queen . . . ? Were I in your place, I would frame high notions of my birth; and the thoughts of what I was should give me courage and dignity to support the oppressions of a little farmer![13]

It is as if Balthus—who read the book repeatedly, at various ages—took this counsel to be aimed directly at him personally.

Heathcliff managed this ascent in part because his history was entirely unknown—not "where he was born, and who were his parents, and how he got his money."[14] By the early 1930s, when his connection with *Wuthering Heights* had flourished to the point of becoming a full-fledged obsession, Balthus was probably already toying with the idea of abandoning at least one side of his past. To have been brought in from the outside, with no facts known, suited him more than his own complications. To come from nowhere was better than to come from Pinsk.

. . .

WHATEVER THEIR ORIGINS, Balthus and Heathcliff shared a sense of entitlement. I had, in the summer of 1994, the good fortune to discuss this aspect of Balthus and Heathcliff along those very lines with the novelist Iris Murdoch.

Dame Iris had long admired Balthus's work but had never before realized his connection with *Wuthering Heights*. After she told me that Brontë was among her favorite writers and one to whom she often returned, I showed her reproductions of *Cathy Dressing* and Balthus's *Wuthering Heights* illustrations. The novelist could hardly get over the drawings; she said that, unlike other illustrations, "they are exactly the way one pictures the book."[15] She also told me her theory that Heathcliff is the illegitimate son of Hindley Earnshaw, the man who brings him home. Although few other people agreed with her, she was convinced of it.

That lineage, of course, meant that Heathcliff was truly entitled to a lot of what he ends up with. This, too, may have struck a chord with Balthus: even if others did not know it, he thought of himself as highborn, and as worthy of a title, as all the rich young people he knew. He had to fight for the position others assumed with ease, but he considered it to be rightfully his.

CATHERINE EARNSHAW made a perfect Antoinette de Watteville.

> She was slender, and apparently scarcely past girlhood: an admirable form, and the most exquisite little face that I have ever had the pleasure of beholding; small features, very fair; flaxen ringlets, or rather golden, hanging loose on her delicate neck.[16]

For the aristocratic Catherine, position and wealth are second nature.

Balthus adored such assurance, and the right to it. Brontë's imperious young heiress has the rank and station of his own resistant inamorata from Bern. Catherine lords her edge of superiority over Heathcliff in much the same way that Antoinette spurned Balthus.

Yet Catherine is no marble goddess; she has just the sort of complexity Balthus craved. Brontë makes her a blend of woman and man, of self and love object. This is what Somerset Maugham is driving at in quoting Catherine saying to her maid that she and Heathcliff are a single being. The crossover, and the sort of obsessiveness that brings it about, was Balthus's home territory.

In the woman in *Cathy Dressing*, who is both Brontë's heroine and his own future wife, Balthus created a blend of confidence and melancholy that was the embodiment of his desires. She was the distant, imperious, haunting seducer he would succeed in conquering; as such, she was also, in female form, the creature he would become.

Cathy Dressing DEPICTS a moment in *Wuthering Heights* when Catherine is blatantly rejecting her would-be suitor (color plate 7). The large oil is based on a China-ink drawing that Balthus identified as illustrating the moment in Brontë's text when Heathcliff asks Cathy, "Why have you that silk frock on, then?" Cathy has just managed to inform Edgar Linton that the coast is clear for him to come and visit her at home. Then, while she is beautifying herself for Edgar, Heathcliff shows up unexpectedly. Cathy lies that she is not busy that afternoon and is staying in because it is raining. Heathcliff, knowing better, feels completely ostracized. Having asked the woman he adores why she is dressed so enticingly, he follows the question with a panicky "Nobody coming here, I hope?" Cathy stammers another falsity: "Not that I know of him." She then further denigrates her despondent listener by telling him that he should, at this very moment, be working in the fields.

Balthus has put his own personal twist on the scene. The fantasy of how the silk frock is "on" is pornographically sublime. In the drawing, Cathy wears a dress—albeit a tight and slinky one rather than the sort of Victorian garment Brontë must have had in mind. In the painting, she sports an item whose sole purpose is to emphasize her nudity. Here Balthus has draped Cathy in silk as if to follow the rules and match Brontë's text, yet in effect he has stripped her naked. He has also shaved her pubis; otherwise a fully mature woman, she is as hairless at the genitals as a preadolescent. This creature completely suits his own taste. She has the curves of a Cranach Venus, the vulva of a ten-year-old, the pose of a slut, and breasts that partially resemble those of a dancing milkmaid but, with their muscular thrust and sideways nipples, ultimately look like no one's at all.

In *Cathy Dressing*, Balthus has transformed a Victorian novel into out-and-out erotica. Not only does the narcissistic, self-absorbed Heathcliff have both his hands wrapped around the wooden chair support in a way that suggests self-stimulation, but Cathy has her left hand on a distinctly phallic wooden mirror support and is fingering its tip. The Count de Rola would surely deny such a reading, yet the more we look at *Cathy Dressing*, especially in the context of Balthus's other paintings of the same year, the more sexualized it becomes. And the more we understand of Balthus and his fantasies, the more pertinent do these particular forms of sexuality seem.

The way the maid combs and pulls Cathy's hair seems a reiteration of the violent hair-pulling of *The Guitar Lesson;* Balthus savors such moments of women in pain. As a youth he had adored *Struwwelpeter* with all its sadistic yanking on long tresses. Now the victim is not a child but a mature female seductress, whose dense and knotty hair eroticizes her face—by accentuating and compensating for the lack of any at her pubis.

That face, however, is a mask. Cathy thrusts her oversized head forward in a way that separates it from the rest of her body. From the neck down, she is earthy, sensuous, and seductive—entirely alive, though unlike anyone we have ever seen before—yet her face is unreal. Its features seem pasted on rather than intrinsic. At the same time, that patently artificial mouth with its downward cast, her flared nose, her arched eyebrows, and her stony, half-shut eyes rolling upward are pained, armored, and ferocious.

Balthus would play down the alien and brutal aspects of his subjects in the years to come—as he would learn to wear his own masks and hide his real self—but this is the vision of the female he would continue to present, in subtler, quieter, softer form, for the rest of his life.

BALTHUS RENDERS HEATHCLIFF, too, just as he wants him. For a field laborer, he is exceptionally well dressed. Brontë makes him an impostor; Balthus sees to it that he is one with tremendous style. Deliberately using his own face—with the knowledge that at least part of the audience for this painting would recognize it as such—Balthus has made the lad as attractive as he is intense, and very dapper even if he is broke.

Consider his shoes. They are earthbound, solid, strong. Balthus might have painted them as mud-covered Wellingtons; instead he shows them as handsome English-style boots with a nice shine. He could not resist giving himself a touch of class.

Yet he is depressed, as all the world should see. Good-looking and well-turned-out though Balthus/Heathcliff is, he has been brutally snubbed. He knows the whole story: that he is being lied to, that he is being deceived and rejected by the goddess in his midst, that he is a solitary outsider. Clearly Cathy is having her glorious hair combed on someone else's behalf. She thrusts her body forward like a parody of temptation, but does so in the opposite direction from where Heathcliff is. Her eyes are focused on someone not visible to us. Balthus/Heathcliff responds by basking in his own anguish—and, it appears, hatching a plot. He sits impassively, but he is nobody's fool. The poor fellow knows without question that he is where he does not belong—and that he is not wanted. He may enjoy the momentary luxury of being in the company of an attractive woman, but he is allowed to approach no further.

The sorry Heathcliff, embalmed in grays and browns, is completely diminished by his position and by Catherine's focus on another. Imprisoned, he yearns for power, while Catherine has all the freedom and confidence he lacks. He is the nobody; she has the appurtenances of wealth. Not only can she afford to have a lady's maid comb her hair, but she has a range of props at her disposal: the well-made vanity table with its ovoid mirror; the fine filmy gown, almost like angel's wings, that circumscribes her nudity; expensive black silk shoes. A coquette and a showgirl, she has the devices as well as the allure she requires to put her beauty on display and tempt her admirers. Heathcliff so far has few such advantages.

Yet the victim is the despot in the making. Balthus himself would ascend to Catherine's position—and had already begun to reach it. As an artist, unlike the hapless outsider with whom he identified himself in this painting, he had, by 1933, developed the skill to attract attention and present visual wonders. The persona from which he showed himself so estranged was, in fact, one whose scheming and sense of detail he himself was mastering.

CATHERINE'S GAUDY SHOES elevate her as if on small platforms. They show how deliberate she is in her wish to entice, to appear delicate and tall. She is conscious of every nuance, just as her creator was.

The maid Nelly, on the other hand, wears slippers that put her flat and heavy on the ground. Those oversized red boats on her feet are just one of the ways in which Balthus has amused himself with this frump. Cathy is an exultant queen bee; Nelly, a pathetic, nasty old spinster. Cathy's hair epitomizes abandon and sexuality; the maid's tight little bun embodies repression and repressiveness. Nelly wears the clothing of servitude, while her mistress enjoys the garb, the nakedness—and the know-how—of freedom.

And if Catherine's tapered thighs turn gracefully, the maid's gigantic and rigid legs have the dimensions of tree trunks. Balthus paints details of this sort the way he disseminates information about his life. He feels free to exaggerate and distort, as well as to spoof, as long as he makes the statement he wants. Here the goal is a mockery of the inhibited bourgeoisie: the teachers who chastised him when he was twelve in Geneva; the character who held the cat so awkwardly in *The Quays;* the round-shouldered old biddy who, twenty years after *Cathy Dressing,* would make her way across *The Passage du Commerce Saint-André.* In his sardonic portrayal, Balthus impales the type forever.

. . .

IN *Cathy Dressing*, BALTHUS has stopped and frozen the action. As in *The Street,* forward progress has been arrested as in a freeze-frame. The locking of time allows for the ambient feelings to smolder indefinitely. The Venus-like Cathy—both Brontë's heroine and Antoinette de Watteville—is thus immobilized, with the body and pose Balthus desires, for luxuriant savoring. If the work of most of Balthus's contemporaries in 1933 was true to the frantic pace of the era—so that looking at it invariably makes us hurry forward, in a full adult rush—Balthus's gets us to linger, at the pace of adolescence.

Not only is this the moment in *Wuthering Heights* when Heathcliff's rejection is at its most palpable, but it is also the point when violence and the struggle for power reach a crescendo. Shortly after Cathy stammers out her lie and instructs Heathcliff to go work in the fields, she confesses that the Lintons

"Why have you that silk frock on, then?,"
1933, China ink, 50.3 x 41.2 cm

may be coming. Heathcliff instantly tries to gain the upper hand. "Order Ellen to say you are engaged, Cathy!" he demands.[17]

Human existence consists of taking every possible opportunity to be the one in charge. The pendulum perpetually swings from subjugation to control. First Heathcliff imperiously denigrates the Lintons as "pitiful" and "silly"; Catherine gazes at him in rage and berates him mercilessly for offering "no company at all" and knowing nothing. Then she humiliates Nelly with a stream of abusive language, pinches her "with a prolonged wrench, very spitefully on the arm,"[18] denies having done so, and slaps the miserable servant with "a stinging blow." A moment later, Catherine boxes one of Edgar Linton's ears.

Yet the result of this outbreak of violence is that it "effected a closer intimacy" between Edgar Linton and Cathy. As if in response to her barbarity, they soon move from the status of friends to lovers. Like the teacher in *The Guitar Lesson*, she is seductive because of her viciousness as well as her looks. Malevolence is sexy.

BALTHUS HAS DEPICTED the fierce scenario with acumen. *Cathy Dressing* is a powerful, arresting canvas. The rhythms are rich, the tonal contrasts vivid. The curve of the servant's apron echoes the lines of Cathy's right hip and thigh, and of the mirror. Everything serves to point up the contrast between the man and the woman. Heathcliff is clothed and dark, Cathy naked and light. He is all compressed angles; she stands free. A void establishes distance between the man and the housekeeper, and isolates him as a loner; this visual device emphasizes that while he is surrounded by a world he finds beautiful, he is not part of it. Cathy—unique in the annals of painting with her large head, exaggerated breasts, hairless pudenda, and hooker's slippers—is spotlighted. This is life as a novel, as theater.

Again the implausible and the real coexist in perfect alliance. Heathcliff, Catherine, and Nelly are fictional, but they are situated in actual space. The complex atmosphere that results from the simultaneous isolation and connectedness of the three characters works only because the action takes place in a familiar and accessible everyday setting. Balthus uses the cupboard in the corner of the room as he does the buildings in the background in *The Street:* to make an eerie and uncomfortable situation entirely real as well as aesthetically appealing.

That cupboard, like the shop fronts in the sixth arrondissement, is post-and-lintel architecture: the well-ordered bourgeois world within which the emotional havoc occurs. Balthus has painted this piece of furniture with impeccable articulation. The shadows within the recesses of the door panels read clearly. The darkness that emanates from the cupboard interior, revealed in the crack of the open door, is a minor tour de force. Here, as in the domestic scenes Balthus would paint for the rest of his life, furniture shows that a sober and convincing artist has been at work. The chair and table legs, the rush seat, and the drawer pull all ring true. We think we might run our hands over the wainscoting and feel its ridges. The sheen of the wood and the cracks between the floorboards are palpable. These real, and reassuringly familiar, surfaces and substances provide a counterpoint to the disarming violence and elusiveness emanating from the three hostile characters in the scene.

The furniture and architecture look as if they have been laid out with a draftsman's tools. Cool and regular, each solidly constructed element has been placed in obeisance to the grid. The people in the painting, however, assume jagged, audacious angles. Cathy sways forward. Nelly is twisted. Heathcliff, in spite of his attempt at repose, is no more relaxed than a contortionist. His legs bend and twist painfully within his baggy pants.

The effect is precisely what Artaud intended gesture to be in the Theater of Cruelty. Antoinette/Catherine's stance epitomizes her aristocratic confidence and womanly power. Nelly's bowed spine denotes her servitude and calls to mind the long years in which she has been bent over her work. The way that Balthus/Heathcliff is hunched over isolates him; crushed by all that surrounds him, he has been forced inside himself. Physically sturdy and big-boned, he seems to hold considerable power in reserve while he cowers and broods. Two years later, he will emerge the vainglorious King of Cats, but he is not there yet.

YET BALTHUS LEADS US to feel that in some ways he is no more successful and confident as a painter than as a lover. His modesty and sense of doubt come through in his painting of Cathy's ankles. He deliberately has us see his waffling. As if to make his indecision visible, to declare himself the struggling painter, he has allowed us to see vestiges of the paint from what must have been an earlier version of both ankles, even while the more decisive painting on top makes them tapered.

The process of painting thus seems an ongoing effort rather than a fait accompli. Instead of seeming smug, Balthus leaves the impression of having finally despaired and said, "Enough, it has the better of me." Neither here nor anywhere else does he give the sense that he has finished a painting to his satisfaction. He wants us to know that as far as he is concerned, he has never gotten it quite right, that the painter's battle to be faithful to appearances and to achieve the desired rhythms and balances is never won.

In occasional details, however, he seems satisfied with his success. There is no doubt or hesitancy in the renditions of Heathcliff's trouser legs or the wooden cupboard. And when Balthus wants to be unrealistic—by enlarging a head, fudging a hand, exaggerating the proportion of limbs—he does so easily. He can be perfectly literal about a shadow, absolutely faithful to its shape and character—and then absurd about a human form.

This is, after all, the same Balthus who will be proper and courtly and rule-abiding when he talks to us on the phone or receives us in his living room—and then will dole out complete lies, or conveniently pretend not to hear, or fire off some deliberately outrageous diatribe. In his art, he jumps from realism to exaggeration, from an old-master technique to the style of a primitive or a child. He makes the shifts discriminately, but according to his own rules. At the dinner table, it is his decision alone when to be decorous and when to turn his back on someone. What matters is that the choices are his own.

II

IN *Cathy Dressing*, BALTHUS'S painterly skill—however much he announced its limitations—again puts emotions at center stage. Everything contributes to the psychological narrative.

Moreover, by casting himself and his beloved as the two central characters, the artist declares the display intensely personal. Thus he invites, and makes inevitable, exactly the sort of assumptions and ruminations he has repeatedly insisted are insignificant.

It seems the most deliberate contradiction: this focus on personal, literary elements and, then, the instruction to disregard the biographical and thematic content of his art and consider only its visual and formal sides. The maneuver is like presenting a deliciously tempting array of foods to ravenous onlookers before insisting not only that they must not touch a morsel of it, but that to desire it or consider taking a taste is a mark of intellectual inferiority and aesthetic ignorance.

Yet we cross the boundary—precisely as we are beckoned. In so doing, we can get to know Balthus quite well after all. Violating his rules, we learn that he is not really so mysterious.

Cathy Dressing SHOWS HOW obsession—wanting to be where we are not welcome, desiring what we cannot have—makes someone alive. Mental gyrations are everything. To the self-enclosed, isolated, and—at this moment—passive lover, although the object of his ardor is only a few feet away, his thoughts and

fantasies about her are even more real than her vibrant body. Longing and plot-
ting are more intense than gratification.

This is, consistently, Balthus's psychological hierarchy. Even in his few
group scenes, his characters are isolated in their private mental universes, usually engaged more by reverie and desire than by action. Bernini and Rodin—
even Cézanne in his early erotic canvases—show their lovers united. With the
exception of one late drawing based on a Japanese print of a copulating couple,
in Balthus's art the male and female invariably remain separate. The central act
is dreaming and desiring. Consummation rarely occurs.

Balthus's paintings render their subjects immobilized, overcome by a mix
of memory and longing, craving something they do not have. And they put
the viewer in a similar state of paralysis: wondering and wanting, rather than
knowing and possessing.

In *Cathy Dressing*, what Balthus emphasized in his mirror image was
Heathcliff's isolation and self-absorption. Though totally preoccupied with
Antoinette/Cathy, the misfit remains in a different sphere from her. This is the
moment to brood beneath his covering, not to make love. Cathy flaunts her
sex with abandon; next to the most flagrant display of nakedness, Heathcliff
remains clothed in somber Victorian style, his white collar still on, his cravat
meticulous. He is on fire but imprisoned.

The preoccupation with unachievable, out-of-reach beauty—the impossibility of the conquest of painting as of this woman—the sense of unattainable riches that belong both to past memories and to the distant future pertain
to Balthus himself as well as to the characters in his art and the state in which
he puts the viewer. In Heathcliff, the artist has, indeed, found his true autobiographical representative: melancholic, insolent, full of desire. Heathcliff/
Balthus reveals himself to be vehement, yet remains like a child who says, "I
have a secret, and I'm not going to tell you what it is."

Clandestine, powerful, craving transformations: Brontë's dark hero was
indeed Balthus's perfect stand-in. The homeless and disenfranchised Jew who
would make himself landed gentry, the forlorn and suicidal lover who would
in time conquer the woman who had rejected him, could hardly have fastened
upon a better match for himself in all of fiction. Driven by the most potent
desire for the unrealistic and unavailable, possessed by an uncanny knack to
make them real, Balthus and Heathcliff were one.

Balthus, and the viewer of his art, can never quite have his feast guiltlessly
and wholly. We are all relegated to the role of unfulfilled voyeur. The artist has
presented beauty in his ideal terms, yet has always kept it unavailable. His
finest landscapes—*Champrovent* (1941–43), *Montecalvello* (1979)—are exqui-

site in their tone and balance, yet we see them at a remove, like a distant dream we cannot unlock. The forbidden Cathy is Balthus's archetype; through the act of painting, Balthus could make everything entirely to his liking. But he, and we, comes no closer than Heathcliff to possessing this ideal.

IN *Cathy Dressing,* BALTHUS WAS declaring himself. We see him as a plotter. At age twenty-five, he seems to be considering just how far he might go.

There is no saying what the people who saw this self-portrait-at-a-remove at the Galerie Pierre may have read into the artist's sullen, scheming face, but those of us who view it today can only marvel at the underdog's ultimate victory. Whatever Balthus as Heathcliff was imagining, he has outdone his grandest dreams. He married the aristocrat. Then he kept her as his wife while for many years invariably having one or another far younger women as his model and living companion. Not only did he eventually wed the wellborn woman whose photo once lay at his side in his staged suicide attempt, but he managed to maintain apparent equilibrium in their marriage while also enjoying his other, completely public, alliances. Then she further complied with his wishes by willingly granting a divorce so he could marry a second time—again to a wellborn woman, only now one who offered the added advantages of being younger and Oriental.

The impoverished artist who once identified with Brontë's anguished field-worker later bought mansions and castles. He has had high society eating out of his hand, and prestigious hostesses desperate for his appearance at their parties. He has lived to see this canvas that once hung unsold in a small gallery, just around the corner from the garret studio on which he could scarcely afford the rent, end up in France's national museum of modern art, where it is safeguarded today as a treasure.

In the 1980s a single canvas by Balthus came to command a price higher than the value of the de Wattevilles' house in Bern. That the artist would achieve all this could never have been guessed by the viewer of *Cathy Dressing* in 1933, but that he wanted all this was patently clear.

THIS CANVAS BASED ON A Victorian novel was, in 1933, also its maker's presentation of himself as old-fashioned. Then as now, Balthus was more drawn to Romantic nineteenth-century life than to the vicissitudes of his own era. The style and subject matter of *Cathy Dressing* were as unrelated to the Paris of the times as his life in Rossinière was removed from the nineties.

He was, however, a traditionalist with temerity. The artist cherished the past, but in his own lubricious way. The manner of articulation was one thing, the object another. So even if the French public might have sanctioned his style, in the few decades since they had attacked Manet's *Olympia* with umbrellas and sticks the majority had hardly come far enough to tolerate Balthus's Catherine. Most viewers were shocked, all the more so because the young man who had turned a Victorian heroine into a modern slut had done so in the politest, most educated manner.

Balthus seems to derive particular pleasure from embracing history and formality and then taking license with them. He has centered Cathy's foot on the rug design in the same construction, and with the same precision, that Jan van Eyck used for the placement of his Holy Virgin's feet within the story cycle told on the floor tiles of their church interiors. But having followed the holy schemata, Balthus then makes his Madonna naked—and seductive according to his own highly personal taste for the haughty and brazen.

CATHY IS LITHE AND LUMINOUS like a Cranach Venus, but her erect breasts are her suitor's unique invention. They dart out. Throughout the paintings of this period, Balthus makes female breasts into aggressive objects that lunge— bearing little resemblance to the real thing.

In his later work, Balthus would reduce breast size; his women would become relatively flat-chested, with the proportions of girls a year or two into puberty. Haze would envelop their bodies. Nothing about their sexuality would be as blatant as in the artist's paintings of the early 1930s. But in *Cathy Dressing* and the other canvases of those young and unguarded days, the women are unabashed about who they are and what they have to offer. And Balthus did not dissemble about how he wanted them.

While Cathy's body is in all other ways mature and fully developed, because she has the hairless pudenda of a ten-year-old, the exposed, reddened crack of her bare vagina is presented with complete candor. Balthus would keep pubic hair off his women forever after, but in his later art the blatancy of this early canvas would give way to blurriness and he would use shadows and impasto to render the crotches vague. Here nothing is in doubt.

III

ALL OF BALTHUS'S INK DRAWINGS for *Wuthering Heights* depict incidents either of torture or escape. The dominant activity is mockery, the prevailing

emotion lust. The anguished characters are either fearful or scowling. No wonder Iris Murdoch declared these, unlike other illustrations, to reflect just the
way one mentally sees Brontë's novel.

Emily Brontë "embraced the Swedenborgians, a sect within the Anglican
Church who believed in sex after death. Heathcliff and Cathy's romance in
Wuthering Heights reflects Brontë's Swedenborgian sympathies because they
consummate their affair only after they have died and are wandering the moors
as ghostly lovers."[19] Balthus, however, dwelled exclusively on the emotionally
charged scenes of torment and subjugation that dominate the first half of
Brontë's narrative. All the images that Balthus chose to draw are a preamble to
that postmortem consummation.

WHEN BALTHUS MADE THESE drawings in the early 1930s, it was easy
enough for him to identify with Heathcliff as an angry, frustrated young man
and outsider. At the point when Brontë's hero grew from being the rough-
hewn misfit, Balthus stopped and his illustrations came to an end. But he must
certainly have hoped that his own evolution would parallel Heathcliff's ascendancy. For Heathcliff eventually takes over Wuthering Heights and becomes
lord of the manor. He is the ultimate victor—and Balthus must have studied
his upward course carefully. Not only does Heathcliff gain wealth and stature,
but he becomes castellan: the governor of the castle.

Castellan indeed. In Poland that word signified the senator appointed by
the king as chief of an entire town. In 1962, when Balthus became director of
the French Academy at the Villa Medici in Rome at the behest of André Malraux, he assumed that very position. For the unhappy boarder in his Jewish
cousins' small Berlin apartment, the impoverished resident of the one-room
attic studio on the Rue de Fürstemberg, the social outsider shunned by the
noble Antoinette and ostracized by her world, to ascend to this seat of power
was a victory that made Heathcliff's rise slight by comparison. The story
Balthus illustrated when he was, above all, a dreamer in 1932, forecast to an
astounding degree his own ultimate elevation—of which the years in Rome
were in many ways the peak.

Wuthering Heights did not merely provide the themes that would dominate his art for the next fifty years; it was the fictional model to which his own
very real course of action ultimately bore an astonishing resemblance.

OVER THE YEARS, OF COURSE, Balthus has gone well beyond his fictional
mirror and has acquired more grace than sternness. The charm and polish of

the Count de Rola leave few traces of Heathcliff in evidence. When I was chatting with the artist in his garden in Rossinière in the spring of 1993, I asked him if he thought that my eleven-year-old daughter, who was playing on the lawn, would soon be ready for *Wuthering Heights*.

In his Missoni cardigan, surrounded by diplomats and bankers from Bern and Paris, the artist now tacitly rejected the book that had once obsessed him. He told me, his most bemused expression on his face, that he had recently reread parts of the novel and found it "extremely strange and puzzling." He could not understand its excesses. No, Lucy should not be exposed to anything so disturbing.

Balthus said that in recently rereading the novel, which, he told me, he had first read at age fourteen in Yorkshire (the point when, I was certain, he was in actual fact sharing his cousin's room in Berlin), he was struck by how "weird" it was. He dismissed Brontë's novel with a shrug of the shoulders. What now intrigued him the most about it was "the landscape—so like the Roman Campagna. A strange, even bizarre landscape—not beautiful but intriguing." He added that he hadn't liked the movie; Olivier was a great actor, but not quite right. Merle Oberon, whom he subsequently met, was, he felt, miscast as Cathy.

Balthus clearly no longer found Brontë's exclamatory style—and her flagrant fury—to be to his taste as they once were. In fact, now he wished to renounce such sordidness. He looked at it as an outsider. But for a very long time, Heathcliff—and *Wuthering Heights*—was the fiber of his being.

CHAPTER THIRTEEN

ALICE

No crime is vulgar, but all vulgarity is crime.
Vulgarity is the conduct of others.

—Oscar Wilde[1]

I

THE MOST OVERTLY SALACIOUS painting of all in the front room at the Galerie Pierre in 1934 was simply called *Alice.* Like *The Guitar Lesson,* the canvas and its title reflect Balthus unmasked—or premasked.

The subject is a leathery young woman who stands before us like a blend of conqueror and sacrificial offering (color plate 8). Her pudenda, and one of her substantial breasts, are on full view. Her scanty, translucent slip is there only for the ineffectiveness of its attempt at modesty. The undergarment has fallen beneath the single breast—which occupies two-thirds of the woman's chest—and its hem is hiked up above her bulging mons veneris.

The woman elevates her left foot on a chair seat. Contrasted with that delicate and fragile piece of furniture, her gargantuan legs and compact body have tremendous strength. Her pose seems designed for the presentation of her vagina. Her dark labia and pubic hair, depicted in graphic detail, are plainly visible near the center point of the painting.

There is nothing pretty about the woman's blatant lubriciousness. She is more daunting than tempting, the suggestion of sex more sinister than pleasurable. She treats her body with full knowledge of its power, but is contemptuous of the world it will sway. Her naked self appears as an effective weapon like Coomaraswamy's bomb. The woman is an unusually introspective aggressor, strangely detached from the sexuality with which she is so bountifully endowed. She baits and titillates the viewer—yet we are made to feel sleazy and embarrassed just to be in her company.

Like a jaded, worn-out tart, this brazen creature offers herself while remaining in charge. If she so chose, she could easily resist anyone who succumbed to her charms. Her legs have the musculature and apparent strength of the pincers on a prehistoric reptile; she could clamp us to death with them if she wanted to.

And what name had Balthus managed to give his snarling hussy? That of the most beguiling and innocent of little girls, the ultimate sweet nubile fantasy figure: Alice. If he can recast the Virgin Mary as the teacher of sex in *The Guitar Lesson,* then why not transform Lewis Carroll's child heroine into a tough hooker getting ready for the evening's work? The beguiling ingenue and ferocious muscle-woman are one and the same.

So the only creature in all of Balthus's art to have pubic hair is named after a prepubescent. In all of his other paintings, the artist returns older women to their girlish state by removing that badge of maturity. Here he has recast a fully developed female as a child. But the end result is the same—a declaration that every female, of whatever age, is a mix of harlot and little girl.

IN HIS LATER ART, Balthus would cloak women's breasts and genitals in shadowy haze and fudge the details. His female subjects would become less forthright, and so would he. The bare floorboards and stark, caned-seat side chair of *Alice* would give way to Oriental rugs and upholstered settees. But what is raw and naked here would always lurk underneath.

Jean Leymarie has called *The Guitar Lesson* the artist's only erotic painting. And the point Balthus made to me more than any other, in all of our conversations, is how mystified he is by the notion of sexuality in his work—which he considers as far-fetched as the suggestion of violence in it. *Alice* makes Balthus and Leymarie's whitewash laughable. The skirts might come down a few inches, and the women assume a look of innocence, yet not only the eroticism but also the mendacity would always be there.

Whether he made it blatant, as in *Alice,* or muted, as in his subsequent work, Balthus could never do other than imbue his subjects with sexual suggestiveness. What is both frightening and refreshing about this canvas from 1933 is that it presents a consuming, troubling libido with such complete candor. At his most psychologically honest, Balthus had immense courage in breaking traditional boundaries of behavior. Brazenly shedding inhibitions, he readily summoned all of his prodigious painterly skills to the fore.

The basis of Alice's existence seems to reside in her genitals and breasts—and to some extent her hair. While other artists tend to depict these body parts more romantically, emphasizing their sensuous charms, Balthus has rendered these female attributes burdensome and traplike. The weight of the exposed breast must be difficult to support; the hair is miserably tangled. Femininity here has none of the softness or grace with which painters ranging from

Velázquez to Matisse have traditionally imbued it. Rather, having a body is an ominous matter.

As is so often the case with Balthus, we witness a form of torture. Balthus's denial of the brutality within his art is ridiculous. Alice is combing her hair in a way that suggests she is coping with terrible, painful knots. This is at the opposite end of the spectrum from hair-combing in, say, Renoir or Degas—where it is a gentle, pleasant, everyday act. Alice holds her hair with her left hand to minimize the sensation, but the process looks arduous nonetheless. Like the combing in *Cathy Dressing* and the hair-pulling in both *The Guitar Lesson* and the first illustration for *Wuthering Heights,* the image makes us wince. It conjures *Struwwelpeter*—that favorite of the Klossowski boys which, in the entire canon of children's literature, is as gruesome and sadistic a volume as could be found. The setting for *Alice* furthers the sense of discomfort: a space like a prison cell, with colors that suggest a military sort of desert fatigue.

BETTY LEYRIS POSED for this painting. When I asked her about the experience—almost sixty years after the fact—she recalled it with a grin. She was a showgirl at the time, and Balthus a close friend. She and her husband considered him a brilliant and exciting painter, and the nature of the depiction did not concern her. Madame Leyris had thick, muscular legs and seemed more amused than fazed that Balthus presented them as such.

Betty Leyris and her husband did, however, emphasize to me that Baladine Klossowska had this body type as well. They characterized Balthus's mother as sturdy and earthy—both in physique and personality. The Leyrises knew her well for a long time. She was, they fondly recalled, a sensible, no-nonsense sort of person—with precise views on how to clean a room, and a figure that suited her nature. The prototype for boldness had existed in Balthus's life long before 1934.

Yet even if the overdeveloped Alice was based on Betty Leyris—and had a body type similar to his mother's—Balthus has designed his model's form to suit himself. With her low-slung left breast so large and pendulous that it seems to weigh her down, the right is so much smaller, and painfully compressed, as to be practically nonexistent. It is as if Alice, even more stridently than the teacher in *The Guitar Lesson* and the victim in *The Window,* has elements of a true Amazon:

The name theoretically derives from the Greek words "*a*" (without) and "*mazos*" (breast). The Amazons were said to be a tribe of powerful warrior women who chopped off one breast to draw the bow more easily. As for the other breast, it was used to nurse any female children they bore; male children were disposed of. "The missing breast creates a terrifying asymmetry: one breast is retained to nurture female off-spring, the other is removed to facilitate violence against men."[2]

Meanwhile, Alice's head—like Cathy's in *Cathy Dressing*—is both over-sized and masklike. And as for those legs, their form and proportions are grotesque. They scarcely taper at all. Either thigh, singly, is practically the width of the woman's waist. The source of this girth, clearly, is more muscle and bone than fat. Balthus has depicted a woman not merely strong and ath-letic but possessed of an animal-like power.

My experience of Balthus in Rossinière—the erudite gentleman, the solicitous and thoughtful host, the passionate spokesman for the complete pri-ority of painterly issues over psychological ones—tempts me to gloss over the ramifications of *Alice*. Having been granted the rare luxury of being able to present Balthus's own point of view—instead of joining the less select group of conjecturers—might I not just let other matters drop? I could avoid the nature of this particular eroticism, declare the approach to women self evident, lam-baste the notion of interpretation, and honor the sanctity of the creator's view-point precisely as Coomaraswamy would have me do.

After all, I cannot abide the small-minded judgmentalists who snicker pruriently at the artist's handling of little girls. Spare me the rejoinder I heard hundreds of times as I worked on this book—from people as sophisticated as John Russell on down—that I must be careful not to leave my daughters alone with the eighty-five-year-old Balthus. Based on both my direct knowl-edge of him and what I have heard from each of "the Three Sisters" as well as his other models, Balthus has conducted himself within the confines of taste and propriety with most of his young female models. The clichés promul-gated by the Humbert Humbert school of Balthus observers obfuscate the gentleness, as well as the humor and genius and inventiveness, of the man, and commit the further sin of ignoring the beauty of the work. Wouldn't it be better, then, to focus only on the purely painterly side of Balthus, and on the artist's own dictums, and dwell exclusively on his marvelous taste and phe-nomenal skill?

And it certainly would have been appealing to maintain my position within a friendly and glamorous inner circle by playing according to the rules.

All I would have needed to do is adhere to the artist's guideline that anything smacking of the psychoanalytical is poison in the approach toward art. It's a nice thought: to stay out of the territory that has been explored ad nauseam in discussions of Lucien Freud and Francis Bacon. A line or two on sexual issues and the artist's attitude toward women would suffice.

But Balthus has, in effect, shot himself in the foot and defeated his own purpose by declaring that the art says it all. For what *Alice* makes undeniable is that Balthus has truly denigrated this woman who violates us. We would have to be like robots not to deal with this sordid, terrifying image in all its complexity.

By pulling down the chemise and hiking it up, the artist has, in his way, raped the woman he has named for a little girl. He has done so while pandering to a preference we have now seen repeatedly: for baring one breast only, thus sexualizing the traditional representation of the Madonna with her solitary mammary engorged for nursing. Time and again, the same ambiguities underlie Balthus's obsessive portrayal: the Holy Virgin as hooker, dispassionate seductress. In *Alice* as in *The Guitar Lesson,* her mix of ferocity, haughtiness, and purely erotic allure—painted as if it is the only truth—blatantly beckons us to consider Balthus's lifelong views on females, and on humanity in general, however much the imagery and its ramifications contradict the artist's verbal declarations of his opinions.

This prey/conqueror is the prototype of all the women in his art. Alice offers herself to us corporeally but looks off abstractedly into the distance. She flaunts her body but seems removed from it. Like most of the characters who populate Balthus's paintings, she is dazed and blitzed while managing to exert considerable power. She poses as raw flesh while not really engaging in life.

Balthus and his amiable spokesman Jean Leymarie would have us discuss the colors and forms and write off the rest as part of a youthful phase. But how can we follow suit? What matters *more* than the up-front sexuality and the sinister cast to it? Why does Balthus put womanliness in this single, monotonous hue, this calculating, dull light?

She is in a corner, trapped—yet ready to attack. The chair on which she rests her foot is ridiculously flimsy beneath her heavy leg; she might easily crush it into splinters. All the material substances, in fact, dissolve in obeisance to some supernatural force; we see through the chair caning, and through Alice's camisole. The ratchet in all of this, the machine at the center, is her dark vagina. There power resides.

The artist who has devoted his whole life to masking and dissembling thrives on ripping off the covering, on throwing all protection to the wind with unparalleled zeal. Calculating, sensuous, capable, and frightening: the

young/old *Alice* is the essential Balthus woman. The object of the artist's obsession, she is also the ultimate expression of the man himself.

Alice APPEARS TO HAVE BEEN the first of his mature paintings that Balthus
sold. Its buyer was Pierre Jean Jouve, the man who had reviewed *Les Cenci* and
written the vivid description of Balthus's studio on the Rue de Fürstemberg.
Jouve was a writer of Baladine and Erich Klossowskis' generation. Born in
1887, he had known Balthus's mother since 1925, when Jean Cassou took him
to her studio on the Rue Malebranche on a visit Jouve found especially memorable because he also met Rilke there.

In the late 1920s Jouve grew to know both of the Klossowski boys. In 1930
he and Pierre collaborated on a translation of Hölderlin's poems. After Balthus
returned to Paris from Morocco in 1932, the writer renewed his acquaintance
with him. Twenty-one years older than Balthus, Jouve came to consider the
young painter a sort of protégé.

Jouve presented himself with old-world formality and deliberateness. He
spoke slowly and precisely and comported himself with the utmost courtesy.[3]
The writer and his wife lived a fashionable life with Chinese servants. Balthus
surely admired this sense of style, particularly as it stood in contrast to Jouve's
work. His writing included pure eroticism of tremendously imaginative beauty
and sensuousness, as well as stories and novels full of dissipated characters,
most of them frustrated in their lust, who found their salvation not in absten-
tion or compromise but by becoming deliberately diabolic. Reality and its lack
perpetually collided.

Jouve's universe was populated by people who consciously develop highly
sensuous, paradoxical images. In *Le Monde désert* (*The Desert World*) of 1927, a
woman whose name, Baladine, is thought to have been based on Balthus's
mother, says, "It's true, isn't it, we become demons ourselves."[4] This notion
that people have something of the devil in them was the essence of the writer's
vision. Jouve regarded sex as laden with evil. His poetry, as characterized by a
recent scholar of his work, "reveals life as an endless, hopeless circle of lust and
despair in a stifling sin-laden climate."

Jouve was married to Dr. Blanche Reverchon, a psychoanalyst who was
central to the initial acceptance of Freud in France. In 1924 Jouve and Reverchon cotranslated Freud's *Three Essays on the Theory of Sexuality*—which,
although it was published only under Reverchon's name, was a joint effort. In
1933 they collaborated on "Moments in a Psychoanalysis," an article that documents a young woman's mental illness and transcribes some of her bizarre
dreams. Jouve believed passionately in the Freudian method as a way of pene-

trating the human mind. For all the antipathy to the classic psychoanalytic approach which Balthus—and, even more so, Setsuko—made a point of repeatedly emphasizing to me, the Freudian approach once dominated the thinking of many of Balthus's closest associates.

Jouve deemed Balthus extraordinary upon their first meeting, when the artist was still a teenager. He was particularly intrigued by the youth's connection to Rilke. Jouve felt that Balthus had benefited profoundly from "the very noble influence" of the poet.[5] When, shortly after Jouve met Balthus, Rilke died, Jouve could see the immeasurable effect of this sad event on the young artist. "At the time, Balthus was a young man, endowed with a singular gravity," Jouve later wrote.[6] It was, Jouve felt, as if Balthus, who had not yet reached his eighteenth birthday (or, rather, nonbirthday), took on, with even more zeal now that Rilke was no longer alive, his mentor's intensity. Painting was, now more than ever, Balthus's life—just as poetry had been René's.

Jouve admired Balthus's disdain and wisdom in rejecting almost all of the current trends. It took brains and independence to shun the latest bandwagon—and instead to grow to know the Louvre by heart. "Already, for this curious young man, the whole lesson was to be relearned. . . . Balthus was beginning as an independent, resolutely apart from any school, though for him the essential was the true school."[7]

In Jouve's eyes, an element of death inspired both the invention of Balthus's paintings and their execution. He found that their candid morbidity provided both authentic grandeur and a constantly tragic character. Jouve revered Balthus's art for this revelation of a world other than the absurd one in which we pretend to live, for its rich mixture of anguish and splendor. With *Alice* hanging where it did—alongside the bed in his wood-paneled bed chamber—he experienced the cold, enticing, nasty lust of Balthus's vision full force, unadorned and unrepentant.

JOUVE WROTE AN ESSAY in the late 1950s in which he conjured *Alice* for his readers and described some of its effects on him.

> Imagine a young woman with blank eyes, dressed in a brief chemise and combing her hair with a determined stroke, while raising one of her legs high on an ordinary chair, quite openly revealing her genitals. This of course was the strange companion of my nights—I mean that she attended my sleep and hence could creep inside. . . . She knew my first morning glance, but also the secret of my nights.[8]

Jouve then tells of a morning when he woke up and, stupefied, discovered that Alice had disappeared from the painting, leaving it nothing but a canvas painted a uniform yellow.

> I flung myself out of bed: Alice, known for twenty years, was no longer on the canvas. . . . For several days I remained under the spell of an event I dared not recount, for fear of seeming deranged in mind and because that would have exposed my nocturnal relations with Alice. . . . The picture was still empty.[9]

Jouve begins to dream of Alice. She gambols beside him "with a certain obscenity." He becomes obsessed. "Once . . . I saw Alice appear beside me"— when he is on his usual route to his young mistress's house. Alice is everywhere. Alice "intervened between life and myself, thereby rendering all actions impossible." She appears in the presence of his mistress, where Alice, "in the pose of the picture, came between myself and the woman, not as an accomplice but as a policeman."[10]

He feels that Alice wants to make love with him. "The sadism of that image sought my flesh and my spirit." The crisis escalates. And then, when his wife believes that she is seeing him die, Alice resumes her place in the picture frame.

With Jouve as with Balthus, art and life, sex and malevolence, all went hand in hand.

IN 1935 PIERRE JEAN JOUVE had dedicated a novel called *La Victime* to Balthus. *La Victime* is thought to have been based on "The Facts in the Case of M. Valdemar" by Edgar Allan Poe—to whom Balthus often referred as one of his very favorite writers. Set in Germany at the time of Martin Luther, Jouve's narrative depicts a sort of living damnation.

The central character, Valdemar, is a satanic creature often in a frenzy of passion. Known for his incendiary kiss, he is a seducer who feels himself in bondage to death. Shunned by the townspeople, he is sentenced to hell.

A woman named Dorothée is drawn to Valdemar. She is similarly cruel and malignant, "soulless, obscene, dumb, bearing about her the odor of corruption."[11] "In a cannibalistic dream she seizes and devours a balloon filled with blood."[12] She is Valdemar's ideal mate; when the two of them get together, they are like sleepwalkers. Dorothée dies almost instantaneously after the onset of their relationship but is then reanimated by a friend of Valdemar's.

Her new life does not last, however. She soon falls back into death. Then Valdemar is tortured and executed.

It was natural enough for Jouve to dedicate a book to Balthus. They were close friends in this period, spending an extended stretch of time together in 1936 when Balthus went with the writer to his hunting house in Soglio— especially appealing because it was in the Grisons, not far from where Giacometti was born. As an old-style gentleman of radical thought, Jouve was both a mentor and a soul mate to the young artist, and must have enjoyed honoring him with a dedication.

Beyond that, *La Victime* demonstrated Jouve's view that spiritual disaster and desire go hand in hand, and that unconscious forces and self-absorption destroy us: phenomena that he deemed the very essence of Balthus's art.

II

> *Extraordinary how easy it is to stick a knife into a woman, he thought, and when he saw the result—that she fell, eyes rolling back in her head, he withdrew the knife just as easily without any hurry, and tossed it on the floor. . . . Now that she was dead, he desired her furiously, and would have liked to kiss her on the mouth and make love to her.*
>
> —Pierre Jean Jouve[13]

SHORTLY AFTER *La Victime* APPEARED, Balthus made a painting with the same name. *The Victim* presents the ashen body of a woman—either unconscious or dead. Seemingly raped, she looks both twelve years old (according to her breast development and lack of pubic hair) and twice that age (based on her face, skin, and size). Her body is spread on a white sheet.

It was the ambiguity of this painting that inspired me to go speak with Linda Fairstein, chief of the Manhattan District Attorney's Sex Crimes Unit; I wanted an accurate diagnosis of the woman's situation. My hope was that this astute criminologist would tell me what Balthus would not. Was the "victim" dead or merely comatose? Could the crime be identified?

Fairstein was a superb source for an understanding of *The Victim*. After cautioning me that she opposed gratuitous interpretation and would probably see a Balthus nude only as a formal exercise, she quickly reversed herself and said, "If you gave it to me, I'd say it's a sex crimes scene photograph." Applying police procedures, she turned the reproduction of Balthus's canvas ninety degrees so as to study the event from another angle.

"She looks like a sex murder victim," the prosecutor pronounced—
"exsanguinated." The discoloration of the subject's skin pointed to her having
been "strangled or asphyxiated"—as if the dagger on the ground may have
been used to threaten, but not to implement the crime. The conclusion was
that this was not the aftermath of a spontaneous act of violence. Rather, it was
a setup, which "looks disturbed" and in which "nothing is natural." The exsanguinated hue, not by accident, was a similar color to the flesh of Piero's biblical
personages and provided the detachment and remoteness that Balthus had
imbibed at age eighteen and would cultivate forever after. Balthus had devised
a scene in keeping with Pierre Jean Jouve's text, but also very much according
to his own taste.

IT SEEMS A COMPLETE CONTRADICTION, looking at *The Victim,* to consider
the second sentence Balthus put forth in the *"propos"* to that 1992 exhibition
catalog for the Musée Courbet:

> Hence nothing is further from me than the taste for horror, a fact
> which separates me from expressionism as from a painter as talented as
> Bacon. On the contrary I believe that no great painter has failed to
> acknowledge this profound truth: painting is made to help us live.[14]

Even a rather simple, seemingly straightforward, and exquisitely eloquent
statement like that opens itself up to multiple readings. First of all, I grin at the
sheer hypocrisy of "as talented" for Francis Bacon. One should give Balthus
credit—he is simply being tactful here—but I know from conversations with
him that he deplored Bacon's work. Yet what immediately precedes the falsity
is perfectly true: Balthus's art is nothing like Francis Bacon's. His violence and
self-revelations are of a different sort than those of the English painter; more
importantly, they approached the technique of art with few of the same priorities. The Francis Bacon who really mattered to Balthus is indeed the sixteenth-
century essayist who pointed out that verbal accounts are never to be
trusted—and that ambiguity is rich.

Yet Balthus must have been well aware that Bacon was the other artist
who, in the 1980s, was periodically called "the greatest living painter," and that
Bacon, too, was linked with Giacometti and the tradition of figurative art.
Balthus invited Bacon to the Villa Medici and certainly knew his work well.

As for Bacon's view on Balthus, here Michael Peppiatt, who has written
about both artists, provides an interesting account suggesting that the English
painter regarded Balthus in some of the same ways that Picasso did:

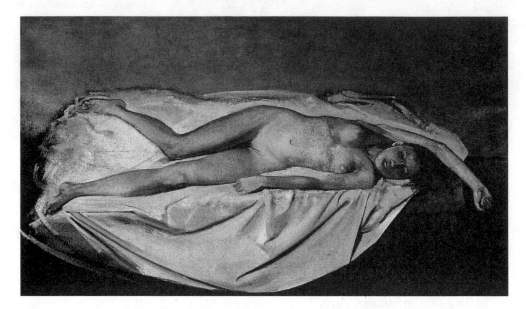

The Victim, 1937, oil on canvas, 132 x 218 cm

Another of the very few contemporary artists whom Bacon admired, albeit with marked reservations, was Balthus, who had already settled into a somewhat ambiguous Old Master status in the French art world. . . . Balthus had been one of a mere handful of painters working inventively with the human figure when Bacon was attempting to find his way, and he had accordingly scrutinized the older artist's work. As so often, he admired only a fragment of the *oeuvre.* "I think Balthus is trying to do something new with an old technique. . . . I myself think you have to break technique, break tradition, to do something really new."[15]

Peppiatt told me that Bacon would subtly disparage Balthus by characterizing him as the person who had redesigned the rooms at the Villa Medici rather than as a painter. Bacon emphatically praised Balthus's expertise in modeling and coloring the plaster wall surfaces there. In this way he made Balthus sound like a first-rate interior decorator—but nothing more. When discussing his or other people's need to refurbish living quarters, Bacon would suggest, as if heaping compliments, "Maybe we should have Balthus do it."[16]

    In spite of Bacon's and Balthus's disparagement of each another—Balthus's being even less subtle than Bacon's—and their completely painterly techniques as well as chosen personas, the two artists shared a macabre sensibility. Although there is much truth in the justification Balthus gives in his Musée Courbet statement for his lack of taste for horror, we must consider that these words come from one of the principal players in the Theater of Cruelty, an ardent fan of Edgar Allan Poe, and the man who painted *The Victim*.

COMPLEMENTARY TO OTHER WORKS in Jouve's book *La Scène capitale,* the novel *La Victime* was ultimately included, in 1946, in a volume called *Histoires sanglantes.* But eventually Balthus's relationship with this man who dedicated a novel to him—and who made that major early acquisition of a key painting— went the route of most of his friendships. The two ultimately feuded so intensely that, in a later edition of *La Victime,* Jouve changed the dedication.

In his anger, the writer also gave *Alice* to a friend in Ireland. Fortunately, however, it did reappear—lent anonymously—at the Centre Pompidou exhibition, where it had to be placed under glass to protect it from possible attack. But until very recently, when it was acquired by the Pompidou, *Alice* had pretty much the fate of *The Guitar Lesson:* it was never on public view, and was reproduced far less than other works.

Balthus's explanation of the turnaround with his former friend and admirer is like his claim to me that the reason for his rift with James Lord, and hence for all of Lord's attacks on him, was entirely because of a social slight he had inadvertently perpetrated. After Jouve died in 1976, the artist took to telling people—including an interviewer for *Le Figaro*—that on one occasion in the 1950s when he was back in Paris from Chassy and had little time to spare, he failed to telephone Jouve. Balthus made himself sound quite pathetic; lamentably, he only had two hours to get through the city. He maintained that, solely as a result of this unintended offense, Jouve wrote to him saying that he knew that Balthus was perverse, but not that he was also a traitor.

According to Balthus, this incident characterized the general atmosphere of the world of Parisian intellectuals at that time. Yet it is hard to believe that one of his most ardent champions and passionate devotees could have cut him off quite so peremptorily.

As always, there must have been another side. The two creators of the blatantly morbid *The Victim* once had a lot in common; now, at least on the surface, they no longer did. Balthus had reached the point of denying and erasing what they had both extolled. And there was no countermanding the whims of a Byronic hero.

CHAPTER FOURTEEN

DERAIN

*All the figures in great paintings induce in us the belief that they
have just been immobilized and that, by a miracle of art, they
continue among the living while ceasing on the other hand to be
perishable.*

—ALBERT CAMUS[1]

I

PIERRE JEAN JOUVE WROTE an account of Balthus in the period following
the Galerie Pierre show. In Jouve's eyes, Balthus was living in Paris as if in the
provinces during an earlier century. In his obsolete surroundings, Balthus had
created an environment that could easily be confused with a dream.

Shortly after his overdose of laudanum, Balthus moved to a new studio.
Jouve writes:

> Since nothing is innocent for a true artist, Balthus's first show
> exhausted him so completely, exposed him to such a degree, that
> a very harsh crisis ensued for him, despite certain signs of success.
> Soon he left the Rue de Fürstemberg for the Cour de Rohan, a site
> more monumental in its sordor, the ruin of the Hôtel de Rohan
> surviving the indignities of time between the Boulevard Saint-
> Germain and the Rue Saint-André-des-Arts. Here he had a huge di-
> lapidated room; the allegory of destruction which he then recounted
> to his consciousness could be given free rein there. It was in this
> seductive and terrible room that the painter produced the scaffold-
> ing for what was to become his first decisive work, during four
> years of efforts and excesses, without a day's respite. The pictures,
> finished with difficulty, left for the Rue La Boétie, or for America,
> without his having to concern himself about them overmuch. But
> similar in this regard to an old master, the illustrious Toscanini, who
> never manifested, after a concert, an uncorroded joy—Balthus was
> never satisfied.[2]

Cyril Connolly, who visited Balthus at the same location at the Cour de Rohan over a decade later, corroborates Jouve's description of Balthus in this studio:

> What he is doing is to carry on in the finest tradition of French paint‑ing in an atmosphere of exacting hard work and solitude. His studio, up several flights of stone stairs in the dilapidated Cour de Rohan, is carved out of the huge vine-clad masonry of Philippe Auguste's fortifi‑cations. The large, quiet room with its bare boards, easels and molder‑ing sofa, seems a symbol of the more somber and melancholy aspect of the owner.[3]

Balthus would keep this space not far from the Boulevard Saint-Germain as a home base for a number of years. On an infinitely smaller scale, it reflected, in the manner of Le Grand Chalet, Balthus's instinct for opulence and his simul‑taneous commitment to his work. The sleeping alcove had in it a grand Renaissance bed with a luxuriant Persian bedspread. But the proportion of grandeur to functionalism was the opposite of what it would become in the artist's later years; most of the space served as austere working quarters.

Like the chalet at Rossinière, to most of the world this hideaway on the Cour de Rohan was an impenetrable domain. Of the few who did get past the door, most joined Jouve and Connolly in finding it grim and melancholy. Only Jean Leymarie could manage to invest these simple digs with aristocratic over‑tones by pointing out that the building they were in was "built over the rem‑nants of the old palace of the Archbishops of Rouen . . . which Henry II had restored for his mistress Diane de Poitiers." This may be the sort of connection to royalty that Balthus prided himself on, but, whatever its history, the walk-up flat in which he conducted the next phase of his life as an artist was fairly spartan.

"HIS STUDIO HAS THE ATMOSPHERE of disorder and bleakness that seems almost calculated," wrote one journalist who called on the painter in this locale that would remain Balthus's primary station until he moved to the countryside in 1953. There was

> an accumulation of rusty kitchenware and old newspapers, one superb sixteenth-century-style bed with a rough beautiful Persian saddle bag flung across it as a coverlet, and two moth-eaten, wobbly armchairs. Balthus himself uses a plain wooden stool.[4]

It all had its effect.

Indeed, it was the artist on that rugged stool whom people noticed more than the setting. James Thrall Soby, who first met Balthus at the Cour de Rohan in about 1935, remarked:

> I guess there is such a thing as an *homme fatale*. He had the lean, compelling looks for it, as every woman I've ever met who knew him has assured me, over and over, over and over again.[5]

Balthus told me that his modest quarters on the Cour de Rohan were a difficult place to work. Reflecting back on the place—just as Virgilio was entering the large living room of the Grand Chalet to announce that tea was now being served in the dining room—the artist made it sound positively squalid. Upstairs in an old building, it was too small and had poor light; nor did his situation improve much in Chassy, where all he had was a large room where he could paint. Lamenting the insufficiencies of these conditions, he furrowed his forehead, arched his eyebrows, and turned down the corners of his frowning mouth in as accurate an expression of melancholy as I have ever seen.

Whatever his circumstances, the period following Balthus's move to the Cour de Rohan was fertile for his work. Those paintings Jouve observed going to the galleries on the Rue La Boétie or to America for exhibition at Pierre Matisse's gallery were among the finest Balthus would produce. In the time between the controversial success of the Galerie Pierre show and the changes wrought by the beginning of the Second World War, Balthus's art flourished. He produced the most powerful portraits he would ever paint—in particular those of André Derain and Joan Miró. He made some of his finest and most riveting paintings of little girls. He completed his monumental group scene *The Mountain,* his ultimate celebration of youth and nature—the painting that, in years to come, he would ask curators to include in exhibitions and writers to feature in publications, since he deemed it exemplary of his artistic goals. Elsewhere, in canvases like *Still Life with Broken Glass,* he gave undisguised and exquisite voice to his premonitions of war.

Balthus in these years in Paris between 1934 and 1939 also cemented the personal relationships that would be a mainstay of his life as he separated himself from Antonin Artaud: his marriage to Antoinette de Watteville, and his close friendships with both Derain and Alberto Giacometti. Moreover, inadequate as the space on the Cour de Rohan was, visitors from the world of art and society were honored to ascend its simple steps. The Vicomtesse de Noailles returned regularly for portrait sittings, as did other figures in the avant-garde art world. People like Jane Cooley were honored to be received in the inner sanctum. Whatever the nature of the despair that had driven him to laudanum, he now began to assemble his world as he wanted it to be.

AT THE COUR DE ROHAN, Balthus began to receive portrait commissions. One of the first of these was for a group portrait of the family of the well-known graphic designer Cassandre. Cassandre, who was seven years older than Balthus, had been born in the Ukraine. His elegant single name—which, like "Balthus," carried a suggestion of wisdom as well as style—was a pseudonym for Adolphe-Jean-Marie Mauron. Best known for his sleek and inventive posters for the aperitif Dubonnet and luxurious French steamship lines, he greatly admired Balthus.

In Balthus's canvas, the bodies of Cassandre's wife and two children twist and turn in a way that is both rhythmic and convincing, and each of the three personages seems possessed of true body weight. The plaid pattern of Cassandre's daughter's dress falls with complete authenticity over its pleats and wrinkles, with its white highlights reflecting a light that seems real. The panel is animated by the arrangement of limbs and its fascinating lack of balance.

But what at first seems plausible—as well as unusually elegant, even sublime—is also sinister. Cassandre's daughter looks possessed by demons. With her sucked-in cheeks and angular jaw, she looks like Artaud in drag. And with his will to distort, Balthus has given this Parisian family heads that dwarf their bodies, and faces that read as blank masks. The woman and her son and daughter each appear to have a secret, to declare that they are moved by emotions and longings and knowledge denied us. In support of that furtiveness, Henri Mauron—Cassandre's son—is reading a text we cannot see. And like the little boy in a virtually identical cap in *The Street,* he seems more like a puppet—albeit an adorable one, the cutest sort of ventriloquist's dummy—than a real person.

Like Jane Cooley, all three of these people are sitting on or near edges. They are penetrated—none of them comfortably. We, the viewers, go on edge as well.

The Maurons' unease prevails in almost all of the twenty or so portraits Balthus painted in the three-year period from 1934 to 1937. In Balthus's vision of humanity, people are compromised, unfulfilled, needy, and awkward—even when they are elegant and well turned-out. They may belong to the upper echelon of society, but something is wrong.

The mixed signals make for provocative art. But when Balthus turned to the painters he supposedly revered—the portrait subjects whose work and

The Mauron-Cassandre Family, 1935, oil on canvas, 72 x 72 cm

nature elevated them well above the world of these outsiders—the results were
more complex still.

II

ANDRÉ DERAIN WAS A SUBJECT Balthus took visible pleasure in discussing
with me. It was a source of rapport between us that I have such admiration for
this misunderstood, insufficiently appreciated artist, and particularly for his
late work.

Balthus told me they first met when the older painter came to see him
shortly after the Galerie Pierre show. Recalling this, Balthus looked as if he

were amazed at the impact of that relatively modest event. He appeared to be
baffled, and humbly pleased, at the recollection of a success he had only now
come to recognize. "It was very strange, the effect it made on painters. Derain
came to see me after that first exhibition. Picasso also came to see me because
of it. He wanted to buy *La Rue.*"

Yet just as there is no corroborating evidence that, although he bought
The Children in 1941, Picasso ever wished to own *The Street*, there is no certainty that Balthus initially encountered André Derain because Derain came to
see him as a result of that show.

Balthus's exhibition of seven paintings when he was twenty-six years old
did, however, stir interest from artists of the previous generation. In the course
of the 1930s, Picasso, Derain, Giacometti, and others came to develop enormous respect for the creative power and originality of this younger painter
whose name was inextricably linked to Rilke's. Even if Balthus was almost certainly embellishing the truth in saying that Derain and Picasso took the initiative in seeking out the younger artist out of admiration for the show at the
Galerie Pierre, he was not exaggerating their genuine affinity for his work.
Moreover, Balthus played the part beautifully. However contrived his "recollections," it was extremely touching to see the world-renowned octogenarian
close his eyes—like someone delving into territory he has not entered for many
decades—and think back on those early years. In his retrospective journey, he
seemed to realize, as if for the first time, how extraordinary it was that those
older, highly esteemed artists had sought him out, much to his surprise. His
childlike pleasure and hint of embarrassment bespoke a lovely, if completely
contrived, modesty.

DERAIN AND BALTHUS'S introduction to one another probably came either
through Giacometti or through Artaud. By the time Balthus painted Derain's
portrait, they had many mutual friends, and both of them were discussing
New York representation with Pierre Matisse—common ground that gave
them, and Miró, an aspect of being brethren. The older and younger artist saw
each other a lot, and Derain's influence on Balthus's approach to art in general,
and on the specifics of his painterly technique, was considerable. The affinity
helped define Balthus's position in the current art world.

The convictions that drew Balthus to André Derain in the 1930s, and have
pertained ever since, not only announced his distinction and differentness
from the main artistic current but made clear his central concerns as a painter.
Whatever the psychological elements of his art, and however emphatic the sexuality, from the visual and technical side Balthus was obsessed with the classic

problems of painting very much as Derain approached them. There was a libertine spirit to Derain's salacious vignettes for Artaud's *Héliogabale,* a naughti-
ness that must have made Balthus comfortable, but it was Derain's serious
return to the traditions of French painting and his insistence on nature as the
starting point of his art that drew him to the older artist. By contrast, other
current styles were of little interest.

For Balthus to have embraced Derain and his work at that time was to
stand apart. This would be a lifelong fealty—still strong in 1976, when Balthus
mounted, at the Villa Medici, one of the most significant Derain shows ever,
twenty-two years after the master's death.

Derain and his work were extremely controversial, his worth hotly
debated—most especially in the 1930s. Knowing this, Derain characterized his
own position:

> I am not attached to any principle—except that of liberty—but my
> idea of liberty is that it must be related to tradition. I do not wish to
> expound any theories as to what ought to be done in the arts. I simply
> paint as best I can. The point is that there are too many theories run-
> ning around and not sufficient passion to make them work.[6]

That primacy of painting also attracted Alberto Giacometti, André Derain's
other great advocate at the time and Balthus's other primary mentor and
friend. Giacometti cited 1936—the same year Balthus labored over Derain's
portrait—as the year of his discovery of the older artist. The Swiss was swayed
by the honesty of Derain's painting, the bravery of his attempt to capture
appearances, and the depth and subtlety that Derain's work continuously
yielded:

> But, as a matter of fact, from that day, I might even say from the
> moment of that day in 1936 when a canvas by Derain seen by chance
> in a gallery—three pears on a table against a huge black background—
> stopped me short, struck me as something wholly new (here I had
> really seen a painting by Derain for the first time beyond its immedi-
> ate appearance), from that moment all of Derain's canvases without
> exception have halted me in my tracks, all have compelled me to con-
> sider them at length, to seek what was there behind them.[7]

Giacometti, Derain, and Balthus became a sort of triumvirate.

· · ·

Beyond admiring Derain's work, Balthus also relished the older artist's personal magnetism, his larger-than-life personality. Balthus told me that from the start he considered Derain "a wonderful man. He was like a cloud— changing every minute; that's what I always thought." Balthus emphasized that in that time period they had very different statuses—Derain extremely well known, Balthus just starting out—and that as a younger artist beginning to find his way, he looked up to Derain as a mentor.

Whenever we talked about Derain, Balthus wore a warm look on his face. At the same time, he always made a point of keeping himself one step removed, of emphasizing a certain space from our subject. "I can't say I was an intimate friend. We saw each other very often—I think he liked me—but there was still a distance between a very famous painter and a young man. He was a very much older man, and I never wanted to disturb him. Giacometti was very fond of him." Balthus often invoked Derain when we took our after-dinner coffee in front of the large open hearth in the library, where a small Derain watercolor costume design hung behind the sofa, but his admiration always had just a soupçon of reserve.

For all his purported fondness for Derain, Balthus often seemed to damn him with faint praise. He repeatedly mentioned their age difference—twenty-eight years—in a way that he never did when discussing Rilke, who was Derain's elder by five. And he constantly made the cloud analogy. The impression was that Derain was splendid yet detached.

> I knew him very well. He was one of the most extraordinary men I have ever met. He made the impression of a cloud—a cloud changing, moving. He changed his mind very often, contradicting himself. A conversation with him was very interesting and nourishing. But people think I was influenced by him. I never was; he was out of my reach.

Balthus emphasized the distinction between Derain's quick and spontaneous working method and his own deliberation.

> His idea was Frans Hals, wonderful strokes, immediate success in one stroke—which is basically the contrary of myself. I am building up. . . . Derain was a painter of the *premier jet*. What is typical for Derain is the brushstroke. He was immensely clever. And I am not. I am terribly unclever, and always have been. He does a child in one sitting.

He continuously repeated that idea of Derain being "*du premier jet*"—an expression Balthus used both in French and in English, where he made it "of the first jet." Derain's "beautiful drawings" and his "beautiful still lifes" were, Balthus remarked, of a piece: the first, spontaneous sketches and his "final product," the oil paintings, amazingly similar.

Balthus said that Derain's quick working method and virtuosity stupefied him, but that he, on the contrary, always labored slowly, which had been the case ever since his youth. "He wanted to make at once a painting. I can't do anything at once. It takes a long time to get where I want to get. The whole difference between Derain and me was his speed, my building up. From that point of view," he and Derain—for all their rapport otherwise—"did not understand one another."

This difference pertains not only to their work but to their approach to life. Derain, the son of a creamery owner, was a robust and utterly forthright man known for his unaffected ways. Although he had a preference for an English style of dressing and drove a silver Bugatti—both of which must have appealed enormously to the young Balthus—he evinced no premeditation or artifice in his presentation of himself any more than in his work. For Balthus, reconstruction and constant refinement have been essential not only when he makes paintings but also in the development of his persona. If Derain lived as well as painted with the abandon of the first sketch, Balthus has planned and deliberated everything—his name and ancestry as much as his oil paintings. Spontaneity would be laden with peril.

BALTHUS QUOTED DERAIN as having said, "All comes from nature and all returns to it," and then added, "I am not sure I agree with the 'returns to it.' " But Balthus concurred heartily that "the richness of painting comes from the observation of nature." In a number of our conversations, Balthus stressed to me that visual observation of the real world was "absolutely essential" to his work. He decried modern art today, saying that many paintings and sculptures ring false because their creator did not have this starting point. "If you try to invent things and it is not nourished by the observation of things around you, the painting turns very often and very quickly into a sort of mannerism."

Mannerism, of course, is a word that most of us would apply to Balthus's work as well. But this was neither the first nor the last time I heard Balthus accuse someone else of exhibiting his own most salient qualities. In retrospect, that maneuver seemed a ploy—a means of throwing us all off his own scent— but at the time it worked completely.

.   .   .

"IF YOU LOOK INTO A MUSEUM catalog today, you see immediately that something is lost," Balthus allowed in the course of his ruminations on the sofa of the main salon one afternoon. "From the moment one doesn't look anymore, it becomes boring. A research of something personal, the deliberate quest for originality, is one of the main weaknesses." The chief problem, Balthus insisted, derived from "that necessity to make something astonishing."

The observation was as duplicitous as it was intriguing. Because even if Balthus was justified in regarding himself as an artist who started with the observation of life, there has rarely been an artist so singularly personal in his approach or so bent on originality.

Surely Balthus knew that his art has had such success because of its unique psychological impact. It does, indeed, derive from nature, and much of it is well painted, but the "something personal" is the main reason Balthus's work ultimately became better known and more popular than Derain's—and continues to fetch significantly higher prices.

It was as if by criticizing certain characteristics—another person's manipulativeness, someone's immersion in his own psyche—Balthus intended to prevent me from realizing the extent to which those selfsame traits applied to *him.*

III

There are times when fatigue is the great aphrodisiac, annihilating all other thoughts, granting sensuous slow motion to heavy limbs, urging generosity, acceptance, infinite abandonment.
—IAN McEWAN, *Enduring Love*[8]

GUILLAUME APOLLINAIRE WROTE in 1916 that Derain's study of the masters gave him "an unparalleled audacity. . . . It is such audacity which is the true measure of discipline."[9] Balthus cherished that mix of courage and self-control, the ability to abide by rules while entering uncharted territory.

With their close mutual friendship, Giacometti, Derain, and Balthus were also on common ground in their shared view that the attempt to make art was a struggle in which total success was impossible. Giacometti wrote, "Derain was continually being overtaken by his surroundings; impossibility terrified him, and every work spelled failure for him before it was begun." This applied to all of them, and was part and parcel of their mutual goal of rendering the true look of places and people and things.

Additionally for Giacometti, part of what was so exciting about Derain was that none of the issues of contemporary painting—abstract art, Tachism, or other current movements—had any meaning for him. This gave Giacometti occasion to repeat Apollinaire's adjective "audacious" forty years later. "Perhaps he only wanted to capture a little of the appearances of things, the marvelous, fascinating, inscrutable appearances surrounding him. Derain excites me more, has given me more and taught me more than any painter since Cézanne; to me he is the most audacious of them all."[10]

For Balthus, who has always despised trendiness in any form, that indifference to the latest art-world whim in deference to higher goals was also paramount.

And Derain gave Balthus approval. According to Derain's biographer Pierre Cabanne, this was why Derain "granted the young man long sessions of posing, which he had never done for anyone else, and virtually filial relations were established between them."[11] The commitment for Derain was considerable; Balthus was "the only young painter with whom he was closely linked."[12]

How, THEN, DID BALTHUS paint this artist he so admired and who esteemed him equally? What image did he give to the "extraordinary, immensely clever man" he likened to a cloud and who demonstrated filial feeling toward him? He portrayed him as a cranky tyrant (color plate 9). His beloved André Derain looks like a corporate tycoon with heartburn. The older artist is shown to be brutal and imperious. He seems also to be in pain—and slightly ridiculous.

Derain is not Derain; he is Derain transformed by Balthus. As with virtually all of his portrayals, Balthus has put himself, implicitly, in a position of superiority through the simple technique of catching and revealing some essential flaw and weakness in his subject. Presenting Derain as a bombast in apparent discomfort, the younger artist has gained the upper hand.

Moreover, since the painting now hangs virtually all the time at the Museum of Modern Art in New York, this is how much of the world has come to see Derain. MoMA hardly ever shows any of Derain's actual work, but Balthus's provocative portrait of the demonic artist is almost always in place. Not only did Balthus choose the image he wanted for his so-called mentor, but he did it so skillfully that he stole the audience.

PART OF WHAT MAKES THE PORTRAIT such an eye-catcher is that it looks as if Derain has just had passionate sex with the model behind him. I write this although Balthus specifically denied the point to me and called it an absurd assumption. It was he who brought up the notion in our conversation, only to refute it ardently.

Balthus laughingly told me that in her Metropolitan Museum catalog, Sabine Rewald had claimed "that Derain had just gone to bed with the model behind him"—but that this was sheer nonsense. What Mrs. Rewald actually wrote was, "Derain was known for his appetite for sensuous pleasures. Rather than underplaying these inclinations, Balthus exaggerated them. . . . The model, her face numb, slumps in exhaustion, as if worn out by Derain's demands." Balthus assumed that Mrs. Rewald meant "Derain's demands" to be those of vehement lovemaking, and scoffed at the idea as outrageous. He asked me how anyone could even imagine such a thing.

I certainly had not thought to discuss the sexual connection between Derain and his model. It seemed, on the other hand, that Balthus delighted in it. The octogenarian Balthus was clearly preoccupied with the eroticism he was denying so vociferously.

WHEN I HAVE LOOKED at the Derain portrait at the Museum of Modern Art, I have often thought of Balthus's question, "Who could imagine such a thing?" Seeing the model's bedroom eyes, hiked-up skirt, and half-pulled-off top, who could not? And given that the woman is in Balthus's favorite, one-breast-exposed-just-below-the-nipple, short-tight-skirt getup, there is little doubt that he, too, had once imagined it easily.

I said none of this when I was talking with Balthus, however. I must admit that I sat there on the living room sofa like a perfect toady—willingly inhaling his cigarette smoke secondhand while convincing myself I did not mind it (so content was I to have direct access to the oracle), placidly agreeing that it was foolish to think that Derain had just had sex with the wanton creature behind him. But every time I have seen the painting since that occasion, there has been no question in my mind as to the connection between Derain and his model. Derain's lust and engagement with the woman are tacit; if they have not actually just had intercourse, the idea is still everywhere in the air.

Pierre Cabanne not only recognized the sexual scenario here but saw this autobiographical significance: "Derain, eyes staring, expression tormented, hand on his heart, wanted to confess or to boast of having disturbed the very young and partially undressed model sitting, eyes lowered, behind him. This admirable work is a double portrait, that of Derain painted by Balthus, and of Balthus painting Derain as he recognizes himself in him."[13]

. . .

AGAIN THE FACTS ARE HAZY, the boundaries nil. Balthus could not paint a
subject from the world outside himself without interjecting his personal narcissism. He did not make a portrait of André Derain as Derain was; nor did he
simply use Derain as a guise for a self-portrait. Rather, he made Derain into his
fantasy: Derain as Balthus would have lived if he were Derain.

Yet, as when he discussed the neighborhood of *The Street,* Balthus
approached his portrait of his mentor like an elderly person looking through
an old photo album—both with an interest in recapturing simple truths and
with the wish to sanitize. On the first occasion when we were looking at a
reproduction of the painting, Balthus identified the model as a "Jewish girl
who disappeared, and who posed for Derain occasionally." He appeared
unable to recall her name, but clearly considered it important to do so. The
reconstruction of facts and the precise identity of faces and locations from the
distant past were all that mattered, it seemed.

Several days later, Balthus's memory sharpened. "That girl was a charming Jewish girl whom we all knew and who was deported at the end—she was
sent away and never heard of again: Sonia Mossé. She came and sat when I
painted the portrait. She was fair, very fair," Balthus reminisced. Sonia Mossé,
I subsequently learned, was an intimate of Artaud's, someone whose relationship with Artaud took such a turn that in 1939 he tried to cast a spell on her, an
episode of which evidence exists in the form of a sinister document in wax
crayon and burned paper.

The artist never told me that Sabine Rewald had identified the model
otherwise. But I now think that one of the reasons he was so determined to
come up with Sonia Mossé was his usual eagerness to pinpoint Sabine
Rewald's factual errors. Ms. Rewald has written of the model, "She was Raymonde, Derain's mistress and the mother of his son. Raymonde actually suffered from an ailment that made her fall asleep at odd moments, just as she
does here."

Balthus, of course, knew Mrs. Rewald had said this. By implicitly pointing out that the Met curator had the wrong person—and once he had recollected the name of Sonia Mossé, Balthus repeated it to me on several
subsequent occasions—he was therefore further dispelling her theory, or the
notion he attributed to her, that the model had been sexually exhausted by
Derain. How could we give any credence to someone who could not even
identify the person in a painting correctly? By his account of this painting,
Mrs. Rewald had also misidentified a poor beleaguered Jewess as an Aryan. If

Sabine Rewald could make such an error, it was further indication of how wrong she was in her notion that Balthus was Jewish.

Yet in 1936, the year of this portrait, the model André Derain was painting more than any other was his mistress Raymonde Knaubliche. And the woman in Balthus's painting does, indeed, closely resemble Derain's contemporaneous paintings of Raymonde. The model in the background in the Balthus has the identical nose, drooping eyelids, shoulder-length hair, square shoulders, and ample bosom as Derain's images of Raymonde. Sonia Mossé was probably a ruse—another attempt by Balthus to lead me into his camp.

I COULD BE WRONG HERE. Perhaps poor Sonia did, indeed, pose for this picture. Maybe the idea of sex is in my mind only. But whoever the actual sitter was, Balthus has reconstructed her in his usual way. Not only does a solitary nipple rest exposed on the top of her filmy undergarment, and not only does she have her skirt hiked up and pulled tight across her hefty thighs—as if Balthus anticipated by decades the 1990s style of large women in very short, very snug miniskirts—but Derain's model has the classically Balthusian over-sized, masklike head.

This depiction has far more to do with Balthus's personal taste than with his portrait subject. Derain's way of showing women was to make them totally nude, soft and sensuous, content rather than tortured. They look entirely alert, not in the fatigued, anesthetized state often preferred by Balthus. Derain's females, Raymonde and others, look as if they are naked of their own volition, not as if they have been raped; they are bucolic types in the classical tradition. With a light, cheerful touch, Derain imbues his nudes with lyricism. The pose of his 1935–36 *Nu au canapé vert* may be similar to that of Balthus's *Victim*, but Derain's lady is basking in glory. Pleasure pervades; there are no complications. Life is a happy bacchanal in the tradition of Renoir. As Balthus has pointed out, the creator of these figures painted easily and with alacrity; his creations enjoy the same beatitude.

Denys Sutton wrote of Derain and the opposite sex:

> True descendant of a Courbet or a Renoir, he became the enthusiastic recorder of femininity. . . . He responded, happily, devotedly, to women. . . . Slowly and gently, the brush seems to stroke the canvas, as if the real body lay there to be awakened by the artist's touch.[14]

Yet Balthus has, insistently, rendered Derain's model tough and slutty. Instead of luxuriating in a sylvan ideal as she would have been in one of Derain's own paintings, she appears used-up, as if she has just been violated. Unable to resist taking *his,* not his subject's, approach, Balthus has turned the woman into his usual, preferred mix of victim and culprit.

What the older artist exalted, the younger one deprecates. Balthus uses his brush to assault, not to caress.

IRRESPECTIVE OF HIS actual personality, Derain emerges as a true Balthus type: a hedonistic, mendacious troublemaker.

Derain's eyes roll upward—as if into one of the clouds to which Balthus has repeatedly compared him—making him inaccessible. Like most of the characters in Balthus's paintings, he averts our gaze and will not directly engage with us; he is in his own private universe.

Yet with his massive body, his gangster's bathrobe, and the spent and wanton woman behind him scratching her knee, Derain is also intensely earthy. His bodily needs, and all the milk and cream of his childhood, have made him who he is: a physical giant. To add to his massiveness, Balthus, the chronic enlarger of people's heads, has this time made his subject's visage, bulbous and jowly though it is, proportionately too small for his torso.

People in Balthus's paintings either rule or seem diminished. Derain is a monarch; yet, ironically, he is also Balthus's underling. By portraying the older painter as a modernized, bohemian Louis XIV—gigantic and amusing, a force to be reckoned with—Balthus has made him bombastic and silly in spite of his visible greatness. In short, by saying "Look how powerful he is," Balthus has said, "But I, of course, am really far more intelligent than the old cad."

BALTHUS TOLD ME THAT ANY psychological elements of his painting of Derain, or his other portraits, are entirely inadvertent. He maintained assiduously that there is no symbolism whatsoever in these works. The pose is the pose that was taken; there is nothing more to it. The visual elements of the painted canvas are all that matter. The tonality, the composition, the relationship of the angle of the crook of Derain's left arm to the waves of the model's hair, the working of the vertical bathrobe stripes against the diagonal floorboard cracks: these were the issues of concern to the painter.

Yet when we meet up with Balthus's Derain face-to-face at the Museum of Modern Art, how can we fail but react to the personality and psychological draw of this sociopath who stands there glowering at us? For Balthus to insist that we regard this portrait only as a design scheme and an exercise in physical

illusion, while downplaying the emotional nature of the encounter, is like asking us to listen to a wartime speech of Winston Churchill's and only notice the
word usage and the nuances of his Oxonian accent.

How, for example, can we not wonder why one of Derain's talonlike fingers is tucked into his shirt? Is he checking his own heartbeat? The artist who
has positioned his subject in this manner might merely laugh or shake his head
in amazement at our responses, yet the gesture invariably begs countless questions. This is an unusual hand gesture for a painting of a close acquaintance,
even if there was ample precedent for it in eighteenth- and nineteenth-century
portraiture. Moreover—whoever Balthus has since become—it was painted by
someone whose closest companions at the time were all steeped in psychoanalytical theory and preoccupied with violence as the themes of their art. Is
Derain meant to be imitating the act of someone shooting himself, in a mock
suicide? Is the single finger penetrating the open slit analogous to the sexual
act? This second interpretation seems especially likely—in part because of the
way Derain's finger connects visually to the model's hand between her bare
knees, so close to her crotch that we feel as if we have been invited to investi-
gate beneath her lifted skirt. Balthus may have also posed Derain in this way as
an echo of the way his beloved Jean-Louis David showed Napoleon—hence
suggesting imperious determination.

The Balthus I got to know would, of course, declare that Derain happened to put his finger through the slit of his shirt, and he happened to paint it
that way. But by now we should know better than to count on it.

ON THOSE INFREQUENT OCCASIONS when he has painted men, Balthus
never seems as at home as in his depictions of women. An encounter with the
Derain portrait at the Modern subsumes us with its awkwardness. Derain
looks labored upon, as if Balthus has not resolved the nature of their connection or how to paint him.

The older artist stands painfully rigid. The impression he makes is accentuated by the wood support on which Balthus painted this portrait. Derain's
head looks truly wooden. Ashen-faced, he is like a corpse; the eyes rolling
upward are those of a dead person. What Jouve terms Balthus's essential morbidity is evident here.

The secondary figure of the female model is rendered with Balthus's more
typical style of painting: easy and assured. She assumes her pose gracefully.
Alluring and violated, luscious but dazed, she is a type with whom he is at ease.
The painter knows where he stands with her, and paints her accordingly.

Is Derain, however, quite literally, a stiff? Are we meant—by these frozen eyes and the revolverlike hand gesture—to feel that he has battled in agony as an artist to the point where he has killed himself? At the time Balthus was painting him, Derain's work was the subject of such hot debate that there was an entire publication called *For or Against Derain.* Was Balthus declaring that Derain's much lambasted tenacity about painting nature—his traditionalism in an unappreciative world—was a form of suicide? Were his integrity and commitment to the real values of painting beyond toleration? It was a despair with which Derain's portraitist readily identified.

ONE AFTERNOON WHEN WE WERE sitting on the settee in the living room, Balthus told me through his smoke rings that he greatly admired Picasso's portrait of Gertrude Stein. Derain's totemic head—symmetrical, stolid, masklike—resembles that image. Derain's wide and flattened face, like Picasso's rendition of Stein, is severe, grand, and discomfiting. Even the features are similar. And in both portraits the viewer is confronted more with a fabricated presence than an actual person.

Derain's female model, however much softer she is, is also not quite real. Her face is tacitly a painting of a face rather than a face itself. While Balthus has opted for an extremely realistic effect in his detailed rendering of Derain's skin, with the model's skin he has used a painter's signs and given the impression of a fuzzy, even haphazard, brushwork. This results in the girl being dehumanized, so that her presence is very similar to that of cats in a number of Balthus's canvases. She exists as an object: a thing to be painted, or to be used for companionship. The slight haze that envelops her—similar to the way in which dream sequences are rendered cinematographically, slightly out of focus in contrast to the clarity used for everyday events—supports our impression of her as a fantasy. A woman to be used for art and for sex—one breast popping out, her skirt clinging to her hips, her limp arms making her seem relaxed in her submission—is everything Balthus wants a model to be.

Derain, on the other hand, belongs to the pageant of life as much as Piero's figures in the procession at Arezzo. The blocklike figure, unreal and strange though he is, has a totemic power. Balthus has articulated the oversized cretin with consummate skill. Derain's bathrobe falls easily; its folds billow with authentic fullness. The graceful knot of the bathrobe belt floats before us; the shadow of its free-falling end has been positioned with supreme know-how. In his areas of strength, Balthus is a sublime craftsman.

As in *The Guitar Lesson,* he again gets the floorboards perfectly, making the spaces between them plausible. He knows how to capture the shine on the toes of Derain's shoes. But where he is at sea as a painter, he is totally lost. In

André Derain as elsewhere, Balthus is helpless with hands. Derain's are certainly not human. The backs of the palms are too big, the fingers too tapered, the spaces between these sticklike digits too precisely like V-cuts. There is not enough differentiation at the wrist. These hands are barbaric and animalistic. The question is why. They may be ill formed quite simply because Balthus was unable to show them otherwise. But perhaps he painted hands as he did—whether consciously or not—in order to give Derain, as well as so many other subjects, the attributes of vultures and other birds of prey. Derain's head, too, is not really human; it is, rather, like the hands, a scary transformation of person into beast.

A LARGE REPRODUCTION OF THIS portrait by Balthus hangs at the entrance to Derain's studio in Chambourcy, a village on the outskirts of Paris. Looking at it there, I discussed the bathrobe with Derain's niece, Geneviève Taillade, who lived with her uncle and has extremely fond memories of Balthus's visits to him. She told me that Derain never actually wore such a robe.

Of course, it is possible that if it wasn't Derain's, the robe was Balthus's—all the more plausible since Balthus told me he painted this portrait of André Derain in his own studio at the Cour de Rohan. But even the loosest robe of as thin a man as Balthus would be unlikely to fit on the frame of the corpulent Derain. The robe is probably pure invention. It adds to the conundrum of the painting. It makes Derain seem like a stylish lord. It also suggests intimacy. Balthus's assertions to the contrary notwithstanding, Derain appears to have thrown on the robe because he has just emerged from being in bed with the woman behind him. The billowing garment is also essential to our impression of Derain as a figure of overwhelming mass.

In addition, like the pageboy outfits in which Balthus has periodically clad young boys over the years, the robe introduces an element from an earlier era into a scene of modern life. It is a costume, and life an act of theater. The bathrobe furthers a sense of tension. We feel that with one slight tug, or if Derain were merely to step forward, it might untie and the robe fall open.

This particular detail will show up repeatedly in Balthus's work. Derain's bathrobe belt is the precursor of the wide, bowed sashes wrapped around the naked midriffs of the Japanese women of two large canvases done between 1967 and 1976. Like ribbons around packages, Derain's belt and those sashes hold and wrap. In a subtle way, they harness their subjects. Yet if the tension slackens just a little, they will release.

It is in part because we sense this possibility that Derain's robe might easily come undone that the painting puts us on edge. All propriety could dissolve in an instant. Balthus would, of course, call this my hang-up, not his: my obsession, while all he was doing was trying his humble best to paint a loosely tied bathrobe. But surely few people have better known the effect of details, and the sexuality that lurks in clothing.

THE OLDER ARTIST CAME every morning to pose. "It was quite a walk"—so Balthus recalled—from the studio Derain was sharing at the time with his friend Léopold-Lévy on the Rue d'Assas near the Jardin du Luxembourg.

We do not, however, picture the portrait as having been done on Derain's sojourns to his young admirer's digs. We assume that the setting is Derain's own studio—and that those are Derain's own canvases behind him. Not that it really matters, of course, on whose actual possessions Balthus based these turned paintings; after all, only the backs are visible on these canvases facing the wall. They serve their purpose of stating Derain's profession, regardless of what was on the other side. They are signals, just as the half-naked model is a general announcement of Derain's passion.

By having their stretcher sides on view, not only is the issue of the authorship of these canvases avoided, but those backs also remind us that there is a lot we don't see. The stacked paintings are like the black or shuttered windows in Balthus's great urban scenes: a deliberate holding back. In a studio interior by Matisse, by contrast, everything is plainly visible and the viewer can invariably identify the many paintings within the painting.

BALTHUS, HOWEVER, SPECIALIZES in keeping the visible invisible. He adds details he need not necessarily put in, only to render them secretive. There is a closed door at a right angle to the painting backs in the Derain portrait which also seems to prohibit knowledge. It, too, is a framework with its contents off-limits. Throughout Balthus's work, we are left wishing to see faces and surfaces and rooms that are denied us; and we are reminded that Balthus determines what we get to know and what we don't.

Balthus has accomplished this act of control—his declaration of where we are allowed and where we are forbidden—with consummate skill. He has evoked the shut door and the backs of the canvases impeccably. The light that bounces off their stretchers is a masterpiece of verisimilitude. We believe the truthfulness of what we see.

So it is easy enough, viewing this portrait, to accept the harmless lie that the paintings with their backs to us in this studio are by André Derain. One might well say that the minor deception doesn't matter; why shouldn't Balthus have used his own work as stand-ins? Yet in a way, it is very significant that the canvases before which the older painter is shown standing were Balthus's own.

After all, he converted Derain's model into *his* preferred variety—a Balthusian half-clad vamp—whereas Derain himself was inclined to paint women entirely nude. The boundaries between Balthus and his subject have, as usual, been made to evaporate. Yet again, Balthus wants to be the creature before his eyes, and, at the same time, wants the subject to be Balthus.

Not that Derain resembles Balthus physically; in build and features they are opposites. But the portrait of Derain looks like an imagined self-portrait as much as a painting that one person has done of another. We picture it as having been created by someone standing before a mirror.

This impression emerges in part from the pose and the glasslike hardness that is intensified by the wooden surface of the picture. It is furthered by the degree to which Balthus has painted here very much in the style of Derain, using Derain's palette of that period and incorporating Derain's style and sort of luminosity.

Balthus who became Artaud, Balthus whose female adolescent models were in some ways versions of himself, Balthus the teacher in *The Guitar Lesson:* here, too, in his portrait of an older artist whose integrity and independence and flair he admired, he inextricably merged himself with his subject.

SOME OBSERVERS HAVE SAID that Derain actually taught Balthus. James Thrall Soby—who collected the work of both these artists in the 1930s, knew them personally, and studied their art closely—wrote that Balthus was "under the tutelage of André Derain."[15] He credited Derain with the marked change in Balthus's work following the Galerie Pierre show, resulting in Balthus's progress toward "a new finesse of technique and to a gentler lyricism" in his work of the late 1930s. Derain, according to Soby, was responsible for Balthus's departure from "the Anglo-Germanic turbulence of an earlier Romanticism" and his consequent route toward Frenchness. But it was probably a case of discipleship more than a student-teacher connection.

Derain's and Balthus's pictures are not likely to be confused; as Balthus told me, Derain's have visibly been painted spontaneously, whereas Balthus's have been labored on. Yet many aspects of Balthus's art stem directly from Derain's. The sweeping gestures and lively motion of arms and legs in Balthus's canvases from 1935 on are closely akin to what we find in Derain's pictures of the preceding two decades. Balthus took up Derain's manner of casting a warm glow on well-lit flesh against a somber brown background. The younger artist's palette of the mid to late 1930s is much the same as Derain's in its depth and the austerity and the predominance of old-master hues. It may well be from Derain that Balthus got the determination to opt for the traditional coloring and dense surfaces that are such a far cry from the post-Fauve, Cubist, and Surreal modes prevalent at the time.

On occasion Balthus seems to have quoted the older artist rather precisely. Lady Abdy's pose is like a dramatized version of some of Derain's figures. A number of Balthus's portraits—particularly his commissions of rich women—appear to descend from Derain's c. 1930 *Blond Italian* and related canvases. There is also a strong resemblance between Balthus's kitchen still lifes and those by Derain that preceded them.

Balthus's 1937 *Still Life* looks remarkably like Derain's paintings of similar subject matter in the 1920s. Balthus has placed his objects on virtually the identical wooden French country kitchen table as the one Derain used—thin-legged, rough-hewn, with a single drawer. The younger artist has followed his

André Derain, *The Laden Table*, 1921–22, oil on canvas, 97.1 x 163.2 cm

mentor's lead in bringing Chardin into the twentieth century, giving the total mélange a fullness while clearly articulating each individual object. Bulbous carafes are carefully juxtaposed with shallow serving vessels, rhythmically angled dishes with pieces of bread. Balthus has used Derain's somber palette as well as Derain's method of gently lighting the objects and table against an earthy green background.

Yet for all his dependence on Derain, Balthus has made a Balthus. On the one hand, he has painted a kitchen still life as they have existed in France for centuries: a basket heaped with bread; a lovely flask and handsome goblet filled with refreshing drink (although we are unclear whether this is water or white wine). On the other hand, something different is going on here. In the center of the composition, lying on the table, there is a hammer. It has just struck. A second, thin-necked decanter lies shattered on its side. Broken-glass fragments—an extraordinary feat of painting—surround the hapless vessel. The fork that spears a potato does not hold the vegetable; it impales it. And the sharp knife that pierces the half loaf of crusty country bread looks like an agent of destruction, more a weapon than a kitchen implement.

Balthus and I talked about this 1937 *Still Life* on several occasions, in part because I have admired it and known it well for most of my lifetime. The painting has been owned, since 1940, by the Wadsworth Atheneum in Hartford, only fifteen minutes from where I grew up. This connection pleased its painter. A. Everett Austin, Jr.—the museum director who acquired it for the Atheneum, and was a close friend of James Thrall Soby's—was one of Balthus's earliest supporters anywhere. I felt as if my origins in the community of the Atheneum put me up a notch.

But Balthus maintained to me that there was no aspect of aggression or destruction in the painting. "There's no violence in the knife. It's just the angle that I liked. It has no other meaning." He said he had no idea why it is sometimes called *Still Life with Violence.* He assumed that I agreed that this concept of destruction was as ridiculous as the notion of eroticism in his work.

Yet the painting itself leaves no doubt as to the violence. As Linda Fairstein pointed out, in traditional painting, "usually a knife is passive. But here it is actually used as a cutting instrument . . . the way you would stab an object. The bread is impaled." Every detail reflects the Balthusian emphasis on power and dominance. Additionally, Balthus's denials notwithstanding, the 1937 *Still Life* seems to reflect the social disorder that was beginning to tear apart European life at the time. The treachery and tumult redolent in Balthus's painting align it with Joan Miró's 1937 *Still Life with Old Shoe*—a painting whose maker was unequivocal about his wish to depict the forces of death. Miró had his studio directly above the Galerie Pierre. Balthus had seen him working on

Still Life, 1937, oil on canvas, 81 x 99 cm

this composition in which a chunk of bread resembles a dismembered body part, and an armlike fork pierces an apple as if to decimate it. Balthus's approach is more understated than Miró's—the Spaniard's colors are lurid and chemical-looking, while Balthus's are earth-toned and restrained—but his own *Still Life* has some of the macabre and haunting aspects of the Miró.

The malignant forces of war were clearly present. However assiduous his denials, Balthus incorporated the prevailing violence into his work. Derain might use art to provide an alternative, but for all the surface resemblance of his work to Derain's, Balthus never strayed far from the themes of dominance and defeat, mastery and victimization. Even his children—at an allegedly innocent stage of life—look crafty, devious, and willful. Balthus cannot help being sinister. Everyone, even inanimate objects, succumbs to, and exerts, a wily power.

IV

ON SOME OF THE MANY occasions when Balthus and I talked about André Derain, my host digressed to the subject of G. K. Chesterton's novel *The Man*

Who Was Thursday. Derain, Balthus explained, always struck him as being just like the character named Sunday from that book. From the first instant of his meeting Derain, he had noticed the artist's resemblance to this odd individual who was the president of the Central Anarchist Council in the novel. Balthus's associations often rambled in such a way that it was hard to tell whether it was Derain or Sunday about whom he was talking.

Balthus's affinity for Chesterton fits. The novelist embraced amorphousness and obscurity and prized the human potential for transformation. His comments in an essay on *A Midsummer Night's Dream* could equally well describe *The Street* and other Balthus paintings.

> Here is the pursuit of the man we cannot catch, the flight from the man we cannot see; here is the perpetual returning to the same place, here is the crazy alteration in the very objects of our desire, the substitution of one face for another face, the putting of the wrong souls in the wrong bodies, the fantastic disloyalties of the night.[16]

The Man Who Was Thursday, which Balthus said had first impressed him when he was a child, was beloved by the intellectual elite. J. R. R. Tolkien, C. S. Lewis, W. H. Auden, Jorge Luis Borges, and T. S. Eliot all praised it. The saga embraced by this admirable roster of writers centered on an unsolved mystery involving seven anarchists of whom Sunday is the president. It was—the description is Garry Wills's—a tale of "compelling inconsequence" in which "the impossible becomes inevitable. Tyrannic accidents [occur in] the despotic mood of dreams. . . . The book is all a chase, an evasion, and dream; a benign nightmare prolonged, page by page, beyond our waking."[17] Part of what made its followers into a sort of cult is that as many puzzles remain when the book is over as develop at the beginning.

Chesterton's men in the Central Anarchist Council have sworn to destroy the world. The anarchist poet Sunday leads them in this effort, yet although his role is pivotal, his identity remains a mystery. Who Sunday really is is the central, unanswered question of *The Man Who Was Thursday.*

André Derain in Balthus's painting is, in many ways, this fictional character with whom he was so inextricably linked in Balthus's thoughts. Consider these descriptions of Sunday:

> His face projected something broad and brutal, the chin carried forward with a look of cockney contempt. . . . He seemed like a walking blasphemy, a blend of the angel and the ape. . . . [His] big bull's eyes blinked suddenly like those of an angry lion. . . .[18]

His neck and shoulders were brutal, like those of some apish god. His head had a stoop that was hardly human, like the stoop of an ox. In fact, I had at once the revolting fancy that this was not a man at all, but a beast dressed up in men's clothes.[19]

Perhaps *this* was Balthus's Derain—and he based his portrait subject more on a figment of G. K. Chesterton's imagination than on the man who made that long walk each morning to his studio.

THE REAL ANDRÉ DERAIN was neither like Balthus's portrait nor like Chesterton's character. Photographs make clear that while the older artist was as enormous and jowly as Balthus showed him to be, his head was not proportionally small, and it did not sit so squat on his shoulders without a visible neck. Of Derain's body, Balthus made a parody, creating Chesterton's beast more than the man before him. But it is Derain's personality that Balthus distorted the most. In real life, Derain, often seen with a half smile, was the image of the amiable old Frenchman. In his more serious moments, he looked intensely pensive and sensitive—not haughty or arrogant. Alexander Liberman compared him to one "of the great actors of the Comédie-Française."[20] Very much the *crémier*'s son, Derain had a "simplicity, ease, and naturalness, as well as an intense and subtle dignity in his bearing." Denys Sutton reported of Derain that "the large, imposing, robust . . . figure reminded one of a warm and comfortable country house."[21]

Yet Balthus made him forbidding and despotic. His often repeated statement that people impose their own cravings and neuroses on their vision of the world, rather than view that world objectively, applies equally to how he invokes his subjects. Yet again, what he lambastes in other people is what he did in extremis himself. His portrait of Derain expresses Balthus's own needs and personal psychology more than any more objective outside truth, something on which he placed little value.

THERE WAS LITTLE Balthus resented so much as the feeling of being beholden. This probably explains why Balthus painted the object of his reverence as such a despot and brute.

"If you make a portrait and you are trying to find the style of a person, the psychology comes in by itself," Balthus maintained to me with a quiet air of authority. And so he portrayed Derain—his alleged hero and friend—with the older artist scowling, rolling his hyperthyroid eyes with an intense look of dis-

André Derain

pleasure, looking practically like a murderer. The older artist is gruff, impenetrable, and arrogant. Balthus claims not to have had any interest in psychology,
yet he has made an intensely revelatory character portrayal. The problem is
that the dominant mentality is that of Balthus more than his subject.

THE IMAGE OF DERAIN as a cloud—the comparison Balthus repeated so
many times to me—did not, in fact, originate with Balthus as its spokesman or

Derain as its inspiration. The person who initially was like a cloud was Sunday. "The Professor" in Chesterton's novel tells his listeners:

> My early life, as you know, was a bit too large and loose. Well, when I saw Sunday's face I thought it was too large—everybody does, but I also thought it was too loose. The face was so big, that one couldn't focus it or make it a face at all. . . .
>
> But put it this way. Walking up a road at night, I have seen a lamp and a lighted window and a cloud make together a most complete and unmistakable face. . . . Yet when I walked a little farther I found that there was no face, that the window was ten yards away, the lamp ten hundred yards, the cloud beyond the world. Well, Sunday's face escaped me; it ran away to right and left, as such chance pictures run away. And so his face has made me, somehow, doubt whether there are any faces. . . . Sunday has taught me the last and the worst doubts, the doubts of a spiritualist.[22]

Are there any faces? There are, after all, no cats.

BALTHUS TOLD ME THAT several years after he moved into the Cour de Rohan, Derain took space there also. The older artist had come to know the building both during his posing sessions and on his frequent subsequent visits. Balthus said that when the large room below his own became free, he went to see the proprietor on his friend's behalf and helped make arrangements for Derain to rent it. The space had previously been used by a man who repaired tapestries. It was very dark, but Derain said he could manage there. Discussing this, Balthus made the slightly smug smile that often accompanied the use of his favorite adjective, and said that "Derain found it very amusing there, a strange life, very popular; for Derain it was a kind of a gighole."

This all sounded charming to me. There were Balthus and Derain in that same hidden Parisian courtyard, their studios stacked like nests. Balthus had kindly facilitated it all. The only problem is that, with subsequent research, I have learned that this was not the case. In the late 1930s, when Balthus was in the army, Derain did sometimes use Balthus's studio space on the Cour de Rohan. But Derain never rented a room there for himself.

Balthus also told me, more than once, that he completed his painting *The Mountain* in Derain's studio opposite Braque's on the Rue du Douanier. Whenever he mentioned this fact, he annotated it—with the precision of a gazetteer—by adding the information that the Rue du Douanier is now the

Rue Braque. This meticulous attention to detail made me feel that Balthus was doing his utmost to help me get the facts straight. He often gave me the impression that clarity—and my education—was among his primary concerns.

Subsequent to Balthus's elucidation of this bit of geography, I learned that Derain and Braque did, indeed—in 1928—build houses opposite one another's at 5 and 6, Rue du Douanier, which was near the Parc de Montsouris. Derain, however, sold that house in 1935. And Balthus did not complete *The Mountain* until two years later. In all likelihood, the place where Balthus worked on his large painting was the studio that Derain had taken, in the year he gave up the place on the Rue du Douanier, with Léopold-Lévy on the Rue d'Assas near the Jardin du Luxembourg. The studio on the Rue d'Assas would have been available for Balthus both because Léopold-Lévy had virtually stopped going there and because Derain had, in 1935, purchased La Roseraie, his lovely farm in Chambourcy, about an hour outside Paris, and, ever since giving up his place on the Rue du Douanier, had been spending most of his time at his studio out there.

Simple enough. Balthus's error about the location of Derain's studio probably reflected nothing more than an old person's memory lapse. It seems perfectly natural for him to have conflated the two locations of Derain's Paris studios.

Yet when someone as sharp as Balthus, and as capable of fabrication, commits even such a minor lapse, it becomes suspect. Perhaps the error reflected some personal agenda. Maybe it was just one of those things he said because it appealed to him.

FOR BALTHUS, ENTERTAINMENT—for himself and his audience—mattered more than facts. In the many interviews with the artist that appeared in 1994—all, of course, with the usual claims about his unwillingness to grant interviews—he readily embellished his family's connection to both Bonnard and Matisse; by 1996 he had thrown Monet into the group as well. With me, his purposes were best served by beefing up the Derain stories.

In the course of his Derain reminiscences, Balthus also told me that—having married Antoinette de Watteville in 1937—he had left her and their two children at Derain's house in Chambourcy during the war when he joined the military. This, too, may have reflected a genuine memory lapse rather than conscious maneuvering, but with Balthus it is impossible to disregard the possibility that it came from a wish to reconstruct history. For when Balthus left Antoinette at Derain's house in 1939, the couple did not yet have children. By

the time their first son, Stanislas, was born in 1942, Balthus had long been discharged from the army—he served for only a few months—and the couple
had moved to Bern, which is where they were still living when their second son
was born two years later. In the meantime, in October 1940, Derain's house
was occupied by German soldiers—who tore it to shreds. The other person
Balthus left with Antoinette in Chambourcy in 1939 was his mother, Baladine
Klossowska.

GENEVIÈVE TAILLADE, André Derain's niece, told me this when I visited her
at La Roseraie in 1991. This eighteenth-century manor house where Derain
lived was one of the grandest structures in the small Ile-de-France village. With
its rough plaster walls, gentle mansard roof, large windows, and scrollwork
railings, it had a picture-book charm. There were gardens, gigantic chestnut
trees and smaller limes, and an artificial pond with ducks and geese. Farmland
surrounded it all. Derain had goats and rabbits as well as numerous cats and
dogs. The artist lived in this bucolic atmosphere with his wife, Alice, her sister
Suzanne—Geneviève's mother—and Geneviève.

Before wartime, Balthus had been something of a regular at Derain's high-
spirited Sunday lunches, at which there were generally about ten guests. The
others at the table included Georges Braque—droll and enchanting in spite of
the debilitating effects of the head injuries he suffered during World War I; the
designer Paul Poiret, who lived within walking distance; Serge Lifar, who had
performed with Diaghilev; and the filmmaker Jean Renoir, who, as Pierre-
Auguste's son, relished the conversation with artists.

Derain's favorite foods were served, which meant that these events
attended by Balthus were true country feasts. In his childhood in nearby Cha-
tou, the heavyset Derain had developed certain culinary passions typical in the
house of a *crémier-glacier*. These consisted of *matelotes d'anguille* (eel stew), rich
vols-au-vent, and special cuts of mutton chops. But Balthus's presence threatened to disrupt the carefully planned meals. "The tall, slender Balthus would
regularly engage in such long, erudite conversations with Derain that the cook
would fret that they would never come down from the studio to eat," Madame
Taillade recalled. "The kitchen help would become very impatient and irritated waiting for them to come to the table while Balthus and Derain would
stay in the studio and talk and talk and talk." Her annoyance, of course, was
good-humored. "Balthus was very nice and charming to everyone in the
household, and everyone loved his knowledge of literature, and of paintings."

Any occasion when Balthus visited was exciting for the young Geneviève.
For a long time she had found Balthus exceptionally good-looking, and he

9. *André Derain,* 1936, oil on wood, 112.8 x 72.4 cm

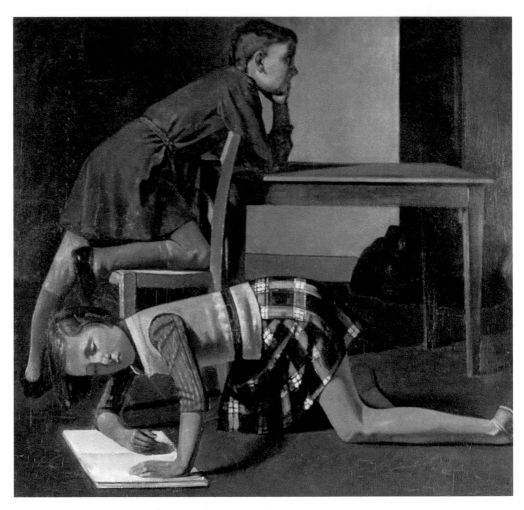

10. *The Children,* 1937, oil on canvas, 125 x 130 cm

11. *Thérèse Dreaming*, 1938, oil on canvas, 150.5 x 130.2 cm

12. *The Three Sisters,* 1954–55, oil on canvas, 60 x 119 cm

13. *Bouquet of Roses on a Window Sill,* 1958, oil on canvas, 134 x 131 cm

outdid himself as a young soldier; he was especially dashing because of the boots he wore, which were, she says, like those of a spahi. At least at the start, the realities of wartime presented their more positive aspects to Balthus. Not only was he a smart and handsome soldier, but he had found an idyllic refuge for his family.

No wonder he might now choose to remember that he had left his children at La Roseraie. It was the same sort of sylvan ideal he liked to imagine, in retrospect, as the milieu in which he had spent his own childhood in uninterupted bliss.

V

ONE EVENING WHEN we were talking about Derain, Balthus suddenly lapsed uncharacteristically into complete earnestness. Sitting before the library fire, he addressed a subject that has long puzzled me greatly. When I think back on the conversation, I am still struck by the rarity and bravery of Balthus's independent stance. He was so accurate and moral—where most people buy into nasty clichés—that it was hard to believe he could ever be otherwise.

The issue was André Derain's role in the war. In the fall of 1940, German troops tore apart La Roseraie and destroyed much of Derain's work. They threatened to shoot the artist, whom they accused of having done obscene drawings representing Hitler, and claimed he was Jewish. He was not. Some seventy soldiers occupied the house.

That December, Derain heard that the Germans had vacated the house, but when he and Alice tried to return, they were turned away by machine-gunners. They ended up back in Paris.

Later that month, the Gestapo interrogated the artist. A few days afterward, an officer asked if he wanted the house back, but he declined. The officer then told Derain about an upcoming artists' trip to Germany—but Derain explained that he never traveled.

In late 1941 a former model of Derain's—at that point married to Arno Becher, a sculptor favored by the Nazis—came to see him and informed him he was on the list for this trip. Then a Gestapo officer began to visit daily. He told Derain to pack his bags.

Derain felt that he had no choice in making the trip to Germany—which the Gestapo hoped to use for publicity purposes. His first response was to move, quickly, the work of Léopold-Lévy, who was Jewish, from the studio they shared on the Rue d'Assas; Derain believed that the Germans would destroy it. His apologists say that he then endeavored to use his time in enemy territory to work toward the release of French prisoners of war, and to try to improve the welfare of members of the Société des Indépendants and students from the Ecole des Beaux-Arts who were imprisoned there. As a result of that trip, however, Derain has been accused ever since of being a collaborationist.

The artist's Jewish friends and Braque were among the many people who jumped to his defense when Derain was vilified upon his return. But right after the war, he was asked nonetheless—by the ad hoc Comité d'Epuration—to provide an explanation for why he went to Germany when he did. Incensed, he would not heed their request. Because of the government's failure to condemn the activities of this "Purification Committee" after the restoration of the Republic, he ended up refusing to have any dealings with the French government. This decision cost him dearly, and it has affected his reputation—and a number of people's attitudes toward him—to this day.

Balthus lamented Derain's fate to me, saying that he was extremely upset by the way the artist's work had virtually been banned after 1945. "He couldn't expose anymore, and people avoided seeing him. Yet he was forced to go to Germany. There was a group who went to Germany with the conviction that their group was helping prisoners to come out. Derain went to Germany only to obtain the release of artists who were there." Balthus was probably overstating Derain's altruism here—Derain made the trip primarily because he felt he had no option—but he was quite right that Derain then did his best to put a miserable, unwelcome journey to good purposes, and has been unjustly maligned. Balthus's stance on all of this was loyal and generous. Rather than succumb to the usual gossip-mongering, he wished to set the record straight.

Balthus at times displayed such steadfast integrity that I felt guilt at ever impugning his character, and craved the luxury of being able to believe and admire him always.

VI

IN 1938 MARGUERITE YOURCENAR'S book *Nouvelles orientales* (*Oriental Tales*) was published. In reminiscing about Derain, Balthus told me that one of his strongest memories was of recounting to the older artist the first story in it. Derain loved Yourcenar's tale fervently.

The recollection made Balthus beam—both because of the pleasure he had brought to someone so close to him and because of the story itself. He told me that Yourcenar's book—and this tale in particular—has remained among his favorite works of literature throughout his life.

The story is called "How Wang-Fo Was Saved." Wang-Fo is an old painter with a disciple named Ling. For both of them, painting is the most precious thing on earth. Wang-Fo is described as loving "the image of things and not the things themselves";[23] the only objects he cares for are his art supplies. Ling, who carries a heavy sack of his master's sketches on his back, does not consider them a burden because for him "the sack was full of snow-covered mountains, torrents in spring, and the face of the summer moon."[24]

We learn that Ling is the son of a banker and the grandson of a jade merchant and lives with his beautiful wife in a house painted vermilion. But one night he meets Wang-Fo in a tavern. Wang-Fo has been drinking rice wine "in order to better paint a drunkard. . . . Thanks to him, Ling got to know the beauty of the drunkards' faces blurred by the vapors of hot drink, the brown splendor of the roasts unevenly brushed by tongues of fire, and the exquisite blush of wine stains strewn on the tablecloths like withered petals."[25] In this flashback, Ling pays Wang-Fo's bar bill and invites him home; by the end of their walk, during which he learns that the house he thought red was more the color of a rotten orange, Ling feels that Wang-Fo has given him "a new soul and a new vision of the world."[26]

Wang-Fo paints Ling's wife, after which Ling prefers the portrait to the woman. Because of this change in her husband, she dies, leaving her looking "even more delicate than usual." Wang-Fo does one last painting of her "because he loved the green hue that suffuses the face of the dead. His disciple Ling mixed the colors and the task needed such concentration that he forgot to shed tears."[27]

From then on, Wang-Fo and Ling travel all over the Kingdom of Han. As they move from village to village, Ling takes care of Wang-Fo's art supplies and sees to his meals, while Wang-Fo paints constantly. The two are then taken by soldiers to the Imperial Palace, where, after going through countless rooms, they reach an exotic garden in which the emperor sits on a jade throne.

The emperor reveals to Wang-Fo that he was brought up in the most secret chamber of the palace. He was raised there in solitude except for the collection of Wang-Fo's paintings his father had assembled to be his companions. All his impressions of the world came to him through these pictures. And when, at age sixteen, the doors were opened for him and he began to see the real world from the balcony, he discovered that it was not nearly as beautiful as it looked in this art. "You lied, Wang-Fo, you old impostor," laments the emperor.

> The world is nothing but a mass of muddled colors thrown into the
> world by an insane painter, and smudged by our tears. The Kingdom
> of Han is not the most beautiful of kingdoms, and I am not the

Emperor. The only empire which is worth reigning over is that which
you alone can enter, old Wang, by the road of One Thousand Curves
and Ten Thousand Colors.[28]

As his punishment for having filled the emperor with disappointment and disgust at everything he owns, Wang-Fo is to have his eyes burned out and his
hand cut off. Hearing this, Ling attempts to stab the emperor—and instantly
has his head cut off by one of the emperor's guards. Wang-Fo responds to the
slaying of his companion and would-be savior by admiring "the beautiful scarlet stain that his disciple's blood made on the green stone floor."[29]

The emperor then demands one last task of Wang-Fo before the artist is
deprived of eyes and hands. He must complete to the very best of his ability a
landscape of mountains and sea. The work is still unfinished, but the emperor
already considers it to be far more beautiful than such scenes in actuality. If
Wang-Fo does not do as ordered, the emperor will burn all of the artist's work.

Wang-Fo, assisted by slaves and eunuchs, goes about the task. As he does
so, the sea in the painting becomes real and the small rowboat on which he is
doing the finishing touches becomes an actual boat.

Then Ling comes to life and helps Wang-Fo into the boat. Everyone
around them, including the emperor, drowns. And then, as the rowboat with
Wang-Fo at the helm and Ling at the oars fades into the distance, they all
revive. With the finished painting at his side, the emperor watches the tiny
boat disappear. "The painter Wang-Fo and his disciple Ling vanished forever
on the jade-blue sea that Wang-Fo had just created."[30]

It is easy to imagine Balthus eagerly telling Derain the tale—and the two
of them relishing it. No wonder "How Wang-Fo Was Saved" was a clear memory over half a century later. The first time I met Balthus, he told me that when
he looks at something, his immediate response, whatever it is, is simply to
imagine how it can be painted. His art makes clear that he, too, thought death
could be an exquisite sight. He and Derain wanted to create in their art something more powerful, and more palpable, than life itself. For Balthus especially,
the painted world could certainly have more reality than the actual one.

CHAPTER FIFTEEN

MIRÓ

I

Wⁿᴇɴ I ASKED BALTHUS about Joan Miró, whose portrait he began the year after Derain's, he offered nothing about Miró in his own right but immediately quoted the Spaniard as saying, "Je suis entièrement pour Balthus."

This was how Balthus measured the people around him: whether he has felt them to be partisans or foes.

Esteemed like a god by Baladine and Rilke, Balthus has been unable to satiate his appetite for admiration since his youth. The craving for fealty has been the focal point of all of his relationships.

A joint interview with Balthus and Harumi appeared in the September 8, 1996, *London Times Magazine.* Color photos bespeak their glamorous life. The text dwells on the father and daughter's shared fondness for amusing dinner parties and Barbara Cartland novels. But then Balthus issues the statement:

> She had one great stroke of luck in her life—that her philosophy teacher took a keen interest in her. He was an admirer of my work, and when he discovered Harumi was my daughter he completely changed his attitude towards her. Through him she got interested in my art for the first time.[1]

Balthus does not think to mention his daughter's own sense of fulfillment or happiness beyond the context of his own position. The vital issue is his own standing.

Yet it is understandable that it mattered considerably that Miró, an esteemed artist and a modernist, defended Balthus when he was not yet thirty

years old. Having made incendiary paintings guaranteed to stir up intense controversy, Balthus knew that some people snickered at the mere mention of his
name. Others denigrated him as a child molester. His supporters emerged as
people of courage. And Joan Miró was one to be proud of.

AT THE TIME BALTHUS PAINTED Miró, both artists were represented by
Pierre Loeb in Paris and Pierre Matisse in New York. Miró, fifteen years
Balthus's senior, was forty-five. He painted in a very different way than
Balthus, but he had many qualities that Balthus greatly admired. Miró was
witty and artistically adventurous. He had tremendous powers of invention
and was certainly willing to jolt his audience. Like Balthus, he was roughly
affiliated with Surrealism but not devoted to it. Moreover, the Spaniard was
steeped in tradition.

Miró's early style would visibly nourish Balthus's work over the years. The
1919 *Woman Before the Mirror* gave a prototype, in reverse, of the layout
Balthus used for various late works, among them the 1963–66 *Turkish Room*
and the various versions of *Cat at the Mirror;* Miró's representational early
landscapes also had their echoes in Balthus's work at Chassy.

When he painted Miró's portrait in 1937, Balthus did not consider his
subject either a close friend or an artistic comrade the way he had Derain, but
there was nonetheless a genuine rapport between them. This was already
apparent in the resemblance between his own 1937 *Still Life* and Miró's *Still
Life with Old Shoe.* Both Miró and Balthus were clearly preoccupied with the
fragility and struggle that often lay beneath the surface of visual grace. Each
had painted a canvas suggesting that pears and bottles of wine and kitchen
ceramics might no longer be allowed to stand unimpeded in simple kitchens,
that people might not continue to partake of daily life as they had. Each recognized the tenuousness of life and the havoc being wreaked on civilization.

When he and his young daughter Dolores sat for Balthus, Miró had only
recently arrived in Paris as a refugee from Spain. The artists came from different worlds, but each knew what it was to be buffeted by circumstance, to be
forced into exile, and to fight to survive.

As for Miró's personality, Balthus told me he could not verbalize it. Miró
was "indescribable." Beyond that, Balthus's recollections were quite terse: "He
looked very intense. He was a very curious man. He never spoke a lot. He was
probably very shy. And so was I. The little girl moved all the time."

But then Balthus added an extraordinary remark. He said that "Miró's art
describes him very well." The statement completely contradicted Balthus's
often repeated assertions to me about the separation between a person's private

self and his artwork, and about the need to accept paintings aesthetically rather than as guides to their creators. Having perpetually battled the idea of his own art as autobiography, he had no trouble applying the forbidden procedure to Miró.

THE FIRST TIME BALTHUS AND I ever talked about his Miró portrait—when he was telling me his horror story about how Pierre Loeb had tricked him into selling it at a low price—he told me that Miró had come to him for posing sessions "every day for an entire year." In subsequent conversations, he reduced the number to "forty" or "over forty." He worked and reworked the painting, Balthus explained, in order to get the artist's face more precise and the painting more complete. "I was fascinated by the expression of Miró. It was astonishing and childish. He was charming; I liked him very much; and yet he never said a word. . . . What was strange with Miró was that he never said a word and you did not feel embarrassed by his silence."

After each of these descriptions, Balthus reiterated that a large part of the pleasure he took in painting the taciturn Spaniard derived from his awareness that Miró was both such an unlikely and genuine partisan of his work. Balthus said that Miró's positive judgment surprised other people. His feeling of gratification probably contributed significantly to the uniquely serene ambience of *Joan Miró and His Daughter Dolores*. The portrait of the father and daughter betrays mixed emotions—and is fraught with the usual Balthusian undertone of mockery—but it displays profound tenderness and dignity. A beatific calm pervades. Miró is odd and funny-looking, and Dolores anxious and restless, yet clearly Balthus held his subject in rare high regard. Miró emerges with the inner strength of a saint, the painting an icon.

THIS DOUBLE PORTRAIT IS among Balthus's most beautifully painted works. Thanks to James Thrall Soby's public-spiritedness, as previously described, it now belongs to the Museum of Modern Art in New York. For many years, it was regularly on view there. As of this writing, it is no longer in favor and is consigned to storage most of the time, but when we are lucky enough to see it, this magisterial picture is remarkable for the quiet strength that suffuses the viewer. John Russell, in his Tate catalog, accurately compares its composition to a sculpture of a Madonna and child. Joan and Dolores are statuesque. They exert a powerful dual presence. The lack of extraneous detail contributes to their aura of religiosity and purity; the stable, tranquil composition provides an atmosphere of grace and balance.

The canvas is a precisely halved rectangle with light gray-green above and a subtle charcoal brown-black below. The mutual boundary between those two colors is a wonderful Balthus touch: luminous, like a distant horizon line. By allowing a narrow stripe of canvas to be seen here and at the bottom, the artist keeps this background both light and distant. If the striped wallpaper in *The Guitar Lesson* suggests emotional conflagration, this setting conveys resolution and reserve. It soothes us, so that, in spite of Dolores's distinct restlessness, equanimity prevails.

Yet for all its restraint, the portrait of Joan and Dolores Miró presents the relationship of father and daughter as emotionally loaded. While looking desperate to break free, Dolores also clings to her father—with a child's instinctual longing for her parent's protection even in awkward circumstances. Although he is extremely stiff and awkward, Miró holds her gently and protectively.

The two are further linked by their close resemblance to one another. Their thin mouths match. They both have unusually symmetrical faces, similarly flat. His cheeks are hollow whereas hers are like boards, but they have the same angled jaw. Up close, these features seem exaggerated, and Joan and Dolores are like porcelain dolls: emblems of people as well as people. Yet when we stand at a distance from the painting, the faces are real.

Balthus's evocation of the actual world is remarkable. We know the degree to which Miró needs a shave. We are apprised of the spread of his collar, the thickness of his tie knot. We feel the pull of his suit jacket, the way his trouser legs wrinkle below the knee. Not only are the details distinct, but they have a poetic effect. Miró's suede shoes, muted in tone, soft in form, convey their wearer's quietude. Dolores's, however, shine. They are the essence of a little girl's Mary Janes, evocative of dressing up and important occasions—even if in this instance they are rendered absurd by Dolores's huge legs, which dwarf them completely and would crush such delicate footwear in only a moment's wearing.

Shoes of this sort are almost a signature element of Balthus's work. Slippers like these gleam in his art of every period. They embody the light steps of girlhood. They are also one of those subjects Balthus could paint with consummate skill. Similarly, the patches of white light on Dolores's dress and knees are among the artist's fortes. Such luminous squares, very much like those in Derain's later work, appear consistently throughout Balthus's art. They succeed in making the act of seeing a miracle.

Yet while Balthus's strong points are sublime in this portrait of Miró and his daughter, his problem areas are equally apparent. Miró's right hand looks worse than arthritic; it is either a highly deformed human hand or not human

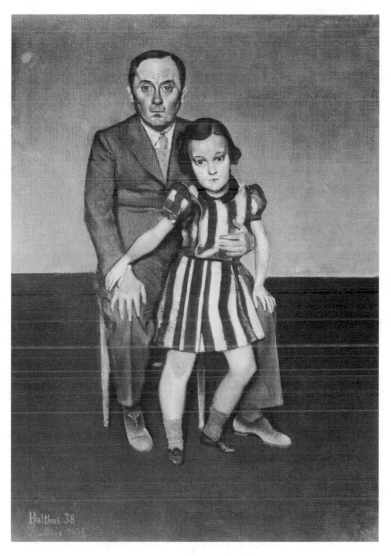

Joan Miró and His Daughter Dolores, 1937–38,
oil on canvas, 130.2 x 88.9 cm

at all. The relationship of Dolores's left thumb to the finger next to it is completely wrong. Again we ask if the reason for these distortions is that Balthus really cannot paint hands or if, perhaps unconsciously, he wished to imbue people with a beastly side.

The sleeves—whether of the man's suit coat, or short and puffed for the girl's dress—are, however, painted impeccably. And the hair of both Mirós is rendered with exactitude and flair. With this painting Balthus emerges, to a new degree, as a master craftsman of supreme patience and unerring eye.

II

No wonder James Thrall Soby, Alfred Barr, and other contemporary observers all felt as they did about *Joan Miró and His Daughter Dolores.* Its quality is so high that, shortly after Balthus completed it and it was shipped to Pierre Matisse's New York gallery, not only was the painting snatched up by the Museum of Modern Art, but it was also selected to appear in color on the April 1938 cover of the American magazine *ARTnews.* The attention to this canvas is particularly unusual in that its painter was, until that moment, unknown to all but a handful of people, and this exhibition on Fifty-seventh Street, his second solo show anywhere, was his first ever in America. But Balthus had won his success deservedly. Just thirty years old, he had mastered a sublime blend of restraint and richness—both visual and psychological.

In *Miró and Dolores,* Balthus has carefully evoked emotional complexity. Having distilled his impressions, deliberated without hurry, and worked and reworked his matte surface, he has imbued his imagery with a mixture of intense filial connectedness and anguished loneliness. The painting summons the qualities that drove writers like Jouve and Artaud and Camus to a frenzy of excitement about Balthus. Like the *View of Montecalvello,* which the artist completed forty-one years later, it is one of those occasions when Balthus has come to grips with both the longings and the comforts of earthly existence.

Here Balthus's reverence for life, alongside his poignant revelation of the exigencies of human experience, is so palpable that the elements that disturb us in so much of his work—the trickery and insistent deception, as well as the pounding theme of domination—are naught compared with the genius.

But Balthus's particular slant is clearly in evidence as well. Linda Fairstein pointed out to me that "Miró is cupping what is about to be his daughter's bosom." Even though she is only eight and her breasts have not yet developed, this is not generally how the father of a girl that age would hold her. Beyond that, the girl is not just sitting on his lap; she is pressed against his inner thigh. The scenario is all the stranger—again this is Linda Fairstein— because of "the gross distortion of Dolores's ungainly, misshapen legs."

The play for power is a primary component of the sexual innuendo in *Joan Miró and His Daughter Dolores*—even if the tone is now far more muted than it was in Balthus's paintings of a few years earlier. Freedom and its constraint meet head-on. Balthus's Dolores is torn between the poles of childhood with her mix of restlessness and dependency, her eagerness to run loose and play coupled with the yearning to be warmly nestled by a parent. The artist evoked the cravings and pleasures, as well as the awkwardness and anxieties, of both of his sitters. Meanwhile, he imposed his own steely grip.

Balthus told me that Miró "loved to pose and didn't move at all." With a slightly sadistic grin, he added that Dolores behaved so badly that he "had to put her in a coal bag." In the painting, rather than gloss over the painful truth of the child's discomfort, Balthus illustrated it in its full intensity. Dolores appears not just a little bit fidgety; next to her stolid and resigned father, she is visibly anguished. It is as if Balthus delighted in stressing both the restlessness he inflicted and the curbs he imposed on it.

Reflecting back on Dolores Miró, who was seven when he began the painting and eight when he finished it, Balthus said that the child's single redeeming trait was that on one occasion in the course of those more than forty posing sessions, she asked her father why he didn't paint the way Balthus did. Quoting her, he raised his eyebrows in satisfaction. But otherwise the child was simply a nuisance because of her inability to hold her pose.

The battle of wills between the little girl and her thirty-year-old portraitist had the makings of legend. James Thrall Soby has written in his unpublished memoirs that Miró's wife, Pilar, told him that "Balthus got so upset by Dolores's restless energy that he held her dangling out his studio window until she promised, sobbing wildly, to hold still when she and her father posed again." According to Soby, Pilar would forever after suffer palpably at the mere mention of Balthus's name. How the kindly Miró tolerated Balthus's mistreatment of his daughter—or why Pilar did not prevail in rescuing Dolores from her misery—remains an open question. It may only be a matter of the difference between the current regard for children's rights and the virtual lack of it in the 1930s. But for the girl's mother, this was not just a case of a child being kept in line; it was torture.

IN NOVEMBER 1993 I MET with Dolores. She had traveled to New York from Majorca for her father's large exhibition at the Museum of Modern Art. Fifty-five years had passed since Balthus painted her.

We agreed to rendezvous in the lobby of the Parker Meridien Hotel. After phoning her room, I awaited her opposite the elevator bank, assuming I would readily recognize her as an older version of the person in Balthus's portrait. But it was she who spotted me first; I was unable to identify the small, awkward child wearing that starched English dress in the woman who now introduced herself to me as Miró's daughter.

The elegant creature before me looked like a cross between Marlene Dietrich and Paloma Picasso. Her carefully made-up face was fine-boned and strik-ingly exotic. Her hair was a tangerine gold. More diamonds sparkled off her than I had ever seen at 10:30 in the morning. She wore a white silk blouse under a stylish black jumper. In one hand she held a cigarette with its ash dan-gling; in the other a supple leather clutch that, when she later opened it, proved to be full of makeup.

Her jewelry conjured store windows in Cannes and Palm Beach: large earrings in which the ovals of small diamonds framed enormous, softly rounded corals; rings and bracelets from a treasure chest. But there was nothing haughty or pretentious about the artist's daughter. The diminutive Dolores was affable and outgoing. If Balthus had painted her to be an awkward and inhibited child, the grown woman was gracious, friendly, and helpful.

We sat in the hotel restaurant. Immediately she wanted news of Balthus. Her father had seen little of him since 1938, and she and her mother—who was still alive—had completely lost touch with him. Dolores had the impression that "Balthus was a Russian prince before the Revolution." She had read about his large house and his young wife in the French *Vogue,* and she was curious to learn more.

But for all the warm inquiry, there had been nothing happy about the experience of posing for him. "He was quite awful." She recalled how restless she had been, at ages seven and eight, during the sittings of two to three hours' duration, and remarked that Balthus did nothing to put her at her ease. In fact, he made it worse. "He had a big sack—a sailor's bag" into which he threatened to stuff her if she did not keep still. I told Dolores about the artist's claim that he had actually put her into a coal bag. This, she laughed, was an exaggeration. But he had, indeed, terrified her, for she really thought he would put her in that sailor's bag. "Il m'a menacé. It was a joke, but he was a very serious man and I was very scared. He was not easy. He had a very rough voice. He was very hard. He never joked with me. He never entertained me. He only gave me a few cookies."

The main difficulty with the pose for this painting, Dolores recollected, was that she had to sit on her father's lap at such an angle that it was impossible for her feet to stay stationary. It was "a very uncomfortable position—I was slipping. I remember that he had parquet"; it was too slippery for her to steady her feet on it.

Simply thinking about it brought a look of consternation to Dolores's face. She then demonstrated her problem for me by stretching out her legs at the angle required by Balthus and showing how her feet were perpetually slid-

ing from underneath her. She illustrated this, as if the wretched experience had
only occurred yesterday.

After a few sessions, Dolores explained, Balthus developed a system
to keep her from moving. He put down nails on the floor against which
she braced her toes. This contrivance, of course, made her all the more miserable. Telling me so, she now splayed her legs forward uncomfortably. Not
only was she locked in a physically uncomfortable position, but she felt very
much alone, because her father would generally sleep while she sat there. For
him, it was an ideal way out of the situation, but Dolores had no means of
escape.

WHEN DOLORES IMITATED her painful pose, I expected to see beefy legs—
proportioned like those in the painting. The considerable girth of the child's
bare legs is plain above the schoolgirl's shoes and ankle socks in her portrait. It
came as no surprise that the sophisticated woman before me now sported sheer
black stockings and very delicate, sharply pointed, soft black leather high
heels, but I was amazed when I observed her dimensions. Dolores was such a
tiny woman that her legs were not much longer now than they had appeared
when she was eight, but they were remarkably slender. The girl could not, in
truth, have had anything remotely like the beefy limbs she has in the painting—given how delicate her legs were now, when she was in her sixties.
Balthus had taken considerable liberty with her proportions when he painted
her. It was clearly part of his agenda to render her graceless.

Referring more to the atmosphere than to details like her shape, Dolores
told me that she felt that the impression given by Balthus's painting was not
accurate. "I wasn't a sad child. I was gay." The outfit that to her eye Balthus has
made look like a stiff uniform was, in fact, a source of considerable pleasure to
her. "It was a very smart dress. My mother dressed me very well. I was very
spoiled by my parents. They bought me the best things; this was from a very
smart boutique run by two English ladies."

Glancing at a glossy reproduction of the double portrait, Dolores Miró
also commented on the inaccuracy of the representation of her father. "He
looked like a cat there. He was so tired. It's not the normal expression of my
father, because he had alive eyes." Nor was he, in fact, catlike.

But the dour tone of the double portrait had its elements of truth. Recalling that time period, Dolores said she felt she had no choice other than to do
what was expected of her. Looking at her own glum face in the painting, she
recalled that this was a different era from now—a time when children simply

did as they were told. "I did not ask questions. That's the way it was. I was posing for Balthus!"

In a similar vein, she said that although her father was very kind, if she
was uncomfortable, it did not especially concern him. "He was a very tender
father. But he didn't play very much with me. Parents were very severe back
then. You did what your parents wanted you to do." And so, after school,
although she was tired and unhappy, day after day she sat for Balthus with her
feet braced. "I was nailed to the spot. I couldn't move."

BEYOND BEING UNCOMFORTABLE during these posing sessions, it was a generally awkward time in Dolores's life. Her family had fled Spain for Paris earlier
that same year because of the rise of Franco in the Spanish Civil War. Paris was
difficult; she was at a new school and did not speak French.

Balthus, indeed, makes Miró and his daughter look like refugees. They
are out of place. Dolores appears not only ill at ease but also, appropriately, in
flight. Yet she looks worse off than she was. Not only did Balthus make her legs
clunky, but he also flattened her face; he chose to render her grotesque.

And while Dolores appears about to take off—with her knee bent in a
familiar Balthus posture, as if she is trying to get off the stage—she is held captive. Captive by her father, and captive by Balthus.

Why are they so frontal, so formalized? Why must Balthus invariably distort the world? Of course he paints beautifully. Dolores and Joan are an
impressively stolid, sculptural pair, like an Iberian wooden statue but with the
massing nicely broken up by all the little rhythms. The visual harmonies are
delightful—his tie is the same orange as the piping of her dress. But they are
somehow mocked and dehumanized, belittled, for all the triumphant visual
beauty.

AS ALWAYS, BALTHUS RENDERED the world more according to his own
vision than in response to how it really was. He made Dolores miserable, and
then painted her as such. It was his choice to present a lithe, high-spirited child
as stocky and depressed, and to immobilize and dull a normally bright-eyed
man. In effect, he subjugated them. At the same time, by gratuitously rendering the unfeline Miró as catlike, Balthus was giving the older painter the image
he generally reserved for himself.

Again Balthus had to transform his subject in order to possess it. Having
literally exhausted Miró father and daughter in the sessions at the Cour de
Rohan, Balthus has shown them exhausted; he has also made them restrained

and uncomfortable. While hinting at Miró's actual pleasantness and gentleness, Balthus also made the Spaniard much that he was not: more tired than
his daughter knew him to be, stiff and tense when in life he was lively and animated. Miró's suit, which in truth fit perfectly well, becomes too small and
taut; it pulls at the waist. Dolores's beloved dress here seems to bind her. To
present the facts was not what interested Balthus. He would rather blend reality with fiction to suit the dictates of his personal taste.

Balthus may have cherished Miró's support, but—perhaps because he
could not bear to feel beholden—he chose, at least unconsciously, to overpower both the artist and his child. The subject was not Joan Miró and his
daughter Dolores as they were but, rather, as Balthus would have them. So
Miró emerges as a painter not unlike himself: holding firm—across her breast,
no less—to a squirming young girl who has been nailed in place.

WHEN I ASKED BALTHUS whether he and Miró had kept in touch after the
1930s, he told me a story that was anything but what I wanted to hear. It's a
familiar sort of frustration: you are counting on an old person to dispense a
nugget, and you get, instead, a worthless bauble. Worse, the old person treats
the bauble as a gem. Balthus retold the story with equal gusto on a number of
occasions when Miró's name came up.

One evening in the 1960s, Balthus went to have dinner with his two sons
in Paris. They were meeting at a Chinese restaurant near the Rue de Rivoli. He
arrived ahead of Stanislas and Thadée and saw that Miró and Pilar were dining
there. Balthus was chatting with them when a waiter came and said, "Elles
vous attendent dans le bar."

Balthus told me that when he walked into the bar, he thought he saw, in
his words, "two American lesbians" standing there. A moment later, he realized
they were his sons, both of whom were sporting long hair at the time.

The anecdote had no bearing, of course, on Miró. But something about
this incident filled Balthus with sophomoric pleasure. His sons' mistaken sexual identities, and his repeated reference to this incident when Miró's name
was in the air, have little to do with the Spaniard, but to Balthus the misappre-
hension had irresistible charm.

CHAPTER SIXTEEN

SURREALISM À LA

COURBET

I

THE PORTRAIT OF MIRÓ and Dolores also appeared in the *New York Herald Tribune.* This was the image that initially brought Balthus before the American public, the audience that for many years would be a mainstay of his life.

But there were a number of other major paintings with which Balthus made his imprint in 1938 with that first New York show. Besides the Miró and Derain portraits, there was the 1935 *Brother and Sister* (later known as *The Children*); *The Street* and *Cathy Dressing,* both lent by James Thrall Soby; and several other portraits. The works most conspicuously missing were *The Guitar Lesson* and *Alice.*

Although *The Guitar Lesson* would have its first public presentation in that same space forty years later, the American audience back then clearly was not ready for it; Soby was its owner at the time and could have lent it, but he and Pierre Matisse must have decided this would be ill advised. *Alice,* equally unsuitable, had already been purchased by Jouve.

Balthus's work arrived on the American exhibition scene with a splash. Soby—one of the major critical voices of the era—wrote in his catalog essay:

> When a painter in his twenties can communicate original ideas with such terrific force, and on such a large scale, as Balthus has done, he must be appraised as a painter who may give direction to a whole epoch in art.[1]

The mainstream did not agree, however. Carlyle Burrows, in the *New York Herald Tribune,* derided the artist for his "queer streak of fantasy" and "the individuality earnestly claimed for him by the aesthetes of Paris."² The critic declared, "The portraits are unflattering, to say the least. Several of them, no doubt, have a subtle psychological connotation, but for a portrait painter of reputation, his portraiture is not very skillful nor very clever." Burrows characterized Derain in his dressing gown as "very self-conscious and bilious looking."

And if Soby was touting Balthus as a leader in modern art, E. A. Jewell, in the *New York Times,* allotted him no more than a single paragraph that concluded with the words, "It may be felt that much is as yet potential rather than in full measure 'realized.' "³

BUT JAMES THRALL SOBY was not the only observer to recognize Balthus as a young master. By electing to reproduce in full color the portrait of Miró and Dolores as the cover of *ARTnews,* Alfred Frankfurter, its prescient and influential editor, instantly elevated the thirty-year-old artist.

Positioning the painting as such, Frankfurter put on center stage a look and mood fresh to the art of that epoch. In spite of the flawed technology of color printing in the 1930s, the somber greens and blacks of *Joan Miró and His Daughter Dolores,* and the aura of hierarchical distance established by the sitters' statuelike pose, had both a drama and a restraint new to the American scene. The father's and daughter's haunting stares and the palpable awkwardness of their bodies captivated the art cognoscenti. Layers of civilization, and a supreme knowledge of painting in the greatest European tradition, were evident in this painting by the thirty-year-old Parisian.

Frankfurter chose to review the show himself. His lengthy piece made Balthus's Pierre Matisse exhibition one of the pivotal events of the season, along with shows of British masters and mainstream American sculpture. He gave his text the ambiguous headline THE IMPORTANT PREMIERE OF BALTHUS: NOUVEAU SACHLICHKEIT A LA CELINE. The words suggested a rare blend of French and German cultures, both provocative and obtuse. If their meaning was somewhat hazy, however, the thrust of the opening sentence was clear enough: "You can take it or leave it, but you can't overcome the impact of Balthus in the paintings that look at you—stare at you would be a better phrase—from the walls of the Pierre Matisse Gallery which is presenting his American debut." This scholar of the contemporary art scene believed that "it will be hard to reckon without [the young Frenchman], pro or con, in any future estimation of the vital subject of painting."⁴

· · ·

YET FOR ALL Alfred Frankfurter's excitement, virtually everything he wrote is contrary to what Balthus, at least in his discussions with me, would have one believe. The editor, like several other writers of the period, declared the young artist a "pupil of Derain"; Balthus says this was not so. Frankfurter pointed to the "stylistic affinity of *Neue Sachlichkeit* practitioners like Dix and Schrimpf": a comparison Balthus vociferously rejected when we spoke—in spite of its having been frequently aired in the literature on him. Frankfurter also wrote that "Monsieur Balthus is in his motivation half sensational journalist, half clinical psychologist." Balthus would more willingly have been compared to a simple tradesman like a sign painter.

Frankfurter, however, stressed his subject's "analysis of morbid psychology." He noted it in Balthus's response to *Wuthering Heights,* "the macabre elements of which he had enthusiastically perceived and emphasized." The artist's alertness to the underside of life was an essential factor in Balthus's attraction. The *ARTnews* editor used a marvelous painting based on one of the Heathcliff and Cathy drawings to launch into an analysis of the painter's diabolical sensibility:

> *Frère et soeur* is the beginning of the delineation of Freudian realities on a series of extraordinarily horrid children who, one dreads, are, like the very closely related precious heroine of the play called *The Children's Hour,* the superterrible infants of the future. The painter Miró and his daughter somehow escape this uncomfortable sort of survey, to become a Gallicized and softened New Objectivity and the best painting in the exhibition. But Madame la Vicomtesse de Noailles, leader of the newer and madder Paris intelligentsia, patroness of Dalí, and so forth, does not fare so well: she is one of Balthus's bad little girls with curls quite grown up, with the gangling dreams of adolescence turned into a full-fledged libido. The conclusion, one supposes, is that everyone, from Bernardo Daddi to Balthus, paints the devil as he finds him; it makes little difference whether he is called Satan or Sigmund.

The vehemently anti-Freudian Balthus I know decries all these ideas, of course: that the girls were bad, that we sense anything of the Vicomtesse de Noailles's libido, that he was painting the devil. Yet what primarily attracted others was the liberating effect of his work. They applauded, and themselves felt emboldened by, Balthus's courage.

The American art scene at the time was largely dominated by Impressionistic renderings of ladies with parasols. Art we now consider innocent like

Alexander Calder's upbeat circus figures or Picasso's Dinard paintings was deemed too spontaneous and personal.

Balthus was even more daring than his fellow moderns who garnered such opprobrium. Painting his subjects realistically, yet distorting and exaggerating the contortions of their minds as well as their bodies, the young artist evoked themes that most people kept fiercely private even if the power issues and yearnings permeated their fantasies or dream lives. Balthus may choose for his own reasons to downplay what was in effect his own tremendous bravery, but he was as candid and insightful in his psychological observations as he was skillful and original in his grasp of the beauty of painted canvas. With supreme artistic eloquence, he boldly laid bare the dark inner workings of the human mind. Herein rested his acclaim and his future.

II

BOTH ALFRED FRANKFURTER'S and James Thrall Soby's essays for that Pierre Matisse catalog included a quotation from Balthus that has been repeated more than any other. This was, "Je fais du Surréalisme à la Courbet." That remark has shed a light on Balthus's work to which numerous observers have been drawn as if to a beacon in a fog. If one understands the tenets of Surrealism and the painterly priorities of Courbet, this straightforward explication pulls Balthus's work out of obscurity.

Its illuminating quality may be the very reason Balthus told me he never made the statement. He acted as if it were just another falsification of art history. More than once, he maintained to me that someone else invented the remark. He wore a mischievous, transparent smile on each of the several occasions when he disavowed it; he looked like a teenager feigning innocence when no one could possibly doubt the child's guilt. But he was resolute that he had never uttered the rubric so often applied to him.

Beyond rendering his complexity comprehensible, what must further irritate Balthus about "I do Surrealism in the style of Courbet" is that it suggests the deliberate evocation of the unconscious that the artist now so vehemently decries. Naturally, he is eager to dismiss an association that values the life of dreams and esteems fantasy and free association in the same way that psychoanalysis does. Surrealism recognizes the difference between reality and its subterfuges; rather than just pretend, it allows for the ramifications of imagination. To Balthus, today these distinctions no longer exist. But then they did.

.   .   .

To FURTHER THE NOTION that Balthus never had any interest whatsoever in Surrealism or its objectives, Jean Leymarie provides the explanation that this "persistent misunderstanding about his initial alliance" originated because the Galerie Pierre was primarily a showplace for Surrealism. The public at large lacked the discernment to recognize that an artist who showed there might not be part of the group. If we, on the other hand, wish to make clear our higher intellectual stature, we must disregard the old Balthus doctrine and comply with the artist and his loyal minions on the new rules.

Yet even if Balthus today denies having said "I do Surrealism in the style of Courbet" and Leymarie follows suit by declaring that the linkage had nothing to do with the artist himself, numerous witnesses quoted him as having said and believed the statement in the 1930s. And the artist's displeasure notwithstanding, when he uttered "Je fais du Surréalisme à la Courbet," the erudite, perceptive Balthus had beautifully elucidated the formulation of his art.

James Thrall Soby extrapolated on Balthus's words in his 1938 Pierre Matisse essay: "It was the Surrealists who first reintroduced the anecdote to art by painting pictures in which Freudian and post-Freudian symbols unfolded a dream-life scenario." The suggestion is that Balthus's imagery is profoundly connected with his personal emotional makeup and the childhood experiences and perceptions that underlie it. The Balthus of the 1990s would have us believe that nothing personal is going on in his art; *The Street* is merely the good old neighborhood, not a dream; anecdote is overrated as an aspect of his work. But the psychological, autobiographical aspects inherent in that word "Surrealism" were something he once openly acknowledged.

IT IS NOT, HOWEVER, correct to classify Balthus as a practitioner of full-fledged, doctrinaire Surrealism. That claim, put forward in various books, overreaches the truth. Balthus accepted certain tenets of Surrealism as if they were second nature to him, but was at complete odds with it on the vital issue of the technique of painting. Then as now, he considered Max Ernst, René Magritte, Salvador Dalí, and most of their confreres to be rather poor painters. Balthus has come, in retrospect, to disavow the movement with which he once tangentially aligned himself both because of its emphasis on the psychological, storytelling side of art and because of the thin, flaccid painting styles of many of its proponents.

This is where "à la Courbet" comes in. Courbet embodied a range of painterly skills that Balthus admired and believed in—so much so that Balthus studied and borrowed from the nineteenth-century Frenchman to an extent only exceeded by his dependency on Piero. Soby writes, "It is significant, too, that Balthus's idol among his elders in Paris is the man who in our time most nearly represents Courbet's forceful lyricism, André Derain—the best painter in the business."

The Balthus I came to know would not acknowledge Derain as an "idol" any more than he would accept his connection to Surrealism. Like a number of painters in old age, Balthus had managed to disclaim most of the influences pivotal to his artistic development. But his allegiance to Derain—and, through him, to Courbet's technique—was as vital as "Je fait du Surréalisme." No wonder he ultimately scrapped the whole slogan.

III

BALTHUS TOLD ME ABOUT a visit he had in 1934 from some of the leading practitioners of Surrealism. They "came to see my painting. Among them was Giacometti—this was the first time we ever met. We started talking about painting. It was Breton, Eluard, and another. We didn't agree. They didn't like painting. When they left, Eluard said to Giacometti, 'You can count a new enemy among your friends.' Alberto told me this when I saw him in Bern just afterwards. That gives you a good idea of the atmosphere among those people. They hated painting, and they had a disastrous influence on painting."

When Balthus said this to me, there was no context for Eluard's remark except the general suggestion that it was clear to the Surrealists that at age twenty-six, when other young artists were clamoring to be considered part of the movement, Balthus stood in complete opposition to their outlook. James Lord puts a different slant on the comment in his book *Some Remarkable Men*. Lord reports that on this occasion of their first meeting, Giacometti was highly outspoken in his criticism of one of Balthus's small paintings, which is the reason Breton—not Eluard—said he had just made an enemy. Given that both Lord and Balthus are capable of inventing information to suit their agendas, it is hard to know which of them to believe.

Why would Giacometti have been so harsh on a first encounter? On the other hand, if Giacometti was indeed so critical, in his version to me Balthus would deliberately have eliminated such a distressing detail.

HOWEVER MUCH HE WOULD later disparage Surrealist art, in the thirties Balthus was happy enough to join its practitioners at some of the most amusing and elegant social events in Paris. He often left his simple digs on the Cour de Rohan for luncheons or dinner parties at the enormous home on the Place des

Etats-Unis of Charles and Marie-Laure de Noailles. Renowned hosts, adventurous supporters of contemporary culture, and powerful personalities, the
vicomte and vicomtesse were the talk of Paris. With history and wealth behind
them, they backed outrageous art, including Surrealism at its most scandalous.
The most hidebound snob or groundbreaking modernist could feel at home
with them, and Balthus, for one, relished the connection for over two decades.
The de Noailles gladly returned the favor. Starting in the mid-1930s, they were
good friends and champions of Balthus, and would remain so for many years.

By the time the octogenarian Balthus reminisced about the de Noailles to
me, he put all the emphasis on the traditions they embodied and the sense that
he and they were in the same social orbit. Balthus made no mention of the aristocratic pair's engagement with the avant-garde—the main point for almost
anyone else discussing them. He described them, rather, as "great patrons, with
very good taste; they had beautiful Delacroix, two beautiful Watteaus, and
above all the beautiful Goyas." This was, fair enough, the art that Balthus liked
the most. But it also represented the de Noailles's wealth, and the impressive
background from which they inherited these trophies—as opposed to the rad-
icalism of their leaps into recent filmmaking and art. And it was because of
their courageous modernism—rather than his trumped-up links with aristocracy and the world of money—that Balthus was included.

Balthus told me that the de Noailles were friends of his parents. It seems
unlikely, however, that this was the case. The affluent art patrons were virtually
Balthus's contemporaries—not Erich and Baladine's—and I feel that he
claimed this only to emphasize his parents' connections with the Parisian aristocracy during his own childhood. This is probably the same reason Balthus
made a point of telling me that Charles, more than Marie-Laure, was his close
friend. Of the two, Charles had, by Balthus's standards, the more impressive
lineage; moreover, unlike his wife, Charles did not have the taint of being part
Jewish.

According to everyone else's recollections and all the evidence, however,
Balthus's real companion of the two was Marie-Laure. Ned Rorem, Claus von
Bülow, James Lord, Bernard Minoret, and others of the de Noailles' circle with
whom I have spoken all laugh at the notion that Balthus would now rather be
affiliated with the quieter, stuffier, more impeccably aristocratic Charles. For
Marie-Laure was truly Balthus's champion and his liaison to another world.

THE ONLY REMINISCENCE of Madame de Noailles I could elicit from the
revisionist Balthus was that she was "extraordinary, quite mad." Indeed, Marie-
Laure's extremism, like Artaud's, probably explains why Balthus now mini-

mized his involvement with her. The formidable vicomtesse had a spice from which the Count de Rola had come to wish to disassociate himself.

"Brilliant, talented, and perverse . . . she looked like Louis XIV and was as autocratic as he with friends and lovers."[5] Her maternal grandmother—the Duchesse de Chevigné, an eminent beauty—had been one of the two people on whom Marcel Proust had based his Duchesse de Guermantes. Moreover, the Duchesse de Chevigné, born Laure de Sade, descended from "the divine marquis." This meant that when Marie-Laure de Noailles purchased the original manuscript of *Les 120 Jours de Sodome*—the volume of prison writings in which Sade unleashed his sexual imagination with greatest abandon—she was acquiring not just an extraordinary and scandalous object but also an ancestral heirloom.

It could hardly have escaped Balthus's notice that Marie-Laure's sizable financial fortune came from an American Jew. Bernard Minoret—a Parisian writer who was a close friend of the de Noailles' and remains the preeminent authority on them, and who also knew Balthus well—put together the different pieces of her background for me. "With a prestigious title but no money to support it, the Duchesse de Chevigné had sold her daughter, Marie-Thérèse de Chevigné, to the family banker, Maurice Bischoffsheim." These were Marie-Laure's parents, and when Bischoffsheim died while Marie-Laure was still a baby, she became a great heiress.

Bischoffsheim's early death had been caused by tuberculosis, for which reason Marie-Laure was sheltered in her childhood—the assumption being that she, too, had fragile health. Meanwhile, her mother married another Jew—Francis de Croisset—also a source for one of Proust's characters, Bloch. "He was," said Minoret, "a homosexual, as would be Marie-Laure's own husband, but in neither case did this detract from a happy marriage." When the Duchesse de Chevigné had argued with Marie-Thérèse about this second match, Marie-Thérèse replied, "You made me marry a Jew the first time for your pleasure. Now the second time I marry a Jew for *my* pleasure."[6] Balthus skirted the issue of his own Jewish lineage as early as the 1930s—although with his mother on the scene it was harder to deny—but he probably noted with envy this case in which Jews married into the top ranks of French society.

At age seventeen, Marie-Laure Bischoffsheim had fallen in love with Jean Cocteau. Cocteau's sexual preferences, however, were too singularly defined for anything to come of it. Then, at twenty-one, she married the Vicomte de Noailles. The brother of a duke, he descended from a family that was what the French call *la noblesse du court*—their favors having come directly from the king. The Vicomte de Noailles was, according to Bernard Minoret, polite to the point of inaccessibility: secure in his family rank, and suitably aloof and unknowable. No wonder Balthus claimed the de Noailles as friends of his parents, and Charles as the one of the pair to whom he was closer.

Most people assume that Charles de Noailles was never in love with his wife. He and Marie-Laure led fairly separate lives. "Early in their marriage, she found him, to her great surprise, enjoying an affair with their handsome male gymnastics instructor," Bernard Minoret explained. Nevertheless, the vicomte and vicomtesse produced two daughters and functioned effectively together as extraordinary art patrons.

In the 1920s Charles and Marie-Laure de Noailles built a house in the latest International Style overlooking the sea at Hyères. They had tried to hire Walter Gropius, then the director of the Bauhaus, to design it. When Gropius said he was too busy, they settled on the designer and architect Robert Mallet-Stevens, who came up with a design in keeping with Bauhaus form: streamlined, ornament-free, frankly industrial, and machine-made. It was an unusual choice for French aristocrats. The villa featured a Cubist garden with lawns and shrubs shaped into rigid blocks of varying heights. The de Noailles quickly placed sculpture by Henri Laurens and Jacques Lipchitz amid those living cubes, and then commissioned Giacometti to create a piece. Giacometti made many plaster maquettes for this abstract design, which he completed in 1932. It was the largest sculpture he ever created. His sole big work in stone, it is ambiguous while distinctly phallic, and rather forbidding. The de Noailles soon put a Brancusi in the garden at Hyères as well. And although they kept most of the spaces inside the villa lean and spare, in one room they packed— "like books in a library"—major oils by Paul Klee, Joan Miró, Pablo Picasso, Georges Braque, Marc Chagall, André Masson, and Max Ernst. They became friends and key supporters of most of these artists, as well as of André Gide and Francis Poulenc.

By the time Balthus was part of the de Noailles's circle, they had made the Surrealists the focal point of their patronage and collecting. Salvador Dalí became their close friend and painted a major portrait of Marie-Laure. The couple acquired many of the Spaniard's paintings, and financed his and Luis Buñuel's film *L'Age d'or*. In their grand house in Paris on the Place des Etats-Unis, the de Noailles showed the film in the screening room they had created in their grand and ornate salon that was entirely in Louis XV style except for the movie projector and screen. The event was a scandal. The film's sequences include a son being murdered by his father, an old lady getting slapped, and a blind man being abused. The heroine rapturously sucks the naked big toe of a statue of a pope. Near the end of the film, the Marquis de Sade's protagonist from *Les 120 Jours de Sodome* appears in the guise of Jesus Christ. As Balthus told me with a look of profound fascination on his face, for this reason Charles de

Noailles was kicked out of the elegant and prestigious Jockey Club. He was also threatened with excommunication. Balthus delighted in both the vicomte's position in the social establishment and his cheerful willingness to offend.

Balthus first encountered Charles and Marie-Laure de Noailles in their Paris house on the Place des Etats-Unis. Whatever his views on Surrealism, it must have been thrilling for the artist, not yet thirty, to be welcomed into their world. The opulence of the setting and the courage reflected in its collections were extraordinary. Ornate chambers full of eighteenth-century furniture abutted Art Deco rooms designed by Jean-Michel Frank. A Dalí hung between the two Goyas. There was a Rubens among canvases by the young hell-raisers of the art world.

In 1936 Balthus painted a portrait of Marie-Laure, and it soon hung there as well. Bernard Minoret told me that the vicomtesse was passionate about Balthus in this period. Ardent about art and literature, she adored this erudite, intense, immensely knowledgeable, and handsome painter. Decades later, Marie-Laure de Noailles "told friends"—this is also according to Bernard Minoret—"that she had wanted to go to bed with Balthus, who did not return the interest, but she was still thrilled to have him paint her portrait."

CONTEMPORARY DIARIES CAPTURE the impression Balthus made as one of the habitués—along with Dalí, Giacometti, and Cocteau—at the Place des Etats-Unis. Claude Mauriac writes in his journals of "Balthus, a young painter with a strange, quite handsome, anguished face,"[7] and "the romantic, swarthy countenance of a young wolf."[8] But if he struck others as somber, Balthus made his visits to the Place des Etats-Unis all sound like fun and games of which he enjoyed every minute. His recollections of the many occasions when he frequented the great house always made him grin. Salvador Dalí was "extremely amusing . . . frightfully amusing." Cyril Connolly was "a most amusing man . . . frightfully funny." On one occasion at that house on the Place des Etats-Unis, Connolly "told us that he had a dream about his father. He was fishing and caught a large fish, which he discovered was his father. Then the fish said, 'Put me back at once.' " Connolly's own account of dinners with Balthus simply calls the artist's companionship "depressing"—but Balthus gives the impression that these occasions consisted of nothing but hijinks and laughs.

Balthus also told me that he met Luis Buñuel at the de Noailles's. Buñuel, he claimed, wanted to do a film of *Wuthering Heights* with him. But their "conceptions were too different" for them to agree on the details.

Balthus mentioned, too, that Philippe de Montebello, the director of the

Marie-Laure, Vicomtesse de Noailles, at the Futurist Ball in 1927

Metropolitan Museum, is the great-nephew of the Vicomtesse de Noailles. This is probably the reason the artist went to such pains to spare criticism of de Montebello when he made his diatribe against the Met at the time of his show there. Aristocrats, after all, should stick together.

BALTHUS'S PORTRAIT OF Marie-Laure de Noailles transforms the flamboyant vicomtesse into a Balthus. The doyenne of the modernist villa at Hyères and the lavish, ornate chambers overlooking the Place des Etats-Unis—the lively socialite we see beaming ebulliently in Man Ray's photo of her at the Futurist Ball—is now a melancholy creature in austere dress and plain surroundings.

The mountain went to Muhammad. Rather than pose in her own lavish surroundings, Marie-Laure sat for her portrait in the spare and rugged setting of Balthus's studio at the Cour de Rohan, the starkness of which subsumed her. If no name were attached to the portrait made of her there, we might think it

The Vicountess de Noailles, 1936, oil on canvas, 158 x 135 cm

showed an exhausted shopgirl recuperating in her modest digs after a hard day's work. Not only is the setting lean, but—in true Balthus fashion of the time—the brilliant hostess and patron looks downtrodden, troubled, and victimized by her situation in life. Depicting her as one of his own, Balthus established his mastery over her. It must have satisfied him deeply to extricate this free and rich woman from her world and make her succumb to the rigors and darkness of his.

Marie-Laure's black suit looks like a uniform. She might be a policewoman, or a prison matron. The vicomtesse looks grim and mannish.

Whether or not by plan, in painting this mistress of two splendid houses attired so soberly in his own plain garret, Balthus has given her an aspect of her most renowned ancestor in his jail cell. Marie-Laure de Noailles has about her something of the Marquis de Sade—exiled from the splendor of his château in Lacoste to the wretched prison, but still with his imagination and mental power intact.

For all the sobriety of the scene, Marie-Laure maintains a touch of her reputed élan. In this she is helped immeasurably by her shoes. As Balthus made clear in *Cathy Dressing* and other paintings, few artists in history have ever done as much with footwear. He shows what a marvelous contrivance it can be. Shoes are a vehicle of coquetry, a symbol of confidence and esprit. With their pointed toes and thick high heels, the vicomtesse's rich black velvet pumps remind us that she is a society person. Her posture is awkward and defeated; her hair looks as if it has been treated with a hot iron; her gaze bespeaks discomfort and trouble; but she is a woman of the world.

IV

THE PERSON WHO INTRODUCED Balthus to the de Noailles was, in all likelihood, Alberto Giacometti.

Even before they commissioned the large sculpture for their garden at Hyères, Charles and Marie-Laure had, in June 1929, been among the first people to acquire work by Giacometti when they bought a plaster plaque he had left on consignment at the Galerie Jeanne Bucher. The de Noailles were probably also responsible for Jean Cocteau's getting to know the sculptor's work that same year—a significant boost since Cocteau wrote about it with much admiration at a stage when it had few champions. Later on—in the mid-1940s—Giacometti did several portrait busts of the vicomtesse.

In the late twenties and early thirties, Giacometti was steeped in Surrealism. But then the sculptor rejected the movement, which became a source of great rapport between him and Balthus. "Alberto"—the name always rolled off Balthus's tongue slowly and reverently—was "the last really great artist" as well as "a very intimate friend of mine." Balthus recounted how the Swiss had told the members of the Surrealist group that his reason for splitting from their ranks was "that the only thing he was interested in was putting the nose in the right place. He said that this was his aim from then on. When André Breton said, 'But everybody knows what a head is,' Giacometti said, 'Well, I don't know what a head is.' " Balthus could imagine no better articulation of the concerns of a real artist.

Alberto Giacometti, photographed by Rene Burri, 1960

Giacometti's break from Surrealism revolved, in part, around the connection with Charles and Marie-Laure. In the early 1930s he had created lamps, andirons, sconces, and other practical objects for their designer, Jean-Michel Frank. In that same period, the Swiss would dine from time to time with his fellow Surrealists. One evening, at the end of the meal, André Breton suddenly attacked him for accepting these commissions from Frank, which Breton declared to be contrary to the spirit of true art. When Giacometti argued that he had been happy to combine beauty and comfort in people's lives, Breton accused him of being bourgeois and anti-Surrealist.

"Everything I've done till now has been no more than masturbation," Giacometti retorted. He then left the room, severing forever his connection with most of his Surrealist comrades.[9]

ONE OF THE PRECIPITATING reasons for Giacometti's departure from Surreal form and his return to the model was his exposure to the art of Balthus. In this regard, it now seems ironic to me that Balthus never mentioned the profound impression his Galerie Pierre exhibition had on Giacometti—about which I learned from other sources—given his exaggerated reports of the effect of the show on Picasso, Miró, and Derain.

Giacometti visited Balthus's Galerie Pierre exhibition repeatedly. After one of those occasions, he told his friend Anatole Jakovsky, "On perd le temps à continuer"—meaning, in the context in which it was said, that it was a waste of time to devote another moment to Surrealism.[10] Balthus's art definitively showed him just how exciting the issues of representation could still be. Not only did the young artist make clear the real point of art, but he did so with a skill the Swiss esteemed. In particular, Giacometti admired Balthus's draftsmanship; the Swiss told his friend Eberhard Kornfeld—who did not share this admiration for Balthus—"Lui, il peut dessiner; moi, je ne peux pas dessiner."[11]

Balthus told me that shortly after Breton and Eluard brought Giacometti to meet him for that first time at the Rue de Fürstemberg, he and Giacometti encountered one another by chance in Switzerland. Balthus was in Bern, where he had an appointment to see Paul Klee, who was a friend of his father's. He stopped at the Bear Pit on his way to Klee's house. "I was looking down at the Bear Pit. Suddenly someone touched my shoulder. It was Giacometti who was also there to look at the bears. Giacometti asked, 'What are you doing here?' 'I have an appointment to see Klee.' 'So have I,' Giacometti replied." They were both scheduled to arrive at Klee's studio at the same time. "We had three-quarters of an hour. We were on the terrace and started talking," Balthus told me. It was not until many hours later that they realized they had forgotten all about Klee. In the excitement of their conversation, they had entirely missed their appointment.

The truth of the incident may never be known. In James Lord's account of it, only Giacometti was en route to Klee. But the story—which Balthus told with evident pleasure—makes its point charmingly. He evinced no regret whatsoever that he and Giacometti had stood up Paul Klee. Even though

Balthus told me on various occasions that Klee is one of the few twentieth-century artists he really admires, he clearly felt that his and Giacometti's intense rapport took precedence over anything they might learn from Klee. The offense and inconvenience of forgetting an appointment was not an issue.

FROM THAT POINT FORWARD, Balthus and Giacometti would see one another at the de Noailles', and also often had lunch together at Derain's house in Chambourcy. The triumvirate were not only united in their attachment to the art of the past and their opposition to most modernism, but they also had in common that they were all represented by Pierre Matisse in America. Derain, however, was in effect a mentor. Balthus and Giacometti, for all of their differences, were more or less on an equal footing.

Their relationship ultimately developed its full share of complexity, but even if it did not last until the end of Giacometti's life, it endured for a number of years and would reemerge significantly, as did the connection with Marie-Laure de Noailles, after the hiatus of the war.

CHAPTER SEVENTEEN

THE CHILDREN

"Now sit down on the footstool."
To do so, Gilberte folded up under her the heron-like legs of
a girl of fifteen. Below her tartan skirt, she revealed ribbed cot-
ton stockings to just above the knees, unconscious of the perfect
oval shape of her knee-caps.

—COLETTE, *Gigi*[1]

Picasso lived off other people . . . he cannibalized them. He
would do anything to "get" your devotions. . . . His friends were
all, to some extent, his victims.

—JOHN RICHARDSON, IN AN INTERVIEW ON PICASSO[2]

I

IN OCTOBER 1941 Pablo Picasso bought, from the dealer Pierre Colle, one of Balthus's most enticing, most splendidly executed paintings ever: *The Children* (color plate 10). Picasso was the giant of the century—the measuring stick for inventiveness, passion, and artistic skill—and the endorsement was significant.

Based on one of Balthus's sexiest illustrations for *Wuthering Heights, The Children* grapples with themes that would preoccupy the artist all his life—the power plays of teenagers, heightened concentration, an erotic attraction both repressed and fiery. It addresses the anguish and nirvana of adolescence with authenticity and force. The approach is pure Balthus: bold yet furtive, passionate yet hesitant, raw yet impeccably tasteful.

It is no wonder that Picasso—so versed in the history of art, so intent on the aesthetic and psychological possibilities of painting—would want and treasure this large canvas. Like Picasso's own work, it deals with issues of the libido as perceived by a canny dramaturge. And *The Children* is painted with finesse and depth. Both the solitude and the interdependence fundamental to human experience are palpable in this picture where the folds of material and the reflection of light come alive in stunning verisimilitude.

Picasso and Balthus in Picasso's studio in the late 1940s, by Cecil Beaton

WHEN BALTHUS TALKED TO ME about Picasso, it was the same as when he talked about Miró: what mattered was what the other person thought of him. By being one of the first people ever to buy a Balthus painting—and among the earliest Europeans, since most of Balthus's collectors of the 1930s were American—Picasso rated virtually as a hero. For the most esteemed painter of the day, a generation older, to acquire one of his paintings was a momentous development—not unlike the praise he had received and perpetually relished from Rilke.

Yet I could not substantiate—and, in fact, doubt—Balthus's repeated claim to me that Picasso told him, after visiting the Galerie Pierre show, that he had wanted to buy *The Street*—but presumably did not do so because he did not have enough money. John Richardson, the Picasso biographer, has assured me that Picasso could afford what he wanted at that point. The Spaniard had already purchased, in 1930, his splendid Normandy Château de Boisgeloup as a country house; he had the space for *The Street*, and no lack of funds. Besides, none of the many witnesses to Picasso's life ever reported him claiming to have wanted *The Street*. But Picasso's acquisition of *The Children* in 1941—in and of

itself, without the embellishment that he had wanted a larger painting earlier—represented tremendous commitment.

And Balthus's account of his warm rapport with Picasso seems plausible.
Picasso and Balthus had much in common even before they met. Each had
both the fickleness and the intensity of an adolescent, a characteristically
teenage irresponsibility as well as a completely mature level of accomplishment. Once successful, each wielded power over his coterie and over numerous
women.

Motivated above all by their own imperatives, neither gave much credence to the notion of objectivity. It was fine to dissemble; all that seemed to
matter was that their audience responded as intended. Both Balthus and
Picasso were cognizant that by its very nature the art of painting was an act of
deception with every brushstroke; they treated human relationships similarly,
and forever offered up different selves as if they were constructing a canvas.

Picasso also had a tangential connection to Rilke, which may have helped
alert him to Balthus. In the summer of 1915, when Rilke had lived in the
Munich house of Hertha von Koenig, the poet had come to know Picasso's
Family of Saltimbanques, which was in his hostess's collection. This large 1905
"circus period" canvas inspired his fifth Duino Elegy, with its reference to
"these acrobats—wrung by our (oh, for the sake of whom?) never-contented
will."[3] Picasso had met Rilke on at least one occasion. A generation apart, the
Spanish painter and Balthus had many reasons to feel a natural affinity.

Yet Balthus recalled only one instance of their talking at length. He told
me that this was in the summer of 1947, when Balthus was spending two weeks
in Golfe-Juan at the house of the psychoanalyst Jacques Lacan.

Lacan was "the psychiatrist whom Picasso consulted for every kind of
medical problem, including the common cold."[4] Since 1945 he had been analyzing Dora Maar, who, besides being the "sometime mistress of Georges
Bataille," had been Picasso's mistress.[5] Dora Maar was one of Balthus's closest
friends in that same period. Lacan had been treating her following a dramatic
incident in which she had furiously barged in on Picasso and Paul Eluard and
"grabbed both men by the arms and tried to bring them down on their
knees."[6]

Balthus almost invariably mentioned Jacques Lacan to me in the course of
his frequent diatribes against psychoanalysis. Balthus told me more than once,
and always with pride, that he had consulted Lacan about the hallucinations
he had experienced as a result of malaria fever. Yet he always emphasized that
that was the full extent of their discussions; he would have tolerated nothing
more. Moreover, Lacan could not help him understand these deliriums that
had been brought on by fever and illness. Balthus belittled Lacan; he said that

Dora Maar had told him that the renowned doctor slept too much during their sessions for the treatment to be effective.

Yet there are reasons to believe that Balthus and Lacan might have enjoyed a certain rapport. When Lacan wrote his dissertation at medical school in 1932, his subject had been "the case history of a provincial woman, a postal worker, who had criminally assaulted a well-known actress with a knife."[7] Balthus would have been intrigued by such a study, just as he would have been sympathetic to Lacan's effrontery to the psychoanalytic establishment with his practice of shortening sessions to a few minutes and of sometimes treating patients in taxicabs.

Lacan, on the other hand, could hardly have failed to see Balthus as an exemplar of one of his central concepts of human development. "Lacan rooted the origin of selfhood in the 'mirror stage': one is the image of oneself, with which one tries, like a perpetual child, to catch up."[8]

Even if he was subsequently skeptical about Lacan professionally, Balthus enjoyed the holiday on the Mediterranean he spent with the psychoanalyst, his stepdaughter Laurence Bataille (daughter of Georges), and Laurence's mother, Sylvia, now married to Lacan. To his great pleasure, during those two weeks in Golfe-Juan, he and Picasso saw each other every day on the beach. It was in the course of that period that they had their one extended conversation.

The occasion was an evening when Balthus and Picasso and Laurence were sitting on the terrace of the Restaurant Marcel and discussed art for about two hours. They talked, Balthus told me, about modern art, which both of them disliked. And modern architecture, which they loathed. Picasso said he preferred great châteaux and fine furniture to the latest, ornament-free, streamlined style of building. The younger artist was, of course, in full accord. And, Balthus recalled with a proud face, Picasso spoke to him about *The Children*. Balthus told me that "Picasso said the reason he loved *The Children* was because I was the only artist at the time not doing Picassos."

Balthus uttered the marvelous words slowly, savoring each syllable. This tribute to his independence gave him immense satisfaction.

But Balthus has subsequently spun Picasso's dictum in such different forms that it is hard to discern the real one. In one of those interviews with "the artist who never grants interviews" which Balthus gave to *Le Monde*—on May 8, 1991—Balthus referred to this same exchange in Golfe-Juan and Picasso's comments on his work by telling his interlocutor, "I can't repeat what he told me, he was too generous to me." Then, in an interview in the July 18, 1991, *Le Figaro* when the artist was recalling the atmosphere of the Deux Magots in the 1930s, Balthus cast it very differently. Reminiscing about the writers, painters, musicians, and filmmakers at the café, he said that "Each one was curious about the others. That's why Picasso took the trouble to go see one of my first shows: Boris Kochno had accompanied him. Everyone was doing Picasso, except me. That's what must have interested him. We became intimate friends very quickly." Here this notion of everyone other than Balthus doing Picassos originated with Balthus, not Picasso.

Did Picasso, in fact, actually utter that charming observation which Balthus refused to repeat to the French papers but proudly quoted to me at least five times? Perhaps the reason Balthus was so reticent in his *Monde* interview is that this, too, is a tale Balthus fabricated because he wished it were so. When he had given me the scoop a few months earlier, quoting Picasso with full weight on the portent and magnitude of these unforgettable words of encouragement, he probably felt that I, as a naïve young American, would not question the authenticity of Picasso's remark. Too many readers of *Le Figaro* and *Le Monde,* however, would. So, much as Balthus wanted Picasso to have made the pronouncement, in one public instance he coyly—under the pretext of modesty—kept it secret, while in another he put forward the sacred idea but without going the extra step to claim it as Picasso's.

Picasso's distinguishing of Balthus in this way is, after all, an extraordinary concept. For one of the creative giants of our century to have singled out the young artist for his independence and courage is no small matter. When Balthus "quoted" the remark to me, he seemed fully to believe that Picasso had made it to him. It was as if Balthus had carried it in his thoughts as a mental talisman ever since.

This may be why in his 1996 statement to the *New York Times* ("Reclusive Balthus . . . Still a Man of Mystery") Balthus recalled, "Dear old Pablo. Personally I loved him very much. . . . He said he was intrigued because everyone else was making Picassos except me. He covered me with such compliments that I can't repeat them."[9] The ploy, of course, was brilliant; if one assumes he modestly isn't repeating greater accolades, one would hardly doubt the praise he does quote.

PICASSO HIMSELF SENT OUT mixed signals on the subject of Balthus. Picasso truly admired the younger painter, yet at the same time he apparently disparaged Balthus's resistance to modernism—rather than revered it as Balthus would have had me believe.

The photographer Brassaï, an intimate of Picasso's, reports:

One day Picasso was standing in front of a canvas on which he had sketched in some figures, talking with the painter Balthus, whose

British stolidity he enjoys, and I heard him say: "I have done the figures; now you are going to paint the interior for me. You have the
secret of creating an intimate atmosphere. I don't." It wasn't meant
entirely as a joke.[10]

Yet Picasso—châteaux or not—was apparently critical of the extent to which
Balthus deliberately lived outside his own time. In *Life with Picasso*, Françoise
Gilot, Picasso's lover of the 1950s, writes of Dora Maar, following an exhibition
at Pierre Loeb's gallery:

> After that period, she began to have conversations about painting with
> Balthus. Once after Pablo had called on her and looked at the work
> she was doing, he told me he saw in it the results of those contacts with
> Balthus. That disturbed him.
>
> "One can't work toward a tendency that lies ahead and then do an
> about-face toward something that is another world entirely," he
> [Picasso] said. "That kind of painting may not be outgrown for
> Balthus but it certainly is for someone who has been working against
> the tradition that Balthus is working. Balthus began with Courbet and
> never got very much beyond him. For Dora Maar it's an anachro-
> nism."[11]

Balthus brought up this remark to me—over twenty-five years after Gilot's book
was published—by saying that the "pretentious" Gilot had written that Picasso
had claimed he "was not a modern painter." Picasso had been greatly bothered,
Balthus told me. Picasso wrote him "a strong and furious letter insisting that
he had never said it." But Françoise Gilot was probably a reliable source, and
there is no certainty that Picasso actually wrote that "furious letter" to Balthus.
It is even possible that the remark Balthus claimed had so angered Picasso was
the basis for Balthus's declaration that he was the only one not doing Picassos,
with Balthus having twisted it in order to turn criticism into a compliment.

John Richardson, who knew both Picasso and Dora Maar well, told me
that "Picasso liked the work," but, in the same vein as the remark quoted by
Gilot, Picasso would qualify his judgment by saying of Balthus, "il n'est pas
comme nous."[12] Balthus's failure to engage in the adventures of modernism
was troublesome to the Spaniard.

Jean Cocteau gives a slightly different slant to the issue of Picasso's feeling
for Balthus. Cocteau writes that Picasso was initially an enthusiast of Balthus's
work. But, sounding quite spineless, Picasso waffled in response to his cohorts'
contempt for the younger painter:

In Paris Picasso found Balthus's picture admirable. Now, at Vallauris, he finds it "not bad," as a consequence of all the reproaches made to him for admiring that canvas.[13]

What is certain is that Balthus and his work always exerted a force about which no one could remain impassive. Picasso was no exception in feeling a need to reckon with this artist who was so unlike anybody else. And he recognized Balthus as a painter of prodigious gifts. James Lord describes a conversation at a dinner party at Douglas Cooper's in the 1950s. Picasso quipped sardonically about Balthus being with "some baby girl in his sinister castle" and having a "child bride." Yet the resounding note was one of respect. "I like Balthus and he likes me," Lord quotes Picasso as saying.

> Never mind that he's not a noble, he has an aristocratic hand. Nobody can paint a portrait the way that he can. His portrait of Miró is a masterpiece.[14]

The rapport that emanates from those words is echoed by an account from the sculptor Raymond Mason:

> Picasso, fiercest of judges, admired Balthus (and vice versa, let us remark). He had said that they were the two sides of the same medal. His genius is in that remark. Oddly, they have the same histrionic talent. Two men of the theater. Dramatic, poetic, whatever you want to call it. The theater implies an audience, is addressed to others.[15]

WHEN PICASSO TOLD PEOPLE that Balthus liked him, he was right. But Balthus had mixed feelings about Picasso's art. He told me that he was "not equally comfortable with all aspects of Picasso's works," did not like the "blue period," and felt that "Picasso became himself only from the Dinard period on." Yet when they were both in southern France and Picasso was working on ceramics at Vallauris, Balthus developed considerable respect for what Picasso was doing. That period of commitment to clay pottery appealed to Balthus far more than other aspects of Picasso's career. Here Picasso "became engrossed with the material, not with Picasso." Similarly, Balthus admires Picasso's tapestries. He told me that when both Picasso and Braque did their collages for these textiles, they immersed themselves in the tapestry process admirably— for which reason Balthus showed these pieces in Rome.

It struck me as strange that whereas Picasso, in buying *The Children,* had tacitly embraced Balthus's work at its most profound and serious, Balthus favored Picasso's art in its more frivolous strains. On the other hand, to judge Picasso in this way was in keeping with Balthus's unpredictability—and to his consistent fondness for amusement above all else. In any event, by buying *The Children*, the painting genius of our century had endeared himself to the younger artist forever.

II

The Children IS BASED ON Balthus's 1933 illustration for the line "Because Cathy taught him what she learnt..." from *Wuthering Heights*. Brontë's Cathy personifies worldliness and education. She knows the riches contained in books; she represents refinement. With her, the ruffian brute Heathcliff will acquire—or disdain—civilization.

The full sentence in Brontë is: "Heathcliff bore his degradation pretty well at first, because Cathy taught him what she learnt, and worked or played with him in the fields."[16] Yet in Balthus's illustration Heathcliff does far more than bear his degradation. Balthus has transformed his alter ego. With his right knee elevated on a chair, his elbow on the chair back, and his chin resting in the palm of his hand, the lean, strong boy has a look of supreme confidence. However low his social status, he positions his beautiful body with pride and vigor. Swarthy and sexy, he lords himself over Cathy, who is sprawled suggestively on the floor beneath him.

In the drawing, the twenty-five-year-old Balthus drew Heathcliff, of course, as a self-portrait. The rendition is pure fantasy—both in regard to *Wuthering Heights* and in regard to his own situation; it accommodates Balthus's image of himself as surly, commanding, and in very tight pants. He poses like a well-built hustler in a porno magazine. Flashing his muscular buttocks, swaying his triangular back with cavalier competence, he is very much the same shirtless fellow who stokes the fire in *Les Beaux Jours*. Cathy, in her tight and slinky dress, is leggy and slender, with the wanton hair of a wench. Balthus would probably insist that the observation derives entirely from my fixation rather than his intentions, but the position of her head beneath Heathcliff's crotch invites the prospect of fellatio.

The drawing captures Balthus's spontaneous, unguarded image of the episode. Heathcliff looks as if he might crush Cathy. His left knee appears to lean on her head, while his right one is conveniently supported by a chair seat so that it rests neatly over her back. The illusion is that he is digging his knee into her and might even kick her in the head, although on close viewing you realize that he is not actually touching her. The sadistic element corresponds

"Because Cathy taught him what she learnt," 1933, China ink, 50.4 x 41 cm

with Balthus's first illustration for the novel—in which Cathy huddles at Heathcliff's side on her knees, looking as if she were praying to him, chastened by his hand outstretched over her head at the same time that his hair is being pulled.

In the 1937 painting, a lot that Balthus laid bare in pen and ink four years earlier is now elegantly cloaked. The raw emotions and the physical immediacy have been replaced by more depth and obscurity. In the illustration, the boy stares, albeit sideways, at the girl. In the painting, he looks away. On paper, he leers; on canvas, he is in a reverie, with his profile blurred in shadow.

What was earlier a violent scenario is now relatively sedate. The boy and the girl have retreated to their own separate universes though they occupy the same room. The tumult of Brontë and the drama of Balthus's own relationship with Antoinette no longer pertain. Here Balthus has used his young neighbors Hubert and Thérèse Blanchard as models. Hubert and Thérèse, Balthus told me, were from a large family, then out of work, who lived near the Cour du Rohan.

The nubile wench in a cocktail dress has been replaced by a dour creature with severely cut hair. She is clad in a rather unflattering, English-style school-girl's uniform of sleeveless jumper, blouse, and plaid kilt. The strapping young man who was formerly swinging his backside in our faces is now in a school-boy's smock that looks fit for a monk. Rather than dominate or submit, the brother and sister scarcely affect one another.

The boy gazes dreamily into space. Intensely serious, he appears mindful of situations and possibilities a million miles away. He leans with one knee bent underneath him on a chair and the other leg twisted and stretched awk-wardly behind him. His elbows rest on a tabletop, with his left hand support-ing the dead weight of his chin. The contortions and the inertness of his lithe body belong authentically to his stage of life. No one but a teenager could sus-tain such a position, locking himself in his own insular world.

The girl arranges herself even more unusually than the boy does. She may be perfectly comfortable, but her pose is quite implausible. A gangly teenager, she kneels on her hands and her knees—with her back arched, her buttocks high, and her ankles elongated. She looks as if she has been pushed around like putty by a demanding choreographer or exercise master. Her long limbs have been made to assume positions that appear agonizing even for the most supple of bodies. Her situation is awkward; using her hands for support as she does, she substantially covers the surface of the pages of the book that she is suppos-edly reading.

The girl holds her head—which, in the usual Balthus fashion, is about the width and length of her chest—at such an odd tilt that she is really not doing what she is supposed to be doing. Allegedly she is reading, but if she can see the pages at all at this angle, it is only out of the right-hand corners of her eyes. More probably, what she is really doing is looking off into the distance. One can't be sure—her eyes are nearly shut and her pupils invisible—but she cer-tainly meets neither her book nor the world head-on. She is tricky and decep-tive. With her pursed lips, the girl is, like her companion, lost in her own private world. Her personal agenda is her sole obligation; reverie is reality; her thoughts are known only to her.

Thus *The Children* is a perfect encapsulation of adolescence. As any observer of teenagers knows, they really can read and relax in implausible posi-tions. They often would rather dissemble than reveal. They are full of sensu-ous, sexual feelings—about themselves and the people they know—without being clear about what to do with the awareness. Overwhelmed by instincts and emotions beyond their grasp, they develop personal armor. And they willingly inhabit their own clandestine universe. Sagely and skillfully, Balthus evoked the period of his own life where he has always remained.

HUBERT BLANCHARD IS THE FIRST of Balthus's young men to wear one of those traditional smocks that were a staple of French life before World War II. The resemblance of the one-piece garment to the outfits worn in Piero's frescoes was certainly not lost on Balthus. But what this clothing really meant to him is hard to determine. Balthus, of course, would ascribe no particular meaning to Hubert's garment; it's what boys wore. Yet it has a significant effect. Because it is a uniform, a prescribed costume, it casts the child in an assigned role; his thoughts are elsewhere, but he is locked into a situation with its rules and expectations. His outfit becomes a subterfuge, a disguise of sorts—even if it was imposed by school authorities rather than chosen by Hubert. While Thérèse's short plaid skirt announces that the painting is a modern-day scene, the odd getup on her brother makes him appear to have dropped in from another century. Like the colors of the painting, the tunic is a declaration of the "old-fashioned."

The impact of this deliberate conjuring of an earlier culture—both through the character's costume and through the style of painting—is similar to that of André Derain's 1909 oil on linen *The Bagpiper*. In that important large painting, Derain depicted the actual landscape of the region of Carrière Saint-Denis, where he and Braque were working at the time, and then clothed the central character in the medieval garb a jester or troubadour might have worn. Not only did Balthus and Derain paint the modern world in decidedly retrograde styles, but they peopled it with beings who belong as much to earlier centuries as to our own.

The gray tunic also adds a female aspect to the male. I say this with full knowledge that Balthus would disagree; the artist would maintain that this is what Hubert wore, period. Yet—in his kneesocks and black pumps and this garment that is like a belted dress—the soft-skinned Hubert is slightly feminized. He certainly is no longer the swashbuckling Heathcliff of the early drawing. He is, rather, one of the many weak male characters in Balthus's art.

III

WHEN WE LOOK AT THE 1937 *Children* in the Musée Picasso today, we see why its distinguished owner considered Balthus his superior at rendering an interior. In this articulate painting, the distant floor molding neatly establishes the perimeters of the space. A broad range of elements—the light on the chair seat beneath Hubert's right leg, the shadow cast by the tabletop on its support, the recession of the floor—makes the architectural environment solid and real.

Not only is the setting plausible, but, for all its starkness and simplicity, it is enchanting. The man who would make such a fuss about châteaux could extract a truer magnificence from bare wooden furniture and a sack of coal than from all of his aristocratic trappings. Humble, functional substances have rare luster here. The details that give the scene its verisimilitude also help provide its omniscient grace. The black line under the edge of the table articulates the structure; it also works visually against the light vertical that abuts the black pillar, making a lively crisscross that moves back and forth like a grid by Mondrian. The bright white expanse of the book plays against the plane of the chair seat, and then against the flat tabletop, to create a well-ordered processional.

Balthus has composed the picture with the mastery he acquired in part during that long winter of copying Poussin at the Louvre. This is a neatly constructed universe. Thérèse in the foreground assumes center stage just behind the picture plane. Hubert is locked in position distinctly behind her. The bag of coal and well-lit rear wall neatly carry us beyond the two figures and establish the space of the room. They also provide both an anchor and a welcome visual resting place, necessary because of all that is going on with the two children.

For—engaging as the interior and its objects are—what dominates the surface of this painting is the vibrant rhythm established by the two young people both individually and in tandem. Balthus's intimate canvas concentrates on its focal figures much as Poussin's *Echo et Narcisses* does. Thérèse and Hubert define the picture space; between them, they practically touch all four boundaries. What matters in this environment is that they occupy it. The quiet grid of verticals and horizontals provides an orderly basis for the high-speed contrapposto of human existence; the inert wood and weighty mound of coal are a foil for the pulsating life of the two teenagers.

Studying the boy's head up close, it reads so abstractly that we can hardly fathom it. But when we step back, the flesh coheres. The way the boy's chin sits in his right palm makes us feel that, physically and psychologically, this is what it means to be alive.

With Hubert, Balthus, as usual, eradicates many of the differences between adults and children. Ages merge just as genders do. We have considered how, as a mature artist, Balthus sees from the child's point of view; conversely, his children have adult experiences. Grown-ups may thrive on the enchantment of childhood, but children are overexperienced.

Thérèse, too, has a ferocious intensity—and so does Balthus in his responses to her. The artist notices everything, and makes it come alive. The light that splashes the girl's left leg and anklebone is both authentic and wondrous. The way her kilt cascades from her hips is entirely convincing. This short wrap skirt—the perfect schoolgirl item—is a masterpiece. Its black and gray and light-reflecting white interlock in a way that honors every fold and wrinkle, while at the same time providing a splendid passage of visual animation. The red windowpane overplaid reads as a nice subtle detail. (Almost lost in reproduction, it is distinct in the actual painting.) Like a panoply of materials in Balthus's work—tablecloths, dress materials, bedcovers, the Japanese textile in *The Turkish Room* of 1963–66—the tartan shows the artist's eye for surfaces and his ability to record them. The brown stripes of Thérèse's blouse undulate down her sleeve in obeisance to every crease; her vest catches the light or darkness in shadow where it should, and hangs just so. The color tone of every thread is impeccable. None of this is achieved through mechanical precision, but, rather, by a deeper and more subtle feeling for the true nature of appearances.

Balthus chooses when to dwell on details, but also when not to. He captures every slight dip in Thérèse's hem, yet he has left the pages of the girl's book entirely blank. The book is emblematic—of the world of words—yet its text, like Balthus's own, is kept invisible and unknowable.

THÉRÈSE AND HUBERT HAVE SOLID, earthy bodies; their poses make them seem even stronger. Thérèse stretches out her gangly, nubile frame and arches it mightily. She places her limbs as only a child might—flattening her lower leg, bending her foot, and twisting her arms in a way that tenses her body like a coiled spring. It looks unnatural, yet children are sometimes endowed with this flexibility. Thérèse's hands offset one another across a void so that, in addition to supporting her, they impart a certain bounce—and help give her élan.

The shadow made by Thérèse's left arm makes her all the more real. This shadow also curves in a way that takes us forcefully from the foreground and under her skirt into the interesting shadowed area beneath her crotch. The chair legs, in turn, cast straight, staccato shadows that accentuate the richness of this curve. Balthus would maintain that all these shadows are what they are and nothing more—that the notion of the shadow formed by Thérèse's arm being a path toward her sexuality has to do with my hang-ups, not his intentions—yet *The Children* gains considerable excitement because of the way we are drawn into the dark and unknown world lurking beneath Thérèse's kilt.

After a while the table legs and their shadows begin to seem phallic—the straight and hard shafts very much part of the world of the boy—whatever the disclaimers may be.

Hubert knows his own strength. He rests forcibly on that right knee and leans hard on his elbow. Like Thérèse, he bends and angles his body with a savoir faire lacking in toddlers and an elasticity lost to adults. With his waist held in like a springboard by the rope belt that encompasses his tunic, his body takes off north and south of it. Consciously or unconsciously, Hubert adjusts himself in counterpoint to Thérèse; he bends his right leg and twists the left in neat relationship to hers. Yet for all their gyrations, Hubert and Thérèse, unlike the figures in so many of Balthus's paintings, are not artificially contorted. For while Dolores Miró has been bent so that she cannot maintain her balance, the woman in *The Window* squashed as if under glass, and the characters in *The Street* manipulated like marionettes, these two people are simply being true to their age.

PICASSO, NOT SURPRISINGLY, had acquired for himself the quintessential Balthus. *The Children* is somber to the point of melancholy while at the same time exultant of both human existence and the act of painting. It is a better painting than *The Street:* less self-consciously strange, more anchored in reality, surer and not so contrived. It makes interior space—both physical and psychological—real. Light, air, enclosure, masses, shadows, voids: they all exist, palpably, before our eyes. The textures are plausible, the rhythm enticing. And it is a painting about adolescence: its tenor and excitement, the intense bodily awareness, the engagement and impenetrable distance.

Whatever the variables in his means of depiction, the predominant subject in all of Balthus's subsequent work—right through to his last large painting of the 1990s—would remain, give or take a couple of years, the stage of life in which he captured Thérèse and Hubert Blanchard. Balthus makes his teenagers the key players in their universe. Matisse's sons, Picasso's children, are, by comparison, ancillary, diminished, minor. Like Renoir's little girls, these characters are secondary objects within the domestic life made by their parents. Balthus's, on the other hand, soar in their private fantasies and have bodies with the power of Bernini's. They rule the universe.

CHAPTER EIGHTEEN

THÉRÈSE

*"Milk is for the pussy, isn't it?" said Simone. "Do you dare
me to sit in the saucer?"*
"I dare you," I answered, almost breathless.
— GEORGES BATAILLE, *Story of the Eye*[1]

*It is indeed a question as to what arouses us most in erotic works
of art. For some it may be an excessive amount of pubic hair, for
others the complete absence of hair. . . . Sometimes it is the
expression on a woman's face, the contortion of features
expressing complete abandon. . . . Everyone has his Achilles'
heel, to twist a cliché. Certainly one of the most successful
methods of animating the spectator is to give the impression
that he is observing the performance through a keyhole. . . . The
most important thing, it goes without saying, is that the artist
be an artist. Just as a good pornographic novel depends on the
writer's ability to write, so it is with a painting or piece of
sculpture. Even in "obscene" works of art we look for the touch
of the master. The work of a hack leaves us cold or derisive.*
— HENRY MILLER[2]

I

EXCEPT FOR THE OCCASIONAL portrait or character in a group scene,
Balthus rarely included men or boys in his paintings. The males who strike us
as most real—three-dimensional and alive in the way that the women are—are
mostly self-portraits, or self-portraits at a remove. Hubert Blanchard in *The
Children* is the rare exception.

In 1937 and 1938 Balthus went on to paint three major oils of Thérèse
without him. Painting the young women alone, he focused utterly and
achieved his most authentic voice.

The three paintings of Thérèse show Balthus at the apogee of his strength.
For the rest of his life, he would return to images of daydreaming girls in

domestic interiors, and to personality-filled cats, but rarely again would he summon his powers so effectively.

Balthus told me—as he has many other people—that he regards his large multifigure compositions as his most successful paintings. In these big and panoramic canvases of people whose lives overlap but don't interlock, the artist has, he says, left his greatest mark. Even if Balthus attained his own objectives, I disagree that they are his finest work. It seems to me, rather, that his close-ups of adolescents are his ultimate accomplishment.

It is in his chamber music—of which the portraits of Thérèse are primary exemplars—that Balthus has made his most significant contribution to world art. These more concentrated paintings cohere better than the larger, more stilted pictures; the details ring truer. They are to his body of work what *Echo et Narcisse* was to Poussin's.

The subjects of these less complex compositions are real people, not somnambulists. Visual and emotional truth is nearer, even if still in a mist. Balthus's celebrations of females between the ages of twelve and twenty-two fulfill his goal of awakening. Both the viewer and the subjects come alive—to glorious if frightening possibilities.

BALTHUS HAS CREATED unique imagery in these intimate paintings of teenage girls. In his more schematic art, people look posed and anesthetized—as if someone had to dull or numb the excitement; this is not so for the close-ups. The gimmickry is less cumbersome than in works like *The Street*. There is—in the technique as well as in the characters invented—the superb linking of childhood with adulthood that marks Balthus at his best.

A supreme example of all the paintings of teenage girls is the 1938 *Thérèse Dreaming* (color plate 11). The canvas is as well painted, and in its subtle way as provocative, as anything Balthus has ever done. It belongs to the time period when he was unabashed about who and what he was—when he tried no guises and perpetrated no fluff. It arrests us because it is painted so richly and convincingly, because it betrays such unembarrassed convictions, and because the subject, whether it attracts us intensely or makes us extremely uncomfortable, is alive in all its complexity.

A SIGNATURE BALTHUS, exquisitely crafted, tasteful to a fault, *Thérèse Dreaming* presents the nubile schoolgirl exposing herself coyly but shamelessly. Because of the girl's age, her clothing, and her apparent indifference to the effect of her fierce sexuality, the image is more laden with libido than

Titian's Venuses, Goya's Mayas, or Ingres's bordello scenes. Thérèse emanates eroticism while looking blithely unaware of that fact.

Balthus poses the young adolescent with her legs spread wide and her skirt and petticoat thrust back. Her crotch, scantily clad in white underpants, faces us in full view. The lack of modesty or embarrassment is completely out of character for a young woman at this point in her maturation, when she has just begun to develop breasts. Her attitude suits either a mature seductress or a younger child who does not know any better. Or perhaps she is asleep and is not aware that we are seeing her in this indecent way. In any event, either out of his allegedly deliberate attempt to shock or, more likely, because of a desire to satisfy his own longings, the thirty-year-old artist has not just been risqué in having Thérèse display herself this way; he has been remarkably salacious. Thérèse's sexuality may be dormant for her, but it is rampant for us.

In *Thérèse Dreaming,* the man who claims to revere the idea of privacy has invaded someone else's. Balthus demands that we honor the walls and constructs of his life; but no aspect of Thérèse is off limits. We feel, with this painting, that we are being taken into the world of sights to which we are not meant to have access: that thin strip of material covering the genitals, the inside of the petticoat, a rather personal view of the girl's armpits. The bulge of her inner thigh is ours to study. So are the shadows within her joints. We even have an inkling of the secret of her dream—that it must have to do with her burgeoning body and incipient womanliness.

Linda Fairstein's take on *Thérèse* is that she is "unabashedly erotic. These little girls in seductive poses are titillating to anyone attracted to adolescents. Stimulation is invited." What I wish Balthus would realize is that to acknowledge this truth is in no way to minimize the wonder of his artistry—or to denigrate his achievement.

That Balthus could, on every occasion when I ever saw him, be shocked and appalled that anyone might call his work erotic—and that his campaign against the notion of eroticism in his art has been the rallying cry of all his recent interviews—at times seem laughable, and at other moments odd and pathetic. It is as if, like his teenage subject, he has deliberately closed his eyes to what is obvious to everyone else.

In *Thérèse Dreaming,* SUNLIGHT caresses this scarcely developed young woman's naked legs. It shines off the back of her left thigh up to the point where it begins to bulge into her pale buttock, and illuminates the inside of her right thigh as high as her pubis. Her skin is alive. Thérèse's soft young flesh—

which we see in such amplitude—glows with more clarity and warmth than any other substance in the canvas.

The narrow folds of underwear, however, make the actual center of her sexuality less brazen than in *The Guitar Lesson, Cathy Dressing,* or *Alice.* In *Girl with a Cat,* his painting of a similarly positioned Thérèse done one year earlier, the slightly younger child—viewed from the same angle in almost the identical pose on the same chaise—has underpants so tight that the crack of her vagina reads as a dark crease. Now she is, technically, accorded a bit more modesty. Yet the imagery is "dirtier"—and more mischievous—than if Balthus had painted a straightforward nude. Had he taken the approach of a Matisse or an Ingres— overtly erotic, a mature man savoring a mature woman who looks entirely comfortable with the nakedness she celebrates—there would be nothing to talk about. Instead Balthus has us looking up a schoolgirl's skirt—and makes the act feel clandestine and naughty.

The bareness of the child's legs is accentuated by her shoes and socks. Balthus is up to his old tricks: the covering of one part of the body to call atten- tion to the revealing of another. But in *Thérèse Dreaming* and *Girl with a Cat,* the shoes go further still in augmenting the eroticism: the left one points directly at her genitals. The firm and rigid shoe assumes a subtly phallic role as if it is about to penetrate the girl.

Balthus would probably declare this idea even more far-fetched than Guy Davenport's observations in *A Balthus Notebook* that if the man in *Les Beaux Jours* were to turn around, he might look up the woman's skirt. Balthus brought up Davenport's assertion as an example of the ridiculous things people say about his work. How absurd, the artist laughed; "one does not see how the boy can turn around."

In *Thérèse Dreaming,* Balthus spread his nubile subject's legs in a way that threw them open for imaginary penetration and took it further with that per- fectly angled foot. Balthus's often repeated claim to me that he simply painted teenagers the way they sit in their usual poses is about as likely as Lord Byron being his grandfather. Dolores Miró and Jane Cooley confirmed that Balthus situated his models solely to suit his very precise goals—with scant concern for his subjects' comfort or the issue of naturalness. Thérèse sits the way Balthus wants to see her.

The girl lifts her arms with her elbows out and her fingers crossed at the top of her head. Pressing her hands into her cranium, she seems to contain her thoughts—and pull herself together, figuratively and metaphorically. Her arms bring all the lines of energy full circle and home again; she is reaching within— rather than toward anyone or anything. Stretched backward in this manner, her arms also render her defenseless and leave her body available, with her developing breasts free and clear. The motion of the twelve-year-old's limbs thus has all the power Antonin Artaud wished for.

Balthus often used arms this expressively. In *The Mountain,* the central female figure raises her arms and interlocks her fingers as if in a fantastic stretch or ritual dance. We know it means *something,* but we do not know exactly what. The limp arms of the unconscious figure in the foreground, like those of *The Victim,* imply a state somewhere between sleep and death. Other Balthus women painted through the years extend their arms in front of them almost as if they are swimming—indeed, they look as if they are underwater—or drop them in abandonment, or bend them as if they are possessed by demons. The gestures are generally extreme, the arms often disproportionately long. The meaning is ambiguous, but the effect is substantial.

LIKE THE MAN WHO PAINTED HER, Thérèse appears to reveal a great deal and to open herself to us, but remains remote. We will not get past the barriers. Her mouth is clamped shut, her eyes closed. She will not speak; we have no idea what she sees.

But we do know that her left nostril—her face is in profile, so it is the only one we see—is dilated as if she is having a rich experience, even if its precise nature is kept from us. That evocative swelling of her nose is more apparent in the actual canvas. I visited *Thérèse Dreaming* when it was in the collection of Natasha Gelman. The painting was then hanging in Mrs. Gelman's elegant, old Fifth Avenue apartment in the company of Matisses and Mirós and Cézannes—except on those periodic occasions when it was on view across the street on loan to the Metropolitan Museum of Art. (Mrs. Gelman has since died, and *Thérèse* has gone permanently to the Met.) The unsalable artistic escapade of the 1930s had been elevated to the blue-chip artwork of the nineties; Thérèse, like the man who painted her, had been transplanted from plain and rugged digs to surroundings of splendor. But whatever space she, and he, may now occupy—however much their audience has grown, and however much Thérèse and her creator now bask in glory—they still keep their fantasies and pleasures secret. The sensory thrill suggested by that swollen nostril, exposed though it is to any onlooker, has a source that is Thérèse's—and, perhaps, Balthus's—alone to know.

In *Girl with a Cat,* a cat stares out at us from the foreground. Scowling and protective, he looks like Thérèse's bodyguard. The spectacular feline holds the world at bay. In *Thérèse Dreaming,* a very different sort of cat—in the same position in the painting—laps a bowl of milk. The earlier cat sits there imperi-

Girl with a Cat, 1937, oil on wood, 87.6 x 77.7 cm

ous, while this one stands, its tail stretched behind it, semirigid, in a position of action. This second cat smiles. Cartoonlike in execution—with a goony, merry facial expression unlike one ever worn by a real cat—it is a far less realistic image than the brown tabby in *Girl with a Cat*. It is, rather, testimony to Balthus's whim.

The devilish animal, its smile pure mischief, appears overcome with pleasure. It squints its eyes as if it is intoxicated. With its bright red tongue, it devours the contents of its bowl—milk or cream, we assume—gleefully. At the very least, the image suggests the thrill in taking sensuous pleasure. More specifically, in *Thérèse Dreaming* the cat—always a stand-in for the artist him-self, the self-declared "H.M. the King of Cats"—is Balthus salivating. Not just salivating but partaking. He is lapping up the young girl whose legs are spread and crotch presented.

THE REJOINDER I HEARD Balthus utter as much as any other was, "Everyone is excited because you can see the little girls' underpants."

To this he would nod his pale, marvelous head in tired agreement, inhale deeply from yet another long white Dunhill, and acknowledge, "Well, one does see them." And then he would utter the same refrain: "The problem is the viewer's longings and interests, not mine." With a voice betraying just a hint of mockery and condescension, a look of puzzlement on his face—and the sug-gestion that he is the victim of forces that have nothing to do with him—he would complain again that his paintings "are awakening strange obsessions." I heard this day after day, as if the refined old man simply could not fathom the perversion that seems to be running rampant in the world.

As a boy Balthus must have been perpetually aware of the blatant sexual charge between Baladine and Rilke. Invited into their passionate universe, he was also made to keep his distance from it, neither to respond nor to appear to notice. Now he could be the one to display his longings and demand that others act as if nothing was there.

But a crotch is a crotch. And Thérèse fascinates and terrifies—as her cre-ator perfectly well knows.

Is it too much to say that the crack within the human body—the biologi-cal crevice with its pleasures mysterious yet infinite—was akin to the "Crac" about which Rilke had written the young Balthus: analogous, according to Rilke's "Mr. Blackwood," to the nonexistent moment between midnight of February 28 and the start of March 1 in non–leap years? Three-quarters of the time, the anniversary of Balthus's birthday occurred but did not occur, and as such was his alone, the domain that only he could enter. "What is private must remain so," Balthus wrote to John Russell in the statement that became his credo. Furtive, personal territory—known but unknowable—was the best of all.

THE SEXUALITY OF *Thérèse Dreaming*—her fantasies of genital pleasure; our fantasies of her imaginary, perhaps masturbatory, sequence of stimuli—gives the work much of its strength and beauty. Balthus would change his style—

and dissemble in myriad ways as both a man and a painter—for over half a century to come, but where his heart and ultimate talent were and would always be is clear in this painting. Balthus truly loved young girls (the jump-ropers on the Piazza Santa Croce, Laurence, Setsuko, and others). He also tortured them (Dolores Miró, Elsa Henriquez) with a cruelty edging on sadism. In either case, the obsession is indisputable.

Balthus's repeated disclaimers about the significance of this subject matter do him the great disservice of adding to, rather than dispelling, the idea that he is a painter of "dirty" pictures. By protesting what is obvious, he denigrates it. His only real perversion is in depriving himself of the acknowledgment of the excitement of neurotic thought that is so central to his being and his work. For the abandon and lack of self-consciousness of Balthus's art at its best testify to aliveness and offer the thrill of feeling. If, on close viewing, the eroticism begets more eroticism—and so the chair legs become phallic, the cat's bowl vaginal, the vases uterine, the clothing fetishistic—then this sensuous deluge should be celebrated, not disparaged. In the pervading intelligence of his art, Balthus elevates these soaring libidinal feelings from the sphere of the merely animal to the unique arena of human sexuality.

Looking at almost all of Balthus's art from the 1930s, we believe that every decision about clothing, gestures, and postures has to do with our sexual selves, our sense of who we are in our own eyes and whom we might attract, of what we want or else wish to avoid.

Balthus may have told me dozens of times that all comparisons to Nabokov are entirely off base, yet like the worldly and erudite author of *Lolita*, he, too, has had the bravery and magnificent effrontery to acknowledge that grown men can be sexually attracted to young girls, and to make great art of that taboo. In a disarmingly tasteful style of painting, he has tackled without equivocation an apparently tasteless subject. Like Nabokov, he has brought intense culture and intelligence to the revelation of raw emotion.

The price has been high. I have had people tell me that Balthus was arrested because of his activities with young girls. The word that gets thrown around in random conversation is "pedophile." Indeed, he has had a series of relationships with teenage women, married someone thirty-four years his junior, and painted young girls. But we live in a world where middle-aged women sport baby-doll dresses and twelve-year-olds wear miniskirts. Junior high school girls try for the effects of fully sexualized women; women in menopause present themselves as little girls. Balthus has simply gone further than most in revealing all of this—and committed what for some is the transgression of treating his fantasy as reality.

· · ·

BALTHUS'S TEENAGE GIRLS represent, I believe, both the object of the artist's
love and his narcissism. Those unyielding, secretive girls—lost in their own
reverie—resemble Balthus himself. Like him, they are alluring and unavailable. On one level his women are himself in female form. The adolescence
with which Balthus has always been most obsessed with is his own.

These girls are also, in part, an evocation of the mother with whom he
identified: the love-struck young woman whom he wanted as his own. And
having probably been tortured in ways by his mother's affair with Rilke, he
now inflicted reciprocal pain on her stand-ins. The teenage girls of Balthus's
paintings are Baladine overwhelmed by Rilke, Baladine punished by her son,
as well as Balthus as a teenager overwhelmed.

Of course, they are also, quite simply, teenage girls. The species in general
has rarely had a greater admirer. Based on the look I saw on Balthus's face when
he met my own young teenage daughters—I will get to this—attractive young
women are his intoxicant. That said, at least in old age, he was the most harmless Humbert Humbert imaginable; he knew how to behave.

BALTHUS, OF COURSE, is quite right that the craft of painting is pivotal. His
brother's renditions of eroticized women—weakly drawn, overtly sexual without any of the same art—are a mockery by comparison. *Thérèse Dreaming*
grips us so, and has its ravishing impact, because of its power of representation,
the triumph of its colors, and the pulsing movement that is as alive and
charged as its subject's nubile body.

In this canvas as in his life in his marvelous chalet, Balthus as set designer
and couturier has displayed unerring, impeccable taste. The wallpaper behind
Thérèse has, with its lustrous colors, the resonance of a deep yet quiet voice.
This is virtually the same paper as in *The Guitar Lesson,* although Balthus
painted them in different studios. Its design is probably a product of the artist's
imagination, more than a reproduction of an actual object. It reveals the inanimate ability to invest inanimate objects with maximum impact. That know-
how is equally apparent in the still life on the wooden table with its
Morandi-like reserve, clarity, and magisterial articulation.

Balthus makes all the elements plausible and rich. In what will consistently be one of the strong points of his work, he has painted the draped white
material in *Thérèse* so that every fold reads easily and rhythmically. The position of the table in the space of the room is distinct. The angle of each chair is

as exact as Dolores Miró's feet were when the poor child had to buttress her toes against nails. The way the light falls is masterful: providing a soft tone to the background, intensifying shadows, highlighting Thérèse's flesh.

The 1938 canvas contains most everything Balthus is best at: a cat, country furniture catching the light, folded material, women's knees, a pillow, naked flesh. And it further validates Picasso's statement that Balthus was the master of interiors. How authentically the shadows of the furniture fall on the floor. We believe that what we see truly exists. The chaise legs, like Thérèse's shoes, seem as real as the details of a Jan van Eyck. And beyond the agglomeration of details, Balthus composes the painting as a totality. He gets the surfaces right, and establishes an embroidered hem as fact, but he also understands objects in space in a more profound and generalized sense, making them, in a large and noble way, forms and light and shadow.

At the same time, *Thérèse Dreaming* avoids Balthus's problem areas. The artist has navigated his way around the troublesome issue of the hands by interlocking them. And there is no thought of including a boy or man, except by implication. The painting does have, however, the usual element of Balthus's bizarreness of scale. Although it is not particularly noticeable at first, the girl has a disproportionately large head. This is yet another successful contrivance: like the chair caning, it works without our necessarily being aware of it. Rather than having us think that we are looking at something that does not scan when we see this oversized head, Balthus convinces us that we are in the powerful presence of a real personage. Supremely conscious of effect in his art as in his life, the artist formulated the proportion for its impact. Thérèse's vast face and skull have the effect of absorbing us in her thoughtfulness. Quite literally, her mind looms large before our eyes.

THE SOLID, STATUESQUE STILL LIFE on the table—the immobile vase, flacon, and canister, with their shapes rigid, the hardness of their metal and glass palpable—exists in counterpoint to Thérèse's large and wide cheeks. The order and separateness of the neatly placed objects on the tabletop are like a foil to this alive, complicated creature.

Yet Balthus has evoked the child's features with extraordinary economy. Thérèse's closed eyes and eyebrow are painted with utter simplicity. The pursed lips and rounded nostril are achieved with a minimum of brush. A simple interplay of thin, opaque tans and rouges establishes the luminous flesh. Their maker knows the devices to create precisely the living presence he wanted.

Thérèse's body, meanwhile, is a mixture of repose and action. With her solid, powerful upper body—a Balthus trademark—she leans back, her weight centered on her buttocks. Yet her back is poised; she does not allow herself to sink into the pillow. She is resting yet perched: comfortable but at the start of something. Similarly, with her legs relaxed yet braced, her arms comfortable but active, she combines being asleep with being alert.

These confluences create tremendous rhythm and visual motion. The composition moves in and out with a pulsing energy. The left leg, starting at the foot, shoots up to the knee, then drops down slowly as it widens to the thigh and crotch. The elbows jut. As with Giacometti's figurines, Thérèse's sturdy, powerful limbs endow her with vitality and potency. The total effect is the perfect physical representation of the mixed state of being that is adolescence. Balthus says today that each of his paintings is "a prayer"; it is, by most standards, an offbeat form of religion, but this art is indeed a celebration, an homage to human capability and complexity.

This self-taught artist could outpaint almost anyone of the day. At age thirty, he evinces the extraordinary skill that, while not consistently at the same level, would distinguish him for years to come. He folds a towel on the table with the expertise of Velázquez. He makes a country chair and table exist as vividly as the brothers Le Nain did. He captures the way the unfinished dark wood of a country table absorbs light. He brings off the caning of the chaise—not by any tedious verisimilitude but by inventing just the right sawtooth effect for the wrapped stretcher at the end. Up close, the caning of both the chair and the side chair are really very simply painted: in a creamy beige true to straw, accented by aptly colored shadows. At a distance, the rendition works so well that we know the precise extent of the indentation and sagging. Psychologically ambiguous, Balthus was visually utterly exact.

The majesty of forms and light and shadow is, indeed, a mainstay of all his art. He evokes physical truth. We know what his chairs are covered with; we feel them as solid surfaces, strong enough to sit on. His furniture has adequate strength and weight and substance. Balthus, like all the great painters, attends to the rudiments of life. People live and breathe, stretch their bodies, occupy space. They have weight. They dream. Chairs and beds support our bodies; tables elevate the accessories to our existence.

And art heightens sensation. In *Thérèse Dreaming*, the color relationships have been as carefully constructed as the composition. Few painters of our century have taken such pains with the formulation, such care with every sequence. Having kept the color range minimal—with that self-imposed discipline Balthus told me he enjoys—he has worked it to full effect. The warm orangy red of the wallpaper stripes is picked up by Thérèse's skirt and shoes, and by the cylindrical container on the table. The only other colors are browns, whites, the tones of flesh and straw, and a range of greens. It is all rich and subdued at the same time, simply balanced.

In making these aesthetic choices Balthus was taking a solitary stance. Even with the similarities to Derain and Giacometti, he made himself as different from everyone around him in the 1930s as he has since the Second World War by choosing to be an old-world aristocrat. The Surrealists were painting bright. His beloved Bonnard was all pastel. Picasso's dominant hue was a Mediterranean blue; Matisse's canvases shone with the sunshine of Nice. Balthus's palette is deeper, more resonant—deliberately layered with weighted colors.

The green he has chosen for the pillow is evidence both of Balthus's perfect sense of visual pitch and of his exquisite tastefulness. It is the same sense of style that prevails in his house in Switzerland: in the handsome country antiques, the aged vases full of local meadow flowers, the impeccable porcelain accoutrements in the bathrooms, the fine old prints in the guest rooms, the baronial iron lamps that Balthus had had made in Italy. Balthus has a judgment and a sense of history in a way that, even in our international world, seem quintessentially European. That green cosseting Thérèse's back is darker than sea foam, but similar; it is velvet, but it seems indigenous to nature. This is a rich, masterful color: a color that conjures age, that belongs to a society where we sit on materials that have preceded us by centuries—and presumably will outlive us by as much. Balthus knew the effect of things: of color as of limb position. In *The Bernese Hat*, the yellow of the hat gives the painting a note of light Mozartian esprit; this green has the depth and resonance of Beethoven's *Appassionata*.

II

SINCE LITTLE INFURIATES Balthus more than the "idiotic" comparisons between his work and Vladimir Nabokov's *Lolita*, it is odd that the second portrait of Thérèse—the 1938 *Girl with a Cat*—appears on the cover of the Penguin Twentieth-Century Classic edition of *Lolita*, a much circulated paperback. When I was with Balthus, I saw him turn down a request for one of his paintings to appear on the cover of a book by Josephine Humphries; he did not know Humphries's work, but explained to me that he disapproved of having his art on a piece of fiction. Yet Penguin got the permission of DACS, the organization that controls Balthus's reproduction rights, to have the alluring Thérèse symbolize precisely what the artist says she does not.

This particular Balthus is a full crotch view. It presents a sinister, uncomfortable-looking child. In fact, she *is* all wrong for Lolita, but not necessarily for the reasons Balthus would claim. For one thing, the old-master colors of the painting, the daybed, and her clothing make her too purely old-fashioned European. She is from the wrong culture; Nabokov's book is rooted in America in the 1950s, and Lolita is too much part of that world for the Balthus to work. More importantly, *Lolita* is a book emphatically about self-knowledge, about unabashed delight in one's own obsessions, about the celebration of neurosis. Balthus, on the contrary, may hint at private feelings, but then he denies them and makes a halfhearted attempt to cloak them. He does not know how he feels about his feelings, or at least he does not let you know; he plays games with you. He is no more up front about what is really going on emotionally than he is about the facts of his background, whereas Nabokov's writing extolls impassioned delight with tumultuous honesty and frankly depicts an obsession with obsession.

It is for this reason that, even if Balthus has repeatedly insisted on denying any link in sensibility with Nabokov, the novelist practically flaunted their similarities. Once, when a group of people were visiting the filmmaker Billy Wilder, whose art collection included major paintings by many of the best-known twentieth-century masters (Picasso, Matisse, etc.), the guests were all musing about which picture they would take as their own if they could choose just one. Nabokov had no doubt as to what his selection would be, and was proud of it. He pointed to the Balthus frontal nude of a teenage girl and said with unabashed delight that he would pick that one.

In *Lolita,* rather than lay the groundwork for speculation, Nabokov tells all:

> As greater authors than I have put it: "Let readers imagine," etc. On second thought, I may as well give those imaginations a kick in the pants. I knew I had fallen in love with Lolita forever; but I also knew she would not be forever Lolita.[3]

Humbert deliberately affronts us. He assumes guilt, and from time to time addresses an imaginary jury. Unafraid to be funny, he leaves few questions begging: "She was all rose and honey, dressed in her brightest gingham, with a pattern of little red apples, and her arms and legs were of a deep golden brown, with scratches like tiny dotted lines of coagulated rubies, and the ribbed cuffs of her white socks were turned down at the remembered level, and because of her childish gait, or because I had memorized her as always wearing heelless shoes, her saddle oxfords looked somehow too large and too high-heeled for her."[4] Nabokov's book is a shameless partaking of delights: a deliberately all-or-nothing engagement. Humbert refers to himself as "a maniac with pederosis."[5] He sets forth his ardor unequivocally: "Lolita, Lolita, Lolita, Lolita, Lolita, Lolita, Lolita, Lolita, Lolita. Repeat till the page is full, printer."[6]

Humbert, who in fact has murdered someone, knows the connection between who he really is and how he behaves, and is capable of being witty and worldly and ironic about it. Balthus, on the other hand, perpetually equivocates. In his paintings of young girls, he presents them as sexual presences but then has them deny their sexuality; the girl being groped in *The Street* looks as if nothing is happening, as if she is some otherworldly religious figure heading off into a spiritual world. No one engages one hundred percent in what he or she is doing. The artist invites emotions only to take them away. With Matisse and Picasso, however different their voices, we know where they stand—be it lusty and appreciative, or angry and deprecating—while with Balthus we are in tenuous territory. Studied and contrived, the paintings, like their teenage subjects, need to give mixed signals in order to keep their secrets and hence their power.

CHAPTER NINETEEN

BATTLEFIELDS

AND CHÂTEAUX

It was said, though I do not know where the story originated (it may even be true), that he had been ordained a Catholic priest and had served in the Great War as a chaplain in the Austro-Hungarian army; when I asked him once about this period of his life he would say nothing and only gave me one of his studiedly enigmatic smiles. He had suffered a shrapnel wound—"in a skirmish in the Carpathians"—which had left him with an attractive Byronic limp. He was tall, straight-backed, with glossy blue-black hair, soft eyes, an engaging, if somewhat laboured, ironical smile. He could have been one of those Prussian princes out of the last century, all gold braid and duelling scars, so beloved of operetta composers. He claimed he had been captured in battle by the Russian army, and when the Revolution came had joined the Reds and fought in the civil war. All this gave him the faintly preposterous air of fortitude and self-importance of the Man Who Has Seen Action.
—JOHN BANVILLE, *The Untouchable*[1]

I

THE TIME WAS ENDING when artists or their subjects might calmly lean back and dream. *Thérèse Dreaming* would soon seem like a memory of easier times. Everything changed irrevocably with the onset of World War II.

Having installed Antoinette and Baladine at Derain's, Balthus went off to fight for France. On September 2, 1939, he was mobilized. In a letter dated October 17, 1939, the woman who was then Pierre Matisse's wife, Teeny (later Mrs. Marcel Duchamp), wrote Chick Austin, "Pierre writes Balthus is at the front. The whole situation is very frightening—no one here even guesses how 'real' war can become almost overnight."

The war became real soon enough. But Balthus's days as a soldier were few. The artist told me that he was "blown up on a mine in Savoie just at the beginning of the War" and was immediately demobilized for that reason. Balthus has mentioned the injury in several interviews as well. It is why, he explained one afternoon as we were slowly making our way down the corridor of Le Grand Chalet, he has had to walk with a stick ever since. This accident probably saved his life, he said philosophically, shrugging his shoulders as if this were yet another strange twist of fate. It was one of the many examples he gave me of circumstances beyond his control—and of his resignation to them.

John Russell, Jean Leymarie, and Sabine Rewald all handle the issue of Balthus and the war by reporting, in their published texts on the artist, that he was called to service when fighting broke out, and demobilized about three months later, in December 1939. They provide no additional details. However, in her doctoral thesis, Rewald goes further. Balthus's wartime experience is yet another of his inventions, it seems. Whereas the artist has for years been telling people that he was hit by a mine which severely damaged one of his legs, Pierre Leyris, according to Rewald, told her that Balthus's leg problems were the result of an operation he had had before the war—and which he later used as an excuse to prevent him from being remobilized.

James Lord, who knew lots of people Balthus knew during the war, and spent considerable time with the artist shortly thereafter, maintains that Balthus was stationed only on the inactive front, where there was no real fighting—and got through the war unscathed. On the concept that Balthus's limp was the result of an injury incurred on the battlefield, Lord told me, "I never saw him limp,"[2] even though Lord pointed out that, more recently, as an old man, Balthus has come to depend on a walking stick. Lord also said that, until I told him about it, he had never heard that Balthus had claimed a war injury. "All of that is completely untrue. He was never in any active service or any real danger. . . . Of course he wasn't wounded; he didn't do any fighting."[3] When I told Lord that Balthus had come to say he had caught shrapnel in various parts of his body, Lord responded, "I think that's absolute pure bullshit. If that were the case, everyone in Paris would have known it. Alberto [Giacometti], Pierre [Klossowski], Dora [Maar]: all kinds of people would have known. We all saw one another at Marie-Laure's. If Balthus had been badly wounded, he would have gotten a decoration."[4] But, like Pierre Leyris, Lord felt that the myth-making had to be treated with understanding: "He was a great maker-upper, and the more power to him."[5]

James Thrall Soby also suggests that the land mine in Savoie was a fabrication. Soby, who knew Balthus fairly well and had many friends in common with him, treads lightly, as in his handling of the artist's Byronic ancestry claims, but is careful to avoid inaccuracy. After referring to "the intestinal infection which has plagued him" ever since he developed it during his military service in Morocco, Soby writes, "In 1939 he was called up and sent to the front in World War II. His health broke quickly, he was demobilized and spent the remainder of the war with his wife and children in Switzerland."[6]

A version of these same events that requires some reading between the lines is given by Jean Rodolphe von Salis. Von Salis first met Balthus in the 1920s, when he was writing his book on Rilke's years in Switzerland. Von Salis had access to correct information about Balthus from Antoinette de Watteville's brother, with whom he was friends in Bern, and over the years he periodically ran into Baladine, Pierre, and Balthus in Paris. Von Salis writes:

> In May 1940, in the worst of the battle of France, when the German armored divisions were approaching Paris, I was astonished to see Balthus enter the Café de Flore limping and apparently suffering. He had been wounded, he said, on the Maginot Line, and the army had discharged him.[7]

Given that this account appeared in a sanctioned publication—the catalog for Balthus's 1993 exhibition in Lausanne—it has an amazingly sardonic tone, not just for the use of the word *pénétrer* to depict Balthus's manner of entering the Flore, but also for the suggestion that Balthus's suffering and report of being wounded may not have been a hundred percent authentic.

A letter that Pierre Matisse wrote to Chick Austin in December 1939 clarifies this matter of Balthus's fate as a soldier. Russell, Leymarie, and Rewald are accurate in saying that he was demobilized, even if, probably deliberately, they are vague about the reason. Leyris and Lord are also apparently correct that the leg injury about which Balthus spoke so resignedly to me was a ruse. Indeed, as Soby said, Balthus's "health broke." Matisse wrote Austin of the great misfortune of Balthus having been in the war from the very start, and then referred to him "picking up remains after the battles until it got the best of him. Now he is in Switzerland trying to recuperate after being temporarily discharged."

In April 1997 I visited Pierre and Teeny Matisse's daughter, Jacqueline Matisse Monnier, and asked her for her recollections of Balthus's war experience or of her parents' discussions about it. Jackie, who posed for Balthus as a teenager, has always very much liked the artist in spite of his having made her hold awkward poses for many hours, a discomfort she took in stride because "this is how life was": children did what was expected of them. But when I told her that Balthus was now claiming war injuries, and that they were getting more severe by the interview, she raised her eyebrows with dismay. "He never

talked about anything of the sort in conversations with my father or Giacometti," she recalled. For of course they would have recognized the lie. "But
he did often speak of his malaria, which is what we all thought his limp came
from."

It seems to me that Balthus's "war injuries" may have been inspired in part
by what actually happened to André Malraux, whom he met shortly after the
war and greatly admired. In order to help some English parachutists escape a
unit of Reich soldiers, Malraux ran across a field to divert attention from the
fleeing Britons, getting shot in the thigh and incurring further injuries in the
process—as a result of which he continued to suffer from leg wounds after
the war. Consequently Malraux was awarded the British Distinguished Service
Order by King George, given to him by Ambassador Alfred Duff Cooper at
the British Embassy in Paris. Surely Balthus would have been pleased to have
such accolades fall on him.

THE IDEA THAT THE EMOTIONAL agony of the battlefield, rather than any
physical woes, is what prompted Balthus's swift discharge suggests that the
man who painted *The Victim* could not bear the sight of real victims in the
flesh. I believe this to be so.

My sense is that Balthus is someone for whom violence is enchanting as
the stuff of imagination, but intolerable in reality. He has, time and again,
painted scenes of aggression; he has an appetite, like that of a child playing
with guns, for extreme power. His look of sheer adulation when saying how
much he admired Saddam Hussein "as a genius for his ability to hold up the
world at gunpoint" was, I believe, not evil but merely perverse: a pleasure in
being outrageous, an infatuation with the fantasy of tyranny. Balthus also
described himself as "*derangé*" by the realities of the Persian Gulf War, which
was then taking place in part thanks to the same Hussein. Balthus declared
himself incapable of understanding why one paints in a world where such horrible things happen. Having witnessed two world wars, he said he was distraught at the thought of a third.

Balthus's aggressiveness, even his lies, are in all likelihood a mask he has
developed to cover up the extreme sensitivity and vulnerability to which Pierre
Matisse referred in that letter. The same duality can be seen in Balthus's paintings. On some level, he is impelled to mutilate his subject, to treat women like
circus acts and put them on display, to show schoolboys as cruel and manipulative when they play their games, to shatter a glass and spear a piece of bread.
On the other hand, he is the most sensitive of appreciators; the man who
evokes the beauty of a landscape and flowers so palpably that it takes our

breath away. Known for having delivered the cruelest snubs, he is also warm, gracious, and generous.

Both as a person and as a painter, Balthus savors and destroys, cherishes and diminishes. Those few lines of Pierre Matisse's—revealing, as they do, the dichotomy between the artist's response to real victims and his creation of painted ones, between his fragility and his boldness, between his vulnerability and the myths in which he has encased himself—help us to understand the pronounced duality that gives such tension to Balthus's work.

That dreadful experience of seeing bodies on the battlefield chastened the artist profoundly. The struggle to grapple with violence—especially since he connected it inextricably with sex—and the essentially unresolved question of who he really was in the modern world have dominated Balthus's life ever since those tumultuous events of 1939.

Indeed, one of Balthus's recent accounts of his war experience, while probably a whopper, evokes the psychological impact of war on him with trenchant accuracy. In his November 1994 "elusive," "never gives interviews" interview in *Art & Antiques,* he amplified the story of his war injury to a new degree. Now, according to his innocent interviewer, the artist had stepped on a mine near the Maginot Line and "caught shrapnel in his spine, right leg, and stomach." Balthus touchingly explains: " 'I often dream of that experience . . . not seeing the others, completely alone, just hearing the sound of airplanes and having the feeling they want to hear you.' "[8] It's very moving, and perhaps I am a monster for believing Pierre Leyris and all the other available accounts of Balthus's contemporaries in 1940, rather than this tale from the artist himself. But it sounds far more like an invention than the truth. The scene is not unlike the report of the solitary Balthus in the mountains after Rilke's funeral. Like all of Balthus's snippets of autobiography, it may distort the facts, but it is entirely accurate in depicting the artist's thoughts and emotions, his fears as well as his hopes.

IN JUNE 1940, SOME SIX MONTHS following his demobilization, Balthus moved to Champrovent, in Savoie. Savoie at the end of 1939 and in 1940 was under Italian military administration, for which reason a number of Parisians—Gertrude Stein among them—were refugees in the area. Balthus and Pierre had previously visited Pierre and Betty Leyris at their large farmhouse there, and now he took a house nearby for himself and Antoinette.

Balthus quickly began to paint again. He did a pair of domestic interiors called *The Living Room,* for which the local farmer's teenage daughters modeled. Both of these works show a girl reading in a pose like that of Thérèse in

The Children, with a second girl, her skirt hiked well up her thigh, sprawling on the sofa. To escape the realities of the world around him, Balthus had quickly retreated to his favorite fantasies.

In late 1941 the Wehrmacht took over Savoie and Balthus and Antoinette fled to Switzerland. They stayed briefly in Bern, and in 1942 they went on to Fribourg, where they remained until September 1945. In 1942 Stanislas was born; in 1944 Thaddeus.

It was in this period after Balthus had actually left Savoie that he painted his marvelous *Landscape at Champrovent*—the painting that Guy Davenport interpreted as a direct counterpoint to the horrors of Treblinka.

MOST POLES, WHETHER JEWISH or not, were in exile from Paris during the war. Between February 1, 1933, and May 31, 1944, Erich Klossowski found refuge in Sanary, where he lived, along with his female companion Hilde Stieler, in the house of the Cavet family.

Erich
Klossowski,
in his late
years

Balthus would never have given me information about the trauma of the war for his parents; nor would he approve of my revealing it. However, Serge and Beate Klarsfeld, the renowned experts on Nazism in France, generously filled me in here—both with information on the effects of Balthus's Jewish lineage and with material on Erich. They provided a reminiscence by Marcelle Cavet, the daughter of the people who ran the *pension* in which Erich Klossowski spent those eleven years, which reflects the reality of this time period in the life of Balthus's family. Erich Klossowski

> was a man of extraordinary culture, very subtle, very refined, and very pleasant. He was discreet, affable, calm, he came down the path very deliberately, returning in the same way, always at the same time. He was always dressed in black, with a silk foulard tie. He loved France passionately and was particularly devoted to Chateaubriand. . . .
>
> Klossowski was very fond of this house which had, for him, the charm of the old Provençal farms with its terrace and its arbor. One of Hilde Stieler's friends had complimented her on her choice of residence by saying: "You live in a fairy-tale house!" They did a lot of painting in those days. . . .
>
> I can still see Monsieur Klossowski in the kitchen corner, listening to the news on the radio, his expression so attentive and anxious. After the defeat, in 1940, he virtually stopped painting. In the course of 1939 a Dutchman arrived in Sanary, Monsieur de Wilt, who became very close to the Klossowski couple and was able to help them a good deal. That really permitted them to survive. . . .
>
> Toward the end of the war—it was after May 1944—they were billeted in a residence like the other Sanary émigrés (in the Haut-Var). This was a general measure. So they left the *pension,* but they returned to Sanary after the Liberation. They lived then in a little house in the Rue Barthélemy-Dedon. That was where Klossowski died, in 1952.[9]

In his cultivation and pace, the elder Klossowski was remarkably like Balthus in Rossinière. He countered the anguish of life by immersing himself in culture and maintaining his immense personal dignity.

II

She was closed in dream, a princess in a tower, scarcely a flesh-and-blood woman at all. Did he then desire her not for herself but for all that was unawakened in her, all that had not yet

come into being? His mother had read him that story: at the
Prince's kiss, Dornröschen opened her eyes. Then the fire leaped
in the fireplace, the horses in the stables stirred, the pigeons on
the roof took heads from under their wings. And a mournful
desire moved in him, for the princess in her chamber, as he
imagined her young body stirring, the ribs moving under the
skin, the wrists turning, the eyes, dark with dream, slowly
opening after their hundred years sleep.

—STEVEN MILLHAUSER, *Martin Dressler*[10]

IN SEPTEMBER 1945 BALTHUS and Antoinette and their young sons moved
to the Villa Diodati near Geneva. Lord Byron had stayed in this house in 1816;
Balthus's year or so in the same auspicious setting must certainly have helped
the development of his imaginary descendancy from the English Romantic
poet.

André Maurois, whom Balthus knew, described the Villa Diodati in his
1930 biography of Byron. "It was an old house and well placed, standing halfway up the slope of the hill, with grass and vineyards below, and it had a splendid view of the lake with its flowery shores, and across to Geneva and the
Jura."[11] When Byron had lived there, Percy and Mary Shelley were in a peasant's cottage just below.

At the Villa Diodati, Balthus completed his most significant painting of
the epoch: *Les Beaux Jours* (color plate 2). This is the single Balthus painting of
which I am leaving the name untranslated. *The Golden Days*—as it is known at
the Hirshhorn Museum and in various English texts—imposes an inappropriate tint of nostalgia and distances it too much in the past; adolescence and its
sexual intensity—the subject of this painting—are perpetual. Both Balthus
and Setsuko voiced their skepticism to me about "Golden." They made me feel
as if I, as an American, were a party to the travesty—simply because I came
from the heathen culture that devised it. "*The Golden Days*," Setsuko would
say, with a bemused expression on her face. She emphasized the "*Golden*" with
the same hint of contempt she used for the name of the television show "Dal-
las," which at that point was reaching the Swiss mountains. Balthus would
assume a similarly ironic voice whenever he would say to me "*The Golden
Days*, I think it is called now, Nicholas"—as if he had no more control over it
than the painting that fell off the roof of his car.

Setsuko and I often talked about this particular painting. Its image was
present in the detail of a superb tea cozy she had painted on silk and that adds
its playful touch to the elegantly appointed service table in the dining room at
Le Grand Chalet. This charming object, while managing to evoke a rather sin-

Balthus in 1953 at a rehearsal of *L'Ile des chèvres* by Ugo Betti,
for which he designed the sets

ister painting, cleverly transforms its imagery and renders its tone lighthearted. In Setsuko's version, the vain young woman has been transformed into a horse, and a humanoid cat reads up on art auctions. She told me she made it in part to compensate her husband for the absence of one of his favorite paintings. She and I were both of the opinion that *Les Beaux Jours* is one of Balthus's masterpieces. And—by dint of my having come from that alien land on the other side of the Atlantic—I was in the rare position of knowing more about its ultimate fate than did its maker in his Alpine retreat.

The painting's situation at the Hirshhorn is, in fact, grotesque. Like the "murderous" lighting conditions at the Centre Pompidou—or the deadening glazing imposed by the Metropolitan on *Nude in Front of a Mantel*—the setting seems practically designed to obliterate the true quality of the art. No wonder that Balthus despairs at the "blindness" of current museum administrators. In the white, airport-style doughnut-shaped Hirshhorn Museum on the Washington Mall, *Les Beaux Jours'* nearby companions for the past few years have been large canvases by Francis Bacon and Fernando Botero. Presumably this is because the three of them are figurative paintings of the same generation, but the alphabetical closeness of the painters' names would be no less valid a reason. The viewer must screen out the work of the other two painters in order to let the Balthus have its effect, and their proximity makes the process difficult. Yet the tonality of *Les Beaux Jours* is so different from that of its neighbors that the effort pays off. Balthus's painting is darker and more matte, the palette more somber. His sensibility is adventurous, playful, and understatedly haughty; their works look like outright screams. Balthus's canvas appears as if it has been nurtured for centuries; Botero's and Bacon's, comparatively, seem to have just sprouted. Balthus's art is subtly audacious; theirs, not the least bit subtly, goes for the quick shock.

With *Les Beaux Jours*, it is, indeed, the tone, and the success of the illusions, that strikes us first. The flames positively glow in the darkness of the fireplace, while staying precisely where they should be in the background. Balthus ranks with Velázquez in his *Forge of Vulcan* for his ability to paint the mysterious substance of fire. In *Les Beaux Jours,* the luminosity originates within the

Balthus and Silvia Monfort, 1953

flames. Elsewhere on the canvas, light caresses materials or brings objects into sharp focus. The rich russets—and the green specific to tarnished brass—come and go in intensity, with shimmering whites adding the occasional accent mark. As in a theatrical production, the elaborate lighting system creates both singular moments and prolonged passages.

On one level, you can see why Balthus shrugs his shoulders at the various analyses of the subject matter of the painting and disparages the thematic context. Clearly he went to as much trouble in articulating the white bowl at the left-hand border of the canvas, in delineating its graceful contour and in making its lustrous shadow, as he did in playing out the silent male-female dialogue—or, rather, the two monologues—that was his starting point. The light that pours in through the open, windblown curtains—Balthus's usual source of awakenings—helps delineate the rim of that bowl, rendering it a thin and uneven gray, restrained and imprecise. We could study that bowl for hours to understand the craft of painting. The deep brown-black behind its right-hand lip accentuates its whiteness and provides a backdrop to the splash of sunlight on the table.

The more we look, the more that bowl becomes a female form, a uterine symbol of the type we know from Flemish paintings, its whiteness an analogue to female purity and virginity. These linkages may be entirely inadvertent on Balthus's part—the result of his having imparted meanings over which he had no more control than the details of a dream—yet that bowl and the curves of the young woman and her chaise in *Les Beaux Jours* are as sensuous as in an Ingres. One can hardly blame the viewer who can't get sex off his mind.

Were we to follow the artist's guidelines, of course, Setsuko's tea cozy would represent the level of interpretation at which we should stop. Yet *Les Beaux Jours* is, to most of us, everything Balthus says his work is not: intensely erotic, loaded with portent, full of symbolism. Yes, its initial power derives from its visual strengths—the workmanship is brilliant, the shadows palpable, the forms anchored and weighty, the surfaces and light intensely lush, the sequence of curves against the grid a feast. The artist's disclaimers do not, however, cancel out the obvious meaning of some of the subject matter. I, among other people, am convinced that the blazing fire represents the supine young woman's burning sexuality, and that the shirtless man stoking the fire—a Balthus-as-Heathcliff self-portrait—is vicariously performing, with those phallic logs, the act he would like to be performing in actuality. The woman has multiple readings. Looking in her mirror, she is as transfixed as Narcissus—which makes her a sort of female self-portrait of Balthus, to whom Rilke dedicated his poem "Narcissus." She also looks—consider the way her right arm hangs—partly anesthetized or in a trance.

The swarthy, sexy Heathcliff type stoking the fire epitomizes maleness in counterpoint to the sheer womanliness of this modern goddess with her hiked-up skirt. His face is turned so we cannot see it, but his shirtless torso and active pose suggest great virility. A presumed self-portrait, Balthus makes himself look fit and competent.

He also looks hungry for what he cannot have. One imagines each of these personages in a private sexual universe: as aware of self as of the "other," full of longing more than satisfaction.

BALTHUS HAS, WITH PAINSTAKING deliberation and care, created the massing of the woman's hair, its bulk as well as the individual strands, and then let his brush pass over them with a certain abandon. And he has painted her large, flat, dramatic face—part in dark shadow, part in lustrous sunlight—to make it exquisitely beautiful. World War II was raging through Europe in its final days when Balthus began this painting. The artist, in the small neutral country that was like the eye of the storm—with Germany, France, and Italy all touching its borders—was, whether he was conscious of his agony or seemingly unaware of it, for whatever reasons of avoidance or escapism, immersing himself, as if nothing else in the world mattered, in porcelain bowls and beautiful hair. He celebrated life as it was being threatened all around him, and basked in a world that was going up in smoke. He coped with the vulnerability associated with his Jewishness by lying about it; perhaps the only way he could deal with the reality of war was to avoid it.

But this painting is a commentary on violence as well as an escape from it. Destruction and the will to overpower are very much at its essence. The flames, after all, are visible.

The woman's right hand—a classic Balthus failure, it looks as much like the foot of a dead chicken, or a rubber puppet, as a human hand—hangs limp from her arm. It suggests that she is in a fugue state. She wraps the left one, however, around the mirror handle; she is competent and in control. Her head is inclined toward us; she knows her audience. Yet her eyes aim only for the mirror. The woman exists exclusively for herself. Aware yet unaware, playing to the crowd with single-minded vanity, she is the ultimate teenage girl—and very much like the man who painted her. The world may be on fire, but at least she has self-contemplation to fall back on, and the ability to withhold her charms.

This woman seems oblivious to the way one of her breasts is exposed and her thighs are visible almost to her crotch. Meanwhile, the row of tacks along the wainscoting, the clock and elegant container on the mantel, the gold mirror frame, all lend propriety to the setting. There is so much geometric order, and such a successful impression of reality, that the disorder (emotional and sexual) and the artifice (her waist is half the width of her head) affect us only gradually. Yet the painting abounds in psychological disruptions and tension. The fire tongs seem not merely powerful but almost like instruments of torture. The sphinx and fire irons imply secrets held within. The phallic logs thrust toward the warm hearth. The fire, meanwhile, can be seen to symbolize the war itself: a conflagration created by men.

A dozen years had passed since Balthus first began drawing himself as Heathcliff. But this is Heathcliff still: the working man in the presence of the lady, the outsider in the drawing room. An outcast, he has supernatural strength. His bare hand is in the coals. Stripped to the waist, he shows himself muscular, broad-backed, sexy. The deep red-brown of his back is almost the same color as the fire wall. He is taut and strong, with the hue and intensity of flames. Like the Heathcliff of the earlier drawings, he poses with his lean but solid buttocks aimed directly at us. Balthus has painted the skintight pants, and the rope holding them up, impeccably—with the same force and know-how of his subject stoking the fire.

IN 1946, WHILE HE WAS STILL living at the Villa Diodati, Balthus drew a portrait of Honoré de Balzac for the cover of a special edition of *Les Marana: Vengeance d'artiste,* published by Albert Skira. That spring Balthus collaborated with Skira and the French ambassador to Switzerland, Henri Hoppenot, in organizing an exhibition called "Ecole de Paris" at the Kunsthalle in Bern. He wrote to the conservator at the Kunsthalle that his goal was to show "the great precursors"—Cézanne, Seurat, Manet, Renoir, and van Gogh—an important group of recent pictures by Bonnard, Braque, Picasso, and Matisse, and "a few contemporary masters." He included his own *Beaux Jours.* It was the first time a painting by Balthus was ever exhibited in a museum.[12]

The world has certainly come around since. A guard at the Hirshhorn told me that this is one of the most visited paintings at the museum. No wonder. In a society that savors Calvin Klein ads, *Les Beaux Jours* has some of the same appeal. Intensely male-female, its sexuality more salacious than satiated, it rivets us.

And reproductions do no justice to it. The angles of limbs make a march into the space. Abandon and wildness soar in this ordered world of firm horizontals and verticals. As with Balthus himself, we get a European feel for structure, a sense of history, a system. But what dominates is the unfathomable: raw, untempered, and beyond our grasp.

III

IN 1946 BALTHUS RETURNED to Paris with Antoinette and the boys. The unit of mother, father, and their two sons, however, lasted for even less time than in Balthus's own childhood. It wasn't a year before the young Swiss mother returned to her homeland with the children, aged three and five. Thus began the generally amicable separation that did not turn into an actual divorce until nearly twenty years later, to facilitate Balthus's marriage to Setsuko.

Balthus used his studio on the Cour de Rohan, but for a while lived in the apartment of the Princess Caetani at 7, Rue de Cirque. His routine often consisted of an end-of-the-day drink at the Parisian café Les Deux Magots. A contemporaneous observer depicts him there in the Rilke mold: aristocratic, aloof, and independent.

> He is a mild, thin, younger man, conventionally dressed in a slightly dusty, dark brown suit. He is very well-bred looking with a small, neatly cut head, a sharp-featured, incisively lined face. He sits there with feline detachment and sardonic ease, completely united to the Parisian scene around him, yet somehow apart from it.
>
> His paintings are similarly distinct from current fads and schools. . . . The work of Balthus is eminently hard to pigeonhole.[13]

Ten years later, in another rare firsthand account of the artist, the journalist Georges Bernier, well versed in all the latest rages in painting, wrote similarly:

> The first thing that struck me about Balthus when I met him was his elegance. . . . There is a certain element of dandyism inspired by Baudelaire, for whom he has a profound admiration. But there is no dandyism in the fact that for over thirty years he has worked in a style that is in direct opposition to contemporary trends; in this respect both his life and his work have an exemplary value.[14]

In that period following the war, the editor Judith Jones also spent some time at the Princess Caetani's. She remembers Balthus as being so weakened by what she was told was a bout with the aftereffects of malaria that on some days he could not get up. "He seemed terribly alone; yellow, gaunt, and fragile."[15]

When he was well, however, he came and went quietly. It was in one of these stronger moments that Jones witnessed what she called his "tender, good impulse." Another resident of the house, Paul Chapin, was inclined to epileptic fits. One day he went down with a seizure; it was Balthus who cradled his head and calmly held his tongue.

Balthus at this time went daily to the Café de Flore, a favorite Left Bank hangout for artists. Sporting his tweed jacket and Scotch plaid tie, sipping black coffee, he would generally sit by himself. But he soon took up again with old friends like Giacometti, Jean-Louis Barrault, and Marie-Laure de Noailles and came to know André Malraux and Albert Camus, while also occasionally spending time with Bataille, Lacan, Eluard, and Picasso. Claude Roy tried in this period to turn him again toward the Communist party but had no success.

Georges Bataille was also staying at the Princess Caetani's in 1946. Balthus had first gotten to know Bataille in about 1937, when the writer and Pierre Klossowski had founded the Collège Sociologique in Paris—to pursue Nietzschean studies and the relation between eroticism and death. Now the thirty-eight-year-old Balthus became involved with Bataille's sixteen-year-old daughter Laurence.

Laurence's mother was the beautiful actress Sylvia Bataille—now married to Jacques Lacan—and her uncle was André Masson. The girl would maintain her position as Balthus's main model and companion until Balthus moved from Paris in 1953. If his wife offered him access to the aristocracy, Laurence provided more colorful access—including that trip to Golfe-Juan which featured the evening with Picasso.

IN 1946 BALTHUS HAD HIS SECOND Paris exhibition. It was held at the Galerie Beaux-Arts—run by Henriette Gomès, who had formerly been a secretary at the Galerie Pierre. The show was deemed a failure, with two hundred visitors at the most and no reviews whatsoever. Balthus did a bit better, however, when Pierre Matisse, who had last given him an exhibition in 1939, showed his work again in 1949 in New York.

Balthus was just scraping by financially as a painter. His situation stabilized further in the early 1950s, when Henriette Gomès set up a syndicate to support him. Besides Gomès, its members included Claude Herseint, Pierre Matisse, Alix de Rothschild, Marie-Laure de Noailles, and Maurice Rheims. They covered Balthus's essential expenses, in return for which he periodically paid them in artworks. Their organization guaranteed the artist's meager financial survival for several more years in Paris and then when he moved to Chassy.

Balthus's work in the late 1940s consisted substantially of nudes of Laurence Bataille. With her large, globular head and awkward, flattened, stick-figure body, the unnamed Laurence appears at an awkward, in-between moment of development. Balthus accentuated rather than minimized her boyishness. It is yet another highly personalized vision of femininity.

The naked Laurence generally appears as if she is a misty vision in a

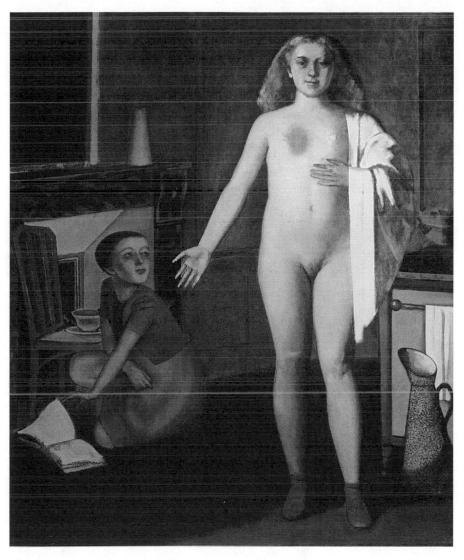

The Room, 1947–48, oil on canvas, 190 x 160 cm

dream. The 1947–48 *Room*—at the Hirshhorn Museum—shows the dazed teenager in a state of deshabille similar to that of Balthus's prewar nudes, with her feet and a single shoulder covered to accentuate the nudity of her breasts and genitals. But if her predecessors seemed like hussies, she has the look of a saint: otherworldly, more resurrected than earthbound.

Oddly proportioned as Laurence appears—her breasts too high, her stocky torso rigid like a tree trunk—and bizarre as her moonlike face is, the painting as a whole still offers a haunting truthfulness. Up close, the flesh has the texture, the absorption of light, and the variables of real, living human skin. The curvature of the limbs is plausible. However, the nude woman's admirer—the child who sits on the floor reading—belongs only to the realm of imagination. Her head is flattened and oblong; her face is contorted like a mask. Again we jump between the realms of truth and invention. The painting is a mix of the quotidian and the extraterrestrial.

Balthus has invested every detail of the setting with poetry, in the Rilkean mode. He seems to have scattered the elements of a Morandi around the composition. A cup and saucer, and two pitchers, exist in counterpoint as objects of heightened presence. The metal pitchers, noble in aspect, appear to move heavenward, purifying their setting. The open book is both a marvelous thing

The Week of Four "Thursdays," 1949, oil on canvas, 97.7 x 83.8 cm

and a source of mental riches. Yet the babyish woman—exultantly anesthetized—and her demonic admirer are unfathomably creepy.

It was a period in which Balthus was painting in a manner increasingly
disjointed from reality. The 1949 *Week of Four "Thursdays"*—Thursday was a
holiday in French schools—has an eerily artificial flatness. The wide-eyed cat
has its upper lip stretched tight in the manner of a feline smile. The central figure is so papery that she looks as if she has been put through a duck press.
Balthus has deformed her—and then knocked her out. The situation and its
painting are a contrivance, but the materials are superb; Balthus has, as always,
painted the hanging folds of fabric with utter conviction and skill. We are left
both incredulous and believing.

LAURENCE WAVES CRAZILY from a small kayak in *The Méditerranée's Cat*.
Balthus painted this work as a signboard for the interior of a seafood restaurant
on the Place de l'Odéon—not far from his studio on the Cour de Rohan—
that he frequented with Eluard, Camus, and Malraux. Françoise Gilot traces
the imagery to the evening with Picasso at Golfe-Juan two years earlier. Gilot
has written that Balthus was seated at the table at the Restaurant Marcel with
her, Picasso, Marie-Laure de Noailles, Lacan, Sylvia Bataille, Laurence, and

The Méditerranée's Cat, 1949, oil on canvas, 127 x 185 cm

other friends. "Balthus kept observing Laurence and obviously found her quite to his liking. Soon she got bored with sitting there or of being so carefully observed and left the dinner to go rowing in the harbor in a turquoise blue canoe moored at the front of an open-air terrace. The sight of this charming girl affirming her independence by veering away from the adults on her small skiff charmed him so that it became the theme of *The Méditerranée's Cat.*"[16] The ocean-fresh fish, on the other hand, have lost their independence. But as these creatures leap from sea to plate, one is convinced of the quality of the food at the Méditerranée.

The mad, hedonistic, human cat belongs to a tradition that goes back to ancient Egypt. The details, however, are pure Balthus. With his carving knife and long-tined fork, this imperious cat-man owns the world. His legs splayed, he sits like a swarthy gangster; clearly he is the kingpin. A giant, nicely cooked lobster awaits him; so does a bottle of young white wine catching the sunlight. His napkin is tucked in place; he is ready, with unequivocal delight, to take the world as his oyster.

The perfectly crafted, simple awning post that divides the picture in half confirms the truth of the scene and brings us right up to it. The cat's authority is thus assured.

THE BOY IN THE 1948–50 *Card Game* has a head that is large even by Balthus standards. This flattened globe, seemingly neckless, bears little relationship to the rest of him. His body is further disjointed—almost mermaidlike in its division. From the knees up, the boy is strong and muscular, with broad shoulders and an impressively tapered back—just like that of the shirtless hunk, the self-portrait-as-Heathcliff, in *Les Beaux Jours.* But his lower legs could belong to an aristocratic lady, ending as they do in delicate ankles and tiny feet clad in something like ballet slippers. He twists his bifurcated figure in a manner that might, realistically, be possible, but that would induce excruciating pain. The boy seems all the more awkward, and violent, because of the way he holds his playing cards uncomfortably at the small of his back—as if they are a secret weapon he is about to deploy.

This fellow is practically the mirror image of Hubert Blanchard in *The Children,* or, even more precisely, of Heathcliff in the 1933 drawing on which that 1937 oil was based. If you consider *The Card Game* next to that drawing which preceded it by fifteen years, the two characters look as if they are meant to be on a stage facing one another, their positions choreographed for their symmetry. They flaunt their muscular yet trim buttocks in pants so formfitting that the curves and crack are precisely legible.

Self-portrait, 1943, crayon,
40 x 40 cm

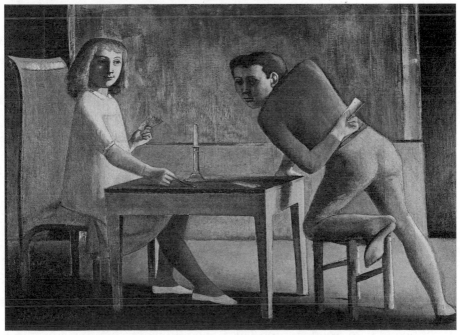

The Card Game, 1948–50, oil on canvas, 140 x 194 cm

These young men assume their poses with narcissistic zeal. The expressions on their faces make them secretive and unreadable: plotters who conceal their schemes. But they gladly let us know that they relish their sexy, adolescent bodies. Variations of Balthus himself, they are intensely attractive, yet armored and slightly malevolent.

When I went to see *The Card Game* at the Museo Thyssen-Bornemisza in Madrid, however, I had a great surprise. The girl, too, is a version of Balthus. She has the identical face, and the same whisper of a smile, as his 1943 self-portrait drawing. Exquisitely posed and feline, she is, except for the hair, the artist's perfect double.

So Balthus has given his face to one of these two card players, his chosen body image to the other. The artist has both penetrated his characters—putting himself into them and creating them out of his own flesh and blood—and transformed the "outsiders" into extensions of himself.

AT THE THYSSEN-BORNEMISZA, *The Card Game* hangs on a salmon-colored wall—the matte hue of a postmodern hotel lobby—at the end of a vast and grandiose gallery. A relatively large Balthus canvas—55 by 76⅜ inches—it shares the space with an Edward Hopper of almost equal size, as if they were companion paintings. The Balthus-Hopper comparison is one that a number of people have made over the years. Balthus told me he had never heard of Hopper, which may or may not be the case. In any event, the equation of the two artists is highly superficial. They painted different worlds in dissimilar styles. By comparison, Hopper is straightforwardness itself, a paean to American directness, while Balthus, visually and psychologically, offers a sea of complexity.

Yet in spite of all the weirdness, *The Card Game* is rare among Balthus's work in the success with which the artist has painted a male. Strange as the lad's body is, its surfaces pulsate and the frame and musculature look authentic. His legs capture the light splendidly. Even his more visible hand is painted convincingly—a rarity in Balthus's art. The thumb structure, however, is truly a disaster. The area beneath the thumb bulges out of all proportion, and there is inadequate differentiation between this puffy mass and the actual thumb, which is too short and flat. Yet the card it holds is one of Balthus's masterpieces of verisimilitude. And the boy's strange hydrocephalic head is rendered superbly.

There are patches of genius throughout *The Card Game*. The blue Empire chair that is like a throne for the girl is a fascinating passage of painting, a juxtaposition of hard wood and soft fabric. The strong green of the tabletop—which diminishes in reproduction—soars back in space, glowing vibrantly for a fine touch center stage. The candle stand is excellent. The overall composition—an elaborate series of movements and responses, all carefully orchestrated within a balanced, geometric plan—is subtly stunning in its muted palate and velvety, layered texture.

The psychological life of the painting parrots the visual: intricately layered, alternately clear and hazy. After my own time with the painting, on returning to it with my daughter Charlotte, by now eleven years old, I had occasion to see it through the eyes of a near-contemporary of the subjects of the painting. Here was a viewer herself in the throes of Balthus's golden age, that period of complexity between childhood and adulthood. First she remarked that the boy is naked. He is not, of course, but the sight of his buttocks is so startling, the seat of his power so palpable, that he might as well be. Then she pointed out what the painting is really about. "He looks as if he's about to make a pass at her. Who cares about the cards?" Charlotte added that the boy is a cad; the girl, on the other hand, "is pretending to be stupid and ignorant."

The observations seemed especially valid because they came from a child who loved to play actual cards and did so all the time. She read the painting as being like the scene now revised in *The Street:* the demonic, aggressive boy making moves on the girl in never-never land, the brigand and the anesthetized angel. By instinct, my daughter, almost the same age as these two characters, saw this painting as a scene of attempted sexual conquest.

As far as the card game goes, the conclusion is not quite clear. The girl smugly fancies herself to have played the winning card, but the boy may trump her yet with what he is holding folded behind his back. Victory is dicey, but determination is rampant. That phallic candle at the center of the composition, its light taper thrusting into the darkness (forgive me, Balthus; laugh and deny as you will; but I'm not the one who devised this scene that so patently depicts the drive "to dip your wick"), symbolizes the goal.

It is, of course, what Balthus's art virtually always evokes: the powerful male and the crafty but captive female—in a rarified, enchanted world of deceptive equipoise and visual lushness fraught with ambient tension. Often the dominating man assumes the form of the invisible artist; on rarer occasions like this one, he actually faces us—even if he deliberately avoids meeting our eye. Regardless, Balthus himself is both the love object and the successful master.

IV

BALTHUS IN PARIS in the late forties and early fifties was making quite an impression. Robert Craft describes an evening with Igor Stravinsky—they were also friends of the Caetanis—and the artist in 1952:

May 10. After a dinner in a bistro near the Invalides, we go with Balthus to the Deux Magots. Slim, pale, handsome, bittersweet, dandyish, he is femininely conscious of his clothes, which are evidently meant to identify him as a Hebridean laird, or, at any rate, to conceal that his work could have anything to do with paint. He will say nothing about art, except to vent scorn on "the latest daubs of Chagall," but to steer him away from music, Schubert's above all, is difficult. . . .

What about Balthus's portrait of Eros? Do his open-legged, mirror-fixated, pubescent girls represent joyful innocence, as Camus and Artaud have claimed? Or do they, as I think, project a lesbian fantasy, for it seems to me that the girl in *The Guitar Lesson* openly dreams of being fingered by an older woman. And all of Balthus's girls are either flushed with desire or pale with satisfaction (or is it the other way around?). They are definitely not little girls to gratify boys of any age, but then, those barely budding bosoms and itchily self-conscious pudenda, girl-bodies with acromegalic boy's heads, stubby legs, edematous calves, puppy-fat ankles, teeny feet are a long way from my vision of volupté.

I also fail to glean any insight from the man concerning the other oddities of his artistic eidos. Why, master of technique that he is, does he seem at times hardly to know how to draw? And why, apart from juvenile would-be-delinquents, is his work in no way concerned with the contemporary? A list of influences would read like a catalog of loans from the Louvre: Piero; Carpaccio; Velázquez (the dwarfs, duennas, cats, mirrors, goldfish bowls); the French seventeenth century; Corot; Courbet; Ingres; Seurat; Cézanne. Whatever the answers, Balthus is peerless among living portraitists . . . [and] stands no less alone in another dimension, the representation of Evil. I am thinking of *La Chambre,* in which, surely, the sexually ambivalent Satanic dwarf cannot be ignored, the picture meaning far more than, as I.S. would have it, spatial architecture and chiaroscuro.[17]

This was characteristic of Balthus's relationship to the world around him. At the de Noailles', at the Catalan—a popular artists' bistro near Picasso's studio on the Rue des Grands-Augustins—and at cafés like the Dôme and the Deux Magots, Balthus met many of the most interesting avant-garde composers, writers, painters, and patrons of the time. Yet the lean, somber artist— contemporary accounts feature the adjective "dandyish" more than any other—was also removed from that milieu and often harshly judged by it. His acquaintances recognized his skill and intelligence, but many of them regarded him as slightly suspect.

Balthus soon opted for a lifestyle that further announced his separateness. In 1953 the artist followed Rilke's example in seeking a rural retreat that would enable him both to work in isolation and to fulfill his fantasies of life as an old-fashioned aristocrat.

He had recently been given to remarking to his close friend Alberto Giacometti that "he needed a château more than a workman needed a loaf of bread."[18] Balthus's listeners mocked his upper-class pretensions, but he scarcely cared. If the notion of living decorously like a feudal lord was offensive to some people when spareness and bohemianism were the order of the day, so much the better. A rural castle was a tool for work as much as a ploy for grandeur; it was also another means of echoing the life of his companion and hero Rainer Maria Rilke.

HAVING DECIDED TO LEAVE PARIS, Balthus scoured the countryside in search of his own equivalent of Muzot. But the reality was that he had relatively less money to spend even than the pittance Rilke had. Dora Maar—Picasso's mistress of the 1930s, and now one of Balthus's closest friends—helped him in his search. She suggested a small château not far from where she lived in the lovely Lubéron village of Ménerbes. But even though the price tag was next to nothing, it was beyond Balthus's reach (the château sold shortly thereafter to the painter Nicolas de Staël). Like Rilke, Balthus could only afford to rent, not buy, but unlike Rilke, he had no angel in the background—beyond the members of the syndicate who were acquiring his art.

When he was with Georges and Diane Bataille near Vézelay, Balthus at last found a suitable place. The dilapidated structure he settled on as his first château, near a tiny town called Blismes in the Nièvre region of the Morvan, in Burgundy, was called Chassy. When he took up residence there in 1953, it had neither electricity nor running water—which had also been the case initially with Muzot. But the rent of approximately $200 a year was hard to beat. And Balthus could indulge in the perquisites of rural life; he told me he had thirty cats there (ten fewer than his hero Delacroix), as well as one dog—a Bouvier des Flandres.

An austere structural block, Chassy was distinguished mainly by four huge round towers at the corners. There was no central heating for the large rooms inside; the roof leaked; and there were gaps in the woodwork and plaster. Once it was electrified, the fittings consisted of bare lightbulbs hanging from the ceiling. And at first there was no telephone.

In Chassy, Balthus was initially as much like Heathcliff the humble field laborer as the ruler of the fief. One winter night in Rossinière, he launched into a reminiscence. Virgilio had just stoked the fire in the library. As the butler refilled his demitasse, Balthus—with the slightly lecturing quality that affluent parents have when wanting to remind their children that they were not always rich—proudly told his wife that at Chassy he often chopped firewood on cold winter days when this was the sole heating fuel. Part of the appeal may have been that in his childhood he probably heard Rilke describe the period in 1897 when the poet had regularly chopped wood in the Berlin suburb of Wilmersdorf while adopting the deliberately earthy lifestyle of his mistress Lou Andreas-Salomé and her husband, Friedrich Andreas. Balthus, too, lent romance to his tasks; explaining to me that it had been his job to patch the roof and bring in electricity, he beamed in fond recall.

Whatever the struggles, the move facilitated a great period for Balthus's work. Chassy offered a view of a farmyard and of fields sloping into a valley, which—for the eight years Balthus lived there—would provide the subject matter for many of the finest paintings he ever did. His achievement at Chassy reflected a tranquillity and equanimity that had nothing to do with the rugged living conditions reported by visitors.

In moving to his château, Balthus had opted not just for links to a noble past and for impressive architecture, but also for a degree of daily hardship as the price to pay for the ability to paint those rural reaches with all the privacy and concentration possible. The goal was to have time to look out the window at the countryside, to notice all the stages in which flowers bloom, and to cultivate one's art at a remove from the modern world: just as, in his youth, he had known Rilke to do.

IN THE 1950s, when Balthus was in his château, *Life* magazine and other publications ran articles that portrayed him as the epitome of landed gentry. While most well-known artists of that epoch could be seen at the Cedar Tavern or in rugged garrets, Balthus was more the precursor of the artists of the eighties whose homes resemble the villas of nobility and movie stars. Looking at those photos of Balthus standing like a confident country gentleman in front of the turrets of his castle, the public had no sense that the few dishes inside were chipped and that a single bare bulb illuminated the dining room. The handsome, impeccably groomed artist posing defiantly before his splendid abode gives no doubt that he was to the manor born.

Indeed, after several years of struggle at Chassy, Balthus began to sell more work at higher prices. He gained the wherewithal to improve his lot in life. The artist soon began to develop a new, upper-class existence that was like a pream-ble to the grandeur that would follow in Rome at the Villa Medici. For the first time since his early childhood, he had servants. And it was in this rural corner of the Morvan that the locals began to call him by the title that became so inor-dinately significant to him and to the world's perception of the previously dis-enfranchised youth.

V

EVER SINCE SHORTLY AFTER the end of World War II, the story that Balthus has been more eager than any other to get people to swallow concerns his use of the title "the Count de Rola." In my time with him, Balthus was busier denying his Jewishness than defending his nobility—but this was only because he treated his title as if it were a fact rather than an issue he would deign to argue.

In his construction of his chosen image, Balthus has achieved his goal with resounding success. Perpetuating his aristocratic fantasy, the once impov-erished grandson of a cantor from Pinsk has scored a victory.

From the time he shed "Baltusz" in adolescence, the artist has always been "Balthus" to his close friends and in his professional life. However, for official and business purposes, until the late 1940s, he was Balthazar Klossowski—the name on his birth certificate. "Balthazar Klossowski" also often appeared in parentheses following his *nom d'artiste* in museum catalogs and on painting identification labels. Then, at about the time of his fortieth birthday, he began to be Count Balthazar Klossowski de Rola. It is the name he has insisted on—in private as well as in public—ever since.

Balthus's title of "Count," however, has no historical basis. The Klos-sowskis were minor nobility and were one of the seventy-three Polish families that bear the Rola coat of arms, but they never held a title. "Rola" was a heraldic appellation that any number of families might use, but it conferred no right to be a "count."

Polish nobility emerged in the fourteenth century, at about the time that the native kings of Poland died out and were first replaced by foreigners, with the French Louis of Anjou being crowned in Cracow in 1370. The highest-ranking nobles were the members of the king's council, which evolved into the upper house of parliament; there was also a huge, unwieldy landed class that was a lesser rank of nobility called the *szlachta,* and this was the group to which Balthus's paternal ancestors belonged. The *szlachta* included members of the king's army, who received land as payment for their services, and its members were equal before the law and enjoyed more freedom than other citizens did.

However, at no point was the *szlachta* entitled to use titles. There was no peerage, and Polish law did not recognize the use of "prince" or "count" or "baron" for anyone in this group.

By the eighteenth century there were about 725,000 members of the *szlachta* in this country of just under ten million people. They were scattered over the 282,000 square miles of the vast kingdom. Laws kept changing as to who was noble. At one point, servants of magnates and Jewish converts became noble en masse. But then, in 1775, there were new regulations requiring that possession of land be a condition of nobility, and it is possible that at that point Balthus's ancestors were declassified; since there was no Klossow, there is no indication that the Klossowskis had the requisite land. Sources that list over 1,000 noble families of Poland do not list the Klossowskis at all.

There was no precedent for Balthus's title in his family. Not surprisingly, neither Balthus's father nor his older brother was ever anything but Erich or Pierre Klossowski. Although my attempt to meet Pierre through an intermediary failed—as I expected it would because of his well-known reluctance to discuss his brother—I have been told by mutual acquaintances of his and Balthus's that he considers the title of "Count" to be nonsense, not only factually unjustifiable but also embarrassingly pretentious.

Yet how natural it is that the once homeless Balthus would want a title that conferred not just social position but also land. By becoming "the Count de Rola," he compensated with a vengeance for previous hardships.

Rilke had similar pretensions. The poet had encouraged a belief that *he* descended from an ancient, aristocratic family from Corinthia. Claiming to be the scion of that distinguished line, the poet designed a coat of arms to be engraved on his tombstone. While the right of his family to use it was questionable at best, and he was often taken to task for his insistence on it and on his aristocratic origins, none of this seemed to trouble Rilke—in spite of all of his legitimate claims to fame. It was not enough that he was infinitely more accomplished than his friends of higher lineage; he wanted their pedigree, too.

It makes perfect sense for Balthus to have borrowed his self-definition from the mentor whose values he had imbibed. Moreover, Rilke and Balthus had similarly unusual, multinational backgrounds. Rilke grew up as a German in Prague with a French-speaking mother; Balthus was raised in Paris and Germany by parents who spoke the languages of both places. Rilke was born in Bohemia, held an Austrian passport, considered Russia to be his emotional home and Paris his intellectual one, had lived in Italy, and ultimately found sanctuary in Switzerland. Balthus, a French citizen at birth, is from a Polish family, found Japan in many ways to be his spiritual home, Italy his source of inspiration, and Switzerland his refuge.

These men also had in common that much of their character was sculpted by their mothers:

> It is true that Rilke's sense of form (which extended even to the externals of his bearing and attire) and his tendency to project an aloof, aristocratic image may have been handed down to him by his mother, along with a passing interest in spiritualism and a strong need for social acceptance. . . . Even the suppressed but powerful erotic element in his nature may be traceable to her.[19]

We know the extent to which Balthus's nature similarly derived from his close companionship with Baladine. And then there was the issue of physical resemblance. Rilke had a noticeably enormous mouth from his mother; Balthus the nose from his. As if to compensate for their distant fathers, each trumped up claims of his paternal lineage.

The Count de Rola had followed Rilke's example, as well as the poet's mandate for him, by choosing the realm of invention over the oppressiveness of facts.

INITIALLY BALTHUS had to disregard people's reactions to his use of the title. Or at least he chose not to be bothered by how appalled they were.

> To those who were listening . . . the utterance sounded strident beyond belief, and they happened to include Derain, Giacometti, Picasso, Artaud, Albert Camus, the Viscount and Viscountess de Noailles, Princess Caetani, et al. Some laughed, some sneered, some smiled indulgently, and everyone took it for granted that the artist had no legitimate claim whatsoever to a title.[20]

Derain, a close friend, was supposedly so disgusted by Balthus's snobbery that he wanted to sever all connections with him, until he was persuaded to relent.

Ned Rorem was particularly disparaging about the artist's title and its trappings. Rorem used to encounter Balthus in the de Noailles's blue marble dining room, where the painter and Dora Maar were lunch guests as often as twice a week, or at dinners at the Catalan hosted by the vicomtesse.

> Balthus, single-named like Colette or Fernandel, was a count because he said he was. Born in Poland, romantic to the teeth, emaciatedly attractive, a self-pitying scold, and far more widely versed—including

in music—than most painters who never read and so hang out in cafés all winter when night falls early (especially in northerly Paris) and it's too dark to paint, Balthus had a little-boy whine that counterbalanced his pedophilic paintings and an opportunistic way of denigrating Marie-Laure that got results (what's money for if not to nourish genius, etcetera). He longed to legitimize his bogus nobility by buying a castle. This he did, with a ramshackle fifty-room ruin. . . .[21]

Balthus succeeded. In the area of France near the château as in Rossinière, the villagers all refer to him as "le comte." When he was director of the Villa Medici in Rome and he and Setsuko issued invitations from "Le Comte et La Comtesse Klossowski de Rola," no one quibbled. Starting in the 1960s, major magazines and newspapers in France began to follow suit. In *Réalités, Paris Match, Le Figaro,* and *Le Monde,* the artist has been called—with no one openly questioning it, even in a country that has a detailed understanding of such matters—"Le Comte Balthazar Klossowski de Rola," usually with his title in bold type right at the top of any article about him.

Even someone as sharp as John Russell unequivocally referred to Balthus as "the Count of Rola" when he wrote a piece for *Art in America* at the time of the exhibition of Balthus's work he organized at the Tate. Subsequently Russell has come to belittle Balthus's use of a title—talking with me, he treated it as an utter joke—but once upon a time he bowed completely to the notion. The American popular press has also perpetuated the claim. *Life*—once the most widely read magazine in the world—declared Balthus in his château to be the Count of Rola. When Balthus had his major exhibition at the Pierre Matisse Gallery in 1977, two of the most savvy and influential art journalists in America presented the painter to the American public unequivocally as "the Count Balthasar Klossowski de Rola"—the only variable from French accounts being that now he was Balthasar rather than Balthazar. Mark Stevens, in *Newsweek,* not only used the title in association with Balthus's Louis XIII château in Chassy but likened the artist to "an émigré from the *ancien régime.*"[22] Robert Hughes, in *Time,* introduced the artist as "Count Balthasar Klossowski de Rola, a French aristocrat of Polish extraction better known by the name of Balthus."[23]

I am no innocent in this matter of reiterating unsubstantiated information. In my book *Patron Saints,* which was published in 1992 and where I discussed Balthus's early patronage by James Thrall Soby, I, too, perpetuated the idea that the artist was "Balthazar Klossowski de Rola," and—even though I had the sense not to use "Count"—referred to him as "a privileged European nobleman." But by the time I wrote an article about Balthus for the *New York*

Times in 1993, I knew better. My editor instructed me to add the information that Balthus's real name was the Count Balthazar Klossowski de Rola—it said so in the computer—but when I argued the point, she accepted the evidence that Balthus was not really the Count de Rola. However, this did not prevent the Sunday *New York Times Magazine*, less than a year later, from identifying the artist, in bold type, as "The Recluse Balthazar Klossowski, Count de Rola."

Naturally, no one has been more diligent in pushing Balthus's noble lineage and its significance than Jean Leymarie. It's surprising that Leymarie—an art historian of remarkable scholarship, intellect, and breadth—would permit himself to be so trapped by this nonsense. But he is in there all the way, chronically overstating the case far more than Balthus or Setsuko would ever deign to do. So in the catalog for the 1992 Balthus exhibition at the Musée Gustave Courbet in Ornans, Leymarie—in a text set in the sort of bold italic type generally used only for listings of elaborate concoctions on fancy French restaurant menus—begins with the claim:

> Balthus, unlike Courbet, was born in Paris, his family distinguished and cosmopolitan, but his whole Polish ancestry is linked to the land, and the etymology of his double patronymic, Klossowski de Rola, evokes the soil and a sheaf of wheat.[24]

Why Balthus has perpetrated this scheme is questionable. It is a matter of hot debate among a handful of people who know the artist well. But in any event, the weapon detonated entirely according to his design. When, in 1993, Balthus's illustrations for *Wuthering Heights* finally appeared—sixty years after he had made them—in a limited edition of that novel, the Rola coat of arms appeared as a watermark in the text. As in Brontë's novel, the wanderer had triumphed.

IN OUR CONVERSATIONS, I had a chance to observe, firsthand, the count's highly effective technique for convincing others of the validity of his bogus appellation. His ploy is to act as if he would not even dream of stooping to justify his noble rank: it is simply a fact of which he tries to appear so certain—and, perhaps, *feels* so certain—that he does not give a hint of acknowledging that it might be questionable. Talking with me, Balthus simply laughed at the way James Lord tried to rob him of his right to the title in the *New Criterion* article. He treated Lord's antics as being so childish that all he could do was curl up his face and grin at the ridiculousness.

Listening to Balthus speak about his various detractors with his air of bemusement and superiority, watching his head turn in instinctive response when his servants address him as "Count," seeing him open the letters addressed to "Le Comte et La Comtesse Balthazar Klossowski de Rola," I realized that by this point in his life he had probably come to believe his own myth entirely. Pierre Leyris agreed with me; having seen Balthus in virtually all of his incarnations, this sage observer imagined that in all likelihood Balthus no longer had any idea that he was lying.

I discovered that another family member who has clung to the idea of the family's title—and seems genuinely convinced of it—is Balthus's son Stanislas. Stash happily elucidated "the facts" to me when I was in Rossinière. He explained that the name of "de Rola" goes back to the tenth century and figures in Polish folklore as the equivalent of Merlin—someone with magical powers, who understood the language of the birds. His grandfather did not use "de Rola" and the title that went with it only because he felt you should not do so if you were not rich. (How someone who owned a Delacroix and other art masterpieces was not rich is a question I didn't bother to ask.) And the reason the title was not recorded on Balthus's birth certificate is that there was an administrative mistake in Paris. Art historians and journalists may be too dumb to recognize the point, but there is no question in Stanislas's mind as to his father's right to use "Count." And he admires Balthus's use of it as a kind of defiance, a flying in the face of the ordinary way of doing things.

The tale about the reason for the absence of the alleged title on Balthus's birth certificate is consistent with an account Balthus gave the musician David Bowie in a long interview in 1994 ("rarely interviewed and enigmatic . . . the last Legendary Painter") that reads like a transcribed tape recording. The early part of the story—which explains the variations of Balthus's first name—may have some small kernel of truth to it, but the second part, though it corresponds completely to what Stash told me, seems less likely. My sense is that this was Stash's fabrication, and that Balthus liked it so much that he tried it on for size. It is yet another one of Balthus's bittersweet tales in which he is the victim of some wrongdoing.

> I was born on the 29th and my parents forgot to inscribe me to the *état civil* [registry office], so I was born with a fee of 200 French francs gold and since then I have never been in order. I was born in Paris and they had no name—they expected a girl and they had no names for a boy and so when friends came and they asked what is the child called: "Oh we call it baby." But at the *état civil,* what is he called. "*État civil,* my god, we forgot to register him." Next day they ran to the *état civil* and

my father happened to be like many Poles—he was born in Germany because from Poland there were Poles everywhere in Austria, Germany and in Russia. And my father happened to be born in Germany which has now become Poland again. And, so he was ashamed and he said, well, there's a boy and we want to call him Balthus. Baltusz in Polish. And the man said: *"Mais, ça n'existe pas." "Alors quoi?" "Appellez-le Balthazar,"* and nobody calls me Balthazar for all my life. . . . And it was very funny because my father was so embarrassed and ashamed that he didn't even say that he was a Count."[25]

Stanislas has occasionally gone so far as to elevate himself to "prince." One old friend of Balthus's, roaring with laughter, described an evening when he and Giacometti were together and read "that Stasha was a Prince of Marengo." The friend and Giacometti were both fairly drunk when Giacometti telephoned Balthus, who was in Rome at the time. Giacometti chided his old companion from their days in the Paris cafés, "I hear that your son is a Prince of Marrons Glacés"—at which point Balthus, furious, simply hung up the phone. His rage was not at his son's pretense, only at the mockery of it.

Another friend of Balthus's told me of an intimate dinner at which the artist seriously enumerated the noble origins of everyone present. "Setsuko is a Japanese princess," Balthus allowed. "I am a count. And you," he said, pointing to another guest, "are from a very old family of Ravenna. And you"—now Balthus pointed to Pierre Matisse—"are the son of a famous painter." It went on for about five minutes. Setsuko was the only listener who looked remotely respectful; the others at the table masked their smirks, but nothing could deter the proud speaker.

Balthus has become so mistrusted that his usage of "de Rola"—legitimate even if Pierre and Erich never bothered with it—gets treated as suspect. I have had people insist to me that Balthus picked "de Rola" up from a character in the writings of Alfred de Musset. John Russell maintained to me that Antoinette—who was, after all, a true aristocrat—had told people that the artist came up with "Rola" from Rolle, the Swiss city she lives in.

Whether or not he gleans the mockery of much of his audience, Le Comte Balthazar Klossowski de Rola persists. As in his art, he requires fantasy in order to survive.

I BELIEVE THAT THE REASON Balthus invented, and has so voraciously embraced, his title, is that, like his refutation of Judaism, it makes him feel less vulnerable in a world where he has been buffeted about. Like the portrayals of humankind in his paintings, he suffers from a profound level of fear and sadness which has made him develop a mask. The upper-class cover-up that he finds so intoxicating is a protective encasement around his own fragility.

To be Jewish meant one was at high risk of death. Most Polish Jews ended up in the crematoria at Auschwitz. For someone so sensitive that the disappearance of a pet cat obsessed him as an adolescent, the possibility of the total annihilation of a civilization must have been intolerable. During the Second World War, he escaped to a mountainside in Switzerland and immersed himself in painting utterly pastoral landscapes; his response to tragedy was not to face it squarely but to turn from it. Following the war—knowing that his own mother might have been one of those people in a cattle car bound for a concentration camp, and certainly remembering that he had once been dirt-poor—he became non-Jewish, rich, and, finally, titled. His own self was too terrifying.

In his art, too, Balthus's real persona has ultimately proved too discomfiting. No wonder he was willing to paint out the assault in *The Street,* and has prohibited *The Guitar Lesson* from ever again being seen.

When he was fourteen, Balthus's own mother was so puzzled by him that she lamented that she had no idea who the real boy was. "Qui est Balthus?" she asked, half in despair, half in amusement. When Balthus was eighty-seven, I happened to be present when his twenty-one-year-old daughter said, with a bright smile, to David Bowie—whose interview had recently appeared—that she would like really to understand Balthus. A grinning Bowie, opening his arms with both palms forward in a gesture of questioning, asked, "Who does?" Balthus's primary task—in the substance of his art and his person—has always been to keep the questions unanswerable.

BALTHUS HAS CONVINCED the world that there are no apprehensible facts. Then, contradictorily, he has disseminated considerable information of his own choosing. His machinations have guaranteed excitement and confusion. Even his own family has encountered too much obfuscation and received too many mixed signals to sort him out. The puzzle, however, is not really so hard to unravel.

Having disobeyed Balthus's instructions that he remain "an artist of whom nothing is known" so that the art can stand on its own, I have found that my knowledge of the man—his compulsive mythologizing as well as his erudition, his chicanery alongside his personal magnetism—has led me to an understanding of his work. Conversely, the paintings themselves—gorgeous, narcissistic, seductive; paeans to visual beauty and to the escape route of fantasy—have brought me nearer to the real person than living at his side ever permitted.

Balthus is the same as a painter and as a person: a brilliant connoisseur of impeccable taste, a deceiver bent on covering up the truth. Just as, in his art, he has invariably, and with exquisite judgment, mimicked his well-chosen mentors, blending Piero and Hogarth and Courbet and Seurat, in his life he has modeled himself on a series of heroes—fictional and real, ranging from poetic wild men to dandified aristocrats. For his persona his choices have been dicier than for his work, but in neither case has his own substantial genius ever been enough for him. He has always had to worship, and be, someone else. Having always craved, and stimulated, excitement, it is as if he has himself become so excited and tantalized by his experience that he has had to resort to role playing to anesthetize himself.

Not since *Mitsou* has Balthus allowed himself to relax and remain his own true self. His consummate understanding of painted and natural beauty has not sufficed. The excessive lengths to which he has gone to compensate for some sense of shortcoming complicates his work and gives it its perpetual air of tension.

In his finest works—*The Children, Thérèse Dreaming, Bouquet of Roses, Montecalvello*—he has achieved a sublime level of painting. Even at his weakest, he has always displayed immense skill: the most contrived of his canvases manage to be charged up and lively at least in part, with some wonderful passages if only in the drapery folds. But the work suffers for its lack of personal release. It always has an overstudied aspect. One longs for the oneness between the painter and his art we get with Giotto, Renoir, Giacometti. Unlike them, Balthus—in his paintings as in his life—is creating a stage play.

As Pierre Klossowski wrote of the Marquis de Sade, the pivotal experiences for this creator occur not in life itself but in the artworks. Balthus may have lived, to some extent, according to his desires, but it is thanks to his art, like his title, that he has been able to enjoy his ultimate fantasy in its purest form. His paintings, like his life, are an imaginary universe: his dreams of choice. Thus comes the sense of distance we experience when we look at the work: these are constructions, always at a remove, lacking in spontaneity or unity.

The photographer and writer Brassaï observed of Picasso and Paul Eluard, "To the most realist of painters and the most visual of poets—neither of whom can imagine life without love—art is the act of living and seeing and not of imagining and dreaming."[26] So Picasso, like Cézanne, did his utmost to seize, whole, the reality before his eyes. Balthus, on the contrary, perpetually engaged in the process of re-creating.

That said, whatever his personal foibles, Balthus merits the often made claim that he is, at the end of the twentieth century, the single greatest living artist. When, standing in front of various works by the old masters, we ask ourselves if anyone in our time understands the mystery of painting as they did— and even approaches their technical brilliance and their ability to transmit the miracles of human existence, visual and physical, aesthetic and sensuous—we quickly conclude that it is he more than anyone else.

VI

An extreme cat-like softness; it was the voice of the unseen observer, of the eternally silent superior servant.
                                        —IRIS MURDOCH,[27] *The Italian Girl*

MARIE-LAURE AND CHARLES DE NOAILLES were also among the most indulgent of Balthus's friends when he assumed his new persona after World War II. If the former clone of Antonin Artaud was now a highborn nobleman, so be it. Bernard Minoret told me about a lunch in the house on the Place des Etats-Unis in the late 1950s when most of the de Noailles's dozen or so guests were all making fun of Balthus for having become Le Comte de Rola. Charles de Noailles would have none of their mockery. "Ça ne fait rien," he told his guests. "Ça lui fait tant plaisir."[28] A member of the *"noblesse du court"* could afford to let Balthus have his fun; Balthus was a fine painter and had earned the privilege.

Creators were Marie-Laure's gods, and she considered it her role to serve them. After a brief affair with Edward James, the great British patron of ballet, she had become involved, at age thirty, with the musician Igor Markevitch, ten years her junior, for whom she bought Alfa Romeos. She might not have provided for Balthus as lavishly as for her lovers, but she would always relish her role as Balthus's model. According to Bernard Minoret, in her later years— almost until the time of her death in 1970—the vicomtesse delighted in telling people, "I was Balthus's Lolita."

In 1958 Balthus painted a portrait of another doyenne of Parisian society, the Baroness Alain de Rothschild. As opposed to the painting he had made of Marie-Laure twenty-two years earlier, this large canvas looks almost as if it had been done by one of the Deauville or Palm Beach portraitists who advertise in glossy magazines. The setting is true "Style Rothschild"; the baroness, in a plush robe and fine jewelry, her hair looking as if it were just coifed by Alexandre, relaxes in a large armchair surrounded by the accoutrements of her luxurious life. There is a classical bust on the mantel; she is flanked by a golden urn with a black cupid on it, elaborate candelabra, and glistening objets d'art. In 1936 Balthus had been the circus trainer with a whip who summoned nobility to his garret; now he willingly immersed himself in every nuance of the titled world.

The Baron and Baroness de Rothschild gave a large cocktail party late one afternoon in their enormous house on the Avenue de Martigny to unveil the portrait. (This imposing residence is now used by the French government to house prominent world leaders visiting Paris.) Balthus, typically, was not there. But lots of chic Paris was, and they were clucking—even if the elegant canvas looked more like a lightly painted society portrait commissioned by a wealthy

Portrait of the Baroness Alain de Rothschild, 1958,
oil on canvas, 190 x 152 cm

husband than a full-fledged effort by the artist of *The Children* and *Thérèse Dreaming.*

Charles de Bestégui—who in 1951 had hosted, in his Venetian palace full of Tiepolo frescoes, a beaux-arts ball that many considered the greatest social event in Europe since the war—could be heard voicing his admiration for the regal portrait. At over six by five feet it was Balthus's largest portrait ever, and to most of the guests it was a status symbol with great cachet.

Marie-Laure de Noailles was not to be outshone by the haut monde, however. She showed up for the occasion in the same simple black suit she had worn when Balthus painted her. And while others leaned into the Rothschilds' velvet and brocade-covered armchairs, Marie-Laure insisted that she could only sit on a simple, cane-seated wooden side chair—precisely like the one on which Balthus had shown her. She asked the servants for one, and it was brought in from the kitchen.

In stark and telling contrast to her graceful hostess, the Vicomtesse de Noailles perched on that plain side chair in the middle of the gathering and, in her austere clothing, assumed the same uneasy pose and taciturn expression as in 1936. Having been painted by the *real* Balthus, she would not succumb to this frivolity. She remained one of Balthus's most loyal supporters, but always on her own terms.

FROM THE TIME OF HIS RETURN to Paris in late 1946 until his move to the Morvan in 1953, and then on his periodic returns to the capital for the rest of the decade, the artist often had lunch or dinner in the great dining room of the house on the Place des Etats-Unis or would go with Marie-Laure to the Catalan, where their regular dinner companions included Ned Rorem, James Lord, and Bernard Minoret.

In a diary entry Rorem wrote in the fall of 1951, he describes a viewing of *The Room* at an early stage. The account provides a rare glimpse of Balthus's working method as well as a highly personal take on the work:

> Today lunch with Balthus at the Catalan and afterwards a visit to his very messy studio (it resembles what must have been the interior of the Collier brothers' home) in the adorable Cour de Rohan just off the rue Jardinier. Balthus is working on a most frightening oil. The canvas is enormous, four yards wide, and high as the ceiling. On this are nothing but two curious girls: one, a naked dead doll in false light stretched on a couch awaiting love; the other, a vital little idiot sister in a green sweater opening the curtain and exposing her rival to the real

light of the sun. There is also a vase and cat. All this in colors hitherto uninvented. . . . I had to shiver! Poor great Balthus: so Jewish and sorry for himself; so rich, so poor.[29]

WHEN I MET WITH ROREM in his Upper West Side apartment in the spring of 1995, he described Balthus's everyday behavior in the early fifties. A picture emerged of how the lean and melancholy artist, solitary yet sociable, struck the people with whom he came in regular contact. Rorem spoke with annoyance of Balthus's insistence on speaking English during their initial meeting at Marie-Laure's. John Richardson and several other English people and Americans told me the same thing; it bothered all of them to be at a dinner table where everyone else was speaking French—in which they were also proficient—and to be made to speak English against their will. They and the other guests found Balthus's use of the language forced and phony, but he continued nonetheless. Adding to the discomfort, according to Rorem, Marie-Laure would then try to join the conversation in the language in which it was taking

Ned Rorem in 1951, photographed by Henri Cartier-Bresson

"Ceux-ci sont mes ancêtres," c. 1955, pencil, 10 x 12.7 cm

place, and Balthus would tell her how lamentable her English was. And while Balthus's command of English was commendable, it clearly was not his mother tongue.

In spite of that, Rorem found Balthus polite and attentive. Balthus listened patiently to Rorem's unaccompanied choral pieces. "I remember that he was in no way condescending to me," the composer reminisced.

Yet everything Balthus said seemed to have a subtext. Balthus remarked of these new songs, whose creator was eager for a response, "They remind me of Nathaniel Hawthorne." Rorem "thought that Balthus was name-dropping that he knew Hawthorne as no one else in France did. And I was fascinated that he thought I was New Englandish when I thought I was heart-on-my-sleeve and erotic."[30] Rorem then quipped, "He acted Jewish to me because he wanted to get his way."

Rorem and Marie-Laure de Noailles often discussed Balthus. The composer confirmed Bernard Minoret's report that the viscountess was quite kind on the subject of Balthus's ascendancy to the ranks of the nobility when other people were derisive. "Marie-Laure did not talk about his title; she would have thought that was condescending. Of course, she was not impressed by lineage but by talent. Balthus was impressed by lineage as well as talent."

On the other hand, even if Marie-Laure would not stoop to mocking Balthus's social pretensions, Rorem told me she loved to gossip about his "thing for little girls." She also said, of her own sexual relationship with the painter, "Nous avons fait l'amour à papa." Rorem explained, "That meant heavy necking. They might have kissed under a piano—for one second or twenty minutes. He wouldn't discuss it, but she was a real gossip."

While Balthus never talked openly about his own sexual experiences, he sometimes enjoyed taking a teasing, hypothetical tack with the openly homosexual Rorem. The composer recalled, "Balthus once said to me, 'I'm not queer at all, but if I were I would like to be *encoulé* by Jean-Louis Barrault.' And I thought to myself, why? They look exactly alike: thin and mannered—although Balthus is not quite as theatrical, and a little more melancholy. Look at Barrault in *Les Enfants du paradis*. They're both gaunt, and effete." It's as if Balthus's fantasy was to be buggered by Balthus.

ON ONE OCCASION WHEN the Viscountess de Noailles and Ned Rorem and Balthus were all at the Catalan restaurant, Balthus made some pencil drawings on the paper tablecloth. One is a woman's head in a simulated oval frame. Almost comic-book-like, it mocks a traditional eighteenth-century portrait of an aristocrat, complete with her proper curls and elaborate necklace; we picture the deep colors of history even though it is only in pencil. The other is of a man with three faces. His round head, sitting atop a sort of globe, has a left profile, a right profile, and a third set of features we see head-on. Each face is a variation of the others. The man looks important and imperious—as well as, quite literally, multifaceted.

After making the drawing, Balthus turned to Marie-Laure and Ned Rorem and remarked, *"Ceux-ci sont mes ancêtres."* Marie-Laure carefully cut them out with a scissors and gave them to Rorem with instructions that he should take good care of them.

When I visited the composer, I was intrigued by the small sketches—which I subsequently purchased from him. How perfect that Balthus would make one of his ancestors look like a fictionalized Scottish grandmother—while the other, with his three faces on the same head, might as well be a Romanov, a Poniatowski, and a Radziwill all wrapped into one.

VII

A HANDSOME AND DASHING Danish college student named Claus von Bülow was also part of Marie-Laure de Noailles's circle.

Balthus mentioned von Bülow to me one afternoon in Rossinière. They had had lunch together with Lucien Freud about a year earlier in London— during Balthus's trip there for the opening of Setsuko's exhibition. "Poor Claus," Balthus said with utmost sympathy, "I don't think he could possibly have murdered his wife; I can't imagine that he murdered anyone at all." He delivered the pronouncement with an incredulous grin, injecting cheer into the word "murdered" the way Boris Karloff might have.

Like Ian Fleming, Claus von Bülow was another of Balthus's "amusing" friends with an apparent penchant for S&M. Ned Rorem told me about an occasion in 1952 when von Bülow proudly invited the young composer to see his whip room.[31] Rorem reported with sparkling eyes that it was full of "jewel-encrusted, gold-handled" bull- and horsewhips and cat-o'-nine-tails.

You might well ask my reason for repeating Rorem's tales about the world's most renowned and colorful murder suspect in a book on Balthus. It is because there is a certain alliance of taste. Starting with *The Guitar Lesson*, Balthus had evinced his own interest in sadism in elegant quarters. The well-dressed dominator who showed himself as the whip-bearing "H.M. the King of Cats" also indulged, in his art, in the related fantasy of desanguinated, nearly comatose women.

This sort of thing was the ordinary parlance of the de Noailles set. At Marie-Laure's, houseguests might merrily pore over the original manuscript of *The 120 Days of Sodom* knowing that its author was their hostess's illustrious ancestor. What was a game and what was reality—or to what extent imagination and everyday conduct converged—I cannot judge. Humor and the thrill of being outrageous may have counted more than any deeper instinct.

Another reason Claus von Bülow's whip collection is of concern is that von Bülow's own proclivities may have colored his views on his old friend from Paris.

VON BÜLOW HAD BEEN EXTREMELY accommodating when I phoned him to set up a date to discuss Balthus. He received me on the appointed April after-noon in 1995 in the overstuffed, elegant living room of his house on a large square in the Chelsea section of London. We sat surrounded by nineteenth-century paintings, family antiques, and beautiful photographs of his wife,

Sunny, in the early and seemingly happier years of their marriage, and of their ravishing daughter Cosima.

My host looked completely different than in the days of his trial. Very svelte in the era when the world was trying to figure out if he had set out to give his wife a fatal injection, he had gained a lot of weight since that time. Impeccably dapper whenever the television or newspaper cameras were on him, he now exposed a roll of bare stomach between the bottom of his small and tight bright red polo shirt and the top of his unbelted corduroys. He was growing a beard, which was coming in white and was still at the seedy stage.

The other noticeable change since the time of his trial over a decade earlier was that now von Bülow seemed relaxed and content. His animated demeanor and ebullient conversation were a far cry from the persona he evinced during his ordeal at the Rhode Island courthouse. When he periodically referred back to this period of "shall we say, my troubles," he furrowed his brow, but otherwise he seemed to be completely ensconced in the good life. Based on the phone calls I heard him receive concerning luncheon parties and travel plans, and his references to current girlfriends and dates to attend the opera, he was, indeed, suffering from no lack of amusement.

Perhaps because he had himself been the object of so much gossip and conjecture, the cheerful and perpetually entertaining Claus von Bülow was careful to avoid drawing any spurious conclusions about Balthus—toward whom he felt a mix of compassion and rapport. Even more than Balthus, von Bülow has suffered from the experience of other people projecting their own conclusions and fantasies about his character. The opprobrium extends beyond the obvious arena; some of his fellow members at his London club consider his use of "von" as bogus as Balthus's title. Yet while I would have expected von Bülow, based on his common ground with Balthus, to voice wholehearted support of the count's masquerade, the contrary was true. His similarities to the artist seemed to heighten his alertness to the reality behind Balthus's shams and complexities.

Von Bülow gave new perspective to the worldly—and world-weary—side of the friend he had known for over forty years. He also had a clear grip on the artist's approach to women—both personally and in the paintings. More often than I could possibly have anticipated, the erudite and sharp-focused Claus von Bülow proved to be among the most astute and original firsthand observers of Balthus I have encountered.

WHEN VON BÜLOW INITIALLY entered the circle of Marie-Laure de Noailles, he was not yet the cosmopolite he would become. As if describing a country yokel, he laughingly recalled himself as "a nineteen-year-old Scandinavian in my wooden shoes."[32] In Paris for an interval between his undergraduate studies at Cambridge and his preparation for the bar, the charming young Dane had found his way to the opulent house on the Place des Etats-Unis—where he was very much to Marie-Laure's liking. "She took me under her umbrella, but not into her bed—for which I'm grateful." Von Bülow said that the vicomtesse invariably tried to seduce any new and eligible acquaintance within the first weeks of their meeting. If that did not work out, however, she gave the man a chance to prove himself in other ways.

Since he felt Marie-Laure resembled "Louis XIV in drag" and did not relish the thought of being his hostess's lover, von Bülow was fortunate in having the spark and wit to stay on in a chaste role. Today he credits the Vicomtesse de Noailles with having helped him develop a trait of great significance for his subsequent way of life: "If I have any discipline in dinner table conversation, it is her to whom I am grateful." The Dane was by instinct witty and erudite to a fault; with Marie-Laure's fine-tuning, he fit in well with his hostess's social scene and cast of characters—among whom Balthus was one of the key players.

What drew Balthus to Claus von Bülow was the background of the tall young man from Cambridge. "My mother was the mistress of Prince Raimond von Thurn und Taxis, whose family owned Duino," von Bülow explained to me on that spring afternoon. Raimond was the grandson of Marie von Thurn und Taxis-Hohenlohe, one of Rilke's closest companions and most ardent supporters; Duino was the setting for Rilke's best-known elegies. When von Bülow first mentioned this connection to Balthus at the de Noailles's dinner table, "Balthus was clapping his little hands. He had this nostalgia for *la vieille Europe*." So declaimed the renowned bon vivant with an amused chuckle.

Claus von Bülow spoke to me about Balthus's portrait of Marie-Laure, and I told him the story of the vicomtesse insisting on the simple kitchen stool at the Rothschilds'. He had, he said, the "perfect pendant" to that incident. It concerned the time he took Sunny—"my new American bride"—to the house on the Place des Etats-Unis for the first time. "You could see Marie-Laure eyeing her little Balenciaga suit. And then Marie-Laure said to Sunny, 'Of course, I couldn't afford anything like that.' And you could see Sunny looking all around her—at that fantastic house—and wondering. Then Marie-Laure said, 'What I mean is, you're very beautiful. So you can afford to wear clothing like that. But I'm very homely. So I can only wear these plain clothes. That way, people just look at me and think that the reason I don't look better is because I dress so poorly.' "

It was the sort of brilliance the young Scandinavian esteemed in the doyenne of this illustrious household. He equally admired her coterie of artists. The leader of the vicomtesse's impressive constellation of creative geniuses was Picasso. On one occasion, in response to von Bülow's mention of his upcoming legal studies, Picasso did a drawing of a bewigged barrister on von Bülow's "tummy." The law student saw a motive behind the act beyond pure entertainment: Picasso knew that the man bearing this drawing would cease bathing for quite some time in order to preserve the art—"thus making me a nuisance to my hostess," the Dane remarked.

Balthus—who was almost a generation older than von Bülow and was also "in the top half dozen" of Marie-Laure's circle—offered a far more refined form of companionship. At the de Noailles's own table, or at meals the group would take at La Méditerranée, what was most striking in von Bülow's "privileged exposure to Balthus" was Balthus's emphasis on aristocracy and European traditions. The artist was often in the company of Madame Villabova—of the same name as one of the ladies-in-waiting to the last czarina. "With her, the conversation was a little bit old Europe—a lot of inside-track name-dropping. Balthus would sound nostalgic: 'We are now all *déposé*.' "

You should have heard the glee and condescension with which von Bülow thus quoted Balthus. "The Romanovs were no longer at home; nor were the Klossowskis," he added with a mocking sneer.

VON BÜLOW SEES BALTHUS as having always been very much an observer of the "haut monde." Similarly, the artist struck him more as a perpetual voyeur of women than as an active lover.

He amplified. In recent years, a mutual acquaintance of both of theirs has been a prince from "one of the tremendously grand Black Roman families: you have the whole of the papacy" with a family castle near Montecalvello. The prince has both "won a poetry prize and made a profession of sexual intercourse. He is, reputedly, exceptionally well endowed, and is a great lover of beautiful women who tend to be a great deal younger than him." For Balthus, in von Bülow's eyes, part of the appeal of the friendship with this high-living man with his impressive title is "a certain voyeurism—of both the prestigious family and the sexual prowess." Von Bülow feels that this is very much Balthus's approach: to look at life from a distance and take pleasure in seeing more than in doing.

That space between himself and things, and the concomitant degree of control, seemed to be present even when Balthus drove a car. Von Bülow described the artist as driving "like an Italian bus driver, well back from the wheel, arms straight out in front." We talked about the similar critical distance in his work—about why so much of Balthus's art, for all the eroticism (of which von Bülow considered Balthus's denial laughable), is nonseductive. Velázquez or Matisse presents women to be made love to; Balthus puts them there more to be observed.

Von Bülow remarked that with Picasso's females, you feel that the artist has had sex with them. The entire experience is present. With Balthus's, however, the activity is almost all mental. Von Bülow linked Balthus's attitude to women with his relationship to the social scene. "Balthus may be a voyeur sexually; so he is a voyeur of Gstaad. He could have been mundane in his life; he chose not to be, but he is in his gossip." With those in the upper echelon of society—the world known all too well to Claus von Bülow—as with the staff at the Villa Medici and the townspeople in Rossinière, Balthus knew every name and had a handle on all the personalities; von Bülow saw this degree of engagement as more of a diversion for Balthus than a sign of any more profound connection. "If you are patently a great artist, you've got to let your hair down from time to time. Gossip, where there's nothing else, is appalling. But in perspective it makes you human."

What von Bülow unearthed for me was Balthus's simultaneous immersion in and distance from everything. His portrait of his longtime acquaintance depicted a narcissist and a chronic observer—brilliant and creative, but personally removed. Others of Balthus's friends had suggested the same: the artist as a fantasist, more masturbatory than sexual, more narcissistic than amorous. It is his actual detachment from others that helps facilitate the fierce internal engagement.

BECAUSE OF CLAUS VON BÜLOW'S own history and reputation, I asked him what he thought Balthus had done to the subjects of those paintings who seem most clearly comatose or victimized. With this in mind, I showed him reproductions of *The Guitar Lesson, The Window, The Room,* and *The Victim.*

In all four of these pivotal paintings, von Bülow saw the subservience and apparent helplessness of most of these females as an extension of their usual role in the sexual act. "The fact that the man physically takes the woman: when you go to the next step, she's the victim. Sadomasochism is the natural taken one step further."

Then, looking at the 1936 *Victim,* he unequivocally declared that the woman had been raped—rather than murdered. Studying this ashen white nude with the dagger at her side, he added, "Victim? I think that's perfectly all right by me. One finds women who are inviting, who have very strong personalities, but in bed want the roles reversed."

I made no comment. Given who the speaker was, I listened to it all with rapt attention, while furiously writing down every word. Von Bülow told me that, in light of some of his experiences with the press, he generally insists that interviewers tape-record him and provide him with copies of the tapes. He said, to my surprise, that it suited him to have me transcribing his comments instead. I could not, with my pen, keep up with every utterance— the countless references to history, or to someone's genealogy, the deep admiring remarks about historian Simon Schama—but I missed little concerning his theories on Balthus's treatment of women. I also managed to transcribe all of his utterances pointing to Balthus's subjects as renditions of the artist himself.

"Is he doing anything to women that he isn't doing to himself? There's a melancholia." To von Bülow, the grimness and intensity of Balthus's teenage girls gave them a strong resemblance to their creator. He saw Balthus as the quintessential, brooding, tragic Pole, and the adolescent girls as having been made very much in the artist's own image.

"At the crisis moment in my life, I was criticized for not showing emotion. Well, you can't help your physiognomy. I look like a stand-in for Curt Jurgens as a U-boat captain. Balthus looks like Chopin. And his girls are calculated images of his own profile. Happiness is very distracting."

Claus von Bulow saw the persona of Balthus's girls to be that of their maker, and the world of his paintings—like that of his life—to be his chosen Eden. "Every one of his pictures, though representational in style, is fantasy. You have to honor your fantasy." In a noticeably slow cadence, von Bülow precisely enunciated the nature of Balthus's realm of desire: "The absence of pubic hair and the visibility of the labia major: why shouldn't he live, himself, in fantasy?"

VIII

NOT ONLY DID CYRIL CONNOLLY let Balthus have Byron as an ancestor, but he invested Balthus with some of the artist's chosen ancestor's most endearing personality traits. In an essay for a 1952 Balthus exhibition at the Lefevre Gallery in London, the English novelist wrote, "We see that the exterior of the gentle dandy and witty cosmopolitan conceals a strong will and deeply original mind." Connolly was a sage Balthus observer. He understood the interplay of the contrasting sides of the artist's character. "As a personality Balthus is one of the most delightful companions in Paris and one of the most sought after, his iconoclastic sallies are both provoked and relished and it is perhaps to be

regretted that he never takes his charm and irony with him into the studio. . . .
It is clear . . . that he may incorporate . . . all those lighter qualities which have
endeared him to his friends into his fastidious, virile, and somber imagination."[33] It was a prescient view of the man who had painted *Alice* and *The Victim*—but who would soon enough be making society portraits like the one of
the Baroness de Rothschild.

On the other hand, in his diaries Connolly declared Balthus "depressing"
and "melancholy." And his and Balthus's friendship ultimately went the way of
most of the artist's relationships. In 1948 Connolly had acquired Balthus's *The
Cherry Tree.* Lord Derwent—a friend of the writer's—had offered to take over
payments if Connolly could not make them, but then Peter Derwent died
before the painting had been paid for in full. According to a letter Balthus
wrote James Thrall Soby, Connolly carefully began to avoid running into the
artist. Balthus meanwhile observed his former friend managing somehow to
live well on no income. Then Connolly sold *The Cherry Tree.*

Balthus sarcastically quipped to Soby how "wonderful" it was when Connolly, after selling the painting, offered Balthus half the amount. Here it is not
clear whether he meant half the amount for which he had sold the work or half
of what he still owed, but in either case Balthus felt that the "crook" deserved
"not a cent" for himself.

They made a settlement—about which Balthus gave Soby the most cynical explanation. The artist felt that by agreeing to Connolly's terms he had succumbed to reprehensible values that were perfectly suited to the current world.
It is yet another story of a wound inflicted on Balthus where the details will
always remain elusive and subject to more than one explanation.

For it seems that none of Balthus's close relationships with writers or
other artists endured. With the friend whom Balthus saw more than any other
in these postwar years—Giacometti—there was, similarly, a schism at the end.

BUT WHEN THE SCULPTOR LIVED in the Elyssia quarter and Balthus was
on the Cour de Rohan, the two got together nearly every day. Life revolved
around cafés, and they most often met at the Deux Magots—even more than
at lunch parties at Derain's or the de Noailles's. Balthus told me that, except for
an interlude during wartime, he and Giacometti saw each other in this way
until he left for Chassy in 1953—although even after that point Giacometti
continued to visit him at the château in the Morvan.

In a relationship that James Thrall Soby calls "one of the strangest friendships in the world of modern art," Balthus and Giacometti were soul mates
and complete opposites.[34] Soby, who knew both of them fairly well, writes

about the numerous, deep bonds between the two men, but also describes "how they jabbered like magpies, fought, embraced, quarreled again and always ended in some curious affinity of spirit."

Whenever Balthus talked to me about Giacometti, he lowered his eyelids as if he were talking about a holy person. There was no one else whose name came up in our conversations who garnered quite the same respect, or seemed possessed by the same purity.

Balthus's voice took on that quasi-religious timbre on the afternoon he led me to a fine Giacometti bronze in one of the lesser-used sitting rooms at Le Grand Chalet. He reported proudly that Alberto had told him he was the first person who ever liked it, and so the sculptor had given it to him. Looking on the brink of tears, Balthus implied that there was the most perfect sympathy between them.

Balthus told me that when, in the late 1950s, Giacometti saw his large *Passage du Commerce Saint-André,* the sculptor said "he thought it had the same subject as *The Palace at 4 a.m.*—people crossing an outside room." Balthus then stressed that he did not see the link—because his goal was not to express loneliness. "I never want to express anything at all," he announced definitively. Yet the comparison of Balthus's *Passage* to Giacometti's earlier *Palace* makes sense. And although Balthus now repudiated the notion, he had brought it up with considerable pride.

Balthus and Giacometti, after all, were certainly unified in their determination to portray human isolation—even if the Balthus I knew disavowed that intention. Aspects of the Surreal agenda linked them even if they disparaged the movement itself. Antonin Artaud had been profoundly affected by Giacometti's Surreal work; *The Cage* of 1930 was said to have anticipated the Theater of Cruelty. Giacometti's emphasis on alienation and emotional distance—on the voids as well as the presences—was central to Balthus as well, and would continue to dominate Balthus's art, whatever his disclaimers.

Yet for all their rapport, Balthus and Giacometti favored entirely different ways of life. Giacometti was known to say, "I want to live in such a way that if I became destitute tomorrow it would change nothing for me."[35] It was a far cry from Balthus's "I have a greater need for a château than a workman has for a loaf of bread."[36] By James Lord's account—and Lord did spend a considerable amount of time with Giacometti and Balthus together—

Balthus . . . [was] the artist to whom Alberto was most bound in friendship and in a mutual commitment to aesthetic purposes opposed to contemporary taste. Yet the two were very different as artists and very, very different as men. . . . Alberto desired to live and work in circumstances of austere simplicity, whereas Balthus yearned for pomp. . . . Alberto wanted to be left alone to pursue his work as best he could, convinced in advance that his best would probably turn out to be evidence of failure. Balthus desired not only the homage due to a successful artist but also the deference due to an accredited aristocrat.

[Giacometti] disapproved of Balthus as a person but enjoyed his company. He did not admire his work but was sincere in his esteem for the artistic resolve which engendered it. This esteem was well deserved. . . . High standards of integrity prevailed for both.[37]

THE YOUNG AMERICAN PAINTER Leland Bell—for whom Derain, Balthus, Léger, Giacometti, and Jean Hélion were all mentors verging on gods— periodically discussed Balthus with Giacometti in Paris in the late 1940s and 1950s. In conversations we had in the mid-1980s at his house in New York, Bell provided a firsthand account of Giacometti's views on Balthus's work. Bell and Giacometti both revered Balthus's artistic talent and were frequently annoyed when talk about this artist they so ardently admired would turn to prurient snickering about "Balthus and his little girls." Yet they also agreed with one another that Balthus's denial of the sexuality of his art was nonsense. They considered it as ridiculous as, and not dissimilar to, his obsessive class consciousness.

Giacometti was entirely matter-of-fact on this issue. He remarked to Bell that the erotic element "was always there in Balthus, as if Balthus simply could not help but include it." It was undeniable; it was seminal to the work. Giacometti admired Balthus above all for "his use of space, the marvelous totality of his pictures, his freedom from gimmicks"—precisely the qualities for which Balthus would want to have been esteemed by the man he told me was "the last great living artist." But "Balthus a sa mauvaise audience, et c'est sa faute," Giacometti remarked to Bell.

On one occasion when Bell and Giacometti were discussing Balthus in the mid-1950s, Bell complained to the Swiss about the Museum of Modern Art's decision to hang Balthus's work alongside Pavel Tchelitchew's and Peter Blume's. Together they lamented this pairing of work by "a real painter" with "these decadent minor realists." But whereas Bell expected Giacometti to discuss Balthus only in purely artistic terms, Giacometti, sounding more like most other people than Bell anticipated, was preoccupied with Balthus's pervasive eroticism and his social shenanigans.

The Window, Cour de Rohan, 1950–51,
oil on canvas, 150 x 82 cm

Bell began to tell me about a painting he had seen in Balthus's studio which showed both the studio interior with its still life and the view out the window into the courtyard. "He made big changes, and the paint would run. He was always trying to get the big planes to relate, and he maintained the articulation," the younger artist observed. These were the elements that excited Bell—and still thrilled him as he resurrected the studio visit over thirty years earlier. But to Leland Bell's surprise, what Giacometti emphasized about the canvas was its sexuality. The Swiss said that the buildings across the way reminded him of a woman—as if the dark window openings were female orifices—and that the still life within also had aspects of genitalia. "Even a piece of fruit by Balthus had something erotic about it," Giacometti told Bell. The surprise is that the observation came from someone Balthus would now have us believe was his complete soul mate.

Giacometti also made a point of telling Bell about a recent trip he and Pierre Matisse had made to see Balthus in the Morvan. They had gotten lost near Chassy in their chauffeured car, and asked a peasant where the château of Balthus was. "Balthus, qui ça?" replied the peasant. Pierre Matisse explained, only to hear, "Oh, Le Comte de Rola!" The artist's old friends could hardly believe their ears.

On the other hand, Leland Bell saw Balthus's assumption of this rather silly social position as a partial consequence of the artist's more justified sense of his own status in the intellectual hierarchy. Visiting Balthus in Paris in 1953, Bell encountered Cyril Connolly's friend Peter Derwent in the studio at the Cour de Rohan. Bell began to argue with Derwent about Arp and Mondrian, neither of whose work the wealthy English collector particularly cared for. Balthus took this completely coolly and was silent until Derwent left, at which point he turned to Bell and said, "My dear, you're absolutely right, but you must never bother to argue about art with a layman."

BALTHUS AND GIACOMETTI AGREED about many issues of painting, but differed significantly on the matter of human relationships. When Balthus first moved to Chassy, Giacometti arranged for a friend of his, a woman in her midtwenties named Léna Leclerq, to be the artist's housekeeper. Balthus had little money—his work was not yet selling well, and he lived solely off his regular stipend from the consortium—but even though he didn't have a franc to spare, he needed someone to help with cooking and with cleaning the decrepit château. A country girl whom Giacometti had met in a café, Leclerq was a poet, and Giacometti had the idea that by taking the post she would be able to write while Balthus painted.

Laurence Bataille had remained in Paris, and Antoinette and the boys were in Switzerland. Balthus was on his own. The idea of companionship as well as service suited him perfectly.

Once they were alone in the Morvan, Leclerq—like many women—succumbed to her employer's charms. And for a while she thought she had the lean and intense painter to herself. It was not an easy relationship, however. A fairly dour and defeated person to begin with—as Balthus emphasized in his paintings of her—she suffered from his mockery. When the sardonic Balthus once asked her who in history "she might have liked to be" and she replied Trotsky, he quipped, "You might have chosen Lenin. He, at least, succeeded."[38]

Leclerq's greater agony, however, began when Balthus's fifteen-year-old "niece"—in fact his stepniece, the daughter from a previous marriage of Pierre Klossowski's wife—moved into Chassy. Leclerq attempted suicide. Giacometti and his wife, Annette, who rushed to the scene, were distraught. Balthus, apparently, was not.

Giacometti was put off by his friend's indifference. And their relationship suffered further when Balthus's fortunes changed following the 1956 Museum of Modern Art show. Now a uniformed butler appeared on the scene at Chassy to greet the count's visitors. By the time the Count Klossowski de Rola moved to Rome to assume his position at the Villa Medici in 1961, the rapport of the old days at the Deux Magots was gone.

It seems that Giacometti even lost his feeling for most of Balthus's work. David Sylvester reports a discussion with the Swiss in the following way: "Once in the 1960s I asked him what he thought of the work of Balthus, an old friend to whom he remained devoted; he answered discreetly, saying he liked some of the drawings."[39] Only a loyal politeness remained from the vibrant camaraderie and sense of a mutual battle Giacometti had felt when he and Balthus had championed Derain in the 1930s.

SINCE ALBERTO GIACOMETTI's death in 1966, Balthus, however, has resurrected their friendship—and erased the distance and froideur that marked their relationship in the last decade or so of his former companion's life. This is not unlike the way he managed, when I was present, to depict a nonexistent closeness to his mother in this same period of the fifties and sixties when his social ascendancy had such primary importance that he severed many of his earlier, expendable connections.

That skillful restitution of what was not really there emerges in the longest text Balthus has ever published: a three-paragraph essay about "Alberto" which he wrote in Rome in 1975 for a catalog of a show of Giacometti drawings held at the Galerie Claude Bernard in Paris. The writing style is terse, but the sentiments about Giacometti are eloquent and deeply felt. Given Balthus's usual disinclination to extend himself—he rarely writes letters or makes phone calls: the world must come to him—it was a major act to have committed his words to type in this way. The effect was to establish a sense of his inseparable closeness to "Alberto."

In that brief essay, Balthus dwells on Giacometti's death nearly ten years

*Léna with
Her Arms
Crossed,*
1954, oil on
canvas, 101
x 65 cm

earlier. He treats it as the basis of a rather peculiar, highly personal event.
Balthus describes going to a foundry and seeing a Giacometti bust, of which
the owner wanted to change the bronze patina. Balthus considers this explanation of why it was there to be bizarre and specious. But regardless of the validity of the reason given for the presence of the sculpted head, he became
absorbed in contemplating it. He describes Giacometti's bust very dramatically: as meteoric, charred, fashioned by fire in a breakneck—vertiginous—fall
through an infinite void. Balthus writes that he watched the piece avidly
devour the space around it.

Balthus then claims that, in viewing the sculpture, he came to anticipate
Giacometti's death. After the trip to the foundry, he felt a heavy sadness for
twenty-four hours. It was an invasive, alarming worry. He went home in a
dream.

Shortly after this experience, he heard that Giacometti had, in fact, died.

It is on this note that he concludes the essay—before announcing, warmly, that he wrote these lines for Alberto's brother Diego.

It is a totally narcissistic essay—like the sort of eulogy in which the speaker recalls the deceased only in relationship to himself and his own experience. As in his portraiture, Balthus reveals more about himself and his own vision than about his subject. And he depicts himself as being like the characters in his own large figure compositions: overcome by their personal dramas, full of premonitions, in a sort of fugue state. The effect is dramatic, but Giacometti is lost.

IN CONVERSATION WITH ME, Balthus frequently reiterated that, beyond being "the last great living painter," Giacometti was admirable for having written and published as much as he did. Balthus himself felt that he lacked this ability. He also commended Giacometti's perspective on the world: "Alberto was like two persons. One person who was himself, another who was amused by himself." When Balthus said this, I wrote it down verbatim and accepted it at face value, but in retrospect I wonder if it was not Balthus rather than Giacometti about whom he was talking.

The large photo of Giacometti I had observed in Balthus's studio seemed to keep the Swiss near. Giacometti, after all, was the sole person with whom Balthus used to be able to talk, day in and day out, about the craft of painting. They had similar artistic aims, and shared a sense of the futility and mystery of the battle. Each felt estranged from art historians, critics, and others who observed rather than made art themselves. Balthus told me—naturally with no hint whatsoever of the rift in Giacometti's last decade—that he had never found "the equal of Alberto." He might still discuss art with former students from the Villa Medici—most especially with the painter François Rouen, who periodically visits from Paris—and with Setsuko, but it was not the same.

For whatever strength there is in Setsuko's rather tepid art rests on the apparent ease behind its creation. What Balthus and Giacometti had most in common at the height of their closeness was that certain things did *not* come naturally or easily. For both of them art was—at least back then—a ceaseless, ongoing struggle in which satisfaction was impossible.

IN 1991 BALTHUS GRANTED *Le Figaro* an interview on the subject of Giacometti. Balthus declared, "I was very fond of Alberto, for he was one of the most interesting and exciting men you could ever meet."[40] Recalling Gia-

cometti's break from the Surrealists and elaborating on the subsequent priorities of his art, Balthus was completely adulatory.

For the *Figaro* reader, Balthus described the routine of his visits to
Alberto's studio:

> Very often he continued working during my visits. He would show me
> a sculpture and shifted from the most absolute pessimism to the most
> absolute enthusiasm. He was an anxious man, an artist who perpetu-
> ally doubted what he was doing. He was never satisfied with what he
> produced. He would talk all the while he was drawing, painting, or
> sculpting. I never heard him say that he thought any of his sculptures
> were completed. He had a need for an inner truth which he never
> managed to fulfill.

This sounded remarkably like Balthus's account to me of his own dissatisfac-
tion in taking years to finish single paintings, changing them perpetually, never
feeling done.

There is one good moment in painting, Balthus announced—with an
expression, however, that was anything but satisfied. That is when you think it
is finished. But the sensation quickly evaporates.

For with painting you could go on forever: "As you don't know how to
paint; no one really knows how to paint." At times one of his own pictures
might momentarily seem nice to him; on other occasions he doesn't know
what more he can do; and then there are the moments when he simply stops
out of fatigue. But no matter what, the process of painting seems endless, its
goals unachievable, its process as futile as for his beloved Alberto. Like the precious cat that fled from Balthus when he was eleven, art is exquisite, compelling—and beyond human grasp.

IX

FRÉDÉRIQUE TISON, BORN IN 1938, was the daughter of Denise, the wid-
ower whom Pierre Klossowski married in 1947. Her father, who was in the
Resistance, had been killed by the Germans; her mother had been deported
during the war. When she was about ten, she began to pose for Balthus.

Balthus probably first met Frédérique in Champrovent, where Pierre
Klossowski and Denise had begun to go in 1945. Jean Leyris, Betty and Pierre's
son, used to play with the girl and her brother Jean Charles at that time. Leyris
told me Frédérique was "a wild kid, up to mischief, a naughty child in the
nicest way." She did things like "taking plugs out of water barrels and stealing."

Her "uncle" Balthus soon came to find her irresistible. "When she was four-teen, he used to show up at her lycée with boxes of chocolate to court her."

It was not long before Balthus achieved his objective. In 1954 the sixteen-year-old Frédérique arrived in Chassy. For a while Balthus lived with her as well as Léna Leclerq—just as, eight years later, he would live with both Frédérique and Setsuko in Rome. By 1956 Leclerq was long gone, however, and Balthus took his new young mistress along to Rolle for Christmas with Antoinette and the children. He molded his life according to his whims.

Looking at Balthus's work of the period, one can hardly tell which of his female companions Balthus was painting. Both Léna and Frédérique served as his model, but the work was neither personal nor biographical. It was the opposite from Picasso, whose every new relationship brought a different man-ner of painting and characterization of women in general. Individuals might come and go in his life, but whether his subject was Léna, Frédérique, or another of his models, they all became "Balthus girls."

From the time he returned to Paris after the war, Balthus had been paint-ing the naked female figure as if she were the essence of renewal and salvation. Reality might periodically intrude on his life, but in his art he was free to feast upon females at the stage when he seemed to love them best. Adolescent and blossoming, they appear lost in reverie, enjoying endless time as if life was one extended summer afternoon.

These nudes of the late 1950s are variations of creatures we have long known. Their breasts are developed but they have no pubic hair. They present themselves unabashedly for the taking, yet conceal their mental worlds. Their legs gargantuan, their hands malformed, their skin soft and luminous, they descend not so much from the individuals who posed for them as from the mind and experience of their conqueror.

CHAPTER TWENTY

THE THREE SISTERS

I

SHORTLY AFTER HE MOVED to Chassy, Balthus began a series of paintings of three teenage sisters together. The girls were the daughters of the Paris art dealer Pierre Colle, a friend who had died in 1948. The artist started painting the Colle girls when he was visiting their mother in Biarritz in the summer of 1954. He worked and reworked the theme until 1957, and would again take it up in the early 1960s.

These riveting canvases, like the 1938 *Thérèse Dreaming,* show Balthus at his most eloquent and revealing. Looking at them, and talking with their subjects—now three dynamic and intelligent women—we get closer to, yet at the same time grow all the more confused by, the deliberate enigma of their maker.

I HAVE LONG HAD A PERSONAL connection with these paintings of sisters. In the summer of 1976, my future wife and I were in Geneva when we bought a pencil sketch for one of the mid-1950s *Three Sisters.* We were both strapped for money, and I still don't know how we came up with the funds, but we were united in our passion for that drawing.

Part of what captivated us in this study of two of the girls was how it evokes, in a rough way, the posture of teenagers. The arrogant ease of the slightly older sister—leaning back on the sofa with one foot resting on the cushion—contrasts with the more childish curiosity of the younger one curled up on the floor. The girl on the floor gazes with fascination up her sibling's dress and between her legs. The drawing, while complete and telling, is a feat of legerdemain. Balthus's engagement is visible in every pencil stroke, yet his lines betray effortlessness.

Balthus in his studio in Chassy, 1957, by Loomis Dean

When I wrote Balthus in 1990 telling him I had been asked to write a book on him, I mentioned that we owned this sketch and that our own two young daughters had grown up in its presence. Indeed, the *Study for "The Three Sisters"* seemed an integral part of our lives. What I now realize is that this information that I was, however modestly, a collector in the right camp was probably a central factor in Balthus's initially agreeing to meet me.

IN THE SPRING OF 1991, John Russell telephoned one morning to say that one of Balthus's "Three Sisters" was in New York and would see me two days later. She was the eldest of the trio: Marie-Pierre Colle—an editor for *House & Garden,* living in Mexico City.

Marie-Pierre is the girl on the sofa in Balthus's five paintings of the *Three Sisters* series, as well as in numerous sketches, ours among them. When we made our plan to meet at the Upper East Side apartment of the friend with whom she was staying, I told her about our drawing, which she asked me to bring along. The sight of the sketch opened the floodgates of reminiscence. Marie-Pierre was about eleven years old when she started posing at the Cour

Study for "The Three Sisters," c. 1955, pencil and blue wash, 31 x 38 cm

de Rohan; unlike her sisters, she not only sat for the group paintings but sometimes modeled alone. Balthus was "a friend of the family's," she told me. Ever
since her own father's death, the artist had become "like a father" to her and
the others.

As she was recounting this to me forty years later, she was seated, as in her
childhood portraits, on a sofa. I was on an elegant side chair at a right angle to
it. We were completely alone in her friend's vast apartment; the living room
where we were talking resembled an elaborate Parisian salon.

Marie-Pierre was an arresting sight in a very tight and short miniskirt. She
kept changing the position of her legs—sometimes tucked underneath her
buttocks, sometimes crossed in front of her. She appeared to be trying to keep
from revealing too much thigh, yet the effort was exposing a provocative
amount of leg.

Balthus was "tender, gracious, loving," she told me. He "felt responsible"
for her. She went out of her way to make it clear that now he was very much
misunderstood by the public at large. Neither she nor her sisters "felt any
erotic connection with him; he was completely paternal, and in no way
improper."

As she was saying this, suddenly this attractive, youthful woman—impressively svelte and smooth-skinned at fifty—began, with her right hand, to massage her left breast: the one nearer to me. She was wearing a loose-fitting, silky blouse that was unbuttoned to mid-chest, and she had reached through the opening and under her bra. She looked unconscious of the act, as if she were in a trance.

Fascinated by the way she was rubbing herself, I tried nonetheless to give the impression that I did not notice. Our eyes hardly met. Once or twice in the course of our conversation, I said—defensively—that unfortunately I could not stay long. But I was not sure if this reaction to her seductiveness was necessary, since to this day I do not know if she was trying to lure me or if it was the memory of Balthus that was prompting her to fondle her own breast in front of me.

Marie-Pierre continued with her memories. Balthus was always gentle and caring. When she was fourteen, he gave her phonograph records of the Brandenburg Concerti. She had never once found him angry or rude. The only time the artist had ever reprimanded her, he had done so with incredible gentleness. He had told her that when she changed position even slightly, it was a problem for him. She responded that she couldn't see the difference in how she was seated from one moment to the next; in order to demonstrate the change, the artist had "kindly"—shown her "a drawing to indicate otherwise." Meanwhile, she continued to stroke her breast, although now her legs were in a fixed position crossed at the ankles.

Marie-Pierre recalled those times when she was aged eleven to thirteen and modeled for the artist alone, prior to the period of *The Three Sisters*. In that period of the early fifties, she would accompany Balthus to the Louvre with André Malraux, who had arranged those visits on days when the museum was closed to the general public. They would spend the entire morning in front of Poussins and a Courbet.

Then, in 1954, Balthus came to visit her family in Biarritz and began to paint the three Colle girls together. Hearing about this process, asking the occasional question, I simply took notes as if I were unaware of what was going on before my eyes.

Marie-Pierre said that her father was an art dealer and had introduced Balthus and Derain. The Colles owned *The White Skirt*. This provocative 1937 Balthus shows Antoinette, whom Balthus had married earlier that year, looking like a drugged lingerie model. The artist's bride is clad in a translucent bra—through which her nipples show—and an old, full-length white tennis skirt that belonged to her mother. Balthus had told Pierre Colle's widow that if he could have the painting back, he would paint her three daughters and give

The White Skirt, 1937, oil on canvas, 130 x 162 cm

her their group portrait in exchange. And so Madame Colle asked the artist
down to the country house that her parents, from a prominent Mexican family, had in Biarritz. The artist came with Léna Leclerq, with whom he was then
living in Chassy.

"We didn't pose for Balthus because he was the great painter of the century. We posed because he was a friend of the family." The girls wanted to go to
the beach, but instead had to sit still while the artist sketched. Marie-Pierre
stressed to me that it was all in the context of "ordinary life." To keep the children attentive, Balthus put a box of chocolates on the floor—in one painting
he has transformed it into a basket of flowers—from which they could select a
reward if they kept still.

A decade later, she became more of a professional model for the painter.
In November 1963 Balthus invited Marie-Pierre Colle to come to the Villa
Medici, where she posed again for him and stayed for five weeks. She recalls it
as the time when Frédérique was "on her way out, Setsuko in—a turning
point." But in the studio it was business as usual. Every morning Marie-Pierre
posed for hours, while Balthus sketched; he would work on the oil painting
later, with no one there. During these sittings, the artist "never spoke."

The memories brought on the smile people sometimes make when recalling past loves. Meanwhile, Balthus's former model continued to fondle her own breast. And then this beautiful woman stood up and concluded our meeting by going into the bedroom, from which she emerged with a poem Balthus had written for her. As if transfixed—at that moment she looked like one of the women in Baladine's images for Rilke's *Windows*—she read, in a soft voice and measured cadence, the words penned on a small paper she held in her fingers. "Pour la fleur/d'entre les fleurs/l'adolescent Marie-Pierre, /son adorateur." As she reflected back on herself as "the adolescent Marie-Pierre," and the painter/friend-of-the-family as "her adorer," her face lit up even further.

II

SYLVIA COLLE LORANT, the youngest of the three sisters, presented a very different situation than Marie-Pierre. I met her in Paris in November 1992. Her spacious Left Bank apartment offered much visual stimulus to our conversation with its splendid late Derains as well as a version of *The Three Sisters* Balthus painted in the mid-1960s when he revived the series at the Villa Medici.

Sylvia works in the National Museum of Modern Art at the Centre Pompidou and has, for a number of years, been writing a book on Balthus as a set and scenery designer. A scholarly, matter-of-fact art historian, she is exceptionally bright, crisp, and outgoing.

Indeed, Sylvia told me, Balthus had been a father figure to her and her sisters after their father—a wonderful, innovative art dealer—had died so tragically young. But the man who had had even a larger role in bringing them up was Christian Dior. Dior had been a friend of Pierre Colle's, and Madame Colle had been in charge of Dior's boutique. The girls' dolls had clothing by the designer, and it was he who often supplied the boxes of candy that sat on the floor when Balthus painted them.

In Biarritz, she recalled, Balthus would sketch the girls for an hour or so every morning, from ten to eleven or eleven-thirty. He made a lot of drawings of them, but painted the actual oils back in Chassy. He captured the family scenario as it really was: with Marie-Pierre like a queen on a throne, Béatrice always playing, and Sylvia herself totally lost in a book—generally Dostoyevsky, but sometimes Dumas or Hugo.

At that time in their lives, they reacted to the finished paintings just the way one would expect of girls their age. When Baladine Klossowski asked Sylvia what she thought of the version of *The Three Sisters* then owned by Henriette Gomès, Sylvia's main response was that she hated having such big legs.

Yet even if she did not like her oddly proportioned limbs, Sylvia found nothing strange about the whole experience of posing for Balthus. "As a person, he was tender, present. He amused himself with us; he joked a lot. The paintings were enigmatic, but he was not. There was never any danger: the sexuality was in his head. His cerebral world was different from the world out there in the painting. He had the audacity to express his ideas in his art."

The Colle girls knew him well enough to speak with authority. Once Balthus was living in Chassy, he regularly stayed in their apartment on the Rue de Varenne when he visited Paris. Sylvia, even as a child, perceived his layers. She distinguished his behavior as a man from the revelations of his art. She and her family took their old friend's use of a title in stride: "He always knew how to comport himself like a count, and he was always just that." They had perspective on his eroticism. "*Lui,* he exaggerates the theme of provocativeness. And he shows things. But he's no dangerous child molester." In his art, "Balthus deliberately disorients us. He's provocative in presenting a situation which is the projection of the viewer."

The wide-eyed Sylvia—in middle age bearing an uncanny resemblance to

The Three Sisters, 1966, oil on canvas, 130.5 x 175 cm

her adolescent self in Balthus's paintings—amplified her points as she looked up at the painting she owns. She noted "the ambiguity that is always there"—and the hints of eroticism that show up in details like Balthus's placement of white gloves on a little girl. Sylvia explained that this particular *Three Sisters* was based on a combination of models. Balthus had in mind the Colle girls as they had been almost ten years earlier; he had also depended on his other, younger models in Rome, and had now set the scene at the Villa Medici. Sylvia observed, with a deep laugh, that the girth of the legs which so bothered her as a child gave the work expression. And she concurred that in this otherwise marvelous composition, the hands fall apart completely.

And then Sylvia Lorant, perhaps as much as anyone I have ever spoken to except for Pierre Leyris, seemed to capture the true nature of Balthus. "He's never in one situation or another. But always at an intersection of ambiguity—the passage between one time period and another—there at the beginning of adulthood." She suggested that Balthus and his subjects were the same. With all their undercurrents of feelings, the latent yet soaring emotions, they combined dissemblance and candor in equal mixture.

III

IF SYLVIA COLLE LORANT EVOKED the ambiguity of adolescence, Béatrice Colle Saalburg, the middle of the three sisters, represented another side of Balthus's teenage girls: the seer, the observer who could peel away the layers and recognize the core. When I saw her in Paris a couple of days after I spoke with Sylvia—a year after my encounter with Marie-Pierre—she spoke with an impeccable grasp of our elusive subject.

Béatrice and I met one morning at my hotel in the sixth arrondissement—a short walk from Balthus's old neighborhood. Like her sisters, she was quite extraordinary-looking—half Spanish-Mexican, half French—and intensely animated. More than any of his other former models, she was in real life truly a girl from a Balthus painting. Now a grown woman, Béatrice had not lost an iota of her teenage vitality. With her well-defined features and noticeably strong hands, she radiated aliveness and energy.

Possessed of a grace and generosity similar to Sylvia's, Béatrice—who studied with Cassandre and teaches graphic art—provided an account of Balthus that, while human and personal, was as measured and proportionate as a layout sheet. First she meticulously provided historical data—in greater detail than her sisters had. Balthus had been one of the most important artists in her father's gallery in the 1940s and had remained a close friend of Madame

Colle's after Pierre died young. He stayed with the widow and three daughters periodically in Paris after his move to Chassy in 1953.

Béatrice's account of the arrangement between Balthus and Madame Colle concerning *The White Skirt* matched Marie-Pierre's, but then she went further.

It was easy to see why Balthus wanted *The White Skirt*. For one thing, like a hunting trophy, it shows the prey vanquished. The aristocrat—wearing that white flannel tennis skirt which to the young painter must have symbolized her easy way of life—is exhausted on her throne. Through some form of power, sexual or otherwise, her portraitist has reduced her to semiconsciousness. It was also probably a painting Balthus now wanted out of circulation because it revealed his wife in her tight bra in a manner that—while allegedly a concession to her modesty, since she had insisted on the undergarment in preference to total nudity—allows her nipples to show and seems to cheapen her and hold her captive. Or he may have negotiated to get the painting back because he knew he could now get a better price for it.

Meanwhile, to Madame Colle's consternation, once the widow gave *The White Skirt* to its maker, the painting promised by Balthus never arrived. The artist had made any number of sketches of the Colle girls, who had posed as instructed, but neither his three young models nor their mother knew if he had used them for the oil that was to be his half of the exchange. After ten years—by which time Balthus had evolved from the impoverished painter at Chassy to the esteemed director of the Villa Medici—Madame Colle was truly annoyed. "Where's the picture?" she demanded.

Madame Colle had come to realize that Balthus had, indeed, completed canvases of her daughters. She had seen one dated 1954, another 1956, and there were several substantial oil paintings that showed just one or two of the girls. But rather than going to Madame Colle as promised, these canvases had all been sent to dealers, or to members of the syndicate, to help the artist pay off his debts.

Now, however, Balthus had begun his second *Three Sisters* series—albeit in his new Villa Medici style. Marie-Pierre was the only Colle daughter still modeling for the artist, but the others were clearly there in memory, in partnership with the new actual models for these later works. This second group of *Three Sisters* canvases, in pastel tones that reflected Balthus's work on the frescoes at the villa, were—the observation is Béatrice's, but reflects her mother's response as well—"colder, and more aesthetic." But at least Balthus finally sent one.

Madame Colle, however, did not like it. Eventually she selected another painting from the series: the version I saw over Sylvia Lorant's sofa. But even then, it was a far cry from one of the original 1950s *Three Sisters* for which her daughters had actually posed, and which she had been promised.

What happened to Carmen Colle called to mind other stories I have heard about Balthus. It made me wonder if Balthus was actually rooked by Pierre Loeb and Cyril Connolly—or if, for all his tales of woe and wrongdoing done to him, the trickster was Balthus himself.

"He's very weak," Béatrice told me. "He has these two sides. He's someone who escapes, and avoids things. When he sees a problem, he runs around it. He doesn't face the situation.

"He has always lied." This was said with understanding, even fondness: the same voice that Pierre Leyris used when he characterized Balthus as having a "mimetic personality." It was as if this were all beyond Balthus's control, part and parcel of what made him both wonderful and emotionally inaccessible. "He knows how to avoid obstacles. To protect his independence. He has a sense of mystery."

BÉATRICE CONTINUED WITH her general reminiscences. From the start, Balthus "made a strong impression; he was the man in the house." She and her sisters "felt fear and admiration." Everything about him, and every experience, was a bit extraordinary. Like Marie-Pierre, Béatrice remembered the visits to an empty Louvre, not open to the general public: at nine in the morning, when they would concentrate only on Delacroix. In every encounter, the lean, sallow artist was "someone one could not forget—fascinating, a bit animal. He looked at everything, always with a little smile."

And he put a unique twist on every observation and act. "He dominated the situation"—which, in Béatrice's free association forty years later, came easily both because Balthus was "very beautiful" and because he was possessed of "a mélange of profound intelligence." Nothing was by accident in Balthus's behavior. "He was very conscious of this slightly ambiguous side; he always turned reality." He saw the world with a certain "derision." And both his art and his everyday existence were, as much as anything, "like a dream."

PART OF WHAT I LIKED about the clear-headed and good-natured Béatrice Saalburg was that she reported all of this without animus. What James Lord so vehemently deplored, and Jean Leymarie so sheepishly adheres to, she simply accepted as an integral part of someone she both admired for his talent and enjoyed as a person.

Although "it got stronger with Setsuko," in this period in the 1950s when the Colle girls were seeing Balthus regularly, "the Comte de Rola came progressively." It was just another way in which the artist transformed the world around him and initiated his own metamorphosis. Reality was rough enough to require some softening. The artist was "very poor at Chassy"—so much so that he "had to go to friends' houses to get enough to eat." There were "not enough potatoes."

Balthus's companion in this rugged existence was, of course, Léna Leclerq. Béatrice recalled Leclerq as seeming to have evolved out of Parisian café life—as if she simply emerged from nowhere one day at the Deux Magots or the Flore—before she was introduced to Balthus by Giacometti. When Balthus went to Biarritz in July 1954 to begin to fulfill his half of the deal with Madame Colle, he stepped off the train with the young poet and introduced her to the Colle girls with the line, "Voilà ma gouvernante." At about the age of twelve, Béatrice was immediately struck both by how pale Léna was and by her wrists with the slits that had still not healed from her recent suicide attempt.

Léna was—in the French sense of the word—"*formidable.*" She had "yellow eyes" and was shaped "like a Giacometti sculpture . . . very thin, and with a big bust and big calves." Béatrice recalled her as "straightforward"—and as intense as her lover, although their passions lay in very different directions. The daughter of Communists, the poet "remained an anarchist"—which was notable in part because "Balthus had no political conscience at all." After her affair with Balthus, she ended up in a tiny apartment where she hid arms for Algerians.

The teenage Colle girls had all been shaken when Léna tried to kill herself in response to the ascendancy of Frédérique. Even if for Balthus, Léna was nothing but "a little adventure," for Léna, the artist was "her whole life." Indeed, eventually she did succeed in committing suicide.

But in a way this was not surprising. Balthus's effect on women was, by Béatrice's account, extraordinary. "He took them up completely. He was beautiful, young, and irresistible. Laurence, too, was very much in love with him. And other women were overwhelmed. They were at the mercy of Balthus. They posed, and became totally fascinated with him; while he made them part of his life.

"He looked at them like a sibyl. He was like a cat. Once he chose his prey, no one could resist him. It was this that was fascinating: when he desired something, he got it."

To the three young Colle girls, however, he was simply part of life. Dancers and artists came and went in their house; they were used to the extraordinary. What they wanted to do that summer was go to the beach. "Balthus was there each morning with a box of chocolates"—but they wished only to play. Yet they did what they were supposed to, and sat while their parents' friend sketched and made watercolors because, as was the case for Dolores Miró, you did not challenge the rules—especially when the taskmaster was Balthus.

BÉATRICE SAALBURG REVIEWED the stages of Balthus's existence as if they were a sequence of atmospheres and attractions that had no reality beyond the artist's vision and desires. To look out the windows at Chassy is to see the vistas as he painted them; Béatrice remarked that Balthus so completely evoked the atmosphere of that house that she could not figure out whether the pictures gave their atmosphere to the building, or the building to the pictures. The main difference, she told me, between Chassy and the art showing it is the overwhelming cat smell of the actual place.

Frédérique—who still lives in this château that she and Balthus inhabited together—was obviously well suited to the rural existence in that corner of the Morvan, but less able to fit into the next phase of her lover's life, in Rome. "She likes horses, animals, country." I pictured the way she looked at age seventeen on the sofa in *The Dream,* and in *Young Girl in White Dress,* and two years later in *Girl at a Window.* "With her hair to her shoulders, she is now like a woman who prolonged her girlhood. She would have liked to marry Balthus and have children. She was very jealous when he left."

But what suited one stage of Balthus's evolution was inadequate for the next. At the Villa Medici, Balthus would need a woman lofty enough for his new post. "He opened the door for Setsuko. She's very fine. Very intelligent. Perfect for that life"—both in Rome and in Rossinière ever since. I thought of Setsuko on the phone organizing a visit with Mrs. Goulandris in Gstaad, of Setsuko planning dinner with the servants, of Setsuko's tremendous alertness and intelligence and chic, and recognized how right Béatrice was.

"Balthus went from a precarious country situation to civilized life. Frédérique was a bit adolescent, wild, marginal. . . . She isn't entirely reasonable—she is still *très sauvage.*" Thus Balthus had to abandon her.

THIS MATTER OF THE SUBLIMATION of the *"très sauvage"* prompted Béatrice and me to discuss *The Guitar Lesson* and Balthus's repeated assertion that he wished he had never painted it. Balthus's former model had pointed out during our conversation that in all of his other paintings the artist had held himself back as the spectator. "He is always gazing as an outsider—looking at the

Balthus in
Chassy, 1957

*Young Girl in White
Dress,* 1955, oil on
canvas, 116 x 88.9 cm

world like a cat. At the same time, he is spectator and actor. It's the moment between the scene—*le spectacle*—and the action—this little period—that he comes to paint." In paintings like *The Three Sisters,* the views out the window at Chassy, and the earlier canvases of Thérèse, it is as if Balthus is the one looking out the curtain—"always a little bit secret," Béatrice commented. We feel Balthus's presence both as the participant and the observer, but aren't exactly clear about who is who and what is where. There is a tremendous self-consciousness—as if the subjects are observing him observing them—but a lot is furtive, and we know that the world of secrets is what matters. To reveal all would be to lose one's identity: as a liar, an inventor, one's own creator. This is true of Balthus's teenage girls, and of Balthus himself.

Béatrice continued. "In his other paintings, he stopped. *The Guitar Lesson,* however, is the real one. The painting troubles him now because it's too honest." Its subject, of course, is conquest, power, blatant seduction. It does not waffle about the wish to be man and woman at the same time, victor and victim. It reveals the subsuming role of sensuous pleasure—of striped wallpaper and silky upholsteries, of the world of form, as well as of genital sex. For while savoring the texture of satin, it focuses unambivalently on erotic desire, the allure of flesh so strong that everything else in the world ceases to matter.

This time Balthus laid his cards on the table—rather than hiding them with a twisted wrist behind his back. As his former teenage model understood all too well, ultimately he preferred haze.

IV

I SAW THE GREATEST OF ALL the variations of *The Three Sisters*—the one that Sylvia Lorant had seen at Henriette Gomès's—in the sprawling West Hollywood house of Mr. and Mrs. Emilio Azcárraga (color plate 12). The mansion is a vast open-plan building composed of arcades and glass walls and terraces in which inside and outside merge. This Spanish colonial palace with state-of-the-art media equipment is set on a well-tended private park in the middle of a densely packed residential section overlooking Los Angeles.

Like Niarchos's apartment, this enclave belonging to the greatest television magnate in Mexico seemed like a secret lair. Now the work of a struggling artist of the 1950s who could scarcely afford the bare bulbs that were his sole source of lighting was in the inner sanctum of wealth.

Emilio Azcárraga, who died in April 1997, was yet another of the Balthus collectors who seem the stuff of the fiction Balthus read as a youth and dreamed of making his reality. Azcárraga "usually travel[ed] with an entourage befitting the most powerful media mogul in Mexico. With his baronial bearing and distinctive appearance—a stripe of white hair bisect[ed] his jet-black mane—Mr. Azcárraga live[d] up to his nickname, 'El Tigre.' "[1] Thus it was in "the Tiger's" den that *The Three Sisters* and two other masterpieces by the King of Cats had come to rest.

El Tigre wielded power in a way that must have drawn him instinctively to Balthus's work. An obituary of the "Billionaire Who Ruled Mexican Broadcasting" reports:

> His decision making style was as autocratic as it was bold. Televisa employees tell of the tall wooden chairs he kept for visitors to the offices he maintained in Mexico City. . . . The chair was so high that the adults who sat in it could not touch the ground with their feet and so seemed childlike. Whenever he wanted to reprimand or belittle someone who worked for him, he was said to have offered a seat in the notorious chair.[2]

Balthus's portrait subjects would have been right at home.

EVEN THOUGH I HAD MET Sylvia, Béatrice, and Marie-Pierre by the time my wife and I saw the Azcárragas' *Three Sisters,* this painting struck me not so much as a group portrait of these specific girls as an emblem of a particular time in life. It reveals generic types of female adolescents and their connection to one another. Marie-Pierre, on the sofa, is the haughty one, the seductress, infinitely self-assured; Sylvia, on the left, is the girl who deals with life by losing herself in the world of books; Béatrice, on the floor, is the squirmy child. Those distinct personalities emerge from one of Balthus's most well-conceived canvases.

The Three Sisters is among Balthus's masterpieces—completed at a moment in his life when the artist was everything he could be, true to his passions personal and painterly. Subtle yet authoritative, and unique in its delicacy—the picture is neither too weird nor too mannered—it encapsulates a realm of human existence into which few observers have so daringly or skillfully ventured.

The figures—which exist in a Pieresque hierarchy, with Marie-Pierre the Queen of Sheba—function as a frieze. When we examine the canvas closely, we marvel at the way the artist has brought it all off. The girls' faces, much as they seem to belong to living beings, are deliberately blurred: concealing and distanced. Marie-Pierre's right leg, which is like the linchpin of the composition practically dead center, a bold vertical beat in the horizontal flow—makes us feel that Balthus is asking us just how much he can get away with, it is so disproportionately massive. It *should* turn the lithe girl in her orangy-red dress into some sort of monster—yet somehow it does not.

The figures, posed and studied, are frozen in time, suggesting a religious permanence. Similarly, each still life—the basket of apples, the bouquet of flowers, even the solitary apple Béatrice is eating—is an event. A sense of age and experience emanates from the amazing textures of *The Three Sisters*. The flesh, different from all the other substances, is a network of little lines, like a porcelain glaze that has developed craquelure. The dominant dark greens and browns look carefully plotted and worked and reworked, bespeaking a centuries-old tradition of art. These earthly colors seem based in the fundaments of existence, with their deep, quiet tones offsetting the ceaseless rhythm.

On top of this tonality that makes us feel that the artist took years to achieve it and apply the paint, Marie-Pierre's flower, her red shoes, the sole of Béatrice's yellow slippers, and other small details provide bright accents, fresh and young. This color scheme suggests the perpetual newness and spark of youth against the layers of civilization: the ability of children—even in the most antique-laden and cultured settings, redolent of history and rules—to offer sharpness, freshness, and energy.

Meanwhile, Balthus has worked his way around the scene brilliantly. He has painted the folds and cascades of Marie-Pierre's dress in the manner that Morandi paints a seashell: it exists. The cushion shapes on the sofa back echo the three heads and provide a powerful setting. The little orange geranium Marie-Pierre holds has been painted with the delicacy of a Fabergé egg.

At a distance, this is real space. The figures occupy it with a Giacometti-like reality. The wood frame truly supports the upholstery of the armchair, and Sylvia really sits there. Yet there is, of course, something anatomically wrong with Béatrice. Where her buttocks should be divided beneath her yellow garment, the flesh reads as a single continuous mass. Whereas we feel that in many ways Balthus has re-created everyday life in the canvas, here we are left questioning.

This artistic puzzlement has that same dichotomy as the bright paint within the subdued whole, or the bold children in an urbane setting. It is, simultaneously, inordinately sophisticated and childlike—perhaps faux naïve. *The Three Sisters* is not so much the real world as Balthus's version of the real world. Therefore its personages must be contorted, their heads too big (and hence babylike), and their hands disastrous (he has practically painted them out). The art that emerges is serene but tense, totally languid yet charged up.

Energy, myth, imagination, and restlessness all prevail. Puzzles and frippery—
and a high-degree of game-playing—are there like a kid's prank in this extraordinary semblance of earthy reality.

ELEVEN- AND TWELVE-YEAR-OLD girls sit in unusual positions. Or, at least,
seven- and eight-year-olds do. What Balthus did in repeated paintings—his
variations of *The Three Sisters* and of *The Living Room*—was to show girls who
look to be young teenagers but sprawl in a way more characteristic of slightly
younger children, who really do not care or notice if the rest of the world can
see their underwear.

The artist would, of course, attach no significance to his having given the
attributes of seven-year-olds to adolescents. He would say that he was simply
showing children.

But when we consider the actual art as evidence—more than the gospel
preached by Balthus himself or by his spokesman Jean Leymarie or the prodi-
gal son Stanislas now making good—it appears that even in work as subdued
and tasteful as *The Three Sisters,* Balthus was still making powerful young
women his prey. He was no longer depicting them as rapees or murdered
corpses as in *The Victim,* or as the girls under direct genital attack in *The Street*
and *The Guitar Lesson,* but he still had his girls where he wanted them: displaying their sexuality, both offering it and denying it.

As such, the three sisters are like Balthus himself—presenting an irresistible form of beauty and then keeping their secrets and denying access. On
one level, they show all. On another, like cats who purr on your chest when it
suits them and then flee and elude your grasp, they steadfastly maintain their
distance.

CHAPTER TWENTY-ONE

AN OBSESSION

IN DISGUISE

I

Wɪᴛʜ Laurence, Léna, and Frédérique, Balthus had made clear his fondness for the company of young women.

In his art, however, he grew more evasive about his taste. By the time of the 1955 *Woman in a Bathtub* the forthrightness of *Thérèse Dreaming* and other paintings of the 1930s had given way entirely to innuendo and implication. The earlier works are darker, their figures more sculpted, and their forms and colors more heavily weighted. Balthus's paintings from Chassy are comparatively light, with a silvery air that casts his solitary teenage girls in soft ethereality. A fugue atmosphere has replaced the previous drumroll.

In the paintings of the thirties, we could read the expressions on the girls' faces—and see their gritted teeth and sinister glares. Balthus's girls of the fifties are more emblematic—with their features muted and in a haze. Their physical reality as well as their emotions are inaccessible. Refinement has supplanted terrorism.

Iɴ ʀᴇᴘʀᴏᴅᴜᴄᴛɪᴏɴ, *Woman in a Bathtub* seems a contrivance, bizarre and stylized. I was lucky enough to see the actual painting, however, and its true effect is very different. The canvas hangs in the crowded penthouse at the top of a New York skyscraper where a real estate tycoon stores much of his art collection. Even the low ceilings, canned light, and unsympathetic company of totally unrelated abstract art—like someone's stock portfolio in which the oil shares are listed next to the medical research companies—do not manage to deaden the Balthus.

Woman in a Bathtub, 1955, oil on canvas, 200 x 200 cm

To be human is to have vast power and energy in *Woman in a Bathtub.* The creature—based on Frédérique—is possessed of supernatural force. She looks like a Bonnard bather who has now died and been resurrected. Having earlier painted people totally earthbound, kneeling or sprawled or heavy of limb, now he has made a creature who soars, weightless and angelic. Her body flies forward in marvelous contrapposto; the rhythms of the painting are like Nijinsky dancing.

This unbridled energy is built on a solid foundation. A pencil grid shows through the thinly applied paint; the sole of Frédérique's right foot rests heavily on the rim of the tub. Balthus has again painted his specialty of folded towels with immense skill; draped on their tabletop, they have both élan and gravity.

The consummate orchestrator, in *Woman in a Bathtub* Balthus has worked the light tans and chalky greens in perfect concert. These tasteful colors are all possessed of the same, otherworldly pallor. At the same time, the

Caravaggio, *Amor Victorious,* 1602, oil on canvas, 156 x 113 cm

light that illuminates the right profile of the woman's body makes her flesh as real and seductive as it is dreamlike.

The canvas is a paean both to actual life and to inventiveness. No one else would have thought to do a bathroom nude with this unfettered animation and make it ring true.

As both Pierre Klossowski and John Russell have already pointed out, another of these seemingly resurrected women—in the 1955 *Getting Up*— derives directly from Caravaggio's *Amor Victorious* the painting that influenced Balthus far more than any German work during his Berlin years. But what a personal style of borrowing this is. For Balthus has transformed Caravaggio's male cupid into a woman. The folds above the creature's navel are virtually the same in the 1955 painting as in the one from 1602, and the legs are splayed and weighted identically, but where there is a visible penis at the pivot of the earlier painting, now there is—on a mature female form—a shaved vagina.

Getting Up,
1955,
oil on canvas,
162 x 130 cm

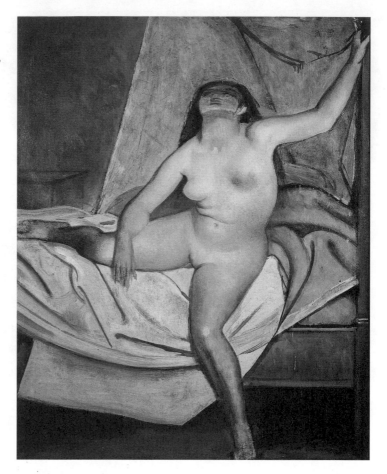

The difference, of course, does not account for all that much in Balthus's world. The boundaries of age and gender are readily crossed. Artists like Derain and Matisse paint women as viewed by the men who lust after them; Balthus, on the other hand, makes ambiguous, androgynous, self-absorbed creatures who befuddle rather than enchant. The agenda is his alone.

LIKE FRÉDÉRIQUE IN THESE 1955 canvases, the woman in *The Moth,* completed five years later, looks as if she has just flown in from another realm or is being launched into a splendid life after death. Balthus reclines some of his women comfortably in armchairs; he also likes them on tiptoes. The springy ones—of which Iya Abdy was perhaps the first—move from sphere to sphere of living.

The Moth, 1959–60, casein and tempera on canvas, 162 x 130 cm

The woman in *The Moth* has a body made real by the modeling of its flesh but artificial by its pose. The warm, bright glow of the oil lamp is convincing, and other details ring true. One superb, highly finished vignette of painting—the upside-down drinking glass—is fixed and immobile, the air trapped within it, the light established inside as well as out. But then everything is thrown into disarray. A tempest-like force has blown into the normal world. The bed-clothes are freshly rumpled. The woman and the moth disrupt the stasis.

This is the painting that Balthus told me had dropped off the roof of his car. Incomplete elements—the side chair that has not been resolved in the right foreground—demonstrate the artist's point that a painting is never really finished. We reach; we lunge with all the energy we can; but we also face our limitations, the hopelessness as well as the necessity of illusion.

II

BY THE 1950S GOOD TASTE and traditional French style had come to the fore in Balthus's paintings. And their maker had gone from being the melancholy double of Antonin Artaud, struggling in his garret, to the Count de Rola at his elegant command post in the Morvan.

The new grace of his art may have been a by-product of his worldly success. In 1956 James Thrall Soby had accorded Balthus major recognition with the exhibition at the Museum of Modern Art which was the artist's first solo museum show anywhere. Soby's selection included thirty-one oils. There were also fourteen ink drawings from 1933 for *Wuthering Heights*—owned by Mrs. Marcel Duchamp, who had formerly been Mrs. Pierre Matisse. By current standards, this was a relatively small show, but for that time period it was substantial.

The catalog that the Museum of Modern Art produced showed that Balthus's work, while not yet in any French museums, had been acquired in America by both the host institution and the Wadsworth Atheneum. Private collectors on both sides of the ocean included the Vicomtesse de Noailles, Pablo Picasso (his address given as Cannes), A. M. Cassandre, Cyril Connolly, Mr. and Mrs. John Hay Whitney, Pierre Matisse, Claude Herseint, and the Reverend James L. McLane, the Los Angeles minister who had acquired several of Balthus's recent canvases.

The show did not receive a lot of attention from the press. But the mere fact of it, and the prestige of the collectors, was reason enough for the increased ease and confidence that began to come through in the work that followed.

Balthus's paintings twenty years earlier had a brave ferocity; their sharp focus highlighted the fantasies behind them with unabashed candor. Now that the Count of Rola had arisen and erected a facade behind which to hide himself, he invested his work with the same obfuscating courtliness as his self.

WHILE THIS CHANGE IN THE 1950S is a loss for those who prefer the most direct confrontation with physical and psychological reality, it also brought its gains.

The 1957 *Girl at a Window* has a quietude lacking in Balthus's earlier work. The large canvas renders simple experiences sumptuous. A tree is in its

Balthus and Frédérique in Chassy, c. 1957

first blush of springtime; a farmyard glows under the sunshine; a meadow shimmers in the distance. They, and the girl viewing them, are in their initial blossoming.

The tonality is pure Piero. This is oil on canvas, but it has the translucency of fresco. And the forms exist as a simple frieze, almost in two-dimensional relief. Grace and lightness pervade.

The atmosphere is different from that of Balthus's art of the 1930s, but the sheer quality of composition is consistent. How well he had learned the lessons gleaned from Poussin at the Louvre. A well-defined geometry and careful per-spective arrangement order this large canvas. The course of the wainscoting and the open shutters delineate the corner of the room so that the viewer, too, feels encased by it. Beyond the window casement that palpably separates interior and exterior we feel the strong presence of the outdoors. The farmyard wall lopes along in an orderly, regular procession.

In a century in which so many artists have deliberately succumbed to, or exulted in, the disorder of their psyches, Balthus has regulated and proportioned the world. With his light, evenhanded touch, he allies himself with Seurat and other great organizers of visual experience. He has lent permanence to impermanence.

The painting has the sun-infused quality of Balthus's early admirer Bonnard. But a shimmering haze slightly veils the world as it never does in Bonnard, so that *Girl at a Window* has the substance of floating chiffon. At the same time, it has staying power. The paint looks baked on. The plaster powder in it—which, to the untrained eye, resembles sand in its granularity—has grit and substance. Thus the pale, pastel lightness seems fixed absolutely.

Balthus's vision, so harsh two decades earlier in paintings like *The Victim* and *The White Skirt,* is now lyrical and idealized. The leaves of the nearby tree are like an airy spray. More is left for the viewer to fill in than was the case in the early work. The girl's body is a summation of human form, the hands a code, the face invisible.

It is the path taken by so many artists, composers, and writers in the course of their lifetimes: this move toward lightness and simplicity, from the earthbound to the heavenly sphere, from the tangible to the amorphous. Rembrandt, Beethoven, Henry James: each progressed toward abstraction and ethereality, from the specific toward the general. But with Balthus, the development stems not so much from a drive to get closer to the essence of truth as from his wish to throw others off. Balthus not only vacated the city with his retreat to Chassy; he also left behind his wish or willingness to flaunt the more disturbing aspects of his psyche. Candor became passé.

Yet the girl in Balthus's painting has no lack of strength. Frédérique—the model here—is shown with torso identical in shape to that of the Heathcliff character we saw shirtless in *Les Beaux Jours.* This is Balthus's generic type, male or female: broad-shouldered and slim-waisted, with the back triangulated and hips sturdy. It is a body with force.

Now, however, the elements of threat and danger—so central to the earlier work—are gone. *Girl at a Window* presents Balthus's world very much as the artist would have me, and his other interlocutors, believe him to be: straightforward, celebrative, entirely absorbed in artistic technique and visual experience devoid of psychological innuendo. The painting, superbly, reveals the bounty of an open window in early spring. The dance of the tree branches

Girl at a Window, 1957, oil on canvas, 160 x 162 cm

and the marvelous lacy effect of the young leaves are the artist's primary concerns. We smell the verdant yard. We feel the warmth of sunlight on brick. The distant landscape might offer a nice walk. If there is an erotic scenario here—if the girl is captive or victimized by her situation—now it truly derives from the viewer's imagination.

A Balthusian secretiveness remains, however. Everything is perfectly organized and extremely attractive—that exquisite back of an Empire chair is as refined as a china teacup—but the details are at a remove from us, not all painted in. We don't see the girl's face, and we never will. To give sumptuously yet to withhold, to order and cultivate while dissembling: this is Balthus's way.

. . .

WHEN I SAW *Girl at a Window,* I found myself wishing that Balthus had managed to curtail his American sales as he told me he had wanted to do after he saw one of his recent works in a cluttered, overdesigned interior featured in *House & Garden.* Having been painted in the rough pile at Chassy where the luxuries were nil, the large 1958 canvas was also at the Azcárragas' house. It was displayed there on a tinted, mirrored wall that represents the worst of Southern California taste. *Girl at a Window* is *about* daylight, and—as the artist so often insisted to me—like all of Balthus's work it requires natural light to be properly seen. Yet it was lit by a combination of fluorescents recessed in nearby window niches and sunken ceiling canisters: the frozen illumination of a department store display. A silver glitter in the "antiqued" mirrored glass shimmered around the painting. The former refugee who painted *Girl at a Window* might have delighted in the sheer opulence of the setting, and in the personal benefits to him of the wealth it represented, but the tastelessness and aesthetic disparity from the artwork were disconcerting.

FORTUNATELY, THERE WERE no such problems in the setting in which the Azcárragas installed the 1959–60, Chassy period, *Landscape with Cow.* The painting itself depicts a rather ordinary sight: a foreground of trees, some ever-green and some deciduous; a cow behind the trees; a barn and farmhouse and other outbuildings in the distance. The sky is a perfect powdery blue with a hint of clouds. Balthus's tribute to the simple rural life in France—to the world that then surrounded him—was hanging on a brick wall and under a wooden ceiling. Those textures suit it well.

Landscape with Cow is one of Balthus's uneven achievements, typical of the Chassy work in both its excellence and its shortcomings. Painted splendidly in part—the wispy pine boughs, sun-drenched fields, and well-constructed barns—it is so studied and contrived in other places, and so lack-ing in the spontaneity required by its natural subject matter, as to be a bit irritating.

At its best, the painting has certain elements of first-rate Impressionism: the rich textures infused with daylight; the ambiguity of the pine needles that are so near we cannot focus on them; and the splendid clarity of the distant building complex. This could be an illustration of Yorkshire for *Wuthering Heights.* The bare-branched, wintery trees are windblown, suggesting that a storm may be brewing, lending fury to the foreground, which is like a screen over the calm behind it. Madness prevails in front on a blustery day, while the distant farm enclave enjoys complete calm and tranquillity.

Landscape with Cow, 1959–60, oil on canvas, 162 x 130 cm

Yet the resemblance to the recognizable world evaporates just behind the trees. The cow at that spot resembles a metal weathervane; it is more an emblem of an animal in relief than a plausible living creature. The man next to him is like a little homunculus in an Annunciation. A stick figure with the physique of a sack of potatoes, he is scarcely taller than the cow. He seems to wave at us wildly, although perhaps he is herding the cow. He is faceless, but the gesture is sufficient to make him seem crazed and ecstatic. With his dome-like hat and scarecrow's limbs, the miniature man is totally weird. As with his later *Large Composition with Raven,* Balthus, in one of his rare paintings of a male, has diminished him absurdly.

The textures of the painting are as varied as its weather conditions. It is painted quite flat on top, while the bottom is thick, seemingly porous like seafoam, with the impression of grit in the paint. In all of this—the strange farmer, the incongruous elements—we feel that Balthus is having his way with

Balthus in Chassy, c. 1956

us. The foreground suggests that a tempest is taking place, but the sky is as tranquil as can be. One tree is placid, but another jumps up as if in a primitive rite. The mood in some places is Morandi; elsewhere, it is Poe or Brontë. And in a painting that by and large is visually sublime, we keep coming back to that oddball clad in blue signaling to us like a lunatic. "I do Surrealism in the style of Courbet."

III

THERE WERE MOMENTS in my initial encounters with Balthus's art of the Chassy period when I was unequivocally seduced. The paintings reduced me to the very state that Balthus's adolescent models are in: overcome by sensuous pleasure to the exclusion of all other thought. Willingly destabilized, I was transported to some other sphere. The most profound of these events occurred on a pilgrimage to the large 1958 *Bouquet of Roses on a Window Sill* (color plate 13) in the Indianapolis Museum of Art.

You would have thought I'd be on my guard that afternoon; I had spent the morning with Balthus's disconcerting *Window* in Bloomington—a painting that clearly warns you about its maker's compulsion to subjugate. At midday driving north on the interstate in my enormous rental car, I felt as if the person about whom I was writing was a charlatan par excellence: a brilliant trickster who had cultivated his skills and honed his technique so skillfully that, sequestered in his opulent European mountain retreat, he had managed to plant perpetual bombs in the American heartland, thus permanently shattering the innocence of this vast country that has been his mainstay and that he has never visited.

But when, a few hours later, I stood in front of *Bouquet of Roses,* I felt as if Balthus had done nothing so much as bestow upon America the most glorious French beauty. Everything else disappeared from my thoughts as I succumbed to the vision before me. It eradicated from my consciousness my own preoccu-

Joan Miró, *View of a Farm,* 1918, oil on canvas, 64.5 x 80.5 cm

pations, the rest of the art in this large and excellent museum, the flat grid of streets I had just negotiated in a city I had never visited before, the concerns about car returns and flight schedules that normally fill a traveler's mind.

When I tried to move from my feeling of intoxication to an ability to make cogent observations, I came to believe that it was completely stupid to write about this paradise in front of my eyes. To be there with pen in hand seemed like standing on a beach or a mountaintop and taking notes about the vista. Yes, I could be a proper art historian and note the sources: Baladine Klossowska's *Fenêtres* illustrations, quite precisely, for the subject matter; Joan Miró's early landscapes, for color and tone and aspects of the construction. But these mental segues felt like silly escapes from the real, hard-core emotional experience. The painting is evanescent. It emits a pink and green glow so gorgeous as to be heavenly. The flowers in their pitcher are like a splendid chorus: each blossom a single triumphant voice, the counterpoint among them impeccably balanced and metered. Balthus is correct: he *is* a religious painter. He had every right to say to me that if I did not understand what he meant by that word, then he could not explain it.

Moreover, if Balthus was genius enough to paint this, then I should believe him about everything. There *is* no violence in his work. At least not here. Possibly his finest painting ever, *Bouquet of Roses* is a complete celebration. Nor is there any eroticism. How could I question anything he said?

ALAS, I SOON BEGAN TO FIND the dark opening in the flower pitcher erotic, and to see the velvety flower petals as imbued with sexuality. So the problem really *was* mine; Balthus was correct that the viewer's hang-ups were to blame.

But *Bouquet of Roses* is, above all, a celebration of the unique possibilities of nature and painting in happy combination. The row of yellow-topped shrubs that bifurcates this view out the window at Chassy is unlike anything else that has ever existed. It is foliage bathed in sunlight on a flawless afternoon; it is impasto and dappled oil paint as miraculous as in a late Monet. The field beyond it recedes so tellingly that we can mentally walk it; yet it is as deeply satisfying for its gritty texture, achieved through Balthus's use of plaster dust in the paint, as for representation of the outdoors.

Balthus always lets you know that even if you are looking at nature, you are looking at an artist's evocation of it—in a win-and-lose struggle. Thus the flower stems have been overpainted—with the landscape, which should be behind them, in front of them as a flurry of paint strokes. This acknowledgment that we are looking at an illusion becomes Balthus's confession that he could only go so far: the artist's sympathetic expression of humility.

It must have heartened Balthus immeasurably at age fourteen to have *Mitsou* embraced by Pierre Bonnard. Now, almost half a century later, he was showing himself to be Bonnard's heir. *Bouquet of Roses* reflects Bonnard's ability to frame nature—a very organized and European form of it—within a domestic setting. It, too, offers bounteous light and reveals the courage to express plenitude. And Balthus has Bonnard's sort of true audacity, the sky, seemingly baked on, is an unblemished powdery blue that few would dare.

BALADINE USED TO WRITE TO Rilke about the flowers he had sent and which she would place on the windowsill. In Balthus's rendition of the subject, each of the roses is at a different stage, from a tight bud to the last full moment of blossoming. The gnarled cherry tree with its springtime flowers on their ancient support system poignantly evokes the wonder of beginnings in a short-lived season. *Bouquet of Roses* thus presents the passage of time, and the juxtaposition of youth with age.

The only adjective of praise I ever heard Balthus apply to his own work was "Mozartian." His use of the term came to mind as I stood in that sprawling Midwestern museum. The deep purples and violets play against the jade greens like high and low notes. The whole is a feat of organization, full of gorgeous passages that flow into one another. The gray plaster of the window ledge, the earthenware of the simple pitcher, and the flat wooden shutters are a totally different timbre from the seafoam and flesh and shimmering pink tones above—providing a Mozartian fullness and balance.

Seeing is rendered divine in this painting that Balthus created in his retreat in the Morvan. At Muzot, Rilke extolled orchards. Now Rilke's protégé guides your eye toward the fertile, practically moist darkness beneath the louvered shutter on the right, the crevices between the rose petals, the darkness inside the jug handle. The shadows of tree trunks are miraculous; so is the act of painting.

IN THE MIDST OF MY EUPHORIA in Indianapolis, I suddenly noticed that the painting was flanked by a Max Beckmann and a Wilfredo Lam. It was as inappropriate as the juxtaposition to Bacon and Botero at the Hirshhorn. It seems that no one knows what to do with Balthus. Unless there are some Derains or Giacomettis around, he certainly does not belong with most of his fellow figurative painters of his century.

This is in part because—like Balthus's objections to the uninhabited weekend houses that have come to clutter the hillside in Rossinière—*Bouquet of Roses* is a nostalgic cry to preserve fleeting beauty. How dare one mar the undulating field, or blemish the splendor of the earth, with the gratuitous marks of mankind? Nature should be left unsullied—plowed, cultivated, and harvested, yes; but not impaired or destroyed.

Contemplating the mauve horizon line of *Bouquet of Roses,* I was struck not just by Balthus's evocation of that passing world but also by his sheer courage. In a soft, quiet voice, with consummate refinement, he hazards what others would not dream of. Like Wang Fo in Marguerite Yourcenar's story, he could at one moment seem the most humble and ordinary man, at another be an insider at the palace—and all the while paint like a magician.

CHAPTER TWENTY-TWO

THE VILLA MEDICI

I

THE VILLA MEDICI IS AMONG the grandest, most prestigious residences ever inhabited by humankind. It offers luxurious seclusion within a vibrant metropolis. A large palace near the top of the Spanish Steps—at the base of the Pincian Hill—it seems a command post, from the north, for all of Rome. Overlooking the city in one direction, it opens onto spectacular private gardens in the other; the total complex is a walled oasis, its small park as quiet and verdant as its interior is opulent and grandiose. The compound is isolated by its walls and off limits to the general public: an inner sanctum.

The sixteenth-century building, the design of which Michelangelo is said to have advised on, has large public rooms as well as a magnificent private apartment for its director. Here the ambassador of French culture to Italy resides in the same bedroom and sitting rooms that during the Renaissance housed cardinals clad in velvet and ermine. These potentates in the almighty Church wielded inestimable power. To live in their former apartment and preside over the Villa Medici—with a beautiful young wife who might glide through the front door in her splendid kimono and descend the Spanish Steps as if they were her private domain—would be to realize the ultimate fantasy. For the former outcast to inhabit the capacious two-story-high cardinal's bedroom in one of the grandest palaces in Rome, overlooking gardens he would transform and a city where he enjoyed celebrity status, would be a colossal feat of Heathcliffian magnitude. Balthus managed to achieve it in spades.

Not that the cardinal's chambers, or the villa itself, were in good condition when Balthus arrived there in 1961. Or that he yet had his perfect fairy-tale wife. Like everything else in his life, these developments required careful, imaginative, diligent maneuvers. It would take skill and energy, and Balthus's innate sense of style, to give the French Academy in Rome the beauty and the theater he—and his employer there, André Malraux—wanted for it. Balthus succeeded not by groveling and conniving but through his serious and conscientious devotion to art, and the further refinement of his already exquisite taste. His goal, of course, was also won through his careful navigation in the world of power and his unfailing instinct for grandeur.

In the city of the popes, the beleaguered grandson of a Breslau cantor reached his social peak. To rule over the great villa—with his second (and, so people said, nobly born, descending from Samurai) wife loyally at his side— was to make Heathcliff's worldly ascent his reality. He could turn the stuff of novels into everyday life as readily as he could cloak deeply guarded truths with fiction.

AT THE TIME ANDRÉ MALRAUX selected Balthus for the job, the influential writer and statesman was Charles de Gaulle's Minister of State for Culture. Like de Gaulle, Malraux knew what ceremony and refined elegance were all about. But he had his work cut out for him in Rome. The French Academy at the Villa Medici was down at the heels in 1961.

The institution had deteriorated significantly in prestige as well as in physical condition since its days of glory in the previous century. Its building, however, came with impressive credentials on which Balthus might surely capitalize. The villa had been started in 1564 by the Cardinal Giovanni Ricci, and considerably enlarged and embellished in 1576 by Cardinal Ferdinando de' Medici, a counsellor to several popes and the Third Grand Duke of Tuscany. Under the guidance of their architects—Nanni de Baccio Bigio and Annibale Lippi for Cardinal Ricci, with the more flamboyant Bartolomeo Ammannati to give it its Medici splendor—it had developed into a structure with a massive and imposing core, two belvedere towers, a gallery for antiquities, garden loggias, a sprawling wing, noble entry portals, and an impressive collection of sculpture. Its facades were covered with friezes, bas-reliefs, the emblems of the noble Medicis, and statues in niches. It had a chapel, a library, and hidden rooms.

Over the centuries, the villa had enjoyed an astonishing history. Velázquez had stayed there, and included its loggias in his views of Rome that now hang in the Prado. Montaigne had frequented the gardens, and Caravaggio and Guido Reni had designed some of the sculpture there. This was all before the building became an outpost for France. As Jean Leymarie pointed out in the pages of a 1984 *House & Garden* article about Balthus's reign at the villa,

"Among the illustrious guests [were] popes, sovereigns, princes and dignitaries, scholars and poets, artists and musicians."[1]

Meanwhile, in 1666, the Academy of France had decided it needed a place where its students could study in Rome; with Bernini the international arbiter of taste, the Italian style had become all the rage at Versailles. Louis XIV's minister Jean-Baptiste Colbert initially acquired a building in central Rome.

The rulers of Italy honored art as a high function of the state, and treated the artists at the academy as official ambassadors. The Romans made a number of the artists at the academy nobility and awarded them titles. In 1725 the academy installed itself in the Mancini Palace, constructed by Mazarin's nephew the Duc de Nevers, and soon artists like Boucher, Fragonard, Hubert-Robert, Houdon, and Coustou were making themselves at home.

All this changed, however, with the French Revolution. The Italian authorities, indignant over the execution of Louis XVI and the spirit of atheism that seemed to take over the Mancini Palace, expelled some of the French artists. In France there was a move to retaliate, and to abolish academies. This rebellion was led in part by the painter Jacques-Louis David—ironically, one of Balthus's heroes in his Artaud days. For a while France sent forth no ambassadors.

Then, in 1799, under Napoleon, the French Academy in Rome was reinstated. The Royal Academy was now replaced by the Académie des Beaux-Arts, and was made to include music as well as sculpture, painting, and architecture. In 1801, in this expanded role, it acquired the Villa Medici. By 1803 enough work had been done there so that the academy could move into the building.

At the start of the nineteenth century, the French Academy in Rome was backed by the full force of the state, yet controversy dominated its ranks. The disputes were much the same as those that would surface when Balthus was appointed. Horace Vernet, the painter who was the academy's first director at the new location on the Pincian Hill, participated in almost as many battles as he painted. The main issue was his insistence that he—and the other visiting artists in Rome—were better able to judge what was right for the academy than were the authorities responsible for it in Paris. Some people felt that the academy should represent French tradition as it had prevailed since the era of Louis XIV, while others thought an art institution needed to embody more radical values. Meanwhile, artistic endeavors at the villa were compromised by other preoccupations; in 1830 Vernet proposed to the authorities in Paris that he be replaced by an obstetrician, given the number of babies being born at the institution.

The reputation of the French Academy soared throughout Europe, however, when Ingres was its director between 1835 and 1842. The academy thrived as a place where recipients of the Prix de Rome could live and pursue their work under idyllic conditions.

Even when the situation there became arduous, the academy held strong. A cholera epidemic ravaged Rome in the course of Ingres's directorship, and the fearful pensioners wanted to return to France for safety. While not forbidding them to do so, Ingres successfully persuaded them to remain right where they were and accept his prescription that, as preventive treatment against the terrible illness, they read Plutarch.

After Ingres's tenure, however, the academy grew stodgy. It turned its back on Delacroix and Courbet, and then on Cézanne and Manet. It recognized Impressionism only to challenge it. It shunned modernism, and stressed formalism when Cubism was the rage in Paris. When the architect Charles Garnier went from Rome to Paris to study an industrial city, he was reprimanded. By the time André Malraux asked Balthus to get involved, most intellectually sophisticated people disparaged this institution that had once been so prestigious. They felt that the competition in Rome destroyed the spirit of young artists and made them conform to flawed and dated artistic standards. By the early 1960s, winners of the Prix de Rome, rather than flaunt their titles, concealed them.

TO MALRAUX, THE SOLUTION to these problems was Balthus. He had met the artist on December 21, 1946, at dinner at Albert Skira's house in Geneva. The two talked about art all evening long, and a friendship began. They had seen more of one another when Balthus was still living in Paris with his studio at the Cour de Rohan, and continued to meet when Balthus visited the capital from Chassy.

Malraux was yet another character in the Balthusian pantheon who bore some resemblance to the painter—without being in the same league of kinship as Artaud or Barrault. Janet Flanner described the Minister of Culture as "nerve-wracked, intense, slender, elegant, and slightly bent, as if from too much reading. His hair is dark and his eyes are deep green; he has an impressive head and, with its dramatic lines and shadows, the cold, impassioned face of a Renaissance *condottiere*."[2] The two men also had in common a professed attitude toward personal publicity. "Malraux himself is hermetic where his private life is concerned. The confusing legends about him have swelled like balloons to fill in his silence. He assumes the position that his private life is actually his and actually private—a large, exclusive territory. It is taken for granted in Paris press circles that if a question of a biographical nature is inadvertently asked in an interview, Malraux will reply by saying *'Vie privée,'* and nothing more."[3] But, like Balthus, he took no little delight in cultivating his own image. "In France, Malraux is regarded along with Lord Byron . . . as one of the flashing company of great modern literary adventurers who make tours of personal destiny . . . and wrote parts of their own legends."[4] And, equally in tandem with Balthus, Malraux had developed a strategy to invalidate critique unfavorable to him and slightly denigrate those who question any aspect of his chosen myth: "Malraux says mordantly, 'There are no heroes without auditors. Adventurers are assumed to be impostors. Most of the letters I receive from strangers are slightly inquisitorial in tone.' "[5]

Malraux and Balthus often spent quiet hours together in the Louvre. Accompanied only by Marie-Pierre Colle, they made these visits either before it opened in the morning or on the day when the museum was closed to the public. Impatient though it made their fourteen-year-old companion, the two men would often linger for as long as an hour in front of a single work.

Only a few years before Malraux appointed him, Balthus was still an indigent artist struggling to put food on the table. But Malraux knew that in summoning his friend to the post of director, the controversial painter would both elevate the artistic tenor of the academy and restore its stature. The minister was certain that, with his eye for quality and passion for creativity, Balthus would be able to restore to the Villa Medici the life and spirit that had once reigned there but was now nearly extinct.

Other voices in 1961, however, expressed great indignation at what they perceived as Malraux's arbitrary selection of an artist as unpopular in some circles as he was beloved in others. The Parisian news magazine *L'Express* referred to Malraux's appointment of Balthus as "a siege." It mocked the connection between the two men, depicting Balthus and Malraux as two eccentrics who were old friends. The polemical, eloquent, and persuasive Malraux had always fascinated the taciturn painter, the paper sniped.[6] The tongue-in-cheek account implied that Malraux and Balthus were rarified elitists at a complete remove from mainstream French culture. Four years prior to appointing him, Malraux had told Balthus, in the course of lunch in Paris, that when General de Gaulle made him minister at some future date, Le Grand Charles wanted the country to have more men in power "like you." To this, the news magazine reported, Balthus had evasively replied, "Oh well, like me . . . you know . . . ." Readers learned that Balthus then returned to his reclusive existence in his sad and beautiful château, where he continued to paint priceless paintings that were available only to a handful of exclusive collectors.

The readers of *L'Express* were treated to the Balthus myth in all its glory— although there was scarcely a word of truth in it. This was the moment when the artist became "the illegitimate son of Rainer Maria Rilke and of a Polish countess, and great-nephew of Lord Byron." The magazine's account of a telephone call that came after de Gaulle became president and actually appointed Malraux his minister as he had previously discussed may or may not have been more accurate. Malraux asked Balthus if the artist remembered their last conversation, to which Balthus replied, "Hmm!. . . . yes . . . of course. . . ." When Malraux then told Balthus that the composer Jacques Ibert, director of the Villa Medici since 1937, was leaving and that Balthus was going to succeed him, Balthus replied that he had never won a Prix de Rome, had never followed the direction of the Ecole des Beaux-Arts, and was not even a member of the Institut de France. As Malraux insisted and Balthus reflected, the artist was ultimately persuaded when it was pointed out that at the Villa Medici he would have a real studio of a type he had never had before; "that was his life-long dream."

In Rossinière, Balthus reiterated this claim to me: that his work space at the Villa Medici was his first true studio. It makes a charming story—that what attracted him to Rome was not his longing for power and grandeur but, rather, the wish of a humble, deprived artist to have a decent place to paint. Yet it does not add up: the Cour de Rohan had also been a real studio, and if Balthus had wanted different light or other windows in his work space in Chassy, he would not have had to accept a position as director of the Villa Medici to find them.

WHEN MALRAUX APPOINTED BALTHUS director of the French Academy in Italy, the painter's primary obligation was ostensibly to oversee the activities of some twenty-two winners of the Prix de Rome during their two-year stints. Under idyllic conditions, the pensioners were free to pursue further work on their painting, sculpture, music, or writing. Malraux also asked Balthus to be an ambassador of French culture in Rome—not just of painting, sculpture, graphics, and music, as one would expect at the academy, but also of literature, theater, cinema, science, and philosophy. The minister wanted conferences and receptions; he also intended for Balthus to restore the building and its gardens. Fired up by all the possibilities, Balthus accepted.

But the institute that ruled the Villa Medici did not buy the idea. They pointed out that when Ibert had been appointed in 1937, it was only after the minister of culture had consulted the academy. The reason Malraux's appointment of Balthus caused an uproar was in part because, although Ibert's ill health made it clear that he needed to be replaced, there was some question as to who was in charge of the appointment. L'Académie des Beaux-Arts—one of the five academies that constituted the Institut de France—believed that it should fill the post; Malraux, the minister of culture, felt the decision was his to make.

The question of who should have authority in Rome had long been a subject of controversy in Paris. In 1863 Prosper Mérimée and Viollet-le-Duc had convinced Napoleon III that the teaching at the Villa Medici had become sterile, so the emperor rescinded the privilege formerly held by the Académie des Beaux-Arts whereby that institution could designate the winners of the Prix de Rome and appoint the director of the villa. Shortly thereafter, however, the Republic paradoxically increased the academy's power to confer this directorship. The question of who really held the reins had never been resolved. In 1959 a law had been passed stipulating that the director of the Villa Medici would be chosen from a list of three names proposed by the institute. But by the time Malraux tapped Balthus, the institute had come up with only one name: the painter Yves Brayer, one of its members. Brayer would have kept the Villa Medici pretty much as it had become—a place where artists like Rouault or Matisse had no role, where competent, unimaginative academicians would be turned out.

The prospect seemed dreadful to many people, but with impeccable form Balthus calmly let out the word that he considered it legally correct. And so this time, according to *L'Express*, it was he who telephoned Malraux. Having gone to Paris to iron out the details of the new post, he now informed his would-be employer that he was leaving the capital immediately. The epitome of delighted restraint, Balthus announced, with no suggestion of hardship, that he would return to the seclusion of Chassy and that the job was Brayer's.

FOLLOWING THIS FAUX DEBACLE, of course, Malraux confirmed Balthus's appointment and cleared the way. Balthus then granted one of his rare newspaper interviews. Heathcliff might become lord of the manor, but he did not have to stop being surly or give up his fun.

The correspondent for the Lausanne-based *Gazette Littéraire* described the circumstances of this exclusive interview. When Balthus had been tracked down in Paris the day after the announcement of his nomination as director of the Villa Medici, he escaped via hidden staircases each time a journalist approached. It was only because of Balthus's esteem for Switzerland and for this particular publication that he had granted this sole interview to a foreign paper. In exchange for the privilege, *La Gazette* did as it was told. Probably thanks to a helping hand from the artist, the paper got its background information wrong. The fifty-three-year-old Balthus was presented as being fifty. Bonnard and Matisse, slight acquaintances of the Klossowskis, were now elevated to the status of friends of his parents. The artist issued a statement on his Swiss connection in which he referred to having lived in Fribourg during the war but completely left out the longer period in Geneva during the years of his parents' separation and the family's insolvency. He also made the odd remark: "To be quite frank, there are some de Watteville members of my family." Indeed there were—his long-estranged wife, their sons, his in-laws—yet this vague way of phrasing it to the journalist from Lausanne suggested that the aristocratic family might have been his own ancestors, not just relatives through marriage.

His silence with the press and his disappearances had been a result, Balthus told the writer from Lausanne, of his wish not to aggravate the quarrel surrounding his appointment and complicate the task ahead. He considered himself above the fray: "I am not the man of a party, or of a clan. I am free."[7] Articles written with the best intentions could create problems, the artist warned. He feared favorable commentary as much as negative press—because even praise seemed to imply the existence of an opposing point of view. Balthus sounded like a mix of philosopher and savvy press agent.

Balthus told the journalist from Lausanne that six years earlier he had run into André Malraux, who had asked him if he would help out if de Gaulle ever regained power. Balthus had spontaneously answered Malraux with a yes, but had not really known what he was saying. Now, Balthus lamented, he was in the situation he was in simply because, as a man of honor, he could not possibly go back on his word. Balthus laid it on thick. He declared himself to be someone who was ready to uproot himself entirely rather than be guilty of having lied.

Malraux liked Balthus's paintings, and Balthus liked Malraux's books, the artist explained. They had once taken "a very Stendhalian walk through the columns of the Palais-Royal, during which we found we thought the same on many important issues." He was "honor-bound" to such a soul mate. Balthus presented himself as an unassuming servant of the state who now must fulfill the goals for the Villa Medici established by Malraux and by Gaëton Picon, the director of arts and letters.

Balthus declared that the first person he would invite to Rome would be "Hergé, Tintin's father." Then—in that humble, resigned tone I knew all too well—he offered, "They tell me I can be useful there, just as I am, so I'm going." His interlocutor was appropriately affected:

> The answer is laconic. The rest vanishes into the smoke of the cigarette Balthus lights. I observe his face: that of a man of refinement, lean as his young man's body, with calm, pale eyes and an aquiline nose slender as an antenna. The very image of a freedom that knows itself, and

values itself. The forehead under the gray clumps of hair suggests culture, the thin-lipped mouth wit and humor.[8]

II

BALTHUS MIGHT CLAIM TINTIN as the essence of French culture, but Malraux had picked the right candidate to restore the shabby and decrepit Villa Medici and raise it to unprecedented heights. He had the right combination of diplomacy and imperiousness. The American journalist Milton Gendel provided this firsthand account in 1962, the year following Balthus's takeover:

> Like his painting, Balthus, at fifty, has changed very little in his main features over the decades. He is handsome, youthful, tall, lean, well-constructed, polished, refined, elegant, measured, elusive, allusive, warm and affable.[9]

His aesthetics were as suitable as his manners. Balthus's first primary task at the Villa Medici was to renovate the building. He made it a Balthus. Its interior design acquired the subtle luminosity, as well as the precision and orderliness, that for three decades he had been developing in his art.

The villa became like a stage set: the ultimate palace, not so much the real thing as a series of artificial backdrops, almost parodically refined and mannered, in which every detail suggested an ancient noble past.

When I visited the Roman complex long after Balthus had left, I had been warned by him and Setsuko that a lot of the qualities they had installed there had been destroyed in the 1980s. Now there were—the Klossowskis uttered the word as if it were the deepest, darkest perversion—"televisions" all over the place. Clearly it had become more like any other dormitory than an ancient palace. Nonetheless, to my eyes Balthus was still very much in evidence. The sense of pose and contrivance that pervaded the interior design made the Villa Medici of a piece with its director of the sixties and seventies, and with the art he produced after his arrival there. In 1961 Balthus's canvases began to acquire the same muted patina he was applying to the villa's walls—and an elegance bordering on decadence. This premeditated look of antiquity, the deliberate courtliness, the mannerist formality were evident in the building he redesigned at the same time he was redesigning his art and himself.

In renovating the historic structure, Balthus kept the essential layout of the interior but changed most everything else. First he removed the false ceiling and relocated many of the doorways, thereby altering the flow of space and creating a different atmosphere. He added necessities, like more toilets. Then, working with old Italian artisans, he redid the walls of most of the villa's rooms. Balthus developed a system whereby they removed the whitewash and oil paint that had been applied during the course of the preceding two centuries. Once these skillful workers had achieved the texture and hue necessary for the first stage of the process and Balthus had approved it, they would complete the work of simulating the look of old frescoes. To get the desired matteness and mottling without sacrificing the vibrancy of color, they utilized a technique Balthus had devised of brushing on multiple layers of paint and then rubbing them down. This culminated in a process of polishing the last coat of paint with sandpaper and broken bottle shards. The resultant colors are rich but chalky. When it was all done, one had the impression that it had always been as it now looked.

Trompe-l'oeil effects predominated. Some of the rooms were painted to achieve the illusion of elaborate, waist-high wainscoting with raised molding and recessed paneling. The floor molding was marbleized. At the top of the two-story grand salon, there was a false window—like a Renaissance theater backdrop of blind windows similar to those in *The Street*. As in that canvas painted thirty years earlier, the solid blank panels suggest more about what you cannot see than what you can. The results of this carefully plotted visual chicanery are charming yet theatrical.

Balthus repaved the floors as well. He used terra-cotta tiles fashioned as they had been in the sixteenth century, and coordinated their tones with the ochers, greens, and lilacs he had designated for the walls. He also had the ceiling beams and doors stripped to their natural wood tones. In some cases, he had his artisans decorate doors with false graining—the type you know is false, where the impression of design is more important than that of nature. And he replaced the door hardware with weighty and impressive hinges.

Balthus also managed to uncover, beneath multiple layers of paint, some biblical frescoes bearing the arms of Cardinal Ricci. The splendor of the sixteenth century was reborn much as the villa's tenacious director was.

To furnish the rooms of the renovated Villa Medici, Balthus took off for the countryside and searched out treasures from antique dealers whose prices were within reach. Here he used his connoisseur's eye to further his goals as a ceremonialist. He found a range of suitable objects within the academy's rather limited budget.

Balthus's goal was to have a country-house mix of unmatched furniture and accoutrements that ranged from formal to rustic. Individual objects were

Salon-library of the director's apartment at the Villa Medici
after Balthus's redecoration, as it appeared in *House & Garden*

quite impressive, but the general impression was of homey irregularity. There was no clutter, however. Balthus placed the chairs and tables sparely and precisely so as to invoke a feeling of ceremony and openness. The rather theatrical arrangement—the rooms became an artificial setting more than spaces to be lived in—provided a visual rhythm as well as a look of historical portent.

There was a seventeenth-century waxed wood Florentine desk, some eighteenth-century Genoese painted yellow side chairs upholstered in brown leather, rococo armchairs, dining room chairs from Lucca polychromed with floral designs, other upholstered seating covered in velvet, ornate side tables, and imposing cupboards. Whenever possible, Balthus had selected pieces on which the antique surfaces and coverings were original. And when something original was unavailable, he ordered the perfect copy. The Sardinian rugs were based on ancient designs. The wrought-iron lamps—tall, graceful, with wonderful S-shaped stands and supports—were made by a blacksmith. Although new and carefully wired, they looked like ancient candelabra from a cathedral apse; at the same time, they harmonized with the busts by Giacometti that would stand near them. Lamps of the same style provide most of the lighting today inside the Grand Chalet and contribute significantly to both its visual charm and the pervading sense of history.

In the vast rooms that Balthus made so regal in his renovated villa, the only sound might be the echo reverberating off the plaster walls of one's own steps on the terra-cotta floors. The dramatic emptiness of a high-ceilinged chamber was punctuated by little more than the deep note of a massive armoire against one wall and the staccato of a gilded side chair on another. Truly this was a royal abode.

THE YEAR AFTER HE ARRIVED at the Villa Medici, the fifty-four-year-old Balthus went to Japan, at Malraux's request, to organize a major exhibition of Japanese folk art to be held in Paris. The journey led to Balthus's winning a far greater trophy even than the iron teapots and wooden ware he was eyeing for the French public. It was on this occasion that he met Setsuko Ideta. Like his and Antoinette's older son, she was twenty years old.

The day following the opening of Balthus's Lausanne exhibition, in June 1993, by sheer happenstance I found myself, during a lunch party at Le Grand Chalet, next to the wife of the man who had been the French chargé d'affaires responsible for Balthus during that journey to Asia. Perhaps our gossip about our illustrious host was the norm at all large social events chez Balthus, but it still took me by surprise.

Portrait of Setsuko, 1962, crayon, 28 x 26 cm

I had on many quieter occasions talked with Balthus and Setsuko about their initial meeting, and I had also read their official versions of the event in several interviews. But what I learned over our barbecued chicken and assorted salads—a surprisingly American menu in a garden overlooking the Alps—put a very different slant on things.

My luncheon partner gave me her husband's version of Balthus's first visit to the Orient in reality—as opposed to those journeys he had been taking in his imagination since his childhood. Upon his arrival at the airport in Tokyo, Balthus immediately informed his guide "that one of the goals of his journey was to acquire a young Japanese wife to take back to Rome."

As the chargé's wife quoted Balthus's conversation with her husband, she scanned the festive lunch party of about fifty people. This woman who had devoted much of her life to the diplomatic corps grinned approvingly at Setsuko, who presided over the buffet table. She then focused in the direction of Balthus as he held forth to elegant young women and bright young business types from Geneva who surrounded him. This event, thirty-one years after Balthus had initiated that quest for a wife in Japan, seemed to be evidence of the success of the scheme. The chargé had served his country well by leading the ambassador of French culture not just to any young Japanese wife but to the ideal one.

As was so often the case, Balthus got precisely what he wanted. Setsuko was the embodiment of much that he cherished: female beauty, youthful vitality, piercing intelligence, and the charms and diffidence of the Orient.

At the time of Balthus's trip, Setsuko was in her first year at a Jesuit university. She knew Western culture unusually well. In her youth, she had taken classical ballet with an instructor trained in Moscow. Now she was studying French and participating actively in the university's English theater club. Like Balthus, she was passionate about Russian, French, and English novels. A friend who was working for the cultural department of the newspaper *Asahi* approached her to see if she would like to join Balthus's group to serve as an interpreter on their visits to rarely seen temples near Kyoto, where they were selecting art for Malraux's exhibition.

Presumably that invitation was part of the French chargé's initiative. He had found the right candidate, for the cosmopolitan Setsuko was steeped in her Japanese heritage as well as that of other cultures. Setsuko came from the Samurai family of Kyushu, originally from Kyoto, and was well versed in Oriental literature and ceremony. And like Balthus, Setsuko was more than the product of her culture and education. She was poised and confident, and extremely alert. She had tremendous natural intelligence, as well as a wit and sense of mischief that matched Balthus's. I have found Setsuko to be warm and kind, but clearly she was, from the start, someone who would have no trouble playing the Count de Rola's games. She, too, could choose her own role in the world.

I write this, of course, in the context of having seen the Countess de Rola day in and day out some thirty years after she arrived as a young student at the Villa Medici. In my time with her, I witnessed her managing her complex household competently, organizing visitors' appointments, and quietly but effectively steering her notoriously imperious but now aged husband in the directions she thought would be good for him (studio time, rest periods, conversations with me: always interspersed with the fixed schedule of four substantial meals planned to strengthen him without irritating his fragile stomach). I also had ample time to chat with her informally—about art, novels, people, music, and a full gamut of subjects—and always found her to be knowledgeable and extremely quick on the uptake. We were, after all, two members of the same generation in the household of someone almost old enough to be our grandparent—even if she happened to be married to him—

and I felt that she enjoyed having someone else there who did not have to deal with infirmity and could hear and walk easily. When relaxed, Setsuko was funny, opinionated, and full of pleasure. On the other hand, when she was navigating in the upper social strata, she suddenly seemed to go onstage—and not very well. On the phone with a millionaire collector from Gstaad, her voice became like that of a schoolgirl on the stage playing the part of a socialite, her enthusiasm and giggles too forced, her intensity betraying a certain discomfort.

That feeling of Setsuko swimming in unfamiliar seas was, I have been told, all too apparent during one memorable moment when she visited New York in 1995. The countess and some friends were dining at the fashionable restaurant Le Cirque. Shortly after they were seated, the Queen of Spain arrived with an entourage and was given a table near the entrance. Setsuko told her friends, "I must go say hello to the queen." The others had downplayed the royal arrival, and suggested to Setsuko that she should just continue to enjoy her dinner. "No, I *must* go say hello," Setsuko insisted, explaining that Balthus was soon to have an exhibition in Madrid, the queen knew about it, and so on. Finally someone at the table had to explain to her that you never approach royalty, but wait for them to greet you. They tried not to make the countess feel chided, but deemed it essential that she understand the protocol.

In spite of their counsel, they were unable to stop Setsuko on the way out of the restaurant. She charged toward the queen's table, warmly proffering greetings. The Queen of Spain, of course, was friendly and cordial, giving Balthus's wife full respect. But, as when Balthus flaunted his title, close friends felt a tinge of embarrassment.

THE LANGUAGE IN WHICH BALTHUS and Setsuko got to know one another was English. This was what she spoke for Balthus's group as they toured the temples of Kyoto. But in my presence they mainly spoke French—except when they used Japanese, which they spoke whenever they didn't want me to understand what they were saying.

In their first encounters, however, they mainly argued. Setsuko and Balthus told me that they quarreled almost as soon as they met—about education. When Balthus declared to the young woman that he did not believe in schools, she was scandalized. Yet—as she later told David Bowie—she "fell in love with that crazy man immediately."[10] Even if they disagreed and neither was using his or her native tongue, they seemed made for each other. From July to September—the duration of Balthus's trip—they were together constantly.

Balthus and Setsuko's reminiscences to me about that summer were colored by the keen pleasure that underlies every detail of incipient romance. They both roared when recalling an evening when Balthus got drunk on sake and had to be carried down a long corridor—especially awkward for his porters, he told me, because he was taller than most Japanese men. It was so cold in northern Japan that they had to continue walking in a snowstorm just to keep warm. "It was all like a nightmare," Setsuko said—"we couldn't believe it was happening"—but the memory seemed enchanting. They slept in their overcoats between days of looking at iron teapots and handwoven shoes.

Laughing their way through these memories, they described a visit to a Japanese collector who kept boasting about his Foujitas. They had to see him as part of their quest for popular art. As Setsuko was politely voicing admiration to the collector for his Foujitas, Balthus stood there telling Setsuko in English that he couldn't stand them.

In little time, Balthus asked Setsuko to join him in Rome. At first she demurred. Setsuko told me she knew that Balthus was still married and had a mistress as well. But the third time he asked her, she thought, "This is the man of my life. I didn't know him well, and I didn't know his work, but I felt this." She did not return with him immediately. But later that year, she accepted his invitation to the opening at the Japanese Culture House of a show of Tesehiragaa, the master of flower arrangement. And so she went to Italy.

WHEN SETSUKO ARRIVED at the Villa Medici that fall, Frédérique, who had accompanied Balthus from Chassy, was also on the scene. For a while she and her Japanese replacement overlapped. And Balthus was, indeed, still technically married to Antoinette.

The ability to sustain multiple love relationships at the same time was neither new nor problematic for Balthus. He had long realized that he had the charm and power to carry it off. Moreover, it conformed to the Rilkean model. Rilke had courted Paula Modersohn-Becker at the same time that he was preparing to marry Clara Westhoff—while managing to keep Lou Andreas-Salomé still on the line. The poet had been a consistently unfaithful husband and had enjoyed various other liaisons during his years with Baladine Klossowska.

An artistic genius, after all, was entitled to follow his own rules. But it was a juggling act. Whatever the reactions of the principals, the arrangement with Setsuko and Frédérique—with occasional guest appearances by Antoinette—created consternation among some observers.

Antoinette by now was set up in the large house in Rolle where she was to remain for the rest of her life. At that point she was already living with "Monsieur Matossiani"—as even her sons called the man who became her long-term companion. But she still did periodically visit her husband in Rome.

Frédérique, however, was initially "in charge of everything" at the Villa Medici—according to a friend of Balthus's who was there at the time. Having lived with Balthus for quite a few years, Frédérique had come up with her own means of coping. "Contemptuous of his moods and whims," she was a powerful, coercive presence. Now she had to assume a different role.

There was a dinner one night at the villa at which Setsuko, Frédérique, and Antoinette were all present, along with a few pensioners and outside visitors. Some of the other guests simply sat there gaping, and the three women were closely observed. Antoinette was the most relaxed, holding forth with aristocratic ease. Setsuko—relatively young, and very new to the scene—was quiet. Frédérique, the least educated and sophisticated of the trio, was the quietest of all. But in subsequent weeks her ire began to surface. "Many resented Setsuko as she worked her way in—especially when she began to paint pseudo-Balthuses. And Frédérique became very jealous, making great scenes. She was given an atelier . . . but eventually she had to leave."[11] Just as Léna Leclerq had ceded her position to Frédérique, Balthus's stepniece, however reluctantly, stepped aside with Setsuko's ascendancy. "Balthus gave her the château at Chassy as a compensation present."[12] She returned there, and has remained at Chassy ever since.

At the Villa Medici, Balthus and Setsuko occupied the vast and history-laden "chambres de cardinal." This private enclave consisted mainly of a sitting room flanked by two bedrooms. The grandeur was fit for royalty. Under ornate coffered ceilings, frescoed and gilded, each had a room with an imposing, thronelike bed surrounded on all four sides by draperies. From these beds the gaunt director and his stunning young girlfriend looked through large windows at the quiet gardens. The Count de Rola and his future countess appeared not to be bothered by the lack of coziness, and met the challenge with all the majesty and aplomb it required.

BALTHUS'S INITIAL RENOVATION of the Villa Medici drew general approval, but a couple of years after he and Setsuko settled in, he made some changes that sparked considerable controversy. In 1964 Balthus set about improving the library facilities. Few people argued when the director designed stacks for book storage and hired a full-time librarian, but then Balthus moved a number of plaster casts from the space he was taking over for the library. After letting it be known that he neither liked nor cared about these fragile objects, he exiled them to the basement. Distressed observers cried out that the move virtually destroyed the casts.

In 1973 Balthus offended even more sensibilities when he began the restoration of the villa's gardens. These grounds were dominated by large flowering bushes and palms that were vestiges of nineteenth-century horticultural taste. Balthus desired a look that was far more formal and controlled.

The artist studied engravings that depicted these same gardens at various stages of their history, and decided that he wanted them to be as close as possible to the way they had been when they were laid out at the start of the sixteenth century. He moved the palms, threw out the overgrown bushes, and uprooted magnolia trees that had flowered behind the villa for over two centuries. Balthus transformed the dense profusion into a sequence of empty squares of neatly mown grass—bordered only by low, well-pruned hedges.

Balthus then had some of the pensioners at the villa make synthetic resin copies of statues formerly owned by the Medicis, the originals of which were in the Boboli Gardens near the Palazzo Pitti in Florence. He placed the copies with tremendous precision in the interior of the garden loggia.

It was a very Balthusian move: emphasizing the noble past by reproducing it artificially. And the artist did not stop with the statues in the loggia. Ferdinando de' Medici had been an ardent collector of the Hellenistic antique sculptures known as Niobides. Balthus had copies made from the originals of these in the Uffizi. He carefully installed these reproduction Niobides in a vast rectangle, walled by hedges, in a distant corner of the Villa Medici's gardens.

As of this writing, these statues are still in that garden precisely where Balthus positioned them. But one has to walk some distance behind the villa to find the grassy rectangle that houses them. Even once one has located it, the small lawn is practically inaccessible: framed by a six-foot-high hedge in which there is only one narrow opening at the corner where one least expects to find it. When the viewer has wended his or her way into that isolated garden with its invisible entrance, the statues, clustered theatrically under a tree, look like forbidden fruit. In that location, they resemble a vision in a dream: a treasure that is virtually hidden. With their highly contrived arrangement, they are juxtaposed like a theatrical pageant.

Balthus told a number of people that the originals of these Niobides now in the Uffizi had been at the Villa Medici in the sixteenth century. The implication was that all that he was doing in the garden, therefore, was trying his humble best to restore a glory that rightly belonged there. A number of listeners accepted his information at face value. But others were not so sure.

Copies of the Niobides as arranged by Balthus in the garden of the Villa Medici,
as photographed for *House & Garden*

There is, in fact, no historical record indicating that the Niobides had ever been at the Villa Medici. The notion that they had been here on the Pincian Hill is almost certainly a fabrication. Balthus was treating the villa's past like his own—by inventing it. To "reconstruct" what had never actually been in the gardens was like "restoring" a title that had, in truth, never stood before a name.

III

THE MERE TITLE OF "COUNT" was no longer enough for Balthus once he was director of the Villa Medici. Ensconced on the Pincian Hill, he now made a valiant attempt to convince people of his direct descent from the last king of Poland. In his first few years at the Villa Medici, he let it be known that one of his ancestors was Stanisław August Poniatowski. The last gasp of the ancient régime, Poniatowski had been King Stanisław II from 1764 until his abdication in 1795 following an insurrection that brought an end to all royal authority in Poland.

Stanisław II was a splendid choice as a forebear. He was esteemed for having collected art and invited numerous artists to his court, and for having reconstructed the royal castle in Warsaw and built the elegant palace of Łazienki. Stanisław II was also an accomplished and progressive administrator—a perfect model for the director of the Villa Medici in his diligence and intellect as well as in his lineage and imperial ways. He was known as a reformer who modernized the state government and improved the parliamentary system while at the same time strengthening the royal power.

But then, in 1967, a friend of Balthus's married a member of the Poniatowski family. The jig was up. The friend noticed that Balthus suddenly grew very cool toward him, and did not answer his phone calls. This was a great surprise since the friend, who has asked to remain unnamed, was someone who had known Balthus for as long as he could remember.

The friend, however, quickly grasped what the problem was. For one thing, he was married to a genuine Poniatowski, of whose lineage Balthus probably was unbearably jealous. Worse still, the man and his wife knew enough to refute Balthus's latest claims, and so the artist had to stay clear of them.

This man's attitude exemplified that of Balthus's most forgiving friends. Since he loved and admired the artist in spite of what the dealer regarded as "Balthus's strange weakness," he did not take offense. He considered Balthus a brilliant and wonderful person who suffered from a sort of illness that in its worst guises—when it led the artist to arrogance or anti-Semitism—was disgusting and contemptible, but that should be treated as an addiction and peculiarity out of control.

Like other Balthus loyalists, the friend learned to turn the other cheek. He was resentful on the two occasions when he sent the artist large shipments of paintings—in one case by Baladine Klossowska, in another by Erich—that he owned because of the connection of their families but for which Balthus never so much as said thank you. He understood, however, what it was in Balthus that sometimes made common courtesy beneath him. The friend recognized that the breach in manners derived from Balthus's inability to cope with the memory of Baladine and Erich being in such desperate straits that someone else had to store their paintings for them since they did not have their own roof over their heads.

In any case, the friend ultimately concluded that there was no winning with Balthus. A year or so after the man married a woman with the last name of Poniatowski, the woman's brother, who was the interior minister of France, asked him for advice about this "artist called Balthus." The problem, explained the new brother-in-law, was that he was regularly receiving letters from someone seeking to have his name put into the family records; he realized that this "Count Balthazar Klossowski de Rola" was the same person as the Balthus whom the man knew. The man found himself standing up for the poseur, assuring his relative that Balthus was a wonderful individual and fine painter in spite of his ridiculous persistence about this bogus claim. So the scion of the Poniatowskis—whose position in the French government made the idea of a connection to him that much more appealing to Balthus—wrote Balthus back saying that it would in fact be a tremendous honor if they could have him as a family member, because he was such a great artist, but unfortunately there was no blood-line basis for the claim.

Not that this stopped Balthus. In spite of the minister's letter, he has continued to greet the woman whose maiden name was Poniatowski with an enthusiastic "Ma chère cousine" as he embraces her, while doing "Mon cousin" with her husband—disregarding their fatuous grins and palpable discomfort. The couple has always found this laughable, but have been determined not to humiliate their friend. They feel that the claim is so important to him that to comment on it would be like pointing out someone's alcoholism while watching him take a drink.

WITH ME, BALTHUS TOOK a different slant on the Poniatowski theme. He never claimed direct lineage from the Polish king, but shortly after I asked him about his Jewish relatives—not yet aware that I was entering into such treacherous territory, nor recognizing his answer as a lie—he mentioned to me, in his general ruminations on the subject, that "just by the way, for a while it had been the fashion even to claim that the last king of Poland, Poniatowski, was part Jewish." The notion of such a rumor is probably yet another of Balthus's inventions; I know of no case in which the issue was raised about the king; nor does Balthus's friend married to a Poniatowski. But it seemed to console Balthus to reflect that the poor king—whom he sometimes fancied as his relative—had also suffered the same ridiculous plight as he.

Balthus once complained rather bitterly to the woman who was a Poniatowski that he "hated" her husband—because when her husband would phone him he would ask for "Balthus" rather than for the Comte de Rola. The artist was counting on the woman's understanding about the matter; he said that he expected her to agree on how important it was to maintain the stature of "the house." She did not, however, give him the satisfaction of an affirmative answer. Yet like her husband, she "did not want to bring Balthus down too much." For even though she found his pretensions laughable and his anti-

Semitism appalling, she, too, recognized his need to live in his myths. Like many of us, the woman and her husband have only one main question—which is what Setsuko really thinks.

In 1992 this same old friend of Balthus's was approached by representatives of the Polish government in Switzerland in the hope that he could be a conduit for them to Balthus. In Poland there were great celebrations in honor of the centennial of the birthday of the novelist Bruno Schulz, and the authorities said that their dream was to have similar festivities and an exhibition of Balthus—claimed by the Poles as their greatest twentieth-century artist—in Warsaw.

One of the people pushing for this show was extremely proud because she had located a cousin of Balthus's. Documents had been found in the town of Pinsk. Balthus would be so proud; his grandfather had been a revered *hasam*—a cantor—there. The Polish ambassador to Switzerland wanted to visit Balthus and present him with a gift of copies of the historic papers showing this. Balthus's old friend was roaring as he told me the story. As a member of a Polish family, he declared this to be the funniest Polish joke he had ever heard. Could I imagine how Balthus would have reacted? The man did not mince words when telling the ambassador to forget the whole thing.

IT IS HARD TO KNOW how many people at the Villa Medici believed Balthus in his claims of direct descent from royalty. But many witnessed him exercising a truly despotic will. In Rome the artist reached a new peak not just of grandiosity but also of imperiousness.

Pierre Leyris told me—in a voice of resignation more than anger—that Balthus in those years was "practically pathological" and "able to be very cruel to people." Leyris said that Balthus closed the villa's door on his own brother at a time when Pierre Klossowski "was very poor." On top of the difficulties attendant upon Balthus's treatment of Pierre's stepdaughter Frédérique, it is little wonder that the brothers virtually severed all connections from that point forward.

Not only old friends and family members but also visitors from afar often had a hard time with the count. This was when Pierre Matisse would wait for days on end nearby in his room at the luxurious Hotel Hassler, ordering room service, afraid to leave because Balthus had insisted that *he* must be the one to call the dealer first, at *his* convenience, to let Matisse know when he might visit the studio and perhaps see something available for the marketplace.

Various American collectors of Balthus's work who went to Rome in those years and also stayed at the Hassler, expecting to be able to meet the painter next door, fared even less well than Matisse. People not accustomed to hearing no for an answer were told by Balthus's secretary that the artist was too busy to receive them. Joseph Hirshhorn described such a snub to me with a look of amused disbelief. The collector owned Balthus's beloved *Les Beaux Jours* as well as two other important canvases, but the artist could not spare him even a few minutes. S. I. Newhouse told me of a similar rebuff. Unused to having a door closed to him, he nonetheless took it in good temper, as if he were dealing with a moody teenager. Balthus, indeed, demonstrated that adolescent insistence on having the upper hand. And he seemed particularly keen to disparage other people whose ancestors came from places like Pinsk.

But high-ranking French government ministers did not necessarily fare better. Balthus's secretary told me that, more than once, she heard her boss, upon being notified that one such minister had come to call, explode, "I don't want him here!" It was her unpleasant task to show the disgruntled official around the gardens—a role she especially disliked on days when she was dressed in old jeans and felt ill suited to be in such a position.

BUT INSIDE THE VILLA'S WALLS, the artist was thoughtful and benevolent. His living quarters and attitude to the outside world befit a feudal lord, yet not just the students but also the employees revered him for his insights and general kindness—in spite of the occasional lapses.

To the maids and gardeners at the Villa Medici, Balthus was unfailingly gracious and solicitous. Like a true aristocrat, he deemed himself superior to the bourgeoisie—however haute—while maintaining great delicacy and politeness toward the lowest echelons of his staff. Balthus knew everyone's name, and how many children each of them had. Years later, long after he left his post in Rome and had retired to Switzerland, he would occasionally return to visit the villa, and would astonish people by having forgotten none of this information. Balthus's former chauffeur and a handyman at the villa both told me how touched they were on these visits when Balthus not only would ask for each of their family members by name but would clearly remember where their wives had worked and what their children had been doing years earlier.

Balthus had gotten to know some of these staff families especially well during his years of tenure at the French Academy. Michelina and Katia, the young teenage daughters of his cook, had become his most regular models. They posed for the new variations of *The Three Sisters* as well as for drawings and oils in which they were shown individually, reading or lolling about. Here the extent of the artist's relationship to his models is hard to assess. Jean Leyris—who spent a lot of time at the villa—told me that there was sufficient innuendo to raise the hackles of the girls' mother. On account of work sessions with Michelina that "were not completely innocent," the levelheaded cook "came around and said 'basta basta.' " Yet like the daughters of Pierre Colle, the cook's daughters have always claimed they considered Balthus to be, above all, paternal: fatherly and protective in a traditional way. By their account, he eroticized them in his paintings but not in the way he treated them.

I found this to be equally true of Balthus's approach in the early 1990s to another of his young models, also a servant's child. Maria Sanchez, the daughter of one of the Filipino couples working for Balthus and Setsuko, and a friend of my own daughters, always found the count unfailingly gentle and easy to be with when he sketched her. He had come quite some distance from his days of threatening Dolores Miró, and the era of his model being his mistress was long since over.

IV

TO A NUMBER OF SERIOUS and committed younger artists, Balthus was *the* living master. His devotees included many of the best-known figurative painters in America and France, art students all over the world, and a lot of the pensioners at the Villa Medici. Few were blind to his personal pretensions, but they took them with a grain of salt. Balthus might insist on a silly title, but he could paint, and talk about art, as no one else could. And if his work had a disturbing eroticism and a cruel edge, to the other practitioners of his craft, Balthus's abilities and genuine love of painting overrode everything else. For those who focused above all on the artist's ability to see and glean beauty, and his sheer expertise at brushing pigment on canvas, he was without equal.

As director of the Villa Medici, Balthus gave students a sense of possibilities they might otherwise never have felt. André Barelier, a Parisian sculptor who arrived at the villa as a young pensioner, described to me what it was like to work under him. Fresh out of the Academy of Beaux-Arts, Barelier was feeling lost and unable to create. Then, Barelier recalled, Balthus recommended that he try sculpture over painting and steered him toward the art of Giacometti. These two leads changed his life.

When Barelier remained unable to muster the self-confidence necessary to keep working, Balthus treated this agony with respect and guided the young artist to overcome it. It helped Barelier that the master acknowledged the impossibility of art and was kind enough to compare Barelier's doubts to Giacometti's struggles in the period when that great sculptor ground head after head into dirt. Barelier was moved when Balthus likened artists to mountain climbers: no matter how they plot their course, they are overwhelmed by the task ahead and their awareness that they may never reach the top. Numerous students felt similarly encouraged by the master in their midst.

Barelier and the other pensioners were reassured that so renowned an artist often felt extremely dissatisfied with his own work and, like them, periodically questioned his route. They learned that after working on a single canvas for months, Balthus would end up covering it completely until it was entirely white again. Moreover, Balthus let the people around him know that, rather than being burdened by this, he felt liberated. He preferred to continue his pursuit of perfection than to sit back smug.

If Balthus was known to be arrogant, superior, deceptive, or mocking to outsiders, with his students and fellow painters he was warm, cordial, easy, and generous. He gave them—as he still does when he receives his favorite young painters at Le Grand Chalet—a sense of equality. He never pontificated or acted the important artist. A number of his former students at the villa report that during studio visits he was kind and gentle, and often complimentary. When he made suggestions, he did so modestly.

Not that Balthus was ever an old pal or a backslapping friend to the pensioners at the villa. Few of them considered him to be someone they could get close to. But even if the director kept his distance and was publicly intimidating, he won the pensioners' sympathies not only because he gave the impression that he and they were all engaged in a similar struggle, but also because, for all his prodigious abilities, he never acted as if he knew how to do anything they did not know.

"THEY ALL ADORED HIM" was the assessment of Beatrice Cazac, an Englishwoman I met who was very much part of the young set at the French Academy—first as a girlfriend of Balthus's son Thadée, who was living in Rome during his father's first few years at the villa, and ultimately as the wife of one of the Prix de Rome artists. As an insider, Cazac got to see the naughty teenager side of Balthus that even the pensioners did not witness. Balthus did not attend his son's nightlong parties in the Chambre Turque—Thadée's digs under his father's rule in Rome—but the artist did preside at intimate lunches and other events where his young audience was duly enchanted.

There was one such lunch on a day "when the whole school was in upheaval because there had been graffiti"—which, unknown to the population at large, had been put on the villa's walls by Thadée and Béatrice and a third friend at about three that morning after a particularly convivial evening. The trio of graffiti makers had used slang scatalogical terms to rename some highly unpopular officials. Among their victims was a math teacher who had just imposed a three-day suspension on a friend of theirs. Balthus, "delighted with this," entertained his son and the other young people by providing a long list of the imaginary graffiti he might add; "he spent the entire lunch thinking up scatological equivalents" for the names of everyone at the villa.

There was also one memorable New Year's Eve—an occasion when the Romans have a tradition of throwing broken and chipped pottery and old pots and pans out the window. Balthus trumped the usual way of doing this by getting some pensioners to take a number of old plasters and line them up on the road in front of the villa in such a way that cars had to slalom around them. It was raining, and by New Year's Day the plasters had completely disintegrated. To the people for whom the destruction of the statues in the old library was heresy, this was, of course, insult added to injury.

But for Balthus, amusement was the goal. At a series of costume parties where the mandate was to appear as royalty, he was King Balthus on the first night, the King of Cats the next. Eventually Setsuko "would help in making Balthus less available,"[13] but in the early years in Rome he lived flamboyantly. During Setsuko's occasional absences, he was known to seduce his sons' girlfriends (without much objection from Stash or Thadée) and other sixteen-year-olds. Even then, he made clear that his true predilection was for girls younger than that. One of his most often quoted bons mots of the time was to call one teenager "un vieux chameau de treize ans"; she was "an old camel" because at thirteen she had passed her period of glory. He also made public his musings as to what toddler girls would be like later in life. Setsuko in those early years was seen as being jealous and possessive, eager to protect her territory. But when one cat was away, the other played freely.

V

POPULAR AS HE WAS in some circles, Balthus encountered severe disapproval in others. The painter and art teacher Bernard Chaet told me of one typically anti-Balthus sequence of events that occurred in the spring of 1963.

Chaet was then a visiting artist at the American Academy in Rome. One day he saw Balthus at the annual concert sponsored jointly by the French and American academies. He asked to be introduced to this artist whom he and a number of his fellow painters so admired.

Chaet summoned up the courage to speak his best French for this encounter. Disarmed by Balthus's use of perfect English, he managed nonetheless to achieve his objective of asking Balthus if he would be willing to pay a call on the American Academy and critique everyone's work. Balthus was receptive. He replied to his young admirer that he would be happy to spend a day as requested. He told Chaet that America was the country where he had received more support than anywhere else, and that he owed it to the academy to pay this visit. Besides, he enjoyed reviewing students' work, as long as he was not expected to discuss his own.

Bernard Chaet was overjoyed. He approached Richard Kimball, an architect who was the director of the American Academy, told him about the wonderful meeting, and suggested to Kimball that he now send an official formal invitation.

To Chaet's dismay, a week passed in which Kimball did nothing. He approached the director again. This time Kimball answered that he had looked up Balthus's work in a book and was appalled; he "wouldn't have an artist who painted pornographic pictures in the building."[14] Anyone who wanted to see Balthus would have to do so at the French Academy, at his or her own peril.

WHETHER PEOPLE WERE FOR or against him, Balthus in Rome was someone everybody noticed and talked about. When he was kind and easy, it was news; when he was haughty, it was even more interesting. William Bailey told me about the vernissage of an exhibition he had at a gallery that also represented Balthus. In keeping with his characteristically generous support of young artists, Balthus graciously attended the opening—and had kind things to say. But then Alberto Moravia arrived. Balthus suddenly switched gears. When someone of equal renown was in the room, Balthus completely lost his air of relaxation. Balthus and Moravia each held court as if the other were not present. The writer was surrounded by one group of people, the artist by another; vying for center stage, neither would yield to his rival. As director of the Villa Medici, Balthus was as he had been as a child: alternately amiable genius and prima donna.

There were occasions when he even turned on the people on whom he generally bestowed his charms. I heard of one such event from his former secretary. She told me that in general, Balthus was unfailingly cordial to her. She had no reason to expect him to behave otherwise at a party given in her honor. Her purpose in working for Balthus had been to pay the tuition at the University of Rome; she was being feted for having at last received her degree there. At the party, Balthus had too much to drink. "What did you learn at your university?" he demanded harshly. It was a rhetorical question. Instantly he provided his own answer: "Nothing."

Everyone knew Balthus scoffed at higher education and disapproved of

degrees, but no one expected him to deny his secretary the pleasure of her celebration. Setsuko tried to get him to stop, but he was relentless. He began to
badger the young woman with questions about artists of whom she had never
heard. Life was the great teacher, Balthus explained, while university titles were
a sham.

This declaration was ironic coming from someone so insistent on his own
title of a different sort. But none of the Villa Medici staff or pensioners dared
interrupt the diatribe. And much as Balthus's secretary liked and admired her
employer, it was a smart she never forgot.

WHEN BALTHUS'S ALTER EGO Heathcliff became lord and master of Thrush
Grange, he took charge of the surrounding countryside as well. When Balthus
wasn't being "le grand seigneur"—elusively perched in the tower with his
beautiful young girlfriend—he was a dazzling public figure. Balthus's and Setsuko's Roman life outdistanced that of either Brontë's Victorian gentry or
Rilke's grandest chevaliers. At Balthus's behest, Setsuko—who had dressed in
Western style in her own country—took to wearing fine kimonos. These stiff,
shimmering garments served in part to support Balthus's claim that she was
related to the imperial family.

The next step, of course, was for Balthus to align himself more formally
with this highborn young woman from Japan. But first it was necessary to
divorce Antoinette. Balthus had never bothered to do so. Antoinette, however,
was delighted that Balthus actually wanted to marry one of his girlfriends; like
her two sons, she was very pleased with her husband's new match. Setsuko was
not merely charming and beautiful but also extremely intelligent and artistically talented. Here was someone alert and confident enough to deal with
Balthus, who absolutely adored him and also understood him. Antoinette and
Thaddeus and Stanislas probably sensed that Setsuko had what it would take
to cope with Balthus into old age; she would play his games, but knew him for
what he was. The divorce went through, and on October 3, 1967, the fifty-
nine-year-old Balthazar Klossowski and the twenty-five-year-old Setsuko Ideta
were married in Tokyo at a Buddhist and Shinto ceremony that was followed
by a party at the French consulate.

Once they were wed, the Count and Countess Klossowski de Rola entertained often and beautifully. "Princes and princesses, cardinals, ambassadors
dined at the count's table, where exquisite foods and wines were served on
plates and in goblets emblazoned with golden crowns."[15] Not only had Balthus
redone the rooms and gardens at the Villa Medici in an approximation of their
former glory, but he restored the institutional decorum.

Not all of Balthus's old acquaintances were as impressed with the Count de Rola's elevated status as he was, however. In Paris I spoke with Pauline Roux, the widow of Gaston Roux—who had been a friend of Balthus's for many years. Madame Roux, in a matter-of-fact-way, recalled a time in the mid-1950s when she and her husband and Alberto Giacometti had had dinner with Balthus in a small bistro on the outskirts of Paris. It was a relaxed and informal get-together of four hardworking people with relatively simple needs in life; Balthus may already have been parading as a count in other circles, but with his old friends he was still the unassuming artist. That night they all shared a couscous.

The next time Madame Roux saw Balthus, it was after she had received an invitation sent in the name of Count Balthazar Klossowski de Rola. Now she and her husband were being summoned to lunch at the Villa Medici. They could hardly believe the transformation. "A valet de chambre," Madame Roux recalled in amazement, "dressed in a traditional uniform, stood behind every chair. There were plates under plates." As Madame Roux pointed out, the other attendee at the Paris bistro meal, Giacometti, "by contrast never had anything more than a simple studio and a small adjoining room"—although he had become even more of a success in the art world. Moreover, Balthus's ascendancy bestowed few advantages on his old friends; for all the panoply of effects and the high tone of the service, the Rouxs were served "only an omelette."

But the Villa Medici itself certainly benefited from its director's energy. Balthus brought in a new, avant-garde playfulness. Balthus's old collaborator Jean-Louis Barrault, as well as his newer friend Federico Fellini, visited from time to time. Le Grand Magique Circus, under the direction of Savary, was performed twice in a circus tent. A range of artists arrived: Italian contemporaries like Valerio Zurlini and Renato Guttoso, and Balthus's friends, among them Miró and Stanley William Hayter. Painters like Francis Bacon—who was internationally renowned even if Balthus deplored his work—also appeared. The president of the Italian Senate came to the villa, and so did Fiat executive Gianni Agnelli, who to the Italians was more royal than royalty.

Socializing with the upper echelon, Balthus and Setsuko were generally treated as friends and equals. On the rare occasion when they were not, Balthus would suffer no Heathcliff-like denigration. At a get-together of ambassadors at the French church in Rome, he was furious not to be seated in one of the golden chairs accorded to the ambassadors. He left in a huff. Balthus could be humble and modest with his students—in front of whom he felt privileged and in command—but if ever he was affronted or made to feel in any way secondary, he would turn the tyrant.

One way to avoid difficulties, of course, was to maintain control. There were few details of life at the Villa Medici that escaped its director. He closely considered the invitation list to each opening and reception. He knew who everyone was. He read every document that left the villa. Yet his secretary found that he did not like signing them, a task he would always delegate to his secretary general. The mixture of engagement and elusiveness was much the same as in the style of his art.

When Balthus and Setsuko weren't in their public roles, they lived very much as they have in their subsequent retirement in Rossinière. Often secluded, they guarded their privacy and maintained tight control of the world around them. The employees and pensioners at the villa considered the director an intensely solitary figure. Part of Balthus's way of keeping in control was always to maintain a critical distance.

LIFE DID NOT ALWAYS GO according to plan, however. Balthus's and Setsuko's first child, a boy named Fumio, died tragically at the age of two. When he told me this, Balthus said that the little boy was "buried in Italy," but mentioned nothing more except that the baby had been delivered by his former brother-in-law, Hubert de Watteville, who was one of the most renowned obstetricians in Rome and who had also delivered the children of Sophia Loren, who was quite a good friend of Balthus's. The artist neglected, however, to tell me that, in the most miserable of ironies, Fumio suffered from Tay-Sachs disease.

This dreadful genetic disorder occurs almost exclusively among the descendants of Eastern European Jews. An autosomal-recessive disorder, it has to be inherited from both parents; these carriers, themselves healthy, each have one normal and one mutant gene. Because the carrier frequency among Ashkenazi Jews is one in thirty, while among the general population it is one in three hundred, it is highly probable that at least one of the parents is Ashkenazi (or French Canadian, the other one-in-thirty group). Here the mother, being Japanese, fell into the one-in-three-hundred group—increasing the statistical likelihood of the father being an Eastern European Jew.

When it struck their son, Balthus and Setsuko discussed the illness openly with their friends—even if they never acknowledged its Jewish aspect. One of its terrible symptoms was that Fumio could never lift his head; it was very moving to see Setsuko, while visiting other friends with infants, as she held their babies and observed the gestures and motions her own infant could not make. Fumio, according to friends of the Klossowskis at the time, became increasingly beautiful and angelic-looking as the terrible illness overtook him and led to his death. A few years after this tragedy, Harumi, also delivered with the help of Balthus's former brother-in-law, was born in 1974.

MEANWHILE, TRADING ON THEIR status in the world by dint of their father's position, Balthus's sons by Antoinette were making their way in the somewhat less intellectual segment of society dominated by rock musicians and fashion designers. They lacked their father's talent and drive but had some of his personal flair and charm as well as his fondness for having a good time among people who were rich and smart.

"The boys were both wildly attractive," Claus von Bülow told me. Thadée was reaping the rewards of this attractiveness in Paris, where, although he never held what could be considered a job, he was writing on Jean-Louis Barrault and other subjects. "Stash" became something of a figure on the scene in London in the Swinging Sixties. As Stash later explained to me, he took up his father's English-speaking side and inclination toward Anglo-Saxon culture, while Thadée went in the French direction.

One account describes Stash at a party given by Christopher Gibbs in 1967. Cecil Beaton was there taking "some puffs of dope" with Jane Orinsby-Gore, waiting for Mick Jagger and Marianne Faithfull to arrive.

> At 10:15 the exotic couple appeared and Marianne made "groovy" conversation. Prince Stanislas ("Stash") Klossowski de Rola (son of the artist Balthus, about whom he later compiled a book) was also there, dressed as Hamlet, with stripes of sequins on his blouse and shoes. He had recently hit the headlines by being "busted" with Brian Jones at his flat in Courtfield Road.[16]

They all went off later to the Baghdad Restaurant in Fulham Road. This was the same time period when, according to James Lord and Gene Thaw, Stash stole that cache of drawings in order to cover personal debts.

While never claiming a title, Thadée also fell in with the international jet set. Described in a biography of Yves Saint Laurent as "improbably handsome with thick curly hair and shabby chic clothes,"[17] he became, in 1965, the boyfriend of Clara Saint, a key figure in Saint Laurent's circle. Saint was a "classically pretty" heiress "with long, straight blonde hair . . . and a sunny demeanor"[18] who had been engaged to André Malraux's son before he died in a car crash on the Riviera, and who had become famous when she helped

Rudolf Nureyev defect from the Soviet Union. Saint handled Saint Laurent's publicity, and she and Thadée were fixtures in the designer's coterie—to which Thadée added a certain distinction both because of his own intelligence and because of his background as Balthus's son and Pierre Klossowski's nephew.

Thadée, Clara Saint, Yves Saint Laurent, Paloma Picasso, and Saint Laurent's other friends would regularly party in the chic apartment of Fernando Sanchez on the Place de Fürstemberg. Practically underneath the simple studio where Balthus had painted *The Street* and where, some thirty years earlier, Artaud and Leyris had found the laudanum-stunned artist with Antoinette's photo falling from his hand, they would loll "on low white sofas with candles burning, incense smouldering."[19] It was here that Thadée first met Loulou de La Falaise—the daughter of a *real* count. Le Comte Alain de La Falaise descended from one of the most distinguished families in France, while Loulou's mother, Maxime Birley, was an English debutante, the daughter of the court portraitist Sir Oswald Birley. Loulou came to the fashion world naturally; her mother had modeled for Elsa Schiaparelli.

Loulou had lived in Ireland during a brief marriage to Desmond FitzGerald, the Knight of Glin, but at age twenty hoped to settle in Paris. Fun-loving and remarkably pretty, she quickly became part of Saint Laurent's circle. Everyone noticed her and Paloma Picasso in their flea-market clothing when others wore couture. In antique dresses, long shawls, and heavy jewelry, Loulou captivated Saint Laurent and his friends, among them Andy Warhol. She began to spend a lot of time in New York at Warhol's Factory and modeled for Diana Vreeland at *Vogue*.

In 1972 Loulou went to work for Saint Laurent as a sort of right hand and ambassador to the world. After settling into an apartment on the Rue des Grands-Augustins with her boyfriend at the time, the Catalan architect Ricardo Bofill, she became a major player in Saint Laurent's business empire. Then, in the spring of 1977, she caused an enormous stir by announcing her marriage to Thadée, whose relationship with Clara Saint had lasted for nearly ten years. It was a scandal in part because

Clara only found out about it when she saw the official announcement in *Le Figaro*. Even the self-absorbed Andy Warhol noticed how unhappy she seemed when he saw her for lunch with Paloma Picasso at Angélina's in Paris that May. Although Clara was already recovering her good humor, managing to laugh at Warhol's suggestion that they should outdo Loulou and Thadée by announcing their own wedding in *Le Figaro*.[20]

People took sides. Paloma Picasso stuck by Clara Saint. But Yves Saint Laurent hosted a ball to celebrate the wedding. This lavish event took place "at the Châlet des Iles, a castle on an island in a lake in the Bois de Boulogne. The island was specially decorated for the night and the four hundred guests were taken across the lake in lantern-lit boats with swans trailing behind them."[21] This marriage of Balthus's son into the heart of the fashion world caused no little excitement. Paris *Vogue* photographed the guests, among them various members of the Klossowski, de La Falaise, and Rothschild families, Karl Lagerfeld, Kenzo, and Bianca Jagger—who had flown in from New York for the event, to which she wore a pink Dior gown that Saint Laurent covered with ferns.

Loulou and Thadée regularly appeared at Yves Saint Laurent's side. At the party to introduce the perfume Opium in New York—the setting was the Chinese junk *Peking*, festooned with hundreds of white orchids and moored next to the Brooklyn Bridge—the designer was flanked by Loulou in a black velvet jacket "with a red and green opium poppy embroidered across it" and Thadée "in the same classic style of evening dress as Yves's with a bright red cummerbund at his waist and a red cotton peasant handkerchief tucked into his breast pocket."[22] As Saint Laurent began to be affected by chronic health difficulties, Loulou increasingly came to function as his representative as well as his muse. She knew everyone: old friends from Warhol's Factory; the habitués of her uncle's posh London nightclub, Annabel's; her mother's associates through Diana Vreeland; and the Hollywood friends of her former roommate, Berry Berenson, who was married to Anthony Perkins. In 1978 Loulou and Thadée hosted a large party at a new nightclub in Montmartre where she went as a fallen angel, he as a cherub, and some of the best-known names in the fashion world as their favorite characters from the stage and mythology. Once Loulou gave birth to Balthus's first grandchild, Anna, she and Thadée retreated to a quieter way of life, but she has remained an essential consultant and adviser to Yves Saint Laurent while Thadée has continued to write—if publishing infrequently.

Their union is yet another way that art and fashion have combined in Balthus's world—and that the artist, through his son, has penetrated into society and the aristocracy.

VI

ONCE BALTHUS HAD FINISHED refurbishing the building and transforming the gardens at the Villa Medici, he oversaw a program of annual exhibitions mounted with the utmost discernment. Shows at the Villa Medici had previously been held in the Grand Salon. Feeling that this setting competed with the work, Balthus restored the old gallery downstairs, where he personally attended to every detail of the exhibition installation and placed each work meticulously.

Federico Fellini gave a vivid account of Balthus's painstaking engagement with the restoration process of the villa in general and the space for these art shows specifically:

> I am continually amazed at the extreme simplicity of such a rapport with things, once the right space and time, the unique caliber have been found. Not perfectionism or abstraction, but a relentless search for the "truth" of every historical thing. I remember, in this connection, the time when Balthus himself was searching for, and finally executed with his own hands, a particular vibrant shade of color to give the plaster of the walls of the Académie's exhibition rooms; the result was a color of time, a most adequate background for the overbearing presences of Ingres, Courbet, Braque and Corot.[23]

Balthus may not have permitted unwelcome visitors to intrude on his private time, but with his exhibitions he opened up the doors of the Villa Medici in an unprecedented way. The vernissages each autumn marked the start of the cultural season in Rome. This meant in part that prestigious visitors like the president of the Italian Republic routinely attended. So did a public that had never before felt as enfranchised. For Balthus initiated a new policy of having no admission charge. Hordes of people now entered this sanctum they had previously considered off limits.

The tasteful and informative catalogs bespeak the exceptional caliber of the exhibition program. The first show, in 1967, was of work by Rodin—which for Balthus must have seemed a personal sort of homage since Rilke had been the sculptor's secretary. Then came "Ingres in Italia," followed by "Chateaubriand: Viaggiatore e uomo politico." The exhibition for the 1969–70 season was of Courbet, while the next year Balthus staged a major show of his hero among more recent artists: Alberto Giacometti. The 1971–72 season featured Bonnard; 1972–73, a show of fifteenth-century European drawings; 1973–74, the French Carravagiesque, until then virtually unknown to the Romans; and 1974–75, Braque.

These exhibitions mounted by Balthus at the Villa Medici represented artistic values that ran counter to the mainstream of the time. For a number of young painters in Europe and in America, their impresario was the standard-bearer of a well-defined point of view important both for its powerful content and for its independence. Anchored in the art of the past, it valued nature and real appearance as the basis of all art. This taste was at the opposite pole from Abstract Expressionism, Pop Art, and other current trends. Reflecting his own passions and taste, the shows Balthus organized at the villa offered a rare alternative.

With a committee of high-ranking officials, the able aid of Jean Leymarie, and the official clout of the French Academy—which, under Malraux, was now at the pinnacle of its importance—it was possible to secure fantastic loans for these exhibitions. Balthus culled and selected each artist's work with tremendous care. With his uncanny memory, he greatly facilitated the organization of each by knowing precisely what he wanted to borrow and where each object was.

These shows at the Villa Medici give great insight into the sources of Balthus's own art. In this respect the most significant was the 1969–70 Courbet exhibition. The five works reproduced in color in its catalog are virtually prototypes for entire groups of Balthus's paintings. Balthus's presentation of them in this manner was an astounding admission. While he readily mentioned, to fellow artists and friends, his passion for Courbet in general, he would never cite individual paintings as pivotal influences in the way that he did by focusing on them in this publication.

The resemblance between these five Courbets and many of Balthus's own canvases is like that of parent and child who not only have the same features but speak and stand in an identical manner.

There was the 1844 portrait of Juliette Courbet. Surely this beguiling girl with her sideways glance and folded arms was the direct ancestor of the Thérèse that Balthus painted in 1937, his Colette of 1954, and the Frédériques of 1955. The nineteenth-century Juliette is dressed more decorously and has better posture than her descendants in Balthus's work, but she, too, has the familial oversized head, minxlike gaze, luminous skin, and intense personality. Balthus mimicked not only what Courbet painted but *how* he painted: the splendid control of space, the weight of flesh, the shimmer of a striped fabric, the attention to the precise way hair pulls.

Next in Balthus's selection of color plates came Courbet's 1865 canvas of Pierre Joseph Proudhon and his daughters. It was as if Balthus were deliberately showing the starting point of his own work. With their large heads and stylish frocks—and, above all, in their total self-absorption and the contortions of their bodies—Proudhon's daughters are quintessential Balthus girls, alluring as well as devious, and the taciturn, enigmatic Proudhon a stand-in for the artist himself.

The third Courbet Balthus reproduced in color, *La Dame en podosople,*

Gustave Courbet, *Portrait of P. J. Proudhon in 1853,*
1865, oil on canvas, 147 x 198 cm

Gustave Courbet, *The Two Friends,* or *Sleep,* 1866, oil on canvas, 135 x 200 cm

also from 1865, served to identify, very specifically, the bizarre girl in a boat in Balthus's 1949 *Méditerranée's Cat*. The fourth was the 1866 *Le Sommeil*, as powerful an image of Sapphic love as has ever been painted. This lewd, gorgeous canvas shows two buxom women lying asleep, their bodies intertwined after lovemaking. Its overtly salacious exposition of lesbian sexuality awakens and provokes: objectives dear to Balthus. At the same time, *Le Sommeil* presents many of Courbet's devices that Balthus used to invoke energy—above all, the limbs that swing and fly exuberantly.

Balthus probably showed the nineteenth-century canvas in his Villa Medici catalog for its combination of courageous subject matter and sumptuous painting, Beyond that, *Le Sommeil* served another purpose. If he wanted to present evidence that other great painters besides himself have been unabashed in the brazen display of their most ardent fantasies, he could have found no better example.

By the time we get to the fifth of the Courbets Balthus reproduced in color, the 1869 *Passage of Interlaken,* its apparent innocence and lack of eroticism comes as more of a surprise than would have, say, a reproduction of the artist's infamous *Birth of the World*. That view of female genitals as seen from between her spread legs, displayed for years in the same secretive manner as *The Guitar Lesson,* is what the public might have expected from the naughty Balthus. The Interlaken scene, on the other hand, served Balthus's purpose of demonstrating that the painter of *Le Sommeil* was also a naturalist of divine power. Balthus wanted to be identified similarly.

But in the context of the Villa Medici catalog, the Interlaken scene has another effect as well. In part because of what we have just been looking at, the trees and mountains read as phallic symbols more than as pure landscape elements. Every detail is sexualized. It is precisely what happens with Balthus's Swiss landscapes; we feel that the apparent innocence is a subterfuge.

Courbet was a painter's painter: fiercely independent and technically splendid, in love with both earthly reality and the artistic possibilities of appearances. Balthus's presentation of his art was a tremendous coup. His other exhibitions in the Eternal City were also breakthroughs. Before 1974 there was scarcely a person in Rome who knew who Georges Braque was. Then, in one of the last exhibitions Balthus organized before leaving the academy, people desperate to see the Frenchman's work flocked there in droves. The lines extended all the way to the Church of Trinità dei Monti. André Malraux could hardly have scored a greater success in his choice of ambassador of the most refined and inventive sides of French culture.

· · ·

THE ENGLISH PAINTER Graham Nicksen told me about a conversation he had with Balthus in Rome in the 1960s. Nicksen asked Balthus how his work was going. The world-weary count replied that he was so busy with the restoration of the villa and with his administrative responsibilities that he did not have a moment to paint. Balthus seemed bewildered by this, as if he scarcely understood how such a predicament had befallen him, while at the same time making clear his sacrifice—both for France and for the students. He presented himself very much as a victim, consistent with his stance that he was there out of friendship for Malraux and because he had said he would do it. Wanting his sacrifice known, he sounded resolute rather than resentful; he had to give up his own work entirely in the service of the villa, but it was worthwhile.

Nicksen was duly sympathetic, until he learned soon after, from others at the villa, that Balthus in this period was working away for hours every day at his painting—that even if his output had shrunk significantly, he was still making his second series of *The Three Sisters, The Turkish Room,* the monumental *Katia Reading,* and other paintings. Whatever story he gave to Graham Nicksen, he often remained at a quiet remove from the other activities at the villa, and worked alone in his studio every day.

Balthus's choice of work quarters at the villa had startled a number of people. At the far end of the studio wing, they were considered the least comfortable of all of them—nearest the roadway that goes through the Borghese Gardens, in which the villa's property is set. Because of its poor location, this space had less light and more noise than anyone else's. It also had no heating. But Balthus made it clear that the other, more desirable studios were for the pensioners. Such graciousness fits his pattern: when Balthus feels in command, he is hospitable and self-sacrificing to a fault. Moreover, it probably suited the villa's director to remain a bit of an outsider—so long as the terms were of his own choosing.

The two contrasting spaces used by the director fit both aspects of Balthus's personality. In the rugged studio, he could pursue his serious work. From the grand cardinal's apartment, he could rule his kingdom. The same mix would later be provided by the straightforward studio in Rossinière with its good northern light and the palatial chalet across the road. The grand seigneur and humble artist could live as one.

A telling description of life in that studio at the Villa Medici is provided by Fellini in his reminiscence of the very first time he met Balthus:

> I knew him through Alain Curry—who interpreted the *La dolce vita* character as an intellectual suicide—in 1962 or 63—I don't remember. Alain Curry came to Rome to ask me to give him a hand with a film;

Balthus and Federico Fellini in 1992, by Scalfani

he wanted to bring to the screen *L'Annonce faite à Marie,* the text of
Paul Claudel that had already been done in theater; counting on my
intervention with the state institutions, l'Ente Gestione Cinema or l'I-
talnoleggio, for a financial contribution. We considered via Sistina,
Hôtel de la Ville, and talked about it. Then he told me that he was
invited to a dinner by a friend, un grande amico. We left and took the
road together to Trinità dei Monti. Arriving at the Villa Medici, he
said to me: "My friend lives here," without saying the name. . . . On
the intercom he spoke with someone, then we went up. On the stairs,
turning toward me, he said: "He is the most important living painter,"
always without saying the name. At once I found myself in the middle
of ancient walls, magnificent balconies, ceilings high and precious,
domestics in white gloves, a butler in livery. I heard a high and
sonorous voice say: "Caro Alain, come, come." "Caro Balthus,"
responded Alain, and only then did I know who I was in front of.

A grande, grandissimo character, between Jules Berry and Jean-
Louis Barrault: tall, lean, aristocratic profile, dominating eyes, mas-
terly gestures, with something enigmatic, fiendish, Mephistophelian.
A prince of the Renaissance, or a prince of Transylvania. . . . In the

magical climate that prevailed at Villa Medici was born between us a true friendship, authentic, full of feeling. One day he invited me to his studio where no one ever entered, inaccessible like an esoteric temple. "Do you want to visit my studio?" he asked me unexpectedly. . . . We went down to the garden, proceeding into the most wild part of the park up to a building in ruin: his studio was here. There prevailed a breathtaking disorder: paintings leaning against walls, old tables cluttered, dusty and tattered screens, shredded fans, pots, hammers, African masks, Japanese and Chinese objects, mannequins, boxes, vases, stills, scales, bottles, flacons, acids, poisons: a true laboratory of a witch doctor, of an alchemist, of *demiurgo*. An atmosphere of magic that my caution had never known in the legendary studios of Courbet, Picasso or of Chagall.[24]

In Balthus, Fellini had met his match. The film director "was always the most assiduous creator of myths about himself—his pathological lying was legendary." Fellini has been quoted as saying, "We change our accounts of events continually so as not to bore ourselves."[25] But it seems that at least in relating the impression of his soul mate's studio, Fellini found no cause to distort.

It was in that "atmosphere of magic" that Balthus took his work to its next, even more obsessive stage.

VII

> *"She lifted her clothes up an' showed me—you know what.*
> *They wore them split drawers then, girls did. . . . She wanted*
> *me to come an' feel. But I never knowed afore then as women*
> *had hair there. Black hair! An' I don't know why, it upset me*
> *and made me hate the thoughts of women from that day."* . . .
> *"And you hated the thought of women because they have*
> *hair where some men do?"*
> *"Yes! I know now I was a fool. But that was it."*
> —D. H. LAWRENCE, *John Thomas and Lady Jane*[26]

BALTHUS'S ARTISTIC APPROACH to women and to the surrounding world entered a more extreme phase once he got to the Villa Medici. Now more than ever his females were like the artist himself: absorbed in their own fantasies while remaining unavailable to the rest of us. Enveloped in mental and physical clouds, these scantily clad or naked ladies are both stirring and inaccessible.

Balthus's female subjects continued (the sole exception was *Alice*) to lack even a trace of pubic hair. That hairlessness is a way of keeping the girls young—not yet as advanced as their male admirers, assuming those admirers have reached puberty—and of extending their virginity. Sade's view of virginity was that it was a state that had to be destroyed; his ideal form of incest consisted of giving the father a first go at deflowering the girl child. Balthus, presenting his sensuous young creatures as innocent (as suggested by their biological prepubescence) yet vanquished (by dint of the way he displays them), seems to have given himself the role of Sadean conqueror.

IN *The Turkish Room* OF 1963–66, Balthus puts his own new young mistress on display as the ultimate sylph: childlike in her lack of pubic hair and the incipience of her womanly figure, worldly and experienced in her attitude. This painting of Setsuko also makes clear how stultified, and stylized, Balthus had become in his move into new spheres of living.

Like *Cathy Dressing, The Turkish Room* is in the collection of the Centre Pompidou in Paris. When I last viewed these two canvases there, both were in storage, and I ended up studying them leaning against picture racks next to one another. *Cathy Dressing* has a sharp focus, somber-colored, bare-bones, wooden appearance: like an early black-and-white film in period costume. Even if its story line is ambiguous, it depicts a vivid narrative. *The Turkish Room,* all pose and no plot, is flatter and brighter. Everything about it is weightless and delicate, less real and more opulent, a case of remorseless embellishment.

The abrupt clarity of the earlier work has given way to an impression of pure luxury such as one expects to find in a posh hotel suite. Where once a stark pine cupboard set the tone, now luxuriant Moorish windows do. Just as the rigors of life in that attic studio on the Place de Fürstemberg were now replaced by the layered opulence of the Villa Medici, the work produced in those different settings had been similarly transmogrified.

Yet for all the differences of surface and appearance, both paintings depict female vanity: a beautiful woman preoccupied with her own appearance, posing for all the world to see her. In both instances, the woman Balthus portrayed so lubriciously would soon become his wife, and the renderings of his two inamorata are remarkably akin. They are naked except for their dressing gowns, which cover mainly their shoulders and arms. These robes are like theater curtains opened to frame the vital action. Each of these women has milky white flesh with a pink cast to it.

The Turkish Room, 1963–66,
casein and tempera on canvas, 180 x 210 cm

Their bodies are a sensuous series of curves that gives them the allure of Ingres's odalisques. They have gently rounded bellies. Their complete absence of pubic hair makes them seem virginal. To many viewers, the only discordant note is their notably strong and massive legs, but to Balthus this, too, is patently part of the ideal. The "artist of whom nothing is known" wants all the world to see the object of his passion in his chosen manner, and the women have complied.

YET EVEN IF BOTH OF BALTHUS's brides-to-be display their bodies freely, they won't meet our eye; they look sideways, with faces like masks. These expressionless, impassive visages that resemble shields over their real heads are framed by thick manes of streaming hair—in marked contrast to their hairless pubes.

Thus, in *The Turkish Room* Balthus exhibits the same taste and fantasy as always, but having opted for an entirely different presentation. Formerly strident, now he is powdery and soft—in hue as well as form. The brooding emotional climate of the 1930s has given way to ambient delicacy, to a deliberately hazy veneer no more readable than the woman's face.

Life had gotten easier. *Cathy Dressing*, after all, is a portrayal of an unavailable woman, brazen and forbidding, whereas *The Turkish Room* displays Balthus's imported luxury, docile and at home in the splendid surroundings to which he has brought her. What an exquisite prize she is, with her bisquelike, porcelain skin.

IN REPRODUCTION, *The Turkish Room* is completely cloying. Too stylized and sweet, it seems cheap in its Eastern affect—like the decoration on a package of halvah. Balthus seems to have gone completely decadent. But in actuality— even in the poor light and unflattering setting of a museum storage room— the painting is surprisingly seductive. In spite of its artifice, it is a sequence of genuine riches: the eloquent, Morandi-like still life on the table; the impeccable dish of eggs, which, although they are big enough to have been laid by ostriches, are superb in their authentic roundness and graceful massing; the panoply of patterns; the articulate fold in Setsuko's left leg where her thigh and calf curve into one another opposite her knee.

Balthus, by the way, denied to me the notion that the cup and vase on the green table were intended to refer to the work of Morandi. Perhaps he so insistently refuted it because the notion is given such credence in the literature on him. Jean Leymarie calls the cup and stoneware vessel "a discreet homage as it were to Morandi,"[27] and Sabine Rewald goes even further, suggesting that the vignette may be "a tribute to Giorgio Morandi . . . who died in 1964 while Balthus was painting this work."[28] For all the times Balthus told me how much he admired Morandi and regretted never having met him, he still insisted that these objects—truly incredibly Morandi like—were in no way intended to evoke the Italian's work, that the assertions to that effect are entirely without basis. I attribute this disclaimer, however, simply to perversity: not unlike those occasions when an adolescent will do whatever his or her parents have just forbidden, solely for the sake of challenging authority.

It is, in fact, the Morandiesque factors—the refinement and understatement—that make this complex canvas successful in actuality even while it is

jarring in reproduction. The painting has a matteness that lends a certain quietude to the intricacies. The surface of the wall and floor tile and brocade are
slightly rubbed and faded. The curvaceous table legs bulge gracefully. The
painter who was openly angry and melancholic thirty years ago is now completely self-possessed.

As in his role as France's cultural ambassador to Rome, in his painting
Balthus has taken firm control of a complex situation. He had given himself a
major challenge by making his setting this highly ornate, Eastern-style room
that Horace Vernet designed at the Villa Medici in the early nineteenth century, and by then posing his new mistress in it. By dramatically foreshadowing
all the three-dimensional elements, he has combined them with the highly
embellished surfaces to make a complex frieze. And for all the emphasis on
detail, he has always maintained his focus on the entire presence of the woman
and the sweep of her body.

The pose—which seems a direct quotation from Miró's 1919 *Seated Nude,*
a similar mirror image that belonged to Pierre Matisse—would reappear in
Balthus's work from this point forward. The hand mirror—a traditional Japanese symbol of the soul—would remain a recurring element in Balthus's art
right up to his most recent work. Here its circular form works with the head,
tabletops, window domes, vase, cup, bowl, and eggs to establish a series of
ovoids. It also raises the issue of self-image—betraying an extreme consciousness of how one is seen from the outside, in a situation that prizes external surface over inner truth.

The Turkish Room SUGGESTS A LINK to the work of Henri Matisse. This is yet
another theory about his work that Balthus brought up only to deny its validity. "It is curious that people see the influence of Matisse. It is quite the opposite," he remarked as we looked at a reproduction of this most Oriental of his
works in the large Skira book opened on the tea table in front of us.

Balthus's swipes at Matisse are legend. The artist told me—as he has, with
variations, told others—that Bonnard lived next door when the family lived in
Saint-Germain, and that he could recall a dinner when he was "ten or twelve
years old" at which both Matisse and Bonnard were present. "Bonnard had
such a sweet face; he looked like a dog a little bit. Matisse said to Bonnard,
'Vous et moi, nous sommes les plus grands peintres de l'époque.' I shall never
forget the expression of Bonnard, who replied, 'C'est horrible ce que vous
dites, Matisse.' "

It is, of course, a lovely story—with the innocent child sympathetic to the

Katia Reading, 1968–76, casein and tempera on canvas, 179 x 211 cm

great Bonnard's disdain for Matisse's boastfulness. But its accuracy is dubious. For one thing, the Klossowskis had been forced to leave Paris and enter their first agonizing exile long before Balthus reached the age of ten. Moreover, there is no other source suggesting that Bonnard lived next door. But for some reason Balthus felt a need to denigrate Matisse.

The painter and writer Andrew Forge told me about an occasion when Balthus and the English art historian David Sylvester were walking through a market square in Paris. The stalls were piled high with produce that looked especially plentiful in the late afternoon light.

"Bonnard or Matisse?" Sylvester asked Balthus.

"Unless we are talking about Bonnard," Balthus answered, "we have nothing to discuss."

And in an interview in *Le Monde,* he went so far as to say, "Matisse? I prefer Tintin. It's just as simplified, but funnier." The quip is over-the-top, like

Balthus's remark to the press about Hans Arp: "I too could have done the sort of things he did—you just have to paint like a blind man."[29] Here provocation more than connoisseurship is the issue at hand.

LIKE THE TRANSITION FROM *Cathy Dressing* to *The Turkish Room,* the move Balthus made from the 1938 *Thérèse Dreaming* to the 1968–76 *Katia Reading* echoes the shift from life in the garret on the Cour de Rohan to the style of the Count de Rola at the Villa Medici. What was raw and immediate has become mannered and couched, yet the original fire lurks underneath.

Katia is in much the same pose as Thérèse, her red skirt folded high on her thighs. Only now her underpants don't show. The new view is sideways rather than straight-on. For many of the same reasons, Balthus's painting technique—which in 1938 was so sharp-focused—has become fuzzier, the layers shielding one another. Subtlety and haze have replaced the earlier forthrightness.

Katia, like Thérèse, is in her own world, seemingly unaware that she is on view. Each escapes to another realm; Thérèse by dreaming, Katia by reading. Whereas Thérèse's eyes are closed entirely, Katia's are locked in the right-hand corners of their sockets. Yet we don't really believe it is with her copy of *Tintin* that the sullen girl is so completely preoccupied; the book is really just a pretext.

The act of making the body comfortable, of suiting one's own needs, becomes a supreme human endeavor in Balthus's work. The artist has simplified everything in *Katia Reading* to solidify that sense of physical ease. He has reduced the elements and cast them in a uniform glow that makes the setting magisterial and creates a profound hush. Escapism and repose are rendered holy.

THESE EFFECTS, ALAS, ARE NEARLY lost in the painting's current setting. In the same modern New York office penthouse as *Woman in a Bathtub,* the large *Katia Reading* looks unfortunately compressed as it practically touches floor and ceiling. Katia seems like an old-fashioned Roman child misplaced in midtown Manhattan. The business furniture and buzzing telephones impart the wrong style and pace.

But if one can screen out the setting and hubbub that surround the canvas, the painting itself becomes a calm sanctuary. Air circulates freely between the picture plane and the simple backdrop. And while the floors and walls are impressively solid and inanimate, Katia is radiantly alive. The dynamic rhythms of her body are as convincing as her pensiveness. Her left foot is so firmly planted on the ground that we believe its weight; the right is angled for maximum comfort. Her slouch and the unfortunate curve of her shoulders and back ring true even if they seem exaggerated.

Katia's head is greatly enlarged in the usual Balthus manner. Not only is it as wide as her shoulders, but it is almost as long from temple to chin as her chest is from neck to waist. Yet we accept the contrivance; it leads us to zero in on the girl's mind. Her large face provides her with true adolescent hauteur, brought near by the light that sparkles gently off her lips and in the whites of her eyes.

With her veritable moon-face, Katia is a direct descendant of the creatures in *The Street*. The continuous plane of her forehead into her nose, her deep philtrum, and her full lips also liken her to Piero's characters at Arezzo. She further resembles those biblical personages in seeming like a character from the past viewed in the present.

Meanwhile, the setting also belongs to a past era. Balthus's rendition of the wall behind Katia connects with his treatment of the Villa Medici interior. The surface is rich, complex, and suggestive of history. The real victory, however, is in the slip-covered boudoir chair that is Katia's throne. Probably no one else in the history of art has ever painted upholstered furniture in this way. The texture produced by Balthus's technique of glazing makes the chair as solid as plaster, yet the billowing folds of its skirt give the cream-colored fabric a summery lightness. The convex folds and recesses between the pleats endow ordinary reality with profound sanctity.

On one level, *Katia Reading* seems too studied: irritating in its artifice and coy in its degree of restraint. Yet at the same time, certain elements—the slip-covers, the weight of the girl's foot—are extremely impressive. In the subject matter and emotional climate of the canvas, Balthus seems to have been imitating his former self, now annoyingly disguised; yet the older man's grasp of certain simple and absolute visual truths is moving. This luscious, secretive adolescent girl—seated like a seductive, if elusive, noblewoman—could have come from no one else's hand.

VIII

BALTHUS IN THE POSTWAR YEARS painted even fewer males than before. And except for the occasional portrait and self-portrait, representations of men or boys tend to be oddballs: bald babies with globular faces, the waving farmer in *Landscape with Cow* who looks like a study for the movie *The Coneheads*. A single bather in a sort of jockstrap, painted in 1960, seems a parody of a Cézanne: one of Cézanne's youths as a doctor's doll.

But he did again turn to male subject matter in a second painting of two card players which he painted between 1968 and 1973 (color plate 14). Its protagonists, however, are completely bizarre. Stranger yet, the painter himself told me I was the one with the problem in not recognizing them simply as ordinary boys playing cards. We were seated with a reproduction of the painting in front of us. In retrospect, it seems a ruse, but when Balthus at that moment claimed that these were the sort of kids you see every day, I believed that he believed it. For a while, I, too, ceased questioning them—as if I were in a dream.

The boy on the left—who kneels on one leg in a precise echo of Hubert's position in *The Children*—has a moon-face that is flattened like a relief mask. He is a complete demon. His squint is positively evil; his body is like an assemblage of disjointed parts; and his pose is self-consciously theatrical.

The longer-haired figure in *The Card Players* is even more puzzling than this artificial young man. I studied the canvas in Rotterdam, where it hangs in the Boymans Museum. After fifteen minutes of conversation with a friend who had accompanied me there, we suddenly realized that while he assumed this creature on the right-hand side of the painting to be female, I thought it male. My friend was adamant that everything about the gesture and pose, as well as the clothing, justified his conclusion. Indeed, Jean Leymarie—who can be counted on to tell the gospel according to Balthus—calls this "a woman." Yet there were reasons why I instinctively thought otherwise, and still question the child's gender. For one thing, this creature's bangs and pageboy hairstyle are almost identical to those sported by Balthus as he appeared with his mother and Rilke in Beatenberg in the photograph I studied so often in the living room at Le Grand Chalet. Moreover, the character's tunic-style dress closely resembles, with minor variations in its collar, the outfit worn by the boy in *The Children*. And its features are so close to those of the other child in *The Card Players*—the one who is unquestionably male—that they appear to be two variations of the same person.

Linda Fairstein—admittedly an unusual source for the study of artworks, but someone who has observed maleness and femaleness with forensic expertise—concurred with me that the questionable card player is male. Fairstein reads the character as being of the same gender apparent in the face and torso, if not the skirt, of the dwarflike curtain holder in *The Room*—Balthus's "She's just a little girl, Nicholas" notwithstanding. Balthus, after all, knew how to paint women, painted them all the time, and made them extremely womanly. This character is not a girl according to the artist's own established pictorial vocabulary.

When I raised the issue of this person's gender with John Russell, he told

me that for years he had assumed this was a girl. But once I suggested otherwise, he agreed that my view was plausible. "Sexual ambiguity," Russell said,
"is the essence of everything to do with Balthus."

I believe that, by intention or not, the card players are Balthus and Pierre.
These are two brothers: competing, holding secrets, posing, playing for keeps.
One holds his cards close to his chest. The other—clearly the younger one—
plays the winning card with unabashed glee. He has won the title and the fortune—and the international acclaim. Maybe he has won their mother, too.

This feline, impish androgyne is one of the characters who have proliferated in Balthus's art since its beginnings. He closely resembles Mitsou. By
being, at the same time, innocent and culprit, as well as revealer and concealer,
he is a familiar type. He also descends directly from the multifaceted seductress of *The Guitar Lesson*. With her female breasts and male face, and her features those of her creator, the music teacher too, had a dual persona: the
conqueror of young girls who was both Balthus and his mother. In the
younger child in *The Card Players*, the concealing, game-playing Count de
Rola has, yet again, painted himself, and in so doing has merged male and
female, young and old.

FOR RAINER MARIE RILKE, androgyny was a natural state. In his majestic
Letters to a Young Poet, Rilke had declared:

> Perhaps the sexes are more akin than people think, and the great
> renewal of the world will consist perhaps in this: that man and
> maiden, freed of all false feelings and aversions, will seek each other
> not as opposites but as siblings and neighbors and will join forces as
> *human beings* in order to bear in common, simply, earnestly, and
> patiently, the difficult sex that has been laid upon them.[30]

Balthus's males have more femaleness than the females maleness, but the interplay is always there.

Ages merge just as genders do. The girls consistently appear to have the
wisdom of the ancients. Conceived as they are out of his love, the most childlike of his nubile adolescents have the years of the substantially older man who
painted them. And the hussies among his older women—especially those of
the 1930s—are like young male warriors.

So this teenage victor at the card game—youthful and wizened, masculine
and feminine—is both the summation of his characters and the perfect
Balthus self-portrait. However insistent his verbal denials of his own remark-

able achievement, Balthus shatters boundaries and gives splendid voice to the multiplicity of the human soul.

THE COMPLEXITY OF THE individual characters and of the interplay between them in *The Card Players* is no less profound because Balthus chooses to deny it. Maintaining that all that matters is the visual orchestration, he wears the same mask as the androgynous, smirking youth who proffers the winning card but avoids the world with his squinting eyes.

Indeed, in the actual surface variations as well as the implicit textures, the rhythms, color play, and spatial movement, this canvas is among Balthus's most enticing creations. It is a remarkable technical accomplishment, especially in the context of other twentieth-century art. But more than its construction and visual complexity, its ability to delve into the world revealed and liberated by Balthus's much disparaged Freud is what distinguishes it above all.

BALTHUS APPEARED TO OPEN UP more than usual when we discussed *The Card Players*. He told me he painted it the same way as his 1979 *View of Montecalvello*—the subtle masterpiece he knew I loved. He had worked on *The Card Players* "endlessly" over a five-year period using a technique he referred to as "glazure." This consists, he explained, of building up layers of crazzé arte, a plaster and casein mixture, which he mixed with oil—and on top of which he applied color. Balthus said he was "always fascinated by glazure. You get a substance which has a body: thickness and transparency." This way of working was given up by the Impressionists and therefore is no longer practiced today; he added with visible pride that his method was both dated and out of fashion.

One of the by-products of this technique is that the painting weighs hundreds of pounds. Another result is that *The Card Players* has an extraordinary texture and sequence of forms. The dark green background is a sea of paint. It does not disguise how worked it is, yet for all the apparent labor behind it, it remains supremely graceful. The painting frankly reveals the process of re-creation that constitutes the making of art. It announces the physical act of applying paint to a support as clearly as a marble sculpture flaunts its stone. The artist's loving but struggle-filled relationship with his materials is plain to see.

The appearance and function of the spare, rugged furniture in this large canvas renders them virtually sacred. The table is like an altar; we expect the sacraments to appear on it. Its cloth covering, while squashed flat as in a Japanese woodcut, is folded dramatically at the corners, as if a holy rite has been performed. The empty chair has a quiet nobility to it, thanks both to the splay of its legs and the regal legerdemain with which it has been painted. This is Balthus's power: to make the most of something so simple, to extract the magic from the commonplace.

With his impeccable light touch, Balthus gives the progression of legs—both human and furniture—a force and sanctity. The bottom portion of the painting—the horizontal band that stretches all the way across at a height of about two feet—is a sequence of elements delicate and convincing. The legs, each with its shadow, are like the tree trunks in a forest by Derain: rhythmically rich and entirely real. For Balthus understands not just the nature of matter; he imbues it with poetry.

The boy on the left who resembles Hubert in *The Children* follows Hubert's example of resting the substantial weight of his upper body on his right arm. We are completely convinced of his mass and his three-dimensionality; his presence is as real as that of the chair and table legs. Yet Balthus has then gone on to distort him according to his own taste and inclination. His chest and back are disproportionately elongated. He arrives with the just-blown-in force of the Annunciate. But rather than looking like the angel Gabriel, he wears a Japanese mask.

Compared with this thick-boned, massive lad, the other character—the one of indeterminate sex—is pixyish. Full of graceful, gentle twists, he/she is both lighter and refreshingly still. While the personage on the left emanates brute strength from his wide trunk and gargantuan jacket, this younger being is mignon as well as clever.

Meanwhile, its outfit has been painted with impressive dexterity. Up close, the blue and reddish brown subtly suggest pleats. But they also read as pure abstraction and as forged iron. There is nothing Balthus doesn't venture with textures. He has integrated a pale grid—invisible in reproduction—into the checkerboard pattern of the tablecloth, by drawing it in with pencil and etching it with a fine metal point. The reason for this seems to be the artist's caprice—the same factor governing the way that one corner of the cloth reveals the pattern that is intended as the public face of the object while the other shows the underside that is meant to be its secret. The curving scrollwork chair has the roughness and soft luminism we associate with Braque. The character's hair reads like blocky sculpture. Everything devolves into a work of art.

THE MATTE, MUTED COLORS OF *The Card Players* have all been related with the authority and confidence with which that contented creature has played the winning card and will enter its score on the open pad. Pink comes through in the larger fellow's hand. His robust coloring contrasts with the other's pallor. In both cases, the rendering of their features recalls late Rembrandt; up close, you cannot possibly understand what you're looking at, but from afar it is clear. These heads have not been drawn and then colored sequentially. Rather, they have been constructed from scratch; the areas of light and dark, the pinks and tans, all emerge simultaneously.

When you are very near to the painting, the notepad, too, is just rough pigment. But at a proper distance it is a little miracle of painting. Its cover is folded just so. The shadow on its bulge and under the top sheet and the light on the top of the cover near its stitching make it not just plausible but terribly significant.

Balthus has eschewed the facile approach of artists like Magritte and some of the other Surrealists and opted instead for a more difficult, but also more convincing, route. You realize, just looking at this notebook, that if on one level he is the biggest phony in the world—I write this just after the appearance of a particularly self-serving picture story about him and Harumi in the *London Times Magazine,* with especially contrived photos—on another he is completely sincerely in love with painting, not just with its illusion and invention but also with its celebration of the seeable.

For if in its subject matter, and in what that imagery says about its maker, *The Card Players* is completely weird, in its craft it is testimony to humility and dedication. The points where the back supports of the empty chair lock onto the side posts have total verisimilitude. An unexpected purple, like a dusty lavender, appears at the top and bottom of each of these boards because such are the miracles of vision. Throughout the painting, light falls so that we imbibe its glow, and paint magically evokes sunshine. A hollow palm emits its shine, while fingers cosset the darkness they create in their folds; these are the experiences that make life unfathomably wonderful. When Balthus's line wavers, it is because ambiguity is a truer state than clarity is. We see his changes—thin paint next to thick, light pencil on the surface next to lines incised deeply within—because their course mimics the vagaries of the human mind.

Contrast and change are fundamental. The thrusting thigh of the heathen in red is angled dramatically against the strong central axis and the rigid armature made by the bold vertical and horizontals. That limb lives, its power both aesthetic and sexual. Daring and audacious, Balthus takes us on his journey.

BALTHUS STARTED *The Card Players* after seeing a Kabuki play in Japan. He said that the painting was inspired by a scene in which two clan chiefs are in a standoff that precedes a lethal battle. Therefore—although it was not his intention, he remarked—"*The Card Players* is like a fight somehow. Yet it's misleading to say too much. The why and the how don't help. One has to look at the painting and see it."

The Kabuki reference sheds light—albeit an ambiguous, Balthusian light on the gender issue in the painting. This form of Japanese theater is performed by an all-male cast. When there are female roles, males impersonate them. *The Card Players,* of course, is not meant to illustrate Kabuki, but it was, nonetheless, inspired by the form. Even if the figure on the right is to be considered a girl, its prototype was a man in the guise of a woman.

How like Balthus to have cast teenage children in the roles of warriors. His adolescents on some level have always been doing battle. Evil and violence, manipulation and control—themes that his brother Pierre embraced more openly—have long lurked in his work, even if cloaked under all those carefully studied layers. These boys playing their card game are no less calculating than the music teacher in *The Guitar Lesson.* Virtually all of the children in Balthus's work have, in fact, lost their sweetness a long time ago. They have an agenda whose precise nature may be hidden but whose ferocity is not.

Indeed, teenagers scheme. They dissemble. They have their own inner world, their selfish ambitions, their simultaneous need for privacy and for provoking their audience. Balthus simply trumps their mendacity.

I HAD SEEN *The Card Players* twice before my viewing of it in Rotterdam. *The Card Players* had been in the 1977 Pierre Matisse exhibition and the 1984 show at the Met, yet on both occasions I had found it so discomfiting, compared with the female figures and landscapes nearby, that I had practically rushed away. I now think that this is because the cattiness of the standoff—the stench of sheer, unadorned hostility that emanates from the painting—repelled me. The majesty of its painting technique was not sufficient recompense for its nasty atmosphere. Whereas the sex-laden violence of *The Guitar Lesson* riveted me, the froideur of these two hideous-faced boys did not.

Even when I journeyed to Rotterdam to study this large canvas and felt I had no choice but to linger over it, its redolent spirit of antagonism overpowered its extraordinary visual serenity. The mixture of sweet and sour baffled me. But after about half an hour, the charms began to outwit the ugliness. The lush, subtle textures and orchestrations of form gripped me. That empty wooden chair took on a spiritualism, a lightness and equanimity so moving that, viewing it, I clearly understood, as I did before *Montecalvello,* what Balthus meant when he called himself "a religious painter."

I came back repeatedly to that simple piece of country furniture bathed in its holy light. Balthus's tender rendition of a few pieces of wood and the miracle of their joints is an ethereal vision of earthly reality. The sight of it in Rotterdam made me breathe deeper and slower. The processional aspect of the table legs, the slow folds of the tablecloth corners, moved me as I have been moved by Piero at Arezzo.

The mix of transparency and mass throughout this large composition is remarkable. A golden light suffuses the entire painting—lightly, tastefully so. The objects belong plausibly to the earth, yet to another world as well.

Then the masklike faces of the two demons took over again. It was as if the devil himself was present. The flattened moons with their beady, slit eyes are as smug and conniving as anyone I have ever met. They betray unabashed selfishness. Yet at the same time, wearing masks like those employed in Oriental theater, they are completely artificial. Truly this is what Artaud meant, more than thirty years earlier, by "Theater of Cruelty." Malice emerges exquisite.

The Card Players WAS ON BALTHUS'S easel in Rome when Baladine Klossowska died—the occasion when, I learned from Balthus himself, Pierre was present but he was not. Apparently this was the prerogative of genius; Rilke, when faced with the knowledge of his father's impending death, had similarly chosen not to go to the scene.

The director of the Villa Medici was, in any event, scarcely in touch with his mother and brother. His world now safely removed from the old days of panicked exile to Berlin, he had mostly put them behind him. Yet his was a mind that, on some level, would always factor the past into the present. Like anyone confronting the death of a parent, he must, however furtively, have been reliving old issues like sibling rivalry. The antagonisms of childhood were clearly still in his thoughts. If *The Card Players* can be seen as a flashback to Balthus's own youth, in his spite-filled relationship with Pierre he has emerged both the victor and the scorekeeper.

So the cad playing the winning card—male and female at the same time, smirking victoriously, staring at us yet yielding nothing—seems another of Balthus's self-portraits à clef. He has, of course, progressed since his 1930s incarnation as disenfranchised Heathcliff. Now the imperious youth sits on his scrollwork chair as if enthroned—the young dauphin, perhaps. With the same facial structure, flattened nose, and continuous forehead, so Arezzo-like, of the mannequinlike characters in *The Street*, he now calmly assumes the pose of victory. In *The Guitar Lesson*, he wins his battle by brute force; thirty-five years later, he achieves it through craft.

After all, Balthus could now relax. He had become the director of the Villa Medici, a titled count, a friend of the Agnellis and Malraux and Fellini. Yet at age sixty he was still at the psychological stage where he had almost always been. The obsession of his art, that period of human development mirrored his own mind. It was the same as when he painted *The Children.* The most crafty, manipulative, and devious aspects of adolescence were his home territory.

BUT EVEN IF BALTHUS HAD changed little over the years, and *The Card Players* exhibits many of the strengths of his most cultivated art, it lacks the punch and force of those pictures of teenagers Balthus painted when he was at the peak of his skills in the 1930s. Like virtually all of his canvases of the Villa Medici years, the Rotterdam painting is incredibly mannered—as if Balthus, still immensely talented, still disarmingly intelligent, is now pasticheing himself. He does so beautifully, but now we are seeing everything filtered. Intuition and brutal candor have been replaced by style.

Even on those rare occasions when the later work is successful, it recapitulates themes and ideas that the younger Balthus, in the days when he could afford nothing but his humble digs on the Rue de Fürstemberg or the Cour de Rohan, had evoked more honestly and more vividly. *The Card Players,* based on theater, is theater itself. Its figures are actors more than people, its space a stage set more than a room. It is doubly awkward because the issue here is maleness—territory in which Balthus was even less at home than usual. The collision between psychological obfuscation and visual clarity is wrenching.

ONE OF BALTHUS'S USUAL contrivances to separate himself from the subject matter of his art came up in the latest of the sanctioned Balthus publications to date: Claude Roy's large volume published in France in 1996 by Gallimard, in which the flap photo shows writer and subject facing the camera together from the garden of Le Grand Chalet and the descriptive text identifies the volume as a portrait by a friend. A conversation is quoted between Balthus and a guest at the Villa Medici.

> "May I ask if you frequently play or used to play cards?" Balthus has not heard. He asks for the question again, with a nuance of polite ferocity which escapes the visitor. To oblige repetition of a foolish remark, to hear it spoken twice: a subtle pleasure. Balthus does not answer directly. "I'm not sure," is all he says, "that every painter who

has painted the severed head of Holofernes practices decapitation with a saber."[31]

Indeed, the issue of whether Balthus played poker or blackjack is irrelevant; but the themes of malevolence, sibling rivalry, secretiveness, androgyny, and the craving for power that clearly underlie this painting—and their obsessive if clandestine position in Balthus's life—are very much to the point.

IX

BALTHUS SPENT TEN YEARS painting *Japonaise au miroir noir*—translated as *Japanese Figure with a Black Mirror* in Rewald's catalog, and as *Japanese Girl with Black Mirror* in the English version of Leymarie's opus. "Girl" seems a misnomer; the model was Setsuko, and Balthus began this painting, and its companion, *Japonaise avec table rouge,* in 1967, the year he married her at age twenty-five.

Setsuko's arms here define "gesture" as Artaud emphasized it in non-Western theater, declaring its superiority to verbal language. When we see this splendid canvas, these arms immediately ennoble their owner and bespeak her needs and wants. The right one reaches out in the fullest possible stretch, expressing freedom and will. The left provides requisite balance and support, and portrays the spectacular abilities of the human body. Both limbs are painted simplistically—clearly just paint: flat, featureless, a form of code—yet they are animal, plausible, and real.

Japanese at a Black Mirror—my preferred translation—is now in a lavish New York duplex. Although Balthus would hardly approve of the decor, and would like even less the Philip Pearlstein hung nearby, he was pleased when I told him about the brilliant winter sunlight, invited in by the width of Park Avenue, that was bathing the painting when I went to see it. That light enables one to savor the creamy impasto and the underlying prime coat of a tan umber that unifies the range of matte colors. It illuminates such splendid nuances as the bits of blue in the white waist sash and the purple within the black of the lacquer furniture. These, I knew full well, were the elements of the painting its maker would most gladly discuss with me.

What I did not bring up with Balthus, however, was the woman's pose and clothing. In "the Fifth day" of *The 120 Days of Sodom,* the Marquis de Sade describes a "charming little maid" wearing a garment with a "neat flap under which one could slip one's hand and grasp the ass without the slightest difficulty; the flap was held by a ribbon tied in a big bow, and when one wished to have the child completely exposed in this part, one had merely to undo the bow."[32] I doubt that Balthus had Sade's invention in mind when he clad his subject in her bizarre pose crawling toward the mirror, but the idea behind her seductive costume could well have come from his brother's favorite writer. That bowed ribbon wraps its wearer like a parcel or gift to be opened. The wide sash seems to pull upward as we look at it. It keeps the woman's stomach suspended—almost like a ribbon used to hang an Easter egg.

Indeed, this sensuous and elegant painting is not singularly the paean to loveliness it at first purports to be. Janet Hobhouse, one of the most insightful writers on Balthus, remarked that the "Japanese model is depicted crawling like someone wounded trying to reach a phone. Sadism pervades the work like an exotic waft."[33] Balthus would not hear of such a thing, of course, but the flap skirt and sash might be an outfit from a bondage boutique. Wearing it, the lunging Setsuko looks uncomfortable and desperate, yet at the same time she is an irresistible tigress. This is, of course, the mix of victim and tyrant that has been apparent in Balthus's depiction of women since the 1930s—of which his first wife, posing for *Cathy Dressing,* was the seminal type.

Japanese at a Black Mirror, 1967–76,
casein and tempera on canvas, 150 x 196 cm

We know full well that the artist deems such observations to be heresy. Perhaps he has denied the violence of his work for so long and so vehemently that he may even believe it himself. But I think Hobhouse is right when she writes that "there is a consistent double-dealing in Balthus's presentation of time and space. Violence is in the air, and under the cleanest of skies."[34] *Japanese at a Black Mirror* is a beautiful painting, exquisitely colored, its complex components admirably related. It looks completely at home in its plush surroundings, but the more you look, the more it exemplifies Hobhouse's observation that "Balthus imagines disaster, violence and violation . . . [although] he does not depict it directly. Instead he makes his laconic and elegant suggestion, preserves the refinement of his sensibility by the delicacy of his art, allowing us to translate those vibrations in the work into our own shudder, to make (if we insist) our own grosser response to what his art pretends to deny is there at all."[35]

Balthus, in fact, thrives on contradictory messages. In the 1994 article in the glossy American magazine *Art & Antiques* where he denies that he likes to grant interviews or speak out about himself, he then turns around with the dictum, "The idea I am getting across has to do with religion, not at all with eroticism."[36] Inconsistency is second nature to him. *Japanese at a Black Mirror* presents itself one way and then does something else, just as the man does.

The more we look at this seemingly serene, straightforward scenario, the more contrived it is. The woman's proportions are absurd. Her arms are drawn awkwardly: her hand is like guesswork. Nothing is quite right, yet it remains a sensuous, sexy picture.

The opposites coexist visually as well. In a rhythmic space formed by the intersection of bold planes, the exotic woman is an amalgam of curves against the syncopating geometry of the surfaces. The background patterning, like the colors, seems Pompeian, making the canvas feel as ancient as it is modern. The skin is at one moment paint, at another flesh: art and life simultaneously. With Balthus, nothing is ever just one thing or another.

BALTHUS ADORED A STORY I told him about *Japanese at a Black Mirror*. Its owner, whom I met in New York, told me that she had first seen the canvas at Pierre Matisse's exhibition in 1977. She had studied art history at college, genuinely knew a lot about art, and had the courage to buy what she wanted; moreover, she was extremely wealthy. She was any gallery's dream client.

But she was not recognized when a friend brought her into the Balthus show. After she so fell in love with this painting that she inquired about its price, Pierre Matisse simply told her she could not afford it. The woman evinced considerable charm when she quoted this remark to me, since it was well known that she was married to one of the richest men in America. With a look of satisfaction, she reported that within hours of Pierre Matisse declaring her insufficiently affluent, she reached her husband on his car phone and, although they did not collect art in great quantity, the next day they went to the gallery together and bought the canvas.

Balthus was riveted by my account of this speedy purchase. "How *brilliant* of Pierre," he declared with an approving grin. It was as if the collectors had been inspired to acquire *Japanese at a Black Mirror* simply to disprove the gallery owner's claim that they couldn't afford it. The maneuver, Balthus explained, was completely in character for his beloved dealer. Such manipulation—especially of the very rich—was, in Balthus's eyes, the most admirable of achievements.

CHAPTER TWENTY-THREE

ROSSINIÈRE

I

BALTHUS HAD SERVED two terms as director of the Villa Medici before his replacement was named in the mid-1970s. For a while he remained there in limbo: no longer fully in charge, but unwilling to exit completely.

His Roman way of life was hard to give up. There was ample staff to care for his baby daughter, and a chauffeur to drive the family to the ancient castle Balthus had now acquired and restored to perfection at Montecalvello, near Viterbo, some thirty miles away.

He had unfinished business. Balthus wanted to be on hand to continue his exhibition program and to receive visitors he had invited to the villa but who had not yet shown up. He still had his studio in the villa's gardens, where there were several paintings awaiting completion. The task beckoned all the more now that his work was fetching enormous prices on the international art market.

But this was a treacherous time in Italy. Kidnapping was on the rise, and rich and important people were increasingly fearful. Balthus and Setsuko concluded that they needed to live elsewhere even if they retained ownership of Montecalvello. They turned to the mountains. The reason, ostensibly, was that the climate was better for Balthus's health. But the Swiss Alps offered other advantages as well, among them a favorable tax situation. In 1977 the count and countess and their baby Harumi finally left Rome for the Canton de Vaud and made the forty-five-room "Grand Chalet" their new home.

One day at breakfast, Balthus and Setsuko told me the circumstances of their first visit to their future residence, then a hotel. "We were in Gstaad with friends and wanted to go somewhere for tea," Setsuko explained. "We came to

14. *The Card Players,* 1968–73, casein and tempera on canvas, 190 x 225 cm

15. *View of Montecalvello,* 1979, oil on canvas, 130 x 162 cm

16. *Cat at the Mirror III*, 1989–94, oil on canvas, 220 x 195 cm

Le Grand Chalet and had a bad tea, with only water in the pot. The owners, who were running it as an inn, said, 'We're trying to sell, but no one seems to be interested.' " These, of course, were the Devenishes, the other dinner guests on my first evening at Le Grand Chalet.

"Balthus then told me that because he had had malaria he could not stay entirely in our castle near Rome," Setsuko recalled that, on walking into Le Grand Chalet, "I said to my husband, 'This I would like to have as my house.' "

The palatial chalet, which was built between 1752 and 1756, required less major reconstruction than had Balthus's earlier retreats or Rilke's Muzot. The construction was sound, with enormous vaulted cellars, originally used as storehouses for cheese, serving as the foundation for the complex wooden framework topped by the vast sloping roof made of a seemingly infinite number of small nailed planks. In the 1850s, the building had become a hotel, receiving such illustrious guests as Victor Hugo, who spent time there in 1883. Balthus removed the balcony and one of the rooms that had been added during this hotel phase, and stripped all the pine inside so that the hand-planed boards were restored to their original eighteenth-century appearance. A wonderful rustic elegance prevailed, with cracks and splits in the plaster, a well-chosen mix of country and formal furniture. The Klossowskis de Rola put in a new kitchen. By the time the butlers in uniforms were in place and the other staff members lined up, Le Grand Chalet resembled nothing so much as a small and exclusive establishment in the Relais & Château group—except that it was a private abode.

Balthus by now was an international celebrity in a bustling art world. In 1980 a number of his key works—*The Street, The Mountain, The Landscape at Champrovent, Les Beaux Jours, The Méditerranée's Cat, The Room, The Passage du Commerce Saint-André, The Moth, The Turkish Room, Katia Reading, The Card Players,* and others—made the complex journey to Venice, by plane and truck and ultimately through the canals on a cargo boat, where they formed a solo show that was the great drawing card of "La Biennale." The summer tourist crowds and art cognoscenti who flocked to the show were offered an elaborate catalog with texts by Jean Leymarie and Federico Fellini; Balthus was now truly at the forefront of modern culture.

The Venice experience was not entirely satisfying for the artist, however. Several days before the Biennale opened, he was so frustrated when *Les Beaux Jours* arrived from Washington covered in Plexiglas that he threatened to break the covering with a stick. The reflections, indeed, prevented anything close to an adequate viewing of his work. But the courier said he would lose his job if

Balthus in Venice

the protective covering were removed, and Balthus relented. Meanwhile, his presence in Venice that summer earned him a cameo appearance in Erica Jong's roman à clef *Serenissima;* his was a name on everyone's lips.

Yet Balthus was an ambivalent celebrity. In 1982 Giovanni Carandente organized a major retrospective of the artist's drawings and watercolors at the Festival of the Two Worlds in Spoleto. William Bailey described the honoree on the evening of the opening. Following the actual vernissage, people were gathering at a café on the main piazza. Bailey observed a man in a kimono standing silent on the piano nobile of a palazzo, a similarly clad woman at his side, both of them observing all the people through a large window. They simply surveyed the crowd, while most of the throng remained unaware of their watchful eyes.

Later on, Carandente—an art historian who had worked hard both on the show and on a major book that accompanied it—brought Balthus to the café. Everyone stood up to congratulate the seventy-four-year-old artist. Carandente took Balthus's hand and attempted to raise it in a sign of victory— "a very Italian gesture," Bailey explained. "Their clasped hands were to celebrate the success." But before the gesture was complete, Balthus, visibly annoyed, pushed Carandente's hand down with his own.

Nude with Towel,
1981–82, oil on canvas,
163 x 130 cm

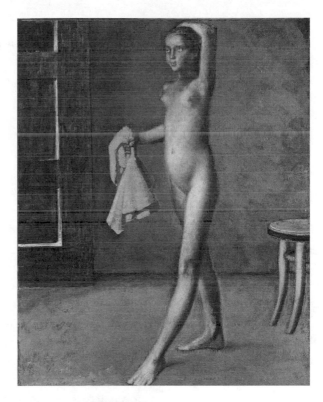

Dozing Nude, 1980,
casein and tempera on
canvas, 200 x 150 cm

This was not, however, a gesture of arrogance from the Count de Rola so much as one of modesty from a serious artist. A few minutes later, Balthus walked into the café, quite simply, to mingle with the young artists and his other admirers, chatting easily and warmly.

The following year, just as his retrospective of nearly a hundred works was opening at the Centre Pompidou, "Balthus, the Mystery Man" was one of the subjects listed on the cover of the sleek magazine *Connoisseur.* It may well have been one of the reasons that Balthus soon earned the nickname "the Garbo of painters." The only current photo with the piece showed him avoiding the camera, trying to shield his eyes from the flash with his left hand. "Balthus does not grant interviews. Period," the writer erroneously started his piece. On the subject of his upcoming Paris exhibition, the dream of most artists, Balthus offered only one statement: "If I could, I'd definitely try to stop the show."[1]

AWAY FROM THE RESPONSIBILITIES of the French Academy, ensconced in his Swiss studio, Balthus began to paint with renewed zeal. Occasionally, he did so very well. But in the late 1970s and into the 1980s, the artist also produced a number of paintings that had the look of weak Balthus paraphrases. Signature pieces, recognizable even across the room to the unknowing viewer as "a Balthus," their essential ingredients are a nubile adolescent girl, in full-crotch view with no pubic hair; a Hogarthian cat; a mirror; and a rich arrangement of textiles. By and large these canvases are extremely stylized and mannered, with a cloying artificiality.

The Comte de Rola—the grand seigneur of Rossinière, the darling of fashion magazines—was still Balthus in his technical know-how, and was still painting adolescent girls in their sensuous reverie, but his art became even more affected than he did. Its details were evidence that a knowing and serious painter was still at work, but the cultivated remoteness renders it irritatingly precious.

Viewing these late Balthus paintings is like seeing a former beauty—one whom you first knew when she was much younger and her appearance was entirely natural—who now wears layers of makeup, has had her skin tightened with a face-lift, and frosts and lacquers her hair. You know that the old face is in there somewhere, and you look for the ingredients that once swayed you, but you cannot quite feel them.

It seems as if Balthus is using every trick in the book to be who he has always been. But for all the stylish disguising, he has lost the power of his youth. At the same time, these late paintings are composed by an expert; beyond the dissembling, they contain some utterly beautiful passages of painting.

II

The body—and this sense comes to consciousness at puberty—is
by definition both a subjective object and an object objectively
perceived. To the adolescent it is, like the analyst in the
transference, the most familiar stranger. In puberty the adoles-
cent develops what can be accurately referred to as a transference
to his own body, what crystallizes in adolescence, what return
partly as excitement through risk, are doubts about the mother
and the holding environment of infancy. These doubts are
transferred on to the body, turned against it, as it begins to
represent a new kind of internal environment, a more solitary
one. That is to say, the adolescent begins to realize that the
original mother is his body.

                                                    —ADAM PHILLIPS[2]

In *Cat at the Mirror I* of 1977–80, the only element that strikes one as real and
genuine is the small detail of the cat. The naked girl—the primary subject of
the painting—is virtually weightless. Floating in space, she is completely
unconvincing as a physical presence. Once upon a time, in paintings like
Thérèse Dreaming, Balthus could get his subjects to sit or stand with complete
authority. We felt we knew precisely where the center of gravity was, where
every joint and muscle was, and could practically measure the body weight.
But the girl in *Cat at the Mirror I* belongs only to the world of the imagination.

The odd creature is all the more implausible because she has the body of
an eleven-year-old just on the brink of puberty—the start of breasts, no pubic
hair—and the face of a twenty-five-year-old. Moreover, she is androgynous.
While predominantly female, she has elements of certain male prototypes: particularly Renaissance paintings of the infant Jesus in which the baby prema-
turely shows his wisdom and age.

In the strange contortions of her body, this clumsily drawn child is like no
one we have seen before. Her shoulders are completely out of kilter; her flat
and lifeless torso is modeled more like plaster than flesh; her left arm is too
long; her head projects unusually far in front of her neck; her misaligned
breasts fail to relate to one another; and her feet are more likely a bird's than a
person's. A creepy, flat light works its way across the scene, making the bizarre
creature look like a waxen corpse; the gray color of her skin further sucks the
life out of her. On the other hand, it seems almost as if she has flown in from
somewhere, and has landed so that she pivots on her crotch. The junction of

her legs at her genitals is, indeed, the focal point of the painting: a V that is echoed throughout her robe lining, the legs of her footstool, and other details.

I do not believe that Balthus consciously set out to make the woman either so strange or so sexualized. I think, rather, that he was a man possessed: not quite knowing what he was doing. He has stretched and contorted and spread-eagled his young lady here, and—to use Linda Fairstein's word for the lifeless hue of Balthus's 1937 *Victim*—desanguinated her. The result is that his idealized blond goddess, smiling contentedly at the golden back of a mirror she holds out for the cat, is tortured and lifeless. But one has no sense that either she or the artist who created her is aware of her state.

The cat, however, is as knowable as the girl is indecipherable. The little feline is three-dimensional and massive—as well as completely demonic. And it is the cat, rather than the girl, who looks in the mirror. If the cat is emblem-

Cat at the Mirror I, 1977–80, casein and tempera on canvas, 180 x 170 cm

atic of Balthus himself—a fair assumption, given the artist's lifetime identification—then is the entire *Cat at the Mirror I,* and not just this detail, also a case
of the cat looking in the mirror? Has Narcissus painted Narcissus? Has Balthus
by this point in his life come to see himself as the little girl whose image the
world associates with him; have he and his obsession become one and the
same?

In SPITE OF THE FLAWS and awkwardness of its central figure, *Cat at the Mirror I* holds the viewer's attention with its carefully balanced, intricate composition. Every color in the elegant palette has been skillfully mixed to have the
same tone and light intensity as the next, whatever its hue.

In his areas of strength, Balthus is in top form here. The plum background has the mottled texture and muted glow of sun-bleached fresco. The
drapery—the ultimate symbol of concealment, and the material analogue to
decorum—is painted superbly. The various encapsulations of surface beauty,
like the robe lining and the bedspread, are completely convincing, even while
the feet and hands are not. The towel around the washstand is perfect.

The textile accoutrements sparkle with light, but the comb and mirror are
brighter yet. These shining symbols of vanity—of consciousness of how one
looks and is perceived by the world—stand out above all. Appearance and presentation are at the center of Balthus's universe.

BALTHUS WAS NOW AT A POINT where most major art historians of the time
felt obliged to comment on his work. If his 1934 Galerie Pierre show had managed to garner only a few brief paragraphs in minor publications—when the
artist was at an apogee of brilliance and originality—now, with his skills
diminished and emotions masked, he had everyone looking. Critical response
varied wildly, however.

Kenneth Clark, perhaps the most esteemed of all commentators, came in
enthusiastic but equivocal. Clark wrote, in 1980, that Balthus

> is a painter of consummate skill and brilliant pictorial gifts. His late
> nudes are ravishing pieces of painting, and will delight the eye of any-
> one who is responsive to the perception of color and the use of paint.
> On the rare occasions when he does a piece of "pure" painting, as for
> example the picture of fruit on a window sill (1956), it excels in sensu-
> ous charm alone almost all the painters of his time.

On the other hand, Clark was far less enthusiastic about the large paintings that the artist himself considers his greatest successes, and that have traditionally preoccupied most of Balthus's advocates:

> Personally I do not like so much his more ambitious compositions. Some of them, like *The Passage du Commerce Saint-André*, seem too literary in the old deprecating sense. We spend time in trying to interpret the meaning of the figures and lose the feeling of the whole. This also applies to a large picture called *The Mountain*, which was obviously intended as a *masterpiece*, and suffers from the drawbacks of that dangerous genre. It might have won the prize for figure composition in any academy.[3]

Also critical of what he perceived as the academic strain of Balthus's work, but now truly nasty about it, the great British Cubist scholar and Picasso authority Douglas Cooper weighed in with:

> The French painter known as Balthus is a minor, undistinguished, quasi-academic figure . . . : he has a particular ability to decolorise, to uglify and deform, produces paintings which are undistinguished and of little artistic significance, but fortunately has too weak a personality to exert any influence on others. Balthus's pattern of composition results from elaborate mathematical calculations: no element in them is free, and the ultimate effect is artificial, strained, static and awkward. His landscapes are frozen and airless, while his figures are monstrous mannequins which reveal how little understanding Balthus has of human anatomy. Moreover, Balthus lacks the mastery, the penetrating vision, the emotional force and the panache of the great painters from whom he tries to draw inspiration. . . .[4]

In complete contrast to this diatribe of Douglas Cooper's came the evaluation of John Rewald. The ultimate authority on Postimpressionism and one of the sages in the field, Rewald was open with friends about his complete disgust at Balthus's personal pretentiousness and use of a title, but did not let this color his views on Balthus's art. He wrote: "Balthus is a superb draftsman, one of the finest of our time."[5] What was certain was that Balthus had become someone about whom almost everyone had an opinion—however disparate the voices.

The less erudite press, meanwhile, dwelled on those aspects of Balthus's work most certain to win readers' attention. The words that proliferated in the headlines of the various Balthus articles that were beginning to crop up everywhere were "nymphs" and "Eros"; the vocabulary of the texts often belonged more to the domain of the tabloids than to art criticism. "Mysterious" and "elusive" became more than ever the catchwords for the man. In any event, whether the pundits were obediently taking their cue from the master or going their own course, the world was now paying homage.

THE MANNERIST DECADENCE that marked the lesser examples of Balthus's work at the Villa Medici—the weakest of the blurry, stylized nudes—only intensified once he got to Rossinière. There were regular lapses in which his work seems as affected, and as lacking in substance, as his title. But sometimes he made a canvas of inestimable power.

It was because of the strongest of these late paintings that one day in 1991 I told Balthus that I had no business writing about him. I had driven, with Dominique Bozo, from Rossinière to Gstaad to see Balthus's 1979 *View of Montecalvello* (color plate 15) in Basil and Elise Goulandris's chalet there. At tea later that same afternoon, I honestly reported to the artist that, after looking at this large landscape, I considered words and information of no meaning whatsoever next to the visual and emotional impact of his work. Facing *Montecalvello*, I did not see how I could presume that any observations I might make would matter. I felt unworthy. I meant this, and Balthus looked very pleased as I spoke.

I was, of course, aware that the person with whom I had the good fortune to chat at the dinner table that evening was the only living artist to have a painting at the Goulandrises'—alongside world-renowned masterpieces by Cézanne, van Gogh, and Monet. And I knew that its owners regarded Balthus's large canvas as being of equal caliber to their other paintings. These were impressive facts, and I concurred with the Goulandrises' judgment; Balthus's canvas was as sumptuous an object, as knowingly and intelligently crafted, as their Postimpressionist masterpieces. Beyond this distinction, however, I felt that *View of Montecalvello* was something other than a work of art: it was the embodiment of peace itself. It fully justified the statement Balthus had often repeated to me with many variations: "I consider myself as a religious painter. It's not an idea. It's a feeling."

I had previously seen *Montecalvello* in 1984 in Balthus's show at the Met, but in the confusion of that crowded assemblage on mustard-colored walls, it had had no particular effect on me. Now, when I could stand alone, quiet and uninterrupted, in front of the large canvas, I was disbelieving. It wasn't that the Goulandrises' living room suited it particularly—the furniture and interior design were more appropriate for Beverly Hills than for a Swiss mountain dwelling—but there was ideal, high-altitude daylight and a neutral wall color. Moreover, the setting offered a vista of the Alpine valley below which was similar to the sweeping panorama in the painting. *Montecalvello,* of course, depicts the more modest-scaled terrain near Viterbo, but there is still a sense of life as viewed from an aerie.

This feeling of being in the mountains was accentuated at one point when I was studying the work and Basil Goulandris—heir to a Greek shipping fortune, a lean and athletic old man now sadly debilitated by Parkinson's—came over, accompanied by his young male nurse, to join me. Staring into Balthus's misty landscape, he remarked, "That's by our neighbor here." Once I filled in his memory gap by supplying the name, Mr. Goulandris spoke as if he and Balthus and the people they knew in common in this marvelous part of the world lived a life like mythological creatures in the clouds. Gazing at Balthus's painting as if he inhabited it, its owner discussed its quality of peacefulness as a coefficient of the location they all enjoyed up here in the Alps, removed from much else in civilization.

Elise Goulandris—younger and healthier than her husband—was among those people who was simultaneously "on to" Balthus and enormously charmed by him. She and Bozo both expressed their great surprise to me that Balthus was cooperating with me on my book to such an extent. But they attributed it to the artist having mellowed in recent years. Elise was pleased to own this wonderful painting, and supplied the information that its gritty texture came from Balthus's use of dirt in the paint. In fact, it is, I later learned, plaster dust, but whatever its precise content, I was glad that Mrs. Goulandris called my attention to this tactile quality that explains why *View of Monte-calvello,* which always seems limp in reproduction on glossy paper, is so miraculously effective in actuality.

When we discussed this painting in some detail the next day, Balthus elaborated on this texture. His goal was to evoke the mist that arose from the lake. By using crazzé arte and adding oil to this plaster and casein mixture before putting color on it, he built up layers of thick painting and thin painting. Again I heard, verbatim, the statement he had made in reference to *The Card Players*—that he was "always fascinated by glazure. You get a substance which has a body: thickness and transparency."

The result of Balthus's diligent yet graceful scumbling, and of his use of that slightly pebbly plaster powder with the pigment, gives a unique quality to the light of this painting—as if we are looking through a soft and gauzy veil. This is true not only in the valley that Balthus has overpainted with a thin film of white to indicate the mist, but over the whole canvas. Calmly celebrative, the painting is thus elusive: palpable yet misty. The paint both establishes the age and permanence of the scene and creates a sense of distance. The landscape before us is real; at the same time, it is magical.

Serious and somber as *View of Montecalvello* is, it also manages to be intensely playful and high-spirited. The rocks swirl upward; while we believe that these are actual cliffs, they leap, weightless. Balthus told me that these cliffs were "sandstone shaped by rain and water"; he seems to have put that process of their formation into his rendering of them.

Every element is imbued with aliveness. The hills galavant. The geological layers swirl about like lather. Each tree exists as a living, growing being. You feel that you can see the air and are nourished by the very oxygen that makes all this possible.

View of Montecalvello is not just landscape; it is nature transformed. Even more than physical facts, its subject is perception. It is landscape *observed*. The characters on the stone terrace in the right-hand corner are pivotal. They appear to be—in a cartoon rendition—Balthus and a young girl. The painter's vantage point, and hence ours, is different from theirs—he painted this from the top floor of his nearby castle—but we join these people down below in the act of taking in the scene. Balthus explained to me, "I thought that people looking at that landscape gave it another dimension." He felt that "their eyes and presence opened it up more."

Balthus has captured their immersion in nature's pleasures. We join them in being affected by the kingdom of the earth. We perceive the small cottage as the essence of safe refuge. We look toward the distant tower as Balthus and Rilke and Baladine might have, over half a century earlier, scouted out the castle at Muzot. The winding paths and clearings beckon us.

The depth of the space and the softness of the atmosphere are a major achievement. Balthus had, indeed, studied Masaccio and other early Renaissance masters as a young man, and found a way to convey their sort of holy beauty in his own, humorous, playful, twentieth-century voice. *View of Montecalvello* illustrates heavenly quietude; beyond that, it captures the process of imbibing peace.

BALTHUS'S VIEWS OF Montecalvello—both the Goulandris canvas and several large pencil versions—are grand summation works. The vista may be specific to Balthus's castle, but it feels as Swiss and Chinese as it does Italian. It carries the force of mountains, and of Chinese landscape painting: central issues for Balthus since his childhood.

Rilke had given the teenage Balthus the Chinese novels of Victor Segalen, and Balthus made illustrations of classic Chinese literature for the poet. In various sanctioned publications on the artist, the adolescent boy is depicted during one of his long summer holidays in Beatenberg, sitting outside while looking at a volume of Chinese and Japanese landscape painting. He suddenly realizes that the view of the Lake of Thun and nearby mountain peaks is remarkably like the plates in the book. For the burgeoning artist, the Chinese art is a revelation for its ability to evoke the harmony of nature in the form of such peaks.

Balthus's spokesman Leymarie also claims that around this same period Erich Klossowski took Balthus to Aix-en-Provence to look at the countryside around Mont Sainte-Victoire. The goal of their journey was for father and son to consider the importance of Chinese art for Cézanne. But here the ground is shaky; I have yet to find a Cézanne source that attests to the French master's involvement with Asian landscape painting. Nor is it likely that Balthus and his father had either the time or the money to head off to Aix in these years when they were mainly in Germany. Since the trip certainly is never referred to in any Balthus documents (including all the letters that document Balthus's youth) prior to Leymarie's 1979 book, it possibly falls into the category of Balthus's preferred past.

But it is entirely credible that in the summer when Balthus, age eighteen, was in Florence, he went to Siena, where—in front of Simone Martini's frescoes in the Palazzo Pubblico—he met a Chinese student who was "fascinated by . . . connections between the painting of his own country and that of the Tuscan trecento."[6] Leymarie tells us that Balthus and the student noted the similarity between the lunar landscape of China and Tuscan hill country. More profoundly, they realized that what most matters in art—the principles of harmony—has nothing to do, specifically, with location or epoch.

What Balthus captured almost sixty years later in these views from Montecalvello is, in keeping with that observation, both universal and timeless. The painting and drawing convey the feeling of mountain air and the atmosphere of the summit. They reveal the wondrous transcendent possibilities of art that unify Western and Eastern cultures.

IN CHINESE ART, "the power of the mountain . . . is well captured by the composition in which all the components of the mountain—such as hills, peaks, boulders, rocks, and trees—are shown in rhythmical upward movement, their momentum converging on the summit with a crescendo."[7] This is, of course, precisely the movement that Balthus achieves in the *Montecalvello* oil. Landscape floats; the trees open their arms in a gentle reach. Cliffs, usually forbidding, leap cheerfully.

That weightless ascent is, in fact, a pervading characteristic of much of Balthus's late work. Lightness marks drapery folds, the stance of a model on tiptoe, and the rendering of fruit in a basket. Spiritualism overcomes gravity. Mass is minimized; light—physical and emotional—emphasized. Form evokes the feeling of a cosmic ecstasy.

In ancient China, mountains were sacred: the object of worship. They were seen to represent the power of the earth as a whole, and were revered as a source of water—both of streams and of clouds. Beyond that, mountains were the intermediaries between earth and heaven. While it cannot be said that Balthus actively worshiped these natural forms, it is as if they had a religious value for him—and much of the same significance.

To the ancient Chinese—whose ways Balthus has studied and admired since his youth—mountains were where people went "to receive divine revelations and to attain immortality, or at least certain magical powers."[8] Mountains felt nearer to God, and at the same time invited aloofness. High hills were also viewed as a potential source of danger: forbidding; a locale where fearful creatures might be. For all these reasons, they became Balthus's ideal refuge: his aesthetic nirvana, the place where he has often lived physically and always resided emotionally, and where he would ultimately spend most of his time.

In Chinese poetry, mountains exist as a source of seclusion where one can discuss paintings and literature. Away from the world of people, they provide a chance to relish life and admire God. Their remoteness offers a vehicle of escape toward spiritual purity—obtained in part through a respect for nature.

Chassy; the distant studio at the summit of the Villa Medici; and, most certainly, Rossinière: all of these settings afforded that essential isolation—and, quite literally, the elevation—Balthus had first experienced at Muzot. Mountains in Chinese art are a place for spiritual freedom away from the prevailing social order, and they are powerful and benevolent. At the same time, they provide definition, and offer contours and boundaries as opposed, say, to the more carefree aspects of a Mediterranean seacoast. They were Balthus's true environment—and a world whose magnificence he could readily evoke in his art.

III

A SECOND SUCCESS of this late period is the 1980–81 *Painter and His Model.* The French museums only came around to esteeming Balthus decades after their American counterparts did, but in the 1970s the Centre Pompidou began to acquire his work, and this is another of the paintings in their collection.

Like most of Balthus's paintings at the Pompidou, however, it is often in storage there, so it was in a dark cellar in Paris that I developed my deepest acquaintance with this large—about seven and a half feet square—canvas.

Like *Montecalvello, The Painter and His Model* is a grand summation: in this instance of Balthus's position relative to the art of his times, to the world at large, and to his models. In the hustle-bustle of the contemporary art scene—in which this painting now lives by virtue of the collection it is in—*The Painter and His Model* stands out for its gentleness and quietude, the refinement of the sensibility behind it, and the high degree of control evident in its surface and composition. In a century in which the Cubists have disrupted form, and the abstractionists demolished the notion of representation altogether, Balthus has persevered all his life as a traditional picture maker. Just as he applied himself tenaciously to the task of composition when he was sixteen and Bonnard emphasized its importance even though Baladine disagreed, he continued in the same vein throughout the artistic hell and high water of his lifetime.

This canvas also presents further evidence of his meticulous, tender attention to the nature of materials. A gentle, munificent light caresses the wooden dowels of the simple side chair on which the model leans. Balthus has found just the right means of evoking the old wood of the basic kitchen table: scumbling the paint, scratching into the impasto, rubbing and adding. In that simple, rough piece of country furniture he emerges as our century's answer to the brothers Le Nain: of calm and humble vision, realistic and reverent. Flaunting his bogus title and living in his splendid chalet with its bevy of servants, the count still had not lost his feeling for life in its most rudimentary form.

The little stepladder here is an extraordinary feat of painting. The inside of one of its vertical supports glows a luminous orange. Deep shadows form where the steps intercept it. This ladder is so plausible that we imagine ascending it—at the slow, magisterial pace invited by the dignity and quietude with which the artist has rendered it.

Balthus has captured the wire handle of the pail underneath in much the same way as he has evoked the central metal braces of the ladder, so that we believe they are actually there even though we know we are looking at a shorthand contrivance. That simple pail is frozen in place like objects in Arezzo. Piero miraculously flattened and abstracted things while giving them the breath of life; Balthus took his cues accordingly. The bucket is stylized, yet its volume reads clearly. The light on it varies according to where it has fallen on the cylinder, the extruded band, or the bevel. The handle makes the appropriate shadows. Balthus has managed both to convey real appearances and to cast a spell of enchantment. This is truly a painter's studio; it is also, contrarily, a frieze of a mellow, organized world.

The corner of the room is the longitudinal center of this well-constructed canvas. Balthus has precisely and articulately abutted the two rough plaster walls that constitute that corner; the space reads clearly. Moreover, this quiet meeting of walls is an artistic event—quite unlike anything that occurs in the work of other modern painters. A tension arises between the flatness on the canvas of these subtly resonant walls and their palpable three-dimensionality. The simplicity of minimal sculpture vies with the success of the illusion. Anchored in tradition, Balthus is also modern and insouciant in his own way.

NOT ONLY IS THE STYLE HIS OWN, but so is the scenario. The two characters' highly contrived poses are Balthus's own invention. The turbaned artist—with his back to us, standing practically weightless on tiptoe, holding back a single curtain—is without precedent in the art of others. The off-the-heels stance is one in which Balthus has periodically cast his models over the years, elevating and etherealizing them, but it is his alone. The model, resting firmly on her knees and elbows as Thérèse did in *The Children,* is also particular to Balthus's pictorial vocabulary.

In the self portrait, Balthus is actually a synthesis of many of his own prototypes. In Chassy in the 1950s, he more than once painted teenage women seen from behind and looking out the window. The golem/dwarf in *The Room* of 1952–54 grasps the drapery in much the way Balthus does here. Now Balthus has assigned himself all the roles in which he used to cast others: the character who averts his or her eyes from us and chooses instead to explore the unknown; the revealer and giver of light.

These are some of Balthus's favorite themes: the illumination of what would otherwise be dark, the nature of windows as explored by Baladine and Rilke in tandem, the pulling back of a curtain as when a play begins. Revelation and concealment are simultaneous. And then there is the ever present drama of male and female—which in this painting coincides with the relationship of painter and subject. Life and the art that re-creates that life intersect in myriad ways on this canvas—just as they did when Rilke and Baladine wrote to one another. The confluence of art, perception, sex, seeing, and hiding—all in a visually exquisite if austere universe—leaves us enchanted but unsettled.

FOR A LONG TIME, it seemed clear to me that a lot of what I had come to see and understand in Balthus was exemplified by his pose as well as his peculiar getup in *The Painter and His Model.* The turban or head bandage that is like a mummy's wrappings offered distinct readings. So did the stance. But then an

The Painter and His Model, 1980–81,
casein and tempera on canvas, 226.5 x 230.5 cm

event occurred that filled me with misgivings about my own vision, and I developed qualms not only about my presumption to interpret Balthus's costume and position in this painting but also about my views on the symbolism throughout his work.

In the middle of a time period when I was thinking extensively about *The Painter and His Model,* I visited the painter Cleve Gray. I had gone to see his wife—Francine du Plessix Gray—who had touched in an interesting way on Pierre Klossowski in an article she wrote for *The New Yorker* about Maurice Lever's biography of the Marquis de Sade. After she and I had a discussion about Balthus's guises and other aspects of his work, I ended up in Cleve's studio, where I rekindled my earlier admiration both for his painting and for his views on the art of others.

Subsequently—at dinner with the Grays and my wife—I mentioned *The Painter and His Model*, which Cleve also knows well. Cleve, whose well-organized abstract canvases derive from nature, maintained that Balthus shows himself with his back to us for entirely visual reasons. The painter wears a turban only because of aesthetics, he insisted. I could see Cleve's point. By facing *out* the window, Balthus takes *us* that way as well; if he faced forward, we would stop too soon. His extended arm can be explained by its role as a vital linear element that takes us to the edge of the canvas. The turban or head bandage is a splendid compact massing of white on white just where it is needed. These are a painter's decisions, and that's how a painter's mind works.

Listening to an artist, it occurred to me that perhaps all of Balthus's assertions to me were correct—that the basis for everything, indeed, is visual. Yet, finally, I cannot help thinking that every decision behind this painting—although unquestionably informed, as Cleve Gray maintains, by Balthus's splendid eye—is the result of the same program whereby Balthus manipulates his celebrity/recluse image and his elevation in the world.

For I believe that the reason the painter wears a turban—or white bandage—around his head is part of a far more complex psychological agenda. The image hearkens back to Piero. It is similar to the headgear worn by the soldiers engaged in "the discovery of the true cross." In his self-portrait, Balthus has thereby linked himself to the holy crusaders. Moreover, I think that Balthus painted this turban to create an enigma. It covers and disguises. Just as the pose prevents us from seeing his face, the headgear screens his hair. Thus this is the ultimate "of whom nothing is known."

There is the added factor that the turban was so interesting to paint. Folds of white material have long been one of Balthus's specialties. He could handle them with the same spectacular finesse as fruit in a bowl: these are the artist's strong suits. He has painted this intricately folded material so that it reads easily, with the light and shadows hitting just the right places.

As for the outstretched arm, as marvelous as it is in the overall composition, it does not assume its length and sweep solely for formal reasons. Balthus would inevitably claim that he positioned himself as such because he liked the way it looked and it suited the picture needs of the painting, yet the balletic stance is, as for the women he painted similarly in other paintings, significant. In depicting himself in this particular pose suggestive of flying, Balthus has aligned himself with many of his former female subjects and has put himself, like them, in a position not quite of this earth. While Balthus showed many of his people heavily grounded by their gargantuan legs, he made these characters looking out windows weightless—or, in the case of the self-portrait, trying to be weightless. The completely blank and viewless window, its vast flat panes silvery-toned, also implies some heavenly and spiritual sphere.

So, like his teenage subjects, Balthus escapes the normal vicissitudes of human existence. In *The Painter and His Model,* Monsieur le Comte is high and separate: the observer peering from his tower. Like his flying women, he is incorporeal; like great artists and genuine aristocrats, he inhabits a higher sphere of existence.

BALTHUS HAS CREATED the female model according to his fantasy, too. Rilke had said of the fifteen-year-old Balthus that he would thrive according to his own rules, his ways dictated by his creative need. It was his prerogative to paint as he wished. So he has painted his ideal woman: blond and fair, yet with an Oriental, Setsuko-like cast to her. His creature of choice is delicate and small-boned in the upper part of her body, yet Amazonian from the waist down. She is both a schoolgirl in his studio and a Renaissance saint, an earthly being and a doll.

The poor woman is, in fact, one of Balthus's strangest creatures thus far. Her head is far too big for her shoulders, her calves almost the thickness of her head. Her legs are absurdly long. In proportion to the man behind her, she is, at least in her upper body, ridiculously small. But Balthus has painted these distortions as if they are ineffably real. The textures and massing are so plausible that we come to accept the scale. As usual, the artist has done precisely what he wants, and it succeeds because he has rendered it so charmingly and convincingly.

The decisions about proportion and skin tone and the woman's saintly features couldn't be entirely visual. By making the proportions disconcerting and the iconographical elements discombobulating, Balthus exerts his own power. He keeps us guessing and asking.

Yet perhaps, in seeing these factors as deriving from the artist's psychological intent, his craving to dominate, I have brought more of myself to bear here—and too little of him. This, of course, is what Balthus would have me believe.

THE SITUATION IS all the more complicated because, in his art as in his person, Balthus disseminates conflicting information. This still life on the table seems as holy as it is sexy. When we are not dwelling on the eroticism of its recesses and bulges and darkened orifices, it has the sanctity we associate with the most devout spirit of Renaissance painting. The warm light enrobes each pear and apple. These pieces of fruit look locked in place, as if they have been put there by divine plan. Like Derain, Balthus is a celebrant of daily, earthly life.

But whereas Derain is almost slapdash in his brushwork, Balthus resembles an Oriental ceramicist. He attends carefully to surface and form with an eye to the sort of perfection possible only in art. He has modeled the shapes and perfected the contours with much deliberation, getting the sheen just so. The resultant still life has—as do virtually all of Balthus's watercolors of similar subject matter—a profound stillness and sense of repose.

The apples and pear are of this world but also of another: they are painted so lightly that the background beige color of the wall shows through them, as if they are a vision more than actual objects. Yet the brushwork is just thick enough to give weight to this translucent fruit, so that it sits eloquently in its humble vessel. And although that container is primarily an abstraction—we cannot tell for sure if it is wood, earthenware, or straw: an ambiguousness that is Balthus's choice, since he could paint any of these substances impeccably—what matters about it is that it is strong, hollow, and rigid.

A vignette of this sort—and Balthus's art at its best is full of these miraculous still lifes—transfixes the viewer. It entices and calms us; it causes us to slow down. We notice the way light falls on a stepladder; we meditate on drapery folds. Like the two creatures in this painting, we assume a contemplative attitude. All of this suggests why it is so hard to get a handle on Balthus's identity.

In keeping with the principle we first discovered in Balthus's art of the 1930s, design, in the purest, most visual sense, is also a governing factor in this and other paintings. Extraordinarily graceful linear arrangements vie with disturbing psychological themes in *The Painter and His Model*. The curve of the model's dress hem echoes the arc formed by the painter's right profile, neck, and right arm. Every line in the composition corresponds to another. As precisely as if it were drawn with a compass and protractor, the front right leg of the Empire chair extends the curve of that hem. And the drapery in the upper right corner of the composition seems to answer all the other arcs with its broad concave form. Herein lies an essential aspect of Balthus's picture making, a sensuous immersion no less vital than his apparent feeling for human flesh. It is no surprise that one of Balthus's favorite painters was Ingres, the master of curves against the grid. Like Ingres, Balthus first establishes a classical system of order as a setting for organic forms of seductive power. Both artists relished the formal pleasures of art in concert with the palpable allure of the human body.

And the relationship of colors is comparable to that of shapes. The vibrating orange and yellow that are compact and intense in the checkerboard patterns of the metal box on the table (in which Balthus has initialed and dated the painting) exist in more diffuse form, larger-scaled and muted, in the stepladder on the opposite side of the painting. This is as organized as a composition by Mozart in which a motif is stated in one key and rhythm is played out in another. The whole is a complex of shuffles and echoes.

Balthus wrote a friend, when he was eighteen, that the only way he could describe the effect of Piero della Francesca's art on him was to copy it. The experience is so essentially visual and artistic that words, as Balthus later heard Antonin Artaud declare, do not suffice. Tone, form, the way figures exist in a room, the location of walls and objects, the enchantment of curves: these are the issues. The nobility of looking, and doing so patiently—the act in which the artist shows himself to be engaged, in that pose recalling the endless springtime afternoons enjoyed by the adolescent girls who have frequented his art— is embodied in this canvas.

YET IF *The Painter and His Model* so powerfully evokes the process of looking, it also sharply reminds us of what we do *not* see. The painter has his back turned; he is nothing but a form. Full knowledge, as always with Balthus, is as elusive as a cat. We see the artist, yet his true face, any "up front" aspect of him, will be hidden forever. And that turban distances him all the more.

The model, similarly, offers such differing meanings as to be equally ungraspable. Kneeling and angelic, she is almost saintly. Yet as with Ingres, her flesh is luminous, her body lithe, and these give her the charge of sex. This painting is, with every possible implication, about a man and a woman alone in a room together.

Their thoughts and relationship are ambiguous, yet by dint of the way this canvas is painted, every possibility occurs to us. If the support of the side chair begins to look phallic, and the perfectly rounded fruit analogous to the woman's breasts, and its darkened holes akin to the other parts of her body concealed by her loose sheath, such impressions are not merely, as Balthus declares, the product of our obsessions. As Giacometti remarked, the eroticism pervades everything in tandem with, not in opposition to, the other glories of Balthus's art.

IV

EVER SINCE HIS FIRST EXHIBITION with Pierre Matisse in 1938, Balthus had depended on Americans as his most ardent champions. This changed at the time of his show at the Met in 1984. New York from that point forward remained a stronghold of economic support, but less so of critical approval.

Bearing his look of grief mixed with incomprehension—one of his stock expressions—Balthus told me he was "surprised by the amount of hate that burst out" when his retrospective that had done so well in Paris was subsequently reviled on the other side of the Atlantic. I was puzzled to hear this, since I remember the positive excitement that surrounded that exhibition, and the favorable reviews in places like the *New York Times*. But almost a decade later, Balthus was still smarting.

The primary problem, of course, was the issue of biography. It probably mattered far less to Balthus that critics had applauded his work than that he had publicly been identified as part Jewish and his title had been disputed. His lament to an interviewer in 1994 was "One article said I was no more a count than the author was Miss America. Probably I'm a murderer, too."[9]

This was a variation on a theme; Balthus told me repeatedly that one critic actually likened him to a murderer. I assume this stemmed from the Peter Schjeldahl review, in truth not so accusatory, in which the critic quoted Nabokov's declaration in *Lolita* that "you can always count on a murderer for a fancy prose style" as "a way of thinking about Balthus at his more frequent worse."[10] Balthus often cited "the horrible things" said in American newspapers as evidence that "the whole country" had turned on him. In light of the mobs who visited that show and the preponderance of enthusiastic press, it was a remarkable reaction: either essentially contrived or genuinely paranoiac.

Balthus, however, had been displeased by the Met show even before it went up. Two weeks before the exhibition opening, he sent officials at the museum a document entitled "A Misleading Image: A Statement by Balthus." Here he complained both about not having been consulted on the selection of work for the show and, in particular, about the catalog text. "The catalog, whose proofs were never officially sent to me but which I chanced upon, contains a vast amount of biographical detail, most of it irrelevant, indiscreet or untrue. . . . This 'getting to the facts' appears to me a misleading and harmful screen placed between the viewer and the painting. . . . I very much disapprove of the habit of feeding the public with details and anecdotes on a painter's private life together with the implication that the latter somehow explains his paintings. I am not interested in fame and have no wish to be treated as a celebrity. . . . Paintings do not describe or reveal a painter."[11]

Balthus refused to attend the opening. Tensions flared. An angry William Lieberman kept Stanislas, who entered the fray, from attending the official dinner. Afterward, Pierre and Tana Matisse had to prevail upon Stanislas not to go through with his idea of sending Balthus's letter to the press.

It was fairly obvious what the offensive issues were. Sabine Rewald had revealed Balthus's brutality to Elsa Henriquez—the model for *The Window*—

and a couple of his other models, and she had read a high degree of sexuality into the work. Conveniently for Balthus, she had also made a couple of minor errors in her text—thereby giving him grounds for declaring it invalid in its entirety. Worst of all from his point of view, she spelled out his lineage correctly—neither as Byron's descendant nor as a Romanov nor as a count, but as Abraham Beer Spiro's grandson.

On other occasions—when the "facts" were as he liked them—Balthus was willing enough to savor the fame he claimed to eschew. This was the time in which he began to permit himself to be pictured in one chic and glossy magazine after another, and to have the interiors of his private dwellings on display for all the world to see. He was not yet at the point he would soon reach of allowing the makers of TV documentaries to focus their cameras on his family gathered around the dining room table, but the conditions of his privacy were clear. It could be violated—so long as the intrusion was on his own terms.

As always with Balthus, his work had its passionate devotees as well as its ardent detractors. A number of serious young painters felt that this show at the Met was one of the few instances they knew of where an official institution accorded real painting its just position. On the other hand, to some observers Balthus was not the master he and his supporters purported him to be. Hilton Kramer told me that when he and his wife went to the show, they "were dissecting a Balthus landscape we considered especially poor. We were enumerating all the elements we deemed unsuccessful. At that moment Philippe de Montebello came flouncing in. 'I see you share my rapture over my favorite picture,' said Philippe. We hardly knew how to reply, but managed to be polite."[12]

The hordes who filled the exhibition rooms focused more on the subject matter than on the technique. Aghast or thrilled, most found it a revelation. Balthus had certainly inspired "an awakening." And however much he felt himself maligned, in this country he had never visited he was deemed a master in his own lifetime.

V

Between 1983 and 1986 the financially successful, socially prominent Count Klossowski de Rola painted a canvas that was like a polite paraphrase of *The Guitar Lesson,* the painting with which the impoverished Balthus had shown his true colors half a century earlier. But what he had laid bare in 1934 he recapitulated with artifice. Now he would rather give mixed signals than shock with his candor. He had acquired considerable craft since his days on the Rue de Fürstemberg.

The 1983–86 *Woman with a Guitar* is like a highly mannered version of the picture that once had to hide its Sadean themes behind a drapery. Spread for the taking, a young woman has dropped her guitar. But if the more recent canvas shows some of the benefits of a lifetime devoted to mastering artistic technique, it lacks both the power and the honesty of its ancestor. After all, Balthus had learned to say that he now wished he had never painted the canvas that for people like Artaud was such a tour de force.

The irony is that by the time he made *Woman with a Guitar,* Balthus was sufficiently important and famous for the world to embrace it instantly, while when he painted the far better *The Guitar Lesson,* few would even look. Having resorted to artistic and emotional shambling and waffling, he could now instantly score a level of success that had previously eluded him.

IN THE 1983–86 PAINTING, Balthus has removed the image of his mother/himself entirely from the scene. Yet—by the sheer act of having visualized and created this painting—he continues to be palpably present as the observer, seducer, and awakener. And the nude woman remains his glorious and willing prey; Balthus is still making conquests.

This is again the emotional climate of his childhood as he had known it in that small apartment on the Rue Pré-Jérôme. The central character is a woman overcome by romantic passion: an amalgam of Baladine longing for Rilke and the fourteen-year-old son who was privy to her feelings.

Yet the marvelous physicality of *The Guitar Lesson* is gone. In *Woman with a Guitar,* Balthus has either lost or given up the ability to join limbs to a torso. Nor do the guitar, or the woman who has dropped it, stay in place. As with *Cat at the Mirror I,* the elements float. We no longer see reality.

Balthus had an explanation for this, however. He told me that in both *Woman with a Guitar* and *Large Composition with Raven,* another major canvas of the period, he "tried to make a nude which was not a nude. I tried to invent a body which was not a nude: an abstraction of a nude." Yet even if the ephemeral irreality was his intention, it remains to my eye both evasive and visually unsuccessful.

The sensualized female in *Woman with a Guitar* is too small both in relation to the window above her and to the bed that supports her. She looks Lilliputian. If we view the interior details as determining the scale represented by

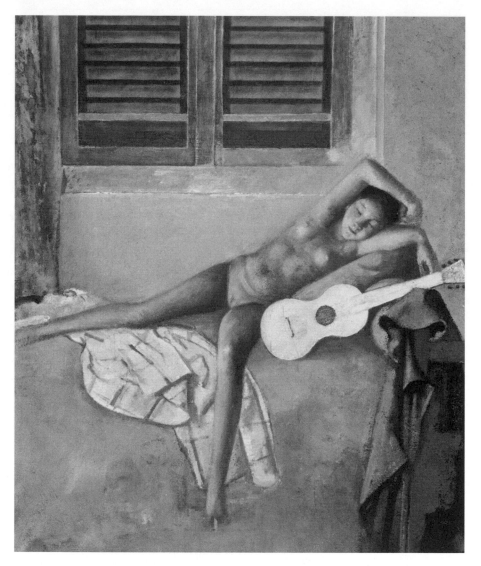

Woman with a Guitar, 1983–86, oil on canvas, 162 x 130 cm

the painting, then the figure, proportionately, should be some twenty feet in the background beyond it—not right on the picture plane as she apparently is. Her nearness feels wrong and unnatural.

And if to some viewers the naked woman may appear utterly relaxed or contentedly exhausted, this creature is also, again to use Linda Fairstein's term, desanguinated. Her body is the color of a corpse, and her legs are splayed so awkwardly that she appears to have been mutilated as much as loved. She is a Bosch-like grotesque: her rigid legs connect to the rest of her body like the limbs of a doctor's doll. This woman's strange body seems flattened and squashed, like a pressed flower. In some ways she is as lifeless as those creatures Balthus had found strewn about the battlefield at the start of the Second World War, the sight of which he found so unbearable; it is as if he could not escape the memory.

Looking at a reproduction of the work, Linda Fairstein commented to me on "the unnaturalness of the pose. She looks absolutely twisted . . . so unnatural. It's very dark and unattractive, not what you do to a woman. Awfully uncomfortable; try doing that."

Once upon a time, Balthus could paint his settings superbly. *The Guitar Lesson, Cathy Dressing, The Children,* and other canvases of the 1930s are successful evocations of interior spaces that truly seem to exist. Now the room has been compressed to a depth of scarcely a yard, and her bed seems more a symbol or device than an object in the real world. What had come to matter in the 1980s for Balthus was surface. The issue is not representation so much as rhythm, color relationships, and the soft textures in which everything is the same. Skin, bed linen, and plaster—once differentiated so successfully in Balthus's work—are now given equal value and appear primarily as painted canvas. Everything is pushed forward to heighten a series of two-dimensional delights—while forsaking truthfulness.

THE ARTIST'S OWN lack of resolve—a sense either that he has given up or recognizes his own incompleteness—is apparent in the woman's left foot. It is blatantly unfinished, as if Balthus simply abandoned the picture in despair; the foot disappears into nothingness. And the woman's right leg practically ends at her ankle.

The rendition is a tacit admission that what the artist is presenting is the *idea* of feet, not the things themselves. It calls attention to Balthus's Giacometti-like awareness of the futility as much as the nobility of art. In this ambivalence and implicit lack of resolve, the confusion of its imagery, and its tentative style of painting, *Woman with a Guitar* places Balthus even further from the artistic mainstream of the 1980s than *The Guitar Lesson* did from the trends of the 1930s.

Its cultivated, white-tie traditionalism makes this canvas equally out of sync with its times. The texture has clearly been nurtured slowly, painstakingly worked and reworked, repeatedly laid on and scrubbed down. The pale and muted colors are deliberately understated. The instant anguish of contemporary narrative painting is like a cheap paperback compared with this old leatherbound tome.

Yet in its aristocratic voice, *Woman with a Guitar* has summoned some extraordinary peculiarities: breast development without pubic hair; a masculine rib cage on a female body; the woman's corpselike hue; an obscenely sexualized guitar; lifeless legs but expressive arms; and the mixture of human weight with total ethereality. Perhaps the idea is one of resurrection—an homage to the fresco Balthus diligently copied in Sansepolcro that summer when Piero's marvels planted the seeds of the artistic approach he would take forever after.

IN SPITE OF ITS STRANGENESS and areas of weakness, this painting is evidence of Balthus's increased skill in specific areas. The handling of the drapery is true to the tradition of the masters, as sure as in a Cézanne still life, yet unique in its particular grace and tone. The folds of the cloth over the bedpost are both convincing and elegant. Balthus has articulated the position and drape of the white towel with its windowpane blue check so that this inanimate object has not only a distinct direction but also a certain languor. While their shape is a product of the artist's willfulness and capriciousness, the bedspread and pillow have a miraculous texture; not only do they generate ambient light, but they absorb and reflect it. In texture and brushiness, they are clearly paint; they are also plaster and linen. Simultaneously tangible and ungraspable, they belong to the highest realm of art.

While *Woman with a Guitar* glows as a whole, certain points on the canvas are still brighter. The window frame shines. And in a focused, less diffuse way, so do the woman's nipples, the underside of her breasts, and her left kneecap—much as Thérèse's kneecaps, and those of the girl in *The Guitar Lesson,* did when Balthus painted them half a century earlier. The artist's savoring of his model's body has a Rilkean intensity. So does his feeling for objects. An iron pot at the lower right has the weight—actual and optical—of deeply charred logs. The darkness inside the guitar is another such note—suggestive, much as Balthus would decry the notion, of sexual mystery. Equally authentic are the folds of the woman's body where her thighs hit her pelvis, those bizarre demarcations that create a sweeping V punctuated at its point by her exposed vagina.

This last detail renders the woman like a mannequin—a facsimile of a woman. Again we move from Balthus's brilliant tonal orchestrations to his unsettling representation of life. What a concept of woman this gray, rippling torso is.

Yet this creature locked in an eerie pendulum between youth and death is

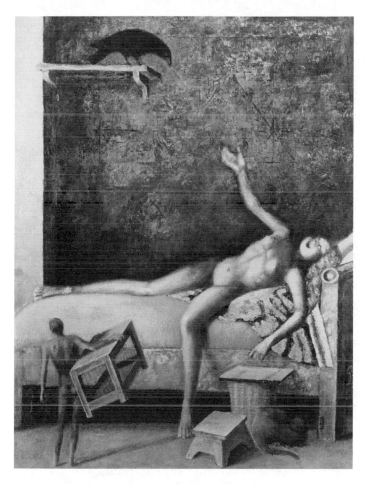

Large Composition with Raven, 1983–86,
oil on canvas, 200 x 150 cm

rendered with subtlety and tastefulness. The canvas is slow and fast, labored and spontaneous, bland and jangling, refined yet abrasive. The sublime, discomfiting *Woman with a Guitar* is both a heavenly seduction and a mordant nightmare.

VI

IN HIS EARLIER ART, Balthus pastiched Piero, Hogarth, Courbet, Seurat—as well as more obscure sources like Reinhardt. For his persona he took on Heathcliff, Artaud, and Byron: poetic despots. Passionate admiration begot brilliant, individualized imitation.

In the later years, the persona he has opted for is that of an émigré noble-man—the denizen of Gstaad or Baden-Baden as we might find him in Ian Fleming or Turgenev. And the painter he pastiched even more than Courbet or Piero was the younger Balthus. Having won his audience and struck it rich, he would create paintings that would be recognizable as Balthuses—that guaranteed a response and consternation while bestowing a certain cachet on their wealthy owners.

His self-referential canvases of the 1980s have passages of excellent painting—their maker was incapable of anything less—but the provocativeness is contrived. In the 1930s he deliberately intended to shock; in the 1980s, when he had achieved—in a form measurable in many millions of Swiss francs—much acclaim in part because of the success of that shock, he now took to jerking around his audience with its echoes. There was a false ring both in the way the paintings were startling and in the way they were tame. But as Baladine had remarked to Rilke after seeing what Balthus had made at the age of fourteen, he remained, as was in the fiber of his being, "a real artist."

THE ABLY CONSTRUCTED 1983–86 *Large Composition with Raven* triumphs in its presentation of objects and space, and offers a rich range of textures and light effects. *Raven* epitomizes aspects of Balthus's style that had been in the ascendancy ever since he began to redo the walls at the Villa Medici; its resonant surface shows how much he could achieve through his use of glazure. And although the subject matter of *Raven* is irritatingly stagy, it remains fascinating because of the kernel of truth that lurks behind it: the connections to the troublesome issues of Balthus's childhood, the artist's obsessional attitude toward women, and his lifelong dialogue with his hero Piero della Francesco.

Balthus and I discussed *Raven* quite a lot on my first trip to Rossinière. "I couldn't explain why," he said. "The idea of this painting. I don't think I had any idea at all; why I was driven to do that, I don't know exactly, but that's how it came. The raven is not a bad omen." The raven itself, while sinister in the poetry of Poe, is sacred in China, Balthus said. At a later date, during one of our phone calls, he added that "in the West the raven is considered a negative sign. It has a sort of sinister meaning in the Western conception, some sort of death message. In the East, on the contrary, and for the red Indians, it is seen as a solar symbol. It represents enlightenment of the Zen sort—sudden enlightenment, on the contrary from Edgar Allan Poe. I think the whole idea of the painting was awakening—becoming aware of things."[13] The duality fascinated him. He told me that the reason he had included the black bird was "perhaps because it had different readings in different cultures."

Balthus maintained that he had no idea why the naked man in the fore-ground is a fraction of the size of the woman or why he's carrying a cage. "It doesn't matter, anyway." This object had once prompted the artist to say to Dominique Bozo—as Stanislas later told me—that it was "a trap to catch art historians." As for the creature I mistakenly called a rabbit, all that Balthus said was that it was a cat. My confusion appeared neither to irritate nor disappoint him—but it seemed as patently clear to Balthus that this animal (plumper and more rabbit-eared than any cat I have ever seen) was a cat as that the golem in *The Room* is "just a little girl." In any event, it carried no symbolic portent whatsoever.

YET BALTHUS'S DENIALS of the weight of his subject matter had a false ring to me. It seemed as staged as the action of the painting itself. There is nothing inadvertent about the way *Raven* puzzles you. And the artist's statements notwithstanding, the painting is blatantly sexual. When you stand before the actual canvas, a strident eroticism is pushed in your face. Almost every detail of the composition aims at, or refers to, the woman's genitals.

The woman's legs are splayed with all deliberateness to reveal her vagina, however hazy and shadowed its representation may be. The raven's beak aims almost precisely toward that same point. So does the corner of the footstool below. The sharp corner of the cage or trap thrusts in the same direction. Moreover, someone as versed as Balthus in the traditions of iconography would have known full well that a trap is a familiar symbol of the female geni-talia; the mousetrap in Flemish painting was code for the uterus.

In *Raven,* the woman's wide-open, darkened mouth is also sexualized. And the side view of the top of the headboard, where a medallion of wood is shown as a circle of light darkened within, is equally analogous to her genitalia. The round basket on the floor, covered with a wooden plank, becomes like a shut womb. Balthus would naturally decry these readings as madness, but it is his canvas that makes them inevitable, even if he cleverly sidesteps the issue by insisting that this emphasis is only in the mind of the viewer.

THE DIMINUTIVE MALE NUDE IN *Raven*—under half the size of the bizarre naked female who dominates the composition—moves away from us. Seeing him from behind, we can make out nothing of his features. This is the way Balthus often showed himself in *Mitsou*—and the position in which the artist has traditionally appeared in his large compositions ever since. We observe him, but cannot read him.

The man is dealing with the cage in a completely unrealistic way. His arm is stretched over the top of it, and it leans against his body. He could not possibly grab it. The image is uncomfortable, and unconvincing. Moreover, the cage, which is very large, appears to float—like an apparition in a dream. It is a ghastly green, which makes it all the more hideous and forbidding.

The cage was more than "a trap to catch art historians."[14] The painting conjures memories of a remarkable letter concerning the Klossowski boys that Rainer Marie Rilke wrote to Simone Brüstlein, in which the poet remarked, "I walk as if I were carrying inside of me a jail—one, not which holds me, but one, rather, which holds my previous existence; it cannot come to me, nor I to it."[15] Isn't that naked man, in fact, carrying his own jail? Isn't this a perfect illustration of the alienation, the sense of distance, described by Balthus's great confrere Rilke?

In *Raven,* the naked man holding his own prison—that analogue to womanliness—has been diminished by a gigantic female in the throes of emotion. That woman is the force that has exposed and entrapped him.

Balthus has given the woman an extraordinary forcefulness, but as in *The Room,* he has also knocked her out and rendered her spent. With her left arm and leg thrown out of kilter, she appears either exhausted or conquered. Is this—the world of beds and traps and naked men and women—a war zone? Is this dominant female, pulverized by her own drama, the enemy—both victor and victim? Is it too much to say that, sixty years after the affair between Rilke and Balthus's mother, this was still the poet's "delicious valley" and "heart's flute," Balthus and Pierre's "third playmate," Baladine?

IT IS BY NO MEANS the subject matter alone that gives *Raven* its breath of life and its sexual vitality. If this same imagery, in the identical arrangement, had been painted without the modeling and textural play and light effects Balthus has given them, it would not engage and unnerve us to such a degree. But the light that bounces off the woman's knees is so luminous that we feel as if she is basking in actual sunshine. The minuscule, naked man whom we see from behind has been painted with both verisimilitude and audacity; his skin that reads so true is an amalgam of green-gray and well-rubbed reds, tans, pinks, and beige. The weave of the basket is plausible in its area of lightness and shadow and in its undulating ripples. The draperies beneath the woman are what they are supposed to be, with high drama in their folds. The darkness under the bed seems so real that we feel we could crawl into it.

The broad, dark expanse of the background wall—a fascinating substance, like ancient plaster—serves as a foil to the sparkle of the scenario in front of it. Similarly, the fiery red, orange, and gold of the bedspread offers a counterpoint to the more natural, matte colors of wood and straw. The red highlights beneath the rabbity cat and the footstool also provide a welcome accent. And everywhere we marvel at the impasto, the simultaneous sheen and weight of the paint.

Indeed, the visual elements—what Balthus purports to be his sole concern—are central. Without the artist's stunning ability to communicate, nothing else would weigh in; he would lack the power to seduce. But to deny the psychoerotic undertones is sheer caprice.

WHAT A MISCHIEF-MAKER this powerful painter is! He has given his female subject the same eerie, lean, muscular rib cage as the figure in *Woman with a Guitar*. It renders her androgynous. And her shoulders and arms, in profile, resemble the wings of a raven in full flight. Those arms are almost as long as her legs, her hands the same size as her feet. Her fingers and toes are like talons. Is she, too, a sacred bird?

These primordial talons, capable of digging in, belong, of course, to a creature of prey. These are the same frightening digits we saw on the dominatrix in *The Guitar Lesson*. They claw at power. They are vehicles of possession: of the most absolute form of seduction.

To seduce and to be seduced—violently as in *The Guitar Lesson*, ever so gently as in *Bouquet of Roses*—is invariably the crux of Balthus and his art. In the pendulum of power, he plays every role: male and female, child and adult, seducer and seducee. Visual, sensual beauty—of which he is the master conjurer—is the means of his conquest. It takes over so that outside "reality" ceases to play a role. Attraction—of the most powerful, magnetic sort—becomes the only truth. To enchant and to hold, or to be enchanted and be held in thrall, are the ultimate human experience. Everything else must be buried, subjected, repressed, transformed. To captivate or to be captivated is the final goal.

I PICTURE, AGAIN, Balthus turning back to me on the stairs of Le Grand Chalet, his face a perfect mix of feline willfulness and the most calculated sort of human intelligence.

He stood there as gaunt and tall—and powerful—as a sculpture by his beloved "Alberto": the name he always uttered slowly and with an emphatically Italian accent. Miles of tweed trousers seemed to encase his lean, lanky legs.

His hollow face, with its great beak of a nose, belonged at that moment to a character from the Poe he adored; his gigantic chalet suddenly seemed a haunted castle. Balthus was very much of this world yet equally from another.

It was the occasion on which, with impeccable word-for-word recall, he quoted his beloved Coomaraswamy: the writer Setsuko had counseled me to take as their *"porte-parole,"* the carrier of the word. With due deliberation, the strength of a tyrant, and the grace and erudition of a young and tender schoolboy, his eyebrows arched as if he were delivering the gospel, he uttered, yet again, the Indian's dictum: "The bomb, for example, is only bad as a work of art if it fails to destroy and kill to the required extent." *Large Composition with Raven* was a weapon successfully deployed.

THE BLACK BIRD AS BALTHUS has painted it in this large canvas is both forbidding and life-giving. As spooky as in Poe and as powerful as in Chinese mythology, the creature holds tremendous power.

What is harder to grasp, however, are the multiple readings suggested by the miniaturized man. Clearly he is overwhelmed by the force of the woman before him. The idea of a female—sexually potent, consumed by her own experience—diminishes him so that he is like a mere mortal at a holy altar.

The humble fellow's scale in relation to this dominatrix is almost precisely that of the worshipers in Piero's *Madonna della misericordia.* The earliest of Piero's paintings, the *Misericordia* was well known to Balthus ever since his visit at age eighteen to Sansepolcro when he copied the haunting *Resurrection* just around the corner from it. In *Raven,* it looks as if he has taken Piero's idea of the oversized virgin—a holy giantess—and sexualized her.

Has Balthus, as in *The Room,* yet again stripped a Piero Madonna so that she can be worshiped on the most earthly terms—and played a little game that both debases and glorifies her?

Going back as early in Balthus's work as *The Quays*—and continuing through *The Passage*—when the artist paints a tall lanky figure from behind, it is traditionally a self-portrait. As for that cage this Balthus image is carrying: if we accept the traditional symbolism of this object as the woman's sexuality and her genitals, then the man carrying it has a grip, albeit implausibly, on the very force that diminishes him. That funny little creature who has escaped from the box—and sits there like the proverbial cat who ate the canary—can also be read as Balthus in command. It is as if the artist deliberately devised a conundrum to which we cannot know the answer, but which he, in his various personae, might solve. Overwhelmed by weird, androgynous female beauty, he has also found a handle for it.

Piero della Francesca, *The Madonna of the Misericordia,*
c. 1460, oil on panel (?), 134 x 91 cm

In 1922 Baladine Klossowska had written Rainer Maria Rilke about an
extraordinary dream:

> The other night I had a dream that was so admirable I must tell it to
> you. I was about to crush—with my finger—some tiny, rather ugly
> creature that was crawling across the table, but just when I wanted to
> kill it, it changed into a dragonfly more beautiful than any I've ever
> seen in all my life. Wings, René, wings of dawn, yes, and illuminating
> the whole room with their luster. Suddenly I exclaim: "But that's my
> soul! Oh, it's my soul!" and I take the dragonfly onto my hand, where
> it flutters. Against the wall, René, was fastened a wonderful yellow
> bird, I think it was stuffed. I had not yet seen it—and just think! how
> symbolic it is, my soul flies away, it flutters up against the bird which it

caresses over and over, its tiny feet crawling over the feathers and its
nervous wings beating with emotion! That was my dream, and now,
darling, dream—dream about it yourself—since this dream is the
image of me and also a certain inexplicable embarrassment in confronting myself—you know what I mean, it was so extraordinary, the
way everything in our love was reflected in that image.[16]

The young Balthus probably heard his mother's account of that dream. Birds
were symbolic; a winged animal could represent the soul. The visions of sleep
were tantamount to reality.

For the young boy on the Rue Pré-Jérôme, the creature that would soon
signify his own being was, of course, the cat. Birds, on the other hand, embodied the possibility of light. The revelation they offered would be thrilling if
ambiguous. Feeling—a burning passion between the sexes—filled the atmosphere. Female emotions predominated.

It is as if *Raven* were a residue of Balthus's childhood and that rich erotic
atmosphere in which the longings of his young and provocative mother, torn
between ecstasy and melancholy, pervaded his world.

CHAPTER TWENTY-FOUR

CAT AT THE MIRROR

I

FROM JANUARY 1991 ON, I was in touch with Balthus only by phone and through our one-way correspondence; periodically I wrote him a letter or card, or sent a gift for one of his nonbirthdays. Initially we tried to arrange for my return to Rossinière, but our plans always fell through. Divided between my hunger for Balthus's own story and my fear of submitting myself to the same old lies, I was not entirely disappointed.

Nonetheless, when, a couple of years into the project, I hung up the phone after one of our rambling conversations, I realized that I had come to love the man. No wonder Rilke adored him so. What a blend he was of sweetness, engagement, intelligence, and talent. As for the mischievousness: that, too, was part of the brightness. And the game-playing: I loved that also—it was intrinsic to the brilliance that put him in the same league as Oscar Wilde and Byron and other geniuses who were outside the norm, in a realm where one was allowed to play by different rules.

This was not the first time I had handled the complex situation of writing about someone by developing an obsessive fondness for him or her and, at the same time, mentally becoming my subject. The person with whom I was engaged on the page turned into my closest family member: the imaginative, brilliant, accomplished parent of my dreams, a friend and brother.

My mental situation could not have been more at odds with the mandate of my many years of all too substantial academic training in art history. Instead of pursuing the course of objective scholarship, I had developed an internal relationship with my subject which had become like that of a volatile teenager with a beloved, or of a conflicted adolescent trying to resolve his views about a difficult parent. It was as if at every moment I had to decide whether I adored or detested this person and his work. And just as I braced myself for battle and lined up all my feelings to support my loathing of Balthus's personal fraudulence and the mannerism of his late painting, I could be catapulted in the opposite direction by a remembrance of some aspect of him I could not help adoring, or by the superb quality of one of his best paintings. This must be how some spouses feel when they are on the verge of divorce but still hopelessly in love with certain sides of their other: torn, confused, always in need of coming to conclusion and resolution when none is possible.

In May 1993 I unexpectedly received an invitation to the opening of Balthus's major exhibition at the Musée des Beaux-Arts in Lausanne. I had not even known that the show was scheduled; the invitation arrived only a week before the event; my wife was out of the country for two weeks and I was in Connecticut alone with our daughters, now aged nine and eleven, and for whom we had no other care arrangements. I phoned my wife, who urged me to take the girls, and then spoke with Balthus and Setsuko, who added an invitation for lunch the day after the opening. And so we flew to Geneva.

BY THE TIME Lucy and Charlotte and I left our Lausanne hotel room to go to the opening at the Musée des Beaux-Arts on that Saturday in May, I felt that the boundaries between my subject and me had all but disappeared. Lucy had donned a short "little nothing" of flowing flowered chiffon over silk; Charlotte a longer, younger, rose-patterned dress of great style. I wore my best suit and favorite English-style shirt. *"Wir waren wie drei Kinder,"* I kept thinking: the ecstatic line that Baladine had written to Rilke. Now I was the opposite-sex parent living amusingly and decadently and ecstatically in the world of beauty with my children. Just having such thoughts, I could picture a bevy of serious psychiatrists in book-lined studies, all shaking their heads in disapproval.

The exhibition looked splendid. Or so I thought. But then Jean Leyris told me that Balthus was not happy with it, which is why a feeling of malaise hung in the atmosphere. Although this prevernissage was scheduled from 10 to 12, and it was now 11 a.m., no one had removed the plastic wrap from the trays of food that were sitting there. The champagne glasses were all lined up perfectly and filled to the same level, but none were touched. Balthus had not yet arrived, Jean explained; worse yet, there was a rumor afloat that he might not appear at all. No one would nibble at a shrimp canapé or sip even an orange juice until the guest of honor showed up. And the word around the large rooms of the Musée des Beaux-Arts was that the master was sulking. He felt that the walls were too white—as indeed they were.

Waiting for Balthus, I looked around. The evidence was palpable; Balthus as a man might rather do anything than own up to the truth, and artistically and personally he never stopped playing games, but he was an utterly superb and brilliant painter. Looking again at *The Méditerranée's Cat, The Passage du Commerce Saint-André,* and above all the Claude-like *Landscape at Champrovent,* I was floored.

Then Balthus arrived. Surrounded by people, with Setsuko on his arm, his entrance was like that of royalty into the court. Over a handsome flannel shirt, he wore a tightly fitted black linen jacket and a flowing scarlet foulard. With his face even more gaunt than two years earlier and his white hair brushed back immaculately, he looked like no one else in the world.

It was not just because it was an exhibition of his work that he seemed the most important presence in the room. Perhaps Balthus could walk into virtually any room and dominate it by dint of his achievement and his reputation, but his magnetic presence had a force all its own. Just seeing him from afar, I was reminded of all that this extraordinary man embodies. In public he was both the quintessential artist and the ultimate count. Like others of us, Balthus was the child the adults worshiped, the prodigy who felt himself the prince. But unlike most other children who felt thus empowered, Balthus never came down in stature. Since his youth, he has nurtured his own prodigious talent and kept his center-stage position while enlarging his audience.

Dozens of people greeted Balthus as he made his entrance. I waited for a lull, but there was none. Finally, at the insistence of my jet-lagged children, we approached. Setsuko, while polite, was slightly posed and formal. She quickly alerted Balthus to our presence. Then, even before saying hello to me, he greeted the girls. Without being either sexual or inappropriate, his gaze as he inhaled my daughters' appearance was passionately reverent.

"My beauties!" he exclaimed—stretching out the noun to three syllables. He leaned down to kiss Lucy and put his hand on Charlotte. "They're *lovely,*" he pronounced with a smile as he embraced me. He was not the first to have said as much, but never before had I witnessed a reaction of such absolute, unadulterated, undisguised engagement. The intensity was the same as in Rilke's and Baladine's letters.

The room was noisy as I made an official introduction following those initial embraces. Balthus wanted to be sure to get the girls' names right, and kept adjusting his hearing aid until it worked. "Lucy" posed no problem, but on the first two tries, he could not get "Charlotte." Then I said, even louder and more clearly, "Charlotte, like Brontë." From then on, he always addressed both by their names correctly; unlike most elderly people, he was never confused about which was which.

The most concerned of hosts, Balthus asked if we were staying for lunch. Would we be there for lunch in Rossinière tomorrow? His presence of mind was heartwarming, especially because he had so much else to consider.

Balthus told me that the exhibition, which he had seen the day before, was "frightfully depressing." Moreover, he did not in the least like the positioning of his last work. (The deficiencies of much art criticism were evident months later when a long, and remarkably self-assured, article about the show appeared in America, where the well-respected and confident writer went on at considerable length about how clear it was that Balthus had personally been responsible for the presentation of this painting in its rather theatrical location.) But, he told me with a look of gentle condescension, "I arrive to assure the lunch."

A LAVISH BUFFET WAS SERVED, and the sizable crowd in attendance ate and previewed the show. My daughters were entertained by the Klossowskis' Filipino staff and their families, and we stayed for a couple of hours.

Then we went to say good-bye to Balthus. Lucy had whispered to me that, whereas she had expected him to be scary, he was "fragile"; it was as if she felt an instinct to come to his rescue.

The artist was besieged by admirers, as was the case throughout the vernissage, but we managed to get close enough to bid our farewells. Again he hugged the girls. And, again, he strongly cupped their chins with his hands and studied their faces.

Balthus's ancient, wizened face and vital stare gave him the intensity of a Giacometti—or of a character from a Camus novel. He resembled a wanderer in the desert who has suddenly seen a lush oasis. Like someone with the deepest thirst who could at last quaff it, he repeated to me how beautiful my girls were. His hearing bothered him, he told me, and the crowded room gave him a headache, but he made me feel as if the three of us offered some form of relief. "You're lovely," he reiterated to Lucy and Charlotte—again with that riveted gaze. He perpetually lifted Charlotte's chin and held it like a precious vase. We agreed how nice it would be to see one another the next day in Rossinière, and then he hugged the girls.

II

THE EXPRESSION ON Balthus's face as he took in the sight of my daughters was more Turgenev than Nabokov: the departing generation drinking in the youth of the emerging one. Tender, yes; erotic, no. The lust that was there was for beauty, for a time of life, for human feeling: not for sex.

For whatever reasons, I had taken my two beautiful children to meet the ultimate connoisseur of little girls. And the man whose lifelong obsession had been female latency had clearly feasted on the sight of these two in their early bloom. The ardor and reverence were spiritual; whatever he may do through the fantasy of his art, in real life Balthus did not want to possess these female children. Youth—and beautiful, radiant youth at that—were his elixir beyond all imagining. Balthus's look was one of worshipfulness and discovery, moving in its sheer vivacity.

By now I had devoted years to trying to understand Balthus's attitude toward young women: its mix of forthright feeling with narcissism and bisexuality, the wavering between far-reaching fantasy and occasional truthfulness. At the same time, I was addressing my own emotional complexity; grappling with my own unclear conception of mental health, I was trying to distinguish who Balthus, and not just my subjective perception of him, really was. In that moment of his meeting my daughters, I saw the object of my quest.

Balthus was an intoxicant, an obsessive, a person for whom sensualness and emotion have always reigned supreme. He has tasted the mountain air as well as the world of salons; he has savored the miracles of art; he has manipulated and played with human behavior—always with richer, if perilous, rewards.

To cope with his own fevers, he has developed certain defenses. As a conjurer and maker of beauty he has outdistanced almost everyone else of his time, but he has needed to build his own code of behavior to survive. His technique has been to make his own rules and keep everyone guessing. Like a snake charmer, he has been so crafty and talented and able that he has had the world at his feet.

Now the fine vintage on which Balthus was drunk was my daughters. But he tempered his engagement with restraint and formality; Lucy and Charlotte's admirer was completely respectful. They immediately saw him as a comrade. For Balthus is one of those grown-ups who has the quality that children most love: a flair for living. Moreover, he met them as equals. For—as has been the case with other extraordinary octogenarians Lucy and Charlotte had had the good fortune to know—he was still young.

THAT AFTERNOON I RETURNED to the museum for the official opening of Balthus's show. The proceedings took place in a large and ornate auditorium filled with sturdy, middle-aged members of the Swiss bourgeoisie who looked like the ferryboat passengers in *Mitsou*. The museum director, executives from Nestlé (the corporate sponsor), and numerous government officials gave speeches. Soldiers stood erect and motionless in front of the government officials. As they spoke, the museum director and others kept addressing Balthus. "Cher Balthus," they repeatedly intoned, looking toward the front row of the audience. Some addressed him with unctuous formality, others as if he were an old friend.

There was only one problem. Balthus had not shown up. It was a repeat performance of the episode at his school in Geneva which had caused Baladine to be summoned to Monsieur Pittard's office. He was playing hooky.

THE NEXT DAY, standing in the garden behind Le Grand Chalet, Balthus and I again touched on some of the subjects we had last discussed over two years before. "The problem is that everyone sees eroticism. My pictures aren't erotic. The problem is psychoanalysis," Balthus again lamented.

As before, Balthus gave me the sense that I was his dearest friend and aide and confidant. I felt this even more so a bit later when Balthus was upstairs at the living room level and Setsuko asked me to help him down the stairs to the garden. At age eighty-five, in his wooden clogs and with his visibly infirm legs,

Balthus, Setsuko, and Harumi in 1990, by Henri Cartier-Bresson

he had to work hard to make this steep descent without accident. Not only was he frail and partially crippled, but as Balthus had told me earlier, in the past few months he had become nearly blind; otherwise he would have wanted to sketch Lucy and Charlotte. I worried with every step, but he balanced himself on my arm and managed his feet with admirable control.

When we got to the lower level, I teased him about his not having been at the ceremony the day before. He grinned the delighted grin of a wicked child who has had his fun. He asked for details about the event, and when I compared the setting to my large junior high school in Connecticut and said it had been hot and airless, Balthus had a look of mischief on his face that both Lucy and Charlotte later remarked upon. They could imagine what sort of boy he had been.

Of course, it would have been nicer and more diplomatic for the Nestlé executive and the Swiss government officials and the director of the Lausanne museum if Balthus had acknowledged them and thanked them and even said a few words about their efforts. Maybe it wasn't right to be elusive and superior and above it all at a public event. But the act of hooky was only mildly naughty—and understandable in a man of his age. Why should someone as brilliant as Balthus be bothered with boring speeches anyway? At least he was affable to his friends. And in any event, his rule was always to have the last laugh

AFTER LUNCH, WE BID our farewells in the garden, full of the early June blossoms that their talented gardener had cultivated with an eye to the wonderful possibilities of the Alpine climate. Balthus needed to know details the way my mother had when I was in college. When was our train? Where exactly were we going? I explained that we would be returning to Connecticut the next day. He had to get this all straight. His last words to me were an ambiguous "Let me know where you are, Nicholas." I felt that he meant this about everything, of course.

After issuing instructions that I stay in touch, Balthus warmly clasped my right hand with both of his and embraced Lucy and Charlotte. Now nearly late, we hurried down the hill for the mountain train back to Lausanne.

In the shaky coach, I chatted with Jean Leymarie, who said he was struggling with his book on Balthus's own viewpoint and that Balthus would not permit the use of a tape recorder. I certainly concurred on the difficulties of our mutual subject. Balthus is like his art—initially enticing and extraordinary, but guaranteed to leave observers anxious and uneasy if not downright melancholy. Even if I was having a hard time with him, I was aware that Leymarie—the anointed insider of long standing—seemed the most hapless victim of all.

But feeling like a renegade son who has just enjoyed the luxuries of a homecoming, I was not sure that my insistence on independence was any better as a solution to dealing with the master of the Grand Chalet.

AFTERWORD

I

THAT SUNDAY CELEBRATION at Le Grand Chalet in 1993 was the last time
I saw Balthus.

I received an invitation to the opening of his 1996 exhibition in Madrid
but learned that he would not be in attendance. In any event, the more I progressed with this book, the more inclined I was to avoid direct encounters.

I did, however, see Harumi and Setsuko in May 1995 at the Asia Society in
New York. The occasion was a reception to celebrate the publication of a book
with a traditional Japanese tale that Setsuko had illustrated. In 1991, when I
was staying in the room next to hers in Rossinière, Harumi had been an awkward teenager who seemed to spend most of the day rearranging her hair while
listening to rock music. When she arrived at the Asia Society, it was clear that
she had been transformed. Hair was still clearly a key issue for her, but now her
black locks were highlighted with red and swept fetchingly to one side. Ravishing with her Asian-Polish looks, her striking profile and willowy figure, and her
carefully cultivated personal style, Harumi had achieved the rare distinction of
being, when she was only twenty years old, one of twelve women on the International Best Dressed list. She had turned into a poised and pleasant young
woman with a high degree of self-command.

Shortly after being cited for her own stylishness, Harumi took a job in
public relations for the Paris-based designer John Galliano and was the subject
of a major article and picture spread in *Mirabella*. Her father's interest in
appearances had taken her far.

It was hard to have a word with the daughter of the Count and Countess
Klossowski de Rola at the Asia Society, however, because she was perpetually
engaged with one or another of her family's very thin, very elegant friends. At

the moment when I wanted to introduce my wife before we had to rush off to another event, Harumi was rapt in conversation with David Bowie and his sleek, leggy wife, Iman. It was while Katharine and I were waiting for a moment to break in that I heard the twenty-one-year-old tell Bowie how she wanted "to learn history, and to try to understand my father," and the singer reply that the second goal was futile.

Setsuko that evening looked like a Kabuki doll. She glided around coyly, in her own orbit, not quite engaging with anyone. Her coat of pale white makeup was thicker than I had seen on her before, and her hair appeared more lacquered. She appeared completely artificial, encased in her stiff and elaborate starched white kimono with its obi. In spite of being so properly Japanese, she carried a Chanel evening bag; the combination made her resemble a rich tourist from Tokyo.

Balthus's wife that evening seemed particularly cold to me—at first polite if formal, but then icy. Considering our long and friendly days and evenings together in Rossinière, this made me feel a bit strange. On the other hand, she had every reason to be distant. This was her first time in New York, and the occasion was her own opening, all of which could have made her nervous. Besides, I had fallen out of touch, and she could well have gotten word from one or another person that my approach to Balthus as a subject had become less than worshipful.

Then Setsuko read to me from her afterword to Izumi Kyoka's "Tale of the Wandering Monk"—the story for which she had made the illustrations on view. Listening to her, I wondered if some of these words had, in fact, been dictated by Balthus:

> It is said that illustrating a great literary work is like adding legs to a snake. While I fully understood the truth of this statement, I went ahead anyway because I wanted to immerse myself in Kyoka's world, to live within its fantasy and if possible to depict it. I lost myself doing so, in much the same way that one falls in love, regardless of whether or not one's love is requited.[1]

Not only was the command of English more at Balthus's level than at Setsuko's, but the legged-snake imagery and the slightly forlorn tone had a distinctly Balthusian aspect, as did the giveaway about living in fantasy.

But what was most memorable was the expression Setsuko wore on her heavily made-up face as she glared at me through her frozen smile and read, with rising voice, the last sentence of her afterword:

Thus, without being aware of it, I was transformed into some kind of monstrous animal who presumed to paint and even to write an afterword.

"You see, I can be an animal," she said to me, her grin broadening. "I am not just an animal but a *vicious* one." Whatever her intention was in making the declaration—which may have been no more serious than when we once all had a good laugh over Balthus handing her a note instructing her to tell a would-be interviewer on the phone that he was "a wicked old man"—I interpreted it as a warning.

ANY PUBLIC APPEARANCE of Balthus or his wife in the nineties was an event. It was rare that they ventured from their mountain retreat into the larger world, and when they did so, people made note. Friends described Balthus's arrival at the opening of the great Poussin retrospective in Paris in 1994; the seventeen-year-old who had once spent long days working away unnoticed copying *Echo et Narcisse* was now the aged celebrity whose elegant outfit—with a silk scarf visible from across the large room—and slow gait attracted all eyes at dinner at Le Grand Palais.

The architect Gae Aulenti provided a marvelous account of the occasion when Balthus was awarded the Imperial Prize in Japan. This event had taken place in the fall of 1991, and Balthus and Setsuko had often referred to it in our phone calls because of Balthus's need to rest up for the journey first, and then to recover from it, which affected his availability to receive me for another long visit in Rossinière, presumably with Jean Leymarie—the trip which in the end I never made. Prince Masahito Hitachi presided over the ceremony—at which speeches were given by, among others, Jacques Chirac and Helmut Schmidt. Balthus, who was receiving the award medal in painting, was the first of the five honorees.

Aulenti, who was to receive the medal for architecture, was struck by the way that Balthus, although naturally "very tall—I think he was one meter ninety," was further elevated by the unusual leather clogs with thick wooden heels that he was wearing with his evening clothes—the same footwear he had had on for the Award Recipients' Audience with Their Majesties the Emperor and Empress of Japan at the Akasaka Imperial Palace. "Balthus went in front of the prince to take the prize, and he had more height because of these shoes. And the Japanese prince was very short." The architect's attention was further drawn to these black clogs because of the "violet socks" Balthus was wearing.

Aulenti and I were having lunch in Milan in January of 1999 when she described this. Balthus's behavior had left an indelible impression. The architect moved a beer stein next to an ashtray to indicate the height difference. She then tipped the empty stein to demonstrate what happened next. "Balthus kneeled in front of the prince at ninety degrees." Once he had lowered himself to the ground, he was down "for two minutes. In the complete silence you could hear his bones: crack, crack, crack. It was like something out of a Japanese play, Noh theater."

Now Aulenti, looking distinguished as ever with her short gray hair and tailored black jacket and pants, rose from the table and, in the middle of the restaurant, reenacted what happened next. From her prone position she explained, "He couldn't get up." The suspense was palpable as the notables assembled in Tokyo looked on, while no one uttered a sound. It was as if Balthus was stuck.

Then, ever so slowly, he rose. By Aulenti's calculation, it took the artist "three minutes to come back." She and everyone else who was present felt enormous relief. As she imitated Balthus taking that seemingly interminable time to straighten up his body, she said it seemed as if he would never rise again. In Gae Aulenti's eyes, "the most elegant man in the world," Balthus, had stolen the show.[2]

ON FEBRUARY 29, 1996, Setsuko gave a masked ball at Le Grand Chalet, in honor, the invitation said, of the twenty-second birthdays of both Balthus and Harumi. Acknowledging her husband's actual number of years, she invited eighty-eight people. Over a hundred showed up, however—among them complete strangers, safely hidden behind their requisite face-coverings. The cats, Pulcinellos, vampires, and American Indians whom the host and hostess actually knew included Balthus's children and their family and friends; Balthus's local physician, Dr. Valli, and his daughter Anna, Balthus's current adolescent model—looking far beyond her years in a slinky low-cut white dress; Jean Leymarie; Tana Matisse; various art dealers; a plastic surgeon renowned for his face-lifts on international socialites; and a few people with impressive titles—like Nicolas Romanov, a *real* Romanov related to the Russian czars. But for the most part the guests were what one old acquaintance in attendance termed "demimondaines." Neither Pierre Klossowski nor any of Balthus's friends of the pre-nobility era were in evidence.

Balthus himself appeared at 9 p.m., when the curtains opened on a theater stage that Setsuko, dressed as a cat, had improvised. He wore "an ancient

Clockwise from left: Balthus, Nicholas Fox Weber, Charlotte Fox Weber,
Lucy Swift Weber, and Anna Valli, at opening in Lausanne, May 31, 1993

red kimono and a gold Venetian mask of the 17th century."[3] One friend who
was there told me that she found the getup frightening, in part because it gave
its wearer a beak even more pronounced than his own real nose, a sort of gross
parody.

What was most apparent was the degree to which the birthday boy was
now in his wife's wraps. "On the one hand, she's good for him, protecting
him," my friend remarked astutely. "On the other hand, she surrounds him
with these mundane people she likes. They are decorative, but very few of the
real old friends were there."

There was a remarkable birthday cake crafted by the cook of the Embiri-cos, wealthy Greek shipping people and art collectors who live in Lausanne. Its topping was a three-dimensional version of *The Méditerranée's Cat*. The mul-ticolored, hardened frosting was sculpted charmingly into a primitive version of the imagery of that painting: the cat tucking into his lobster feast, the girl waving from the boat. Twenty-two candles flanked this playful assemblage.

The main occupation of most of the guests was taking photos, or having them taken of themselves with Balthus and the cake. The shots of Balthus dur-ing dinner all show him next to the woman considered "the real queen of Italy"—Marina Doria di Savoya, the wife of Victorio Emanuelle. With her hair pulled back sleekly, the bejeweled noblewoman looked the epitome of the rich titled Europeans of the nineties. What with the Romanovs also represented, one would be safe in assuming that the artist's mentor, the hero of his child-hood—Rilke—who was equally drawn to celebrities and people with titles, would have approved.

Meanwhile, no one was heard to say "Many happy returns." The guest of honor, who looked painfully tired and haggard, his skin tone a very pale gray, escaped upstairs at an early hour, bringing the event pretty much to a close before midnight.

Writing this in April 1999, I have as recently as a month ago heard from mutual acquaintances that Balthus is still at work. While they claim he is not nearly as robust as reported in the popular press—where the aged artist is cred-ited with daily sessions in the studio—they say he has been working for several years on a still life. But it is a struggle, and *Cat at the Mirror III*—the painting that had its world premiere in 1993 at the Musée des Beaux-Arts in Lausanne—may well prove to be the last large canvas he ever completes (color plate 16). And at least at present it is the only major work he has ever failed to sell.

Cat at the Mirror III is the painting I first saw in the studio in Rossinière in 1991. Then, although Balthus had been working on it for some two years, he had painted in only the child's head, roughly indicated the cat, and sketched a few other details on top of a rudimentary pencil grid. The other major forms were indicated, but only summarily. The raw material had rich potential at this early stage, and it appeared that this large canvas would become another great Balthus.

Finished, it looks more like "paint by numbers." In the period when I saw this picture on its easel, Balthus had told me that he could no longer see well enough to draw. This painting does, indeed, appear to be the work of someone with impaired eyesight. *Cat at the Mirror* has a vibrancy; it is rich in rhythms and full of nonstop motion; but it reflects blunted vision.

The painting has few of the subtleties of most of Balthus's work. It is missing the beautiful little passages, the quiet and precise details. The waist of the central figure is disconcerting: the child's body is severely disjointed, as if cut in two, and its parts do not cohere. The distortion of the child's body is not the typical Balthus maneuvering of the type where we feel there is an agenda behind it. It seems, rather, that Balthus really could not control what he was doing. He filled in the parts of the painting dutifully, piece by piece, but he could no longer achieve the graceful relationship of the different shapes we know from his successful work.

The colors of this awkward composition are those bright tones of the spectrum known by ophthalmologists to appeal to elderly people—generally over the age of eighty—who can no longer respond to more muted tones. Whereas other aged painters made that transition to the advantage of their work, in Balthus the results are unfortunately garish. The only explanation for these Day-Glo colors is that, with the aging of his eyes, Balthus could no longer perceive the subtleties of hue that had always been such a major element of his work.

The results of the clunky forms and jarring palette is that *Cat at the Mirror III* looks in some ways more like a copy of a Balthus than the real thing. There are details that are true Balthus: the catlike cat, at once mischievous and adorable; the child's exquisite face. The underlying verve reflects an impressive life force given the age of the maker. What it is missing, however, is the artist's former taste and quietude. The painting simply does not hold a candle either to the old-masterish works of the thirties, to those dazzling, Mozartian compositions of the Chassy period, or even to the recent misty *Montecalvello*.

But what is inferior artistically can still represent an act of love and devotion. When I first saw the completed *Cat at the Mirror III* in Lausanne, it struck me above all as the achievement of a loyal husband. Friends of Balthus's intimated to me that the artist needed another few million dollars in order to assure Setsuko's well-being after his death, and that he made this large canvas accordingly to achieve that goal. The assumption was that it would invariably attract a lot of attention, and sell.

Certainly in 1993 there were enough rich people who would jump at the chance to buy a painting so unquestionably Balthusian—with the trademark androgynous girl, mischievous cat, and lust under wraps. Even if Balthus's fellow painters, his disciples from the Villa Medici, and other astute viewers would see how flawed the canvas was, there was little question of its marketability in a world that buys Vuitton bags for their emblem and Cartier jewels for the trademark "C." It seems well within Balthus's power to take advantage of such a situation for the benefit of the woman who has brought him such pleasure in the closing epoch of his life.

. . .

THE YOUNG MODEL for this last painting, Anna Valli, attended the opening
in Lausanne. Although she was not in evidence when Balthus arrived, once
lunch was served and the crowd had thickened, she hardly ever let go of the
artist's hand.

When the two of them posed for photographs in front of *Cat at the Mirror III* in its back gallery, Anna was like a parody of a Balthus girl. Her presence
as she clung to the artist turned him into a caricature of the old pedophile. The
nymphet with streaming blond hair wore a black A-line dress loosely laced in
front—far too adult and sexy for her ten years. She looked totally smitten, and
her presence was disturbing. Together they made, like a bad joke, the ultimate
sick Balthus tableau: the old lecher and the knowing Lolita. Grinning as if she
were his trophy, Balthus seemed to cultivate to the fullest the image he had
repeatedly told me was totally without basis.

Naturally, the village girl was proud to be attending this opening and posing with the world-famous Balthus in front of the painting that depicted her.
One could understand her unabashed delight in her stardom. But the sight of
the two of them cavorting together, with Setsuko standing nearby and looking
on approvingly, was alternately ridiculous and nauseating.

What also became noticeable in this public display was that although the
girl had unquestionably been the model for this large canvas of dubious distinction, a great difference existed between the actual child and Balthus's
invention. For the creature in Balthus's painting is androgynous. It resembles
the doctor's daughter, but it looks equally like photos of the teenage Balthus
and some of his early self-portraits. Moreover, gazing at the hand mirror, the
subject is again the Narcissus about whom Rilke wrote the poem he dedicated
to his young friend.

The child in *Cat at the Mirror III* is, also, very feline-looking: a companion and soul mate to the cat who is its opposite number in the canvas. Additionally, in part because of the hair, this is Antoinette. The figure is a perfect
compendium of Balthus's obsessions. A cat, a little girl, himself, his first love:
there are no boundaries between Balthus and his subjects.

One painting depicts both the subject and the creator of *Mitsou*. And it
evokes the stage in his life where Balthus on one level has remained forever: the
age at which he first got to know Rilke—when, as a prodigy and genius, he
first began to savor as well as circumvent his beautiful, unbearable existence.

. . .

ALAS, BALTHUS'S GAMBLE did not pay off. *Cat at the Mirror III* failed to attract a buyer at the Musée des Beaux-Arts, or in the exhibition's subsequent venue in Japan. Balthus had the painting returned to his studio, where he amended its surfaces lightly.

Then, in the summer of 1994, *Cat at the Mirror III* became, to an embarrassing degree, a marketable commodity. For three weeks it appeared in an exhibition of its own at the Lefevre Gallery on Bruton Street in London.

The location could hardly have been more convenient: just around the corner from Old Bond Street where shops like Asprey and Versace sell their high-priced goods to a rich international clientele. It is natural enough for world-class art to be in the same arena as other expensive merchandise, but what was unusual—in fact, astonishing—about the promotion of *Cat III* was the glossy and expensive twenty-page brochure produced as a sales tool for this single painting.

In that brochure, the artist who has repeatedly told the world that he should be someone "of whom nothing is known" is shown in numerous black-and-white photographs. We see him in his Missoni cardigan: in one shot standing in front of his forty-five-room chalet, in others sitting with a cigarette dangling from his mouth, and—in two particularly contrived-looking photos—beaming in the presence of his young female model. In one of these, Anna looks at him flirtatiously with a coy grin, while he leers at her with what seems to be unrepentant desire. In another, she leans on his shoulder, and they both smile lasciviously as if in the throes of romantic passion. It is as if the aim of these photos is to say, "This is Balthus, the Lolita guy; you know, the one with young girls." There are also numerous photographs taken inside Balthus's studio—the place supposedly so off limits—and three commanding shots of Le Grand Chalet in all its splendor.

The text of the brochure reads like a flyer for an expensive foreign car. *Cat at the Mirror III* is presented as the ultimate luxury model, the prize. Underneath a reproduction of the finished artwork appears the following statement: "This is the largest and final version of a series of paintings by Balthus, called 'Le Chat au Miroir.' The first, measuring 180 cm × 170 cm, was painted between 1977 and 1980. The second version measures 200 cm × 170 cm, and was painted between 1986 and 1989." This one measures 220 by 195 centimeters. We expect to learn its wheelbase and 0-to-60-mph speed as well.

The earlier versions of *Cat at the Mirror,* and details of this one, appear in full color in the brochure, interspersed throughout an "introduction" by Jean Leymarie printed in both French and English. Like all of Leymarie's writings on the artist, it touches trenchantly on the real issues of Balthus's art—the rela-

Balthus in 1990, by Henri Cartier-Bresson

tionship of the girl, the cat, and the looking glass; the significance of Eastern symbolism in that mirror; the questions raised. But then there are Leymarie's statements that sound like pure advertising hype. "Almost square, it is the largest of the three works, the most daring, and in his [Balthus's] demanding eyes, the most interesting." Leymarie ends his commentary with a solipsism of the type that might well suit Balthus but serves little other purpose: "Each of Balthus's paintings is an autonomous world, brought slowly to completion, from which we feel the magical spell without being able to solve the mystery. The mystery for him is in the unveiling and the consecration of the real world." Rilke could get away with such contradictions; Leymarie—and, through him, Balthus— does not fare as well.

By the time of the exhibition that Harumi Klossowski de Rola helped organize at the Accadèmia Valentino in Rome, held there at the end of 1996 and into 1997, Balthus had further worked *Cat at the Mirror III*. But the fingers of the right hand, now lengthened, and the right leg—now dangling rather than resting on a stool—still look like cartoons of body parts. The art, like the man, resembles patchwork: appealing pieces put together from hither and yon, but lacking cohesion. The palpable stiffness and sheer affectation of the least successful of Balthus's work done after World War II, especially the post-Chassy paintings and drawings, are epitomized by this picture.

THE ASKING PRICE FOR *Cat at the Mirror III* for the past few years has reportedly been about $4.5 million. There have been no takers as yet, although apparently the marketing effort has widened; at the Accademia Valentino, the canvas was presented "Courtesy Thomas Ammann Fine Art, Zürich, and the Lefevre Gallery London," two of the most effective commercial establishments anywhere. But whatever its shortcomings, I hope the painting gets it and that Balthus succeeds in gallantly providing the lovely and supportive Setsuko with the lifelong financial security he wants her to have. Worse paintings have sold for more money; and for all its flaws and childlike aspects, this colorful canvas reflects an energy and a spark admirable in someone Balthus's age. It also makes clear his decency as a provider who had never forgotten the reality of financial hardship. The hype, the photos, even the painting itself, are probably testimony as much to Balthus's true love for his wife and daughter as to his willingness to manipulate the public any way he can.

> *Puss was now a splendid sight. The high boots with the tops turned down became him beautifully. The hunter's pouch was handsomely embroidered and made him look like a bold and gallant huntsman.*
>
> *He tossed the sack over his shoulder, bowed low, and said: "See you later, master, and you may now call me Puss in Boots."*
>
> *"Where are you going?" Hans asked anxiously.*
>
> *But the cat was already out of the door and had vanished into a field of waving grain.*
>
> —*Puss in Boots* [4]

NOTES

Unless otherwise indicated, all translations from the French were done especially for this book by Richard Howard.

CHAPTER ONE

1. Oscar Wilde, *De Profundis*, in *The Portable Oscar Wilde* (New York: Penguin Books, 1981), p. 7.
2. Robert Hughes, "The Nymphets of Balthus," *Time*, Nov. 28, 1977.
3. It was André Breton who gave him this nickname. *Visions of Excess* (Minneapolis: University of Minnesota Press, 1985), p. xi.
4. *Le Monde*, Nov. 3, 1983.
5. As quoted in Richard Jenkyns, "The Pleasures of Melodrama," *New York Review of Books*, July 11, 1996, p. 10.
6. Garson Kanin, *Remembering Mr. Maugham* (London: Hamish Hamilton, 1966), pp. 46, 69.
7. Conversation between Balthus and NFW, Rossinière (hereafter cited as Conversation), Jan. 20, 1991. All unidentified quotations from Balthus throughout the text come from conversations held at Le Grand Chalet in December 1990 or January 1991.

CHAPTER TWO

1. John Richardson, *Braque* (London: Penguin Modern Painters, 1959), as quoted in *The Penguin Book of Art Writing*, eds. Martin Gayford and Karen Wright (London: Penguin Books, 1998), p. 312.
2. Jean Rodolphe von Salis, *Rainer Maria Rilke: The Years in Switzerland* (London: Hogarth Press, 1964), p. 89.
3. Michael Peppiatt, "Balthus," *Réalités* (English edition), Paris, October 1967, p. 53.
4. Michael Peppiatt, "Balthus: Dreams, Enigmas, and Nymphets," *Connoisseur*, Nov. 1983, p. 100.
5. Conversation, Jan. 16, 1991.
6. Conversation, Jan. 18, 1991.
7. Conversation, Dec. 2, 1990.
8. Conversation, Jan. 18, 1991.
9. Conversation, Jan. 17, 1991.
10. Conversation, Dec. 2, 1990.
11. Thomas B. Hess, "Balthus: Seen and Scene," *New York*, Nov. 21, 1977, p. 97.
12. Wolfgang Leppmann, *Rilke: A Life*, trans. Russell M. Stockman (New York: Fromm International Publishing, 1984), p. 287.
13. John Russell, "Balthus Mesmerizes with his Chilling Imagery," *New York Times*, Feb. 19, 1984.
14. Kenneth Clark, "A Modern Master," *New York Review of Books*, June 12, 1980.

15. Sabine Rewald, *Balthus* (New York: Metropolitan Museum of Art, 1984), p. 12.

16. Pierre Jean Jouve, *The Desert World,* trans. Lydia Davis (1927; Evanston, Ill.: Marlboro Press, Northwestern University, 1996), p. 18.

17. Jean-Jacques Fernier, "Balthus," in *Balthus dans la Maison de Courbet* (Ornans: Musée Gustave Courbet, 1992). The schoolmate of Balthus's at the lycée was André Ostier, subsequently a photographer and editor.

18. *Rainer Maria Rilke et Merline: Correspondance,* ed. Dieter Bassermann (Zurich: Insel Verlag, 1954), pp. 97, 98 (letter of Nov. 21 and 22, 1920).

19. Ibid., p. 100 (letter of Nov. 28, 1920).

20. Rainer Maria Rilke, *Briefe an Nanny Wunderly-Volkart* (Leipzig/Frankfurt am Main: Insel Verlag, 1977), p. 323.

21. Rainer Maria Rilke, "Lettres à un jeune peintre," *Fontaine* (Paris), 1945, no. 44: p. 528 (letter of Dec. 31, 1920).

22. Rainer Maria Rilke, *Letters to Merline, 1919–1921,* trans. Jesse Browner (New York: Paragon House, 1989), p. 28 (letter of Nov. 18, 1920).

23. Rilke, "Lettres à un jeune peintre," pp. 526, 527 (letter of Nov. 24, 1920).

24. Rainer Maria Rilke and André Gide, *Correspondance, 1909–1926,* ed. Renée Lang (Paris: Correa, 1952), p. 196 (letter of Dec. 13, 1920, to Charles Vildrac; originally published in Rainer Maria Rilke, *Les Lettres,* 1952).

25. Ibid.

26. Donald Prater, *A Ringing Glass: The Life of Rainer Maria Rilke* (Oxford: Oxford University Press, 1986), p. 325.

27. Von Salis, *Rainer Maria Rilke,* p. 142.

28. Rilke et Merline, *Correspondance,* pp. 81–82 (letter of Oct. 21, 1920).

29. Ibid., p. 84 (letter of Oct. 20 and 22, 1920).

30. Von Salis, *Rainer Maria Rilke,* p. 89.

31. Rilke and Merline, *Correspondance.* p. 81.

32. *Letters of Rainer Maria Rilke,* trans. Jane Bannard Greene and M. D. Herter Norton (New York: W. W. Norton & Co., 1947–48), vol. 2, p. 240 (letter of Dec. 21, 1920).

33. Ralph Freedman, *Life of a Poet: Rainer Maria Rilke* (New York: Farrar, Straus & Giroux, 1996), pp. 370–71.

34. Yves Bonnefoy, "L'Invention de Balthus," published originally in *L'Improbable* (Paris: Mercure de France, 1959).

35. Rainer Maria Rilke, *Briefe an Schweizer Freunde* (Frankfurt am Main: Suhrkamp Verlag, 1990), p. 196.

36. Rainer Maria Rilke, preface to *Mitsou,* trans. Richard Miller (New York: Metropolitan Museum of Art, 1984), pp. 12–13.

CHAPTER THREE

1. Rux Martin, "Truth, Power, Self: An Interview with Michel Foucault," quoted in David Macey, *The Lives of Michel Foucault* (New York: Pantheon Books, 1993), p. xiv.

2. Honoré de Balzac, *Père Goriot,* trans. A. J. Krailsheimer (Oxford: Oxford University Press, 1991), p. 110.

3. Rainer Maria Rilke, *Letters to Frau Gudi Nolke during His Life in Switzerland,* ed. Paul Obermüller, trans. Violet M. Macdonald (London: Hogarth Press, 1955), pp. 121–22.

4. Ingeborg Schnack, *Rainer Maria Rilke: Chronik seines Lebens und seines Werkes* (Frankfurt am Main: Insel Verlag, 1975), p. 766.

5. *Rainer Maria Rilke et Merline: Correspondance,* ed. Dieter Bassermann (Zurich: Insel Verlag, 1954), pp. 231, 232 (letter of March 1 and 2, 1921).

6. Wolfgang Leppmann, *Rilke: A Life,* trans. Russell M. Stockman (New York: Fromm International Publishing, 1984).

7. Polish government officials in Switzerland have the family papers that prove the facts as reported by Sabine Rewald and James Lord. Balthus and Pierre Klossowski's old friends, as well as Eugen Spiro's widow, have also confirmed the information. Additionally, Rilke's correspondence contains numerous references to Baladine's brother, Eugen Spiro, in Berlin—as well as to other members of Baladine's family, who Rilke not only knew to be Jewish, but whose Jewishness he considered a mark of distinction.

8. Conversation with Beatrice Cazac, New York, July 2, 1996.

9. Barbara Pollack, "Court Rules on Balthus Drawing," *ARTnewsletter,* vol. XX, no. 20 (May 30, 1995), pp. 6, 7.

10. Leslie A. Marchand, *Byron: A Biography* (New York: Alfred A. Knopf, 1957), vol. 1, p. vii.

11. Foreword to *Byron: A Self-portrait* (New York: Charles Scribner's Sons, 1950), p. vii.

12. George Gordon, Lord Byron, "When a Man Hath No Freedom to Fight for at Home," in *A Treasury of Great Poems,* ed. Louis Untermeyer (New York: Simon & Schuster, 1960), p. 698.

13. John Russell, "Master of the Nubile Adolescent," *Art in America,* vol. 55, no. 11 (Nov. 1967), p. 99.

14. Jean Leymarie, *Balthus* (Geneva: Skira, 1978). (There are no page numbers in this book.)

15. Alexander Watt, "Balthus," *Occident* (Paris), Jan. 1948, no. 2: p. 23.

16. I learned this from Kenneth Silver in a phone call on Feb. 16, 1996. Silver learned it from Mrs. Spiro, whom he interviewed in 1983 when he was organizing an exhibition for the Jewish Museum that included work by Eugen Spiro.

17. James Thrall Soby, *Balthus* (New York: Museum of Modern Art, 1956), p. 4.

18. Ibid.

19. *Time,* May 12, 1961.

20. Peter Plagens, "Grand Master of Aloofness," *Newsweek,* Aug. 23, 1993, p. 54.

21. Guy Davenport, *A Balthus Notebook* (New York: Echo Press, 1989), p. 10.

22. Rainer Maria Rilke, *Briefe an Schweizer Freunde* (Frankfurt am Main: Suhrhamp Verlag, 1990), p. 220.

23. Ralph Freedman, *Life of a Poet: Rainer Maria Rilke* (New York: Farrar, Straus & Giroux, 1996), pp. 370–71.

24. Ibid., p. 370.

25. Rainer Maria Rilke, *Briefe an Nanny Wunderly-Volkart* (Leipzig/Frankfurt am Main: Insel Verlag, 1977), p. 328.

26. *Rainer Maria Rilke et Merline: Correspondance,* ed. Dieter Bassermann (Zurich: Insel Verlag, 1954), p. 401 (letter of Apr. 24, 1921).

27. Ibid., p. 195 (letter of Feb. 17, 1921).

28. Ibid.

29. Ibid., p. 209 (letter of Feb. 21, 1921).

30. Rilke, *Briefe an Nanny Wunderly-Volkart,* p. 452.

31. Ibid., p. 724.

32. Rainer Maria Rilke, *Letters to Nolke* (letter of Oct. 31, 1922).

33. Ibid., p. 66.

34. Ibid., pp. 69–70 (letter of Dec. 1, 1922).

35. Rilke, *Briefe an Schweizer Freunde*, pp. 234–35.

36. Freedman, *Life of a Poet*, p. 508.

37. *ARTnews*, vol. XXXVI, no. 27 (Apr. 2, 1938), p. 10.

38. *Rainer Maria Rilke et Merline*, p. 293 (letter of Apr. 1, 1921).

39. Freedman, *Life of a Poet*, p, 327.

40. Ibid., p. 326.

CHAPTER FOUR

1. Stanislas Klossowski de Rola, *Balthus* (London: Thames & Hudson, 1983), p. 8.

2. Ananda K. Coomaraswamy, *Christian and Oriental Philosophy of Art* (New York: Dover Publications, 1956), p. 11.

3. Ibid., p. 27.

4. *Rainer Maria Rilke et Merline: Correspondance,* ed. Dieter Bassermann (Zurich: Insel Verlag, 1954), p. 469 (letter of Nov. 21, 1923).

5. Ibid., p. 472 (letter of Nov. 27, 1923).

6. Ralph Freedman, *Life of a Poet: Rainer Maria Rilke* (New York: Farrar, Straus & Giroux, 1996), p. 574.

7. Rainer Maria Rilke and André Gide, *Correspondance, 1909–1926,* ed. Renée Lang (Paris: Correa, 1952), p. 194 (letter of Nov. 3, 1922).

8. *Rainer Maria Rilke et Merline*, p. 506 (letter of Feb. 29, 1924).

CHAPTER FIVE

1. Rainer Maria Rilke, *Briefe an Schweizer Freunde* (Frankfurt am Main: Suhrkamp Verlag, 1990), p. 289.

2. François Chalais, "Balthus Parle," *Le Figaro,* Mar. 23, 1989.

3. *Rainer Maria Rilke et Merline: Correspondance,* ed. Dieter Bassermann (Zurich: Insel Verlag, 1954), pp. 521, 522 (letter of Oct. 27, 1924).

4. Ralph Freedman, *Life of a Poet: Rainer Maria Rilke* (New York: Farrar, Straus & Giroux, 1996), p. 525.

5. Ibid., p. 519.

6. Harry Kessler, *Diaries,* Apr. 5, 1925, in Ingeborg Schnack, *Rainer Maria Rilke: Chronik seines Lebens und seines Werkes* (Frankfurt am Main: Insel Verlag, 1975), pp. 377–78.

7. Freedman, *Life of a Poet*, p. 521.

8. Ibid., p. 529.

9. Ibid.

10. Richard Verdi, *Nicolas Poussin, 1594–1665* (London: Royal Academy of Arts, 1995), p. 172.

11. *Rainer Maria Rilke et Merline*, p. 549 (letter of Nov. 19, 1925).

12. Ibid., p. 549 (letter of Dec. 29, 1925).

13. *The Complete French Poems of Rainer Maria Rilke,* trans. A. Poulin, Jr. (St. Paul, Minn.: Graywolf Press, 1979), p. 283.

14. Ovid, *The Metamorphoses,* trans. Horace Gregory (New York: Penguin Books, 1960), p. 98.

CHAPTER SIX

1. Bernard Berenson, *Piero della Francesca, or The Ineloquent in Art* (London: Chapman & Hall, 1954), as quoted in *The Penguin Book of Art Writing*, eds. Martin Gayford and Karen Wright (London: Penguin Books, 1998), pp. 464–66.
2. *Rainer Maria Rilke et Merline: Correspondance*, ed. Dieter Bassermann (Zurich: Insel Verlag, 1954), p. 45 (letter of Sept. 18, 1920).
3. Ibid., p. 590 (telegram of July 8, 1926).
4. Ibid. (letter of July 12, 1926).
5. Ibid. (letter of July 14, 1926).
6. Ibid., p. 592 (letter of July 12, 1926).
7. Kenneth Clark, *Piero della Francesca* (London: Phaidon Press, 1951), p. 54.
8. Ibid., p. 71.

CHAPTER SEVEN

1. John Lanchester, *The Debt to Pleasure* (New York: Henry Holt & Co., 1996), p. 32.
2. Ralph Freedman, *Life of a Poet: Rainer Maria Rilke* (New York: Farrar, Straus & Giroux, 1996), p. 547.
3. Barbara Grizzuti Harrison, *The Astonishing World* (New York: Ticknor & Fields, 1992), pp. 54–55.
4. Pierre Jean Jouve, "Balthus," *La Nef* (Algiers), Sept. 1944; in *Balthus* (Paris: Centre Georges Pompidou, 1983), p. 57.

CHAPTER EIGHT

1. Honoré de Balzac, *Père Goriot*, trans. A. J. Krailsheimer (Oxford: Oxford University Press, 1991), pp. 102, 113.
2. André Lhote, "Gromaire à la Galerie Pierre," *La Nouvelle Revue Française* (Paris), June 1934 no. 249, pp. 1045–56.
3. Pierre Loeb, *Voyages à travers la peinture* (Paris: Borda, 1945), pp. 37–39.
4. James Thrall Soby, manuscript of his unpublished memoirs (courtesy of Samuel Childs), chap. 26, "Balthus and Giacometti," p. 6.
5. Rainer Maria Rilke, *Letters to Merline, 1919–1921*, trans. Jesse Browner (New York: Paragon House, 1989), p. 41.
6. Pierre Klossowski, "Balthus: Beyond Realism," *ARTnews*, December 1956, vol. 55, no. 8 (1956): p. 28.
7. Jean Leymarie, *Balthus* (Geneva: Skira, 1978). (This book has no page numbers.)
8. Ibid.
9. Douglas Cooper, "The Writings of Blunt and Others," *Books and Bookmen*, Dec. 1979, p. 41.
10. Gabriele Annan, review of *Balthus*, by Jean Leymarie, *Times Literary Supplement*, Nov. 28, 1980.
11. James Thrall Soby, *Balthus* (New York: Museum of Modern Art, 1956), p. 5.
12. Thornton Wilder, *The Eighth Day* (New York: Harper & Row, 1967), p. 213.
13. Elizabeth Marshall Thomas, "Strong and Sensitive Cats," *Atlantic Monthly*, July 1994, p. 71.

14. Lewis Carroll, *Through the Looking-Glass* (New York: W. W. Norton & Co., 1971), p. 208.

15. Lewis Carroll, *Alice's Adventures in Wonderland* (New York: W. W. Norton & Co., 1971), p. 4.

CHAPTER NINE

1. James Thrall Soby, manuscript of his unpublished memoirs (courtesy of Samuel Childs), chap. 26, "Balthus and Giacometti," p. 3.

2. Ibid.

3. Ibid., p. 4.

4. Ibid., p. 9.

5. James Thrall Soby, "Balthus," catalog essay for exhibition at the Pierre Matisse Gallery, New York, 1938.

6. Ibid.

7. James Thrall Soby, *Balthus* (New York: Museum of Modern Art, 1956), p. 5.

8. Albert Camus, "Balthus," catalog essay for exhibition at the Pierre Matisse Gallery, New York, 1949.

9. Brian Friel, *Dancing at Lughnasa* (London: Faber & Faber, 1990), p. 71.

CHAPTER TEN

1. Baudelaire, *Oeuvres Complètes,* vol. II (Paris: Editions Gallimard, 1976), p. 81.

2. *Aline et Valcour,* in *Sade,* ed. Michel Delon (Paris: Editions Gallimard, 1990), vol. 1, p. 403; quoted in Maurice Lever, *Sade: A Biography,* trans. Arthur Goldhammer (New York: Farrar, Straus & Giroux, 1993), p. 51.

3. Henry Miller, introduction to *Erotic Art of the Masters* (Secaucus, N.J.: Lyle Stuart, undated), p. xi.

4. Federico Fellini, preface to *Balthus,* trans. Luigi Barzini (New York: Pierre Matisse Gallery, 1977).

5. Thomas B. Hess, "Balthus: Seen and Scene," *New York,* Nov. 21, 1977, p. 94.

6. "Family Photos or Pornography? A Father's Bitter Legal Odyssey," *New York Times,* Jan. 30, 1995, pp. A1, B5.

7. Dominique Bozo, preface to *Balthus* (Paris: Centre Pompidou, 1983), pp. 7–8.

8. Paul West, *Lord Byron's Doctor* (New York: Doubleday, 1989), p. 103.

9. Oscar Wilde, preface to *The Picture of Dorian Gray,* in *The Portable Oscar Wilde* (New York: Penguin Books, 1981), p. 139.

10. Sigmund Freud, "Beyond the Pleasure Principle," in *The Freud Reader* (New York: W. W. Norton & Co., 1989), p. 609.

11. James Lord, "Balthus: The Strange Case of the Count de Rola," *The New Criterion,* vol. 2, no. 4 (Dec. 1983): p. 14.

12. Ibid.

13. Ibid.

14. Phillip Knightly, "A Gold-plated Phoney," review of *Ian Fleming,* by Andrew Lycett, *New York Times Book Review,* Oct. 22, 1995, p. 5.

15. Pierre Klossowski, "Eléments d'une étude psychanalytique sur le Marquis de Sade," *Revue Française de Psychanalyse* (Paris), 1933, nos. 3–4: p. 462.

16. Ibid., p. 463.

17. Ibid., p. 469.

18. Ibid., pp. 471–72.

19. Pierre Klossowski, "Balthus: Beyond Realism," *ARTnews,* vol. 55, no. 8 (December 1956): p. 30.

20. Gilles Deleuze, *Logique de sens* (Paris: 10/18, 1973), p. 382; quoted and translated in David Macey, *The Lives of Michel Foucault* (New York: Pantheon Books, 1993), pp. 156-57.

21. Ibid., p. 155.

22. Ibid., pp. 254-55.

23. Ibid., p. 341.

24. Wilde, *The Picture of Dorian Gray,* pp. 305, 353-54.

CHAPTER ELEVEN

1. Ian McEwan, *Enduring Love* (London: Jonathan Cape, 1997), p. 51.

2. *The Complete French Poems of Rainer Maria Rilke,* trans. A. Poulin, Jr. (St. Paul, Minn.: Graywolf Press, 1979), pp. 29-31.

3. Ibid., p. 41.

4. Ibid., p. 49.

5. Sabine Rewald, *Balthus* (New York: Metropolitan Museum of Art, 1984), p. 69.

6. *Le Figaro,* May 5, 1935.

7. Marquis de Sade, *The 120 Days of Sodom,* trans. Austryn Wainhouse and Richard Seaver (New York: Grove Weidenfeld, 1966), p. 197.

8. Sylvia Colle Lorant, "Balthus, décorateur de théâtre," in *Balthus* (Paris: Centre Georges Pompidou, 1983), p. 315.

9. Naomi Greene, *Antonin Artaud. Poet without Words* (New York: Simon & Schuster, 1970), p. 9.

10. Antonin Artaud, "Balthus at the Galerie Pierre" (translator not cited), in *Balthus* (London: Tate Gallery, 1968), p. 33.

11. Antonin Artaud, *Oeuvres complètes* (Paris: Editions Gallimard, 1964 and 1979), vol. 5, pp. 43, 44.

12. Ibid., vol. 7, p. 185.

13. Ibid., vol. 8, p. 125.

14. Ibid., vol. 4, p. 103.

15. Anaïs Nin, *The Diary of Anaïs Nin, 1931-1934* (New York: Swallow Press and Harcourt, Brace & World, 1966), pp. 192-93.

16. Artaud, *Oeuvres complètes,* vol. 4, p. 147.

17. Ibid., 149.

18. Ibid., pp. 198-99.

19. Antonin Artaud, article about *Les Cenci,* first published in *La Bête Noire,* May 1, 1935, no. 2; reprinted in *The Cenci,* trans. Simon Watson-Taylor (London: Calder & Boyars, 1969), p. 17.

20. Ibid., p. 8.

21. Artaud, *The Cenci,* p. 15.

22. Ibid., p. 19.

23. Ibid., p. 29.

24. Ibid., p. 34.

25. Ibid., p. 44.

26. *Comoedia* (Paris), May 6, 1936.

27. Pierre Jean Jouve, "*Les Cenci* d'Antonin Artaud," *La Nouvelle Revue Française* (Paris), June 1935, no. 261: pp. 910-15; in *Balthus* (Paris: Centre Georges Pompidou, 1983), p. 52.

28. Ibid.

29. André Maurois, *Byron,* trans. Hamish Miles (New York: D. Appleton & Co., 1930), p. 476.
30. Artaud, *Oeuvres complètes,* vol. 5, pp. 277–78.
31. Antonin Artaud, "La pintura francesa joven y la tradición," *El Nacional* (Mexico), June 17, 1936; translated into French by Marie Dézon and Philippe Sollers, in *Balthus* (Centre Georges Pompidou), pp. 43–44.
32. Nin, *The Diary of Anaïs Nin,* p. 229.

CHAPTER TWELVE

1. Emily Brontë, *Wuthering Heights* (New York: Random House, 1943), p. 30.
2. Currer Bell (Charlotte Brontë), Preface, in Emily Brontë, *Wuthering Heights* (New York: Modern Library, 1943), p. xi.
3. Antonin Artaud, "Balthus at the Galerie Pierre" (translator not cited), in *Balthus* (London: Tate Gallery, 1962), p. 33.
4. Somerset Maugham, *Ten Novels and Their Authors* (London: Mandarin, 1991), pp. 253–54.
5. Ibid.
6. Ibid., p. 254.
7. Jean Leymarie, *Balthus* (Geneva: Skira, 1978). (This book has no page numbers.)
8. James Thrall Soby, *Balthus* (New York: Museum of Modern Art, 1956), p. 4.
9. Balthus, afterword to *Wuthering Heights* (New York: Limited Editions, 1994), p. 207 (from a photocopy of the text provided by Sidney Shiff, the publisher).
10. Brontë, *Wuthering Heights,* p. 58.
11. Ibid., p. 35.
12. Ibid., p. 60.
13. Ibid., p. 35.
14. Ibid., p. 21.
15. Conversation with Iris Murdoch, Oxford, Aug. 15, 1994.
16. Brontë, *Wuthering Heights,* p. 6.
17. Ibid., p. 43.
18. Ibid., p. 44.
19. Caroline Lees, "Feminists Find Victorian Echo," *London Times,* Aug. 28, 1984, sec. 4, p. 7.

CHAPTER THIRTEEN

1. Oscar Wilde, "Phrases and Philosophies for the Use of the Young" from *Chameleon* I (December 1894), 1–3, in *The Portable Oscar Wilde* (New York: Penguin Books, 1981), p. 740.
2. Natalie Angier, "Goddesses, Harlots and Other Male Fantasies," review of *A History of the Breast,* by Marilyn Yalom (New York: Alfred A. Knopf, 1997), *New York Times Book Review,* Feb. 23, 1997, p. 4.
3. I owe these impressions to the novelist Louis Begley, whose first wife was analyzed by Blanche Reverchon in the era when analysts and their patients socialized together. Conversation in New York, Jan. 11, 1996.
4. Pierre Jean Jouve, *Le Monde désert* (Paris: Editions Gallimard, 1927), p. 146.
5. Pierre Jean Jouve, "Balthus," *La Nef* (Algiers), Sept. 1944, in *Balthus* (Paris: Centre Georges Pompidou, 1983), p. 57.
6. Ibid.

7. Ibid.
8. Pierre Jean Jouve, "Le Tableau," in *Proses* (Paris: Mercure de France, 1960), pp. 45–49; in *Balthus* (Centre Georges Pompidou), pp. 64 66.
9. Ibid.
10. Ibid.
11. As quoted and translated in Margaret Callander, *The Poetry of Pierre Jean Jouve* (Manchester: Manchester University Press, 1965), p. 168.
12. Ibid., p. 167.
13. Pierre Jean Jouve, *La Fiancée*, in *Histoires sanglantes,* p. 836 (from a photocopy supplied by Louis Begley).
14. Balthus, "Propos," in *Balthus dans la Maison de Courbet* (Ornans: Musée Gustave Courbet, 1992).
15. Michael Peppiatt, *Francis Bacon: Anatomy of an Enigma* (New York: Farrar, Straus & Giroux, 1997), p. 288.
16. Conversation with Michael Peppiatt, London, April 21, 1999.

CHAPTER FOURTEEN

1. Albert Camus, "Balthus," catalog essay for exhibition at the Pierre Matisse Gallery, New York, 1949.
2. Pierre Jean Jouve, "Balthus," *La Nef* (Algiers), Sept. 1944; in *Balthus* (Paris: Centre Georges Pompidou, 1983), p. 57.
3. Cyril Connolly, "Balthus," catalog essay for exhibition at the Lefevre Gallery, London, 1952.
4. Alexander Watt, "Balthus," *Occident* (Paris), Jan. 1948: no. 2.
5. James Thrall Soby, manuscript of his unpublished memoirs (courtesy of Samuel Childs), chap. 26, "Balthus and Giacometti," p. 26.
6. Denys Sutton, *André Derain* (London: Phaidon Press, 1959), p. 48.
7. Alberto Giacometti, "Derain," *Derrière le Miroir* (Paris), Feb.–Mar. 1957, no. 94–95 (no page numbers).
8. Ian McEwan, *Enduring Love* (London: Jonathan Cape, 1997), p. 53.
9. Giacometti, "Derain."
10. Ibid.
11. Pierre Cabanne, *André Derain* (Paris: Editions Gallimard, 1990), p. 190.
12. Ibid., p. 188.
13. Ibid., p. 190.
14. Sutton, *André Derain.*
15. James Thrall Soby, press release, 1940, Wadsworth Atheneum, Hartford, Conn.
16. G. K. Chesterton, "Essay on *A Midsummer Night's Dream,*" in ed. W. H. Auden, *G. K. Chesterton, A Selection from His Non-fictional Prose* (London: Faber and Faber, 1970), p. 95.
17. Garry Wills, introduction to *G. K. Chesterton,* p. viii.
18. *G. K. Chesterton,* pp. 9, 13.
19. Ibid., p. 181.
20. Alexander Liberman, *The Artist in His Studio* (New York: Viking Press, 1960), p. 27.
21. Sutton, *André Derain,* p. 51.
22. *G. K. Chesterton,* p. 180.
23. Marguerite Yourcenar, *Oriental Tales,* trans. Alberto Manguel (New York: Farrar, Straus & Giroux, 1985), p. 3.

24. Ibid.
25. Ibid., pp. 4–5.
26. Ibid., p. 5.
27. Ibid., p. 6.
28. Ibid., pp. 13, 14.
29. Ibid., p. 15.
30. Ibid., p. 20.

CHAPTER FIFTEEN

1. "Relative Values," *London Sunday Times Magazine,* Sept. 8, 1996.

CHAPTER SIXTEEN

1. James Thrall Soby, "Balthus," catalog essay for exhibition at the Pierre Matisse Gallery, New York, 1938.
2. Carlyle Burrows, "Portraits by Balthus," *New York Herald Tribune,* Mar. 27, 1938.
3. E. A. Jewell, review of Balthus exhibition at the Pierre Matisse Gallery, *New York Times,* Mar. 27, 1938.
4. Alfred M. Frankfurter, "The Important Premiere of Balthus: Nouveau Sachlichkeit à la Céline," *ARTnews,* no. 36 (Apr. 2, 1938).
5. Arthur Gold and Robert Fitzdale, *Misia* (New York: Alfred A. Knopf, 1980), p. 284.
6. Conversation with Bernard Minoret, Paris, Nov. 10, 1992.
7. Claude Mauriac, *Le Temps immobile* (Paris: Bernard Grasset, 1974), p. 435.
8. Claude Mauriac, *Marek et fils* (Paris: Bernard Grasset, 1986), p. 147.
9. James Lord, *Giacometti* (New York: Farrar, Straus & Giroux, 1983), p. 155.
10. Michael F. Brenson, thesis, Johns Hopkins University, Dec. 1977 (courtesy of the author).
11. Conversation with Eberhard Kornfeld, Bern, Feb. 8, 1993.

CHAPTER SEVENTEEN

1. Colette, *Gigi,* trans. Roger Senhouse (New York: Farrar, Straus & Giroux, 1952), p. 9.
2. "A Discussion with John Richardson," *Art on View* (National Gallery of Australia, Canberra), no. 29: Summer 1995–96, p. 29.
3. Rainer Maria Rilke, *Duino Elegies,* trans. J. B. Leishman and Stephen Spender; in Alfred H. Barr, Jr., *Picasso: Fifty Years of His Art* (New York: Museum of Modern Art, 1946).
4. Arianna Stassinopoulos Huffington, *Picasso* (New York: Simon & Schuster, 1988), p. 300.
5. Ibid., p. 211.
6. Ibid., p. 300.
7. Perry Meisel, "The Unanalyzable," *New York Times Book Review,* Apr. 13, 1997, p. 12.
8. Ibid.
9. Michael Kimmelman, "Balthus at 88, Still a Man of Mystery," *New York Times,* Aug. 25, 1996, p. 32.
10. Brassaï, *Picasso and Company,* trans. Francis Price (New York: Doubleday, 1966), p. 122.
11. Françoise Gilot and Carlton Lake, *Life with Picasso* (New York: McGraw-Hill, 1964), p. 125.
12. Conversation with John Richardson, Bethany, Connecticut, May 17, 1999.
13. Jean Cocteau, *Past Tense,* trans. Richard Howard (New York: Harcourt Brace Jovanovich, 1987), vol. 1, p. 294.

14. James Lord, *Picasso and Dora* (New York: Farrar, Straus & Giroux, 1993), p. 196.

15. Raymond Mason, "Un Témoignage des Années 50," in *Balthus* (Paris: Centre Pompidou, 1983), p. 337.

16. Emily Brontë, *Wuthering Heights* (New York: Random House, 1993), p. 28.

CHAPTER EIGHTEEN

1. Georges Bataille, *Story of the Eye,* trans. Joachim Neugroschel (New York: Penguin Books, 1982), p. 10.

2. Henry Miller, introduction to *Erotic Art of the Masters* (Secaucus, N.J.: Lyle Stuart, undated).

3. Vladimir Nabokov, *Lolita* (London: Penguin Books, 1980), p. 65.

4. Ibid., p. 111.

5. Ibid., p. 255.

6. Ibid., p. 109.

CHAPTER NINETEEN

1. John Banville, *The Untouchable* (London: Picador, 1997), pp. 104–5.

2. Telephone conversation with James Lord, May 2, 1999.

3. Telephone conversation with James Lord, Apr. 30, 1999.

4. Telephone conversation with James Lord, May 2.

5. Telephone conversation with James Lord, Apr. 30.

6. James Thrall Soby, *Balthus* (New York: Museum of Modern Art, 1956), p. 7.

7. Jean Rodolphe von Salis, "Une Amitié," in *Balthus* (Lausanne: Musée des Beaux-Arts, 1993), pp. 66–77.

8. Richard Covington, "Balthus at Home," *Art & Antiques,* Nov. 1994, p. 73.

9. *Zone d'ombres, 1933–1944,* sous la direction de Jacques Grandjonc et Theresia Grundtner, Paris: Alinea, pp. 42–43. The date given for Erich Klossowski's death is incorrect; he died in 1949. (My thanks to Serge Klausfeld for supplying a photocopy of this text.)

10. Steven Millhauser, *Martin Dressler: The Tale of Our American Dream* (New York: Crown Publishing, 1996), p. 139.

11. André Maurois, *Byron,* trans. Hamish Miles (New York: D. Appleton & Co., 1930), p. 340.

12. Balthus, letter sent from the Villa Diodati on Oct. 6, 1945, archives of the Kunsthalle Berne; in Jörg Zutter, "Paysage alpin et conception visionnaire," in *Balthus* (Musée des Beaux-Arts), p. 27.

13. Alexander Watt, "Balthus," *Occident* (Paris), Jan. 1948, no. 2.

14. Georges Bernier, "Balthus," *L'Oeil* (Paris), Mar. 1956, no. 15: pp. 27–33.

15. Telephone conversation with Judith Jones, May 5, 1994.

16. Françoise Gilot, manuscript (subsequently published) of catalog essay for exhibition at the Robert Elkon Gallery, New York, Sept. 1993, pp. 22–23.

17. Robert Craft, *Stravinsky: Chronicle of a Friendship* (Nashville, Tenn.: Vanderbilt University Press, 1994), p. 78.

18. James Lord, *Giacometti* (New York: Farrar, Straus & Giroux, 1983), p. 344.

19. Wolfgang Leppmann, *Rilke: Sein Leben, seine Welt, sein Werk* (Bern: 1981), p. 8.

20. James Lord, "The Strange Case of the Count de Rola," *The New Criterion,* vol. 2, no. 4 (Dec. 1983): p. 17.

21. Ned Rorem, *Knowing When to Stop* (New York: Simon & Schuster, 1994), p. 566.

22. Mark Stevens, "The Connoisseur of Eros," *Newsweek,* Dec. 5, 1977, p. 93.

23. Robert Hughes, "The Nymphets of Balthus, *Time,* Nov. 28, 1977.
24. Jean Leymarie, "Balthus et Courbet," in *Balthus dans la Maison de Courbet* (Ornans: Musée Gustave Courbet, 1992).
25. David Bowie, "The Last Legendary Painter," *Modern Painters,* Autumn 1994, p. 27.
26. Brassaï, *Picasso and Company,* trans. Francis Price (New York: Doubleday, 1964).
27. Irish Murdoch, *The Italian Girl* (London: Chatto & Windus, 1964), p. 116.
28. Conversation with Bernard Minoret, Paris, Nov. 10, 1992.
29. *The Paris and New York Diaries of Ned Rorem* (San Francisco: North Point Press, 1983), pp. 58-59.
30. Conversation with Ned Rorem, New York, Apr. 24, 1995.
31. Ibid.
32. Conversation with Claus von Bülow, 109 Onslow Square, London, Apr. 12, 1995.
33. Cyril Connolly, "Balthus," catalog essay for exhibition at the Lefevre Gallery, London, 1952.
34. James Thrall Soby, manuscript of his unpublished memoirs (courtesy of Samuel Childs), chap. 26, "Balthus and Giacometti," p. 1.
35. Lord, *Giacometti,* p. 170.
36. Ibid.
37. Ibid., pp. 170, 171.
38. Ibid., p. 346.
39. David Sylvester, *Looking at Giacometti* (London: Pimlico, 1995), p. 157.
40. "Balthus: 'Ce qui intéressait Giacometti: Mettre un nez au milieu d'un visage,' " *L'Actualité, Le Figaro,* Nov. 26, 1991.

CHAPTER TWENTY

1. Mark Landler, "A Widow's Pique," *New York Times,* June 16, 1996, sec. 3, p. 1.
2. Julia Preston, "Emilio Azcárraga Milmo, Billionaire Who Ruled Mexican Broadcasting, Is Dead at 66," *New York Times,* Apr. 18, 1997.

CHAPTER TWENTY-TWO

1. Jean Leymarie, "Balthus at the Villa Medici," *House & Garden,* Jan. 1984, p. 63.
2. Janet Flanner, *Men and Monuments* (New York: De Capo Press, 1990), p. 2.
3. Ibid., pp. 5-6.
4. Ibid., p. 56.
5. Ibid.
6. "La Siège de la Villa Medici," *L'Express,* Jan. 19, 1961, p. 34.
7. "Malraux m'a dit: Voulez-vous nous donner un coup de main?," *La Gazette Littéraire* (Lausanne), Apr. 8, 9, 1961.
8. Ibid.
9. Milton Gendel, "H.M. the King of Cats: A Footnote," *ARTnews,* vol. 61, no. 2 (Apr. 1962): p. 32.
10. David Bowie, "The Last Legendary Painter," *Modern Painters,* Autumn 1994, p. 28.
11. Telephone conversation with Beatrice Cazac, June 22, 1996.
12. Ibid.
13. Conversation with Beatrice Cazac, Stanhope Hotel, New York, July 2, 1996.
14. Conversation with Bernard Chaet, New Haven, Conn., Apr. 20, 1994.

15. James Lord, "Balthus: The Strange Case of the Count de Rola," *The New Criterion*, vol. 2, no. 4 (Dec. 1983): p. 22.

16. Hugo Vickers, *Cecil Beaton: The Authorized Biography* (London: Weidenfeld & Nicolson, 1985), p. 513.

17. Alice Rawsthorn, *Yves Saint Laurent: A Biography* (New York: Doubleday, 1996), pp. 81-82.

18. Ibid., p. 81.

19. Ibid., p. 103.

20. Ibid., p. 155.

21. Ibid.

22. Ibid., p. 164.

23. Federico Fellini, preface to *Balthus* (New York: Pierre Matisse Gallery, 1977).

24. "Fellini nell'antro di Balthus: Il regista racconta le sue avventure," *La Stampa*, May 13, 1995, p. 14, translation by Jackie Ivy.

25. Philip Hensher, "True Lies, False Confessions," *The Spectator* (London), June 8, 1996.

26. D. H. Lawrence, *John Thomas and Lady Jane* (Harmondsworth, England: Penguin Books, 1973), p. 230.

27. Jean Leymarie, *Balthus* (Geneva: Skira, 1978).

28. Sabine Rewald, *Balthus* (New York: Metropolitan Museum of Art, 1984), p. 148.

29. Philippe Dagen, "Balthus: Still Striving to Find an Inner Vision," *Le Monde*, Aug. 4-5, 1991; translated in *Guardian Weekly*, Aug. 25, 1991.

30. Ralph Freedman, *Life of a Poet: Rainer Maria Rilke* (New York: Farrar, Straus & Giroux, 1996), p. 193.

31. Claude Roy, *Balthus* (Paris: Editions Gallimard, 1996), p. 18.

32. Marquis de Sade, *The 120 Days of Sodom*, trans. Austryn Wainhouse and Richard Seaver (New York: Grove Weidenfeld, 1966), p. 322.

33. Janet Hobhouse, *The Bride Stripped Bare* (London: Jonathan Cape, 1988), p. 220.

34. Ibid., p. 218.

35. Ibid., p. 220.

36. Richard Covington, "Balthus at Home," *Art & Antiques*, Nov. 19, 1994, p. 75.

CHAPTER TWENTY-THREE

1. Michael Peppiatt, "Balthus: Dreams, Enigmas, and Nymphets," *Connoisseur*, Nov. 1983, p. 100.

2. Adam Phillips, *On Kissing, Tickling, and Being Bored* (Cambridge: Harvard University Press, 1994), p. 31.

3. Kenneth Clark, "A Modern Master," *New York Review of Books*, June 12, 1980, p. 18.

4. Douglas Cooper, "The Writings of Blunt and Others," *Books and Bookmen*, Dec. 1979, pp. 41, 42.

5. John Rewald, "Thoughts on Drawings by Balthus," catalog essay for *Drawings by Balthus* (New York: E. V. Thaw & Co., 1963).

6. Leymarie, *Balthus*.

7. Kiyohiko Munakata, *Sacred Mountains in Chinese Art* (Urbana and Chicago: University of Illinois Press, 1991), p. 63.

8. Ibid.

9. Richard Covington, "Balthus at Home," *Art & Antiques*, Nov. 19, 1994, p. 75.

10. Peter Schjeldahl, "Pretty Babies." The copy of this article in the Artist File at the Museum

of Modern Art does not cite the magazine or date, but it appears to have been concurrent with the exhibition at the Met.

11. "A Misleading Image: A Statement by Balthus," in Sabine Rewald, "Balthus: A Monographic Study," diss., New York University, 1984 (microfilm, New York University).

12. Conversation with Hilton Kramer, New York, Feb. 17, 1995.

13. Telephone conversation, Sept. 15, 1991.

14. Conversation with Stanislas Klossowski de Rola, Rossinière, Jan. 17, 1991.

15. Rainer Maria Rilke, *Briefe an Schweizer Freunden* (Frankfurt am Main: Suhrkamp Verlag, 1990), p. 196.

16. *Rainer Maria Rilke et Merline: Correspondance,* ed. Dieter Bassermann (Zurich: Insel Verlag, 1954), pp. 100, 101 (letter of Nov. 28, 1920).

AFTERWORD

1. Setsuko, afterword to *Tale of the Wandering Monk* (New York: Limited Editions Club, 1995).

2. Conversation with Gae Aulenti, Milan, Jan. 26, 1999.

3. "22 Years for Balthus," *ARTnews,* vol. 95, no. 4 (Apr. 1996): p. 34.

4. *Puss in Boots,* retold by Erich Kastner, trans. Richard and Clara Winston (New York: Julian Messner, 1957), pp. 23–24.

SELECTED BIBLIOGRAPHY

The following bibliography, while not complete, gives the sources I consider of the greatest significance concerning Balthus's life and work. More comprehensive lists of articles appear in the various exhibition catalogs.

MONOGRAPHS

Balthus. Lausanne: Musée des Beaux-Arts, 1993.
Balthus. London: The Tate Gallery, 1968.
Balthus. Madrid: Museo Nacional Centro de Arte Reina Sofía, 1996.
Balthus. Paris: Centre Georges Pompidou, 1983.
Balthus. Venezia: Edizioni "La Biennale di Venezia," 1980.
Balthus dans La Maison de Courbet. Ornans: Musée Gustave Courbet, 1992.
Balthus: Zeichnungen. Bern: Kunstmuseum Bern, 1994.
Carandente, Giovanni. *Balthus: Drawings and Watercolors.* Translated by James Mitchell. London: Thames and Hudson, 1983.
Klossowski de Rola, Stanislas. *Balthus.* London: Thames and Hudson, 1983.
Leymarie, Jean. *Balthus.* Geneva: Skira, 1978.
Omaggio a Balthus. Rome: Accadèmia Valentino, 1996.
Rewald, Sabine. *Balthus.* New York: Metropolitan Museum of Art, 1984.
Roy, Claude. *Balthus.* Paris: Editions Gallimard, 1996.
Soby, James Thrall. *Balthus.* New York: The Museum of Modern Art, 1956.

PERIODICALS

Artaud, Antonin. "Balthus à la Galerie Pierre." *La Nouvelle Revue Française,* no. 248 (May 1934), pp. 899–900.
———. "La Jeune Peinture française et la tradition." *El Nacional,* June 17, 1936.
Bernier, Georges. "Balthus." *L'Oeil,* no. 15 (March 1956), pp. 27–33.
Bonnefoy, Yves. "L'Invention de Balthus." *L'Improbable: Mercure de France,* 1959, pp. 49–74.
Bowie, David. "The Last Legendary Painter." *Modern Painters,* Autumn 1994, pp. 14–33.
Chalais, François. "Balthus parle." *Le Figaro,* March 23, 1989.
Clark, Kenneth. "A Modern Master." *The New York Review of Books,* June 12, 1980.
Covington, Richard. "Balthus at Home." *Art & Antiques,* November 1994, pp. 70–77.
Dagen, Philippe. "Balthus: Still Striving to Find an Inner Vision." *Guardian Weekly,* August 25, 1991. First published in French in *Le Monde,* August 4–5, 1991.
Frankfurter, Alfred M. "The Important Premiere of Balthus: Nouveau Sachlichkeit à la Celine." *The Art News,* no. 36 (April 2, 1938).
Gendel, Milton. "H.M. the King of Cats, a Footnote." *ARTnews* 61, no. 2 (April 1962).
Hess, Thomas B. "Balthus: Seen and Scene." *New York,* November 21, 1977.
Jouve, Pierre Jean. "Balthus." *La Nef,* September 1944.
———. "Le Tableau." *Proses: Mercure de France,* 1960, pp. 45–49.
———. "Les Cenci d'Antonin Artaud." *La Nouvelle Revue Française,* no. 261 (June 1935), pp. 910–15.

Klossowski, Pierre. "Balthus: Beyond Realism." *ARTnews* 55, no. 8 (December 1956), pp. 26–31.

Lhote, André. "Gromaire à la Galerie Pierre." *La Nouvelle Revue Française,* no. 249 (June 1, 1934), pp. 1045–1046.

Lord, James. "Balthus: The Strange Case of the Count de Rola." *The New Criterion* 2, no. 4 (December 1983), pp. 9–25.

Peppiatt, Michael. "Balthus: Dreams, Enigmas, and Nymphets." *Connoisseur,* November 1983.

Perl, Jed. "Balthus." *ARTS* 55, no. 5 (January 1978).

———. "Balthus in New York." *The New Criterion,* May 1984, pp. 7–19.

Rilke, Rainer Maria. "Lettres à un jeune peintre." *Fontaine,* 1945, no. 44.

Russell, John. "Master of the Nubile Adolescent." *Art in America* 55 (November 1967).

Watt, Alexander. "Balthus." *Occident,* no. 2 (January 1948).

ESSAYS

Camus, Albert. "Balthus." Catalog essay for exhibition at the Pierre Matisse Gallery, New York, 1949.

Colle Lorant, Sylvia. "Balthus, décorateur de théâtre." In *Balthus.* Paris: Centre Georges Pompidou, 1983.

Connolly, Cyril. "Balthus." Catalog for exhibition at the Lefevre Gallery, London, 1952.

Fellini, Federico. Preface to *Balthus,* translated by Luigi Barzini. New York: Pierre Matisse Gallery, 1977.

Fernier, Jean-Jacques. "Balthus." In *Balthus.* Ornans: Musée Courbet, 1992.

Perl, Jed. "Balthus: Artist and Model." In *Paris Without End.* San Francisco: Northpoint Press, 1988.

Rewald, John. "Thoughts on Drawings by Balthus." Catalog essay for *Drawings by Balthus* at E. V. Thaw, New York, 1963.

Rilke, Rainer Maria. Preface to *Mitsou.* Zürich and Leipzig: Rotapfel Berlag Erlenbach, 1921.

Salis, Jean Rodolphe von. "Une Amitié." In *Balthus.* Lausanne: Musée des Beaux Arts, 1993.

Schwartz, Sanford. "Heathcliff without Cathy." In *Artists and Writers,* New York: Yarrow Press, 1990.

Soby, James Thrall. "Balthus." Catalog essay for exhibition at the Pierre Matisse Gallery, New York, 1938.

———. "Balthus and Giacometti [c. 1972]." Unpublished memoirs. Library of The Museum of Modern Art, New York.

BOOKS

Artaud, Antonin. *Oeuvres Complètes.* Paris: Editions Gallimard, 1964–79.

Freedman, Ralph. *Life of a Poet: Rainer Maria Rilke.* New York: Farrar Straus Giroux, 1996.

Hobhouse, Janet. *The Bride Stripped Bare.* London: Jonathan Cape, 1988.

Leppmann, Wolfgang. *Rilke: A Life.* Translated by Russell M. Stockman. New York: Fromm International Publishing, 1984.

Loeb, Pierre. *Voyages à Travers la Peinture.* Paris: Borda, 1945.

Prater, Donald. *A Ringing Glass: The Life of Rainer Maria Rilke.* Oxford: Oxford University Press, 1986.

Rilke, Rainer Maria. *Briefe an Nanny Wunderly-Volkart.* Leipzig: Insel Verlag, 1977.

————. *Briefe an Schweizer Freunde.* Frankfurt am Main: Suhrkamp Verlag, 1990.

————, *Letters to Merline, 1919–1921.* Translated by Jesse Browner. New York: Paragon House, 1989.

Rilke, Rainer Maria, and André Gide. *Correspondance, 1909–1926.* Edited by Renée Lang. Paris: Correa, 1952.

Rilke, Rainer Maria, and Merline. *Rainer Maria Rilke et Merline: Correspondance.* Edited by Dieter Bassermann. Zurich: Insel Verlag, 1954.

Schnack, Ingeborg. *Rainer Maria Rilke: Chronik Seines Lebens und Seines Werkes,* Frankfurt am Main: Insel Verlag, 1975.

Salis, J. R. von. *Rainer Maria Rilke. The Years in Switzerland.* London: The Hogarth Press, 1964.

ACKNOWLEDGMENTS

OVER THE YEARS (about eight) that I have been writing this book, a number of people have asked me why I chose Balthus as my topic. Some could not imagine why I picked a subject so patently troublesome. Others wondered why I had willingly entered into a relationship that had me perpetually agonized and excited (emotions by no means incompatible).

The reason is that Victoria Wilson asked me to. The editor of my previous book, she probably had many reasons for proposing Balthus as my topic. But initially she had no idea that I had been fascinated by his work from the time when, at age sixteen, I first began to look at art seriously and there were two Balthuses in the local museum. Nor did she realize that, over twenty years ago, my future wife and I were so enthralled by Balthus's art that only months after we met, we acquired a drawing by him (the first object we owned together—at a time when we could scarcely pay the rent). Having added a watercolor a few years later, we regarded Balthus's vision as part of the fabric of our everyday lives.

Not only did Vicky instinctively recognize a good match, but she nurtured it patiently, generously, and wisely. Once I realized I might be years late in delivering the manuscript, she simply told me to take my time.

Like a wise parent, she was encouraging and tough at the same time. She cautioned against being too conclusive or smug, and led me to realize the importance of being true to my ambivalence. For all these reasons Vicky Wilson is the rarest of editors; it is to her that I owe my first expression of gratitude.

No job description is adequate for Lee Buttala, who works with Vicky at Knopf. He is a master of details, and a paragon of friendliness and support: precisely the qualities one craves when working through complex, and occasionally tense, situations. His apparent unflappability and phenomenal proficiency have, on numerous occasions, been a source of salvation. His enthusiasm has been invaluable.

As is evident in the text of this book, my feelings about Balthus and his family members are complex, but I am extremely grateful to each of them. Would that everyone in the world, whatever his or her nature or motives, could be as gracious and charming, as warm and welcoming, as Balthus himself. Above all—if I may dare to put myself in the same camp as Rilke and Artaud, and as some of the painters who have benefited immeasurably from the artist's integrity and skill at his work—I thank him for being Balthus. To

Setsuko I have deep appreciation for her true kindness and generosity as a hostess and as organizer of her husband's complex existence. Harumi and Stanislas treated me with trust and friendship. And I thank all of them for granting me the permission necessary to reproduce Balthus's art.

Maria Gaetana Matisse has been the most splendid help. She is a person of rare and instinctive insight, and an efficient and effective diplomat. I thank her for her assistance in innumerable ways.

When I met Angela Flowers in the rural reaches of Ireland, I would never have dreamed that her aunt had been one of the first people ever to pose for Balthus. That fact led to my meeting Betty and Pierre Leyris, an encounter that influenced this book substantially, and for which I owe Angela deep thanks.

I also want to express profound gratitude to R. W. B. Lewis for his wise counsel and longtime support; Nancy Lewis for her ceaseless generosity with ideas and friendship; Natalie Charkow for her verve and kindness; John Hollander for the originality of his perceptions; John Eastman for his great intellectual grasp of so many central issues; Phyllis Fitzgerald for her patience and perseverance; John Ryden for his guidance and camaraderie; Barbara Ryden for her unfailing warmth; Stark Canning Whitely for his diligent research on the complex issues of Polish titles and nobility; Julie Agoos for her ever refreshing viewpoint; Brenda Danilowitz for her energy and helpfulness; Sanford Schwartz for his humor and brilliance; Albert J. Solnit for his wisdom and insight; Daphne Astor for her incredible astuteness and compassion; Louis Begley for both questions and answers; Susan Newhouse for her graciousness and thoughtfulness; Pearl A. Weber for her prescience and unique qualities of understanding; and Jackie Ivy for being there in so many ways. Particular thanks go to Nicholas Ohly for his extraordinary gift of friendship as well as his perspicacity.

Additionally, there are the people whose vital testimony informs the text of this book: individuals who not only gave generously of their time but helped mightily in my attempt to understand Balthus. For their thoughtfulness, intelligence, and graciousness, I thank Linda Fairstein, Judith Jones, Claus von Bülow, Pierre Leyris, Jean Leyris, John Russell, Jan Krugier, Hilton Kramer, Serge Klarsfeld, Gae Aulenti, James Lord, Basil Goulandris, Elise Goulandris, Bernard Minoret, Francine du Plessix Gray, Cleve Gray, Eugene Victor Thaw, Ned Rorem, Dolores Miró, John Richardson, Jean Leymarie, Michael Peppiatt, Marie-Pierre Colle, Sylvia Colle Lorant, Béatrice Colle Saalburg, Beatrice Cazac, and Pauline Roux. I am also grateful to the following people, no longer alive, with whom I was fortunate enough to have the chance to discuss Balthus: Jacqueline Kennedy Onassis, Betty Leyris, James Thrall Soby, Jane Cooley Allen, Dominique Bozo, Leland Bell, and Iris Murdoch.

Gloria Loomis has been incredible. As agent for this book, she has functioned like the ideal godparent: protective, perceptive, encouraging, realistic, deeply caring. As a friend she has been profoundly wise and generous.

In researching photos and helping with some extremely complicated logistics, Gwen Smith has been wonderfully capable, tenacious, and imaginative; it is hard to imagine how the project could have been completed without her.

And Suzanne Gray Kelly has been angelic and inordinately helpful in her assistance with some very complex stages of manuscript preparation. I cannot thank her enough for her diligence and support.

For their unstinting helpfulness I also thank Jacqueline Monnier, Janet Malcolm, Rona Roob, Leslie Waddington, Michael Brenson, Eberhard Kornfeld, Kenneth Marcus, R. B. Kitaj, Ziona Kaplan Weber, David Michaelis, Ruth Lord, Terry Tabaka, George Gibson, Micky Astor, Philip Rylands, Carl Leonardson, Sorrel Danilowitz, Laurence Murphy, Paul Overy, Katharine Faucett, Michael Anderson, Florence Giry, Judith Thurman, Martin Filler, Carlotta Hadley, John Banville, Carol Marks, Claudia Kalitan, Ted Van Dyke, Phyllis Rose, Louise Kennedy, Andrea Warburg Kaufman, Steven Marans, Flora Samuels, Corinne Zimmermann, Macgan Pussilano, Barry Svigals, Sidney Shiff, Kelly Feeney, John Bayley, Clare Edwards, Jonathan Galassi, Camilla Lyon, Aaron Hamburger, Charles Kingsley, and Tamerlane Greggs.

The role of Richard Howard in this book is immeasurable. In translating texts by Rilke, Artaud, Jouve, Baladine Klossowska, and others, he managed to evoke their poetry and spark with complete fidelity to the individual idiosyncrasies of each of those brilliant minds. Moreover, Richard always made it seem like fun, and he bolstered my spirits in the homestretch of this project more than he can imagine. He is a rare and wonderful and exceptionally generous person.

For what they gave me long ago, my parents, too, have been central to this project. First of all, they had Soby's MoMA catalog at home, where I found it soon after my discovery of Balthus. My father, Saul Weber, provided a special slant on the artist—even before I knew his work—by often referring to two dour, fascinating daughters of friends of his as "the Balthus girls." My mother, Caroline Fox Weber, a painter, kept me ever aware that paints and canvas, not psychological concepts, were the starting point of art. My mother and father also made me realize that no two people are Jewish in the same way, and they deplored judgmentalism on this issue.

Nancy Weber, my sister, has always been the least rivalrous of siblings, and I trust that by now she knows the value I place on her kindness, her spiritual adventurousness, and her mix of passion and intelligence.

WITH HER INCREDIBLY ORIGINAL mind and passion both for the human comedy and for writing about it, Katharine Weber has, as usual, been the truest of partners. There is, in fact, no adequate way of expressing my fascination with, and love for, this extraordinary woman who is my wife.

As for our daughters Lucy Swift Weber and Charlotte Fox Weber: they have participated in this project from their girlhood into their womanhood. Time and again, each of these wonderful people has provided insight and candor about Balthus as a person and about his work. Charlotte, as always, has had a particular feeling for personal quirkiness and the most subtle nuances of human behavior. Lucy, so remarkably visual, has repeatedly pointed out much in the art that might otherwise have eluded me. Their sketches and journals pertaining to Balthus are among my favorite documents in the world.

Moreover, they have been loving and supportive, funny, intrepid, and alive to the hilt. Each is an inspiration. I dedicate this book to them both with admiration and with love.

INDEX

Note: Page numbers in *italics* refer to illustrations.
Artworks are by Balthus unless otherwise noted.

Abdy, Lady Iya:
  Balthus's portrait of, 258–59, *260*, 264, 334, 478
  in *Les Cenci*, 264–65, 271, *273*, 274
Abdy, Sir Robert, 259
Accademia Valentino, Rome, 603
Adam Announcing His Death (Piero della Francesca), 122
Agnelli, Gianni, 30, 519
Alberti, Leon Battista, 129
Alice, 152, 302–9; *color plate 6*
  author's analysis and interpretation of, 151, 234, 302–7, 391
  ownership of, 307, 313, 358
Alice's Adventures in Wonderland (Carroll), 184–85
Allen, Jane Cooley, 14–16, *15*, 32, 316–17, 391
Alp Action, interview, 91
Amazon, use of term, 304–5
Ammann, Thomas, 213, 603
Ammannati, Bartolomeo, 492
Amor Victorious (Caravaggio), 83, 477, *477*
Andreas, Friedrich, 426
Andreas-Salomé, Lou, 48, 86, 426, 506
André Derain, 316, 358; *color plate 9*
  author's analysis and interpretation of, 324–33, 337–38
  Balthus's views on, 318, 325, 326, 328, 332, 339–40
Angelico, Fra, 108
Annan, Gabriele, 171
Antoinette, 139–42, *140*, 144–45
Antonin Artaud, *261*, 262
Antonin Artaud (Man Ray), *267*
Apollinaire, Guillaume, 323, 324
Arezzo, Italy, frescoes in, 110, 112, 119, 127, 186, 187
Arp, Hans, 452, 536
Art & Antiques, interview, 406, 548
Artaud, Antonin, 259–82, *261*, *267*, 316, 319, 326, 429
  on Balthus and suicide, 279–81, 282
  Balthus's identification with, 17, 117, 147, 260, 262, 269, 277, 287, 436, 480, 577

on Balthus's work, 49, 154, 191, 263–65, 269, 270, 275–78, 279, 352, 424, 570
  birth and background of, 262
  Les Cenci by, 259, 262, 264–65, 270–75, *273*, 307
  death of, 279
  drugs and, 279, 281
  and Giacometti's work, 449
  Héliogabale by, 265–66, 277, 320
  influence of, 266–67, 269
  madness of, 262, 278–79, 364
  in Mexico, 275, 278
  Surrealism and, 262, 275–77, 449
  symbols in work of, 272, 274
  on terror and cruelty as themes, 266, 268, 269
  and Theater of Cruelty, 259, 262–63, 269, 270, 275, 277, 295, 449, 544
Art in America, 430
Artist and the Model (Picasso), 258
ARTnews, 352, 359, 360
Asia Society, New York, 593–95
Asso, Pierre, *273*
As You Like It (Shakespeare), 270
Auden, W. H., 337
Aulenti, Gae, 595–96
Austin, A. Everett, Jr. "Chick," 402
  and *Still Life*, 335
  and *The Street*, 195–96, *197*, 198
  and Wadsworth Atheneum, 14, 195, 335
Autumn (Poussin), 101
Azcárraga, Emilio, 471–72, 484

Bacon, Francis (philosopher), 85, 174
Bacon, Francis (painter), 85, 306, 311–12
  art of, 311, 410, 489, 519
  Balthus admired by, 312
Bagpiper, The (Derain), 384
Bailey, William, 257, 517, 552
Balthus (Leymarie), 169, 170–73, 286, 591
"Balthus et la Suisse" (Leymarie), 131
Balthus Notebook, A (Davenport), 70–71, 391
Balthus Poems, The (Dobyns), 30
Balzac, Honoré de, 414

Baptism of St. John (Piero della Francesca), 118, 129
Barelier, André, 514–15
Barr, Alfred, 164, 192, 199, 352
Barrault, Jean-Louis, 416, 441, 519, 521, 529
    and *Les Cenci,* 271
    and *L'Etat de siège,* 203, *203*
Barthes, Roland, 245
Bataille, Diane, 425
Bataille, Georges, 4, 245, 246
    friendship of, 416, 425
    and Maar, 376
Bataille, Laurence, 377, 452
    as Balthus's mistress, 416, 468, 475
    as model, 416, 419–20
Bataille, Sylvia, 4–5, 377, 416, 419
Baudelaire, Charles-Pierre, 26, 205, 262
Bay, Margrit, 138
Beaton, Cecil, 375, 521
Beaux Jours, Les, 100, 391, 409–14; *color plate 2*
    author's analysis and interpretation of, 410–14
    exhibition of, 409–10, 414, 551
    and Hirshhorn, 410, 414, 513
    self-portrait in, 381, 412, 413–14
    Setsuko's views on, 410
Becher, Arno, 343
Beckmann, Max, 82, 489
Bell, Leland, 450–52
Bellini, Giovanni, 196
Benjamin, Walter, 68
Berenson, Berry, 523
Berlin:
    Balthus in, 81–83
    Eugen Spiro in, 37, 53, 74, 75, 82, 90, 93, 286, 300
    museums in, 83
Berlin Secessionists, 37
Bern, Kunsthalle, 414
Bernard, Claude, 66
Bernese Hat, The, 399
Bernhard, Hedwig, 73
Bernier, Georges, 415
Bernini, Gianlorenzo, 219, 297, 387, 493
Berry, Jules, 529
Berthau, Julien, *273*
Bestégui, Charles de, 438
Bête Noire, 262
Bey, Khalil, 213
Bibesco, Princess Marthe, 98
Bigio, Nanni de Baccio, 492
Birley, Maxime, 522
Birley, Sir Oswald, 522
Birth of the World (Courbet), 213, 527
Bischoffsheim, Maurice, 365
Blanchard, Hubert, 382, 385, 386–87

Blanchard, Thérèse, 388–94
    in *The Children,* 382, 385, 386–87
    in *Girl with a Cat,* 392–93, 399–400
    in *Thérèse Dreaming,* 389–94
Blin, Roger, 271
Blond Italian (Derain), 334
Blume, Peter, 450
Bofill, Ricardo, 522
Bonaparte, Princess Marie, 233
Bonnard, Pierre, *97,* 110, 341, 497–98, 534–35
    on Balthus's talent, 25, 56, 96–97, 154, 489, 564
    exhibit of work of, 524
    influence of, 132, 153, 158, 476, 482, 489
    letter to Rilke from, 19, 20
    work of, 143, 399, 414
Bonnefoy, Yves, 52
Bordone, Paris, *Pietà,* 100
Borges, Jorge Luis, 337
Botero, Fernando, 410, 489
Botticelli, Sandro, 108
Boudin, Eugène-Louis, 201
Bouquet of Roses on a Window Sill, 435, 487–90, 581; *color plate 13*
Bowie, David, 147, 226, 432, 434, 505, 594
Boymans Museum, Rotterdam, 538
Bozo, Dominique, 169–70, 559, 560, 579
    and Centre Pompidou, 169, 210–11, 212
    on *The Guitar Lesson,* 210–11, 213
Brancusi, Constantin, 191, 366
Braque, Georges:
    and Derain, 340–41, 342, 344, 384
    work of, 19, 366, 414, 524, 527
Brassaï, 378–79, 435
Brayer, Yves, 497
Bressant, Cécile, *273*
Breton, André, 363, 370, 371–72
Brontë, Emily, *Wuthering Heights,* 284–89, 293, 297–301, 381, 382, 431
Brother and Sister/The Children, see Children, The
Brüstlein, Simone, 53, 580
Buber, Martin, 147
Bülow, Claus von, 364, 442–47, 521
Bülow, Cosima von, 443
Bülow, Sunny von, 443, 444
Buñuel, Luis, 224, 366, 367
Burckhardt, Carl, 48
Burke, Edmund, 129
Burrows, Carlyle, 358–59
Byron, Capt. John, 67
Byron, Lord (George Gordon):
    as Balthus's idol, 17, 577, 585
    and family connection, 66–69, 70, 409, 447, 496
    at Villa Diodati, 409

Cabanne, Pierre, 324, 325
Caetani, Princess, 415, 416, 423, 429
Cage, The (Giacometti), 449
Caillebotte, Gustave, 153
Calder, Alexander, 361
Camus, Albert:
  on Balthus's work, 49, 50, 191, 202–3, 278, 352, 424
  friendship of, 416, 419
  L'Etat de siège, 203, 203
Carandente, Giovanni, 552
Caravaggio:
  Amor Victorious, 83, 477, 477
  and Villa Medici, 492
Card Game, The, 420–23, 421
Card Players, The, 538–45; *color plate 14*
  androgyny in, 266, 538–39, 541, 543, 544
  Balthus's views on, 540, 560
  exhibition of, 538, 543, 551
  repainting of, 104, 540
Carpaccio, Vittore, 424
Carroll, Lewis, 184, 185, 303
Cartier-Bresson, Henri:
  Ned Rorem by, 439
  photograph of Balthus by, 602
Casarès, Maria, 203
Cassandre (Mauron), 317–18, 465, 480
Cat at the Mirror I, 348, 555–57, 556, 573
Cat at the Mirror III, 120, 598–603;
  color plate 16
  exhibition of, 598
  potential sale of, 599, 600–601, 603
  reworking of, 348, 603
Cathy Dressing, 283, 284, 289–301, 370, 536, 575; *color plate 7*
  author's analysis and interpretation of, 290–95, 296–300, 304, 391, 533
  Cathy depicted in, 144, 145, 152, 234, 284, 289–91, 292, 293, 295, 297, 299, 305, 547
  exhibition of, 152, 298–99, 358
  Heathcliff depicted in, 152, 228, 291–92, 294, 295, 297, 300
  ownership of, 358, 531
  power struggle in, 293–94, 295
  "Why have you that silk frock on, then?," 293
Cavet, Marcelle, 408
Cazac, Beatrice, 515
Cenci, Les (Artaud), 259, 262, 270–75
  Balthus's sets for, 264–65, 270–74, 273
  cast of, 273
  Jouve and, 274, 307
Centre Pompidou, Paris, 169
  Balthus retrospective (1983) in, 4, 5, 210–12, 313, 410, 554

Balthus's work acquired by, 298, 531, 563–64
  catalog of, 263, 279
"Ceux-ci sont mes ancêtres," 440, 441
Cézanne, Paul, 201, 494
  art of, 297, 435, 576
  exhibitions of, work of, 169, 212, 414
  influence of, 160, 324, 424, 537
  Piero and, 112
  Rilke's writings on, 37
Chaet, Bernard, 516–17
Chagall, Marc, 366, 424, 530
Chamberlain, John, 119
Chapin, Paul, 415
Chardin, Jean-Baptiste-Siméon, 112, 225, 335
Chassy, château at, 69, 199–200, 416, 425–26, 430, 448, 481, 486
  Balthus's work at, 475, 486, 488, 565
  Frédérique in, 64, 453, 457, 468, 469, 481, 507
  Léna in, 452–53, 457, 462, 507
  poverty and, 468
  studio at, 316, 459
Chateaubriand, 524
Cherry Tree, The, 101, 448
Chesterton, G. K., 336–38, 340
Chevigné, Duchesse Laure de, 365
Chevigné, Marie-Thérèse de, 365
Children, The, 407, 420, 438, 538, 575;
  color plate 10
  author's analysis and interpretation of, 381–87, 545, 565
  "Because Cathy taught him," 382
  exhibition of, 358
  Picasso and, 319, 374–75, 377, 380–81, 387, 480
  technical achievement of, 384–85, 435
Child with a Cat (Géricault), 105–6, 106
Chirac, Jacques, 595
Chirico, Giorgio De, 64, 201
Christie's, New York, 63, 64
Chroniques italiennes (Stendhal), 271
Cimabue, 277
Clair, Jean:
  on *Passage du Commerce Saint-André*, 27
  on *The Street*, 173
Clark, Lord Kenneth, 34, 124, 189, 557–58
Claudel, Paul, 529
Cocteau, Jean, 365, 367, 379
Colbert, Jean-Baptiste, 493
Colette in Profile, 66
Colle, Béatrice (Saalburg), 465–69, 471, 472
Colle, Carmen, 461–62, 463, 466–67, 468
Colle, Marie-Pierre, 459–63, 472, 495
Colle, Pierre, 374, 458, 461, 463
Colle, Sylvia (Lorant), 463–65, 472

Communist party, 415
Concert (Poussin), 105
Connoisseur, 26, 554
Connolly, Cyril, 67, 367, 467
    and Balthus's personal history, 68, 447–48
    on Balthus's studio, 314–15
    and *The Cherry Tree,* 448, 480
Contat, Anton, 80, 95
Cooley, Jane (Allen), 14–16, *15,* 32, 316–17, 391
Cooley, Paul, 14, 16
Coomaraswamy, Ananda, 88–89, 90, 97, 302,
    305, 582
Cooper, Alfred Duff, 405
Cooper, Douglas, 171, 380, 558
Copeau, Jacques, 93
Corot, Jean-Baptiste-Camille, 149, 424, 524
Courbet, Gustave, 327, 494, 530
    Birth of the World, 213, 527
    La Dame en podosople, 525, 527
    influence of, 108, 150, 265, 361–67, 424,
        435, 525, 527, 577
    Passage of Interlaken, 527
    Portrait of P. J. Proudhon, 525, *526*
    Sleep/The Two Friends, 526, 527
    Surrealism à la, 361–67, 379
    Villa Medici exhibit on, 524, 525–27
Courbet, Juliette, 525
Craft, Robert, 423–24
Cranach, Lucas, 152
Croissot, Francis de, 365
Cubism, 109, 183, 258, 334, 494, 564
Curry, Alain, 528–29
Curtis, Tony, 201

DACS, 399
Dada art, 109
Dalí, Salvador, 224, 362, 366, 367
Dame en podosople, La (Courbet), 525, 527
Dans le parc (P. Klossowski), *246*
Daumier, Honoré, 36
Davenport, Guy, 70–72, 391, 407
David, Jacques-Louis, 105, 264, 493
Dean, Loomis, photograph by, *459*
Degas, Edgar, 156, 304
de Gaulle, Charles, 492, 495, 496, 498
Delacroix, Eugène, 31, 74, 83, 425, 494
    influence of, 104, 149
    work of, studied in Louvre, 467
Delaroche-Vernet, Madame Philippe, 106
Deleuze, Gilles, 245
Della pittura (Alberti), 129
Delvaux, Paul, 276
Denis, Maurice, 96, 97
Denoël, Robert, 259
De Prospettiva Pingendi (Piero della
    Francesca), 129

Derain, André, 318–46, *339*
    The Bagpiper, 384
    Balthus's portrait of, 316, 318, 324–33,
        337–40, *358; color plate 9*
    Blond Italian, 334
    and Braque, 340–41, 342, 344, 384
    Chambourcy studio of, 331, 340–41
    culinary passions of, 342
    family of, 342
    friendship of Balthus and, 119, 316, 319–21,
        323, 341–43, 372, 373, 429, 461
    and Giacometti, 319, 320, 321, 323–24, 373,
        448
    influence of, 16, 319–21, 333–35, 350, 363,
        384, 450
    The Laden Table, 334
    personal characteristics of, 321, 322, 338–40
    work of, 156, 265, 319–22, 327–28, 330,
        333–35, *334,* 384, 399, 478, 489, 541, 569
    and World War II, 342, 343–44
Derwent, Lord Peter, 448, 452
Désormière, Roger, 271
Devenish, Mr. and Mrs., 7, 8, 551
Diaghilev, Sergey, 342
Dior, Christian, 463
Dix, Otto, 81, 360
Dobyns, Stephen, 30
Dozing Nude, 553
Drawing on Catalan Placemat, 23, *24*
Dream, The, 469
Dreyer, Carl, 262
Druet, Eugène, 96
Duchamp, Marcel, 191, 201
Duchamp, Mrs. Marcel, 480
Duino Elegies (Rilke), 32, 46, 76, 90, 376, 444

Echo et Narcisse (Poussin), 98–104, *101,* 105,
    385, 389
Eliot, T. S., 337
Eluard, Paul, 49, 363, 372, 376, 416, 419, 435
Ernst, Max, 155, 224, 362, 366
Etat de siège, L' (Camus), 203, *203*
Express, L', 70, 495–96, 497

Factory (Warhol), 523
Fairstein, Linda, 310–11, 335, 352, 390, 538, 556,
    574, 575
Faithfull, Marianne, 521
Fauvism, 109, 334
Feast of the Gods (Bellini), 196
Fellini, Federico, 33, 208, 519, 524, 528–29,
    529, 551
Fenêtres, Les (Rilke, with Baladine's
    illustrations), 249–50, 251, 255, 488
Figaro, Le, 96, 377–78, 430, 455–56
FitzGerald, Desmond, Knight of Glin, 522

Flagellation (Piero della Francesca), 189
Flanner, Janet, 494
Fleming, Ian, 214, 232, 442, 578
Fontaine, Rilke's letters published in, 58
Forge, Andrew, 535
Forge of Vulcan (Velázquez), 411
For or Against Derain, 330
Foucault, Michel, 245, 246
France, Balthus's identification with, 83
Frank, Jean-Michel, 367, 371
Frankfurter, Alfred, 359 60, 361
Freedman, Ralph, 48, 80
French Academy, and Villa Medici, 70, 300,
    492, 493–94, 496–98, 515, 525
French Revolution, 493
Freud, Lucien, 118, 306, 442
Freud, Sigmund, 86, 87, 229, 233, 307–8, 360,
    362

Gailliarde, Raphael, 89
Galerie Beaux-Arts, Paris, 416
Galerie Claude Bernard, Paris, 453
Galerie Pierre, Paris, 150–57, 259
    Alice in, 151, 152
    Cathy Dressing in, 152, 298
    and critical reviews, 154–55, 263–64, 269,
        557
    The Guitar Lesson in, 150, 207, 210, 213, 214
    impact of 1934 exhibition in, 154, 163,
        239–40, 318–19, 333, 372, 375
    The Quays in, 152
    The Street in, 152–53, 155–57, 191–92, 194
    Surrealism shown in, 150, 164, 191, 362
    The Window in, 151–52, 251
    see also Loeb, Pierre
Gallimard, publishers, 545
Garnier, Charles, 494
Gauguin, Paul, 17
Gazette Littraire, La, interview, 497–99
Gebsattel, Victor Emil Freiherr von, 86
Gelman, Natasha, 392
Gendel, Milton, 499
George, Prince, of Greece, 274
Géricault, Jean-Louis-André-Théodore:
    Child with a Cat, 105 6, *106*
    influence of, 102, 105, 152, 225
    Poussin copied by, 105
German Expressionism, 82–83, 129
Gertrude Stein Gallery, New York, *66*
Getting Up, 477–78, *478*
Giacobetti, photography by, *590*
Giacometti, Alberto, 117, 183, 310, 311, 319,
    370–73, *371*
    Balthus's essay on, 453–55
    on Balthus's work, 450–52, 570
    The Cage, 449

death of, 453–45
and de Noailles, 370 71, 373
and Derain, 319, 320, 321, 323–24, 373, 448
friendship of Balthus and, 316, 320, 323,
    363, 367, 372–73, 405, 416, 425, 429, 433,
    448–56, 468, 519
The Palace at 4 a.m., 449
and Surrealism, 370–72, 449, 456
work of, 61, 366, 370, 398, 399, 435, 449,
    468, 473, 489, 514, 524, 581
Gibbs, Christopher, 521
Gide, André, 93, 95, 110, 233, 366
Gilot, Françoise, 379, 419
Giorgione, 277
Giotto, 277, 435
Girl at a Window, 469, 480–84, *483*
Girl with a Cat, 31, 32, 391, 392 93, *393*,
    399–400
Golden Days, The, see Beaux Jours, Les
Gomès, Henriette, 416, 463, 471
Gordon, Catherine, 67
Gordon, George, *see* Byron, Lord
Goulandris, Basil and Elise, 169, 559, 560
Goya y Lucientes, Francisco José de, 278, 390
Graber, Hans, 108
Grand Chalet, Le, 6–8, 162, 163, 315, 550–51
    artwork in, 12–13, 139, 143
    masked ball in, 596–98
    media articles about, 169
Grande Jatte, La (Seurat), 156, 191, *192*, 202
Grand Magique Circus, Le, 519
Gray, Cleve, 566–67
Gray, Francine du Plessix, 566–67
Greco, El, 278
Grès, Madame, 259
Gropius, Walter, 366
Guitar Lesson, The, 205–32, 248, 265, 330; *color
    plate 5*
    Alice compared with, 302, 303, 304, 306, 313
    author's analysis and interpretation of,
        217–32, 234–35, 237–38, 241, 256, 266,
        350, 391, 540, 543
    Centre Pompidou and, 210–12
    exclusion from public showing, 210–11, 212,
        213, 358, 527
    at Galerie Pierre, 150, 207, 210, 213, 214
    influences and sources of, 225–26
    at Matisse gallery, 207–9, 210, 211, 212, 213,
        221, 358
    MoMA and, 209–10, 211, 212
    ownership of, 207, 211, 213–17, 358
    public reaction to, 207–8, 212, 252, 424
    self-portrait in, 228–32, 234, 237, 333
    sexual violence of, 205–6, 212, 217–28, 285,
        291, 294, 442, 469, 471, 474, 543, 544
    The Street compared with, 219, 222, 229

Guitar Lesson, The (*cont.*)
  Study drawing after, 229–31, *230*
  Woman with a Guitar compared with,
    572–76, 581
Guttoso, Renato, 519

Hals, Frans, 321
Hanson, Duane, 119
Hausenstein, Margot, 56
Hawthorne, Nathaniel, 440
Hayter, Stanley William, 110, 184, 287, 519
Héliogabale (Artaud), 265–66, 277, 320
Hélion, Jean, 450
Henriquez, Elsa, 252, 254, 255, 571–72
Hepburn, Audrey, 117
Herseint, Claude, 416, 480
Herstand, Arnold, 66
Hess, Thomas B., 31, 172, 208–9, 210
Hirshhorn, Joseph, 72, 513
Hirshhorn Museum, Washington, D.C., 410,
  414, 417, 489
Hitchcock, Henry-Russell, 195–96, *197,* 198
Hobhouse, Janet, 547, 548
Hogarth, William, 17, 172, 435, 577
Hölderlin, Friedrich, 233, 307
Honnegar, Arthur, *203*
Hoppenot, Henri, 414
Hopper, Edward, 422
House & Garden, 118, 169, 201, 484, 492–93,
  501, 509
Hughes, Robert, 4, 430
Hugo, Victor, 8, 551
Humphries, Josephine, 399
Hussein, Saddam, 54, 405
Hyman, Timothy, 82, 83

Ibert, Jacques, 496
Ideta, Setsuko, *see* Setsuko
Iman, 594
Imperial Prize (Japan), 595–96
Impressionism, 132, 135, 136, 172, 360, 484,
  494, 540
Indianapolis Museum of Art, 487
Ingres, Jean-Auguste-Dominique, 390, 391,
  412, 532
  influence of, 105, 424, 569, 570
  at Villa Medici, 493–94, 524
Institute of Contemporary Art, London, 243
International Style, 195
Italy:
  Arezzo, 110, 112, 119, 120, 127, 186, 187
  Florence, 119
  Monterchi, 123
  Piero's frescoes in, 107–16, 126–29
  Rome, *see* Villa Medici
  Sansepolcro, 112, 126, 189, 582

Jagger, Bianca, 523
Jagger, Mick, 521
Jakovsky, Anatole, 372
Japanese at a Black Mirror, 30–31, 546–49,
  547
Japonaise avec table rouge, 546
Jeaneret, Alain, 148
Jewell, E. A., 359
Joan Miró and His Daughter Dolores, 163–64,
  215, 348–57, *351*
  author's analysis and interpretation of,
    349–57
  critical success of, 352, 360, 380
  Dolores's reminiscences of, 353–56, 391, 469
  exhibition of, 349, 352, 358, 360
Jones, Brian, 521
Jones, Judith, 415
Jong, Erica, 552
Jouve, Pierre Jean, 307–10
  Alice sold to, 307, 358
  on Balthus's studio, 148–49, 307, 314–15
  on Balthus's work, 154, 161, 191, 272, 274,
    308–9, 316, 329, 352
  and *Les Cenci,* 274, 307
  death of, 313
  influence of, 311
  Pierre Klossowski and, 233
  La Victime by, 309–10, 313
Judas (Piero della Francesca), *188*

Kabuki theater, 542–43
Kandinsky, Wassily, 191, 225
Katia Reading, 187, 528, *535,* 536–37, 551
Kenzo, 523
Kessler, Harry, 98
Key, Ellen, 36–37
Khan, Prince Sadruddin Aga, 91, 117
Kimball, Richard, 517
King of Cats, The, 51–52, 228, 240–41, *242,*
  394, 442
Kippenberg, Anton, 131
Klarsfeld, Serge and Beate, 408
Klee, Paul, 191, 366, 372–73
Klossowska, Anna (grandchild), 523
Klossowska, Antoinette (first wife), *see*
  Watteville, Antoinette de
Klossowska, Denise (Pierre's wife), 243, 245,
  456
Klossowska, Elizabeth Dorothée "Baladine"
  (mother), *39, 77*
  art done by, 36, *39,* 91, 96, 249–50, 488
  in Balthus's paintings, 124, 182, 234, 237–38,
    254–55, 304, 396, 539
  and Balthus's schooling, 56–58
  and Balthus's talent, 53, 57, 74, 75, 90–91,
    96, 102, 154, 578

family background of, 59–60, 62, 68,
   72–74, 237
and *Fenêtres,* 249–50, 251, 255, 488
financial situation of, 40, 53, 74–75, 76, 90
illness and death of, 237, 544
influence of, 108, 250, 488
Junot and, 307
marriage of Erich and, 60
as "Merline" or "Mouky," 19, 40
and Muzot, 46, 67, 75–76, 77, 91, 93, 98
passport problems of, 95–96
personal characteristics of, 147, 304
physical appearance of, 35–36, 37, 62, 234
and Rilke, 6, 19–20, 35, 36–37, 40–47, 45,
   50, 58, 62, 67, 74–80, 90–91, 92–93,
   95–96, 98, 130, 396, 506, 583–84
separation of Erich and, 37, 40, 62
sons' closeness to, 48, 59, 74, 95, 236–37,
   248
in World War II, 68, 342
Klossowska de Rola, Harumi (daughter), 33,
   69–70, 253–54, 434, *590*
   at Asia Society, 593–94
   birthday party for, *596*
   birth of, 521
   and father's work, 347, 603
   media stories about, 347, 542, 593
Klossowski, Erich (father), *38,* 55, 82, 110, *407*
   absence of, 35, 236–37, 255
   death of, 408
   marriage of Baladine and, 60
   paintings by, 36, *38,* 236
   personal characteristics of, 147
   and Piero, 107, 108
   as Polish Catholic, 74
   separation of Baladine and, 37, 40, 62
   as theater designer, 37, 74, 76, 236, 270
   World War I and, 37
   World War II and, 406–8
Klossowski, Fumio (son), death of, 520–21
Klossowski, Pierre (brother), *236,* 522
   adolescence of, 37, 75, 76
   artwork of, *239, 244, 246,* 247, 396
   and Balthus's privacy, 4, 245
   on Balthus's work, 165, 240, 477
   childhood of, *36,* 243, 245, 247
   and Collège Sociologique, 416
   at Ecole Dramatique, 93, 98
   Frédérique as stepdaughter of, 64, 245, 453,
      456, 512
   marriage of, 243
   patrons of, 97–98
   and Rilke, 35, 41, 54, 72–73, 78, 84, 233,
      236, 245
   and Sade studies, 4, 233–34, 236, 237–39,
      243, 245–47, 248, 435, 566

writings of, 4, 52, 146, 165, 233, 243,
   245–47, 248, 307
Klossowski de Rola, Comte, *see* Rola,
   Comte de
Klossowski de Rola, Stanislas "Stash" (son),
   72, 88, 521
   birth of, 342
   and father's work, 63–64, 139, 141–42,
      571
   and use of title, 432, 433
Klossowski de Rola, Thadée (son), 4, 69–70,
   515–16, 521–23
Knaubliche, Raymonde, 326–37
Kochno, Boris, 378
Koenig, Hertha von, 376
Kolb, Annette, 98
Kornfeld, Eberhard, 372
Kramer, Hilton, 207, 572
Krugier, Jan, 111
Kunsthalle, Bern, 414
Kyoka, Izuma, 594

Lacan, Jacques, 85, 213, 376–77, 416, 419
Lachaise, Gaston, 209
Laden Table, The (Derain), *334*
Lady Abdy, 258–59, *260,* 264, 334, 478
La Falaise, Le Comte Alain de, 522
La Falaise, Loulou de, 69–70, 522–23
Laforgue, René, 233
Lagerfeld, Karl, 523
Lam, Wilfredo, 489
Landscape at Champrovent, 71, 297–98, 407,
   551, 587; *color plate 3*
Landscape with Cow, 484–86, *485,* 537
Large Composition with Raven, 485, 573, *577,*
   578–84
   author's analysis and interpretation of, 266,
      579–81, 584
   Balthus's views on, 578–79
Laurens, Henri, 366
Lausanne, Musée des Beaux-Arts, 87, 162,
   586–90, 598
Leclerq, Léna, 468, 475
   at Chassy, 452–53, 457, 462, 507
   as model, 452–53, *454*
Lefevre Gallery, London, 601, 603
Legend of the True Cross (Piero della
   Francesca), 112, 120
Léger, Fernand, 450
Léna with Her Arms Crossed, 454
Le Nain, brothers, 155, 398, 564
Leonardo (butler/chauffeur), 7, 8, 253
Léopold-Lévy, 332, 341, 343
Letters to a Young Poet (Rilke), 539
Lever, Maurice, 566
Lewis, C. S., 337

Leymarie, Jean, 596
  Balthus by, 169, 170–73, 286, 591
  "Balthus et la Suisse" by, 131
  on Balthus's personal history, 68, 403, 431,
     467, 474, 562
  on Balthus's studio, 315
  on Balthus's work, 143, 169, 262, 303, 306,
     533, 538, 551, 601–2
  and Villa Medici, 111, 172, 492–93, 525
Leyris, Betty, 146–48, 304, 406
Leyris, Jean, 456, 586
Leyris, Pierre, 146–48, 465
  on Artaud, 260, 262
  on Balthus's mimetic personality, 260, 282,
     432, 467
  on Balthus's personal history, 147, 148, 281,
     512
  and World War II memories, 403, 406
Lhote, André, 154–55, 157
Liberman, Alexander, 338
Lieberman, William, 72, 571
Lifar, Serge, 342
Life magazine, 426, 430
Lipchitz, Jacques, 366
Lippi, Annibale, 492
Living Room, The, 406, 474
Loeb, Pierre:
  gallery of, 151; *see also* Galerie Pierre, Paris
  and Miró, 163–64, 215, 348, 467
  and *The Street,* 155–57, 158, 161, 162, 192
Lolita (Nabokov), 31, *32,* 395, 399–400, 571
London Times Magazine, 347, 542
Lorant, Sylvia Colle, 463–65, 472
Lord, James, 313, 364, 438
  and Balthus's drawings, 139–41, 521
  on Balthus's personal history, 380, 467
  on Giacometti, 363, 449–50
  and World War II, 403
  writings of, 61, 431
Lorrain, Claude, 105
Louvre, Paris, Balthus's copy work in, 96, 97,
     98–99, 157, 385

Maar, Dora, 376, 377, 379, 425, 429
McLane, Rev. James L., 196, 480
Madonna della misericordia (Piero della
     Francesca), 582, *583*
Madonna del parto (Piero della Francesca),
     123–26, *127*
Madrid, Museo Thyssen-Bornemisza in,
     422
Magritte, René, 276, 362, 542
Mallet-Stevens, Robert, 366
Malraux, André, 79, 416, 419, 461
  physical appearance and personality of,
     494–95

and Villa Medici, 300, 492, 494–99, 525,
     527, 528
  and World War II, 404
Manet, Edouard, 299, 414, 494
Mantegna, Andrea, 191, 277
Man Who Was Thursday, The (Chesterton),
     337–38, 340
Marana, Les, 414
Marc, Olivier, 70
Markevitch, Igor, 436
Marquet, Albert, 96
Martini, Simone, 562
Masaccio, 108, 112, 119, 191, 561
Masahito Hitachi, Prince (Japan), 595
Masolino, 118
Mason, Raymond, 380
Masson, André, 366, 416
Matisse, Henri:
  art of, 225, 268, 304, 332, 387, 391, 399, 401,
     446, 478
  and Balthus's parents, 341, 497–98
  exhibition of work by, 414
  influence of, 534–35
  Pierre as son of, 200
  Poussin's *Narcisse* copied by, 99
Matisse, Patricia, 207, 209
Matisse, Pierre, 452
  as Balthus's U.S. dealer, 140–41, 164,
     200–201, 207–11, 213, 316, 319, 348, 358,
     480, 548–49, 571
  and *The Card Players,* 543–44
  and Cooley portrait, 14
  and *The Guitar Lesson,* 207–9, 210, 211, 212,
     213, 221, 358
  on his father's work, 268
  and *Japanese at a Black Mirror,* 548–49
  and Miró portrait, 164, 348, 352
  and Miró's work, 319, 348, 534
  and MoMA, 209, 211
  in Rome, 9, 512
Matisse, Tara, 200, 571, 596
  and art authentication, 63, 64
  and *The Guitar Lesson,* 213, 215
Matisse, Teeny, 402
Matossiani, Monsieur, 507
Matta Echaurren, Roberto, 207
Maugham, Somerset, 285–86, 289
Mauriac, Claude, 367
Maurois, André, 409
Mauron, Adolphe-Jean-Marie (Cassandre),
     317–18, 465, 480
Mauron, Henri, 317
Mauron-Cassandre Family, 318
Medici, Cardinal Ferdinando de', 492, 508
Méditerranée's Cat, The, 419–20, *419,* 527, 551,
     587, 597–98

Men Carrying the Wood (Piero della
    Francesca), *188*
Menuhin, Yehudi, 60, 72
Mérimée, Prosper, 497
Metamorphosis (Ovid), 103–4
Metropolitan Museum, New York, 368
    Balthus retrospective (1984) in, 33–34, 72,
        200–201, 543, 559, 570–72
    exhibit catalog of, 35, 60, 61, 71, 81–82, 173,
        200–201, 325, 571–72
    Nude in Front of a Mantel in, 122, 410
    Thérèse Dreaming in, 392
Michelangelo, 112, 277, 491
Miller, Henry, 206–7
Milles, Les, Deportation Camp, 68
Minoret, Bernard, 364, 365, 366, 367, 436,
    438, 441
Minotaure, 50–51
Minotaure exhibit, Paris (1934), 191
Mirabella, 593
Miró, Dolores:
    in Balthus's portrait, 348, 349, *351,* 353, 387,
        397
    reminiscences of, 353–56, 391, 469
Miró, Joan, 347–57, 372, 375, 519
    Balthus's portrait of, 163–64, 215, 316, 347,
        348–57, *351,* 358, 360, 380
    influence of, 348, 488, 534
    Matisse as dealer for, 319, 348, 534
    personality of, 348
    Still Life with Shoe, 335–36, 348
    studio of, 335–36
    View of a Farm, 487, 488
    Woman Before the Mirror, 348
    work of, 335–36, 348, 366, *487,* 488
Miró, Pilar, 353
Mitsou:
    Balthus's alter ego in, 134, 240, 600
    Balthus's illustrations for, 20–26, *22, 25,*
        34–35, 47, 54, 55, 56, 131, 154, 489, 579
    contract for, 44
    imagery in, 29, 34, 50, 51, 53, 54, 84, 223,
        238
    publication of, 48
    Rilke's preface for, 21, 34, 46–48, 49, 53,
        54–55, 250
Modersohn-Becker, Paula, 506
Modigliani, Amedeo, 201, 209, 221
MoMA, *see* Museum of Modern Art,
    New York
Monde, Le, 377, 430, 535
Mondrian, Piet, 385, 452
Monet, Claude, 341, 488
Monfort, Silvia, *411*
Monnier, Jacqueline Matisse, 404
Montaigne, Michel Eyquem de, 492

Montebello, Philippe de, 367–68, 572
Morandi, Giorgio:
    influence of, 143–44, 172, 396, 418, 533
    Still Life, 142
Moravia, Alberto, 517
Morgan, Ted, 180
Mossé, Sonia, 326, 327
Moth, The, 478–80, *479,* 551
    loss and recovery of, 51, 168, 479
Mountain, The, 81, *81,* 100, 316, 340–41, 392,
    551, 558
Mozart, Wolfgang Amadeus, 146, 570
Mühll, Dory von der, 72
Murdoch, Iris, 289, 300
Musée des Beaux-Arts, Lausanne, 586–90,
    598, 599–600
Musée Courbet, 166, 311, 313
Musée d'Orsay, Paris, 213
Musée Gustave Courbet, Ornans, 431
Musée Picasso, Paris, 384
Museo Thyssen-Bornemisza, Madrid, 422
Museum of Modern Art, New York:
    André Derain in, 324, 325, 328–29
    Balthus's exhibit in (1956), 69, 197, 199,
        450, 453, 480
    catalog of, 69, 164, 201, 202, 286
    and *The Guitar Lesson,* 209–10, 211, 212
    and Miró portrait, 163–64, 349, 352
    The Street in, 161, 176, 197, 198–200
Musset, Alfred de, 433
Muzot:
    Baladine and, 46, 67, 75–76, 77, 91, 93, 98
    Balthus's visits to, 46, 77, 109
    Rilke and, 46, 67, 75–77, 90, 98, 109, 130,
        425, 551

Nabokov, Vladimir, 588
    Lolita, 31, 32, 395, 399–400, 571
Napoleon I, emperor of France, 493
Napoleon III, emperor of France, 497
"Narcisse" (Rilke), 102–4, 105, 181, 412
National Gallery, London, 118
Nativity (Piero della Francesca), 118
Neri, Grazia, photograph by, *552*
Neue Sachlichkeit painters, 81–82, 360
New Criterion, The, 61, 431
Newhouse, S. I., 513
New York Herald Tribune, 358
New York Times, The, 60, 68, 430–31, 571
New York Times Magazine, The 180, 431
Niarchos, Stavros, 217, 223, 228, 471
Nichols, Mike, 213
Nicksen, Graham, 528
Nietzsche, Friedrich Wilhelm, 416
Nin, Anaïs, 268, 281
Niobides sculptures, 508–9, *508*

Noailles, Countess Anna de, 98
Noailles, Comte Charles de:
   as art patron, 364, 366, 367, 370, 371
   social circle of, 364, 366, 367, 373, 424, 429,
      436, 448
Noailles, Vicomtesse Marie-Laure de, 364–71,
      368
   as art patron, 364, 366, 367, 370, 371, 416,
      480
   Balthus's portrait of, 316, 360, 367, 368–70,
      369, 438, 443–45
   family background of, 73, 365
   personality of, 364–65
   Rorem and, 438–41
   social circle of, 364, 366, 367, 373, 416, 419,
      424, 429, 436, 442
Noli me tangere (Piero della Francesca), 107
Nolke, Gudi, 56, 77–79
Nouvelle Revue Française, La, 154–55, 263, 270,
      274
Nouvelles orientales (Oriental Tales)
      (Yourcenar), 344–46
Nude in Front of a Mantel, 122, 125, 144, 410
Nude with Towel, 553
Nureyev, Rudolf, 521–22

Oberon, Merle, 301
Olivier, Sir Laurence, 301
Olympia (Manet), 299
Onassis, Jacqueline, 70
120 Days of Sodom (Sade), 224, 365, 366, 442,
      546–47
Opium (perfume), 523
Oriental art, influence of, 30–31, 42, 79, 83,
      91–92, 124, 172, 263, 331, 542–43, 544,
      561–64, 601
Orinsby-Gore, Jane, 521
Ovid, Metamorphosis, 103–4

Painter and His Model, The, 563–70, 566
Palace at 4 a.m., The (Giacometti), 449
Paris:
   architecture in, 174
   Balthus's first move to, 93–94, 95–106
   Balthus's oils of people in, 131–34; see also
      Street, The
   bohemianism of, 148
   Cour de Rohan studio in, 314–17, 331, 340,
      368, 415, 496, 536
   Galerie Beaux-Arts in, 416
   Galerie Druet in, 96
   Galerie Pierre in, 150–57, 191, 192, 194
   Louvre in, 96
   Minotaure exhibition in, 191
   postwar years in, 415–19, 423–25
   Rilke in, 98

Rue de Fürstemburg studio in, 148–49, 155,
      167, 169, 255, 279, 307
Paris Match, 8, 169, 430
Passage du Commerce Saint-André, The, 27–28,
      28, 165–67, 292, 449
   author's analysis and interpretation of, 116,
      120, 134, 582
   Balthus's views on, 27, 28, 165–66, 167, 276
   critical review of, 558
   exhibition of, 166, 212, 551, 587
   self-portrait in, 28, 134, 582
   as tableau vivant, 165
Passage of Interlaken (Courbet), 527
Patron Saints (Weber), 430
Paz, Octavio, 49, 278
Pearlstein, Philip, 546
Pei, I. M., 257
Peppiatt, Michael, 311–2
Perkins, Anthony, 523
Persian Gulf War, 54, 90, 405
Picasso, Pablo, 148, 201, 374–80, 375, 416, 419,
      429, 530
   Artist and the Model by, 258
   art of, 156, 330, 361, 374, 380, 399, 401,
      435–36, 445, 446, 457
   on Balthus's work, 319, 372, 377–80, 397
   Bernard Berenson on, 107
   The Children owned by, 319, 374–75, 377,
      380–81, 387, 480
   exhibition of work of, 191, 209, 258, 366, 414
Picasso, Paloma, 522, 523
Piero della Francesca, 107–29, 277
   Adam Announcing His Death, 122
   Balthus's copies of, 112–13, 114, 115–16, 120,
      157
   Baptism of St. John, 118, 129
   composition of, 112, 116, 129
   De Prospettiva Pingendi, 129
   Flagellation, 189
   influence of, 17, 109, 112–13, 115, 120–29,
      145, 150, 186–87, 189, 229, 278, 311, 330,
      363, 384, 424, 435, 481, 537, 564, 567,
      570, 576, 577, 578, 582
   Judas, 188
   Legend of the True Cross, 112, 120
   Madonna della misericordia, 582, 583
   Madonna del parto, 123–26, 127
   Men Carrying the Wood, 188
   name of, 108
   Nativity, 118
   Noli me tangere, 107
   other artists and, 108, 112
   qualities of work of, 108–9, 112, 122,
      126–27, 129, 145
   The Queen of Sheba, 124, 129, 187, 189
   restorations of work by, 118

Resurrection of Christ, 112–13, *114*, 115
The Victory of Hercules, 128, 187, 189
work in museum collections, 118
writings of, 129
Pierre Matisse Gallery, New York, *see* Matisse,
Pierre
Pietà (Duidono), 100
Pitoëff, Georges, 262
Poe, Edgar Allan, 105, 176, 309, 313, 578, 582
Poiret, Paul, 342
Poland:
Jews in, 434
nobility of, 427–28, 509–13
Polignac, Princess de, 274
Pompidou Centre, *see* Centre Pompidou,
Paris
Poniatowski, Stanisław August (Stanisław II),
61–62, 66, 509–10
Portrait of Erich Klossowski (Spiro), *38*
Portrait of Jane Cooley, 14–16, *15*
Portrait of Louise Vernet as a Child (Géricault),
105–6, *106*
Portrait of P. J. Proudhon (Courbet), 525, *526*
Portrait of Setsuko, *503*
Portrait of the Baroness Alain de Rothschild,
436–38, *437*
Postimpressionism, 160
Poulan, Jean, 265
Poulenc, Francis, 366
Poussin, Nicolas:
Autumn, 101
Balthus's copying at Louvre, 97, 98–99,
154, 157, 255, 385, 481
Concert, 105
Echo et Narcisse, 98–105, *101*, 105, 385, 389
influence of, 17, 97, 99–102, 117, 150, 385,
481
other artists copying work of, 99, 105
Paris retrospective of, 595
Piero and, 109, 112
Prix de Rome, 494, 497
Proudhon, Pierre Joseph, 525, *526*
Proust, Marcel, 365

Quays, The, 132–34, *133*, 132, 292, 582
Queen of Sheba, The (Piero della Francesca),
124, 129, 187, 189

Radziwill, Prince "Stash," 70
Ray, Man, *Antonin Artaud*, *267*
Raynal, Tériade and Maurice, 262
Réalités, 26, 430
Reinhardt, Joseph, 136–38, 144, *145*, 577
Reinhart, Georg, 40, 75, 76
Reinhart, Werner, 46, 131
Rembrandt van Rijn, 278, 482, 542

Renaissance art, 126, 186, 187, 221, 266, 277,
555, 561, 568; *see also* Piero della
Francesca
Reni, Guido, 492
Renoir, Jean, 342
Renoir, Pierre-Auguste, 304, 327, 342, 387,
414, 435
Resurrection of Christ (Piero della Francesca),
111, 112–13, *114*, 115
Balthus's copy after, 112–13, *114*, 115–16, 582
Reverchon, Blanche, 307
Rewald, John, 141, 558
Rewald, Sabine, 144
and authentication of Balthus's work,
63–65
on Balthus's work, 35, 180, 326–27, 533
doctoral thesis by, 111, 403
Metropolitan Museum catalog by, 35, 61,
71, 81–82, 173, 325, 571–72
Rheims, Maurice, 416
Ricci, Cardinal Giovanni, 492, 500
Richardson, John, 375, 439
Rilke, Rainer Maria, *43*, 77
on androgyny, 539
and anti-Semitism, 73
and Baladine, 6, 19–20, 35, 36–37, 40–47,
45, 50, 58, 62, 67, 74–80, 90–91, *92–93*,
95–96, 98, 130, 396, 506, 583–84
and Balthus, 19, 41–42, 67, 319, 562, 585
on Balthus's talent, 25, 53–54, 56, 73, 78–79,
93–94, 98, 154, 264, 265, 278, 568
on Cézanne, 37
childhood of, 41, 57
on the "Crac," 57, 84–85, 104, 120, 219, 394
daughter of, 42
death and burial of, 130–31, 308, 406
Duilo Elegies, 32, 46, 76, 90, 376, 444
family background of, 428–29
and father's death, 544
and *Fenêtres*, 249–50, 251, 255, 488
health of, 92–93, 98, 130
on his own work, 32
influence of, 31–32, 42, 44, 46, 55, 58, 79,
83–86, 93–94, 97–98, 160, 165, 250–51,
308, 415, 425, 426, 428–29, 489, 576, 580,
598
and Klossowski boys, 35, 37, 41–42, 54,
72–73, 76, 77–80, 84, 93–94, 97–98, 245,
247, 262, 580
Letters to a Young Poet, 539
and *Mitsou* contract, 44
Mitsou preface by, 21, 34, 46–48, *49*, 53,
54–55, 250
and Muzot, 46, 67, 75–76, 77, 90, 98, 109,
130, 425, 551
and "Narcisse," 102–4, 105, 181, 412

Rilke, Rainer Maria (*cont.*)
  in Paris, 98
  patrons of, 40, 46, 75, 110
  and Piero's work, 107–8
  poetry by, 32, 46, 48, 76, 90, 102–4, 249–51,
    376, 444
  and psychoanalysis, 86
  published letters of, 58–59
  as "René," 40
  and Rodin, 524
  solitude sought by, 19, 40, 46, 76, 93, 165
  Sonnets to Orpheus, 32
  in Switzerland, 404
Rilke, Ruth, 42
Rimbaud, Arthur, 262
Roberte au passage Choiseul (P. Klossowski),
  244
Rockefeller, Blanchette, 209, 212
Rodin, Auguste, 37, 297, 524
Rola, Comte de:
  use of title, 5, 7, 67, 170, 243, 427–33, 436,
    441, 464, 467, 518–19
Romanov family, 62, 70, 596, 598
Rome, Villa Medici in, *see* Villa Medici
Room, The, 29–30, *417,* 438–39; *color plate 1*
  androgynous figure in, 29, 160, 168, 266,
    424, 538, 565
  author's analysis and interpretation of, 30,
    124–26, 168, 184, 417–18, 582
  awakening as theme in, 29, 222
  Balthus's views on, 29, 125–26, 126, 160,
    579
  current status of, 30, 417
  exhibition of, 30, 210, 551
  Piero's influence in, 124–26
Rorem, Ned, 364, 429–30, 438–41, *439,* 442
Rotapfel-Verlag, publishers, 44
Rothschild, Baroness Alain de, 436–38, *437,*
  444, 448
Rothschild, Alix de, 416
Rouault, Georges, 497
Rouen, François, 455
Rousseau, Henri, 155
Roussel, Xavier, 110
Roux, Gaston, 519
Roux, Pauline, 519
Roy, Claude, 416, 545
Ruskin, John, 108
Russell, John, 33–34, 394, 459, 477, 538–39
  on Balthus's personal history, 68, 403, 430,
    433
  on *Passage du Commerce Saint-André,* 27
  on *The Street,* 121, 184, 186
  Tate catalog essay by, 4, 34, 58, 121, 184, 186,
    349

Saalburg, Béatrice Colle, 465–69, 471, 472
Sade, Laure de, 365
Sade, Marquis de, 205, 270, 370
  Gray's writings on, 566–67
  The 120 Days of Sodom, 224, 365, 366, 442,
    546–47
  Pierre Klossowski's writings on, 4, 233–34,
    236, 237–39, 243, 245–47, 248, 435, 566
  on virginity, 531
Saint, Clara, 521–23
Saint Laurent, Yves, 521–22, 523
Salis, Jean Rodolphe von, 46, 404
Sanchez, Fernando, 522
Sanchez, Maria, 514
Sansepolcro, Italy, frescoes in, 112, 127, 189,
  582
Savoya, Marina Doria di, 598
Scalfani, photograph by, *529*
*Scène du jeune ogier et du Commandeur de
  Saint-Vit* (P. Klossowski), *244*
Schiaparelli, Elsa, 522
Schjeldahl, Peter, 571
Schmidt, Helmut, 595
Schrimpf, Georg, 81, 82, 360
Schulz, Bruno, 512
Segalen, Victor, 562
Self-Portrait, 421, 422
Self-portrait (Artaud), *261*
Serenissima (Jong), 552
Setsuko, *89, 503, 590*
  artwork by, 117–18, *119,* 442, 455, 507, 593
  at Asia Society, 593–95
  and Balthus's fragility, 590–91
  Balthus's marriage to, 298, 415, 518
  and Balthus's stories, 4, 6, 50, 72
  and Balthus's work, 169, 409, 516, 587,
    599
  and birthday party, 596–98
  family background of, 433
  and Frédérique, 64, 65, 457, 506, 507
  and Le Grand Chalet, 550–51
  interviews of Balthus and, 6–7, 8, 10, 11,
    89–90
  language and, 52, 505
  meeting of Balthus and, 502–4
  as model, 531, *532*
  physical appearance and personality of, 7,
    504–5, 594
  on psychoanalysis, 86–87, 308
  at Villa Medici, 64, 430, 457, 462, 469,
    506–7, 518, 520
  writings about, 70
  youth of, 33, 82
Seurat, Georges, 414
  La Grande Jatte, 156, 191, *192,* 202

influence of, 17, 108, 150, 153, 160, 191, 202, 424, 435, 482, 577
Shelley, Mary, 409
Shelley, Percy Bysshe, 259, 271, 409
Shiff, Sidney, 287
Signorelli, Luca, 83
Skira (publishing house):
    and *Balthus* (Leymarie), 169, 171
    and *Les Marana*, 414
    and *Minotaure*, 50
Skira, Albert, 414, 494
Sleep (Le Sommeil), 526, 527
Sleep/The Two Friends (Courbet), 526, 527
Soby, James Thrall, 14, 63, 316, 335
    on Balthus's personal history, 403–4
    catalog essays by, 69, 164, 201, 202, 286, 358, 362, 363
    and *Cathy Dressing*, 358
    on Derain, 333
    on Giacometti, 448–49
    and *The Guitar Lesson*, 205, 207, 358
    and *Joan Miró*, 352, 353
    and MoMA exhibit, 480
    and *The Street*, 173, 192–93, 195 96, 197, 198–200, 201–2, 358
Sonnets to Orpheus (Rilke), 32
Sotheby's, New York, 63, 64
Spiro, Abraham Beer, 59, 70, 512, 572
Spiro, Eugen, 59, 147
    in Berlin, 37, 53, 74, 75, 82, 90, 93, 286, 300
    family background of, 60, 62, 66, 72, 73
    in Les Milles, 68
    Portrait of Erich Klossowski, 38
Spiro, Peter, 75, 241
Spoleto, Festival of the Two Worlds (1982) in, 552
Staël, Nicolas de, 425
Stanisław II of Poland, 61–62, 66, 509–10
Stein, Gertrude, 195, 330, 406
Steinlen, Théophile-Alexandre, 36
Stendhal, 271
Stevens, Mark, 430
Stieler, Hilde, 407
Still Life, 334 36, 336
Still Life (Morandi), 142
Still Life with Broken Glass, 316
Still Life with Fruit (Erich Klossowski), 38
Still Life with Old Shoe (Miró), 335–36, 348
Stravinsky, Igor, 423–24
Street, The, 155–62, 189–203, 194, 234, 387; color plate 4
    author's analysis and interpretation of, 119, 152–53, 157–61, 167–68, 176–85, 186–87, 195, 389, 400, 474

Balthus's views on, 157, 161–62, 165–69, 181, 186, 190–91, 193, 194–95, 276, 362
    Card Players compared with, 541
    Cathy Dressing compared with, 293, 294
    early version of, 158–59, 159, 265
    exhibition of, 155–56, 161, 176, 191, 192, 197, 198, 199, 358, 551
    The Guitar Lesson compared with, 219, 221, 229
    Katia Reading compared with, 537
    ownership of, 173, 191–93, 195–97, 198–200, 201–2, 319, 358, 375
    Piero quoted in, 122, 128, 189
    Pierre Klossowski's article on, 165, 166
    repainting of, 153, 158–60, 173, 197–98, 199, 423
    setting of, 156, 168–69, 171–75, 255, 326
    shock value of, 193–95, 198, 199, 285
Strohl, Jean and Frieda, 40, 110–11, 138
Struwwelpeter, 291, 304
Study after *Guitar Lesson*, 229–31, 230
Study for "The Three Sisters," 458–59, 460
Summer Afternoon (Setsuko), 119
Sunday Afternoon on the Island of La Grande Jatte (Seurat), 156, 191, 192, 202
Supervielle, Jules, 98, 270
Surrealism, 225, 256, 334, 399, 542
    "à la Courbet," 361–67, 379
    Artaud and, 262, 275–77, 449
    De Chirico and, 64
    fantasy vs., 361, 362
    Galerie Pierre and, 150, 164, 191, 362
    Giacometti and, 370–72, 449, 456
    Miró and, 348
    and religious mockery, 224
Sutton, Denys, 327, 338
Swedenborgians, 300
Swiss Peasant Costume Cycle (Reinhardt), 136–38, 137
Switzerland:
    Balthus in World War II in, 68–69, 71, 120, 406, 413, 434
    Beatenberg, 76, 77, 79, 91–92, 93, 286, 562
    de Wattevilles in, 136–38
    Geneva, 37
    Le Grand Chalet in, 6–8, 550–51
    Klossowskis in, 35, 37
    landscapes of, 6, 71, 81
    Lausanne, 87, 162, 586–90
    Muzot in, 45, 46, 75, 93, 98, 109, 130
    Rossinière, 5–6, 166, 554, 559
    Villa Diodati in, 68–69, 409, 414
Sylvester, David, 535

Taillade, Geneviève, 331, 342–43
Tate Gallery, London:
    Balthus retrospective (1968) in, 4, 34, 117,
        430
    catalog of, 4, 34, 58, 121, 184, 186, 263, 349
Taxis-Hohenlohe, Marie von Thurn und,
    444
Tchelitchew, Pavel, 450
Tenniel, John, 184
Thaw, Eugene Victor, 140–41, 521
Theater of Cruelty:
    Artaud's purpose in, 262–63, 270, 295,
        544
    Les Cenci and, 259, 262, 275
    reality and, 269, 275, 277, 313
    Surrealism and, 275, 277, 449
Théâtre des Folies-Wagram, Paris, 271
Thérèse Dreaming, 389–99, 438, 475, 536, 555;
    color plate 11
    eroticism of, 389–90
    technical achievement of, 389, 396–99, 435,
        458
Thomson, Virgil, 195
Three Sisters, The, 458–74, 464; color plate 12
    author's interpretation of, 472–74
    Béatrice's reminiscences of, 465–69, 471
    Marie-Pierre's reminiscences of, 459–63
    ownership of, 213, 471, 471–72
    series of, 120, 463, 464, 465, 466, 471, 513,
        528
    sketches for, 458–59, 460
    Sylvia's reminiscences of, 463–65
Through the Looking-Glass (Carroll), 184–85
Time magazine, 4, 430
Tintin, 498, 535
Tison, Frédérique:
    at Chassy, 64, 453, 457, 468, 469, 481, 507
    drawings by, 64–66
    as model and mistress, 456–57, 469, 475,
        476, 478, 482, 512
    as Pierre's stepdaughter, 64, 245, 453, 456,
        512
    at Villa Medici, 64, 457, 462, 469, 506,
        507
Tison, Jean Charles, 456
Titian, 277, 390
Tolkien, J.R.R., 337
Toulouse-Lautrec, Henri, 36, 221
Turgenev, Ivan Sergeyevich, 588
Turkish Room, The, 143, 348, 386, 528, 531–35,
    532, 536, 551
Two Friends, The/Sleep (Courbet), 526, 527

Uccello, Paolo, 277, 278
Uhde, Wilhelm, 155, 158

United States:
    Balthus's art dealer in, see Matisse, Pierre
    Balthus's fame in, 570, 572
    collectors in, 200, 201, 375
Untitled (child on leash), 23, 24

Valéry, Paul, 98, 116
Valli, Anna, 596, 597, 600
van der Weyden, Roger, 256
van Eyck, Jan, 221, 256, 299
van Gogh, Vincent, 17, 169, 414
Velázquez, Diego, 304, 398, 446, 492
    Forge of Vulcan, 411
    influence of, 424
Venice Biennale (1980), 122, 551–52
Vernet, Horace, 105, 493, 535
Via Condotti prize, 33
Vicountess de Noailles, The, 367, 368–70, 369
Victim, The, 100, 310–12, 312, 313, 327, 392,
    405, 474, 556
Victime, La (Jouve), 309–10, 313
Victorio Emanuelle, 598
Victory of Hercules, The (Piero della
    Francesca), 128, 187, 189
View of a Farm (Miró), 487, 488
View of Montecalvello, 352, 543, 559–63, 564,
    599; color plate 15
    author's impressions of, 559–61
    Balthus's views on, 560, 561
    Oriental influence on, 561–63
    ownership of, 169, 559
    technical achievement of, 297–98, 435,
        460, 540
Vildrac, Charles, 46, 47–48
Villa Diodati, Geneva, 68–69, 409, 414
Villa Medici, Rome, 92, 491–99
    artistic standards in, 493–94, 495, 523,
        524–25
    Balthus as director of, 9, 70, 171, 300, 430,
        453, 492–93, 495–99, 514–20, 528, 550
    Balthus's painting at, 528–32, 536–37, 545,
        559, 578
    changes introduced in, 507–9
    exhibitions in, 61, 63, 320, 523–25, 527, 550
    Frédérique at, 64, 457, 462, 469, 506, 507
    history of, 492–94
    Ingres as director of, 493–94, 524
    Japanese trip for, 502–4
    Leymarie as director of, 111, 172, 492–93, 525
    Niobides at, 508–9, 509
    restoration of, 118, 169, 499–502, 501, 507,
        524
    Setsuko in, 64, 430, 457, 462, 469, 506–7,
        518, 520
    social life at, 518–20

staff of, 513–14, 517–18
studio in, 496, 528–29, 530
Viollet-le Duc, Eugène-Emmanuel, 497
Virgilio (servant), 7–8, 426
Vreeland, Diana, 523
Vuillard, Édouard, 158

Wadsworth Atheneum, Hartford, 14, 195,
    207, 335, 480
Warhol, Andy, 119, 201, 522, 523
Warr, Alexander, 68
Watteville, Antoinette de:
    Balthus's divorce from, 298, 415, 518
    Balthus's infatuation with, 144–45, 146,
        231–32, 255, 283–84, 300, 382, 600
    Balthus's marriage to, 298, 316, 341–42, 506
    Balthus's portrait of, 139–42, 140, 144–45
    in Cathy Dressing, 144, 284, 289–90, 293,
        293, 295, 297
    and children, 409, 415, 452, 498
    friendship of, 10, 40, 506–7
    separation of Balthus and, 415
    in White Skirt, 461, 462
Watteville, Hubert de, 520, 521
Watteville, Robert de, 136–38
Weber, Charlotte Fox, 175–76, 423, 586, 587,
    588, 589, 591, 597
Weber, Katharine, 458, 472, 567, 586, 594
Weber, Lucy Swift, 586, 587, 588, 589, 591, 597
Weber, Nicholas Fox, 597
Week of Four "Thursdays," The, 418, 419
Weininger, Andreas, 76
Weininger, Richard, 97–98
Werfel, Franz, 73
Westhoff, Clara, 506
Wharton, Edith, 135
White Skirt, The, 129, 461, 462, 466
Whitney, Mr. and Mrs. John Hay, 480
Wilde, Oscar, 227, 228, 585
Wilder, Billy, 201
Wills, Garry, 337

Wilt, M. de, 408
Window, The, 151–52, 251–59, 304, 571–72;
    color plate 8
    author's analysis and interpretation of, 234,
        254–56, 257–58, 387, 487
    Lady Abdy compared with, 259
    ownership of, 256–57
    sexual violence in, 234, 252, 265, 285
Window, Cour de Rohan, The, 451–52, 451
Wolff, Kurt, 56
Woman Before the Mirror (Miró), 348
Woman in a Bathtub, 475–77, 476, 536
Woman with a Guitar, 572–77, 574, 581
World War I, Klossowskis' exile during, 35, 37,
    53–54, 82
World War II, 402–8
    Baladine and, 68, 342
    and Balthus's exile in Switzerland, 68–69,
        71, 120, 407, 413, 434
    Balthus's military service in, 71, 134–36,
        148, 341, 402–6
    concentration camps in, 73, 406, 434
    Derain and, 342, 343–44
    Erich Klossowski and, 406–8
    and postwar life, 409
    premonitions of, 316, 335, 336
Wunderly-Volkart, Nanny, 74, 76, 93, 131
Wuthering Heights (Bronte):
    Balthus as Heathcliff in, 284–85, 287–90,
        291–92, 297, 298, 300, 301, 381, 577
    Balthus's early reading of, 67, 284, 301
    Balthus's illustrations for, 141, 144, 284–301,
        360, 374, 381, 431, 480

Young Girl in White Dress, 469, 470
Young Woman Getting Ready for the Bath, 144
Yourcenar, Marguerite, 344–46, 490

Ziegler, Richard and Lily, 40
Zurbarán, Francisco de, 278
Zurlini, Valerio, 519

PERMISSIONS ACKNOWLEDGMENTS

Grateful acknowledgment is made to the following for permission to reprint previously published material:

Graywolf Press: "Narcissus" and excerpts from Poems II, III, and XIII from "The Window" from *The Complete French Poems of Rainer Maria Rilke* by Rainer Maria Rilke, translated by A. Poulin, Jr., copyright © 1986 by A. Poulin, Jr. Reprinted by permission of Graywolf Press, Saint Paul, Minnesota.

The Metropolitan Museum of Art: Excerpt from "Mitsou" by Rainer Maria Rilke, translated by Richard Miller. Reprinted by permission of The Metropolitan Museum of Art.

All artwork by Balthus, Antonin Artaud, André Derain, Man Ray, Joan Miró, and Pierre Klossowski is reproduced with permission, © 1999 Artists Rights Society (ARS), New York/ADAGP Paris.

Archives Littéraires Suisse—Berne: 43, 45 (both), 77

The Art Institute of Chicago, Helen Birch Bartlett Memorial Collection, photograph © 1998. All rights reserved.: 192

Bridgeman Art Library, London, New York: 242, 393, 419 (photo: Peter Willi), 464 (photo: Peter Willi), 477 (Scottish National Gallery of Modern Art, Edinburgh), 479 (photo: Peter Willi), 526 (bottom)

Art Resource: 526 (top) (Musée du Petit Palais, Paris. Photo: Erich Lessing)

© Cecil Beaton, courtesy of Sotheby's London: 375

Loomis Dean/Life magazine © Time, Inc.: 459, 470 (top), 481

Edimedia: 334, 532 (Centre Georges Pompidou. Photo: J. Guillot), 566 (Centre Georges Pompidou. Photo: J. Guillot); *color figure 7* (Centre Georges Pompidou. Photo: J. Guillot)

Galerie Alice Pauli, Lausanne: 553 (top)

Galerie Jan Krugier, Geneva: 114

Galerie Lelong, Paris: 236 (photo: Michel Nguyen)

Galerie Thomas Ammann: 260, 421 (bottom), 462; *color figures 5, 16*

© Graziano Arici/Grazia Neri: 552

Harlingue-Viollet: 97

Hirshhorn Museum and Sculpture Garden, Smithsonian Institution: 417; *color figure 2* (Gift of the Joseph Hirshhorn Foundation, 1966. Photo: Lee Stalsworth)

Historisches Museum, Bern: 137

© Evelyn Hofer: 501 (both), 509

Indiana University Art Museum: *color figure 8*

© Indianapolis Museum of Art: *color figure 13* (gift of Joseph Cantor)

The Lefevre Gallery, London: 119

Alexander Liberman: 339

© Lipnitzki-Viollet: 203, 273 (top), 410, 411

Magnum Photos Inc: 371 (© Rene Burri), 439 (© Henri Cartier-Bresson), 590 (© Henri Cartier-Bresson), 602 (© Henri Cartier-Bresson)

The Metropolitan Museum of Art: 81 (purchase, Gift of Mr. and Mrs. Nate B. Spingold and Nathan Cummings, Rogers Fund and The Alfred N. Punnet Endowment Fund, by exchange, and Harris Brisbane Dick Fund, 1982), 125 (Robert Lehman Collection, 1975); *color figure 11* (The Jacques and Natasha Gelman Collection. Photo: Malcolm Veron)

Musée de Louvre/Giaraudon, Paris/Superstock: 106

Musée de Louvre, Paris/Giraudon/Art Resource, New York: 101

The Museum of Modern Art, New York. Photograph © 1998 The Museum of Modern Art: 351 (Abby Aldrich Rockefeller Fund); *color figure 4* (James Thrall Soby Bequest), *color figure 9* (acquired through the Lillie P. Bliss Request)

Nimatallah/Art Resource, New York: 478

© Paris Musée, Christophe Walter: 24 (top)

THIS BOOK was set in Adobe Garamond. Designed for the Adobe Corporation by Robert Slimbach, the fonts are based on types first cut by Claude Garamond (c. 1480–1561). Garamond was a pupil of Geoffroy Tory and is believed to have followed the Venetian models, although he introduced a number of important differences, and it is to him that we owe the letter we now know as "old style." He gave to his letters a certain elegance and feeling of movement that won their creator an immediate reputation and the patronage of Francis I of France.

Composed by North Market Street Graphics,

Lancaster, Pennsylvania

Printed and bound by Quebecor Printing,

Fairfield, Pennsylvania

Designed by Barbara Balch